CONTINUITY
AND CHANGE
IN WORLD POLITICS

Second Edition

CONTINUITY AND CHANGE IN WORLD POLITICS

The Clash of Perspectives

BARRY B. HUGHES

Graduate School of International Studies
University of Denver

PRENTICE HALL, *Englewood Cliffs, New Jersey 07632*

Library of Congress Cataloging-in-Publication Data

Hughes, Barry, (date)-
    Continuity and change in world politics : the clash of
  perspectives / Barry B. Hughes. -- 2nd ed.
    p cm.
    Includes bibliographical references (p.   ) and indexes.
    ISBN 0-13-227000-5
    1. International relations. 2. World politics--1945- I. Title.
  JX1391.H84   1994
  320.9'045--dc20   92-42226
                                                          CIP

Executive Editor: Charlyce Jones Owen
Editorial/production supervision,
  interior design and electronic page makeup: Elizabeth Best
Copy Editor: Stephen C. Hopkins
Cover Design: Violet Lake Studio
Cover art: "Le ciel rouge" (The Red Sky) by Nicholas de Stael, 1952.
  Oil on canvas, 51-1/2 x 64-1/8. Collection Walker Art Center,
  Minneapolis. Gift of the T. B. Walker Foundation, 1954.
Prepress Buyer: Kelly Behr
Manufacturing Buyer: Mary Ann Gloriande
Editorial Assistant: Nicole Signoretti

©1994, 1991 by Prentice-Hall, Inc.
A Simon & Schuster Company
Englewood Cliffs, New Jersey 07632

Printed in the United States of America

10 9 8 7 6 5 4 3 2 1

ISBN 0-13-227000-5

Prentice-Hall International (UK) Limited, *London*
Prentice-Hall of Australia Pty. Limited, *Sydney*
Prentice-Hall Canada Inc., *Toronto*
Prentice-Hall Hispanoamericana, S.A., *Mexico*
Prentice-Hall of India Private Limited, *New Delhi*
Prentice-Hall of Japan, Inc., *Tokyo*
Simon & Schuster Asia Pte. Ltd., Singapore
Editora Prentice-Hall do Brasil, Ltda., *Rio de Janeiro*

To Bernard and Jean Hughes,
who encouraged a boy from Punkin' Center
to grapple with global issues

CONTENTS

PART I—THE WORLD OF POLITICS

PREFACE

Why these are the worst of times to be the author of a textbook on world politics should be obvious. Since the first edition of this book, the communist world largely completed its collapse, the Soviet Union itself dissolved, and the cold war ended. Most textbooks of even three or four years ago seem anachronistic: One geography book recently assigned to some of my students declares that East and West Germany will never reunite. Moreover, it seems unlikely that in the next few years the world will exhibit anything approximating the relative stability of the three decades prior to these recent events.

Why these could be the best of times may be less obvious. First, the excitement of studying global politics infects those of us who write about it at least as much as it does those who will study it in the classroom. It provides a real challenge to review and analyze this period of change. For this author, however, there is the added excitement of asking the following: How well did the earlier edition stand up to these changes? After all, this book is so bold as to use the title *Continuity and Change in World Politics*, thereby implying some capacity to analyze both.

Overall, the answer is that the approach upon which the book rests stood up remarkably well. The first edition did not predict the collapse of the Soviet Union (although it suggested the possibility); it did not forecast a war against Iraq; nor did it foresee the brutality of the civil conflict in Bosnia. Yet the book did discuss nationalism in the former Soviet Union and the former Yugoslavia at length, as it did the geopolitical, nationalistic, and religious bases of conflicts in the Mideast. Little appears to have occurred that a professor could not discuss using the framework of the first edition.

This edition therefore continues to utilize that framework with remarkably little change. It continues its attempt to convey a comprehensive and coherent understanding of global continuity and change in the modern era.

The presentation begins from the premise that an understanding of world politics has four principal elements. The first is an extensive foundation of information including knowledge of the current world and some familiarity with its history. This book provides a significant base of factual knowledge—not abstractly, but as needed to give flesh to a broader framework of understanding. The second element is analysis. Large numbers of important concepts and theories allow a serious student of world politics to move from particularistic description to generalization, from knowledge to analysis. This book extensively and systematically introduces those concepts and theories (**bold type** emphasizes their introduction).

The third element is interpretation. Many books on world politics present information and analysis as if to say, "These are the facts and here is how to interpret them." Yet anyone who reads the opinion page of a daily newspaper or who watches the debates on issues of world politics knows that analysts choose facts selectively and that their interpretations of even the seemingly most basic ones vary. All students of world politics need to understand that the field combines science and controversy, insight and competing interpretations. This text maps the primary competing perspectives on the "big questions" and helps the reader understand that the contributions of scientific analysis have often been within, not across, those worldviews.

The fourth and final element is insight into dynamics. Perhaps because the cold war froze international politics into a fairly rigid pattern for nearly four decades, analysis and interpretation of world politics have frequently failed to emphasize sufficiently how rapidly international relations can change and have neglected to consider the bases of change. This book seeks to convey some understanding of the forces that now transform our world.

I am one of the optimists—we have made great intellectual progress in this discipline during the last few decades. I have tried to write a book that not only collects and synthesizes these growing understandings of the world, but also pushes the limits of them. I have tried to present a comprehensive, coherent, and understandable portrait of global politics.

This and the earlier edition differ primarily in two ways. First, of course, this revision fully updates the information of the volume, incorporating details on the world-transforming events of the last few years. Second, and for this author even more important, this edition has tried to increase still further the coherence and understandability of the concepts, theories, and worldviews it presents. In short, the rewriting sought to sharpen the analytical clarity of the presentation. That effort led to substantial revision within most chapters, especially in the presentation of realism and idealism. Those who used the earlier edition will see little change in the overall framework or the sequence of chapters, but will hopefully notice improvements in presentation throughout.

Since release of the first edition, I have completed a computer simulation model that can help students explore global and regional developments in population, food, energy, economics, the environment, and politics (and interactions among them). The International Futures (IFs) model can be used by itself or as a supplement to this text. See Barry B. Hughes, *International Futures (IFs): Choices in the Creation of a New World Order* (Boulder Colo: Westview Press, 1993).

The Graduate School of International Studies (GSIS) has been an exceptional environment in which to undertake a work that covers as much ground as this one does. The GSIS brings together congenial, intellectually stimulating colleagues from a mixture of disciplines, and it attracts some first-class students with whom to develop ideas interactively. My intellectual debts in the preparation of this book are, of course, much broader than I can give thanks for here. It is only really possible to thank specifically those who saved me from some of my errors and confusions by commenting on substantial parts or all of the manuscript: Mark A. Boyer, *University of Connecticut*; Stuart A. Bremer, *SUNY-Binghamton*; James A. Caporaso, *University of Washington*; Harold Damerow, *Union County College*; Larry Elowitz, *Georgia College*; Scott Gates, *Michigan State University*; Peter M. Haas, *University of Massachusetts*; W. Ladd Hollist, *Brigham Young University*; Joyce P. Kaufman, *University of Maryland*; Yannis Kinnas, Minister Counsellor of Greece to the U.N.; David P. Levine, *University of Denver*; Janice Love, *University of South Carolina*; Michael McGinnis, *Indiana University*; Brian M. Pollins, *Ohio State University*; James Lee Ray, *Florida State University*; Neil Richardson, *University of Wisconsin*; Dale L. Smith, *Florida State University*; Marvin S. Soroos, *North Carolina State University*; and Paul R. Viotti, *USAF Academy*. In addition, James Chung, Steven Durand, and Padma Padula provided invaluable research assistance. Elizabeth Best proved a very supportive production editor.

With more time and additional suggestions, I hope in future editions to correct, develop, and sharpen the argument and the presentation of this book further. I welcome suggestions. Finally, I offer my thanks for the time you spend in reading and thinking about this book, and I convey my hopes that it will reward you.

Barry B. Hughes
University of Denver

Chapter 1

FORCES
OF CHANGE

The political equivalents of earthquakes periodically restructure international relations. For instance, World War II and events of the years immediately following it substantially reorganized the globe. At the beginning of the century the world was highly Eurocentric. Britain was the dominant country in many parts of the globe, but Germany posed an increasingly strong challenge to it. European empires divided much of the world among themselves. The United States and Russia were important but somewhat peripheral powers. Most of the surface features of that early twentieth-century world were still intact in 1938 when World War II began.

Pressures for change had, however, built below the surface throughout the first half of the twentieth century. The outcomes of the war revealed many of the discrepancies between the old surface forms and the new underlying realities. In particular, the United States and the Soviet Union emerged from the war as the dominant military powers. An event in the final months of fighting confirmed the U.S. position: On August 6, 1945, the United States dropped an atomic bomb on Hiroshima, Japan, thereby initiating the atomic weapons era. The Soviet Union exploded its first atomic bomb in 1949. The outlines of a new world order became visible following the earthquake of the war and these two nuclear explosions. Aftershocks of the next few years further clarified and solidified the new structures.

The wartime alliance of the United States and the Soviet Union, formed to combat Germany and Japan, quickly disintegrated. The two new superpowers then rapidly drew much of the rest of the world into new relationships around themselves. By 1949, the United States, Britain, and France forged alliance structures with former enemies Germany[1] and Japan; together they faced former allies, the Soviet Union and China, across an "iron curtain." The **cold war** had begun. The United States led the North Atlantic Treaty Organization (NATO), and the

---

[1]That is, they joined forces with the Federal Republic of Germany, the two-thirds of Germany that they occupied at the end of the war.

1

Soviet Union soon dominated the Warsaw Pact. The two alliances enrolled most of the economically more developed countries of the world.

Among the aftershocks of the early postwar period was decolonization. The war had temporarily reduced or eliminated control by the Western European states over their extensive colonial empires in Africa and Asia; Britain and France acted to reestablish imperial positions as quickly as possible. Nonetheless, the empires crumbled.

The pressures for change did not stop working, however, as new global forms took shape and stabilized. A variety of demographic, economic, environmental, and technological forces continued to operate in ways that once again frequently failed to change surface structures immediately. For instance, since World War II world population had more than doubled by 1990. Germany and Japan rose from the ruins of World War II to engage the United States and other new friends in intense economic competition. Humanity put increasing pressures on its biological and physical environments. New communications technologies linked the peoples of the world as never before. Pressures for change in the new post–World War II surface of global structures continued to build beneath it.

Although the world continued to experience small shocks throughout the 1960s, 1970s, and 1980s, in 1989–1992 another large-scale earthquake rocked it (Chapter 2 describes and analyzes this period). The epicenter was the Soviet Union, which had installed a reforming leadership in 1985, but it rapidly radiated to Central Europe. In 1989 and 1990, Communist parties in the Soviet Union and all of its Eastern allies gave up their dominant role or began to share power with movements for political reform. By 1992 the Warsaw Pact had dissolved and the Soviet Union had disintegrated into fifteen new states.

The ramifications of the new shock spread globally. Rapid movement toward both unilateral and negotiated reductions in arms developed. The United States and the Soviet Union began to see opportunities for cooperation in the resolution of problems around the world rather than only arenas for conflict. Long-standing political configurations in the Middle East, Central America, and elsewhere in the globe began to shift.

Other developments added to the pace of change during this period. Twelve countries in Europe, which had fought an almost uncountable number of wars during the preceding 400 years, moved toward a 1992 deadline for the development of a common economic market. Japan increasingly emerged as the new financial leader of the world: Its foreign aid rivaled that of the United States, and it began to request leadership roles in institutions like the International Monetary Fund. South America completed a movement toward democratization, boasting democratic governments in all countries for the first time ever. South Africa took important steps to loosen the grip of its apartheid system. Given all these developments, there is every reason to expect a period of major aftershocks, not unlike that of the late 1940s and early 1950s.

The sum total of changes wrought by these two extraordinary periods in the last half century is astounding. Yet beneath the mosaic of change, many patterns of continuity persist. Two are especially apparent. First, countries remain the dominant actors in world politics. Some, like the United Kingdom, France, or Portugal can trace their existence back several centuries. Even in the roster of countries there is, of course, change: The United States came onto the scene little more than 200 years ago, Germany has been united for scarcely more than 100 years, and Bangladesh will not celebrate its fiftieth anniversary until 2021. Schoolchildren around the world must now learn the location of new countries such as Croatia, Belarus, and Georgia.

Second, warfare among countries (or tribes or city-states or empires) predates our historic knowledge and appears to be a constant of human existence. In 1990, thirty-one conflicts were under way that together had claimed more than 2 million lives. Not a day passes without a war-related death somewhere in the world. Economic competition among countries is a relative constant, and many of the methods by which countries seek relative advantage today are little changed from those of 300 years ago.

What are the major forces of global change and the primary elements of continuity in world politics? What kind of world are they jointly creating? The years since the end of World War II constitute little more than an average working lifetime. How dramatically might world politics evolve during the working lives of the students reading this book?

This volume cannot foresee the future world, any more than someone in early 1939 could have forecast the world of today. It can convey an understanding of important forces at work, however, and present alternative frameworks for considering the implications of those forces. The rest of this chapter sketches eight forces that appear especially potent in their contribution to global change. Many popular and scholarly works read uniformly optimistic or pessimistic implications into the workings of these forces.[2] Each force, however, has potentially both positive and negative consequences; often the implications for individual human beings will depend on the country of their citizenship or on their social position.

The simultaneous operation of several forces, with substantial and complex interaction among them, presents tremendous difficulty for anyone attempting to understand the present state of world politics or hoping to anticipate its future—it is perhaps impossible to know even the relative importance of these forces, much less to comprehend the product of their interplay. We have seen that world politics is a bit like the surface of the earth, which often exhibits long periods of relative calm, even while massive tectonic plates continue their long-term drift just below its surface. Periodically, and as yet unpredictably, the underlying forces dramatically disrupt surface features. Identification of geologic plates was a critically important step for geologists in their understanding of the effects of plate movement on the earth—it provided a key to finding the location of earthquake zones. Identification of the forces that gradually reshape world politics, and that

---

[2]For almost uniformly optimistic or positive interpretations of major global trends, see Kahn, Brown, and Martel (1976); Naisbitt (1982); and Toffler (1980). For consistently pessimistic or negative perceptions, see Meadows, et al. (1972 and 1992), Lester Brown (1981), and the Council on Environmental Quality (1981).

periodically lead to massive restructurings, has a comparable significance for the political scientist.[3]

DEMOGRAPHIC TRANSITION

People are the core interest of any social science. That fact alone might justify placing demographic change first on our list of important long-term forces. More to the point, the numbers and geographic distributions of populations affect most other patterns of global development. Dramatic global changes in human numbers and distribution have recently occurred and continue. Specifically, *the world is undergoing a demographic transition from small populations with short life expectancies to large populations with long life expectancies.*

A millennium ago global population was a fraction of the 5.4 billion world inhabitants in 1992 (specifically about 250 million or 5 percent of the present world population), and it required high birthrates to offset the prevailing high mortality rates and to allow for a very slow net population growth. Mortality rates of European populations gradually fell, and growth rates accelerated during the last 500 years because of advances in transportation of both food and people, changes in agricultural technology, and progress in sanitation and health care. Yet only in the waning years of the nineteenth century did really dramatic improvement in life expectancy begin. At the end of the seventeenth century life expectancy at birth in England was only thirty-two; by 1860 it had advanced just to forty-five; however, in 1992 it reached seventy-six.[4] In countries like England, birth rates gradually eased in the wake of lower mortality rates until the two again became approximately equal. The European and North American **demographic transitions** from high mortality and fertility rates to low mortality and fertility rates, and the surges of population growth that accompanied the temporary surplus of births relative to deaths, are now largely complete.

The demographic transitions of most non-European peoples began only in the twentieth century, and dramatic declines in mortality did not appear until after World War II. Those mortality declines, because of the rapidity of the transfer of modern medical technology throughout the world, were much more rapid than the earlier ones in Europe. In fact, life expectancies at birth outside of Europe and North America increased from forty-three in 1950–1955 to fifty-four in 1970–1975, and to sixty-two in 1992.[5] As earlier in Europe, mortality declines preceded those

[3]Kirk and others (1956) earlier identified major global forces or trends of importance for international relations. They pointed to accelerating world population growth, the spread of industrialization, advances in technology, depletion of raw materials, the growth of a global economy, decolonization (now fundamentally completed), and the growing importance of Asia (relative to the West). Similarly a collection of studies by Sullivan and Sattler (1971) drew attention to technology, the environment, population, food, raw materials, ideology, and race. That much of what follows is similar to the work of twenty- to thirty-five-year-old studies helps substantiate that these are indeed global "megatrends."

[4]United Nations (1973, 23–24) and Population Reference Bureau (1992). Such progress in life expectancy prolonged the lives of infants and children into their child-bearing years, compounding the impact of mortality declines on population growth rates.

[5]United Nations (1980, 17) and Population Reference Bureau (1992).

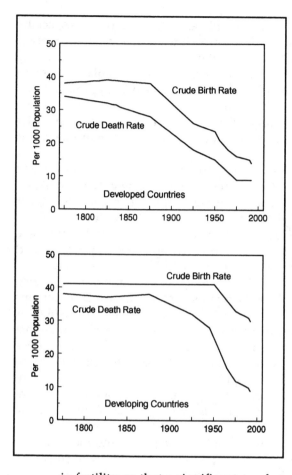

FIGURE 1.1   Demographic Transition
Source: Nancy Birdsall, *Population and Poverty in the Developing World.* World Bank Staff Working Paper No. 404. (Washington, D.C.: World Bank, 1980), 4: Population Reference Bureau, *World Population Data Sheet,* (Washington, D.C.: Population Reference Bureau, 1986, 1988, 1992.)

in fertility, so that a significant gap between mortality and fertility rates opened, and population growth accelerated.

Figure 1.1 portrays the demographic transitions in economically developed and developing countries by showing fertility and mortality rates over time. Demographers measure fertility in various ways. One of the most common is the **crude birth rate** or total annual births per 1,000 population. Similarly, they often capture mortality by the **crude death rate** or total annual deaths per 1,000.[6] The difference between the crude birth and death rates is the net population growth per thousand. For instance, Kenya was one of the fastest-growing countries in the world in 1992. Its crude birth rate was forty-five, and the Kenyan crude death rate was nine. The difference of thirty-six per 1,000 is equivalent to a 3.6 percent annual rate of population growth.

[6]A superior indicator of fertility is the total fertility rate, the number of children an average woman bears during her lifetime, because it is independent of the age distribution of the population. As a measure of mortality, life expectancy at birth is superior to crude death rate for the same reason. Crude birth and death rates, although lacking independence from age distribution, have an offsetting advantage as crude measures of fertility and mortality, namely their direct linkage to population growth rate.

The increasing global gaps between fertility and mortality, driven especially by the post–World War II mortality declines in Africa, Asia, and Latin America, reached a peak near the end of the 1960s. At that time the world passed a critically important demographic **turning point**. Specifically, global population growth rates, which had been increasing indefinitely, reached a peak of approximately 2 percent per year and began to decline (as fertility moved lower and began to catch up with mortality declines). In the early 1980s, the global rate eased to about 1.7 percent, and, although it rests temporarily on a plateau, the growth rate seems poised for further declines.

The world will likely pass a second important demographic turning point near the end of the century. To date, the declines in annual percentage growth rates have been so small that, when the growth rates are applied to higher and higher world population totals, they still yield increasing year-to-year additions to world population (see the bottom half of Figure 1.2). That is, the actual number of people added to world population each year is still growing. Sometime very near the end of the century, however, these annual increments should begin to decrease.[7]

Even after crossing these two critical divides in human demographic history, world population will grow throughout the twenty-first century, reaching perhaps 10 to 12 billion (compared with 5.4 billion in 1992) before any kind of stability is attained. Although future numbers are highly speculative, it is nearly certain that most population growth in the next century will occur outside of North America and Western Europe—in fact, practically all of it will. The demographic transition of the European peoples reshaped the population distribution of the world (increasing their global share), and the demographic transition in developing countries is reshaping it again, even more dramatically (see Figure 1.2). Populations are fundamental to economic and military capabilities, and to pressures on land and other resources; that is, populations influence both the power and the weakness of countries. For better or for worse, Europe and North America will constitute considerably smaller shares of a much larger global population.

Many of the costs of a doubled world population are obvious: a greater congestion and a greater demand on land, air, water, and biologic resources. It should be emphasized, however, that demographic changes will bring both challenges and opportunities. Assuming that fertility rates continue to drop in most of the world, the opportunities include slower growth in pressure on food supplies, raw materials, and employment opportunities. Because younger people require health care, food, and education, while often making little contribution to production, demographers call them the **dependent population**. In general, a large percentage of the population in a rapidly growing country is under the age of fifteen. For instance, that age group constitutes 38 percent of the total in Mexico compared with 22 percent in the United States. Declines in fertility reduce the size of the dependent population relative to the more economically productive population, facilitating economic growth.

[7]Merrick (1986, 13). Brown, Flavin, and Wolf (1988) estimate the peak will be 90 million net births per year.

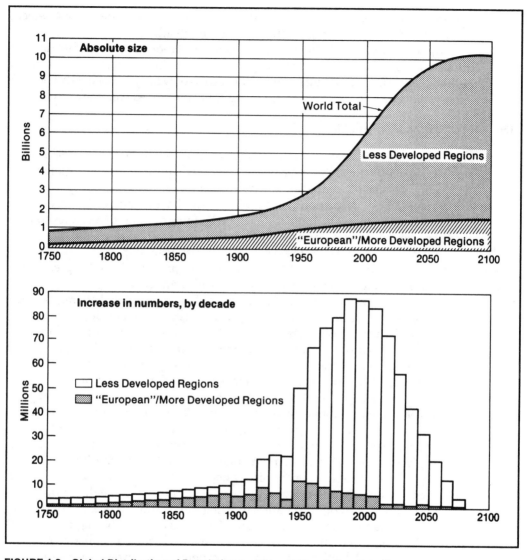

FIGURE 1.2   Global Distribution of Population and Annual Population Growth
Source: Thomas W. Merrick, "World Population in Transition," *Population Bulletin* (Population Reference Bureau, Inc.), 41, No. 2 (April 1986), p.4. Reprinted with permission.

Even the countries that successfully navigate the demographic transition face significant potential problems. In Germany, for instance, population could decline for years, because fertility rates have fallen below mortality. Many European countries may follow this pattern. Declining population shrinks labor forces, whereas the aging, longer-lived population (a second category of the dependent population) simultaneously puts increasing demands for medical care and pension benefits on those who work. In the United States, 13 percent of the population exceeds sixty-five years of age compared with 4 percent in Mexico, and the percentage in the U.S. is rising steadily.

By no means have all countries of the world proceeded any significant distance through this transition. This is especially true in Africa: In Gambia life expectancy at birth is still only forty-four, and in Guinea-Bissau it is only forty-two. Poverty and high fertility may be a trap for several less economically developed countries.

GROWING FOOD SUFFICIENCY

Food is our most basic human need, and *the world has increasingly gained the physical ability to feed itself.* Throughout the post–World War II period growth in global food production persistently equalled or outstripped growth in the global population. In 1990 world food production per capita exceeded that of 1950 by 38 percent. Since the 1950s the **green revolution** has developed strains of grain that can respond to fertilizers, pesticides, and irrigation with dramatically increased yields.[8] Beginning with research on wheat in Mexico under the sponsorship of the Rockefeller Foundation and the direction of Nobel-laureate Norman Borlaug, the green revolution has spread to a variety of grains and to all continents.

Averages, however, can conceal much. Although the global average of food production per capita has increased, the economically more-developed countries, rather than the poorer countries, attained the largest per capita gains. Western Europe, long a food-importing region, now has significant food surpluses and faces food disposal problems comparable with those of the United States. At the other extreme, Africa has experienced long-term declines in food production per capita (see Figure 1.3), offset for consumers only by increasing imports (and gifts) of food. The United Nations estimated that 250,000 died of starvation in the Sudan alone during 1988, when civil war disrupted food production and imports.

Two problems stand in the way of food sufficiency for all humans—and even challenge the gains to date. Environmental constraints pose the first. Although increases in food production increasingly depend on productivity gains on existing agricultural land, rather than on expansion of area cultivated, the pressures that agriculture places on forest areas, grazing areas, and the oceans continue to intensify. For example, increased grazing of animals on neighboring grassland is causing the Sahara and other deserts to expand significantly. Production gains on currently cultivated land come from applications of fertilizers, pesticides, and irrigation water that extend the impact of food production well beyond the farm gates. For instance, fertilizer and pesticide runoffs are the most significant sources of water pollution over most of the globe. Second, great disparities exist in access to food among and within countries. Although surpluses increase in Western Europe, shortages climb in Africa. Although India exported grain for several years in the 1980s, many Indians were malnourished. Food sufficiency requires not only adequate production globally, but adequate incomes locally.

[8]The new strains often have shorter and thicker stalks so that they can hold larger heads without bending over or breaking (lodging).

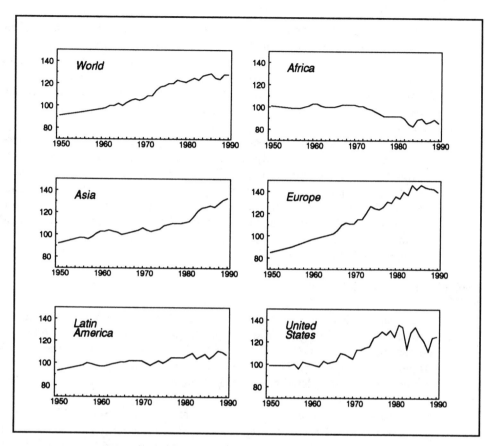

FIGURE 1.3   Food Production per Capita, Percent of 1961–65
Sources: FAO Production Yearbook (Rome: United Nations Food and Agriculture Organization, 1965, 1975, 1981, 1985, 1987, and 1991).

We may be seeing the implications of these two problems in recent data on food production. Whereas global production per capita grew 11 percent in the 1970s, it increased only 3 percent in the 1980s, and not at all in the last half of that decade. The fact that food prices remained low suggests that income was a more important constraint than environmental limits into the early 1990s.

A considerable international effort now focuses on eliminating hunger. For instance, the Hunger Project, a worldwide voluntary organization, decreed a goal of ending world hunger by the year 2000. Because that would require a plunge in the number of globally malnourished individuals from about 300 to 500 million[9] to zero, it appears an unattainable target. Although the world has

[9]United Nations Food and Agricultural Organization (1987, 23) . In 1990 the United Nations Children's Fund (UNICEF) undertook perhaps the most systematic study of malnutrition ever done and estimated that 150 million children in developing countries excluding China suffered from malnutrition (Carlson and Wardlaw 1990, 20).

enough food production capacity to accomplish it physically, the goal runs up against the distributional problem. Massive government-supported or privately supported international and intranational transfer programs could eliminate hunger, but such programs are unlikely. Moreover, a better long-term solution would allow the malnourished to earn income and to buy food on the world food market, not indefinitely converting them into welfare recipients.

The opportunities are spectacular. Nothing is a more basic human need than food. The world can potentially eliminate hunger, that seemingly eternal scourge, within the lifetimes of children today. The elimination of hunger would also assure great progress against the diseases that prey on the malnourished and against the lifelong physical debilitation that can result from a single childhood bout with hunger. If humans were to slay famine, one of the four horsemen of the apocalypse, the impact on our collective self-image and our willingness to tackle other global problems could be dramatic.

ENERGY TRANSITION

In the year 1850, the burning of wood supported approximately 90 percent of the inanimate energy budget in the United States. By 1910, coal provided roughly 70 percent of U.S. energy. In 1970, the United States relied on oil and gas for close to 70 percent of its energy. Thus by 1970 the United States, and much of the rest of the world, had completed two **energy transitions** (wood to coal, and coal to oil and gas), each transition lasting approximately sixty years. *A third energy transition is under way, and the world will largely complete it by 2030.* Since 1970 the global use of conventional oil and gas as a percentage of total energy has declined, whereas coal, nuclear, and solar energy contributions have increased.[10] Because of physical limits on resources of conventional oil and gas, by 2030 they will provide less than half, perhaps near 30 percent of our global energy budget. Although a third energy transition is under way, it is not at all clear what the dominant energy form or energy mix will be on completion.

Important turning points have marked this transition. One that few noted at the time, the peak of oil production in the United States, occurred in 1970. Its significance became clear in 1973–1974 when global oil prices quadrupled, in part because the United States had begun to increase oil imports and compete in the world market. The global energy system will reach another turning point sometime after the year 2000 when *global* conventional oil production will peak. In fact, the rise of global oil production to a peak and its subsequent fall, tracing a bell-shaped pattern like that of Figure 1.4, characterize the energy transition better than most other descriptions.[11]

[10]In 1991 oil and gas contributed about 60 percent of the total (British Petroleum 1992, 34).

[11]The peak of global oil production is, of course, unpredictable. When they include production from extra-heavy oils and oil sands, Chevron Corporation analysts put it as late as 2050 (Chevron 1987, 3). Peak production from conventional oil and gas is very likely before 2025.

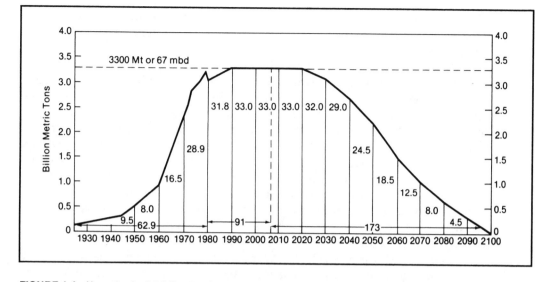

FIGURE 1.4   Hypothetical Oil Production and Resource Depletion Profile
Source: International Energy Agency, *World Energy Outlook* (Paris: OECD, 1982), p. 215. Reprinted with permission.

Past energy transitions had dramatic social and political consequences. Coal is geographically less dispersed than wood. The transition to coal thus led to greater concentrations of labor and of capital (facilitating the growth of labor movements and corporations). The energy quality of coal is also higher, in the sense that it provides more heat per unit of weight; movement to a coal-based economy was necessary for the growth of steel and railroad industries. Oil and gas deposits are even more concentrated globally than coal, and their production requires still more capital and technology. The necessity of mobilizing substantial capital and high technology in the oil and gas industry facilitated the growth of corporations that are among the largest in the world (four of the largest ten corporations by sales in 1988 were energy companies). The political and military importance that the world places on desert real estate in the Middle East (such as in Kuwait) is obviously linked to oil and gas. So, too, is growth in the automobile industry (and in three additional corporations in the top ten), the U.S. interstate and trans-European highways, and the suburbanization of the world.

In short, the nature of the energy system interacts with (it is too strong to say "causes") important developments in economic, social, and political structures. One basis for opposition to the nuclear industry, in addition to the environmental dangers of the plants and fuel cycles, is the linkage between a potentially dangerous, highly capital- and technology-intensive industry (even more so than the oil and gas industry) and government regulation and control. Many nuclear opponents prefer locally distributed energy supplies, such as rooftop solar collectors provide, to the concentrated power (whether electrical, economic, or political) of either corporations or government.[12] Thus the current transition will continue to be a focal point of political debate as well as of environmental and economic argument.

The challenges posed by the energy transition are substantial. Capital investments in existing energy systems, and domestic and international political-economic arrangements based on them, will constitute an anchor that the forces of the transition process will drag along. The anchor will periodically and grudgingly jerk loose, and then grab hold again. For example, rapid and substantial increases and decreases in oil prices (**oil shocks**) have occurred several times, and we can expect them again. Those, in turn, have set in motion massive international movements of capital that are also destabilizing. Although the energy sector constitutes only 5 to 10 percent of the economy of most developed countries, there would be no modern economies without energy. No individual metals, manufactured products, or services can be the source of as much disruption to modern economies as changes in the availability or price of energy.

Opportunities also exist. The world's energy system has become highly concentrated geographically with dependence of the world on the countries of the Persian Gulf. This has been a source of international political instability and conflict for many years. Whatever the newer energy system will be, it appears highly likely that such geographic concentration will decline. It is also possible, although by no means certain, that the intensive research and development efforts that accompany this energy transition will provide environmentally cleaner, less expensive, and even "eternal" energy sources.

INCREASED ENVIRONMENTAL IMPACT

Human beings have long affected their local and regional environments in important ways, but *we now increasingly alter our global environment*. As hunters and gatherers, humans put pressure on, and probably exterminated, some food sources.[13] With fixed agriculture (starting about 10,000 years ago), we began to alter the vegetation of sizable areas. Our reliance on wood for fuel and building materials, and our conversion of forests to fields, caused extensive change in woodland extent. Humans have yet to reverse the large-scale destruction, centuries ago, of forests in Lebanon (the famous cedars) and on the Dalmation coast of Croatia. In recent years forest cover in Haiti declined from more than 90 percent of land area to about 3 percent, and that in Ethiopia shrank from 40 percent in 1900 to 4 percent.

In fact, large-scale **deforestation** may well be the first of the major global changes that humans made to their biological and physical environment. Between the initiation of significant agricultural activity and today, global

---

[12]Solar advocates and nuclear opponents implicitly link political philosophy with energy system preferences (Lovins 1976).

[13]A debate still rages over claims that human hunting (as opposed to climate changes) caused the demise about 11,000 years ago in North America of mammoths, mastodons, mountain deer, giant beavers, dire wolves, and many other large mammals (Bower 1987, 284).

forest area has fallen by approximately 50 percent.[14] Concerns about deforestation have shifted from the more-developed countries, where the process is stabilizing or reversing, to the less developed countries, and in particular to tropical rain forests in the Amazonian basin and in Africa. Why do we worry globally about local rain forests? Shrinking rain forests destroy habitat for local species and can lead to their extinction.[15] Rain forest loss may also change global climate patterns.

With the industrialization of the last 200 years, the ability of humanity to wreak havoc with air, water, and biologic systems grew dramatically. Initial impact was geographically limited, as with the famous coal-based smogs of London and the contemporary petroleum-based smogs of Los Angeles. The impact became regional and global very rapidly, however. Synthetic organic chemical production in the United States grew from 6.7 million metric tons in 1945 to 210 million in 1989, equivalent to almost one ton per citizen. The scope of the toxic waste problem is now global.[16]

Damage to the world oceans was once specific to coastlines that suffered from local failure to control sewage, industrial pollution, and other effluents. Now we see problems (such as oil and plastic pollution) that affect the entire Mediterranean and even appear in the larger oceans.

Burning fossil fuels, especially high-sulphur coal, releases sulfur and nitrogen compounds into the air; in combination with water these create **acid rain**. It is a problem that crosses country borders. Scandinavians complain of damage to their lakes from acid rain originating in the heavily industrialized Ruhr area of Germany and elsewhere in Eastern and Western Europe. The Germans themselves worry that as much as 34 percent of their forest area exhibits pollution-based damage (Postel 1984, 8). So, too, the Canadians complain of acid rain in their maritime provinces, traceable to steel and electric plants of the U.S. Midwest.

British scientists discovered an annually reappearing **ozone hole** in the upper atmosphere over the Antarctic that appears to be growing. Many observers believe that it is a result of increasing global use of chlorofluorocarbons (CFCs) and halons, gases which chemically interact in the upper atmosphere with the ozone and deplete it. Ozone depletion also may be occurring globally. A National Aeronautics and Space Administration study in 1988 reported a 3 percent decline since 1969 over densely populated areas of North America and Europe. Ozone in the upper atmosphere helps protect humans from ultraviolet radiation and the skin cancers that it can cause.[17] Depletion of ozone would damage plants and animals as well.

[14]Forest definitions vary so much across sources that absolute land areas in forests are difficult to specify. This estimate of reduction combines information from the World Resources Institute (1986, 61–62) and the Council on Environmental Quality (1981, 117–118).

[15]Estimates of species loss range from one an hour (about 175,000 over a 20-year period) to a calculation by the World Resources Institute of 5–15 percent of all species (5–30 million) between 1990 and 2020.

[16]Council on Environmental Quality (1991, 304). Between 400,000 and 2 million people suffer pesticide poisoning annually, and 10,000 to 40,000 of these people die (Postel 1987, 7–16).

[17]Ozone near the ground is a local pollutant, not a benefit.

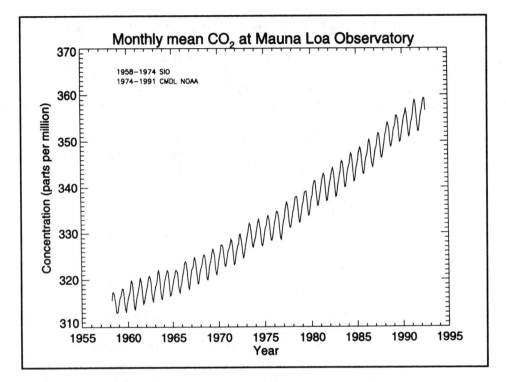

FIGURE 1.5   Increase in Atmospheric Carbon Dioxide
Source: Courtesy of Carbon Cycle Group, National Oceanic and Atmospheric Administration, Boulder, Colorado.

Still another global environmental problem is the increase in atmospheric carbon dioxide (CO_2), to which the burning of fossil fuels contributes the most (Figure 1.5). Atmospheric CO_2 allows sunlight (short-wave solar radiation) to penetrate it, but it traps the long-wave infrared or heat radiation much as glass in a greenhouse does. The **greenhouse effect** is the resultant global warming. CFCs and other pollutants also contribute to lesser degrees. Estimates suggest that a doubling in the atmospheric level of carbon dioxide, which could well occur near the middle of the next century, will cause a 1.5°C to 4.5°C increase in average global temperatures. Six of the world's seven warmest years since 1850 fell in the 1980s, and 1990 was the warmest ever. The greenhouse effect may cause more substantial warming of the ice-covered poles and have somewhat less effect in equatorial regions. In 1987 the U.S. National Academy of Sciences, not typically an alarmist body, released a report suggesting that the earth's heating might well lead to enough melting of ice caps to increase ocean levels five feet by 2100.[18]

[18]*Science News*, January 19, 1991, 36. The world's average temperature is about 59 degrees Fahrenheit and has risen about one degree since 1900. The 1980s were the warmest decade in the history of instrumental records. Much dispute exists, however, as to whether that reflects a greenhouse effect or cyclical variation.

It is difficult to see many opportunities in the increasing scale of human environmental impact. One example, however, is our ability to organize global attacks on diseases (part of our biologic environment) through coordinated vaccination programs. In 1977 the United Nations World Health Organization (WHO) announced that, because of precisely such activity, it had eliminated smallpox infection globally. The virus exists now only in laboratories in Atlanta and Moscow. With a technological revolution occurring in the biologic sciences, other diseases may follow smallpox. "River blindness," which has taken the eyesight of more than 300,000 people, especially in equatorial regions, is a target. In general, the opportunities lie in coordinated international attacks against problems, either those created by humankind (such as polluted water) or those predating our ability to create them (such as disease). As in the global attack on hunger, habits of cooperation, or more concretely the institutional structures set up to manage a problem, could also potentially facilitate international cooperation in other arenas.

The challenges of human impact on the environment are, however, more obvious and are very substantial. With larger human numbers and greater economic activity, the scope of environmental problems must inevitably expand. Only collective international action can handle some, such as the release of CFCs. In September 1987, representatives of twenty-two countries met in Montreal and agreed to reduce the use of CFCs by 50 percent, by no later than the year 1998; they subsequently raised the target to accomplish a complete phaseout by that year. That is an almost unique international agreement and could serve as the prototype for others.

CFCs have substitutes, however, and the economic cost of switching to them is much lower than that of accepting large numbers of additional human cancers from ozone depletion (plus damage to crops and animal life). Reduction in use of fossil fuels and thus in the creation of CO_2 is much more difficult, because the economic costs could be extraordinary. Barring a setback in the momentum of antinuclear forces, or a breakthrough in solar or nuclear fusion technology, humanity is now in the early stages of a global climate experiment. We almost certainly will double the atmospheric level of CO_2 by the end of the coming century, and possibly by its middle. Our scientists now have the ability to measure the increase, the resultant change in global temperatures, and the subsequent rise in global ocean levels. Although some confounding factors (such as changes in atmospheric dust levels) will make direct causal linkages somewhat ambiguous, these scientists will report to humanity before the middle of the next century on the results of this grand experiment. They will report on other ongoing environmental interventions as well.

GLOBAL ECONOMIC RESTRUCTURING

Although it began more than beginning 200 years ago, *the global economic restructuring initiated by the industrial revolution is still very much under way.* The **industrial revolution** refers generally to the social and economic changes surrounding the widespread substitution of complex machinery for the simpler tools of craft production.[19] Many observers of global development would argue that no other force discussed in this chapter is nearly as important as this one, and some would even propose that all others are mere reflections of the industrial revolution and the economic restructuring it set in motion.[20]

The industrial revolution is unfinished in two respects: (1) the diffusion of that revolution to much of the world outside of Europe and North America; and (2) the movement of the economically more developed countries into a new phase of technological advance and economic organization that both extends and supersedes the industrial revolution.

GEOGRAPHIC DIFFUSION

In the late 1700s the early stages of the industrial revolution transformed England and, to a somewhat lesser degree, France. The extension of that revolution to Germany followed its political unification in the latter half of the 1800s. Although beginning earlier, the primary surge of industrialization in the United States occurred after the Civil War (1861–1865). The stirrings of Japanese industrialization followed the Meiji Restoration (1867) and a conscious, revolutionary restructuring of the Japanese political-economic system through the end of the nineteenth century. One of the aims of the Bolshevik Revolution in 1917 was the industrialization of Russia; the Communist government accomplished that. Other European economies and countries of British settlement (like Canada and Australia) also underwent the transformation, primarily in the late nineteenth and early twentieth centuries. In the last half of the present century a new group of industrialized countries has emerged. It includes some additional European and European-settler countries (Spain, Portugal, Greece, Yugoslavia, Israel, South Africa, Brazil, Mexico, and Argentina) and the "four tigers" of Asia (South Korea, Taiwan, Hong Kong, and Singapore) (Table 1.1).

There is substantial debate about which countries might follow, derivative from the theoretical debate concerning the origins of industrialization. Among the possible or probable requirements for industrialization are educated, literate, and technically trained workers; extensive and reliable communication and transportation capabilities; some initial investment in one or more important economic sectors; and a government apparatus that is supportive of industrialization internally and protective of it externally. Countries that will meet these requirements

[19]Maddison (1982), for example, calls the 1700–1800 period that of merchant capitalism and dates industrial capitalism from 1820. He cites increases in the pace of technical progress and fixed capital formation as key characteristics of modern capitalism and distinguishes "machinofacture" from "manufacture."

[20]Social observers as disparate as Karl Marx and Alvin Toffler have focused on the central role of industrialization. Marx placed the nature of production technology in the driver's seat of economic and political development. Focusing on economically advanced countries, Toffler attributes current social developments to the completion of industrialization and to the growth of a high-technology service sector.

TABLE 1.1 World Industrial Production		
Year	Index Value (1913=100)	Average Annual Growth Rate During period (%)
1710	0.6	
1790	1.8	1.4
1840	7.4	2.9
1913	100.0	3.6
1938	182.7	2.4
1973	1,116.0	5.3
1982	1,387.3	2.4
1989	1,788.0	3.7

Sources: W. W. Rostow, *The World Economy: History and Prospect* (Austin: University of Texas Press, 1978), 49, 622; United Nations, *Statistical Yearbook 1983/84* (New York: United Nations, 1986); United Nations, *Monthly Bulletin of Statistics*, assorted issues.

in the waning years of the twentieth century, or in the first half of the twenty-first, may include India and China. China already ranks among the top eight industrial producers in the world, and India is in the top fifteen. Many tallies do not consider them industrialized only because of their large populations and commensurately low average-income levels. When these two giants clearly join the ranks of the industrialized, they will jointly bring nearly one-third of humanity with them, roughly doubling the portion of the world living in industrialized countries.

POSTINDUSTRIAL CHANGE

The second unfinished aspect of the industrial revolution is its continued unfolding in the economically more developed countries. Even in the most advanced economies, the amount of physical capital per worker and the quality of that capital continue to increase (capital consists of machinery and buildings for production). Advanced countries still experience consistent rises in manufacturing productivity (output per worker) and declines in the price of capital relative to the price of labor. For example, annual working hours in advanced industrial countries fell from about 3,000 in 1820 to 1,700 in 1980, whereas per capita output grew by a factor of fifteen, implying that productivity per hour worked increased nearly thirty times during this period (Maddison 1982, 4). Between 1960 and 1990 manufacturing output per hour at least doubled in all major industrial countries; in Japan it increased nearly eight times. The productivity gains and the industrial revolution continue.

The ongoing productivity trend has, however, begun to diminish the relative size of the industrial sector in a fashion reminiscent of an earlier decline in agriculture.

In the United States the agricultural sector's claim on the country's work force declined from approximately 80 percent at the time of the American Revolution to 3 to 4 percent today. The industrial work force increased its share steadily until about 1910 (surpassing the agricultural work force in 1905) and remained near 35 percent of the total until the mid-1960s. Since then the industrial share of the work force has dropped steadily—manufacturing workers (a subset of industrial employees) constituted 31 percent of the U.S. nonagricultural work force in 1960 but only 16 percent in 1991. During the same period, manufacturing as a percentage of the gross national product (GNP) fell from 29 percent to 16–17 percent.[21]

In the last twenty-five years, several other industrialized countries (including the United Kingdom, Belgium, France, and Germany) have experienced relative declines in the share of work force employed in manufacturing and industry (a combination of mining, construction, and manufacturing). Service industries provide most growth in employment in these advanced economies. Services are things you can buy and sell, but not drop on your foot; they include wholesale and retail trade, banking, insurance, advertising, accounting, education, and government. Many observers have shifted their perspective beyond the industrial revolution to what they call, among other things, the postindustrial revolution. Without diminishing the importance of the ongoing industrial revolution, it is critical to emphasize that the service sector has become considerably more than half of the economy in what we still often call the industrialized countries (Figure 1.6).

If there is a "service revolution," it has a somewhat different character than the industrial revolution, or agriculture's green revolution, both of which were clearly characterized by large productivity gains. Great debates rage about the extent to which productivity in the service sector has increased. Some portions of the service sector exhibit many of the same characteristics as blue-collar manufacturing: division of labor into simple, repetitive tasks and relatively low skill requirements. These service jobs, like fast-food processing or dry cleaning, are much like manufacturing jobs and produce or process countable things (like hamburgers). The techniques of the industrial revolution produce clear productivity gains in these services. Many white-collar jobs, however, such as teaching or scientific research, process information and do not have easily measured output. Many jobs remaining in the manufacturing sector (such as automobile design) increasingly also have this character. The centrality of information processing to this employment suggests that we call the new era the **information age**.[22] Computer and communications technologies are espe-

---

[21]*The 1992 Information Please Almanac* (1992, 59). See also World Bank (1991), which indicates slightly slower rates of manufacturing decline in the United States and verifies similar declines in most other industrial countries. Some argue that "deindustrialization" is exaggerated or is not occurring at all. For instance, Drucker (1986, 775) claims that "In the 35 years since the Korean War, manufacturing production in the U.S. has remained a relatively constant 23–24% of the GNP, even as the percentage of workers engaged in the sector declined steadily." The data clearly contradict that assertion. In absolute terms, however, U.S. manufacturing, like agriculture, continues to grow.

[22]To label the new era postindustrial is "rearview-mirror thinking."

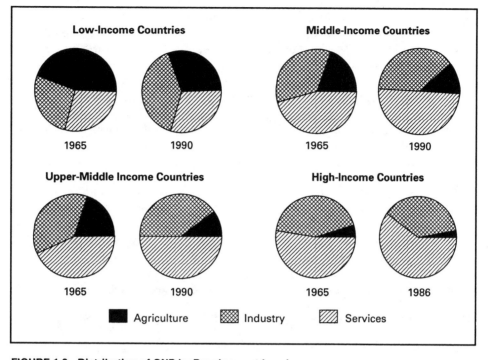

FIGURE 1.6   Distribution of GNP by Development Level
Sources: World Bank, 1992. *World Development Report 1992*. New York: Oxford University Press, pp. 222–223; also *World Development Report 1988*.

cially important to improvements in productivity (however difficult to measure) in the handling of information.[23]

The two extensions of the industrial revolution, diffusion to further countries and a transformation into an information revolution, again present opportunities. The industrial revolution brought some unambiguous improvements in the quality and even the length of life of the inhabitants of the currently industrialized countries. It is likely that few would choose to live almost anywhere, at anytime, before 1700, if they could live in Western Europe or North America today (assuming they could not in advance know their station in life). Thus the extension of the industrial revolution to additional countries appears to offer much promise. It even holds out the hope of closing the income gaps that separate the rich and poor countries of the world. Moreover, the communications technology of the information age is creating a growing sense of global community—it is difficult not to empathize with starving children or war-torn bodies seen on television.

[23]The dividing line between the industrial revolution and the information revolution is not easy to draw, because improvements in processing information often also lead to improvements in making things. Nonetheless, it is clear that modern economies are moving qualitatively beyond the industrial revolution.

The challenges of the global economic restructuring are many. In the more recently industrialized or industrializing countries, environmental quality has suffered. Like Mexico City, with air quality that makes the air of Los Angeles appear pristine, the most polluted cities in the world now lie scattered across the economically less developed portion of the globe. A second major problem is distribution of income, which generally deteriorates in at least the early stages of industrialization. Underlying that problem is inequality in the ownership of the complex machinery or capital so fundamental to the process of industrialization. Social and political conflicts about distributional issues inevitably accompany industrialization.

Increasingly, information-centered societies face a different set of problems, many based in the decreasing size and employment of the industrial sector and the social trauma that process brings. In addition, postindustrial countries like the United States fear dependence on the outside world for basic industrial goods. Less pollution compensates somewhat for these difficulties. So, too, does reduced conflict concerning the ownership of capital. In fact, access to information (and the tools for processing information, such as computers) tends to be fairly widely dispersed in information-age societies and often this dispersal is governmentally subsidized.[24]

THE DECLINE OF THE UNITED STATES AND THE FALL OF THE SOVIET UNION

American power and wealth are not in absolute decline, but because of the gains of other countries, they are in relative decline.[25] Relative decline takes many forms. One source of clout in the world is the strength of a national economy. The United States produced considerably more than 40 percent of the world's goods and services at the end of World War II. Although the wartime destruction of many other economies inflated that number, the figure was still 36 percent in 1960. In the 1980s and early 1990s the U. S. share varied between 22 percent and 28 percent (see Figure 1.7).[26] This economic decline does not reflect a failure of the United States to grow, but rather a persistent, long-term tendency for it to grow more slowly than the rest of the world. Although the U.S. economy has achieved an average annual growth rate of 3.0 percent since 1965, the world economy grew at a 3.5 percent rate.[27]

[24]Because the means of production in the modern age are increasingly information and information-processing capability, rather than land or heavy industrial capital, we may be creating an economy combining collective with widespread, diffuse private ownership of the means of production. In the public sector are government data banks, publicly supported research and development, schools and universities. In the privately owned sector are increasingly powerful computers with relatively easy access to large-scale public and private communications networks and data sources.

[25]Many of the forces and trends of this chapter periodically gain popular attention, normally because of a spectacular event such as an energy crisis. The Reagan era drew much attention to the U.S. world role (see Gilpin 1987b). Consider, for instance, the popularity of the scholarly volume by Paul Kennedy, *The Rise and Fall of Great Powers* (1988). Not everyone agrees that the U.S. position is in decline (Huntington 1988; Kugler and Organski 1989; Nau 1990).

[26]The seeming increase in the U.S. share during the mid-1980s was misleading because it reflected a temporarily stronger U.S. dollar exchange rate rather than a larger economy.

[27]U.S. growth (1965–1989) from the World Bank (1992, 221) and global growth from Sivard (1991, 50).

FIGURE 1.7   World Position: Global Shares
Sources: Assorted Publications of the United Nations, Population Reference
Bureau, U.S. Arms Control and Disarmament Agency, Stockholm International
Peace Research Institute, and the U.S. Central Intelligence Agency.
Note: Soviet/Russian economic and military expenditure estimates are
approximate.

Japanese growth has been especially remarkable (5.6 percent). In 1987 the GNP per
capita in Japan exceeded that in the United States for the first time. While U.S.
manufacturing productivity grew by 130 percent between 1960 and 1989, that in
France, Italy, and Japan grew by 239, 319, and 623 percent, respectively (National
Science Foundation 1991, 111).

Net exports of goods and of capital to the rest of the world also measure global economic influence. Powerful, productive nations typically export more than they import of both goods and capital. The United States capped a long decline in its trade surplus (exports minus imports) with a trade deficit (more imports) in 1971; deficits have since become the rule. Similarly, in 1985 the United States moved from a net capital exporting country to a net capital importer. Residents of other countries have greater investments in the United States than Americans do abroad (about $532 billion in 1989).[28] In 1949 the United States held nearly 60 percent of the world's international financial reserves (mostly gold); that share fell to 6 percent in 1988 (Walters and Blake, 1992, 18).[29] The global portion of foreign exchange held in dollars fell from 80 percent to 52 percent between 1976 and 1992 (*The Economist*, July 25, 1992, 63).

An additional foundation of power is population. Between 1950 and 1992 world population growth averaged 1.8 percent, whereas that in the United States was 1.2 percent. Although 5.9 percent of the world's population resided in the United States in 1950, the figure was 4.7 percent in 1992.

The U.S. lead in technology is diminishing. Between 1965 and 1988–1991, the portion of U.S. patents awarded to U.S. residents fell from more than 80 percent to 53 percent.[30] One study found greater citations by third parties to Japanese patents than to American patents beginning in 1976. Japan's share of global technology-intensive exports climbed sharply from 7.3 percent in 1965 to 19.4 percent in 1985, approaching the 25 percent U.S. share.[31] Whereas in the early 1960s the United States imported less than one-fourth as many high-technology products as it exported, by the late 1970s the imported portion exceeded one-half; and the United States posted its first high-technology trade deficit in 1986 (Burton 1989, 9; Rupert and Rapkin 1985, 167).

When most people think of international power, however, they focus on military strength. In this area, too, the U.S. global dominance has eroded. It was only in nuclear capabilities that the United States ever held a commanding position. From an initial monopoly on nuclear capabilities (which lasted from 1945–1949), the U.S. advantage gradually but steadily gave way to a rough parity with the Soviet Union at the end of the 1970s. In conventional forces the Union of Soviet Socialist Republics (U.S.S.R.) was the premier world power throughout the post–World War II period, with the possible exception of the peak of U.S. buildup during the Vietnam War (around 1968–1970). The United States and China have vied for second place.

[28]Because analysts measure investments at book value, they understate the value of earlier U.S. investments. It is possible that the balance of investment is considerably more even than published figures suggest.

[29]Another interesting financial indicator is that 66 percent of world stock trading occurred in the United States in 1970, but only 31 percent in 1988 (Frank Russell Company data, obtained from T. Rowe Price Investment Services).

[30]Burton (1989, 9); *Business Week*, August 3, 1992, 69.

[31]National Science Foundation data reported in The Christian Science Monitor, April 1, 1988, 13.

American military spending declined sharply after World War II, and by 1950 it was less than 20 percent of the global total (see Figure 1.7). With the initiation of the Korean War, American military spending surged in the 1950s, and the Vietnam War held it above 30 percent of the global total throughout the 1960s. Thereafter the U.S. global share eroded—the Reagan administration's buildup of the 1980s was only a temporary attempt to regain the earlier position.

U.S. citizens recognize the changes that have occurred. In 1963 a survey found that 84 percent of Americans anticipated increases in the country's world influence. At the peak of the Vietnam War that number fell to 62 percent, and it declined further to 58 percent in the late 1970s.[32] In 1987, after the largest peacetime military buildup in U.S. history, only 41 percent of Americans believed the claim that the United States was more important and powerful than it had been ten years earlier (Greenberg 1987, 695–699). Many instead believed that the economic cost of the military buildup weakened the American economy, by contributing to large domestic and international indebtedness, so as to more than offset the military gains.

The emphasis here has been on the United States, primarily because its relative power was so strong at the end of World War II. Its dominant early postwar share of the global economy and nuclear military power made the United States a **hegemonic power** (the term implies an ambiguous combination of leadership and control).

Russia, the other major world power at the end of World War II, has experienced much more dramatic relative decline (see Figure 1.7). Only in total military capabilities, especially with its rise to nuclear parity with the United States in the 1970s, did the former U.S.S.R. once manage to strengthen its global position. The Soviet Union's share of global military expenditures, global economic product, and global population declined slowly, but quite steadily, prior to its collapse in 1991.

The collapse of the U.S.S.R. led many to argue that, contrary to the rumors of its decline, the United States has become stronger than ever. Relative to other great powers, in the global system it is, in fact, exceptionally strong (Kugler and Organski 1989); any potential threat to the United States has greatly diminished with the Soviet Union's demise. The world has, however, become increasingly integrated, and in a global context the U.S. decline continues steadily on most measures. That global decline cannot help but affect its ability to dominate the global system.

Many in the world probably react to declining U.S. hegemony and the collapse of Soviet power with pleasure. Even many Americans may feel more comfortable in a less commanding global role. The other side of the coin is that the U.S. position made it possible to provide important leadership on a variety of environmental, economic, and security issues; no single country can replace it in that leadership role. We will return often to some of the possible consequences of declining leadership ability.

[32]The Reagan presidency temporarily retarded the slide. Whereas 44 percent of the American public in 1982 believed the United States to be less important in the world than ten years earlier, in 1986 that had dropped to 26 percent (Reilly 1988, 47).

GROWTH OF DESTRUCTIVE POTENTIAL

The ability of human beings to injure or kill others continues to increase rapidly. One measure of that "progress" is explosive power. In 1500, near the beginning of the gunpowder era, the maximum explosive power of weaponry was equivalent to about 0.001 ton of trinitrotoluene (TNT). Growth was slow but steady and in World War I the cannon called Big Bertha packed a punch near one ton of TNT. The blockbuster bombs of World War II raised the power to about ten tons (see Table 1.2). The atomic bomb dropped on Hiroshima in 1945, with a force of 20,000 tons of TNT, shifted the explosive power growth curve dramatically upward. The hydrogen bomb quickly multiplied the maximum explosive force again by 1,000. In 1961 the Soviets tested a 50-megaton (50-million-ton) bomb. Weapons of that size actually make little sense, given that much smaller ones can adequately destroy large cities, so countries build primarily warheads of less than one megaton.

"Quality" of weaponry is only part of the story. In 1946 the American arsenal held only nine atomic warheads, and the Soviet Union did not test its first bomb until 1949. In 1992 the United States and the former U.S.S.R. each had more than 10,000 strategic warheads and together possessed more than 1 million times the destructive power of the bomb that killed 140,000 in Hiroshima, Japan

TABLE 1.2
Milestones in Military Potential

Year	Explosive Power (Tons of TNT Equivalent)	Weapon
1500	.001	Gunpowder "bombs"
1914	1.0	Large cannon
1940	10.0	Blockbuster bomb
1946	20,000.0	Hiroshima atomic bomb
1961	50,000,000.0	Largest hydrogen bomb

Year	Maximum Range (Miles)	Weapon
1453	1.0	Cannon
1830	3.0	Coastal artillery
1915	200.0	Zeppelin raid on London
1938	750.0	European bombing formation
1949	5,000.0	Bombing plane
1959	Global	Satellite-launching missile

Sources: Robert U. Ayres, *Technological Forecasting and Long-Range Planning* (New York: McGraw-Hill, 1969), 22; *The Columbia Desk Encyclopedia*, 3rd ed. (New York: Columbia University Press, 1963), 127, 966; Harold Sprout and Margaret Sprout, *Toward a Politics of the Planet Earth* (New York: Van Nostrand Reinhold, 1971), 403.

(McWilliams and Piotrowski 1988, 15; Sivard 1987, 16). There has also been a spread of the weaponry to other countries. Great Britain joined the nuclear club in 1952, France followed in 1960, and China entered in 1964. Together these five countries constitute the declared nuclear powers. In addition, India exploded what it called a "peaceful nuclear device" in 1974. Experts suspect that India, Israel, North Korea, South Africa, and Pakistan have unannounced supplies of nuclear warheads or weapons-grade plutonium (Spector 1988). Argentina, Brazil, and a handful of other countries could mount covert development programs if they wished, and the Iraqi effort was far along when the UN coalition destroyed and dismantled it in 1991–1992.

Atomic warheads are best exploded at some distance from the country deciding to use them. The Soviet Union launched a small satellite named *Sputnik* in October 1957 and thereby announced the impending capability to deliver warheads to targets anywhere on the globe. The most advanced American missile is the MX (called the "Peacemaker" by President Reagan). It carries warheads for ten separate targets and can destroy a combined area about sixty times greater than that devastated by the bomb dropped on Hiroshima (Sivard 1987, 17). India, Israel, Japan, and all five declared nuclear powers have now demonstrated the capability of launching satellites, and several other countries are developing missiles that could potentially deliver nuclear warheads.

The world has passed an important milestone in destructive capability: Sometime in the last twenty years humanity gained the ability to destroy industrial society (and some say humanity itself) with a fairly brief military exchange. Salvos of perhaps 200 warheads could paralyze the economies of the United States and Russia (by destroying, for instance, major energy facilities such as oil refineries). Full use of their approximately 20,000 strategic warheads would extensively burn cities and forests; the resulting smoke in the atmosphere around the world could block sunlight for long enough to create a **nuclear winter** (Thompson and Schneider 1986; Sagan 1983). Many of those whom the initial explosions did not kill would die from radiation burns or starve as crops failed and social structures deteriorated. Few turning points listed in this chapter can be as important.

INCREASED SOCIAL MOBILIZATION

Another important global transition is the *rapid social mobilization of peoples around the world*. **Social mobilization** is the process of transforming the conditions and attitudes of people from the traditional to the modern.[33] Among the many conditions modernization transforms are educational and literacy levels, and the extent of social interactions. Attitudinally, people come to believe that their own actions can improve their conditions of life. These changes frequently precede increased demands for social, economic, and political participation.

[33]Deutsch (1961). Palmer (1989, 60–61) summarizes the wide variety of changes that take place during the process.

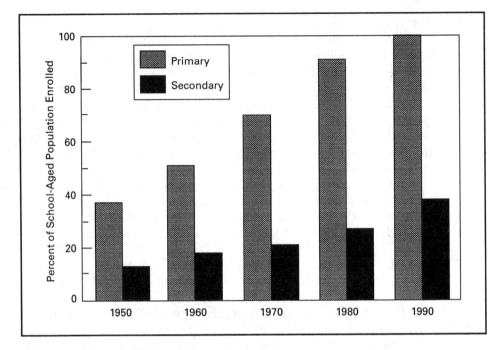

FIGURE 1.8   School Enrollment in Low-Income Countries
Sources: John W. Meyer, Francisco O. Ramirez, Richardson Robinson, and John Boli-Bennett, "The World's Educational Revolution, 1950–70," in *National Development and the World System*, ed. John W. Meyer and Michael T. Hannon (Chicago: The University of Chicago Press, 1979), 37–55; World Bank, *World Development Report* (Washington, D.C.: World Bank: 1979, 1983, 1989, and 1992).

Education is a high priority in societies around the world. Global education expenditures take nearly 5 percent of total economic output, about the same as that absorbed by military spending (Sivard 1991, 50). Globally, in 1960 five of every 1,000 people were teachers, whereas that figure climbed to seven in 1988 (those bearing arms declined from six to five per 1,000). In the poorest countries of the world, only 37 percent of primary school-aged populations attended school in 1950; that number grew to 51 percent in 1960, and in 1989 it reached 100 percent (Figure 1.8).[34] Venezuela illustrates the impact that this can have—between 1958 and 1988 total school enrollments climbed from 800,000 to more than 6 million students. Literacy rates reflect the educational effort. In 1955 a majority of the people in the world older than fifteen years of age were literate for the first time.[35] In 1990 the literate population had reached 65 percent. The advance of literacy in the economically least developed countries is especially rapid; it climbed to 60 percent in 1990.[36]

[34]Meyer and others (1979, 40); World Bank (1979 and 1992).

[35]Deutsch (1988, 313); Cipolla (1962, 116) reports a rate of 56 percent already in 1955.

[36]Sivard (1991, 54); World Bank (1992). Because countries report statistics for their own performance, there is always a danger that they will exaggerate progress; literacy is difficult to measure.

Exposure to print media has increased with literacy. Access to electronic media (radio, movies, and television) is increasing even faster. For instance, the number of radios per 1,000 population globally was 159 in 1965 and 375 in 1989 (Figure 1.9). Televisions per 1,000 increased from 55 to 155 between 1965 and 1989.[37]

The exposure of human beings to a broad range of other humans, and to their ideas, also rises with urbanization. In the early 1990s, for the first time ever, most humans globally were engaged in nonagricultural activities and lived in cities. The portion of humanity dwelling in cities increases by nearly 5 percent each decade. The total is already 77 percent in the most economically developed countries (World Bank 1992, 279).

Karl Deutsch expressed the importance of these changes:

> In all these respects, and many others, the patterns of thousands of years are breaking in our lifetime. Some of these changes seem slow on the time scale of a busy year or two, but they are dramatically swift when seen on a scale of decades or generations. Faster than ever before, humanity is being transformed in its social and economic structures and informed by its mass communications.... The upshot of many of these changes is a thrust of people toward politics. (Deutsch 1988, 313–314)

The implications of social mobilization for political participation are difficult to measure. On the average, however, the societies with the highest levels of social mobilization are those with the most open and democratic political processes. The pressures for greater democracy in South Korea, Taiwan, Russia, and China illustrate how economic advance underlies social mobilization, which in turn calls forth demands for greater control over one's own destiny.[38] Political systems do not always accommodate the increased pressures gracefully. Both violent and nonviolent political protest have been increasing over time around much of the world.

For example, social mobilization often expresses itself in nationalism, a force that both created and destroyed countries during the last 100 years and is not yet spent. Ethnic groups, as they mobilize, often seek to establish control over their own government and sometimes attempt to expel or subjugate others. It is possible that when historians look back on the twentieth century they will describe it primarily in terms of the power of nationalism and the breakdown of the nineteenth-century empires.

Another and generally more peaceful manifestation of social mobilization is the rapid proliferation in developing countries of grass-roots organizations for self-help activities ranging from building a school or health clinic, to reforesting a hillside, to establishing a credit union. The organizations include cooperatives, mothers' clubs, religious groups, neighborhood federations, and many others (Durning 1989b, 155).

[37]Despite advances in world literacy, reading is not increasing at anywhere near the pace of listening and viewing. Global newspaper circulation per 1000 fell from 110 to 104 between 1975 and 1984 (UNESCO, Statistical Yearbook 1987).

[38]Rosenau (1984, 258) makes the related argument that individuals now have improved ability to analyze complex scenarios and that this increases their assertiveness.

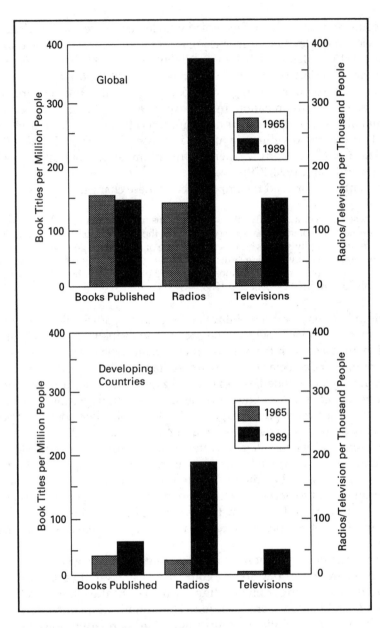

FIGURE 1.9 Exposure to Communication
Source: *Statistical Yearbook 1991* (Paris: United Nations Educational,
Scientific and Cultural Organization), 6–11, 6–19, 6–20.

Social mobilization also spills across the borders of countries. The internationalization of media, and the expansion of global travel and personal communication creates worldwide communities with shared interests and often with

collective political agendas. There are now more global actors, with interests in many issues, than ever before in world politics. Voluntary organizations such as Greenpeace (environmental protection), the Hunger Project (world hunger), Amnesty International (protection of human rights), and Beyond War (nuclear war avoidance) translate increased mobilization into global political pressure. They illustrate an increasing recognition of collective human interests and the degree to which individual countries fall short of satisfying them.

UNCERTAIN IMPLICATIONS OF TRENDS

This chapter sketched eight global forces or megatrends.[39] There is no way to identify the most important global development forces scientifically, so any list will be subjective and probably incomplete. For instance, the chapter mentioned the advance of technologies such as electronics only in passing (and as implicit in other trends). Other analysts might point to the buildup of debt in economically less developed countries or of financial surplus in Japan as important trends. Throughout this book we will direct considerable attention to technology, debt, and still other forces and trends.

The many interacting forces of change, with the multiple opportunities they present and the challenges they pose, create a base on which widely varying understandings of global relations rest. For instance, pessimists point to the growing global population and slowing gains in food supply per capita, the growing human ability to damage the environment, and the growing insecurity that nuclear weapons have brought to the world, an insecurity that proliferation amplifies. Optimists see hope in the declining rate of global population growth, the long-term growth of the physical ability to feed that population, the spread of efficient production and the development of new technologies with ongoing industrialization, and the potential for collective global responses to collective problems.

This book, in addition to presenting the reader with basic information about world politics, constitutes an exploration of such competing understandings of the world—of a clash of perspectives. More specifically, this text presents six images of the global superstructure that rests on the substructure of the eight forces this chapter identified. The six understandings present generally coherent but sometimes quite limited views of the world. Many readers will find one or more of these understandings especially compatible with their own interpretations. This author seeks not to convert you, but instead asks only that you look seriously at the possibility that other perspectives can supplement and enrich your own.

---

[39]Naisbitt (1982) coined the expression "megatrends," but elaborated a very different set from that presented in this chapter.

Chapter 2

ELEMENTS
OF ANALYSIS

Now that we have sketched some of the forces that shape the dynamics of world politics, let us move from the substructures to the superstructures of our subject matter. This chapter defines what we intend to study and how we will organize our approach to it.

SUBJECT MATTER

Scholars of world politics often refer to questions of military and strategic significance—questions of war and peace—as **high politics**. Economic or environmental issues are **low politics**. Stark separation of these issues, and of international politics from international economics, is somewhat recent; for centuries the dominant perspective was that a country's economic performance and international power were highly interdependent. Studies of politics and economics were inextricably linked because government and economy were thought to be closely bound.

In 1776, however, Adam Smith published *The Wealth of Nations* and laid the foundations for the view that the wealth of countries could best be increased without the active intervention of governments.[1] Adam Smith's philosophy of **laissez faire** (nonintervention by the government in the economy) gradually came to be a powerful force in intellectual and policy communities and in establishing boundaries between politics and economics. Simultaneously, European and North American economies industrialized, left predominantly agricultural societies behind, and pushed back threats of starvation. With these developments the once all-encompassing study of political economy split into more and more specialized subdivisions: Not only did demography emerge as a separate field, but politics and economics parted company and further split into subfields such as agricultural economics or international politics.

[1]Smith still emphasized the contribution to a country's power and security that governmental tolerance for actions of firms and individuals could make.

Even as the splintering of political economy occurred, some theoretical perspectives resisted it.[2] For instance, Marxism refused to accept the division between politics and economics, arguing that dominant economic classes are the basis of domestic political leadership and that political relations among countries are firmly rooted in economic interests. In the post–World War II period, and particularly in the last twenty to thirty years, many non-Marxist challenges to the intellectual partitioning of political economy have also arisen.

The forces outlined in Chapter 1 suggest the need to extend the subject matter of world politics even beyond political economy. The onset of the energy transition exposed the linkages between resource availability and the power and security of countries; such linkages had been of great concern to students of politics early in the century but were increasingly ignored thereafter. Moreover, the emergence of the human ability to damage the global environment has created an entirely new and important arena of international policy concern.

This book thus simultaneously returns to the roots of political-economic thought and extends the scope of the field. Three systemic foci or subject matters organize the discussion here: politics, economics, and the broader environment.[3] Figure 2.1 indicates the relationship between the three subject matters and the forces or trends of Chapter 1. Although the figure separates the three subject matters, they are closely related in international affairs.

In fact, separation of the three subject matters only makes sense when each appears to be well under control—when security is relatively assured, economic growth is acceptable, and no significant problem areas emerge from the broader environment. Such satisfaction is most likely to arise in the dominant countries of the interstate system during prosperous periods, for instance in England after the beginning of the industrial revolution and in the United States in the twentieth century, especially after World War II. In contrast, countries that view themselves as militarily inferior may be more apt to rely on economic advance to overcome that status. Countries that consider their economic performance to be inadequate often turn to government leadership to alter that fact. Countries that lack critical raw materials (or that perceive themselves as overpopulated) devote considerable political, economic, and military effort to ensuring adequate supplies of materials and balancing population with land.[4]

One important reason for the reemergence of political economy lies in the disintegration of the earlier colonial empires and the spread of rapid population

---

[2]The study of international relations (as distinct from international politics) has always resisted efforts to narrow it. Sir Alfred Zimmern argued in 1935 that "the study of international relations extends from the natural sciences at one end to moral philosophy...at the other" (quoted in Dougherty and Pfaltzgraff 1981, 6).

[3]Many other divisions of international subject matter are possible. Bell (1987) relies on structural (demographic, technological, and economic), political, and cultural divisions. Braudel (1979, 17) suggests political, economic, social, and cultural.

[4]Japan and Germany, both dissatisfied powers in the 1930s, certainly believed in the close connections among international politics, economics, and resources. As dramatically as they have changed their policies, they have not completely abandoned that orientation.

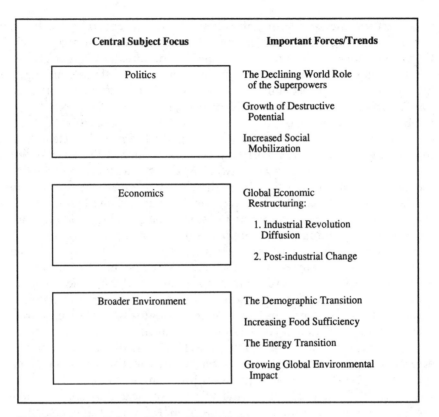

FIGURE 2.1   The Subject Matter of World Politics

growth and industrialization to the former colonies. The linkages among politics, population, food, and economic development are as evident in these new countries today as they were in the new countries of seventeenth-century Europe. Moreover, the same linkages between international power and wealth that were apparent to many in France, when it faced a more powerful and economically advanced England in the 1600s, have become apparent to leadership in economically developing countries now. Like the French leadership then, the former colonies have often concluded in this century that establishing strong central political institutions will help them in their economic and political struggles with other actors and in their internal economic development.

Even dominant countries, generally in control of their military security, economic well-being, and environmental integrity, may face periods historically when they temporarily or permanently lose that control. The United States experienced such a period beginning in the early 1970s: The challenge of Soviet military power threatened security; the erosion of global economic dominance challenged material well-being; and the rise of energy and environmental crises undercut perceptions of their importance to world politics and economics. As a result, the study of these three subject matters increasingly merged.

SOME CENTRAL QUESTIONS

We have not yet specifically identified the issues we want to study. What are the important questions of world politics?

The principal political-military questions center on war (or conflict more generally), peace, and security. What are the causes of war? What brings peace? In a world of potentially dangerous and sometimes hostile actors, how can a people maintain some kind of security? These are not value-free questions, and it is impossible completely to divorce values from the study of world politics. Most of us fear and deplore war and would like to see a much more peaceful world. We might well place desire for peace near the top of our priorities. We should recognize, however, that such a ranking reflects a somewhat conservative orientation to our world. A population that considers itself suppressed and exploited by others (for example, blacks in South Africa or Palestinians in Israel) might share our abstract desire for peace, but actively embrace conflict in the name of freedom and independence, two other important values. Their scholars might write world politics textbooks (or desire to be so permitted) in which the central questions are quite different: How does a people achieve freedom (or justice)?[5] What are the reasons for imperialism? We would be remiss if we paid no attention to these issues.

A different set of economic questions comes to the forefront. For Americans and Western Europeans, one central query has long dominated: How do countries maximize economic growth and well-being? The annual summits of the chief executives of these nations repeatedly show that international relations among Japan, North America, and the countries of Western Europe revolve closely around this question.[6] Again, however, the question reflects a specific set of values and reflects the place that those asking it maintain in the global economy. Many Latin Americans, Africans, and Asians attach at least equal importance to other questions: How might we more equally distribute existing global economic well-being? What is the linkage between economic growth in the more developed and less developed countries? We noted earlier that some scholars characterize these economic questions as low politics in contrast to the high politics of war, peace, and security. Yet that characterization also reflects position in the world— for malnourished or starving individuals throughout the world (nearly 10 percent of the total world population), there can hardly be more important questions.

Still another set of questions focuses on broader environmental factors. In Western Europe and the United States, a central integrating theme with respect to the broader environment has long been in progress—advances in technology for controlling the environment and acquiring resources from it. How can humanity maximize material progress? Other perspectives, however, question whether

---

[5]Bull (1977, 77–98) stresses the tension between the values of order and justice.

[6]The United States, Great Britain, France, West Germany, Italy, Canada, and Japan have regularly scheduled economic summit meetings since 1975. They are known collectively as the Group of 7 or G-7. These countries also struggle domestically and internationally with distributional questions—but with less intensity than do poorer countries.

a continuation of environmentally exploiting progress is desirable or attainable. Some point to ethical issues in the elimination of biologic species. Many others argue that our rush to feed growing populations imposes unsustainable burdens on the environment, and that we exhaust finite resources like oil at excessive rates. These concerns lead to a different question: How can we ensure long-term survival of human society? The famines in Africa in the 1970s and 1980s and the major increases in oil prices during the 1970s temporarily thrust these questions to center stage in world politics.

The division of international subject matter into the three categories of Figure 2.1 (politics, economics, and the broader environment) thus provides a basis for identifying many important questions. The next section shows that the division can also structure an approach to the understanding of particular events or issues.

AN ILLUSTRATION: THE REVOLUTIONS OF 1989–1992

In December 1988 the Supreme Soviet of the U.S.S.R. changed the country's constitution to create a new legislature (the Congress of People's Deputies), to be elected in a partially democratic process involving multiple candidates for many seats. The rewriting also strengthened the presidency. These developments signaled a potential shift of power from the institutions of the Communist party to those of the government proper and to a broad electorate. In January 1989, Poland legalized Solidarity, the trade-union movement that had become an important non-Communist opposition force in the early 1980s and was then banned. These actions, and many others, set in motion a year that only the word "revolutionary" can describe. Subsequent events have dramatically transformed the area that we once called the Soviet bloc and to which we now increasingly refer simply as Central and Eastern Europe: the former U.S.S.R., Poland, the former Czechoslovakia, Hungary, united Germany, Romania, Bulgaria, the former Yugoslavia, and Albania.

In March 1989 opposition and reform candidates stunned the Soviet leadership in the elections for the new Congress of People's Deputies—even many unopposed Communist candidates lost because voters struck their names from ballots. Hungary, already farther along in political and economic change than other countries of the region, began in May to remove the barbed wire from its 150-mile long border with Austria. After this first tangible lifting of the iron curtain, East Germans began to use Hungary as an escape route to Austria and then on to West Germany.

Liberalization spread rapidly and widely. On television the world watched Chinese students occupying Tiananmen Square in the heart of Beijing and protesting for more democracy, even erecting a replica of the Statue of Liberty (which they called the Goddess of Democracy). In June 1989 the hard-line members of the Chinese Communist party won an internal power struggle and used the army to crush the increasingly popular movement.

Elsewhere, however, the forces of reform marched forward. Solidarity made an agreement with the regime that allowed it to contest about half of Polish

Parliamentary seats, and it then swept all but one of those open seats. In August it took control of the government—the first non-Communist government in the region. In November and December the tide of liberalization rose still higher. Protests in East Germany and continued flight of its citizens to the West led to a decision to open the walls between East and West Germany. Massive demonstrations in Czechoslovakia and even Bulgaria swept hard-line leaderships from office; Vaclav Havel, a non-Communist, who not much earlier had been imprisoned, took the presidency in Czechoslovakia. A bloody but quick revolution in Romania toppled the dictatorship there.

In February 1990 the Central Committee of the Communist party in the Soviet Union voted to suggest the elimination from the constitution of Article 6, which guaranteed the leading political and social role to the party. Most Central European leadership had already renounced similar articles. Throughout Eastern and Central Europe, elections and leadership turnover extended into 1990 the revolutionary changes of 1989. Agreements between East and West allowed German reunification at the end of the year. By the end of 1990, economic and political conditions had changed so much that the United States began to offer food aid to its major adversary.

In 1991 events proved as earth-shaking. The United States and the U.S.S.R. began the year with cooperation in the United Nations against the Iraqi invasion of Kuwait. The Warsaw Treaty Alliance dissolved itself in July. The United States and the Soviet Union signed a major conventional arms control treaty with countries throughout Europe and signed a bilateral agreement to reduce nuclear arms very substantially. After a coup attempt by the Communist party and army in the fall, Russian president Yeltsin barred activities of the party. Most dramatic, on December 25, the Russian flag replaced the Soviet flag above the Kremlin, announcing the end of the U.S.S.R.

In 1992 Russia and the fourteen other former republics of the U.S.S.R. joined the United Nations, World Bank, and International Monetary Fund and appealed for a major Western aid package. Fighting intensified between substantial numbers of ethnic groups in the former Yugoslavia and in the former U.S.S.R.

More recent events, as important as they have been, rest on the base of these revolutions of 1989–1992, a period that we therefore want to understand better. Organizing our discussion in three subject-matter categories helps us reach that better understanding.

POLITICAL-MILITARY ASPECTS

This period of revolution demonstrates much that is at the high politics core of world politics. The power of the Soviet Union began to dominate Central Europe following World War II, when Soviet armies remained in place after pushing out the Germans. That military strength allowed the U.S.S.R. to install governments subservient to it throughout the region. Soviet military force subsequently crushed reform movements in Hungary in 1956 and Czechoslovakia in 1968, and discouraged other efforts to escape Communist domination.

Thus leadership changes in the U.S.S.R., and the decreased willingness and ability of that leadership to continue the use of repressive force were critically important factors in the revolutions of 1989–1992. In March 1985 Mikhail Gorbachev took the reins of the Soviet Communist party and increasingly elaborated a vision of economic and political reforms—a vision of peaceful revolution. One debate that will occupy historians for many years is whether the changes would have occurred more slowly, or perhaps not at all, with different top leadership. Another is whether the military buildup of the United States in the 1980s intensified the pressure for reform in the Soviet Union or whether internal forces in that country would have inevitably given rise to it. On one issue there can be little debate: The decreasing power of both the United States and the Soviet Union, relative to many other global actors, had gradually weakened the ability of both to play dominant roles in Western and Central Europe.

The events forced large numbers of new power and security (war and peace) questions onto the agendas of the United States and countries in Western Europe. How should countries sympathetic to the democratic reforms of the East react? How actively should they provide economic support to encourage the process but not imply an attempt to dominate the region? What is the role of NATO after the lifting of the iron curtain? What should be the character of a unified Germany so that it does not threaten the security of its neighbors? What forces, in armies, secret services, or Communist parties, might reverse some or all of the changes and how can the outside world reduce the danger of reversal? It will be many years before answers to all these questions become clear.

A focus on power politics alone, however, cannot help us fully understand the events of 1989–1992 and their aftermath. Ideas and ideals play a critical role. For instance, Communist thought evolved as Communists examined their record of structuring political and economic systems, and found it wanting. Many former Communist parties in Central and Eastern Europe increasingly looked to the social democratic parties of Western Europe for models of success.

A belief by many people in universal human rights was also important. In 1975 the members of both major military alliances (NATO and the Warsaw Pact) and a number of neutral countries in Europe signed an agreement (the Helsinki Final Act) that pledged their attention to such rights as access to communication, freedom of travel, and freedom of political organization. Although the Eastern countries often ignored or repressed these rights, the pressures built both internally and externally for serious commitment to them.

Many ideas and ideals define the appropriate boundaries of community in different ways than do the traditional borders of countries (just as advocates of human rights focus on values they believe are common to a global community, not just to those values found on one side or the other of the cold war). It is impossible to understand the developments of recent years without understanding commitments to both national (ethnic) and religious communities. For example, the Soviet Union forcibly incorporated Lithuania, Latvia, and Estonia, collectively known as the Baltic republics, into the union in August 1939. In August 1989, on the fiftieth anniversary of that occasion, 1 million citizens of the Baltic republics peacefully formed a human chain across the region to demonstrate solidarity and to protest for independence.

Throughout the entire region, many borders fail to conform to the historical homelands of peoples. The pressure for unification of the Germanies originated in the shared belief that the citizens of both were Germans—not East Germans nor West Germans. Non-Russian peoples constituted half of the population in the Soviet Union, and most wanted their independence. After the republics had achieved their independence, minority ethnic groups in most of them began to chafe under new national leaders and a number argued or fought for border redefinitions. The formation of Yugoslavia at the end of World War I unified Serbs, Slovenes, Albanians, Croatians, and others, and pressures for the autonomy of those nationalities date from that event. Ongoing processes of social mobilization increasingly energize various national communities.

Religious communities also crisscross the area. Bulgaria combines a Christian Orthodox majority with an Islamic and Turkish minority. The southern portions of the former Soviet Union contain many Islamic (and frequently Turkish) peoples. Traditional disputes between them and Christian Armenians and Georgians intensified after 1990.

Although many look at the events in this region and see issues of power and security, war and peace, many others look and see issues of autonomy and independence, freedom and community. A relatively complete understanding requires examination through both sets of lenses. Comprehension, however, requires even more.

ECONOMIC ASPECTS

A period of poor economic performance preceded and accompanied the revolutions. Economic growth of the region was weaker throughout the 1980s than it had been earlier. Exact figures are uncertain because the Communist governments often used statistics to trumpet achievements, including some "achievements" that never existed. The fact that the East was falling steadily behind the West was, however, apparent to anyone who could make comparisons through books and magazines, television and movies, or travel.

The Communist governments had many real economic success stories in earlier years. They built heavy industry and infrastructure (for instance, highways, railroads, and power grids). In the mid-1960s the Soviet Union boasted of its achievements in industrialization and pointed to a growth rate that surpassed that of the United States. They proved much less competent, however, as the nature of the leading world economies shifted from industry to services and information. Central planning proved more capable of replicating large industrial complexes than of establishing systems to serve either producers or consumers quickly and flexibly.

In the late 1970s and early 1980s several Eastern European countries began to look to the West for economic assistance in the form of loans to help them overcome relative economic stagnation. Several took on substantial debt. The repression that the Romanian leadership applied to its people, and which required bloodshed to overthrow, grew in part from an effort to repay that debt quickly. Poland and Hungary had especially substantial debt burdens and continued efforts to reorganize their economies so as to repay those debts. That helps us understand why those two countries blazed the trail during this revolutionary period toward market economies, oriented toward the West and exports.

The trade-offs involved in reorienting economies to the West are complex, however. At least in the short term, and perhaps for a considerable period, those countries require aid, investments, loans, and technical assistance; and they are at a significant disadvantage in Western markets. This establishes relationships of some dependence and inequality with Western Europe. There are inevitably some tensions in interactions characterized by such unequal vulnerability.

Many important economic questions thus appeared on the agenda of countries during this period. How rapidly should formerly Communist countries with state ownership of all major economic assets shift those assets and the responsibility for economic decision making to private individuals and firms? How should they balance the benefits of reform against the probable unemployment that would result from it? How rapidly should they open their economies to those of the West, risking dependence to gain the benefits of foreign trade and technology? On the Western side, should the United States and Western Europe provide massive programs of economic aid? What should the conditions be?

These questions raise issues of economic well-being and growth, and of distribution (within and between countries). The ongoing debates about these issues will greatly influence the course of the unfinished revolutions.

BROADER ENVIRONMENT

A fuller understanding of these spectacular events also requires that we look at a broader environment including developments in population, food, energy, and the biologic-physical environment. A focus on demographic factors provides some insights. For example, in Romania a negative population growth rate led the regime to ban abortion and to actively encourage births. The repressive methods it used in this effort were among the factors that encouraged the revolt. Similarly, in the Soviet Union, the greater birth rates of non-Russian peoples, especially the Islamic populations, both strengthened their position and raised Russian fears of becoming a minority in their own country.

Another aspect of the broader environment, food, was especially important in setting the stage for the revolutions. The systems of collective agriculture in the East proved incapable of improving the diets of the people, much less of sustaining the region's traditional position as the breadbasket of Europe. In general, access to a diverse and attractive diet improved as one traveled from east to west in the Communist region and approached the conditions available in Western Europe. The people were aware of this pattern and saw the West as a model for their own agriculture.

Energy was a factor of great importance. The Soviet Union (especially Russia) was the world's largest producer of both oil and natural gas. It still supplies a large portion of the energy of Central Europe and exports some to Western Europe. On the one hand, this provided a basis to Russia for considerable leverage over its neighbors. For many years it has paid a cost to maintain this leverage, because it effectively subsidized the energy systems of its fellow Soviet republics and allies by trading its oil for relatively inferior goods (by world standards) made in Central Europe. On the other hand, however, Russia theoretically had the option of selling its energy, its largest export, for Western currency and then using that currency for imports of food, high-quality goods, and technology from the West. Many have wondered why Russia not only proved willing to allow its former Central European "satellites" and sister republics to improve relations with the West but effectively encouraged them to do so. One reason is that this allowed Russia to begin charging those countries for oil and other raw materials at world prices in Western currency. In short, Russia began to use its energy for the purchase of Western goods rather than for the purchase of political-economic control. This change also allowed Russia to have access to Western technology for its oil fields at a time when its own proved inadequate to sustain production levels.

The condition of the biologic-physical environment also enters into a more complete understanding of the revolutions. The emphasis of Communist governments on heavy industry (using rather old technology), combined with a suppression of mechanisms that people might have used to protest deteriorating local environmental conditions, led to wide-scale abuse of the environment throughout Central and Eastern Europe. Some of the earliest protests against Communist rule emphasized the need to protect the environment. Some of the first opposition parties throughout the region were "greens"—made up of environmental activists. In Bulgaria, "Ecoglasnost" played an important role in overthrowing the communist leadership of Zhikov. In Hungary, the struggle against a dam on the Danube honed political skills later used for more general reform efforts (French 1990).

Only joint attention to strictly political elements (both domestic and foreign), economic factors, and a broader environment can provide a fairly complete understanding of events and issues in world politics. Each of these categories, however, contains a tremendous mass of potential information—this sketch of the background and aftermath of the revolutions of 1989–1992 has conveyed only a small part of it. How can we more systematically approach world politics, so that in attempting to understand a new issue or episode we know what to look for and how to organize it? That is the subject of the next section.

A STRUCTURE OF UNDERSTANDING

A systematic study of international relations cannot consist solely of individual case studies that treat every episode of international relations in isolation. Fundamentally we want to generalize. For instance, we want a more general understanding of dramatic transformations in political relations—one that might allow us to see the similarities and differences between contemporary events and those at the end of World War II (sketched briefly in Chapter 1). We want more general understanding so that we might anticipate such transformations and so that we can make them as peaceful as possible. Similarly, we seek to generalize concerning crises, alliances, treaties, wars, and other interactions among countries. To do so we need some additional tools. We need to reflect on how we understand and generalize.[7]

Figure 2.2 portrays a hierarchy of understanding that structures our knowledge about international relations and our generalizations concerning it. At the most basic level are raw data or unpatterned **facts**: Gorbachev came to power in the Soviet Union in 1985. Reagan advocated and led a substantial U.S. military buildup in the 1980s. The Soviet Union revised its constitution in late 1988. The Hungarians initiated economic reforms earlier than other Central European countries. The U.S.S.R. produced more oil and gas than any other country.

Such facts are critical to our understanding, but they are only a beginning. If our knowledge about the revolutions of 1989–1992 were limited to facts, we might be good at answering trivia questions about them, but we would have no basis for saying anything about the period after World War II. One of the most basic ways in which we organize facts and extend our knowledge is via concepts. **Concepts** are labels for a general category of phenomena. An important concept in both periods (post–World War II and the late 1980s) is power. A discussion of the power of the United States, the U.S.S.R., and countries in Western and Central Europe helps organize facts important to our understanding of the events and outcomes. Defining power satisfactorily and measuring it pose considerable difficulty but are essential for discussion of a broad range of phenomena in world politics. Chapter 4 will discuss alternative definitions and measurements.

Just as facts have little or no meaning without concepts, concepts individually have limited use. Assume for the moment that we have defined power in terms of military capabilities and agree that the U.S.S.R. had several times as much power as the countries of Central Europe in the late 1980s. This concept of power takes on real meaning only when it is linked in **propositions** to other concepts, such as success or failure in the accomplishment of objectives. Voltaire nicely summarized a proposition linking the two concepts (power and success) when he supposedly said that God is always on the side of the larger battalions (Ray 1990, 198). That is, greater power most often facilitates accomplishment of objectives. The fact that the U.S.S.R. failed to sustain its domination of the region seems to contradict this proposition. However, Soviet power had slipped relative to that of countries in Western Europe, which competes in many ways for influence in Central Europe. Such analysis might lead us to a second, related proposition: Third parties often enter into power struggles in support of the weaker party and thereby offset the power of the stronger party.

---

[7]The approach to understanding sketched here and applied in subsequent chapters has deep roots in the positivist, scientific (behavioral) tradition. Although making room for alternative and competing understandings of reality, it ultimately assumes a single objective reality that can be better understood by decomposing that reality, examining the elements of it, and studying the relationships among those elements. Although the approach treats values as appropriate and necessary subject matter, it seeks to avoid value commitments during analysis. While fundamentally behavioral, this book draws also on the philosophical-historical approach of traditionalists. It tries to be sensitive to the radical school (described by Alker and Biersteker 1984). The appendix to Chapter 13 anticipates some of the methodological criticism.

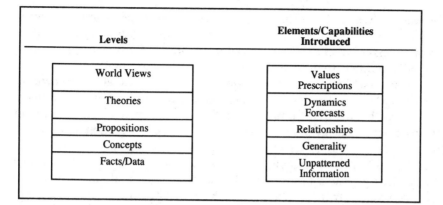

FIGURE 2.2 Hierarchy of Understanding

Propositions, when linked together in clusters and used to explain or predict, constitute **theory**. A theory such as one that clusters related propositions on the utility of power provides explanations of international events. Often it assists in understanding the unfolding of events over time—the dynamics of them. It should, if the theory is "good," also carry some predictive capability, for instance, the ability to foresee the most probable outcomes of future power struggles. This text also highlights names of theories, such as the greenhouse effect (see Chapter 1) or the balance of power, in bold-face type when it first explains them.

Worldviews selectively choose among competing theories. Two bases for the selection stand out. First, alternative worldviews emphasize different basic agents or units of analysis. Although one may emphasize states (countries) and their interactions, another may draw our attention to individuals in communities, and a third to economic actors and markets.[8] Second, and related, competing worldviews highlight different values (both those of agents and those of worldview adherents). Although one worldview may stress the value countries place on security, another may focus on the desire of individuals in ethnic communities for independence or autonomy.

Values add a prescriptive element to worldviews that is missing from theories.[9] Theories explain and perhaps predict, but worldviews also prescribe. When an emphasis on theory concerning the efficacy of power is combined with a value judgment that the use of force is not inherently wrong, the combination

---

[8]Analysis within each worldview often proceeds at more than one level of analysis, for instance at both an individual agent (state, class, individual, or firm) level and a systemic level (state system, class structure, community, or market). That is, levels of analysis do not distinguish worldviews as is sometimes argued.

[9]Worldviews have much in common with paradigms but the typical definition of paradigms (Kuhn 1970) recognizes neither the attention to the different agents nor the role of values. Ferguson and Mansbach (1988) correctly stress the necessity of addressing values in social science (see also Holsti 1985, 132–133). Banks (1984) summarizes how the study of world politics evolved toward the formulation of competing worldviews and how it needs a more integrated perspective; this book seeks to move towards such integration.

becomes a worldview. That particular worldview led some observers of the revolutions in 1989–1992 to interpret them as a successful outcome of pressure applied on the U.S.S.R. by the United States and its European allies during a long period and intensified by the U.S. military buildup of the 1980s.

Conversely, it is possible to reject the utility of a theory based on power in understanding what happened during this period. An observer could instead reasonably argue that the transformation was the result of growing global commitment to basic human rights, including democracy and a communication of that same attachment to Central and Eastern Europe by international agreements and interpersonal contacts, facilitated by ongoing social mobilization and economic decline in the East. These views appeared to strongly influence Gorbachev and many other Communist leaders. In other words, a theoretical understanding of how the world works that downplays power and emphasizes growing global community and protection of individual rights, combined with a value orientation that decries the use of violence, provides a different "understanding" of the period.[10]

CLASH OF PERSPECTIVES: COMPETING WORLDVIEWS

The hierarchy of understanding should make somewhat clearer the constant tension that exists in the study of international relations between facts and interpretation. If our study of the subject matter required only facts, we could potentially all have the same understanding of world politics. *Facts do not speak for themselves, however.* They are organized by concepts, structured by theories, interpreted by worldviews, and evaluated in the light of individual and subjective value systems.

Some argue that this places students of world politics in the position of the blind men and the elephant, each touching a different part of the elephant and interpreting the entire beast in terms of the treelike leg, the ropelike tail, or the fanlike ear. That is a poor analogy. We can exchange facts and thereby gain a broader perspective. We can argue about concepts and definitions, and generally agree on some useful ones. We can build, present, debate, and test theories, ultimately expanding the understanding of all engaged in the enterprise. We can even attempt to identify our own values and the worldviews linked to them, and to communicate those to others. In all these ways, international relations becomes a more scientific, and a more nearly universal, body of knowledge.

We will never all come to share the same values or perspectives, however, and there will always be a clash of perspectives. As a result, in policy debates we will continue to choose differentially among bodies of theory, concepts, and facts. Our task in the study of international relations is complicated. We want to identify as large a body of "knowledge" as possible. We never want to forget, however, that perspectives clash strongly, even in the face of our large and growing knowledge. We clearly need to study competing perspectives as well. As an aid to doing all of that, this text first

---

[10]The meaning, importance, and relationship of concepts, theories, and values deserve much more attention than they can receive in this book. Garnett (1984) provides a valuable treatment.

identifies six worldviews that dominate interpretation of international relations for many North Americans and Europeans. Because individual worldviews are complex and highly differentiated, these are simplified, even caricatured worldviews. Nonetheless, both scholars and practitioners recognize these views to be coherent and important. Identifying them allows us to proceed further to outline the theories, concepts, and facts on which they draw. Each of the three succeeding parts of this volume on international politics, political economy, and the broader environmental context of international politics, presents two primary worldviews.[11]

REALISM AND IDEALISM

Realism portrays the world political system as an anarchic struggle for power and security among competing states (countries). No higher authority (at least none with any real capability to enforce its judgment) exists than these states. Thus states individually, or in alliance with other states, provide for their own defense. Power is the only effective means of assuring security. Because each state's efforts to increase its own power and security pose a potential threat to each other state, regular conflict among states is inevitable. This description of the world also frames the realist's prescription—security and peace follow only from vigilance and willingness to act individually or in concert to prevent any state from achieving a preeminent and threatening position.

If you see the outlines of the stalemated power struggle between the U.S.S.R. and the United States after 1945 in this portrayal of the world, you are right. In the United States, the prevailing wisdom was that it should maintain sufficient military power (in alliances, if not alone) to prevent any significant gains by the U.S.S.R. "The condition upon which God hath given liberty to man is eternal vigilance." (Curran 1790). The U.S.S.R. obviously has had its own realists. A principal lesson that both countries drew from World War II was that power was not mobilized adequately and early enough against the enemy, in that case Hitler's Germany.

Although the realist perspective will hold our attention in several early chapters, it is not without challengers, and they, too, merit our consideration. **Idealism** suggests that there are reasons to believe that the dominant global role of states (countries) might be weakening. The United Nations, as an institution of developing global community, is unable to dictate the terms of agreements among countries, but it brings considerable pressure to bear on some disputes. International law, including a growing web of treaties between the United States and Russia, increasingly constrains individual country action. In addition, international commerce has grown so rapidly in the last thirty years, that it, too, places some limits on individual state action. Thus,

[11]In the remaining pages of this chapter, we present a brief "preview" of all worldviews. There is little agreement in the discipline of international relations concerning the major worldviews or paradigms and their relationships to each other. For a brief but useful summary of proposed typologies see Holsti (1985, 5–7). Lapid (1989) indicates the confusion that alternative paradigms, competing underlying premises, and pluralism in methodology have introduced to the field. The presentation in this volume may help clarify the issue through its specification of the conceptual, theoretical, and value bases of each worldview.

idealists say, we should describe the world not *only* in terms of state interaction but also in terms of increasing community.

It is also questionable whether states actually make foreign policy in the cool, calculated manner, (considering only power balances), that realists describe. The roles of bureaucracy, public opinion, and individual leader personalities are sufficiently important to cast doubt on that rather mechanical image of governmental decision making.

Even among those who see in the realist description a relatively convincing portrayal of the way the world actually works, there are many who question the morality or even sanity of realism as a prescription for action. Especially in an age when war between the states possessing nuclear weapons could unleash mutual destruction, the ongoing power struggle promised by realists appears to many as a disaster waiting to happen. Thus some idealists may not believe that the global community is yet able to restrict state action, but they wish to make it do so.

LIBERALISM AND STRUCTURALISM

Liberalism offers an understanding of economic aspects of world politics. Lest the term be confusing, we should note immediately that it does not refer to "liberal" in the sense of the American liberal-conservative political spectrum. It means liberal in a "classical" sense: those who believe, like Adam Smith did, that markets free of government control provide economic benefits for all participants and maximize aggregate economic well-being.

There is significant overlap between realist and liberal perceptions of the world. Both place a premium on rational, self-interested action by major actors. From the viewpoint of realists and liberals, that behavior not only provides benefits to individual states or producers and consumers, but also provides collective benefits for all. This is best known in the liberal theory of laissez faire. By attempting to maximize profit as a producer or utility as a consumer, these actors assure greater production and more efficient use of resources. For instance, a producer might develop a new technology or discover a low-cost resource from which it profits handsomely, but that also provides real benefits to others who eventually adopt the technology or profit from the low production costs associated with it. Similarly, in international politics, states may attempt to provide only for their own security, but in so doing they maintain a broader balance of power that benefits other states.

There are significant differences as well, however, between realist and liberal perspectives. Realists perceive a relatively fixed amount of security in the system, and view shifts in power and security on the part of one state as mirror images of shifts in power and security on the part of other states. This is called a win-lose or **zero-sum** perspective, because the value of changes sum to zero cross all actors. In contrast, liberals believe all actors can *simultaneously* increase their economic well-being (a win-win or **nonzero-sum** orientation).

Most fundamentally, the two worldviews divide the world in dramatically different ways. Country boundaries are fundamental and essentially impermeable for realists. For liberals, state boundaries are at best a nuisance, and at worst a serious threat to the efficient operation of markets. In fact, for liberals, states pose a threat both internationally, where they often restrict trade and almost always restrict the movement of labor and capital, and domestically, where they frequently interfere in markets through regulation or even state production.

Yet realism and liberalism both constitute highly popular worldviews (at least in some parts of the world), and adherents thus must be able somehow to reconcile their differences. They do so primarily by maintaining a relatively strong intellectual division between politics and economics. For realists, politics is the realm of states and power. For liberals, economics is the realm of producers, consumers, and markets. Thus do realists and liberals easily coexist.

This state-market or political-economic separation is at the core of challenges to liberalism. One can argue that states can, do, and should use the economy as a tool for its own purposes. If economic strength contributes to military capability, and it is difficult to dispute that it does, then perhaps the state should consciously strengthen the economy. The state might accomplish this, for example, through higher tariffs (taxes on imports) to keep the goods of other economies out and to encourage higher production of domestic factories. Although liberals disagree that such "help" actually improves economic performance in the long run, states have a long history of engaging in just such activity. Japan and South Korea are only recent examples of countries where the government has played an active role in building the economy. This challenge to liberalism reintroduces zero-sum thought—one state and its economy can do well at the expense of other states and their economies. Because the emphasis is on state control and objectives, this challenge to liberalism is in many respects an extension of realism. Its name is **mercantilism**.

Another challenge to liberalism does not portray the economy as the instrument of the state but sees instead the state as an instrument of economic agents. Many variations on this challenge have roots in the Marxist argument that the nature of economic production determines social and political relations. A traditional agricultural society generates a feudal division between those who work the land and the aristocrats who own it, and who simultaneously and derivatively hold political control. The rise of capitalism created a division between those who worked in the new industries and the capitalists or bourgeoisie who owned them; the capitalists successfully supplanted the aristocrats in political leadership. Once in control of the state, this class has used state power to protect its domestic prerogatives and to expand its foreign opportunities (markets, raw material access, and investment outlets). Thus, a global structure has arisen in which those who own capital and those who do not remain both bound together and in natural opposition. We call this worldview **structuralism**.

Were this a text written from a realist perspective, we would restrict discussions largely to the high politics of security-seeking behavior and power-based relationships and downplay economic issues. In reality, however, international economic issues are at the top of the agenda in political relationships among North America, Western

Europe, and Japan; and between North and South America. Liberal, mercantilist, and structuralist views on those relationships demand our attention.

MODERNISM AND ECOHOLISM

Modernism is one primary worldview with respect to the environmental context of world politics and global economics. Modernists draw our attention to the concept of progress—to the increasing human mastery of physical and bio-logic environments. Regular breakthroughs in technology play a central role in this advance.

Modernists point to the steady extension of life spans, in Europe initially but now worldwide, as a key indicator of progress. Life spans respond to progress in diverse arenas, especially conquering or controlling diseases and ensuring adequate shelter and food to greater percentages of humans globally. Modernism is nonzero sum, because technology or knowledge is easily transmitted and provides comparable benefits to all who share in it. Prescriptively, modernists argue that states and economic actors should not impede technological progress, and should, in fact, further it.

Challengers to modernism point to environmental problems against which technology appears to be making little progress, or which technology may actually exacerbate, and they emphasize the close relationship between humans and their ecosystem; we call this view **ecoholism**. Of central importance in many challenges is the global population explosion accompanying the demographic transition. According to ecoholists, increased population has created or intensified many environmental problems—not just pollution, but pressure on food production capability and raw material availability. Human beings, they argue, are part of an ecosystem on which they now place demands that are too great.

Ecoholists have a generally zero-sum view of the world. Raw materials like oil, natural gas, copper, and chromium have fixed material endowments, and thus their use deprives others, including future generations, of them. Land, too, is in fixed supply as are the inputs, such as fertilizers, that allow more productive use of it. Clean air and water exist in limited quantity. Both increased population and increased economic activity accelerate depletion or despoliation of the broader environment.

The modernist perspective encourages decoupling of the study of interna-tional politics from consideration of the environment or ecosystem, just as the liberal perspective encourages decoupling of politics from the economy. If the environment places no real limits on human beings, and if, in fact, its fruits are increasingly abundant and easily harvested, then political struggles over the environment can be avoided—we can all (as states, producers, or consumers) take more. If the ecoholists are correct, however, scarcity will intensify rather than lessen, and the environment could become the source of complex interstate strug-gles. After all, what could be of greater interest to countries than inexpensive food supplies or adequate availability of energy? Although some ecoholists believe that states may cooperatively address these issues, many others think that conflict about scarce resources is more likely. In either case, ecoholists argue, international relations cannot ignore the environment.

ORGANIZATION OF THE BOOK

The structure of this book builds on the presentation of this chapter. It has three parts of unequal length. Part One (the longest) focuses centrally on the political-military issues of war and peace. It approaches these issues by first presenting the concepts and theoretical arguments of a realist perspective: states, power, balances of power, and theories of conflict based on these concepts. It proceeds next to elaborate various idealist perspectives, focusing on global, regional, and local communities. In Part Two the spotlight shifts to economic issues of growth and equity, and to their relationships with international politics. That part puts forward, in turn, the liberal, mercantilist, and structuralist views. It thus juxtaposes views of the world centered on markets with those focusing on state interaction and on political-economic structures. Finally, Part Three takes us to the broader environment, to the issues of progress and resource scarcity, and to the linkages between these issues and both international politics and economics. The modernists speak first in that part, expounding on the contributions of growth in knowledge; the ecoholists respond, detailing the human role in ecosystems.

The central place this international relations text gives to the clash of perspectives differentiates it from most others.[12] Some texts first detail international actors (states, international organizations like the United Nations, multinational corporations) and then proceed to discuss interactions among those actors (conflict, diplomacy, trade, aid). A few look in turn at relationships between and within different groupings of countries (Communist versus non-Communist or economically developed versus developing). Still others provide a chronological description of world events, perhaps since World War II. Many books use some combination of these approaches. This book portrays the world in terms of powerful substructural forces (as sketched in Chapter 1) interacting with the more apparent superstructure of world politics. Different observers see that superstructure (and what we know of its interaction with substructural forces) from six competing perspectives—the worldviews outlined here.

There was a period in the study of international relations when the belief in an emerging science of politics was so strong that scholars might have considered the introduction of competing, value-laden worldviews an admission of defeat. There is only one world, the scientist argues, and therefore we need only seek the one accurate description of it.[13] This author, like many others, refuses to abandon the attempt to discover that one true world but must simultaneously recognize two realities. First, the world may be so complex that we can benefit from looking

---

[12]See, however, Viotti and Kauppi (1987), McKinlay and Little (1986), and Frieden and Lake (1987) for texts or readers that present competing worldviews.

[13]That orientation led us to present competing "approaches" or "prototheories" of the world, and to search among them for the most useful.

at it through different lenses or at different angles. Second, accidents of our birth and upbringing (for instance, our country of origin and social position) leave us predisposed to adopt only one perspective and to be certain that we have the best view. Both realities suggest the importance of consciously identifying and separately considering a variety of viewpoints. All you need do is read a newspaper or watch the evening news to discover the ongoing clash of perspectives concerning world politics. This book should help you understand the different perspectives—the worldviews—underlying that clash.

Chapter 3

REALISM
AND IDEALISMS

The world is a dangerous place. In 1990 thirty-one civil and international wars were under way and had claimed cumulative casualties of 2.3 million combatants and civilians. Wars have killed about 142 million people since 1500 (Sivard 1991, 20). Some of the most pressing questions facing humanity are: What causes war? What brings peace? How can we achieve some level of international security?

Two worldviews, realism and idealism, help us address those questions, and this chapter sketches the way in which they do so. The remaining chapters in Part One of the book will detail the manner in which the worldviews introduced here interpret the world.

REALISM

Realism is an influential worldview. The attention scholars of world politics give to this view, its elaboration in the most popular text of the post–World War II era, and the self-conscious attention to its precepts by practitioners like Richard Nixon and Henry Kissinger, attest to that importance.[1]

Realism offers a reasonably parsimonious (simple) worldview that explains a large portion of world politics. Although realists share a relatively simple framework, they elaborate their understanding in individualistic and often complex ways. This chapter portrays this basic worldview, and subsequent chapters will indicate its diversity.

CONCEPTS

Two types of concepts help define realism (and the worldviews to follow): agents or other fundamental units of analysis, and the bases of interaction among

---

[1]See Morgenthau (1973, originally 1948); Lijphart (1981) calls it the "traditional paradigm." Holsti (1985) indicates its influence. Vasquez (1983) identifies and examines its key building blocks. E. H. Carr (1964, originally 1939, vii) also reinforces its importance in his famous study of 1919–1939, written "with the deliberate aim of counteracting the glaring and dangerous defect of nearly all thinking, both academic and popular, about international politics in English-speaking countries from 1919 to 1939—the almost total neglect of the factor of power."

these agents. Theoretical structures within worldviews build on these agents and their interactions.

The unit of analysis at the core of realism is the conflict group, the modern manifestation of which is the **state**.[2] A state is fundamentally what we normally call a country, and we will use the terms interchangeably (and define state more precisely later). Realists portray the state as a unitary actor that speaks with one voice and acts without internal dissension on international issues. In addition, they suggest that states are rational in the pursuit of their **state interests**, primarily security and autonomy.[3] Both the unitary and rationality assumptions are ideals that no state can fully attain. Realists know these to be simplifications of reality but do not view them as brutal ones; moreover, they believe that such simplification adds great power to their theory (see Gilpin 1981, 18–19). Many extensions to the basic realist perspective are friendly amendments to these two assumptions.

Although realist thought begins with the state, much of that thought focuses not on individual states but rather on the structure in which they function, the state system.[4] A **system** is a set of units or actors and the interactions among them; the **state system** is the collection of states in the world and their interactions. For analysts who believe that the system determines the behavior of the individual components, rather than the reverse, the state system becomes the central unit of analysis.[5] Many system-oriented or structural realists (Waltz 1979) emphasize that a state system without central authority is a world of **anarchy**. That systemic condition, and particularly the requirement it places on states to guard their own interests, shapes much of realist thought.

Even fundamentally good individuals, in an anarchic environment, act from self-interest in ways that endanger the interests of others (for instance, by becoming better with a gun, as seen in the early days of the American West). Similarly, an innocent attempt by a state to assure its own security by increasing its weaponry will invariably threaten the security of other states. This inability to protect oneself without threatening others is known as the **security dilemma**.

In economics, money is central to interactions among firms and households, which are basic units of analysis. Realists agree with the popular statement that

---

[2]Even realists question the long-run viability of states. Morgenthau in 1961 wrote of "the contrast between the technological unification of the world and the parochial moral commitments and political institutions of the age" (Smith 1986, 224).

[3]Rationality is often difficult to determine. We generally attempt to measure it against goals that are seldom as simple and as clearly specified as necessary to assess levels of rationality accurately. Common usage sometimes assumes information, for instance about policy outcomes, which is in actuality not available. No realist assumes an omniscient rationality; all accept a bounded rationality, a subject to which we return in Chapter 7.

[4]Each of the worldviews of this text draws attention to an agent and a structure. Relative emphasis on agents and structures varies across worldviews and among proponents of any given one. Hence "structural realism" stresses the state-system level of analysis and more traditional realism focuses on the state. Chapters in the Czempiel and Rosenau volume (1989) emphasize the importance of considering both state and state system.

[5]Kaplan's study (1957) has this general character, as does much of Waltz (1979). Realists often move easily (perhaps too easily) between state and state system as levels of analysis.

"power is the currency of politics." That is, **power** is the basis of interaction among states. (The next chapter defines this central concept.) States use power in pursuit of their interests, on the basis of rational calculations. Obviously, there are times when the interests of states collide, and at such times conflict is possible.

Table 3.1 summarizes the conceptual basis of both realism and idealism. It organizes the entire discussion of this chapter and should be a useful reference throughout.

TABLE 3.1
Political Behavior Worldviews

Worldview Name(s)	Realism	Idealisms: nationalism; religious idealism; universalisms: Marxisms; globalism
Central Concepts Agents/Structures	States; state system; anarchy	Communities
Values of Agents	State Interests: security, autonomy, power	Unity, autonomy
Central Concepts: Bases of Interaction	Power; rational individualistic behavior; security dilemma	Within community cooperation; collective action Outside community exclusion; conversion; conquest
Theories: Systemic Dynamic Descriptions	Balance of power; coalition behavior; hegemonic theory; cooperation on mutual interests	Capture of state; community building; state building
Theories: Typical Forecasts	Same as the past	Consolidation and institutionalization of community
Values of World- View Proponents	Stablility, relative peace	Globalists global community; peace
Typical Prescriptions	Protect, enhance power	Globalists create global community; create global institutions

THEORIES

Theories explain the dynamic interactions of rational, self-interested states in an environment of anarchy. Foremost among these is the **action-reaction dynamic**. States finding themselves in an environment of anarchy and therefore in a security dilemma often view the acts of other states as potentially threatening and react by increasing their own defense. Other states, in turn, can view these decisions as threatening and react with further measures to enhance security. Arms races frequently result.

More than two states interact in most state systems, and they often counter the actions of others not simply with their own actions, but through the building of alliances. Either unilaterally or collectively they seek to balance power with power, to pursue a **balance of power**. Theories of alliances or coalitions among states thus become important in realism. In addition, although the general character of the state system remains stable over time, individual states may rise and fall in power relative to others. In some cases, like that of the United States after World War II, states may even assume a **hegemonic** or dominant position. Realists naturally seek theoretically to explain such fluctuations in position within the state system and their consequences for the conflict level in the system.

Although much of the emphasis of realists has traditionally been on conflict among states, they recognize that even self-serving states can rationally cooperate in pursuit of mutual interests. Cooperation can extend to various security (arms control), economic (trade), and environmental (pollution control) issues. Much realist thought in recent years addresses such cooperation.

Change is important to realists, but they place greater emphasis on continuity. Realist views of history often begin and end with characterizations of power, power balances, and struggles for security. Realists foresee the same kind of interstate struggle in the future.

VALUES AND PRESCRIPTIONS

Values are fundamental to politics, which generally involves struggles over them. To do justice to the subject we must distinguish between the value orientations of the participants in the processes we describe and those of the observer or analyst.[6] With respect to realism, this means identifying both the values of states (the central actors for realists) and the normative orientations of realists themselves.[7]

[6]Discussions of politics frequently omit treatment of values. The failure to distinguish between values of actors and those of worldview proponents (except perhaps with respect to liberalism) further confuses many discussions of values.

[7]The importance of values is a reason this book uses "worldview" in preference to "paradigm." The concern with paradigms in international politics comes from the important work of Kuhn (1970), who detailed a theory of paradigm development and shift in the physical sciences, and suggested that the absence of a substantial base of accepted theory in social science follows from its pre-paradigmatic state. Paradigms in physical sciences, however, normally lack the value and prescriptive elements that are fundamentally important to worldviews in social science (although the clash between Ptolemaic and Copernican universes was not free of religious and secular values). An explanation for the scarcity of *accepted* theory in social science (at the same time that there is *proliferation* of concepts, approaches, and partial theories) is the linkage of social science theories to worldviews with competing value and prescriptive elements.

Realists identify security and the pursuit of autonomy as the central values of states.[8] Because realists emphasize the security and autonomy goals of states, critics sometimes mistakenly characterize realists as being insensitive to the value of peace—even as being amoral. Actually, there are few in this world who do not value peace highly (unless perhaps, as we pointed out before, they feel oppressed). Realists argue, however, that attention by states to peace above attention to power and the preservation of security often leads to the loss of all three. Power deters other states from aggression better than declarations of peaceful intent.

Systemic stability and relative peace are important to realists, and realists (as opposed to the states they describe) are definitely not amoral.[9] Realists believe that self-interested state behavior will lead to a greater degree of systemic peace and individual security than will policies based on universalistic moral standards, which are almost inevitably accompanied by attempts to impose those standards on others. The distinction between the amorality of the prescription for state action and the moral basis of the ultimate aim is not unlike that in free-market capitalism. Although proponents of capitalism expect, even exhort, individual firms and households to act only from self-interest, the "invisible hand" of the market is supposed to produce greater economic benefits for all. Attention to the greater overall economic and physical security of humankind attests to the moral concern of both free-market and realism proponents (although the poor and powerless sometimes doubt their sincerity).[10]

Fundamental to an understanding of the morality of realists is recognition that the clashes of the world often do not involve right versus wrong, or the "good guys" versus the "bad guys," as in a movie about the old American West. They often pit right against right, as in the mutual historical claims of Jews and Palestinians to the same land in the Middle East, or wrong against wrong, as in the war between Nazi Germany and Stalinist Russia. For statesmen, choices may be almost impossible to sort out in moral terms. Moreover, because one side's right is the other side's wrong, attempts to base state action on morality will often create conflict rather than ameliorate it. These considerations drive realists back to security and autonomy as the legitimate basis for state action.

IMPORTANT CONTRIBUTIONS TO REALIST THOUGHT

Thucydides (ca. 460 to 400 B.C.), the chronicler of the Peloponnesian Wars between the alliances led by ancient Athens and Sparta, has become the spiritual father of realism. As Smith (1986, 4) notes, the most often cited sentence of

[8]Realists often claim that states primarily seek power (not security or autonomy). As Keohane (1983b, 515) points out, that assertion is inconsistent with their own balance of power theory in which states "moderate their efforts when their positions are secure."

[9]Bull (1977, 16–20) places "order" at the center of a realist's goal structure. He defines order in terms of preservation of the state system, state autonomy, peace (not universal and permanent, but in the context of state preservation), limitation of violence, and protection of property (including spheres of influence).

[10]Moreover, critics argue that amoral behavior in markets eventually destroys community values, such as trust, which initially provide a social basis for markets (Hirsch 1976; Bell 1976). One could similarly argue that unbridled pursuit of power corrodes the operation of power balancing.

Thucydides is "What made war inevitable was the growth of Athenian power and the fear which this caused in Sparta." Although far more in his writing marks him as a realist, that one sentence emphasizes his attention to power, to the city-state level of analysis (within a systemic context), and to the fundamental importance of security.

This early realist also recognized the highly limited role of moral behavior in the relationships among states. The demands by Athens on Melos, a city-state that refused Athenian demands to contribute to its alliance, stripped away any pretense of morality from the bases of interstate relations:

> We on our side will use no fine phrases, since you know as well as we do that, when these matters are discussed by practical people, the standard of justice depends on the equality of power to compel and that in fact the strong do what they have the power to do and the weak accept what they have to accept. (quoted in Smith 1986, 6)

Thucydides may have had misgivings about that aspect of international relations.[11] The infamous advice that Machiavelli (1469–1527) provided his prince, however, further stamped early realist thought as amoral:

> it is honourable to seem mild, and merciful, and courteous, and religious, and sincere, and indeed to be so, provided your mind be so rectified and prepared that you can act quite contrary on occasion. [A prince is] oftentimes necessitated, for the preservation of his State, to do things inhuman, uncharitable, and irregular.... (Machiavelli 1513)

The interests of the state, fundamentally its security (the *raison d'état*), justified for Machiavelli nearly any action by its leader. A republican in much of his writing, his life experiences best explain Machiavelli's support for a strong and amoral prince. He entered public life in 1494, the year of the French king Charles VIII's invasion of Machiavelli's state, Florence. He eventually served Florence as defense minister and in many other capacities. Looking back for inspiration to the period of Roman greatness, he built a militia based on the citizenry rather than on mercenaries. Throughout his career he faced and opposed the French occupation of Northern Italy and the growing intrusion of Spain. In 1502 he was sent as envoy to Cesare Borgia, then at the peak of his power and cunning. Borgia, despite Machiavelli's early reservations about him, became the model of Machiavelli's ideal prince because he proved successful in consolidating several Italian city-states. In short, Machiavelli believed that Italy needed unification to withstand foreign force, and that realistically this could only come under a strong and sometimes amoral or even immoral prince.

Thomas Hobbes (1588–1679) added a systemic perspective to the realist worldview through his thought experiments concerning a "state of nature." He asked us to imagine the anarchy in a society without central government to provide order, and he described the wretchedness of existence in such a society. His major work *Leviathan* appeared in 1651, following many years of English civil war and

---

[11]Craig and George (1983) characterize such equation of power with license as "vulgar realism."

the execution of the king in 1649. The book called for civil society to give over control to central government, even if that government is a leviathan or monster, in return for an order that makes life not only bearable but also possible. Like Thucydides (whose work Hobbes translated), Machiavelli, and all other political philosophers, Hobbes was influenced by the events raging around him; these led him to propose a strong civil social order (even if not terribly enlightened) as an alternative to anarchy.[12]

Hobbes rooted his thought about the state of nature in an understanding of human nature, which he argued flowed from the working of appetites. Some realists even more strongly tie their thought to a negative characterization of human nature. Theologian Reinhold Niebuhr, who wrote before and after World War II, referred to human nature as "the rock bottom problem" (Smith 1986, 17). He influenced Hans Morgenthau, who in turn wrote the most widely read international politics textbook of the last forty years:

> The history of modern political thought is the story of a contest between two schools that differ fundamentally in their conceptions of the nature of man, society, and politics. One believes that a rational and moral political order, derived from universally valid abstract principles, can be achieved here and now. It assumes the essential goodness and infinite malleability of human nature.... The other school believes that the world, imperfect as it is from the rational point of view, is the result of forces inherent in human nature. To improve the world, one must work with these forces, not against them. (Morgenthau 1973, 3)

Two infamous tyrants, Hitler and Stalin, and the events surrounding World War II, reinforced this common realist emphasis on a fundamentally bad human nature.

The basic concepts and theories of realism do not, however, actually require a negative view of human beings, individually or within states. We earlier discussed the security dilemma. States acting innocently to enhance their own security may threaten that of others and set up an action-reaction dynamic. The insight by realists that structure may matter more than human nature and intentions emerges in a variant called structural realism or **neorealism**. Neorealists introduce two principal elements into the perspective.[13] First, they focus more heavily than traditional realists on systemic structures and the influences these have on state behavior. They direct attention to systemic anarchy, to distribution of capabilities within the system, and to the implications these systemic conditions have for individual state behavior. Second (and related), neorealists take a more theoretical orientation. Rather than simply describing how statesmen pursue state interest (as Machiavelli did), they posit rational, self-serving states interacting in an environment of anarchy, and they seek to deduce typical patterns of interaction.[14]

---

[12]He did not appear to fear broader international anarchy in the same way, perhaps because he did not see the existence of England or the English so threatened by it.

[13]Waltz (1979) has most clearly developed neorealism, without so labeling it. See Ruggie (1983), Ashley (1984), Gilpin (1984), and Walker (1987) for overviews.

[14]Neorealists are thus sometimes called structural realists or structuralists (Keohane 1983b, 1986).

Neorealists need not assume an evil human nature to analyze ongoing conflicts of interest. Greater attention to system structure and theory also provides neorealists a basis for somewhat more extensive consideration of change, an issue to which we will return.

Recognizing that the historic patterns of interstate conflict endanger the very existence of humanity in a world of nuclear weapons, neorealists have also broadened their interests to the study of cooperation. For example, Keohane (1984) has analyzed the implications of changes in systemic structure (for instance, the changing power of the United States) for interstate cooperation on trade and other issues. This attention to cooperation has at times actually blurred the lines between realism and idealism, the worldview we examine next.[15] For the purposes of this text, however, we will initially draw the distinction sharply—whereas all variants of realism begin with self-interested, rational, and unitary states pursuing security in an anarchic environment, idealists direct our attention to communities and community building.

IDEALISMS

Nearly all of the thirty-one wars that raged in 1990 had a domestic or civil war character.[16] Outside actors sometimes fomented or took advantage of the domestic conflict to intervene. Thus realism, which treats states as impermeable wholes (like billiard balls), cannot by itself adequately explain most of those wars. Only one war, the low-level border conflict between India and Pakistan (with an estimated 12,000 fatalities since 1971) was primarily an interstate conflict. Even this conflict had a domestic sideshow in which both adversaries variously used or fought the Kashmiri minorities within their borders.

If "What causes war?" is a central question in world politics, a strictly interstate, power-oriented perspective proves inadequate. Almost all of these wars (civil and interstate) centered on conflicting ideals concerning definition of community and institutional organization of community. **Idealism** is a broad rubric incorporating many variations of belief concerning the appropriate *definition and organization of community*.[17] It helps explain most of these conflicts.

---

[15]Keohane builds on realism and neorealism, but in his attention to institutions moves beyond both, making it difficult to label this school. The introduction of such worldview labels as liberal, neoliberal, and neoliberal institutionalism has increased semantic confusion. "Liberal" frequently appears little more than a synonym for "idealist," adopted probably because of the disfavor in which idealists have found themselves since World War II—the term "liberal" creates unfortunate confusion with the largely economic worldview by the same name, and we will not use it or variants here. Grieco (1988) helps clarify the concepts but draws the boundaries between neoliberal and neorealist more sharply than Keohane (1989, 15), who argues that the former subsumes the latter.

[16]Nietschmann (1987, 7) counts 120 wars with 72 percent being state-nation conflicts.

[17]Alker and Biersteker (1984, 124) prefer "communitarian" to idealist, and define it in terms of a search for "legal, religious, societal, historical or other communitarian bases for international government of some kind." That is a very good label because all of the forms of idealism discussed here do share a focus on the definition of a community. In addition, however, the word "idealism" draws our attention to the political-social organization or governance of community, not just to membership.

Writers often define idealism only in terms of beliefs concerning growth of global community (Herz 1951), what we call globalism. Yet nonglobal communities or identity groups (Burton 1985) attract the primary loyalties of most humans. The best known is the **nation**, an ethnic community with a shared sense of self-identity, such as the Germans or the Palestinians. The conflict between India and Pakistan derived, like that between the Iraqi government and the Kurds, from **nationalism**—from a desire by a people with a sense of self-identity to control their own affairs. Nationalism is a form of idealism. The nationalistic Kurds of Iraq disagree about whether they can accept greater autonomy within the Iraqi state or whether they require their own state. Most, however, are dedicated to some *ideal* of national self-control.[18]

Like the Indian-Pakistani conflict, the one within the Sudan has a religious component as well. The Christians of the south objected strongly when the northern-controlled central government imposed Islamic Law on them. That law violated Christian ideals concerning their community. Although some religious commitment to community ideals is **fundamentalism**, especially when that commitment is to a very strict, limited, and traditional interpretation of the ideal, fundamentalist is too strong a term for those who only seek to protect their religious ideals from outside control. We label this more general phenomenon **religious idealism**.

Still another variant of idealism is **universalism**. When an idealistic commitment is not only to the concept of an extended (ultimately global) community but to a community with a particular form of social organization, whether it be Marxist, capitalist-democratic, or religious, that viewpoint is universalist.[19] Ironically, universalism lies behind large numbers of local and regional conflicts over governmental forms. Universalism periodically also gives rise to some extremely large-scale conflicts. For instance, a clash of universalisms (specifically Marxism versus Western democracy) interacted with the power and security considerations of realists to sustain the cold war. Whether universalisms or power and security issues have been more important in that conflict will be an issue in our subsequent cold war discussion.

Realists frequently portray idealism as a vague, normative striving for peace among states. In reality the peaceful pursuit of democratic global community, a

---

[18]Morgenthau illustrates the relative inattention by realists to the important concepts of nation and nationalism. Not only does he use nation throughout as a synonym for state, but his brief discussion of nationalism portrays it as aberrant behavior:

> The intellectual and political excesses of nationalism and its degenerate offspring, racism, have shocked and repelled the non-nationalistic mind to a much greater degree than have the excesses of geopolitics....The excesses of nationalism...are the logical outgrowth of a secular religion that has engulfed in the fanaticism of holy wars of extermination, enslavement, and world conquest only certain countries, yet has left its mark on many everywhere. (Morgenthau 1973, 161)

[19]With the concept of universalism, the overlap between idealism and ideology becomes obvious. Most definitions of ideology specify that they have a strong action strategy component, centered on a particular vision of the community. Universalisms generally do so. Other idealisms, such as nationalism or globalism, often do not (and are often not classified as ideologies). For instance, many nationalists have little sense of the kind of political community they desire or of how to create it. Universalistic ideologies are a subclass of idealisms.

universalism we call **globalism**, attracts both simplistic advocacy and serious analysis (as does realism).[20] It is important to emphasize the distinction between description and prescription. Realism purports to be primarily a descriptive understanding of the world, portraying and analyzing the reality of state behavior. It fails, however, to describe important aspects of world politics adequately (including the outbreak of war); moreover, it also prescribes how states and their leaders should behave, not being content merely to describe. Various idealisms differ in the degree to which they are analytical or descriptive versus prescriptive, and on the whole they place greater emphasis than realism on elaborating a desired, rather than actual, world. Many globalists, however, conscientiously analyze developments that they believe contribute to global community.

This complex of idealist challenges to realism (*idealisms* not *idealism*) lacks the unity and coherence of thought that helps give realism its power—in part because the challengers are more prescriptive and less analytic, in part because idealists support widely varying ideals. Social scientists often relegate the seemingly "irrational" pursuit of various community ideals to the unexplained fringes of our understanding of the world, preferring assumptions of rational behavior by unitary actors.[21] As George Will (1983, 17) stresses, however, ideas do have consequences and thus the contemplation of ideas is an intensely practical undertaking.

The variety of community ideals (from nation to world community) greatly complicates a focus on idealism.[22] Although various idealisms collectively pose a challenge to realism, largely through their common attention to communities with boundaries that often do not coincide with state borders, the differences among idealisms are often stark. Even the label is problematic, because so many authors equate idealism only with the globalist perspective. After a brief discussion of idealism generally, in which we note both common elements and variations, we will focus especially on globalism. Because it questions the very existence of states and a state system structure, whereas nationalisms seek only rearrangements in current states, globalism is the idealism that most clearly challenges realism.

[20]E. H. Carr (1964; originally 1939) used the term "utopianism" to emphasize even more the gap between the cool and careful descriptive power of realism and the presumed unreality of the globalist alternatives. As a result of the attention to international law and moral behavior by many globalists, Boyle (1985, 17) prefers the label "legalist-moralist."

[21]It is much easier to theorize about a world in which all actors have the same preference structures and values than one in which actors vary dramatically with respect to both. For the sake of simplifying theory, classical liberals and realists both choose to ignore real-world diversity. Realists fundamentally fail to relate their theory to an understanding of human values. Although physical security ranks high among human values (see, for example, Maslow 1970), people have instrumental and noninstrumental needs for community association as well.

[22]Macridis contrasts starkly the elements grouped here in idealism: "Cosmopolitanism [globalism] as an ideology is the exact opposite of nationalism" (1986, 263). His discussion of them, however, even his grouping of them in the same chapter, draws attention to their commonality as belief systems focusing on competing definitions of community.

THE WORLDVIEW IN BRIEF

This section identifies the conceptual, theoretical, and value elements common to various idealisms. Refer again to Table 3.1 for a summary. The **community**, those with whom one identifies, is the central conceptual focus of idealists. For some extreme nationalists or fundamentalists, identification with the community suppresses individuality. For other idealists, especially globalists, emphasis on community is compatible with emphasis on individual human beings and groups.[23] Globalists are, in fact, concerned that the community not swallow the individual—their focus remains on a pluralistic community of individuals. Consider the emphasis on individual human rights by some of the American presidents, such as Woodrow Wilson, Franklin D. Roosevelt, and Jimmy Carter, with idealist (both religious and globalist) streaks.

The values of unity and autonomy drive individuals and groups in their community-building and community-sustaining activities. Within the community, individuals and groups seek to strengthen cooperative and collective action on behalf of the community. Interaction of the community and the outside world depends on the idealism that defines the community. Nationalists frequently draw sharp boundaries (based on race, language, or culture) and seek **exclusion** of those on the outside. Beliefs in the superiority of those within the nation are common and cause conflict with the outside world. Religious idealists and universalists almost invariably have a sense of superiority but, rather than excluding the outside world, may seek to extend the benefits of their beliefs to others through **conversion** or **conquest**. Globalists generally assume a common human interest in global community that enlightened individuals will come to perceive.[24]

Many idealists offer little analysis of how the world works—theoretical elements of their thought are not often strong. Common to many idealisms is a desire to capture a state or to create a new one. Nationalists often need to destroy existing state structures (for instance, by carving a piece of territory from one) and thus must challenge a state to accomplish that. Gandhi used nonviolent protest in his effort to create an Indian state from the British colony, but the power differential between the state and the nation frequently encourages the adoption of guerrilla warfare and terrorist techniques.

Leaders of incipient nationalist movements frequently seek to build a **community consciousness** as a first step in efforts to capture or build a state. Both the Palestinian Liberation Organization (PLO) and the fundamentalist Sikhs of India

---

[23]Many who attempt to find order in the chaos of perspectives in international politics discover it in three levels of analysis: individuals, states, and the international system (Singer 1961). For instance, Viotti and Kauppi (1987) relate three major perspectives, pluralism, realism, and globalism, respectively, to the three levels of analysis. In fact, however, worldviews cut across levels of analysis in complex ways (as with microeconomics and macroeconomics in the liberal tradition; attention to both state and state system in realism; and emphasis on individuals, organizations, and global institutions in globalism).

[24]Globalism, rather than religious idealism, actually motivates many members of American ecumenical religions.

have followed that path. Some globalists similarly attempt to build a sense of global community. Analogously, Marxists strive to create a class consciousness among workers as a prelude to revolutionary efforts.

Many globalists engage not only in global community building but in global state building, the creation or strengthening of regional or global institutions like the United Nations. Religious idealists sometimes also create new, more comprehensive political units—the histories of Christianity in Europe and Islam in the Middle East are replete with examples. Similarly, Marxists (driven by a universalistic idealism or ideology) long tried to maintain within the Soviet Union a state containing many nations.

Unlike realists, who forecast a world in the future pretty much like that of the past, idealists desire and generally anticipate progress in community-building, state-building, or state-capturing activities. That is, they expect to see consolidation and institutionalization of the community. For example, many globalists anticipate gradual extension of a common rule of law and of global institutions.

Globalists have a relatively unique status among idealists—they both participate and observe (as do Marxists). Nationalists and religious idealists shape world politics by their actions, often making the world quite different from the one that realists portray. In their efforts to build global community, globalists also act. Globalists, however, have a more self-conscious worldview through which they also observe and analyze world politics. Just as realists expect the individual actions of states to give rise to systemic stability and relative peace (which they value), globalists expect the actions of those pursuing global community eventually to give rise to global community and a more stable peace. They prescribe conscious efforts to create the new norms, good will, trust, and cooperative patterns of behavior that will bring true global community within reach. It is to globalist thought that we now turn in more detail.

IMPORTANT CONTRIBUTIONS TO GLOBALIST THOUGHT

A belief in the universal rule of law, applicable to all individuals and states, runs historically through globalist thought. Early manifestations of belief in universal law came from religion. For instance, the institutionalization of Christianity brought into being political structures that sought universal domain for religious legal strictures ("catholic" *means* "universal"). The Holy Roman Empire splintered and reemerged many times (under Charlemagne in 800, Otto I in 962, the Hapsburgs after 1438) before Europeans officially separated religious universalism (still represented in the papacy) and local law making (the domain of secular states in the modern world). Islam continues to fight this battle, as the recent claims to universalistic spiritual and political legitimacy by Iran's religious leadership attest.

Although much modern globalism has a secular coloration, the religious roots run deep. For instance, the Dutch jurist Hugo Grotius (1583–1645), a very religious man, made a fundamentally important contribution to modern secular globalism by founding modern international law. He strove throughout his life for the unity of the church, both as a goal in itself and as a foundation for peace (Lauterpacht 1985, 11). The Thirty Years War raged during his lifetime, and he believed that it manifested the failure of religious unity to constrain secular ambitions of states like Spain and France.

Grotius based his thought about international law on both religion and a concept of human nature. Specifically he believed that human beings possess reason, goodness, sociability, and the ability to learn and improve. On these religious and philosophical foundations, very different from those of early realism, he built his belief in the law, applicable to both individuals and to states as groupings of individuals.

Enlightenment thought of eighteenth-century Europe further secularized globalism. The scientific and intellectual advances of the seventeenth and eighteenth centuries shaped the thought of that period (to which contributed Montesquieu, Voltaire, Rousseau, Locke, Hume, and Kant). Philosophers of the Enlightenment saw in the *rationality* of humans the basis for progress, human perfectibility, and the discovery of universal social and political principles. The French Revolution drew on these currents of thought and took on a republican universalism that, along with other factors, motivated the Napoleonic conquest of Europe.[25]

As the French experience illustrated, there has always been within idealist thought a tension between largely voluntary propagation of improved international law and an aggressive extension of the rule of "truth" and "right" to those not yet enlightened. It is to disagreements among universalistic idealists about whose version of the proper international legal-political order is correct (Christian, Moslem, Marxist, or secular-democratic), and the disputes that erupt among competing claimants, that realists point in rejecting idealism as a proper basis for state action. When states adopt a particular view of the proper global world order (the ideal) and seek to persuade others, the disputes can quickly become bloody.

This issue distinguishes globalists from many other universalists. Globalists believe there to be some concept of international order that humans naturally and universally desire. Because all humans will come without coercion (although not necessarily without some education) to understand their common interest, cooperation and peaceful movement toward the new international order is possible. Other universalists also believe there is a natural international order, but not all believe that humans will so easily and automatically agree on it. Therefore coercion may be appropriate—the sword can induce acceptance of the new political, economic, or religious order.

[25]This era and the French Revolution were also, however, watersheds in the evolution of nationalism (Macridis 1986, 250–55). Kedourie declares that nationalism is "a doctrine *invented* in Europe at the beginning of the nineteenth century" (1961, 77). Jean Jacques Rousseau may be the father of that modern nationalism and helped the French create their particular manifestation of it. Both a universalism committed to liberty and French nationalism fueled the Napoleonic wars. A great flowering of ideals based on community characterized the period.

President Woodrow Wilson (1856–1924) was an important figure in twenti-eth-century idealist thought. A lawyer and political scientist, Wilson was generally anti-imperialist despite the clashes during his administration of U.S. forces with Mexico and Caribbean states. He sought to keep the United States nonaligned in the early years of World War I. After the war, he personally led the U.S. delegation to peace talks in Paris and sought to create a new world society. Two important pillars were to be the self-determination of peoples and the League of Nations (recognition of both nationalism and globalism). The League became the first worldwide international organization with a security-maintenance function.

The perceptions of Wilson and other globalists that a lawless state system (with actions by monarchs unaccountable to public desires) caused World War I led in the interwar period to a wide variety of efforts to structure an international legal order. In a golden period for globalism, international conferences and agree-ments sought to codify armament balances and to restrict state actions. The Kellogg-Briand Pact (or Pact of Paris) in 1928 bound fifteen states (among them France, Britain, the United States, Germany, Japan, and Italy) to use only pacific methods for dispute settlement and to renounce war. The failure of this interna-tional superstructure to prevent World War II tainted the entire globalist enterprise and set the stage for the post–World War II dominance of realists.

Nonetheless, globalist perspectives continue to pose a challenge to realism in the last half of the twentieth century. The existence of the United Nations, with international peace objectives and security-maintenance instruments imbedded in its structure, illustrates the continuing importance of globalist thought. So, too, do efforts to create a strong international legal system. In addition, the rapid growth of corporations doing business globally and of international organizations (includ-ing many like Amnesty International, based not on states, but on individual membership) has encouraged the enunciation of a variant of globalism that we can call **transnationalism**.[26] Transnationalists rely less heavily on prescriptions for legal order or institution building than the earlier generations of globalists, and instead describe and analyze what they argue to be an inevitable growth in global interactions and structures, driven in substantial part by advances in communica-tions and transportation technology.[27]

REALISM *VERSUS* IDEALISM

The long-term tension between realist and idealist perspectives on world politics and the possibly cyclical nature of their relative influence in world affairs could imply that there is no truth to be uncovered—that understanding of the world is a purely subjective matter. Mansbach and Ferguson (1986) reached fundamentally that conclusion:

[26]Keohane and Nye (1970 and 1977) helped define the perspective. Maghroori and Ramberg (1982) reviewed its development.

[27]Karl Deutsch (1979) ties both national and international community building to ongoing social mobilization and, in particular, to development of communication capabilities among people.

This brief analysis of the sources and nature of evolving theory in international relations is self-consciously gloomy about the prospects for developing a cumulative science in the discipline. Notwithstanding significant advances in data collection and method, it views the discipline as mired in an unceasing set of theoretical debates in which competing empirical assertions grow out of competing normative emphases that have their roots in a broader sociocultural milieu.

This analysis suggests, therefore, that what we believe to be the dominant theories of an age are more the products of ideology and fashion than of science in the Kuhnian sense. If the natural sciences somehow evolve in linear fashion regardless of their social and cultural context, "knowledge" generation in the social sciences—including international relations—may more closely resemble that in the humanities, which is inevitably infused by the ethos of its era. (Mansbach and Ferguson 1986, 30)

There is, without doubt, some validity in that conclusion and basis for the pessimism it conveys. Nonetheless, greater optimism guides the enterprise here. If states were the only important actors in world affairs, and security and autonomy were the dominant values of all humans, realists would be correct. If international organizations and global community were (or were definitely becoming) more important than states, and peace and unity were the dominant human values, globalists would have a monopoly on truth. In reality a multiplicity of actors has long been with us, and human beings hold multiple values. Over time and in different places the importance of different actors and values varies. More than one perspective can be useful in understanding international relations.[28] Leaving aside the fact that one worldview might be closer, even considerably closer, to the truth than another, it is unlikely that realism and globalism could hold sway for so long over so many, if both did not make important contributions to our understanding of the world.

In the next few chapters we pursue the insights of both perspectives. First, we sketch a largely realist view of global relations, elaborating fundamental concepts and theory. Subsequent chapters further develop idealism, especially globalism.

[28]Herz (1951, 228) attempted a synthesis of "the factual insight of Political Realism with the ideals of Political Idealism" that he labeled "Realist Liberalism." Many others have made peace with both perspectives, or at least incorporated the two into their thought in uneasy coexistence. The author of this volume believes that there is ongoing growth in global community and institutions. Although the dominant role of states will continue to make the realist perspective essential for a long time, globalists increasingly have something to say descriptively and analytically (not just prescriptively) about world politics.

Chapter 4

STATES
AND THE PURSUIT
OF INTEREST

This and the next two chapters elaborate realism. In this chapter we discuss some of the primary conceptual building blocks of this worldview: states, interests, and power. In the next two chapters we use those building blocks to look at the interaction of states.

THE RISE OF STATES

What is a state? According to widely accepted convention, a **state** has four characteristics: (1) territory, with clear boundaries; (2) a population; (3) a government, not answerable to outside authorities, with control over the territory and population; and (4) **sovereignty**, or recognition by other states as a legally equal player in the global environment. In other words, what scholars of world politics call a state is essentially what the rest of the English-speaking world knows as a country, and we will use the terms interchangeably. There is, however, an important reason for the insistence of scholars on precision in definition. Taiwan is a country that many other countries do not recognize as a sovereign equal. Both the Republic of China (ROC) on the island of Taiwan and the People's Republic of China (PRC) on the mainland agree that there is a single China and demand that other states recognize only one of them as the legitimate government of the Chinese state. Governments around the world gradually chose to recognize the government that took control of the mainland in 1949. Taiwan lost its membership in the United Nations to the PRC in 1971 and no longer even exchanges ambassadors with the United States. It falls short of being a full state.

Another reason for making a large issue of a seemingly simple concept is that states have not always been the structure in which people organized themselves. Much of world history is a story of empires. Their boundaries were often less well defined than modern states as they struggled to expand and to fight off the "barbarians" on their periphery. Many such empires viewed themselves as the entire civilized world and had no concept of other basically equal political units with which they interacted. Another large part of world history, not just in Europe but in many geographic areas, has been feudal. Feudal governments are not fully in charge of their own fates—they are embedded in larger units (like empires), answerable in part to a king, an emperor, outside religious authorities, or all of these.

Europe in 1600 was a fundamentally feudal system, officially structured by the Holy Roman Empire. This meant that local "sovereigns" were sometimes in reality, and always in theory, accountable to both the Pope and a secular emperor. This feudal character contributes to the difficulty most of us have in developing strong mental pictures of international politics during the Middle Ages—it becomes a blur of expanding and contracting papal and imperial authority, further complicated by the fact that marriages and heredity merged or divided large pieces of territory. For instance, in 1500, Mary of Burgundy married Maximillian of Austria; in the bargain the Netherlands of today became part of the Hapsburg family domains. Later the Netherlands moved to the control of the Spanish branch of the Hapsburg family. Perhaps it was this kind of sequence that supposedly led Harry Truman to conclude that "History is just one damn thing after another."

In the 1500s societal forces were creating increasing tensions that would ultimately lead to change. One important tension was caused by the increased questioning of papal authority. Martin Luther nailed his Ninety-five Theses to the church door in Wittenberg in 1517. Jean Bodin in France published *Six Books on the State* in 1576, arguing the case for the divine right of the French king to rule in an absolute manner, free of outside authority.[1]

The feudal system broke in the Thirty Years War (1618–1648). A mosaic of warfare engulfed much of Europe—especially the modern German and Bohemian (western Czechoslovakian) territories, where the wars reduced population levels by one-third to one-half. A dramatic restructuring of European politics moved forward rapidly in the course of the wars and the settlements. The participants in the Peace (or Treaties) of Westphalia in 1648 officially created a new system of decentralized sovereign and equal units, responsible to no higher authority. Choice of religion, a central issue of the wars, devolved to local sovereigns.

Thus new European structures formalized one of the key characteristics of a modern state: the dominant and sovereign role of government. At the same time, territoriality advanced. By the end of the 1500s England was a defined and relatively fixed territory with an effective monarch. France, Spain, Russia, and Austria followed.

It may be instructive to consider how the movement from feudal units to states occurred. Tilly (1985) provided a colorful image:

> If protection rackets represent organized crime at its smoothest, then war making and state making—quintessential protection rackets with the advantage of legitimacy— qualify as our largest examples of organized crime.... At least for the European

---

[1]Hinsley (1986) traces the rise and fall of the concept of sovereignty during the Roman Empire period, and the reemergence of it with Bodin.

experience of the past few centuries, a portrait of war makers and state makers as coercive and self-seeking entrepreneurs bears a far greater resemblance to the facts than do its chief alternatives: the idea of a social contract, the idea of an open market in which operators of armies and states offer services to willing consumers, the idea of a society whose shared norms and expectations call forth a certain kind of government. (Tilly 1985, 169)

More succinctly, he said "the state makes war, and war makes the state."

According to Tilly's logic, those with some initial power acted to resist their opponents (competitors in the power and security game) and to expand their own power within their current territory and beyond. New military technology helped them expand. Early in the process, there was little distinction between the violence of bandits, pirates, the king's representatives, regional authorities, and professional soldiers. The emerging king relied on bandits and pirates, used professional soldiers who looted for their payment, and played various regional authorities against one another. Only gradually did he obtain a monopoly on the "legitimate" use of violence.

The logic was largely one of conquest and expansion externally, coupled with consolidation internally. The consolidation process relied on tribute (simply taking from subjects) and protection (the more nearly voluntary arrangement in which citizens were willing to accord legitimacy to governmental violence and to help pay for it in exchange for security). In addition, however, the more successful emerging state governments eventually promoted domestic economic growth to create additional resources.

Successful states provided incentives and examples for latecomers. Portugal, the Netherlands, and England were relatively early. Spain, France, Germany, Russia, and Japan reacted in self-defense and built states through emulation and innovation (Modelski 1978). The colonial process and subsequent decolonization extended the European state system to the rest of the world.[2]

It is not impossible that the world could once again see a dynamic of conquest and expansion like the one that gave birth to modern states. In a world of nuclear weapons and continued proliferation of them, however, it seems unlikely that this historic pattern can realistically serve as a model for the process by which the state might be supplanted or supplemented. We will return later to dynamics that might threaten, or at least weaken, the role of the state in world politics.

STATE SYSTEMS

The modern state system developed during a period of about 300 years, beginning in Europe and expanding around the world. According to one count, there were twenty-three members in 1816, forty-two in 1900, sixty-four in 1945, and 161 in

---

[2]States outside of Europe often prove quite different from those in Europe, however, because the processes of formation differed and close relationships between rulers and ruled frequently did not grow in LDCs (Tilly 1985, 185–186).

1985.[3] In 1992 UN membership reached 175 and few states now remain outside of it (Switzerland is one that does).

Because the state system consists wholly of states, it might seem that analysis of it would simply involve studying the behavior and interactions of individual states. But because of the number of possible interactions (for example, alliance combinations) in even a small state system, that quickly becomes a difficult task; in a system of approximately 180 states it is overwhelming. Thus scholars often make the leap from analyzing individual states to considering the structure of the state system as a whole and considering how that structure influences individual state behavior.

Two characteristics of the interstate system structure are especially important. First, as described previously, it lacks central authorities and is therefore one of anarchy. That is a constant, and it forces states to adopt self-help orientations. Second, the distribution of power in the system changes over time, giving rise to specific patterns of behavior. In the rest of this chapter we review assorted typical distributions of power in the system and consider carefully what constitutes power. In Chapter 6 we will return to a consideration of the implications of alternative distributions for individual state behavior and systemic stability.

Polarity describes the distribution of power in the state system. Polarity first distinguishes between great powers and lesser powers. **Great powers** or **major powers** have systemwide interests and sufficient power to pursue them.[4] Second, polarity identifies the number and relative size of the great powers. Historically, great powers have constituted a limited subset of total states, seldom more than five or six. Third, polarity sometimes specifies relationships between greater and lesser (or minor) powers. Kaplan (1957, 21–85) distinguished six theoretically possible systemic polarities:[5]

1. The **multipolar system**. In this system, only the great powers are serious players, and there are but a handful (often five or six) of relatively equal ones.
2. The **loose bipolar system**. In any **bipolar system**, two great powers stand above all other states in power capabilities. In the post–World War bipolar system, the United States and the Soviet Union had such great nuclear and conventional capabilities relative to other great powers that they became **superpowers**. The system is loose when the two primary poles do not organize the remaining states (greater or lesser powers) into strong alliance structures.

---

[3]Singer and Small data (see Small and Singer 1985) provided by Thomas Cusack. The Singer and Small count has its critics. Bennett and Zitomersky (1958, 2) point out that the Singer and Small interstate system is Eurocentric, requiring that either France or Britain diplomatically recognize all member states. In contrast, Bennett and Zitomersky count 305 "autonomous political units" in 1816, only 76 in 1916 (after the spread of European empires), and 149 in 1970 (data again from Cusack). This count gives a very different image of the global political system and its evolution.

[4]The expression "great power" acquired widespread usage in the mid-eighteenth century and first appeared in a treaty in 1815, at which time it referred to Great Britain, France, Austria, Prussia, and Russia (Craig and George 1983, 3). See Stoll (1989) for definition and discussion of major powers.

[5]Kaplan originally identified these as "equilibrium states" of the interstate system. What we call a multipolar system here, he called a balance of power system.

3. The **tight bipolar system**. When the two dominant great powers do organize the system into strong and opposing alliances such as the NATO and the Warsaw Pact of the late 1970s, the system takes on a tight bipolar character.

4. The **universal system**. When a single political entity organizes or controls subordinate political units, the system is universal. Historically this need not mean a global system. Many state systems (Chinese, Greek, European) were self-contained and universal within a geographically limited environment. Late European feudalism was a universal system.

5. The **hierarchical system**. Should no effective political units exist between the universal government and individuals, the system becomes hierarchical.

6. The **unit veto system**. This configuration requires that all states (at least the great powers) have the ability to defend themselves individually from all others. It would in effect require that all have weapons such as nuclear arsenals, the use of which could not be denied to them. Each actor would have a veto on the actions of all others. Should the current system evolve into a world of many relatively equal nuclear powers, the unit veto system could appear—there is the skeleton of such a system already.

These categories are **ideal types**. That is they simplify, even caricature, reality. Reality is seldom as simple as any of our categories or concepts. Nonetheless, polarities offer a powerful way of grasping the structure of power in historic and contemporary systems.[6]

Kaplan's polarity structures emphasize political-military power relations among states, especially great powers. Other characterizations of world politics exist. For example, world-systems theory grows out of Marxist economic analysis and portrays the world in terms of an economic class structure:

> For these world-system theorists, the fundamental units in their model of world order are high-wage, capital-intensive, developed countries specializing in manufactures—the *core*—and low-wage, labor-intensive, underdeveloped countries usually, but not always, specializing in raw materials for export—the *periphery*. A semiperipheral zone, which is something of a mix of core and peripheral economic activities, is also discussed. (Bergesen 1983, 45)

Such a predominantly economic perspective still emphasizes the power relations among states that are so important to realists. And it potentially supplements the realist military-political polarity characterizations of state-system structure by describing relations between more and less economically developed countries (although in terminology quite different from traditional greater power–lesser power analysis). The world-systems approach, however, clashes with realist understanding of the world for two reasons. First, it suggests that class-based distributions of power globally may be significantly independent of state borders and that classes may be a better unit of analysis than states. Second, it posits that political-military power analysis depends on economic power analysis. Neither of these images fits the realist world. This book will return to the world-systems perspective when we present and evaluate economic perspectives on world politics.

---

[6]Kaplan posited "rules" of state behavior in each of these systems. That is, he presented theoretical statements that link polarity to individual state behavior. We will turn to such theoretical discussion in the next chapter.

Many realists have, however, increasingly accepted some of the emphasis by the world-systems theorists on economics and on a truly global world system, while reasserting the priority of politics over economics and rejecting any implication of diminished state role. Reexamining the interstate system with eyes better attuned than before to economic power relationships, some realists have begun to argue that an important structural pattern is the existence of a single leading or **hegemonic state** that dominates the political-economic system. These analysts describe the United States not as a superpower (one of two) but as a hegemon. We might logically add this situation to Kaplan's categorization and call it **unipolar**.

HISTORIC STATE SYSTEMS

The modern state system differs in important ways from historic ones, especially in the technology available to states. Striking similarities appear in earlier variants, however. We want to look briefly at historic patterns, giving primary attention to polarity characterizations, before returning to the modern state system. Holsti (1988, 23–51) surveyed three earlier systems: the Chinese system of the Chou Dynasty period (1122 B.C. to 221 B.C.), the Greek city-state system (800 B.C. to 322 B.C.), and the Renaissance Italy system (fourteenth and fifteenth centuries A.D.). We draw on his review here.

The Chinese system passed through three distinct stages during nearly 1,000 years. The first was a feudal period called Western Chou, lasting roughly from 1122 B.C. to 771 B.C. A central monarchy created and supported a variety of local feudal units. These began gradually to develop their own power bases and capabilities (for example, irrigation systems) and to expand geographically at the expense of weaker neighbors. In addition, some local "nationalisms" grew with differences in dialects, customs, and religion. The monarch's central role weakened. Local rulers increasingly gained authority through inheritance and began to call themselves princes or even kings. In Kaplan's terms, the system moved from hierarchical to universal (feudal).

In the spring and autumn period, 771 B.C. to 483 B.C., the monarchy remained in place and retained its official central role but lost actual control. In fact, by 707 B.C. a vassal had sufficient strength to defeat the Chou monarch's armed forces. The feudal units increasingly treated each other as sovereign equals, concluding treaties and even using hostage exchanges to enforce mutual obligations. At one point, after 546 B.C., a multilateral treaty of nonaggression assured forty years of relative peace.

The Period of Warring States followed from 403 B.C. to 221 B.C. In essence, a multipolar state system had evolved from an initially hierarchical and transitionally universal one. The number of statelike units normally varied between ten and fifteen, but consolidated to seven greater powers and three lesser ones by 230 B.C. Warfare intensified and became more brutal. In 274 B.C. the forces of one general killed 150,000 enemy soldiers. The system gradually evolved into a somewhat unstable bipolar one with two competing alliance structures (organizing the north and south of China). Warfare weakened both, and they succumbed to a third peripheral power, which established a new empire under the Han dynasty.

The parallels with the European system of the last 1,000 years are striking. Both began as hierarchical systems organized as empires. In both, the feudal units gained sufficient strength to resist central authority and developed local national identities that motivated them to do so. In both systems the intensity of warfare among the new states increased, and the structure moved toward bipolarity.

Similarities characterize patterns of cooperation as well as those of structure and conflict. Both systems relied on balances of power, hostages, and bilateral and multilateral treaties to maintain peace or stability. Moreover, the political beliefs and behavior patterns that evolved with the Chinese state system seem fundamentally realist (Holsti 1983, 37–41).

At least two major and related differences exist between the ancient and modern systems. First, the boundaries of the Chinese system did not expand significantly over time, whereas the European system evolved into a truly global one. Second, the level of military technology was much lower in ancient China— the principal military investment then was in four-horse chariots. In 529 B.C. one state organized a military performance of 4,000 chariots. Technology may be a progressive force in history, underlying otherwise cyclical patterns.

In the Greek city-state system of 800 B.C. to 322 B.C., the basic unit was the city-state or *polis*. Considerable growth in intrasystem and extrasystem trade (especially by the fifth century B.C.) assured regular contact among the units. War was recurrent and frequently brutal. The city-states developed mechanisms such as arbitration and conciliation (reliance on third parties for conflict resolution) to deal with conflict. They normally respected the immunity of diplomats from harm, even during warfare.

The *polis* celebrated a philosophy of independence and small size. Although that might seem to preclude desire for empire, stratification grew. In the period 492 B.C. to 477 B.C., the city-states created the Hellenic League under the leadership of Athens and Sparta to resist the external power of the Persians. Thereafter fear of Athenian imperialism led competitors to form the Peloponnesian League under Spartan direction, whereas Athens established the Delian League to formalize its empire. In addition to the Delian League, Athens held an even more extensive hegemonic position in the system, built on its commercial and naval superiority; the attractiveness of its laws, courts, and currency; and the services it performed for other city-states. The system appeared simultaneously to be both bipolar and hegemonic. The Peloponnesian War between the two Leagues erupted in 431 B.C. and lasted nearly thirty years. Thucydides documented this war, his analysis providing the basis on which others subsequently labeled him the first realist. Athens lost the war. In 338 B.C. the weakened system succumbed to an outside power, Alexander the Great's Macedonia.

We need not probe deeply to see the parallels with the evolution of the modern international system or that of the Chou dynasty period. Again we see a multipolar to bipolar evolution. States developed diplomatic techniques to allow some peaceful conflict resolution. Commerce among units rose sharply over time, with Athens taking on an economic leadership role. If the similarities between the

Greek experience and the post–World War II antagonism seem great, consider this comparison of Athens and Sparta:

> Thucydides has drawn the stylized model of two powers, one based on naval force and the other on territorial force, one with men "addicted to innovation, whose designs are characterized by swiftness alike in conception and execution," the other with men who "have a genius for keeping what they have got, accompanied by a total want of invention…," one open, the other closed to foreigners. (Aron 1966, 149)

We must realize, of course, that our interpretation of history uses categories familiar to us and may impose more similarity than the case merits.

In the fourteenth and fifteenth centuries a set of relatively well-defined political entities appeared in northern Italy, somewhat isolated from the rest of Europe by mountains. Venice had been an important trading state for several centuries. In fact, in terms of the larger, extra-Italian system, it had many characteristics of a hegemonic power.[7] Venice was a republic ruled by an oligarchy that received considerable popular support.

In contrast most city-state governments aroused relatively less popular support and therefore were less stable. They proved fairly easy targets for subversion and political intrigue sponsored from without. Frequent mercenary wars characterized the period. The states invented permanent embassies as a mechanism for maintaining diplomatic contact. Moreover, a rough multipolar balance of military power among actors during this period helped maintain relative tranquility. Like Thucydides earlier, another realist, Machiavelli (1469–1527), developed his political philosophy and chronicled history in a milieu with many similarities to the modern one. The French ultimately destroyed the system by invasion from without in 1494, on invitation by Milan.

This portrayal by Holsti of the history of state systems draws heavily upon the polarities of Kaplan. Adam Watson (1992) surveyed the history of all state systems since ancient Sumer (ca. 2000 B.C.). He argues that state systems fall on a spectrum from absolute independence of states to absolute empire. While the periods of the Chinese warring states, Greek city-states, and Italian Renaissance do fall at or near the absolute independence end of the spectrum (and thereby illustrate the anarchy of realists), more common organizing principles of state systems have been hegemony (the dominant actor influences the internal and external policy of other states), dominion (the dominant actor influences the internal character of states), and empire (the dominant actor incorporates other states). Watson argues that most analysts have underestimated the degree to which interstate order and society historically existed, and he suggests that this is also true today.

Whichever characterization of historic state systems we accept, should we believe our era to be unique in the evolution of the modern state system, history refutes that belief. Should we believe that the history of the last few hundred years

[7]Modelski (1978, 218).

is a story of progress toward an ultimately cooperative, peaceful world, attention to earlier history raises doubt. Realist history is repetitive history.[8]

THE MODERN STATE SYSTEM

Two portrayals of the evolution of the modern state system coexist. The first relies on the descriptive concepts of alternative military-political polarities (bipolar, multipolar, and so on). The second traces changing hegemonic leadership in the modern system.[9] We consider each in turn.

EARLY POLARITY

The modern state system obviously evolved with the modern state. In the polarity view, it grew out of what Kaplan (1957, 45) termed a "universal system," namely the Holy Roman Empire. Although the empire retained pretensions of being hierarchical (dealing directly with individuals), the character of feudal Europe, in most geographic environments, was closer to that of a universal system (overseeing subsidiary units that dealt in turn with individuals).

The birth of the modern state system, meaning the birth of a multipolar state system, is often said to be the Treaty of Westphalia in 1648, which ended the Thirty Years War, the pretensions of hierarchy, and the partial reality of a universal system. Thereafter, at least until World War II, the European state system politically and militarily remained a generally multipolar one. The states of Portugal, Spain, the Netherlands, Britain, and France were fairly well established by 1648 and persisted. Other states rose to and fell from positions as greater or lesser powers.

The Treaty of Utrecht in 1713, which presented terms to France after the defeat of its attempt to dominate much of Western Europe, contained the first explicit reference to balance of power (Craig and George 1983, 8). At the Congress of Vienna in 1815, after the defeat of France again, the great powers gave even more deliberate attention to balance and equilibrium. They established the Concert of Europe to facilitate discussions among governments and efforts to maintain the status quo. The following century encompassed the golden age of multipolar power balancing. For most of that period, Britain played an exceptional role. It was the balancer

[8]Science fiction fans will recognize the same basic pattern in Isaac Asimov's Foundation series—a breakup of the galatic empire, an anarchic period in which local units develop and establish a galaxy-wide "state system," premature and abortive attempts to reestablish a universal system (the Mule is a kind of Napoleon), and even an essentially bipolar system under the leadership of the two foundations. An outside power, Gaia, provides unity once again.

[9]The swiftness of the transition made by scholars of world politics in their characterization of history is remarkable. In the index of Waltz (1979) there are many entries under balance of power and multipolarity and none under hegemony. In Gilpin (1981) there are many under both balance of power and hegemony. In Gilpin (1987a) there are none under balance of power or multipolarity, but many under hegemony. As remarkable as this transition in conceptual and descriptive approaches is, there is little literature that assesses the relative power of the major European states through this period and that would allow us to confidently accept one characterization rather than the other (see, however, Modelski and Thompson 1987). Because of differential emphases on political-military and economic-commercial power, both approaches have value.

in the system, except between 1879 and 1890, when Bismark's Germany competed for that position. In the first half of that century, Britain maintained a flexibility in its dealings with other states that allowed it to meditate disputes and prevent disruptions to the European balance. Germany under Bismark acted to achieve the same ends through a series of secret treaties and complex alliances. Before the outbreak of World War I in 1914, the once flexible system had devolved into two fairly fixed alliance structures.

The apparent failure of balancing mechanisms to prevent World War I (1914–1918) gave rise to a surge of globalist idealism and a search for international cooperation in the period following it. For instance, states established the first global political institution, the League of Nations. Nonetheless, the League of Nation's primary purpose, like that of the Concert of Europe, was to assist in the management of a multipolar balance of power, not to replace it with a universal system. It remained a realist world.

One critical difference characterized the war settlements of 1815 and 1919. Although victors restored France to a place of equality and participation after 1815, they reduced Germany to a position of inferiority and subordination after 1919 (they stripped it of military power and territory, forced it to pay heavy reparations, and did not allow it to join the League of Nations until 1926). Although many reasons explain subsequent German aggression and the reinitiation of hostilities in 1939, the desire of Germans to regain what they had lost ranks high on the list. Realists suggest that two interacting policy failures contributed to the outbreak of World War II: the initial failure of world leaders to allow the new Republic of Germany (the so-called Weimar Republic) its historic place in the interstate balance after 1919, and their subsequent failure to restrain Germany's growth when the Nazi regime moved rapidly to rebuild and then surpass earlier German power.

CONTEMPORARY POLARITY

World War II (1939–1945) again reduced Germany to impotence, this time partitioning it physically among four great power victors (France, Great Britain, the United States, and the Soviet Union). The occupation zones of the first three eventually became the Federal Republic of Germany (West Germany), whereas the Soviet zone became the German Democratic Republic (East Germany). As the sarcastic saying goes, the great powers loved Germany so much that they were glad to have two of them.

The victorious great powers (joined by China) moved quickly to set up a cooperative, multipolar base for the postwar international order. They established the United Nations, in which each would sit on the Security Council and hold veto power. The emergence of conflict, however, between the two largest of the powers, the United States and the Soviet Union, rapidly disrupted the plans of the major powers for the postwar management of international power.

Nuclear capability assured the superior positions of the two superpowers (although their conventional military strength also vastly exceeded that of all other great powers except China). The United States exploded its first atomic weapons in 1945, including the two used to end the war with Japan; the Soviet Union exploded its first in 1949. The United States tested a hydrogen bomb in 1952, and the Soviets followed in 1953. By the time other states acquired nuclear weapons, the lead of the superpowers was overwhelming, and the organization of the globe into two competing blocs was very far along.

The informal organization of Europe into two camps occurred almost immediately after the war. Soviet troops remained in the Central and Eastern European countries that they liberated, and U.S. troops remained in Western Europe. Governments politically acceptable to the two powers emerged quickly in these respective **spheres of influence**.

Formal organization followed, and the system quickly became a tight bipolar one. In 1949, NATO came into being with twelve members including the United States, France, and Britain. In 1951 the United States concluded bilateral security or mutual defense treaties with Japan and the Philippines, and a trilateral one with Australia and New Zealand. Further treaties bound the United States to South Korea (1953) and Taiwan (1954), and established the Southeast Asia collective defense group (1954). The Federal Republic of Germany entered NATO in 1955 (as decided in 1954). Many other agreements and treaties extended the network, centered on the United States, around the globe. On the Soviet side, formalization included establishment of the Warsaw Treaty Organization in 1955, linking the Soviet Union to most of the East European states. Various agreements tied the U.S.S.R. and China together after the Communist revolution in China of 1949.

The subsequent transformation of the interstate system from a tight bipolar to a loose bipolar structure was more gradual. Stalin died in 1952, and already, by 1956, General-Secretary Khrushchev undertook a de-Stalinization campaign. Superpower tensions eased a bit, and they held a summit meeting in 1955. Those changes and the desires of Eastern Europeans for greater local autonomy caused unrest within the Soviet bloc. Both Poland and Hungary sought partial freedom from Soviet dictates, and in Hungary the effort led to the revolution of 1956. The Red Army crushed it.

In the West, Britain remained quite content in its "special relationship" with the United States, but France did not. In the late 1950s de Gaulle challenged the privileged U.S. position in the interstate system, initially through resistance to U.S. economic leadership. When France developed its own nuclear weapons (after 1960), it sought military independence as well. In 1966 it withdrew from NATO's integrated military command (although it remained an observer in NATO) and created its own nuclear strike capability (the *Force de Frappe*).

Breakdown of the European colonial empires further weakened the coherence of U.S.–centric global alliance structures. In the early 1960s many economically less-developed countries, especially in Africa, gained independence. They rapidly raised voices of opposition to domination by either superpower. For instance, in 1960 alone, seventeen new states entered the United Nations, and the U.S. dominance of that institution suffered a blow.

In 1961 the U.S.–sponsored invasion of Cuba at the Bay of Pigs failed to oust the Marxist government and in many respects symbolized the loss of U.S. political-military leadership in Latin America. In contrast, the brutal Soviet invasion of Czechoslovakia in 1968 reestablished an orthodox Marxist government and maintained a tight structure in the Eastern European alliance. Even during the Polish unrest of the early 1980s, the fear of Soviet invasion continued to restrain local action. (In the terms of our earthquake analogy, loosening in the U.S. alliance system relieved pressures of underlying forces, but in the Soviet system the pressures continued to build toward a major quake.)

As a much larger power, however, China began to distance itself in small ways from the Soviet Union by the middle of the 1950s. In 1955, Foreign Minister Chou En-lai proposed the Five Principles of Peaceful Coexistence at the Bandung Conference, itself an important event because it marked a first attempt by economically less-developed countries to establish an independent global voice. The break between the two Communist powers became overt in the early 1960s. The Soviets withdrew their advisers from China in 1960, and the Chinese recalled their ambassador to Moscow in 1962 (Woodby and Cottam 1988, 46). China entered the ranks of nuclear powers in 1964. It now has substantial numbers of delivery vehicles for nuclear weapons, and no other state can easily intimidate it. The United States reestablished bilateral contact with China through a surprise visit by President Nixon in 1972 and established formal diplomatic relations with China in 1979. Chinese-Soviet relations remained cool.

In 1958, six European states signed the Treaty of Rome and began a long process of integrating their economies. By the late 1980s, membership of the European Economic Community had expanded to twelve, and the process of integration was accelerating, leading some observers to foresee a "United States of Europe."

Gorbachev became general-secretary of the Soviet Communist party in 1985, and began to loosen the reigns of control in Eastern Europe and to release the pent-up pressure. His design for controlled change, however, gave way to the sudden shocks that Chapter 2 described. By 1990, all Soviet allies in Eastern Europe had removed hard-line Communist governments and Soviet troops were beginning to depart. On December 31, 1991, the U.S.S.R. formally dissolved. Eastern and Western Europe began to grope toward new relationships and greater unity. The transformation of Europe from cold war battlefield to world power center, one of the obvious structural features of the post–cold war era, is now far along.

The Japanese–U.S. relationship has also changed. Although still friendly, increasing frictions over Japanese trade surpluses have led many Americans in the 1990s to perceive Japan as a more serious long-term challenge than Russia.

Already by the late 1960s the modern state system had become a loose bipolar one. There is now evidence of real multipolarity.[10] The visit by Nixon to China was part of an active strategy to accommodate and even facilitate that evolution. Nixon's secretary of state, Henry Kissinger, was a serious student and admirer of

---

[10]Brecher and James (1989, 36) call the current system "polycentric," with two preeminent centers of *military power* and multiple centers of *political decision*.

the Austrian Chancellor Prince Metternich, who convened the 1814–1815 Congress of Vienna to regularize the nineteenth-century multipolar balance of power. Nixon and Kissinger believed that a new five-power multipolar system was developing, with the United States, the U.S.S.R., Japan, China, and a partially unified Western Europe playing great power roles.

This brief review of the modern state system, emphasizing the evolution of polarity, illustrates the utility of describing the world in such terms. It has been the dominant approach to characterizing the modern state system (Box 4.1).

BOX 4.1   Categories of States

The state system today numbers about 180 states, so that the concepts of great powers, lesser powers, and hegemonic states are inadequate to describe the position of states. Two principal typologies attained wide usage after World War II.

The first divides the world into four overlapping quadrants:

The **West** refers to the traditionally non-Communist countries of the world (primarily in the Western Hemisphere and Western Europe), whereas the **East** designates the countries that had or fell under Communist governments after World War II. Although most of those countries have thrown out Communist governments, they still share common problems in restoring Western democracy and market systems.

The **North** means the economically **More-Developed Countries (MDCs)**, and the **South** refers to the economically **Less-Developed Countries (LDCs)**. It is an interesting phenomenon globally that the more-developed countries are located above the equator and the less-developed countries are often near or below the equator. Exceptions include Australia and New Zealand which are "Northern" countries in the southern part of the globe.

The second categorization is similar to the first:

The **First World** contains economically more-advanced, Western countries (a subset of the West).

The **Second World**, (basically the East) consists of the one-time Communist countries of Central and Eastern Europe, including the Soviet Union. This category is now archaic— economically much of the Second World looks surprisingly like the Third World.

The **Third World** is a residual category, generally equivalent to the South. In recent years the great heterogeneity of the Third World grouping has become increasingly clear to the category makers of the First World; they have therefore given it a subcategory, the **Fourth World** consisting of those countries, like Bangladesh, Haiti, and Burkina Faso, that have experienced little or no economic advance in the post–World War II period.

In addition, a category within the South called **Newly Industrialized Countries (NICs)**, or sometimes **Newly Industrialized Economies (NIEs)**, has emerged. Countries within it, like Spain, Yugoslavia, Israel, Brazil, Mexico, Taiwan, and South Korea, have experienced especially rapid economic growth and have strong industrial sectors.

HEGEMONIC LEADERSHIP

A second characterization of historical and contemporary state systems has gained popularity in recent years. Instead of a multipolar world, several scholars describe the European state system since its birth and, in fact, even earlier than 1648, as a hegemonic one with a single dominant power at any one point in time. For example, Modelski (1978; 1987) argues that Venice was the dominant or hegemonic international state during (roughly) the fifteenth century, followed by Portugal in the sixteenth, the Netherlands in the seventeenth, Britain in the eighteenth and nineteenth, and the United States in the twentieth. Thus he presents even the nineteenth century, supposedly that ideal period of multipolarity, as a time in which a single state (Britain) was more than a simple balancer; it was a leading, dominant, or hegemonic state. Should we try to reconcile the multipolar and hegemonic characterizations, we are left with an Orwellian image of the European state system as a collection of equals, among whom one is considerably "more equal" than others.

The explanation for this shift in characterization lies largely in the movement of realist thought from purely military-political analysis into economic analysis. Britain's military superiority in the nineteenth century (especially in any continental conflict) was not as striking as its economic superiority (especially outside the continent). Britain's overwhelming sea power allowed it to establish a predominant commercial position in the world economy.

Similarly, attention to the concept of economic hegemony changes our perception of the post–World War II period. Instead of seeing the United States as a superpower opposed by one of roughly equal size, we see a world in which the United States unilaterally dominated world trade and finance. The Soviet Union remained a generally autarkic or economically independent state engaging in relatively little trade, two-thirds of which was with other Communist countries (Central Intelligence Agency 1988, 217). The nonaligned or neutral states of the world, from Switzerland and Sweden in Europe through India and most African states in the developing world, traded considerably less with the Soviet Union and its allies than with the United States and its allies. The collapse of the Soviet empire exposed the real hegemony of the United States.

Modelski and Thompson (1987) argue, however, that hegemonic global leadership was always as apparent in military power, especially seapower, as in economic size and trade. Obviously the two are related. Figure 4.1 traces five long cycles in hegemonic leadership using seapower concentration (note that, at the end of World War II, the United States had a near monopoly on seapower).

STATE INTERESTS

Realists posit that states are the key actors in world politics. They further argue that states pursue key interests; while common terminology designates those to be "national interests," we will refer to them as **state interests**. Realists claim that those interests provide the only legitimate basis for state action. Two British diplomats have given us standard quotations concerning the centrality of interests

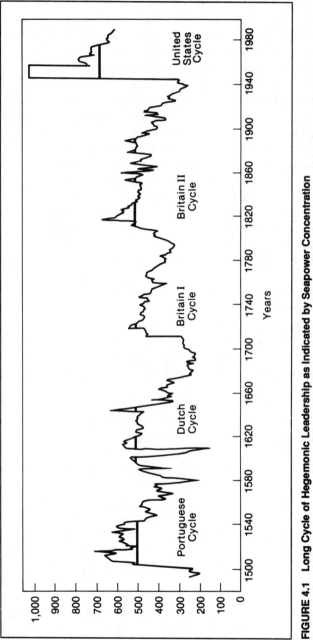

FIGURE 4.1 Long Cycle of Hegemonic Leadership as Indicated by Seapower Concentration

Source: From *Exploring Long Cycles*, edited by George Modelski. Copyright © 1987 by Lynne Rienner Publishers, Inc. Reprinted with permission of the publisher.

to interstate politics. Lord Salisbury claimed that "the only bond of union that endures [is] the absence of all clashing interests" (Morgenthau 1973, 9). Palmerston provided the dictum that "Britain has no permanent friends or enemies, only permanent interests." (*The Economist*, March 16, 1991, 14)

What then are these all-important interests of states? It is interesting and suggestive, given the presumed importance of state interests to the understanding of interstate behavior, that realists seldom devote much attention to defining them. Morgenthau went little further than equating state interest with (1) power and (2) security. A useful first step is to divide state interests into **core interests** and **instrumental interests**. The core interests of the state flow from its desire to preserve its essence: territorial boundaries, population, government, and sovereignty. Territorial disputes are almost certainly the most fundamental of all interstate conflicts, especially when, as in the case of the Iraqi claim to all of Kuwait, they threaten the continued existence of the state. States will, however, resist even the smallest redefinition of borders with the greatest of intensity. India and China fought in 1962 over a remote, mountainous, and largely uninhabitable territory called Ladakh. India and Pakistan have repeatedly clashed over the disposition of the much richer region of Kashmir. In 1992 India and Bangladesh found themselves unable to agree over the use of an area called the Tin Bigha corridor, roughly the size of two football fields, important because it connects (or separates) two population enclaves in each country. Such protectiveness is by no means the preserve of India alone or only of less developed countries. Japan and Russia proved unable to resolve their dispute over the Kurile islands, delaying the kind of post-cold war reconciliation that came with remarkable ease to Russia and the United States, even while their nuclear weapons remained targeted on each other's population.

It may appear cynical to suggest that territory has greater importance to states than do people, but examples of the sacrifice by states of people for territory (for instance, via warfare) come easier to mind than do those involving trades of territory for the security of people. Nonetheless, states also rank protection of their citizenry among their core interests. Israel has been especially willing to take great risks and pay high costs to protect even small numbers of its citizens threatened by terrorism or by state action.

It should surprise no one that states also take threats to their governments seriously; after all, those governments are the democratically or self-appointed agents of the state and take themselves seriously. The Sandinista government of Nicaragua regarded the effort by the United States in the 1980s to overthrow it as the most fundamental threat to core state interests. In the contemporary world more interstate conflicts have their roots in attempts by outside agents to subvert a government than in attempts by external states to change territorial boundaries. In fact, it has been the willingness of Russia and other republics of the former Soviet Union to foreswear such subversion that has made the countries of Western Europe and North America eager to bury old grievances. In this instance, Lord Salisbury appears validated: The elimination of clashing interests once more provides a bond for possible good interstate relations.

Protection of territory, people, and government (and thereby generally of sovereignty as well) thus emerge as fundamental to security and become the bedrock of state interest. Yet as Waltz (1979, 134) points out, "to say that a state seeks its own preservation or pursues its national interest becomes interesting only if we can figure out what the national interest requires a state to do." Unfortunately that is not simple. Consider for example the state interest of Israel and debates over whether or not it should trade land in the occupied West Bank for peace with its neighbors. Although we have already suggested that trades of territory to protect population are historically rare, we have also suggested that Israel places very great importance on protecting the lives of its citizens. What do core interests require Israel to do? For that matter, even if the state were clearly to rank the lives of even a few citizens above territory, would a sacrifice of territory save lives by dampening conflict with neighbors, or would it ultimately cost lives by making the remaining territory of Israel less secure from attack?

States routinely face such fundamentally important uncertainties about the definition of their interest and the demands that definition places upon action. Yet states need to act (even inaction is obviously a choice). Realists help address this dilemma in part by shifting much attention to instrumental interests, notably power. If a state protects and enhances its power, it stands a good chance of deterring threatening action by other states, of maximizing its ongoing options for action, and even of reducing the damage inflicted by mistaken action or inaction. Thus it is easy to understand a shift of the focal point of state interest by realists from core interests to power. We therefore similarly shift our attention to power and begin by considering what we mean by power.

POWER

DEFINITION AND MEASUREMENT

The commonest and most succinct definition of **power** is the ability of A to get B to do X.[11] Unfortunately, it is not at all simple to translate this definition into any clear measurement of power. For instance, should the United States do something Mexico wants (such as signing a free trade agreement), does it indicate that Mexico has power over the United States?

Your first reaction might be "no"—the United States signs such an agreement only if it wants to do so. The United States, however, may pay an economic penalty (for example, higher costs of imported goods) if it did not sign, just as it would pay a penalty if it decided to forego oil from the Persian Gulf. The size of those penalties suggests the amount of power that Mexico and Saudi Arabia have over the United States. That Mexico might pay an even larger penalty if the United States refused

---

[11]This particular definition has a strong relational, even bilateral (two actors) character. Two more general definitions of power in terms of outcomes are "the ability of an actor to influence the outcomes of international events to its own satisfaction" (Jones 1985, 245) or "the ability to prevail in conflict and to overcome obstacles" (Deutsch 1968, 22).

to ratify a free trade agreement suggests that both sides have power, and that it may not be equal.

The extent and complexity of such vulnerability relationships in the modern world are staggering.[12] Moreover, they are highly dynamic. Saudi Arabia had more oil in 1964 than in 1974. Yet the dependence of the world on that oil in 1974 was much greater because the exports of Saudi Arabia were much higher. Relationships of vulnerability can be specific with respect to scope and domain. Mexico has some power over the United States with respect to trade—it does not have obvious power over France on trade or over the United States on arms control.

Frequently when we think of power we focus less on such vulnerability to the withdrawal of a relational benefit than on the ability to coerce another actor with overt force.[13] Clearly, the ability of the United States to bomb Libya or to invade Panama gives it some control of policies in those countries. Here, too, however, power is complex. Libya, although militarily weaker, has the ability to train terrorists for attacks on targets valued by Americans. The presence of the canal in Panama could potentially either deter U.S. military action (for fear of its being shut down) or invite it (because of its strategic importance).

That power is such a central concept to the thought of realists motivates us to measure and compare the aggregate power of various states, despite the fact that power is highly relational, dynamic, and variable in scope and domain. How can we possibly undertake such measurement? Although the linkage is sometimes tenuous, much power grows ultimately out of capabilities: military strength, demographic size, economic production, resource bases, and even geographic position. Because much wisdom lies in the aphorism that "God is always on the side of the larger battalions," let us greatly simplify the issue and look at battalions and other measures of capabilities. We return to the issue of interaction outcomes later.

DEMOGRAPHIC

Table 4.1 ranks states on four capabilities: population, GNP, scientists and engineers engaged in research and development (as a measure of technological capability), and land area. Two states stand above all others in terms of population: China with nearly 1.2 billion people and India with 883 million. The United States ranks a quite distant third. Moreover, the gap between it and the rest of the pack is comparatively narrow; given the high growth rates of countries like Indonesia and Brazil, the gap is also closing rapidly.

---

[12]Caporaso and Haggard (1989) draw attention to elements of the structural relationship between states, asymmetries in particular situations (such as experience), and bargaining capabilities (including information use). Strange (1988) distinguishes between relational and structural power, which refers to an ability to shape the rules of the game. Our later discussion of the structuralist worldview returns to this theme.

[13]Baldwin (1980), however, carefully developed the concept of dependence (emphasizing opportunity costs of breaking a relationship) as a "power term."

TABLE 4.1
Selected Measures of State Power

Population (1992) in Millions		Gross National Product (1990) in Billions	
China	1,165.8	United States	5,392
India	882.6	Japan	2,943
United States	255.6	Russia	1,625
Indonesia	184.5	Germany	1,623
Brazil	150.8	France	1,191
Russia	149.3	Italy	1,091
Japan	123.2	United Kingdom	975
Pakistan	121.7	Canada	570
Bangladesh	111.4	Brazil	414
Nigeria	90.1	China	365
Scientists and Engineers in R&D (Late 1980s) as Percent of World		Land Area in 1,000 Square Miles	
Russia	19.8	Russia	6,593
United States	18.2	Canada	3,852
Japan	12.2	China	3,707
Germany	5.6	United States	3,615
India	2.3	Brazil	3,286
France	2.2	Australia	2,968
United Kingdom	2.0	India	1,269
Italy	1.4	Argentina	1,068
Czechoslovakia	1.3	Kazakhstan	1,049
Canada	1.2	Sudan	967

Sources:(Population and Land Area) Population Reference Bureau, World Population Data Sheet (Washington D.C.: Population Reference Bureau, 1992). (Gross National Product) World Bank, World Development Report 1992 (Washington D.C.: World Bank, 1992) and CIA, The World Factbook 1991 (Washington D.C.: CIA 1991). (Technology) UNESCO, Statistical Yearbook 1991 and U.K. Central Statistics Office, Annual Abstract of Statistics 1992 (London: Central Statistics Office, 1992).

During long periods, other capabilities frequently accrue to states with large populations. For instance, at the end of the last century, the newly unified Germany could boast a population greater than that of the United Kingdom or France. It took little time for Germany to pose an economic and military challenge to the older states. The reunified East and West Germany again boasts a larger population (by about one-third) than either of its two major competitors in Europe.

The nineteenth-century Russian empire did not translate population into systemic influence, however, because of internal weaknesses and because its physical expansion was incomplete.[14] Nor was the United States rise on the world

[14]Peter the Great (reigning 1682–1725) and Catherine the Great (reigning 1762–1776) made significant territorial gains.

stage instantaneous after its population overtook larger European states in the late nineteenth century. Both the United States and Russia, somewhat remote geographically from the core of European politics, and preoccupied with nearer neighbors and expanding frontiers, eventually did translate large population into global roles. The incredibly astute French social observer de Tocqueville foresaw these developments in his study of the United States in 1835. At that time he looked carefully at U.S. census data from 1830 that reported a U.S. population of 12.9 million, including more than 2 million slaves (de Tocqueville 1945, originally 1835, 386f. and 412f.). On the basis of past growth and the amount of land available he argued that:

> The time will therefore come when one hundred and fifty million men will be living in North America,[15] equal in condition, all belonging to one family, owing their origin to the same cause, and preserving the same civilization, the same language, the same religion, the same habits, the same manners, and imbued with the same opinions, propagated under the same forms. The rest is uncertain, but this is certain; and it is a fact new to the world, a fact that the imagination strives in vain to grasp.
>
> There are at the present time two great nations in the world, which started from different points, but seem to tend to the same end. I allude to the Russians and the Americans. Both of them have grown up unnoticed; and while the attention of mankind was directed elsewhere, they have suddenly placed themselves in the front rank among the nations, and the world learned of their existence and their greatness at almost the same time.
>
> All other nations seem to have nearly reached their natural limits, and they have only to maintain their power; but these are still in the act of growth....Their starting-point is different and their courses are not the same; yet each of them seems marked out by the will of Heaven to sway the destinies of half the globe. (de Tocqueville 1945, originally 1835, 451–452)

China and India have adopted much of European technology and increasingly emulate European economic structures. India'sgovernment is a British-style parliamentary democracy. They each have populations two to four times as large as those of Western Europe or the United States. Their economic growth rates are considerably faster than those of the European-based populations. Their natural resources and land areas are extensive. Should we perhaps now foresee that they will come to sway the destinies of the globe?

ECONOMIC, TECHNOLOGICAL, AND TERRITORIAL

Table 4.1 indicates a different structure of global economic capabilities. The United States has a unique place at the pinnacle of the measure. In fact, its economic size is almost twice that of Japan. Japan is nearly twice the size of either Germany or Russia (the Russian GNP estimate is very uncertain). As we saw in Chapter 1, U.S. leadership on this measure has slipped dramatically over time. Nonetheless,

---

[15]He reported 205 million in Europe at that time, in a lesser geographic area; there are now over 255 million people in the United States and about 500 million in all of Europe.

its lead is commanding and reinforces the identification of the United States as an economic hegemon.[16]

GNP may be the best single measure of power because states can fairly readily convert economic capabilities into military ones. In 1940, before the U.S. entry into World War II, Germany outproduced the United States by six to one in combat munitions (Deutsch 1988, 21). But because of the inherent strength of the U.S. economy, American production of munitions thereafter increased sixfold in only three years as the economy mobilized for war. Few doubt today that Japan could similarly turn its economy to military production with remarkable speed, if it made the decision to do so.

Statistically, the United States, Russia, and Japan appear to have an edge over the rest of the world in scientific-technological leadership. Each has a roughly similar portion of the world's scientists and engineers doing research. In the early 1980s nearly 36 percent of all scientists and engineers in the world were Soviet citizens,[17] and the United States placed a distant second. In addition, both the U.S.S.R. and China published more scientific books than did the United States. The U.S.S.R. spent about 4.6 percent of its GNP on research and development, versus 2.4 percent for the United States (Kurian 1984, 383). Yet all of these indicators of technological position were and are suspect measures of scientific leadership. First, countries report these statistics themselves and count scientists and publications differently. Second, access to knowledge may be as important as its generation. Scientists in former Communist countries regularly complain that they lack sufficient access to international journals. Deutsch (1988, 38) reports that the United States accounts for 41.5 percent of total scientific authorship, including authorship in scientific journals. Furthermore, large portions of the global scientific literature are in English and therefore especially accessible to U.S. citizens. With respect to still another measure, applications for patents or inventors certificates, the Japanese led in 1983 with 253,000, as compared to 150,000 in the U.S.S.R. and 104,000 in the United States (United Nations 1985, 511–12). The reality is that we have no good measure of scientific or technological leadership.

Still another basis of power lies in territory. Territorial scope can provide agricultural potential and natural resources. Although simple physical extent cannot guarantee greater physical capabilities (for example, Russian grain-growing areas lie mostly north of the parallel that also marks the Canadian–U.S. border), Table 4.1 includes it for reference. On this measure, Russia is the dominant state (the former Soviet Union sprawled across 8,600,000 square miles).

---

[16]Comparative measurement of economies presents substantial problems, many of which are tied to exchange rates. If the currency of an economy drops 50 percent in value relative to the dollar in one year (after adjustment for relative inflation rates), does that really mean that the economy is 50 percent smaller than the year before? Obviously not. On the problems see Kravis, Heston, and Summers (1982). For adjusted international economic data from 1950–1980 see Summers and Heston (1984).

[17]United Nations Educational, Scientific, and Cultural Organization, *Statistical Yearbook 1987* (Paris: UNESCO).

MILITARY

Military power is more difficult to measure than population or economic size. Military spending often serves as an indicator. Others look at actual capabilities such as military personnel or equipment. We will look in turn at spending and capabilities.

The United States and Russia together account for more than half of world military spending. Before placing much trust in military spending figures, however, consider just two of the problems in comparing the spending of the military superpowers. First, although the United States does not put into its military budget some items that could very reasonably be argued to be military expenditures (for example, veteran's benefits and interest on government debt, much of which it incurred during wartime), the U.S.S.R. long consciously concealed a significant portion of its military budget in other spending categories and the new Russian government continues to have trouble measuring it.[18] Second, the United States has voluntary and relatively high-paid armed forces in contrast to the Russian use of low-paid conscripts. Those who prepared the figures of Table 4.2 attempted to adjust spending for some of these difficulties. For instance, the Central Intelligence Agency calculates military spending in questionable cases by looking at purchases (equipment and labor) and valuing them at U.S. prices. Considering the imprecision of such techniques and the highly politicized environment in which they are applied, debates inevitably rage concerning "true" figures.

TABLE 4.2
Measures of Military Power (1990)

Military Spending in Millions of U.S. Dollars		Military Personnel in Thousands	
United States	249.1	China	3,030
Russia	189.7	Russia	2,437
Saudi Arabia	33.5	United States	2,118
United Kingdom	19.6	India	1,262
France	18.1	North Korea	1,111
Germany	16.9	Vietnam	1,052
Japan	16.3	Iraq	1,000
Kuwait	11.8	South Korea	750
Italy	9.3	Turkey	647
India	8.5	Pakistan	550

Source: International Institute of Strategic Studies, *The Military Balance 1991–92* (London: International Institute of Strategic Studies, 1991).

Notes: Military spending is in 1985 dollars and exchange rates, Saudi and Kuwaiti spending includes estimates of Gulf War costs and contributions. German data is only for former West Germany, excluding West Berlin. Russia is estimated at 61 percent of the former U.S.S.R., using data from the United States Arms Control and Disarmament Agency, *World Military Expenditures and Arms Transfers 1990* (Washington D.C.: U.S. ACDA, 1991), 81.

[18]In 1989 Soviet leadership admitted this and provided estimates (still low) of total spending.

Military spending may understate the military power of countries like China that substitute personnel for money. In terms of military personnel the two superpowers are Russia and China. In general, attention to personnel raises the ranking of Third World countries. But military personnel is clearly an inadequate military power measure by itself.[19]

The two different measures of military power in Table 4.2 suggest quite different global power rankings. Furthermore, we have not addressed the difficulty that nuclear weapons add to the issue. The truth is that we do not really know how to measure military power, as important as it is.

AGGREGATE CAPABILITIES AND POWER

Despite measurement problems, the Correlates of War Project at the University of Michigan added the variables of Tables 4.1 and 4.2 into an overall index of power capabilities; the index provides a sketch of changes in relative power over time.[20] The composite index actually relies on two demographic measures (total population and urban population), two economic indicators (steel production and fuel consumption), and two military figures (personnel and expenditures), combined with equal weight.[21] Table 4.3 reports that index for great powers at selected intervals in the twentieth century (immediately before and after World Wars I and II and in recent years). The absolute numbers have little credibility; we should focus on general patterns and on changes over time.

Several patterns are especially notable in Table 4.3. One is the placement of the United States in first or in a very close second position throughout the century. It has, in fact, been the "American century." Second, the challenge that Germany made to the leading powers and especially to Britain, preceding both world wars, shows clearly in the index. Before both wars German power had risen above British. Coalitions vanquished Germany in both world wars, and Britain re-emerged above all other European states, the same position it had in the nineteenth century. Third, the failure of the European great powers of 1900 (especially Germany, Great Britain, and France) to recover a serious ability to challenge the superpowers after World War II indicates the fundamental transformation of the system that occurred in that war. Finally, China and India, which the Michigan

---

[19]It is also sometimes misleading. For instance, many Soviet "troops" are used primarily for railroad construction and maintenance.

[20]Ray (1987, 193). Merritt and Zinnes (1989) review several composite power measures and find high correlations among them. Tabor (1989) finds, however, that the measures provide inconsistent images of less developed countries.

[21]The 1984 and 1991 calculations by this author replace both steel production and fuel consumption by GNP. Although at one time the former measures were useful indicators of economic power (especially before economists developed GNP accounting in the 1930s), they are no longer (see Oneal 1989, 179–181). Other materials increasingly supplant steel, and high energy consumption can be a sign of economic inefficiency. Continuing to use those indicators overweights the increasingly archaic Russian economy. The analysis here considered all countries of the world for inclusion in the 1980s and 1990s.

TABLE 4.3
Aggregate Power Index

1913 (Pre–World War I)			1920 (Post–World War I)	
United States	26		United States	46
Russia	18		United Kingdom	22
Germany	18		France	13
United Kingdom	14		Italy	11
France	9		Japan	8
Japan	6			
Austria-Hungary	6			
Italy	4			

1938 (Pre–World War II)			1946 (Post–World War II)	
U.S.S.R.	25		United States	45
United States	24		U.S.S.R.	34
Germany	20		United Kingdom	14
United Kingdom	10		France	7
Japan	10			
France	6			
Italy	5			

1984 (Pre–Soviet Collapse)			1991 (Most Recent)	
United States	27		United States	35
U.S.S.R.	24		China	16
China	18		Russia	13
India	10		India	11
Japan	8		Japan	9
West Germany	5		Germany	6
France	4		United Kingdom	5
United Kingdom	4		France	5

Sources: James Lee Ray, *Global Politics*, 3rd ed. (Boston: Houghton Mifflin, 1987), 193–195. Calculations for 1984 and 1991 from sources of Tables 4.1 and 4.2.
Notes: GNP was substituted for both steel production and energy consumption in the index computation beginning in 1984.

scholars did not even consider for inclusion in the power rankings through 1946, ranked above the European states by the mid-1980s. Dramatic global changes marked the "quiet" years after World War II.[22]

[22]The inclusion of India in Table 4.3 contradicts the tendency of most scholars. Levy includes neither it nor Japan. His definition of great power (1983, 16) focuses on military strength and security interests. If we restrict the definition of great power to the traditional one, that is, states that have systemwide (now global) interests and force projection capabilities, there are in reality only two great powers today (the United States and the Russia).

Although not trustworthy, the absolute numbers are provocative. The gap between the United States and all other states is substantial. China ranks high because of its strength on many measures (it appears more powerful overall than Russia), whereas India achieves its position primarily for demographic reasons. Japan surpasses the individual power totals of the traditional European great powers but would fall considerably short of the total for a united Western Europe. It is also interesting that all of the five largest powers in 1991 have Pacific Ocean coastlines (only two of five did in 1913).

In addition to the superpowers and great powers, many other states hold significant military capabilities. Table 4.4 presents some information on the power capabilities of states in regional arenas; it groups sets of states with historic conflicts. Note especially the Asian pairs. In recent years arms expenditures in that region have jumped; Chinese purchases of advanced arms from Russia have even caused Japanese anxiety. In 1992 the Chinese began to apply their power by proceeding with oil exploration in the Spratley Islands, parts or all of which many other Asian states claim.

OTHER CAPABILITIES

The relative ease of quantifying demographic, economic, and military capabilities should not cause us to overlook still others that contribute to overall power. Consider natural resources. Both the United States and Russia have considerable autarky (economic independence), because they possess abundant supplies of many natural resources, especially energy. Germany suffered in World War II from its much greater dependence on outside resources.

Alliances also contribute to power capabilities. The total of alliance strength normally falls short of the sum of strength in individual partners, because of failures of countries to commit fully and the inefficiencies that arise in coordinating two or more separate militaries. Nonetheless, alliances frequently play determining roles in the outcomes of wars. On the basis of demographic and economic size, Table 4.4 shows that Iran should have easily beaten Iraq in their war (Iranian advantages were on the order of three to one). Yet Iran was largely isolated in the international community, whereas Saudi Arabia and others (including the United States) gave Iraq considerable support. The slight edge given the United States over the Soviets in the overall power rankings of Table 4.3 for 1984 did not reflect the important strength of its alliance structure. In the case of an East-West conflict, the Eastern European forces were unreliable allies for the U.S.S.R., even before the governmental changes of 1989–1990.

GEOPOLITICS

Geographic factors make still another nonquantifiable contribution to capabilities. For instance, natural borders, such as the mountains of Switzerland or the seas surrounding Britain, Japan, and the United States, confer advantages. **Geo-**

TABLE 4.4
Regional Balances of Power, 1990–1992

Regions and Competitive States	Population (Millions)	GNP Billions)	Military Spending Billions)
Asia			
India	882.6	254.5	8.5
Pakistan	121.7	35.5	2.8
China	1,165.8	364.9	5.7
India	882.6	254.5	8.5
North Korea	22.2	30.0	5.0
South Korea	44.3	236.4	6.6
China	1,165.8	364.9	5.7
Taiwan	20.8	151.0	5.3
Europe			
Greece	10.3	57.9	2.2
Turkey	59.2	96.5	1.6
Latin America			
Argentina	33.1	93.3	0.6
Brazil	150.8	414.0	0.5
Middle East			
Israel	5.2	53.2	3.6
Egypt	55.7	33.2	2.5
Syria	13.7	14.7	2.3
Iran	53.9	116.0	3.8
Iraq	18.2	35.0	4.8

Sources: (Population) Population Reference Bureau, *1992 World Population Data Sheet* (Washington D.C.: Population Reference Bureau, 1992); (GNP) World Bank, *World Development Report 1992* (Washington D.C., 1992) and CIA, *The World Factbook 1991* (Washington D.C.: CIA, 1991); (Military Spending) International Institute for Strategic Studies, *The Military Balance 1991–92* (London:IISS, 1991).

politics (the role of geographic factors in international politics) heavily influenced both scholars and practitioners in the early part of this century. In 1890 Alfred Mahan attributed the rise of British power to the country's island position and its related development of naval power. His writings encouraged President Theodore

Roosevelt to develop U.S. naval power in the first decade of the twentieth century (Kennedy 1983, 43–85). Sir Halford MacKinder retorted in 1904 that history alternates between land and sea power (which he said had been dominant for four centuries), and he argued that modern industry and the railroad would favor the great land powers in the twentieth century. Moreover, MacKinder described East Europe and Central Russia as the heartland of the world's greatest land mass, which he called the world island (the Euro-Asian-African continental aggregate), and he argued that states could translate control of the heartland into control of the world island and eventually the world. Although Nazi attention to such ideas subsequently contaminated and discredited them, it is of interest that the cold war struggle had its focal point in Eastern Europe.

Neither scholars nor practitioners devote as much attention to geopolitics as they did a century ago. This is as it should be, because industrialization and technological advance reduce the potence of geographic barriers to human movement in commerce or military action.[23] The United States and Russia, separated by the major oceans of the world, are fully able to destroy each other. Yet geopolitical thought still often surfaces. Aron saw the U.S. positioning of troops in Seoul and Berlin as analogous to earlier British policy:

> In relation to the Eurasian land mass, the American continent occupied a position comparable to that of the British Isles in relation to Europe: the United States was continuing the tradition of the insular state by attempting to bar the dominant continental state's expansion in central Germany and in Korea. (Aron 1966, 1)

In evaluating the motivations behind the Soviet invasion of Afghanistan, some observers pointed to the "age-old" drive of the Russians to a warm-water port (a sea port that, unlike those of Russia on the Pacific, would be free of ice throughout the year). They speculated that control of Afghanistan was the first step toward the goal. The second step would be to arouse the nationalistic fervor of the Baluchis in southeastern Iran and southwestern Pakistan so that they would seek their own state, perhaps with Soviet assistance. That overall design would not be so terribly different from the one followed by the United States in facilitating naval connections of its East and West coasts. Early in the century the United States encouraged Panama to declare its independence from Colombia, so that it could build the Panama Canal across the new country.

Most recently, new technologies have led to reassessment of the land- and sea-oriented theories of earlier geopoliticians (Brzezinski 1988). Now they focus on air power and on the "commanding heights of space,"—one of the reasons debates concerning the strategic defense initiative (SDI or "Star Wars") have such intensity. Geopoliticians can reasonably argue that the Soviet Union's urgent

---

[23]More broadly defined, however, geopolitics includes attention to the distribution of industry and technology (not simply geographic features). MacKinder and his contemporaries were observing the decline in Britain's share of world manufacturing from 31.8 percent in 1870 to 14.7 percent in 1906–1910 (Kennedy 1983, 49) and reevaluating sea power in that context. The linkage of decline in American industry to decline in U.S. world role is a successor to this argument.

opposition to U.S. development or deployment of such technology lay in their perception of space as geopolitically central.

POWER AND THE INTEREST OF STATES

We began this discussion of power by noting that realists frequently shift the focus of interstate politics to maintenance and enhancement of power because the instrumental approach appears to offer a definition of state interest with potentially fewer problems that those based on core interests such as territorial integrity, protection of population, and the preservation of a governmental system. In the course of our discussion, however, at least one key problem should have become obvious—it is not at all easy to define and measure power.

Measurement difficulty does not make a concept less important, as a realist would be quick to point out. It does, however, make a concept less useful as a guide to action. For instance, in the 1990s a central foreign policy debate in the United States concerns the appropriate size of the defense budget. What might seem a simple realist argument that the size should be such as to maximize U.S. power runs into the difficulty of measuring power. Clearly military expenditures compete with other governmental and private expenditures and at some point will reduce economic growth. Because both military capabilities and economic health are important to overall power, however, and because we cannot agree on a weighting for their contribution and thus on an overall measurement of U.S. power, we cannot determine an optimal level of U.S. military spending. Many realists, looking at the rapid growth of the Soviet threat after World War II and the military expenditures that the United States needed to counter it, argue for maintenance of considerable expenditures. Many other realists, looking at the growth of the Japanese economy since World War II, probably assisted by low military expenditures, argue for greatly reduced expenditures.

This example leads us to another very important issue with respect to the use of power as a guide to action. States can look at their power in absolute terms (the size of their own military, their own economy, and so on). In reality, however, they more often consider their power *relative* to that of other states. All of the above tables on power have at least implicitly compared the power of states with each other. Our attempt to look at an aggregate measure of power (see again Table 4.3) explicitly divided the overall power of states in the world and focused our attention on relative power.

Much of realist argument understands the world as one of relative gain and loss, as one which is fundamentally **zero-sum** (that is, the gain of one country is another country's loss, so that the *sum* of gains and losses is *zero*). Whether the stakes are power, economic condition, or territory and resources, improvement for one state comes at the cost of another.[24] With respect to economics, Gilpin (1987) argues:

[24]At the power level it is obviously true. The expected utility theory "treats bilateral wars as if they are viewed as situations involving pure competition. *i* believes it can gain as much from a bilateral conflict as *i* believes *j* must lose" (Bueno de Mesquita 1981, 48). And Waltz (1959, 198) claims that "In a condition of anarchy, however, relative gain is more important that absolute gain!"

In a world of competing states, the nationalist considers relative gain to be more important than mutual gain. Thus nations continually try to change the rules or regimes governing international economic relations in order to benefit themselves disproportionately with respect to other economic powers. (Gilpin 1987, 33)

The zero-sum perspective of many realists further complicates the use of power as a guide to action because it requires that we simultaneously consider the actions of other states, including those that are direct counteractions to those of a given state. A zero-sum perspective also leads inevitably to conflict, or at least minimizes the prospects for cooperation, because the gains of one state come only at the expense of another (Grieco 1990). In the remainder of this chapter we begin to explore how states use their power in the pursuit of their interests (including maintenance of that power). In the next chapter we move to consideration of how states interact with each other.

INSTRUMENTS OF POWER: STATECRAFT

The previous discussion focused on power capabilities. Although it would be convenient to continue elaboration of the theoretical argument of realists by assuming that states use their power capabilities skillfully, in reality they do not always do so. Thus many realists take time out to instruct policy makers on the proper use of power. We will similarly digress here to discuss the *art* of statecraft.

Statecraft is the artful application of state power, guided by an understanding of the contemporary state system and a *vision* of desirable change in it. Ideally such understanding and vision should organize the day-to-day reaction to external events that often appears unstructured or ad hoc. From a realist perspective, power realities should inform the understanding of the world, and a stateman's vision should maintain and enhance the state interest (fundamentally its power).[25] The tools of statecraft fall generally into the categories of diplomacy, economic instruments, and the use of force. We consider each in turn.

DIPLOMACY

Simpson (1987: 6) defines diplomacy as "the process by which policies are converted from rhetoric to realities, from strategic generalities to the desired actions or inactions of other governments." **Diplomacy** involves three activities: representation, reporting, and negotiation (Van Dinh 1987, 4). The first two, representation and reporting, center on the conveyance and acquisition of information, of which rational policy making and implementation require large volumes.

REPRESENTATION

It is important to governments that other states adequately understand their policy concerns and objectives. For instance, one factor contributing to the invasion of South Korea by North Korean forces on June 25, 1950 may well have been

[25]See Morgenthau (1973, 5) for such a definition of state interest.

inadequate communication by the United States of its commitment to defend South Korea from attack. On January 12, 1950, Secretary of State Dean Acheson gave a speech to the National Press Club in Washington in which he identified the defense perimeter of the United States in terms of a line from the Aleutians to Japan to the Ryukyus (islands of southwest Japan) to the Philippines (Dougherty and Pfaltzgraff 1986, 80). Although South Korea was not specifically excluded, it was not included in this perimeter. During his presidential campaign, Dwight Eisenhower subsequently argued that this definition virtually invited the attack. The United States has since been more careful not to omit any strategic interest from its public pronouncements.

Nonetheless, the United States perhaps made a similar mistake prior to the Iraqi invasion of Kuwait in 1990. The U.S. ambassador to Iraq, April Glaspie, met with Saddam Hussein on July 25. Although reports of that meeting vary, she may not have conveyed (and may not have been instructed to convey) the clearest and strongest U.S. opposition to such action by Iraq. On August 1, Hussein's forces invaded Kuwait.

States regularly attempt to clarify their policy positions in a variety of ways. One approach in the United States is the statement by presidents of doctrines. The Monroe Doctrine (1823) declared the Western hemisphere off-limits to European powers. The Truman Doctrine (1947) enunciated an intent to support any country resisting Communist pressure. The Carter Doctrine (1980) declared during the Iranian hostage crisis that the Persian Gulf was part of U.S. vital interests. In similar fashion, the Brezhnev Doctrine, formulated with the Soviet invasion of Czechoslovakia in 1967, stated that the Soviets would protect socialism, wherever it existed. On issues of special importance governments also periodically issue "white papers," which generally review a policy problem and state official positions. On a day-to-day basis, foreign ministries routinely brief diplomats from other countries about their policy objectives and intent.

Although states normally wish to communicate clearly, and rely on skilled diplomats to avoid miscommunication, countries also deliberately obfuscate and conceal. With respect to the scope of concerns and intensity of interest, states commonly overstate them to avoid the kind of problem the United States had in Korea. The routine proclamation that a government would "view with serious concern" a particular action by another government deliberately creates some ambiguity about the actual extent of concern and potential counteraction. Similarly, countries may be unwilling to divulge information about their military capabilities. This can sometimes deter action by creating fear of greater retaliation than is actually possible.

Thus governments play a cat-and-mouse game with one another, seeking to inform, misinform, and obfuscate. Still another twist is disinformation, including the propagation of forged documents supposedly originating with one's opponent and intended to discredit that opponent. The Soviet Union once used this technique frequently. For instance, one Soviet forgery of a letter, supposedly from the American undersecretary of state to the U.S. ambassador in Greece, suggested that the United States was willing to support a military coup in Greece, if necessary to maintain its military bases there (Holsti 1988, 211–12). The purpose of the letter was to cause an intense anti-American reaction in Greece.

Propaganda, although tainted by frequent inclusion of untruths, is another form of representation. Diplomatic representation focuses on other governments, whereas propaganda frequently targets foreign populations. The United States Information Agency staffs more than 100 libraries and information centers abroad. More than 100 states broadcast abroad. The United States uses a global radio network called the Voice of America and other vehicles, including Radio Marti, which broadcasts specifically for Cuba, and TV Marti, which began to do so in 1990. The British Broadcast Corporation maintains a World Service that has a well-deserved reputation for accuracy and a large global audience. Germany founded Deutsche Welle in 1953. The future of broadcasts from the former Communist states is in doubt. Ironically, in 1992 Radio Moscow's Vietnamese service, calling itself the Voice of Freedom, began transmitting anti-Communist news about Russia. Like many other countries, Israel supports a foreign radio service; it also relies on an array of organizations and individuals to communicate its message to the U.S. government and public.

REPORTING

Gathering intelligence and providing it to decision makers is a central activity of diplomats and foreign diplomatic missions. When Iranian radicals labeled the American embassy in Teheran a "den of spies" in 1979, they were in a most general sense correct. All embassies seek information on the objectives and interests of the states in which they are located. Much of the information search is open and, as we discussed earlier, the host country facilitates it. Because much information given freely omits or even obfuscates important details concerning intent and capabilities, however, states supplement it with clandestinely obtained knowledge.

Historically, the most important clandestine tool for information gathering was human espionage. The advent of sophisticated electronic eavesdropping extended espionage abilities dramatically. The United States and Russia monitor conversations around the world. American evidence in 1988 that Libya was building a chemical weapons factory came in part from overhearing a telephone conversation between Libyan and German scientists.

The sophistication of electronic measures complicates the relationships between embassies and the host governments. In the 1980s, the United States and the former U.S.S.R. built and sought to open new embassies in Moscow and Washington, respectively. The United States found that surveillance equipment so permeated the structure of its new embassy in Moscow that it could never be secure. The United States had sought similarly to infiltrate electronically the new Russian embassy in Washington, but apparently had less success because the Soviets completed its construction under much stricter controls. To complicate matters, the new Russian embassy sits on a high point within Washington, so that modern electronic equipment can monitor communication in the heart of the U.S. capital.

The United States refused to let the Soviets occupy their new Washington embassy until they resolved problems in Moscow. In late 1991 the chief of the Soviet KGB gave the U.S. ambassador full plans of the "bugging" and the issue moved toward resolution.

The distinction between diplomat and spy is thus fuzzy at times. In addition governments around the world maintain extensive intelligence operations without the cloak of diplomatic function. Among the most famous (or notorious) are the Russian Commissariat for State Security (KGB), the American Central Intelligence Agency (CIA), the Israeli Mossad, and the British MI-6. The bulk of the budgets for such organizations support a range of electronic and human intelligence gathering. Electronic intelligence gathering and protection of communication has become such a large-scale activity that the U.S. Department of Defense also maintains a huge National Security Agency (NSA) devoted solely to it.[26] Electronic intelligence using reconnaissance satellites, spy ships, special aircraft, and ground stations fall into its domain. The outside world may know less about the NSA than about the CIA. The public notoriety of the intelligence organizations comes, however, from their covert actions. The CIA, the KGB, and the services of other states support clandestine psychological, political, military, and economic activities.

In the 1990s economic espionage on behalf of domestic firms moved to a more prominent place on the spying agenda. The French Direction Générale de la Sécurité Extérieure (DGSE) has been accused of bugging airline seats and the hotel rooms of businessmen and of planting moles in foreign companies.[27] IBM is a special target of French, German, and Japanese espionage. The French intelligence budget even increased 9 percent in 1992 (the year after the collapse of the Soviet Union) to allow hiring of 1,000 new employees.

NEGOTIATION

The third diplomatic activity, and the one we most often associate with diplomats, is negotiation. Obviously, an important function of negotiation is to reach agreement among two or more countries on issues in which they have partly overlapping, but also competing, interests. Each side seeks to attain agreement as close to its own position as possible, and the skill of diplomats plays an important role. For instance, diplomats seek to conceal their minimally acceptable position or **resistance point** so as to achieve more. It is partly for this reason that the quotation from Sir Henry Wotton, an English official (1568–1639) is so popular. He defined a diplomat as "an honest man sent abroad to lie for the good of the country" (Van Dinh 1987, 3).

Negotiation most often involves the iterative narrowing of the gap between initial positions—it is hoped in a movement toward the zone of overlap defined by the minimally acceptable positions. In some cases skillful diplomacy even seeks to lower resistance points and to create a zone of overlap where none initially

[26]The U.S. electronic signals intelligence program may employ 65,000 people and the Russians may utilize even more.

[27]*The International Herald Tribune*, June 24, 1992: 6; *Newsweek*, May 4, 1992: 58–60.

existed.[28] For instance, Henry Kissinger flew repeatedly in 1974 between Aswan, Jerusalem, and Damascus and was able to accomplish a lowering of acceptable minimums, so as to secure an agreement among Egypt, Israel, and Syria that defused the military situation remaining from the 1973 Mideast War (Stoessinger 1976, 190–200). His technique became known as **shuttle diplomacy**. President Jimmy Carter accomplished the same feat in 1978, when he brought Egyptian President Sadat and Israeli Prime Minister Begin to Camp David (the U.S. presidential retreat in Maryland) and shuttled between their cabins until an agreement was obtained.

Diplomacy, however, is often a "velvet glove" that conceals the iron hand of power. Weaker powers must frequently make concessions at the table to avoid losses in a test of power. Because powerful states normally prevail in negotiations, states seek to "negotiate from strength." In Vietnam and in Afghanistan, the United States and the U.S.S.R., respectively, found themselves eventually forced to negotiate from considerable weakness (specifically, an obvious lack of will to continue fighting) and both obtained settlements that did little more than cloak their decisions to unilaterally withdraw. The close relationship between diplomacy and force gives rise to a combination that Alexander George (1991) calls **coercive diplomacy**. For instance, the British threatened the use of force against Argentina in the early stages of the 1982 Falklands (Malvinas) dispute, and moved almost in slow motion to apply force, as a part of their search for a diplomatic settlement. The United Nations first imposed sanctions on Iraq and threatened force in an effort to persuade it to withdraw from Kuwait. As these examples illustrate, coercive diplomacy is not always successful.

Negotiation also sometimes has functions other than the apparent one of attaining agreement. It may have a propaganda function. Both superpowers periodically put forward arms control proposals that appeared sincere, but that were patently unacceptable to the other side and that sought only to convey a peace-loving image to publics around the world. Soviet calls over many years for general and complete disarmament fell into this category. Another function is to stall for time in the hope that the external power balance will shift in one's favor.[29] At the beginning of the Vietnam War negotiations in 1969, interminable debates centered on the shape of the negotiating table. Although reflecting some substantive disagreement (notably the identification and status of parties to the negotiation), the delays represented fundamentally the desire of the parties to seek resolution on the battlefield rather than in the conference room. They finally obtained an agreement in 1973, when the United States wanted out of the war.

Negotiating styles differ considerably across time and by country. In the nineteenth century, diplomats commonly conducted discussions covertly and even kept important mutual defense treaties secret. This **old diplomacy** had some

---

[28]Druckman and Hopmann (1989) review the literature and practice of negotiation and conclude that we must relax the assumptions by the realist model of bilateral, unitary, rational, and symmetrical actors.

[29]Negotiation may also simply placate domestic forces or attempt to divide an opposing alliance (Jensen 1988b, 10).

advantages. Practitioners could conduct it in a somewhat genteel atmosphere, unconstrained by the passions of public opinion. The contribution of secret treaties to the spread of World War I (by committing states to actions of which other states were unaware), and the democratization of government in the twentieth century, brought a new, public diplomacy. With few exceptions, like the secret dispatch of diplomats by Bush to China in 1989, diplomats conduct the **new diplomacy** quite openly. Although sessions took place behind closed doors, the press regularly reported progress in the Intermediate Nuclear Forces and Strategic Arms Reduction Talks negotiations between the United States and the U.S.S.R. during 1987–1990.

Bargaining styles also differ across countries:

> Sir Harold Nicolson, a renowned British diplomat argued on the basis of his long experience that the bargaining styles of a country's diplomats reflect major cultural values of their society. He contrasted the "shopkeeper" style of British diplomats— one that is generally pragmatic and based on the assumption that compromise is the only possible reason for and outcome of bargaining—with the style of the totalitarian governments, particularly Soviet Russia in the 1920s and during the height of the cold war, and Nazi Germany in the 1930s. The diplomats of these regimes were known for rigidity in bargaining positions; extensive use of diplomatic forums for propaganda displays; coarseness of language; a strategy of trying to wear down opponents by harangues; interminable wrangling over minute procedural points; constant repeti- tion of slogans and clichés; and, most important, the view that agreements were tactical maneuvers only, to be broken or violated whenever it was to one's advantage (to quote Lenin, "Agreements are like pie crusts: They are made to be broken."). (Holsti 1988, 183)[30]

Although ideology underlies much difference in style, power differentials contribute to the explanation. More powerful states can afford "sincere" and "pragmatic" styles aimed at finalizing agreements. Less powerful states are more likely to bluster and posture, and to rely on tactics to wear down the other side. As the Soviets gained military parity with the West, their negotiating style also evolved toward that of the West.[31]

ECONOMIC POWER

Countries also draw on a wide range of economic instruments in their interactions with other countries (Baldwin 1985, 41). For example, both the former U.S.S.R. and the United States have used their contributions to international organizations as leverage for policy influence. The Soviet Union refused to pay its assessed share of the 1960 United Nations peace-keeping effort in the Congo because UN forces supported an anti-Marxist government faction. In 1990, the

---

[30]Indicating that national characterizations can be dangerous, Barnet (1984) says Lenin was actually quoting an old British proverb.

[31]There remained important differences. Former U.S. START negotiator Edward Rowny stressed that the Soviets had greater patience: "The Russians play chess; we play video games. They like the well-thought through results of step-by-step reasoning; we like the instant results of electronic games." (Jensen 1988b, 16).

United States reduced its contribution to the United Nations Food and Agricultural Organization in protest against its support for the Palestine Liberation Organization. The best-known and perhaps most frequently applied economic instruments are trade restrictions and foreign aid; we now concentrate our attention on them.

TRADE RESTRICTIONS

The commonest trade restrictions, applied with the intent of influencing the behavior of other states, are **boycotts** (the restriction of imports from a country or countries) and **embargoes** (the prohibition of exports) to a country. **Tariffs** (taxes on imports) can also reward and punish other states, but more often raise revenue or protect domestic industry. **Quotas** (numerical limitations) on imports or exports sometimes also constitute the application of economic power.

Trade restrictions have a long and controversial history. Athens applied a trade boycott to Megara, a Spartan ally in 432 B.C. (Baldwin 1985, 150–154). That use of economic power may have precipitated the Peloponnesian War. The League of Nations directed both a boycott and limited embargo at Italy in 1935–1936 in reaction to its invasion of Ethiopia. Analysts almost universally characterize that effort as a failure, and the episode contributed to negative assessments of both the League and economic instruments. Debate continues on the impact of the U.S. embargo on shipment of fuels and goods with military value to Japan during 1940 and 1941. Although that action provided an incentive for the Japanese attack on Pearl Harbor, and therefore was hardly a success (unless its intent was to provoke Japan),[32] it did somewhat weaken Japanese military might.

The United States, the leading economic power of the century, often uses trade restrictions in its foreign policy. For instance, the United States embargoed exports of anything with strategic value to the Soviet Union and its allies (these barriers are falling in the 1990s). In addition, the United States long limited the ability of the Soviet Union and allies to export by refusing to apply low tariffs to their goods. Between 1960 and 1963 the United States gradually raised economic sanctions against Cuba to the level of a total embargo. In fact, one motivation for the invasion of Panama in 1989 was that Noriega had helped Castro circumvent the embargo. Because Cuba had been highly integrated with the U.S. market, the embargo dealt a severe blow to the island economy. It did not, however, achieve a change in the Cuban government. Instead, relations between Cuba and the Soviet Union intensified, as the latter became both market and supplier for Cuba. Cuban economic growth, and possibly Soviet growth as well, suffered from the inefficiency of linking their economies at such a distance. Thus the success of the measure depends on whether the U.S. goal was change in the Cuban government or damage to the Cuban economy.

[32]De Conde reviewed Japanese–U.S. relations in the period preceding the surprise attack. He concluded that:

> Later, isolationists and other critics argued that Roosevelt invited the assault on Pearl Harbor in order to bring the United States into the war against the Axis via the back door of the Pacific. No available evidence shows that he maneuvered the Japanese into attacking.... (De Conde 1978, 173)

After the Soviet invasion of Afghanistan in December 1979, the United States restricted grain shipments to the Soviets to the minimum level allowed by treaty. This embargo forced the U.S.S.R. to turn to supplies from Canada, Australia, and especially Argentina, and it cost U.S. farmers market share and lowered domestic prices. Although the Soviets paid somewhat more for supplies, they had little difficulty obtaining them. The U.S. action could be considered a success only as a symbolic gesture. After Reagan's inaugural in January 1981, he lifted the embargo.

The United States also applied economic sanctions to Panama and Nicaragua in the 1980s. Deterioration of the Panamanian economy facilitated the U.S. invasion in 1989 by lowering support for General Noriega; weakening of the Nicaraguan economy supplemented external pressure for democratic elections and set the stage for an upset of the Sandinistan leadership in 1990.

The former Soviet Union had fewer opportunities to apply trade restrictions, because it had limited trade ties with the rest of the world. It did impose an embargo on Yugoslavia in 1948 in an attempt to bring that Communist but independent country into coordinated action against the West. The result was that Yugoslavia turned its trade quickly and with little difficulty to the West. In contrast, a halt in 1958 by the Soviet Union of imports from Finland (in association with other diplomatic and economic sanctions) resulted in a change in the Finnish government to the satisfaction of the Soviet Union. The sanctions were effective because the Finnish goods were not then competitive in the world market (Holsti 1988, 221). On the whole, however, the Soviet Union held considerably less economic leverage than does the United States.

The United Nations has also sought to organize economic sanctions. Beginning in 1966, it called for a trade embargo against the white minority regime of Zimbabwe (then Southern Rhodesia) in support of the struggle for black majority rule. The sanctions, which were in effect until the change of government in 1979, did not bring the economy to its knees but did worsen economic conditions and helped maintain international attention on Southern Rhodesia as a "pariah state." They probably helped force the change to black majority rule.

In the 1980s, South Africa faced increasing restrictions on its trade and international capital flows for the same reason. A debate raged over whether intensified sanctions would weaken the South African economy and force change, or whether they would create a "bunker mentality" among South African leaders and cause them to resist change even more strongly. Also, some argued that economic sanctions hurt blacks more than whites, and that this was a reason to forego the measures. Others thought that sanctions should be applied even if blacks suffered most in the short term, either because the longer-term benefits would compensate for the pain, or because the pain would mobilize blacks more quickly in the struggle against the white regime. After the decision of the South African government to negotiate with the African National Congress, even some Reagan administration opponents of sanctions (forced upon the administration by Congress) believed in their influence.

Prior to the use of military action against Iraq for its takeover of Kuwait, the UN Security Council ordered tight boycotts and embargoes on Iraq. By some estimates, the GNP of Iraq dropped 50 percent due to the sanctions.[33] In 1992 the UN imposed strong sanctions on Serbia.

EFFECTIVENESS OF TRADE RESTRICTIONS

Although some analysts argue that trade restrictions are effective political instruments,[34] many others conclude that they are not powerful tools. Knorr (1975, 152) reviewed twenty-two cases of trade restrictions and said only four succeeded. In contrast, one comprehensive study concluded that of 115 cases since World War I, they were successful in 34 percent (Hufbauer, Schott, and Elliot 1990, 93). There are two fundamental methodological problems in evaluating success and failure. First, the aims of the sanctions are not always clear. Second, we have no "control" case against which to evaluate the application of economic power—we do not know what would have happened had it not been applied.

Two factors greatly reduce the effectiveness of trade restrictions. The first is that with exceptions such as highly sophisticated technology, most goods are **fungible**. That is, goods produced in one country are nearly indistinguishable from goods originating in another. This is especially true of raw materials like crude oil or grain. Thus restrictions on trade by one or a group of countries often elicits offsetting supplies or markets in others. Governments can easily cheat by simply failing to monitor carefully the actions of companies that can, if caught, be blamed for undertaking actions of which the government officially disapproves. Obviously nearly universal adherence to sanctions, like those imposed on Iraq, have greater chances of success.

The second problem is that governments often apply trade restrictions on issues so important that the states facing sanction will accept considerable sacrifice rather than buckle to pressure. This is a failure in statecraft, because the declared goals are unreasonable. Despite the costs, Cuba was unwilling for more than thirty years to change its system of government to access U.S. markets. In fact, the outside pressure can, at least for a time, be a rallying point for governmental efforts to secure popular support—the "rally around the flag" effect. For instance, the history of U.S. economic interference in Central America is so long and unpopular there that embargoes against the Nicaraguan government aroused some support for it among the population.

Frequently the declared goals (or "apparent" goals, because states often act without a clear goal declaration) differ from the real goals. Many embargoes simply satisfy domestic pressures to "do something," and embargoes threaten all parties less than military action. The U.S. grain embargo against the Soviet Union fell into this category.

---

[33]*The Christian Science Monitor,* April 10, 1991, 9.

[34]Baldwin (1985) believes that scholars underestimate their importance.

FOREIGN AID

Foreign assistance is a second economic instrument available to states and includes monetary grants, commodity gifts, loans, technical assistance, and emergency humanitarian relief. It, too, has a long history. In the eighteenth and nineteenth centuries, European states often provided their allies with financial subsidies. In the 1930s the British originated programs to accelerate the economic development of their colonies (Holsti 1988, 230).

The Marshall Plan was the most spectacular aid program of the post–World War II period. In 1948, three years after the end of the war, the European economies were still in bad shape, with energy shortages and hunger characterizing both the victors and the vanquished. The Soviet Union and the United States were already struggling over the nature of governments in Greece, Turkey, Czechoslovakia, Berlin, and elsewhere; Communist movements in Western Europe were gaining strength. In a speech at Harvard, U.S. Secretary of State George Marshall proposed a substantial aid program for Europe. Although officially named the European Recovery Program, it is much better known as the Marshall Plan. It channeled $12 billion to Europe. Between 1946 and 1952 the United States devoted more than 2 percent of its GNP to foreign aid (Baldwin 1985, 296), compared with approximately 0.2 percent in recent years. The program is universally hailed as a great economic and political success. It helped precipitate the "economic miracles" of European growth in the 1950s and 1960s; it tied Western Europe to the United States politically and economically; and it even provided some initial impetus to the economic integration of Europe by requiring the states to plan the use of aid collectively.

In the 1950s and 1960s U.S. aid shifted from Europe to the Less-Developed Countries (LDCs). The newly recovered countries in Europe increasingly joined in giving aid. The Development Assistance Committee (DAC) now monitors foreign aid programs of major Western donors. Its membership consists of most Western European countries and the United States, Canada, Australia, and New Zealand.[35] According to the DAC, **official development assistance** (ODA) should meet two criteria: It should promote economic development and welfare; and it should be concessional in character, with a grant component of at least 25 percent (Sewell and others 1988, 203). The concessional, nongrant element of aid consists of loans that LDCs can repay during long periods and with low interest rates.

In the 1990s many observers have called for a similar program of aid to the former republics of the U.S.S.R. and to the countries of Eastern Europe. In 1992 Western leaders approved a $24 billion aid package (a fraction of the real economic size of the Marshall Plan), but debates raged on conditions.

Aid Donors and Channels

Because of its strong economy, its involvement in the Marshall Plan, and its early cold war concern about loss of the Third World to communism (especially

---

[35]Eighteen members of the OECD serve on this specialized committee. Greece, Iceland, Luxembourg, Portugal, Spain, and Turkey do not (Sewell, Tucker, et al., 1988, 202).

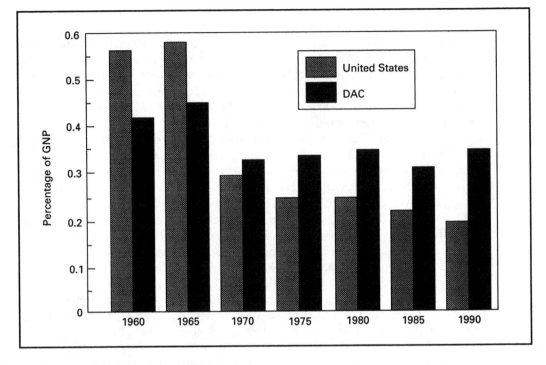

FIGURE 4.2   Foreign Aid Donation Rates
Source: World Bank, *World Development Report 1992* (Washington, D.C.: Oxford University Press, 1992), p. 254.

after the success of communism in China during 1949), the United States was the dominant Western donor of all types of aid through the 1950s and 1960s. In 1970 it still gave nearly one-half of total development assistance, down from 60 percent in 1960 (Hansen and others 1976, 204). As the economies of its allies strengthened and their aid grew, however, the U.S. commitment weakened. In 1990 its share was 20 percent. Figure 4.2 traces the U.S. and DAC aid history as a percentage of GNP.

In an effort to balance its desire to provide aid against the more difficult international economic circumstances in which it increasingly found itself, the United States turned to mechanisms that would help serve domestic as well as foreign interests. For example, to meet the need for food in LDCs, and to simultaneously help dispose of U.S. surpluses, the United States initiated the Food for Peace Program (Public Law [P.L.] 480) in 1954. When U.S. surpluses shrink, routine provisions under this program also decline, but the United States remains the principal source of emergency food relief when starvation threatens Africa or elsewhere in the world. Another mechanism adopted by the United States and other donors facing the same problems is to rely on **tied aid**, distributions that must be spent in the country of their origin. Although recipients lose some value of the aid, tying assures that U.S. aid returns as demand for U.S. goods, and this helps maintain domestic support for the program.

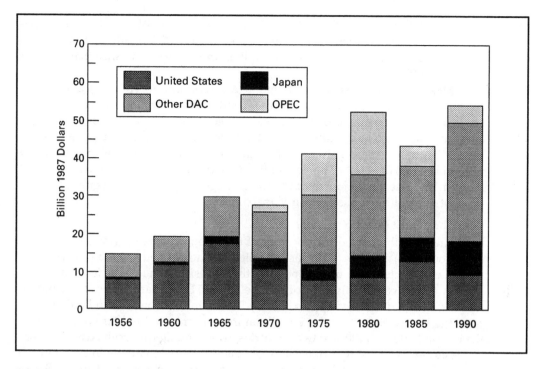

FIGURE 4.3 Foreign Aid Donation Levels
Source: World Bank, *World Development Report 1992* (Washington, D.C.: Oxford University Press, 1992), pp. 154-55.

DAC members other than the United States have maintained fairly constant donations as a portion of GNP. The Scandinavian countries, the Netherlands and France led the ranks in 1990, each directing more than 0.7 percent of GNP to the South. Although traditionally not a large aid donor (giving less than 0.25 percent of GNP throughout the 1970s), Japan stepped up its program substantially in the late 1980s. In 1990 its development assistance budget exceeded $9 billion and it challenged the United States as the world's largest donor of economic aid. Just as the United States translated some of its international surpluses into aid during the 1950s, Japan is doing the same in the 1990s (Figure 4.3).

Several of the wealthier Organization of Petroleum Exporting Countries (OPEC) states (especially Saudi Arabia, Kuwait, and the United Arab Emirates) have similarly distributed surplus funds from increased oil revenues in the 1970s. After the major oil price increases of 1973–1974, Arab OPEC members stepped up development assistance flows as a percentage of GNP from an already generous 2.1 percent in 1970 to 4.8 percent in 1975. As oil prices and revenues slipped in the 1980s, so did the OPEC commitment. By 1980 the rate had dropped to 2.9 percent of GNP, and it fell to 1.4 percent in 1987 (OECD 1988, 60).

Extensive data on former Soviet aid are not readily available. It appears that the Soviet Union gave about 0.2 percent of GNP as development assistance, approximately the same as the United States (Blake and Walters 1987, 140). Between 1954 and 1981, the Soviet Union gave a total of $22.3 billion to non-Communist LDCs in economic aid and $70 billion in military assistance (Saivetz and Woodby 1985, 141).

Most foreign assistance is bilateral aid (country to country) and donor countries distribute it through their own institutions. Both donors and recipients see this as a way of maximizing political and economic control of donors. Recipients have urged greater multilateral aid, support directed through global institutions.[36] Multilateral aid grew from a negligible portion of the total aid effort (5.9 percent in 1965) to about 24 percent of the total in 1975. Since then, multilateral aid has remained near one-fourth of the total, suggesting that donor states continue to want control over this economic instrument.[37]

The Impact of Aid

Aid contributes about 15 percent of the foreign exchange (total funds from other countries) of LDCs.[38] Because it is highly concentrated, it has a much greater impact on selected countries, especially the lowest-income countries, which frequently are not competitive in world trade. In 1985 Egypt earned about $3.5 billion from exports and received approximately $2.5 billion in economic and military aid from the United States. Of the $16 billion in economic and military aid given by the United States in 1990, just two countries, Israel and Egypt, received $5.3 billion. As deserving as these two states may be, the U.S. effort to maintain peace in the Middle East obviously takes priority over economic development in the South (Table 4.5).

The former Soviet Union also concentrated its aid heavily. Large portions of Soviet aid once went to Egypt (when it was a Soviet client state between 1956 and 1972). In 1974 it directed more than 90 percent of its total flows of aid to only three countries: Pakistan, Argentina, and Syria (Hansen and others 1976, 211). From this listing of former aid targets we can see the difficulties that the Soviets had translating aid into long-term development or political commitments to the U.S.S.R.; Egypt and Pakistan subsequently became tied closely to the United States,[39] Argentina today receives little aid and has significant economic problems. In the late 1980s, three-fourths of the Soviet Union's assistance budget went to three other countries: Cuba (perhaps $5 billion in 1989), Mongolia, and Vietnam (OECD 1988, 86 and 228). Those flows have now collapsed.

---

[36]In response to their pressure, the World Bank established the International Development Association (IDA) in 1960 to grant **soft loans** (with long repayment periods and low interest rates) to the LDCs (Riggs and Plano 1988, 319). And in 1966 the United Nations combined earlier and smaller programs into the United Nations Development Program (UNDP).

[37]In addition, nongovernmental organizations (such as the Red Cross societies, Save the Children Fund, OXFAM, and CARE) channel a volume of assistance to LDCs equal to about 10 percent of bilateral and multilateral flows from states—not an insignificant amount (OECD 1988b).

[38]Export earnings account for about 75 percent of LDC foreign exchange (Blake and Walters 1987, 34). A variety of international transfers, including foreign aid and private investment flows, provide the rest of foreign exchange.

[39]Interestingly, Egypt continued to be a prime recipient of Eastern European funds in 1987.

	TABLE 4.5		
	U.S. Foreign Aid by Type and Recipient, 1990		
Country	Total Receipts	Economic Assistance	Military Assistance
Israel	2,987	1,195	1,792
Egypt	2,389	1,093	1,296
Pakistan	587	357	230
Turkey	516	15	501
Philippines	494	351	143
Panama	397	397	
Greece	349		349
El Salvador	328	247	81
Nicaragua	223	223	
Honduras	214	193	21
Bolivia	149	109	40
Morocco	126	82	44
Portugal	126	39	87
Bangladesh	126	126	
Guatemala	118	115	3
India	117	117	
Jordan	115	45	70
Costa Rica	95	95	
Peru	95	93	2
Columbia	94	21	73
Poland	82	82	
Tunisia	75	44	31
Jamaica	74	73	1
Ethiopia	72	72	
Mozambique	72	72	
Total (Twenty-five Countries)	10,020	5,256	4,764
Total (All 108 Recipients)	15,727	10,834	4,893

Source: Agency for International Development, *U.S. Overseas Loans and Grants and Assistance from International Organizations: Obligations and Loan Authorizations, July 1, 1945—September 30, 1990.* Washington D.C.: Agency for International Development, 1991.

Notes: Ranked by amount of total assistance; units are millions of U.S. dollars.

Most OPEC aid helps Arab Moslem countries, and most French aid assists its former colonies in Africa (with which France trades heavily). The bulk of Japanese aid has always flowed to Asian countries (with which it has close trade associations). Some Japanese aid shifted to the Mideast in the 1970s in an effort to assure continued oil flows. In 1990 it announced substantial packages for Eastern Europe— one reason for this was to assure a foothold in new markets. For all of these large donors, political motivations and self-serving economic ones compete actively with humanitarian and economic development reasons for giving aid; Knorr (1975) argues that altruism motivates little aid.

What effect does aid have on the recipients? Partly as a result of the Marshall Plan's success, expectations for success in fostering development within the Third World were high. Studies of the relationship between aid receipts and economic growth, however, are indecisive (Bremer and Hughes 1989, 38–43). Nor is aid a clear political-military success for donors. Recipients understand the mixture of motives behind aid, and they resent efforts to control them. For example, U.S.–aid recipients regularly vote against it in the United Nations. In reality, aid has achieved neither rapid economic growth nor close and enduring political relationships. In this climate of pessimism about aid, the West has exhibited special reluctance about giving large amounts of it to the East.

In retrospect, there are at least four reasons that aid did not meet the expectations of donors or recipients. First, the amount of aid given to the Third World has in reality been small. Annual Marshall Plan aid to Europe during 1948–1952 averaged $13 per capita (Baldwin 1985, 321), whereas the average LDC in 1985 received less than $4 per capita (Sewell 1988, 241). And the 1985 dollar was worth a fraction of the 1950 dollar. Second, Europe had human capital skills—its technological abilities were highly advanced. What it needed was the physical capital of buildings and machinery to put its people to work. The LDCs need human capital as well—for instance, advanced engineering and agricultural skills. Third, the older European states had considerable political and social stability. The new states of the Third World often have experienced social turmoil. Fourth, LDCs have not always used aid wisely. In unstable political environments, aid has frequently facilitated control by oppressive governments and in some cases been appropriated by corrupt officials. At other times aid built grandiose but wasteful projects, from steel plants to soccer stadiums.

It would be inappropriate to end the discussion of aid on a sour note. Many aid donors truly are beneficent, and much aid has saved lives and improved living standards. It is relative to inflated expectations that aid has frequently failed.

MILITARY POWER

States package military force in many ways, including clandestine intervention and subversion, unconventional or guerrilla warfare, limited military strikes, and full-scale warfare. Powerful states select from the full gamut of options, whereas the less powerful more often choose from the menu of clandestine and unconventional instruments. States need not always use force to be effective, and, in fact, they hope to achieve their aims through diplomacy or the threat of force (coercive diplomacy). Actually resorting to full-scale warfare generally indicates a failure of statecraft because the costs for the loser will be greater (because of the costs of the unsuccessful battle) than the costs of a negotiated settlement before defeat. Thus we focus here on lesser force.

Communist forces in China prior to 1949, in Vietnam from the 1950s through the early 1970s, in Nicaragua before the Sandinista victory in 1979, in the Philippines in the 1980s, and in many other instances have used guerrilla or **unconventional warfare** against the established government. In these instances, the inability of the revolutionary elements to apply and win with conventional warfare dictated the kind of force chosen.

Other reasons exist, however, for the use of force short of traditional conventional warfare. The Reagan administration of 1980–1988 significantly increased prior American support for use of unconventional force, directing it against Marxist governments in Afghanistan, Angola, and Nicaragua. In the first case the United States was unwilling to oppose Soviet forces directly and preferred to use Afghan guerrillas as proxies. In the other two cases, the administration did not have congressional or popular support sufficient to allow application of more substantial force.

Even superpowers prefer to use lesser force when accomplishment of desired objectives seems probable with it. Why unnecessarily expend blood and treasure, and why attract more attention and perhaps opposition to actions than necessary? The Soviets helped organize and then supported a coup against the Western-leaning, democratic government of Czechoslovakia in 1948. In a variety of ways the United States encouraged the military coup in Chile that overthrew the Marxist-leaning government of Salvador Allende in 1973. Both actions accomplished intended objectives.

The superpowers in particular also use limited strikes or **demonstration force** as an instrument of policy. In April 1986, the United States selectively bombed Libya in retaliation for Libyan governmental support of terrorist incidents, including a bombing in Berlin. Although the United States denied that leader Muamar Khadafi himself was a target, precision bombing struck his tent and reportedly killed one of his children.[40] Similarly, in 1987 the United States bombed and sank an Iranian oil platform in the Persian Gulf in retaliation for Iranian use of mines against gulf shipping. Only a strong state, such as the United States, appears likely to succeed with demonstration force, because the intention is to demonstrate the capability and the willingness to inflict even more harm.

Gunboat diplomacy is a broader category, into which demonstration force falls. It involves the demonstration, threat, or actual use of limited military (originally naval) force. In an earlier era the Soviet Union used military maneuvers near the borders of Poland and Czechoslovakia to indicate displeasure concerning internal governmental developments and to threaten actual invasion. Again, such behavior is predominantly that of the great powers.[41]

[40]There is still uncertainty about this claim, made by Khadafi's doctor after the attack (*World Almanac* 1987, 902).

[41]In a study of 133 episodes of gunboat diplomacy (limited to naval force) between 1946 and 1978, the United States accounted for 45, and the U.S.S.R. for 10 (Mandel 1986, 64). Another study found that the United States alone used the armed forces for political purposes 215 times between 1946 and 1975 (Blechman and Kaplan, et al., 1978, 23).

CONCLUSION

This chapter elaborated some of the basic elements of realism. Specifically, it defined state and explored the concept of state interest. It pursued the definition and measurement of power in considerable detail because of the centrality of that concept to realism and the deeper understanding power distributions give us of our world. It explored the complexity of translating power into state action by examining the varied instruments of statecraft.

Realism promises much more, however, than this useful but largely descriptive image of states, their power, and their instruments. It potentially offers great insights into their *interactive behavior*. The next chapter pursues that promise.

Chapter 5

STATES
IN INTERACTION

The preceding chapter was the first of three that elaborate a realist, state-centric understanding of the world. It defined and discussed some of the basic components of realist thought: the state, state interests, power, and the tools of statecraft. The discussion of statecraft began to move us away from thinking about states individually to focusing on their interactions. This chapter and the next fully embrace the study of interactions among states. They do so in three stages. This chapter first describes some of those interactions, focusing on conflict, but also considering cooperation. Conflictual and cooperative interactions are the aspects of global politics that we wish to explain (the dependent variables of our investigation). The chapter then moves to an analysis of the interactions of small numbers of states, considering especially bilateral (two-country) relationships. A focus on small numbers of states can make the explanation of conflict and cooperation easier. The next chapter explores the multilateral (many-country) relationships of the broader global system. It will add considerable complexity, but also richness, to our understanding of the dynamics of interstate relations.

FREQUENCY AND INTENSITY OF CONFLICT

In the world of states, conflict will occur. This section examines the historic record of two types of conflict, war and crisis.

STUDIES OF WAR

Lewis Fry Richardson, a mathematician and meteorologist, undertook perhaps the earliest systematic measurements and analysis of war, beginning his work in 1919. He counted 317 wars between 1820 and 1949, in work published posthumously (Richardson 1960a, 1960b).[1] While Richardson worked, Sorokin (1937)

---

[1]Which reminds me. After a lecture by an eminent professor, a student excitedly told him that "the lecture was simply superfluous." To which the professor sarcastically retorted that he hoped "to have it published posthumously." The student had the final words: "Great. The sooner the better!"

published his analysis of 862 European wars between 1100 and 1925. Independent of both Richardson's and Sorokin's efforts, Quincy Wright (1965) identified 200 wars between 1480 and 1941. Given their substantially different war totals, these three scholars obviously defined war differently.

Scholars of world politics have been extremely fortunate to have had a modern, much more intensive project on war measurement and analysis in place since 1963. J. David Singer and Melvin Small have directed the Correlates of War project at the University of Michigan in an ongoing effort to identify and explain international conflict.[2] Defining war as conflict involving at least 1,000 battle deaths, Singer and Small found 224 wars during the 1816–1980 period, of which 67 were interstate, 51 were extrasystemic (that is imperial or colonial), and 106 were civil wars. Leaving aside civil wars, only twenty of those 165 years were free of war. Other studies estimate that no day has been free of war since 1945, and that an average of twelve wars rage at any time in the modern era.[3] The Correlates of War project has also collected data on "militarized international disputes," conflict that may fall short of warfare.

Numbers of wars during long periods are interesting but not very useful. We want to know whether there are any patterns in such characteristics as frequency, cyclic occurrence, and intensity. We look at each in turn.

FREQUENCY

According to the Correlates of War project, the number of total interstate wars has increased irregularly since 1815. Figure 5.1 shows the amount of international war under way between 1816 and 1987. When adjusted by the increasing number of states in the interstate system, however, the frequency of war involvement for an average state exhibits no clear trend in these two centuries. The uncertain trend for overall warfare frequency in recent decades is discouraging for those who value peace. It is, however, consistent with the basic realist belief in continuity of international political behavior.

Another study (Levy 1983) examines only warfare among great powers and finds a clear downward trend since 1495 (see also Wright 1965).[4] Yet, the postwar great powers (identified in Table 4.3) have fought each other on two occasions since World War II: in the Korean War (China versus the U.N. forces led by the United States) and in the Chinese-Indian border dispute of 1962. In addition, the two superpowers warred frequently through support for lesser states that served as their proxies.[5] In brief, the evidence for trends in war frequency is somewhat ambiguous.

[2]Small and Singer (1982, 1985). Another important project focused on 119 wars involving great powers between 1495 and 1975 (Levy 1983).

[3]Kidron and Smith (1983); Sampson (1978, 60).

[4]A particularly quiescent nineteenth century, obvious in Levy's data on great power warfare, could account for the apparent growth in total interstate warfare since 1815.

[5]In the Vietnam War, however, Soviet specialists secretly staffed the anti-aircraft batteries in North Vietnam that shot down many American planes. They publicly acknowledged this in 1989.

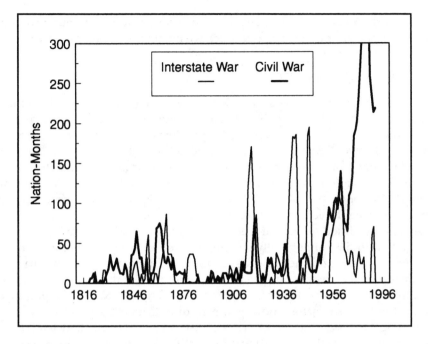

FIGURE 5.1 Annual Amount of War Under Way, 1816–1987
Source: Courtesy of the Correlates of War Project and J. David Singer. Reprinted with permission.

Another and much clearer trend is the near elimination of imperial wars in the post–World War II period. Whereas a high proportion of wars in the late 1800s pitted a great power against a prospective or actual colony in the Third World, that era is largely over. The conflict in 1982 between Britain and Argentina over the islands that the former calls the Falklands and the latter labels the Malvinas (and considers a colonial outpost of Britain) seemed a real anachronism.

Most dramatically, however, conflicts around the world have increasingly become civil wars, with and without intervention from outside. In 1990, armed conflicts (involving 1,000 or more deaths over their entire duration) raged or simmered in thirty-one locations (Lindgren, Heldt, Nordquist, and Wallensteen 1991, 345).[6] Only the conflict between India and Pakistan was fundamentally interstate. Internal conflicts such as those in Nicaragua, Colombia, and the Philippines, constituted more than half. The remaining conflicts centered on state formation, including the Tamil struggle in Sri Lanka and that of Eritrea in Ethiopia.

Realists focus our attention on interstate war, and over the centuries such wars, especially those among the major powers, have been the most violent by a considerable margin. Nonetheless, limiting attention to interstate conflict obvi-

[6]By one count (World Bank 1991, 141) there were 141 civil wars between 1700 and 1989, compared with 63 interstate wars.

ously overlooks very important elements of global politics. Although we continue our discussion here of interstate conflict, we must return subsequently to the issue of intrastate conflict.

CYCLIC OCCURRENCE

The notion that wars occur in some kind of regular cycle has long intrigued scholars and the public. A glance at historic patterns of warfare like that in Figure 5.1 strongly suggests such cycles. The problems are twofold. First, what is the length of the cycle? Suggestions include 20, 30, 50, 100, 165, 177, and 200 years, in part depending on whether all wars, major wars, or polarity-transforming wars are the focus of attention. Singer and Cusack (1981) used the Correlates of War data from 1816 through 1965 in a search for any cyclical pattern of warfare. They found none of any regular length, either for individual countries or at the systemic level. They also identified no secular trend in the frequency of warfare.[7]

Such studies cannot really lay the issue to rest, however, because an important repetitive dynamic need not result in highly regular warfare occurrence. For instance, war outbreak "could be related, among other things, to the time needed to 'forget' the last bloody conflict" (Small and Singer 1985, 13). Forgetting could interact with other factors, however, including leadership personality, weapons technology advance, and the severity of the most recent conflict. Instead of warfare every twenty years, the "forgetting dynamic" could contribute to increased conflict propensity in as little as ten years or as many as forty. In short, the absence of clear-cut cycles does not invalidate a cyclical logic of war explanation.

Thus, a second problem surrounding cyclical-war hypotheses becomes central (Thompson 1988): What is the explanation for the cycles? The generational memory explanation has an appeal to Americans because they can look back on the Spanish American War (1898), World War I (1914–1918), World War II (1939–1945), the Korean War (1950–1953), and the Vietnam War (ca. 1964–1973). Without the Korean War the cyclical pattern is remarkably regular.

The Soviet economist Kondratieff identified fifty or sixty-year economic cycles, and others have associated warfare with the economic cycles, in some cases arguing that warfare peaks in every second economic cycle (Goldstein 1985, 123–141). In reference to this cycle length, the famous political economist Kindleberger said that "Kondratieff is like astrology."[8] Beck's analysis (1991) finds no such cycles in warfare. Pollins (1992) not only identifies warfare cycles, but finds them linked to economic ones. The number of competing explanations for this and other cycles does, in fact, suggest that we lack firm understanding of the underlying dynamics (see Chapter 16). That makes the complex charting of war cycles reminiscent, as Kindleberger suggests, of discovering our fates from the stars.

---

[7]In contrast, Denton and Phillips (1968) claim a twenty- to thirty-year pattern. Small and Singer (1982, 156) note a fifteen- to twenty-year cycle in the amount of war underway (as opposed to initiations of war).

[8]*Forbes*, November 9, 1981, 166.

INTENSITY

Many trends in interstate warfare frequency are ambiguous (although great power warfare appears to be falling). Cycles in warfare outbreak are too irregular and poorly understood to provide either explanatory or predictive capability. Much study of warfare, however, agrees on one long-term and powerful trend: The intensity of the severest wars has increased (albeit irregularly) during several hundred years.[9] Table 5.1 lists the numbers killed in warfare in France, England, Austria-Hungary, and Russia during nine centuries. Especially large increases in casualties relative to population occurred in the seventeenth and eighteenth centuries (related both to technology and to social mobilization within new nations) and again in the twentieth century. The twentieth century easily takes the prize for bloodiest. Major participants suffered 8.4 million military deaths in World War I, and 17 million of their troops and 34 million civilians (2 percent of world population) perished in World War II.[10] Estimates of potential deaths in a full-scale and nuclear World War III range widely, but 1 billion from a global population of more than 5 billion is perhaps conservative.

TABLE 5.1
War Casualties in Britain, France,
Austria-Hungary, and Russia

Century	Casualties	Population Mid-Century	Casualties as Percent of Mid-Century Population
Twelfth	29,940	11,500,000	0.26
Thirteenth	68,440	15,500,000	0.44
Fourteenth	166,729	21,500,000	0.78
Fifteenth	285,000	30,000,000	0.95
Sixteenth	573,020	40,000,000	1.43
Seventeenth	2,497,170	55,000,000	4.54
Eighteenth	3,622,140	90,000,000	4.02
Nineteenth	2,912,771	171,530,000	1.70
Twentieth	33,522,550*	288,717,000	11.60*

Sources: (Compilation of Sorokin Data) Francis A. Beer, *Peace Against War* (San Francisco: W.H. Freeman, 1981):, 45; (Subsequent twentieth century casualties) Ruth Leger Sivard, *World Military and Social Expenditures* (Washington D.C.: World Priorities), assorted issues; United Nations, *World Population Trends and Prospects by Country, 1950–2000* (New York: United Nations, 1979).

*Note: Through 1992 only.

[9]Small and Singer (1982, 141) conclude, however, that "Whether we look at the number of wars, their severity, or their magnitude, there is no significant trend upward or down over the last 165 years." In all cases they control for system size. Table 5.8, examining a much longer period, contradicts that conclusion only for the four states it represents. Levy (1983) concludes that warfare between great powers in general has changed little in severity, but that the most severe wars have become more violent.

[10]Beer (1981, 37–38). Kegley and Wittkopf (1985, 431) claim 65 million total civilian deaths in World War II.

The United States has generally not suffered as much as Europe in the great wars of the last two centuries. Table 5.2 shows U.S. casualties in all its wars since independence. In total numbers of deaths, and especially in the percentage of population dying, the Civil War was the greatest catastrophe the United States has ever suffered. In percentage terms, the Revolutionary War follows and World War II is in third place. For reference only, and not to minimize in any way the suffering of Americans in war, we should compare those numbers with the casualty totals suffered by the U.S.S.R. in three wars of the twentieth century. They lost 6 million in World War I, 800,000 in the 1918–1920 civil war, and about 15 million in World War II (Sivard 1987, 30).

<table>
<tr><td colspan="4" align="center">TABLE 5.2
U.S. War Casualties</td></tr>
<tr><td>War</td><td>Battle
Deaths</td><td>Total
Deaths</td><td>Percent
of
Population</td></tr>
<tr><td>Revolutionary War
(1775–1783)</td><td>6,824</td><td>25,324</td><td>0.645</td></tr>
<tr><td>War of 1812
(1812–1815)</td><td>2,260</td><td>2,260</td><td>0.031</td></tr>
<tr><td>Mexican War
(1846–1848)</td><td>1,723</td><td>13,283</td><td>0.057</td></tr>
<tr><td>Civil War
(1861–1865)</td><td>214,938</td><td>498,332</td><td>1.585</td></tr>
<tr><td>Spanish American
(1898)</td><td>385</td><td>2,446</td><td>0.003</td></tr>
<tr><td>World War I
(1917–1918)</td><td>53,513</td><td>116,708</td><td>0.110</td></tr>
<tr><td>World War II
(1941–1945)</td><td>292,131</td><td>407,316</td><td>0.311</td></tr>
<tr><td>Korean War
(1950–1953)</td><td>33,629</td><td>54,246</td><td>0.036</td></tr>
<tr><td>Vietnam War
(1964–1973)</td><td>47,321</td><td>58,021</td><td>0.029</td></tr>
</table>

Source: The World Almanac and Book of Facts 1987 (New York: World Almanac, 1987), 321, 337.

The increased severity of the worst wars may explain the possible decrease in frequency of general war among great powers (as exposed to probing or proxy wars where the great powers are involved only indirectly). Upward trends in the abilities of states to mobilize populations and economies in war efforts and continued "progress" in military technology should give pause to rational, unitary actors—apparently it does.

CRISES AND SERIOUS INTERSTATE DISPUTES

Although the frequency of full-scale war among great powers may have declined as the consequences become less acceptable (the evidence is, as noted earlier, somewhat mixed), crises among great powers, with the threat of war, remained frequent throughout the cold war. They have more than once taken the world to the brink of nuclear war. Hermann (1969) developed the most widely used definition of **crisis**:[11]

> Crisis is a situation that (1) threatens the high-priority goals of the decision-making unit; (2) restricts the amount of time available for response before the situation is transformed; and (3) surprises the members of the decision-making unit when it occurs. (Hermann 1969, 29)

Scholars have undertaken several extensive analyses of multiple crises, comparable with the projects they devote to war. The study by the Brookings Institution of *Force Without War* found that the United States used force or the threat of it to achieve its objectives 215 times between World War II and the late 1970s, whereas the Soviet Union did the same 156 times.[12] All such instances were crises for some other state, and many constituted crises for the opposing superpower.

Other work focuses more sharply on crises. Lebow (1981) undertook a comparative case study analysis of twenty-six crises between 1897 and 1967. Brecher and Wilkenfeld (1989) profiled 323 crises between 1929 and 1985, and intensively studied selected crisis participants. Another substantial project compiled a data base of 960 "militarized disputes" between 1816 and 1976 (Gochman and Maoz 1984, 590).

Crises are of great importance because they can lead to war (Gochman and Maoz found that one in ten disputes did so). On June 28, 1914, a Serbian nationalist in Sarajevo assassinated the Austrian Archduke and heir to the Austro-Hungarian throne, Francis Ferdinand. Austria sent an ultimatum to Serbia on July 23. Although Serbia met most demands of the ultimatum, Austria declared war against it on July 28; Russia, Serbia's ally, mobilized its army, and Germany, Austria-Hungary's ally, declared war on Russia (August 1) and on France, another ally of Russia, (August 3). Within a relatively brief time after the beginning of the crisis,

---

[11]Snyder and Diesing (1977, 6) argue that the definition should emphasize the interaction of states and the conflict of interest: "An international crisis is a sequence of interactions between the governments of two or more sovereign states in severe conflict, short of actual war, but involving the perception of a dangerously high probability of war."

[12]Blechman and Kaplan et al.(1978) and Kaplan (1981). Interestingly, they found that the outcomes were more often unfavorable for the United States in the early postwar years when the strategic balance was 100-to-one or more in its favor. Outcomes became much more often favorable for the United States when the balance fell below ten-to-one.

a global conflict was under way. It is possible that better crisis management after the assassination could have avoided war. We will never know.

Historians have raised the same issue with respect to the German demands on Czechoslovakia in September 1938. German-speaking people inhabited a portion of Czechoslovakia, the *Sudetenland*. Nazi elements there, encouraged by Hitler, demanded incorporation of the region within Germany. A crisis ensued from German demands that Czechoslovakia cede the region. An international conference in Munich at the end of the month agreed to appease Germany and support the transfer of territory. In retrospect, critics have condemned the British Prime Minister Neville Chamberlain for deciding not to resist German aggression. At the time, however, most Britons applauded him. This may have been a turning point at which Britain and France could have avoided war or fought one against Hitler before the full development of German strength. Again we will never know.

It is said that generals learn the lessons of the last war and then misapply them in the changed circumstances of the present. The same danger exists with respect to crisis management. One can see in the handling of the *Sudetenland* crisis before World War II a desire to avoid repeating the intransigence that seemed to have led to World War I.

TRENDS IN CRISES

Crisis management may have improved, and we return to that subject later. Improvements are important because the number of crises has been increasing. In their study of militarized disputes since 1815, Gochman and Maoz (1984, 593) discovered an increasing trend in absolute numbers. After controlling for the number of states in the system, no clear long-term trend remains; however, even then crises surged during the first twenty-five years of the post-World War II period. Brecher and Wilkenfeld (1989) studied crises since 1928 (Figure 5.2) and identified a slight upward trend, but with much variation over time.

Which countries are most often involved in crises? Since 1815 the ten countries most likely to have initiated or to be the target of disputes are all major powers except one, Turkey (which, as the "sick man of Europe," was long a particularly vulnerable target). Great powers were involved in about two-thirds of all disputes, with Great Britain, the United States, and the U.S.S.R. leading the list (Gochman and Maoz 1984, 609).[13] Surprisingly, great-power participation in disputes since World War II may have actually increased relative to their numbers in the interstate system—they have become regularly embroiled in (and have often caused) the problems of the lesser powers.

The end of the cold war could have a substantial impact on the trend in numbers of crises. Some observers expect that military crises among great powers will decline sharply in number, perhaps replaced both by crises among lesser powers and by trade crises among the greater powers (like the dispute in 1992 between the United Staes and European Community over agricultural trade).

---

[13]Cusack and Eberwein (1982, 9) report that disputes among major powers have a one in five chance of leading to war, compared with one in twenty for minor power disputes.

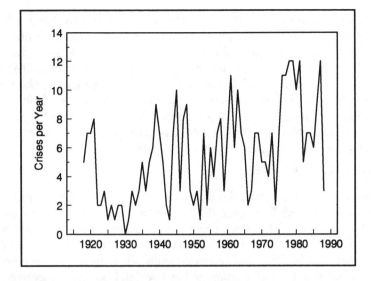

FIGURE 5.2 Frequency of Crises, 1918–88
Sources: Courtesy of Michael Brecher and Jonathan Wilkenfeld, "International Crisis Behavior Project, 1918-1988," ICPSR Study 9286.

Many realists, however, expect that new political alignments will ultimately lead to a resurgence of military crises even among great powers.

OBJECTIVES OF CRISIS INITIATORS

Lebow (1981) classified crises into three major categories according to the objective of the initiator. Some crises justify the broader hostility of the state beginning them. For instance, in 1964 the Johnson administration in the United States had decided that it needed to bomb North Vietnam, if it were to pursue the war in South Vietnam successfully. Although uncertainty lingers over the degree to which the United States provoked and anticipated North Vietnamese patrol boat attacks on U.S. destroyers in early August,[14] the administration used the attacks to garner the domestic support necessary to launch the bombers (Lebow 1981, 30–31).

Many crises are "spin-offs" of activities pursued for other objectives. For example, the German submarine campaign against British shipping in 1915 was a blunt instrument and sunk many neutral ships in the war zone. The Germans believed that the danger of confrontation with neutral powers, like the United States, was less than the advantage to be gained by cutting British sea lanes. On May 7 a U-boat sank the Lusitania with many Americans on board. This was the first of several German-American crises that ultimately helped bring the United States into the war on the British side in April 1917.

[14]Weather conditions and visibility were poor; the attacks, monitored electronically, may not even have occurred. Johnson later quipped that "For all I know, our Navy was shooting at whales out there." (Foster and Edington 1985, 148).

Many crises, and often the most dangerous ones, involve aggressive **brink-manship**, in which "a state knowingly challenges an important commitment of another state in the hope of compelling its adversary to back away from his commitment"(Lebow 1981, 57).[15] Iraq created such a crisis for Kuwait in 1990 when it moved troops to the border and demanded territorial concessions. The United States created such a crisis in trade during 1992 when it challenged fundamental policies of the European community. Two superpower crises, perhaps the two most dangerous of the postwar era, also fall into this category. They were the Berlin blockade and Cuban missile crises. We should sketch each.

BERLIN AND CUBAN CRISES

After the defeat of Germany, the four victorious allies, Britain, France, the United States, and the U.S.S.R., carved Berlin into four occupation zones, as they did the entire country. Unfortunately, Berlin was located deep within the Soviet zone of Germany (which became the German Democratic Republic), and the U.S.S.R. therefore controlled the land access to Berlin, allowing the Western powers to transport goods through East Germany to West Berlin. Cooperation between the Soviets and the other three powers in governing Berlin deteriorated rapidly. In early 1948 the U.S.S.R. rejected the introduction of a new West German currency in West Berlin, but the Western powers went ahead anyway in their zones, prompting the Soviet representative to walk out of the Allied Control Commission, which theoretically governed the entire city. The Russians began to disrupt Western ground transport to Berlin in May and halted it in June.

The exact objectives of the Soviet challenge were unclear, but the Western powers interpreted it as an effort to drive them out of the city. A truly remarkable airlift operation maintained supplies to West Berlin through the fall and winter, until the lifting of the blockade in April 1949. Soviet brinkmanship did not succeed. Several other crises involving Berlin erupted in subsequent years, including that following the building of the Berlin Wall around the Western sectors in 1961. That was essentially a spin-off crisis, because the primary objective in the East was to maintain control over its own territory, rather than to challenge the West. No Berlin crisis after the blockade placed such a serious strain on superpower relations.

By almost all accounts, the most dangerous crisis of the post–World War II period was the Cuban missile crisis. After Castro came to power in 1959 and Cuba moved into the Soviet orbit, concern welled in the United States that any Soviet nuclear weapons on that island could strike U.S. targets without warning, leaving no time for retaliation. The Kennedy administration explicitly warned the U.S.S.R. against placing such weapons there and received assurances that the Soviets would not do so. Apparently in an effort to overcome a position of nuclear inferiority (they had only twenty operational missiles on Soviet territory), and because they believed that an American invasion of Cuba was a serious threat, the

---

[15]Synder and Diesing (1977, 23) emphasize that international crises almost always illustrate "redistributive bargaining"; twelve of sixteen they studied involved (like Cuba) a response to an attempt to change the status quo.

Russian leadership decided to install nuclear missiles there secretly. The action directly affronted the United States and depended for success on the completion of the missile sites before the Americans knew about their construction and could act to stop it.

After discovering construction of nuclear missile sites in October 1962, the United States issued an ultimatum demanding their dismantlement and a guarantee that no missiles would be put into Cuba in the future. (Chapter 6 discusses the U.S. policy approach in more detail.) A naval blockade of Cuba and the threat to use nuclear weapons reinforced the ultimatum. After a few tense days, the Soviets backed down, securing a guarantee against U.S. invasion of Cuba. Many of the U.S. participants in the crisis decision making reported later that they felt the world to be quite near nuclear war—one assessment was a 50 percent probability. Conferences at Harvard in 1988 and in Moscow in 1989 brought together some of the principals from both countries to talk about the crisis. The Soviets revealed that their leadership had actually given the order to run the blockade, and that they countermanded it only an hour before the confrontation. In addition, they had completed delivery of twenty warheads to Cuba.[16] The world has almost certainly never been closer to nuclear war.

Brinkmanship, the willingness to go to the brink of war to achieve an objective, has not been limited to these two crises, nor has only the Soviet Union relied on it. After the Korean War, the United States decided that it could not risk further involvement in Asian land wars. During the 1950s, when it held clear nuclear superiority, Secretary of State John Foster Dulles was especially inclined to use nuclear brinkmanship in interactions with Communist governments. For example, in 1955 the administration publicly raised the possibility that it would use nuclear weapons if war erupted between the mainland Chinese government and that on Taiwan.

States resolve most crises, about 90 percent, short of war (Gochman and Maoz 1984, 601). Happily the superpowers have achieved a perfect record in their direct confrontations. The memory of that remaining 10 percent, however, when deep-seated hostility, unintended consequences, or brinkmanship did lead to war (including World Wars I and II), haunts anyone who thinks about it seriously. With the end of the cold war, the hot spots have changed. Crises are perhaps more likely to involve Iran and Iraq, India and Pakistan, Venezuela and Brazil, China and Vietnam, the Ukraine and Russia, and perhaps even Japan and Russia. These hot spots remain, however, very dangerous.

THE PREVALENCE OF COOPERATION

As important as conflict and war are, they account for only a small fraction of the interactions among states. Although by one estimate England has been involved in wars for fifty-six of every 100 years since A.D. 901. (Blainey 1988, 3), Small and

---

[16]*The New York Times,* January 29, 1989, 1 and 12; *The Christian Science Monitor* January 12, 1989, 7.

Singer (1985, 15) point out that more than one-half of the states that existed at some time between 1816 and 1980 fought no interstate wars at all during that period.

The realist worldview does not ignore cooperation. Realist emphasis on cooperation is limited, however. It portrays much of world politics as zero-sum, and when the gains of one state imply the losses of another (for instance, in relative power or in security), the basis for cooperation is limited. In addition, much of the cooperation on which realists focus is a kind of masked conflict. For instance, when realists characterize war as politics by other means, or see diplomacy as the sheathing of an iron fist in a velvet glove, they portray neither politics nor diplomacy as fundamentally friendly activities.

The self-interested behavior of realist politics can, however, be the basis for fairly elaborate forms of cooperation. Just as we can explain most individual human behavior, even seemingly altruistic action, as self-serving (by establishing mutually beneficial patterns of reciprocity), we can similarly portray elaborate interstate cooperation as fundamentally selfish. Perhaps the largest single number of state interactions involve cooperation to facilitate trade. Few if any states can produce all of what their citizens demand. They thus have mutual interests in the exchange of goods and services.

There are patterns of cooperation and even individual state actions, however, that strain at the limits of realist explanations. Does the high level of Scandinavian foreign aid to LDCs (nearly 1 percent of GDP) really provide access to markets or security greater than that achieved by Switzerland, which gives about 0.3 percent? Is it better to explain the infatuation of the United States with the Peace Corps as an attempt to build prestige and achieve leverage within the Third World, or as an expression of the idealistic urge of individual Americans? Did the invasion of the Falklands by Britain (after their capture by Argentina) represent power politics (based on residual colonial urges and a desire to protect prestige) or the support of a people's right to determine their own government?

It is, as we shall see very clearly in the next chapter, impossible to clearly delineate the boundary between cooperation as extended self-interest and as the expression of global community. In fact, there may not be a boundary, because global community, like local community, appears intimately related to extensive cooperation growing initially from self-interest. Although we have sharply contrasted the realist view of a world based in competing states with the globalist image of a peaceful world community, we could also draw a continuum between the two conceptualizations and the next chapter begins to do so.

The remainder of this chapter will, however, continue to build upon the traditional realist view of cooperation as strictly self-interested. We shift our attention now from the overall extent of conflict and cooperation to the underlying behavior that gives rise to them. Specifically, we begin exploring the dynamics of state interaction by considering bilateral (two-country) patterns.

INSIGHTS FROM BILATERAL ANALYSIS

In the pursuit of their own security interests, states seek to increase their power. We saw in Chapter 4, however, that power is relative. Thus as one country increases its power, the power of others automatically decreases. Even if the attempts by the Ukraine to secure as large a portion of the former Soviet military as possible (including the Black Sea fleet) are purely defensive, such an increase in Ukrainian power poses a threat to the capabilities of Russia. Such countries find themselves in a classic **security dilemma**. That is, actions intended defensively appear offensive to another state. They do not seek conflict, but the zero-sum character of power pushes them into it.

The security dilemma often sets up an **action-reaction dynamic** between the two parties. The action of one state to improve its security elicits a reaction of comparable magnitude from its rival. The most common manifestation of this pattern is the **arms race**. Often each country sees itself as threatened by the other and as acting purely in its own defense by increasing its military capabilities. The other state has the same perception.

States sometimes recognize the influence of the security dilemma on them and the mutual harm it can cause. When they do, they may adopt strategies to dampen the action-reaction dynamic and to reassure their opponent/partner that they intend no threat. Such strategies rely on the recognition that the action-reaction dynamic can also work in reverse—that reductions in threat to an opponent can give rise to matching actions by that state.

Consider the parallel with human beings who also interact repeatedly and find it useful to abide by a variety of rules (such as not hitting each other), even when interacting in the absence of any authority to enforce those rules. They do so because they know that violation of the rules would destroy an existing pattern of cooperation that is a basis for further beneficial interaction. They live in the "shadow of the future" (Axelrod 1984). Individuals therefore often apply the principle of **reciprocity**, as codified in the Golden Rule of "do unto others as you would wish them to do unto you." A large portion of cooperative human behavior involves expectations of reward in the form of reciprocated cooperation. States find themselves in the same situation.

The Golden Rule is balanced in human interaction by the principle of "an eye for an eye, a tooth for a tooth." When we behave cooperatively, we expect cooperation in return, and we are often prepared to retaliate when it is not forthcoming. The deeper the relationship (implying a long historic record of cooperation), the greater the temporary deviation from cooperative reciprocity we will accept.

Axelrod (1984) examined the benefits of this pattern of reciprocity in behavior—behavior that involved reciprocating in either a positive or negative way. He did so to answer fundamentally important questions for those directing the foreign policy of any state:

> When should a person cooperate, and when should a person be selfish, in an ongoing interaction with another person? Should a friend keep providing favors to another friend who never reciprocates?...How intensely should the United States try to punish the Soviet Union for a particular hostile act, and what pattern of behavior can the

United States use to best elicit cooperative behavior from the Soviet Union? (Axelrod 1984, vii)

For instance, how should the United States respond to an action like the Japanese restrictions on imports, so as to avoid escalation but simultaneously to discourage such action?

In an analysis (involving a computerized tournament) of a variety of strategies for two-party interaction, Axelrod found the reciprocity-based strategy that encouraged the most cooperation in the long run to be the simplest one tested: **tit-for-tat**. Beginning with a cooperative stance toward the other party, this strategy rewards cooperation with further cooperation and punishes (once) each negative action by the other side.[17] Moreover, Axelrod argues that this "winning" strategy tends to evolve naturally in many situations of repeated interaction, implying social learning that eliminates other, less successful strategies. That evolution occurs even in unlikely situations, such as in the trench warfare of World War I. "Cooperative" behavior often grew without communication between the infantrymen of the two sides, despite efforts by officers to suppress it. A British officer noted that

> It was the French practice to "let sleeping dogs lie" when in a quiet sector...and of making this clear by retorting vigorously only when challenged. In one sector which we took over from them they explained to me that they had practically a code which the enemy well understood; they fired two shots for every one that came over, but never fired first. (Axelrod 1984, 61)

We can, however, make a further distinction between **specific reciprocity** and **diffuse reciprocity**. In situations of specific reciprocity "partners exchange items of equivalent value in a strictly delimited sequence" (Keohane 1989, 134). The cooperation across the trenches of World War I illustrates specific reciprocity. Diffuse reciprocity involves more delayed and less precise exchange, in which obligations accrue and greater trust exists. "In personal life, bargaining over the price of a house reflects specific reciprocity; groups of friends practice diffuse reciprocity" (Keohane 1989, 134). The trade relations of the United States and Canada illustrate diffuse reciprocity.

While tit-for-tat interaction implements specific reciprocity, a second strategy for interacting with other states, **graduated reciprocation in tension-reduction (GRIT)**, builds on the concept of diffuse reciprocity. Charles Osgood (1962) made the argument that states could elicit cooperative actions from other states by announcing and undertaking a series of unilaterally cooperative steps. He proposed the policy specifically to reduce the arms race of the cold war. We will discuss later some limited attempts to implement this strategy.[18]

---

[17]Hamburger (1979, 232–236) reports earlier work by Rapoport and Chammah on the tit-for-tat strategy. They found that a benevolent version, in which a player tries cooperation every fourth play when mutual defection has been "locked-in," works even better than simple tit-for-tat.

[18]Goldstein and Freeman (1990) examined post–World War II interaction among the United States, U.S.S.R., and China and found that an extended GRIT most successfully established cooperation.

In summary of this discussion, states often find themselves trapped in a security dilemma and a cycle of increased arms spending or even of increased overt violence. They can, however, attempt to dampen such cycles via reciprocity-based strategies such as tit-for-tat and GRIT. We want to move the discussion now to a specific bilateral relationship, that based on the mutual possession of nuclear weapons.

THE NUCLEAR RELATIONSHIP

Although the global system may now be evolving toward a multipolar one (or may find itself in a prolonged unipolar stage), the primary task of managing the current system remained in the hands of two nuclear superpowers for a significant portion of the twentieth century. They have faced each other with weapons so devastating that their use could actually threaten the survival of humanity. Other pairs of countries, notably India-China and India-Pakistan, have more recently entered into similar bilateral nuclear relationships. The probability that nuclear weapons will ever be used in a large-scale exchange is unknown, but however small that probability is, responsible governments must devote great resources to reducing it still further. In this section we review first the status of the weaponry. Then we consider the strategies that states have developed in the complicated effort simultaneously to make the weapons appear "usable" (and therefore useful instruments of power) and to minimize the chances that they will be used.

THE PLAYERS AND THEIR EQUIPMENT

Nuclear forces have two components: nuclear warheads and delivery vehicles. Five states officially have and plan to maintain nuclear warheads. The United States tested its first bomb in 1945 and used two of them against Japan that same year. The U.S.S.R. followed it into the era of nuclear weaponry (1949), as did Great Britain (1952), France (1960), and China (1964). Each of these states has moved from the simpler and less destructive atomic bomb technology, which the United States used against Hiroshima and Nagasaki, to the much more devastating power of hydrogen bombs. India openly exploded a "peaceful nuclear device" in 1974 but claims to have no warheads.

In 1992 the United States and the former Soviet Union each deployed about 11,000–12,000 strategic warheads.[19] The average Soviet warhead was larger, and the total **equivalent megatonnage** (the equivalent explosive power as measured in millions of tons of TNT equivalent) of the former Soviet force was larger. Together the superpowers maintained more than 16,000 megatons in their strategic arsenals, more than three tons per human. The French possessed about 450 warheads, the British about 300, and the Chinese about 350.[20]

---

[19]International Institute for Strategic Studies (1989, 212). Both sides also have "tactical" or battlefield warheads. Total warhead numbers were perhaps 25,000 to 28,000 for the United States and 33,000 for the U.S.S.R.

[20]The bomb dropped by aircraft on Hiroshima could devastate about three square miles. The most recent generation of American ICBMs, the MX (officially, the Peacekeeper), carries ten warheads with sufficient combined explosive power to level an area of 240 square miles (Sivard 1987, 17).

Russia inherited most of the warheads of the former Soviet Union, but Kazakhstan, the Ukraine, and Belarus found themselves with about 2,300 war- heads. Those three new states agreed in early 1992 to disable their missiles within three years and to eliminate them within seven, but we should not forget the similarity of agreements and pie crusts.

Several countries may now be in the category of **undeclared nuclear powers**. Israel may have crossed the nuclear threshold in the late 1960s and may have fifty to 100 atomic warheads and hydrogen bomb technology (Spector 1990, 6).[21] South Africa announced in 1993 that it once had weapons. India may hold the material for forty to sixty bombs. Pakistan possibly crossed the nuclear threshold in 1986–1988 and could possess material for five to ten warheads. Iraq apparently was well on its way to nuclear capability when Israel bombed and destroyed its Osisraq test reactor in 1981 (exactly for that reason), and Iraq was again far along in 1990 when it invaded Kuwait.[22] Argentina and Brazil both have the basic capabilities and had classified nuclear programs. In 1985 they signed a mutual inspection agreement to ease fears of a regional nuclear arms race. The United States pressured Taiwan in 1988 to stop work on a secret nuclear facility that could have produced plutonium for warheads.[23] North Korea may be very close to having nuclear weapons material. Several other Third World countries (including Libya) have indicated interest in nu- clear weapons but appear years away from the capability to develop their own. Almost all First World countries have the technology to produce nuclear weap- ons but refrain from undertaking programs.

International measures exist in an effort to restrict the spread of nuclear capabilities. The International Atomic Energy Agency (IAEA), founded in 1957, requires reporting on nuclear installations in 100 member countries and relies on material audits and on-site inspections to verify that the facilities are not supplying materials for domestic or foreign weapons programs. More than 130 states have signed the 1968 Treaty on Non-Proliferation of Nuclear Weapons (NPT), which requires acceptance of IAEA controls. Argentina, Brazil, India, Israel, Pakistan, and South Africa have not signed and all have facilities not under IAEA safeguards (Spector 1990, 6).

Two difficulties face efforts to prevent nuclear proliferation. First, the tech- nology is very widespread. Second, it is not outrageously expensive. The United States devotes only about 10 percent of its total military expenditures to nuclear forces. Most of the Newly Industrialized Countries (NICs) have the wherewithal to become nuclear powers. To do so, however, they need to obtain or develop delivery systems as well as warheads.

---

[21]See Cobban (1988) for detail on the Israeli program. Although the evidence concerning undeclared nuclear powers is unofficial, it is too strong to ignore and much research on it has been careful.

[22]Israel claimed in 1989 that Iraq still had plutonium for a very small number of warheads and was proceeding to assemble them.

[23]*The New York Times*, March 23, 1988:1.

Delivery vehicles fall into three classes: land-based missiles, submarine-based missiles, and aircraft. The United States and Russia maintain all three types, and the United States refers to its delivery system as the **triad**. Table 5.3 shows the delivery vehicles in each leg of the superpower triads and also indicates the warheads dedicated to them. Historically the Soviet Union relied more heavily on the land-based leg of its triad, and the United States put more warheads on submarines and bombers. In recent years, the configuration of the Soviet triad had come to more closely resemble that of the United States, although the former U.S.S.R. still did not emphasize aircraft. The United Kingdom depends on submarines for potential delivery of its warheads, whereas the French and Chinese maintain land and sea-based missiles. Many of the sometimes confusing acronyms and initials that surround nuclear weaponry identify delivery vehicles or capabilities of them. Box 5.1 defines the most important.

TABLE 5.3
Declared Nuclear Strategic Capabilities (1990)

	U.S.	U.S.S.R.	U.K.	France	China
Delivery					
Vehicles					
ICBMs	1,000	1,334	0	62*	89–130*
SLBMs	608	914	48	96	24
Bombers	268	106	0	0	180–200
Total	1,876	2,354	48	158	293–354
Warheads					
ICBMs	2,450	6,280	0	88*	115–175*
SLBMs	5,216	3,626	96	416	26–38
Bombers	4,300	974	0	0	200+
Total	11,966	10,880	96	504	341–413

Source: Stockholm International Peace Research Institute, *SIPRI Yearbook 1991: World Armaments and Disarmament* (New York: Oxford University Press, 1991), 16,17, 25.
Note: Total of ICBMs, IRBMs, MRBMs.

All potential undeclared nuclear powers have combat aircraft such as U.S. F-15s and F-16s or Soviet MiGs that they could modify to carry nuclear warheads into neighboring states (Spector 1988, 25). Missile technology is advancing rapidly in most. Although the United States and six other industrial countries established a "control regime" in 1987 to slow the proliferation of missile technology, it may not succeed. India (1980) and Israel (1988) have launched satellites, joining the declared nuclear powers and Japan in that exclusive club. In 1989 Iraq demonstrated a missile with that capability. Such states have the capability of delivering nuclear warheads by missile for distances of at least 1,000 miles. Brazil may be next

BOX 5.1 Nuclear Acronyms

DELIVERY VEHICLES

ALCM   Air-launched cruise missile —see cruise missile

ABM   Anti-ballistic missile system —a system designed to detect and destroy
            incoming nuclear missiles

CEP   Circular error probability —a measure of missile accuracy indicating the radius
            of a circle around a target within which 50% of missiles will fall

C^3I Command, control, communications, and intelligence — the system for
            maintaining control over nuclear capabilities during both peacetime and war

CM   Cruise missile —a pilotless, air-breathing missile which flies relatively slowly and
            at low elevations.

GLCM   Ground-launched cruise missile — see cruise missile

ICBM   Intercontinental ballistic missile — range normally exceeds 5,500 kilometers

IRBM   Intermediate-range ballistic missile — range between 1,850 and 5,500
            kilometers

MIRV   Multiple, independently targeted reentry vehicle —a missile with two or more
            warheads which can be directed to separate targets

SLBM   Submarine-launched ballistic missile — either intercontinental or intermediate-
            range

SLCM   Sea-launched cruise missile—see cruise missile

CONTROL EFFORTS

INF   Intermediate nuclear forces treaty — the U.S.–Soviet treaty that eliminated these
            weapons

NPT   Nonproliferation treaty —completed in 1968, it obligates the more than 100
            signatories not to transfer nuclear materials or technology to nonnuclear powers

SALT   Strategic arms limitations talks (I and II — the forum in which the U.S. and
            U.S.S.R. limited strategic missiles

START   Strategic arms reductions talks —the series of discussions in which the U.S. and
            U.S.S.R. agreed to reduce strategic forces

Sources: Christopher J. Lamb, *How to Think about Arms Control, Disarmament, and Defense* (Englewood
Cliffs, N.J.: Prentice-Hall, 1988), 276–278; Teena Karsa Mayers, *Understanding Nuclear Weapons and Arms
Control*, 3rd ed. (Washington D.C.: Pergamon-Brasseys's 1986), 90-91, 112–116; Richard Smoke, *National
Security and the Nuclear Dilemma*, 2nd ed., (New York Random House, 1987), 307–314.

in line. The availability to still additional states (like Libya and South Africa) of nuclear-capable missiles with shorter ranges, provided by the former Soviet Union and Brazil, further adds to the complicated picture of nuclear delivery capability. Proliferation of nuclear capabilities is proceeding more slowly than some feared in the 1950s and 1960s, but it is nonetheless continuing.

The focus here has been on nuclear weaponry. Yet at the beginning of the 1990s, NATO and the Warsaw Pact also faced each other with a vast array of conventional weaponry. For instance, NATO had over 30,000 main battle tanks and the Warsaw Pact fielded close to 70,000. Nearly 5,000 attack aircraft supported NATO forces, and about 3,500 backed up those of their adversaries. We later discuss agreements that began to reduce those stocks.

The former Soviet Union also maintained the world's largest arsenal of chemical weapons, although the United States and Iraq were known to have them, and many other countries were suspected of maintaining arsenals.[24] The dangers of these weapons came to the attention of the international community when Iraq used them in its war with Iran. Although the Geneva Protocol of 1925, to which the United States and the Soviets are signatories, banned the *first use* of such weapons, it did not prohibit production.

Several countries also had, and continue to maintain, stocks of biologic weapons including toxins (poisons of cobras, rattlesnakes, and scorpions), bacteria (the plague, anthrax, meningitis, and typhoid fever), and viruses (yellow fever, dengue fever, and encephalitis). A United Nations treaty in 1972 prohibits development, production, and stockpiling of such weapons. Under the conditions of that treaty both the United States and the former U.S.S.R. report several sites at which they conduct defensive research on biologic agents. Each superpower suspected the other of secretly engaging in the illegal production of those substances. The treaty has no provision for the inspection of research sites. Recent advances in biotechnology, notably cloning and recombinant deoxyribonucleic acid (DNA) techniques, greatly increase the scientific potential for biologic weaponry development. Such weaponry may appear foolish, because it could so easily damage the country that developed or used it. Yet nuclear weapons have the same characteristic.

STRATEGIC CONCEPTS AND THEORY: STATE BEHAVIOR

A state has a **first-strike capability** when it can preemptively launch nuclear weapons against an opponent. It also has a **second-strike capability** when it can launch a devastating attack after absorbing one itself. A second-strike capability requires that the warheads available for retaliation be protected in hardened missile silos, in submarines at sea, or in planes aloft. A second-strike capability greatly reduces the possibility during a crisis that a country will fear losing its retaliatory capability, should the other side strike first. Because of this, a country

---

[24]*Newsweek*, September 19, 1988, 30–31 also claims France to be a known possessor. *The Christian Science Monitor*, December 13, 1988, B1–B16, puts Iran into the category.

with a second-strike capability may be less tempted to launch first. When either or both sides harbor such fears, there is an **unstable nuclear balance**.

Imagine a large-scale border conflict between India and Pakistan, for instance, after both sides have developed nuclear weapons, but before they have protected them in some way against a first strike from the other side. Might not Indian decision makers seriously consider using that country's weapons first, so as to deal a devastating blow against Pakistan and simultaneously eliminate the possibility of a Pakistani nuclear attack on them? They could find the thought morally abhorrent, but fear that Pakistan, facing the same decision problem, would not hesitate to use its weapons first. What can India do in advance to avoid facing this dilemma?

Every country with nuclear weapons wants to convince its actual or potential enemies that it is willing to use those weapons (for self-defense). It also wants to minimize the danger that either side will actually use them. These two objectives have led to the development of a deterrence strategy called **mutual assured destruction** (MAD). It requires that both sides have second-strike capabilities. Thus both sides can destroy the other, but they can also afford to wait and see how the other side handles a crisis situation. This creates a relatively **stable nuclear balance**.

It is no accident that each of the five declared nuclear powers has a force of missile-launching submarines. These are the least-vulnerable leg of modern triads. Improved missile accuracy has put even hardened missile silos at risk in a first strike, and antiaircraft defense makes survivability of bombers en route to targets uncertain. Thus even secondary nuclear powers have a second-strike capability that could, as France has said, "tear off an arm" of a superpower.

The military superpowers themselves have substantially greater second-strike forces (even after steps to reduce nuclear weapon stocks). It was estimated that 3,550 U.S. warheads (with 1,060 megatons) and 820 Soviet warheads would survive first strikes from the other side (Posen and Van Evera 1987, 81–82). In a study done during the 1960s, when strategists formalized the concept of MAD, they estimated that 800 megatons could kill 40 percent of the Soviet population and destroy three-fourths of their industrial capacity (Enthoven and Smith 1971, 207).[25] Thus both the United States and the Russians can do much more with second strikes than "tear off an arm."

The most serious threat to second-strike capabilities today comes from the vulnerability of what are called C^3I systems—command, control, communications, and intelligence systems. Both sides worry that the other side could "decapitate" them and eliminate their ability to launch in retaliation. Both spend huge sums to maintain C^3I capability and thus the credibility of deterrence.

The undeclared nuclear powers currently do not have second-strike capabilities. Thus any regional conflicts that might threaten to escalate to nuclear weapons (such as ones between India and Pakistan or Israel and Iraq) face the instability problems associated with first-strike capabilities. In addition to possible concern about international public disapproval, this is one reason for undeclared powers

[25]Posen and Evera (1987, 106f) say only twenty to forty megatons would kill 21 percent of the Soviet population.

to remain covert. As long as both sides in such conflicts can pretend the weapons do not exist, it may be somewhat easier to control pressures for preemptive strikes. Should such states develop second-strike capabilities, it would rationally be in their interests to announce their ability to retaliate and thereby to deter first-strike action by others.

Students of world politics study the logic of deterrence and MAD with the help of techniques from game theory. A game called the **prisoner's dilemma** illustrates the instability of solely first-strike situations.[26] In one hypothetical example, a district attorney seeks to convict two suspects, Boris and Bill, of armed robbery. He keeps them apart to eliminate communication and offers each the same deal. (Ignore any ethical and legal restrictions the district attorney might face in this example.) Should either confess and the other not, the district attorney will request freedom for the confessor and ten years imprisonment for the other. If both confess, he will ask an eight-year sentence for both. If neither confesses, he will prosecute both on the charge of illegally carrying concealed weapons (found when they were arrested) and should be able to send each to prison for one year.

The matrix of Table 5.4 indicates the payoffs for the two prisoners, dependent on whether or not they confess. The first payoff in each cell is for Bill. Thus should Bill confess and Boris not (bottom left corner), Bill will go free and Boris will spend ten years behind bars. Bill considers his options, based on what Boris might do. Should Boris confess (second column), confession would better serve Bill, cutting his losses from ten years to eight. Should Boris not confess (first column), confession again better serves Bill, improving his prospects from one year in jail to none. Thus no matter what Boris does, Bill improves his prospects by confession and decides to do so. Unfortunately, Boris faces exactly the same logic. They both confess, and both serve eight years. Had they been able to somehow cooperate and avoid any confession, they could have cut their prison terms to one year each. The dilemma is that without being able to communicate and somehow assure each other that they will not confess (or threaten each other should they do so), they cannot reach the superior outcome. Even with communication, trust may be so low that each will defect to confession in a vain attempt to cut their losses.

	TABLE 5.4	
	The Prisoner's Dilemma	
		Boris
Bill	Not Confess	Confess
Not Confess	-1, -1	-10, 0
Confess	0, -10	-8, -8

[26]Presentation of stability in terms of the prisoner's dilemma has become common. See, for example, Russett (1983); Ray (1987, 277–281).

	U.S.S.R.	
TABLE 5.5		
An Unstable Nuclear Balance		
United States	*Wait*	*Attack*
Wait	-10, -10	-1000, -5
Attack	-5, -1000	-800, -800

If the United States and the Soviet Union (or any other pair of nuclear powers) had only first-strike capabilities, they would face the same kind of situation that Bill and Boris did.[27] Table 5.5 portrays a payoff matrix for the two powers in an unstable nuclear balance. Although some readers may think such a portrayal trivializes the stakes of mutual destruction, it is nevertheless helpful in understanding the logic of the situation.

In this gaming representation, both parties can choose to wait (not attack at least for now) or to attack now. If both wait, there are costs because they prolong the tension and expense of the arms race, and continue to live under the threat of future destruction. Should they both attack, the destruction is devastating on both sides. If one should attack and the other not, the aggressor damages the other side even more heavily than in a mutual attack (which prevents some planes and missiles from getting through), while suffering limited damage because the other side is (in this example) unable to retaliate. The reader should analyze the matrix in Table 5.5 and verify the pressure of "rationality" on both sides to strike immediately.

Should both sides develop perfect second-strike capabilities (obviously not really possible), there is still a cost involved in waiting and living in the shadow of nuclear destruction. Nonetheless, the ability to retaliate after being attacked, with the same force available in a first strike, changes the payoffs and pushes the logic of the situation strongly toward delay.

We will return to the interactive logics of nuclear balance later in a discussion of arms control. Short of eliminating nuclear weapons, the best hope of avoiding destruction that the best minds have to date discovered appears to lie in (1) maintaining the relative stability of MAD, (2) attempting to maximize communication and trust, and (3) avoiding major crises that raise the tension levels among the nuclear powers.

STAGES OF THE NUCLEAR POWER BALANCE

The nuclear balance between the U.S.S.R. and the United States evolved through several structural stages that affected the strategies and broader relation-

[27]Hamburger (1979), in an excellent overview of game theory, represents the decision to use or not use nuclear weapons as a game of chicken, not as prisoner's dilemma. In the chicken version, the cell in which both strike is the worst outcome for both countries, rather than the third-best outcome. He reserves prisoner's dilemma to represent arms races.

ship of the two parties.[28] The United States had either a monopoly or a tremendous preponderance of nuclear power between 1945 and 1957. Although it could wreak havoc on the Soviet Union, that country had limited nuclear retaliatory power because of inadequate delivery systems. Both sides knew it. The United States adopted the strategy of **massive retaliation**. It threatened devastation should the Soviets transgress the limits of its sphere of influence (even with just conventional weaponry). Secretary of State John Foster Dulles even talked about rolling back the boundaries of that sphere and liberating the countries of Eastern Europe, threats that seemed credible when backed by U.S. nuclear superiority. The failure of the United States to intervene on behalf of the revolutionaries in Hungary in 1956, when some expected it to translate rhetoric into action, marked the end of such credibility.

In the second period, from roughly 1957 until about 1970, the United States maintained dominance in the nuclear balance but was no longer almost invulnerable to Soviet threat. The 1957 launching of Sputnik demonstrated that the Soviets could send large payloads on missiles. In fact, the United States, which had not yet lifted a satellite, became concerned about a "missile gap." In reality, the Soviets, not the United States, lagged. Apparently, at the time of the Cuban missile crisis in 1962, the Soviets had only twenty ICBMs, and the American nuclear superiority was about fifteen to one.[29] That encouraged Khrushchev to attempt to narrow the gap by placing forty missiles in Cuba.

As both sides developed extensive intercontinental missile delivery capabilities, they enshrined the theory of mutual assured destruction in their thought and doctrine (beginning in the United States). The United States also moved in the 1960s to a doctrine of flexible response rather than massive retaliation. Massive retaliation was no longer a credible threat against conventional-weapon Soviet action when it would elicit a massive second strike from the U.S.S.R. The **flexible response** doctrine tailored response to provocation more carefully, retaining the possibility of using nuclear weapons in retaliation against conventional aggression, but threatening limited nuclear action initially and escalation only if the other side persisted. The United States refused to forswear the first use of nuclear weapons, preferring to retain that option to offset the Warsaw Pact conventional-weapon superiority in Europe.

Since 1970, the two military superpowers have maintained **essential parity** in the nuclear balance. The U.S.S.R. closed the earlier gap in delivery vehicles and proceeded to gradually pull ahead in equivalent megatonnage, despite continuing U.S. superiority in warhead number (Figure 5.3).

MAD remains central to strategic thought on both sides. Because of improvements in the accuracy of missiles and the ability of single missiles to carry many warheads, however, the United States began in the late 1970s and early 1980s to move toward a counterforce strategy; it had earlier focused on destroying population and industry in its second strike (a countervalue strategy), whereas it

---

[28]Russett (1983, 6–17) and Bretton (1986, 349–357) outlined these general stages.

[29]*The New York Times* January 29, 1989, 12.

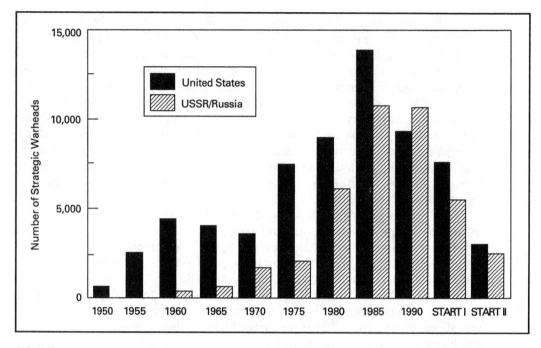

FIGURE 5.3 The Nuclear Warhead Balance
Sources: John P. Holdren, "The Dynamics of the Nuclear Arms Race: History, Status and Prospects," in *Nuclear Weapons and the Future of Humanity*, eds., Avner Cohen and Steven Lee (Totowa, N.J.: Rowman and Alllanheld, 1986), 41–84; International Institute for Strategic Studies, *The Military Balance 1989–90* (London: International Institute for Strategic Studies, 1991), 219–220.

now saw the technological possibility of eliminating some Soviet missiles before their launch.[30]

Ronald Reagan's 1980 election campaign recognized the probable movement of Soviet strategy, as well, toward counterforce. He decried the "window of vulnerability" in the same way that John F. Kennedy had attacked the "missile gap" twenty years earlier. That is, he argued that the large number and size of Soviet warheads, coupled with their increasing accuracy, put U.S. land-based missiles at risk. Because air defense improvements threatened also to eliminate the ability of U.S. bombers to penetrate the Soviet Union, only the submarine leg of the triad offered relatively certain retaliatory capability. Should Soviet submarine warfare continue to improve, he argued, the entire second-strike capability could become vulnerable. His administration's response was to argue for new and technologically advanced bombers (including the B-2 or Stealth bombers, which are nearly invisible to Soviet radar), for advanced and more secure land-based missiles (his Peacekeeper missile), and for increased reliance on the rapidly devel-

[30]Posen and Van Evera (1987, 89–91). Well-developed and protected C^3I systems and counterforce capabilities give rise to speculation that controlled nuclear wars can be fought short of massive exchanges. Keeny and Panofsky (1982) label such thought "nuclear utilization theory strategy" (NUTS).

oping cruise missile technology. Aircraft (or other platforms) outside of the air-defense perimeter could launch cruise missiles at the Soviet Union, and with their advanced electronics and built-in maps, they would move to targets slowly, but at low altitudes and safe from defenses. The United States undertook a large defense buildup in these areas.

The drift of both sides toward counterforce strategies provides some context for the debate over the Reagan proposal for a Strategic Defense Initiative (SDI), better known as "Star Wars".The debate began with a presidential speech on March 23, 1983:

> Would it not be better to save lives than to avenge them? Are we not capable of demonstrating our peaceful intentions by applying all our abilities and our ingenuity to achieving a truly lasting stability? I think we are—indeed we must.
>
> After careful consultation with my advisors, including the Joint Chiefs of Staff, I believe there is a way.... It is that we embark on a program to counter the awesome Soviet missile threat with measures that are defensive. Let us turn to the very strengths in technology that spawned our great industrial base.... I know this is a formidable technical task, one that may not be accomplished before the end of the century. Yet, current technology has attained a level of sophistication where it is reasonable for us to begin this effort. (Payne and Gray 1984, 820)

The United States and the Soviet Union had not seriously reviewed strategic defense since both considered developing ABMs in 1968–1971. After much analysis, they then concluded that such systems were technologically difficult and expensive, and that success with them could limit the effectiveness of a second strike by the other side and thus undercut the deterrence logic of MAD. A treaty in 1972 sharply limited superpower efforts on ABMs.

After Reagan's speech, National Security Directive 6–83 mandated study of technology (involving satellites, lasers, and other advanced weaponry) to eliminate the nuclear threat to the United States and its allies. Two blue-ribbon panels suggested that it would be a twenty-year, $250 to $500 billion effort (some estimated $2 trillion). The SDI or Star Wars proposal draws many criticisms. First, the financial cost would be high. Second, there is no prospect in the foreseeable future that both sides could really have an impermeable defense, capable of defending against first strikes, as Reagan seemed to hope. Third, and perhaps most significant, SDI might allow one side to strike first, and to eliminate most capabilities of the other side (overwhelming any missile defense it had). The initiator might then rely on its own missile defense system to "mop up" the limited retaliatory strike.[31] The result of deploying such a defense would thus be to leave one or both sides with only first-strike forces and to destabilize the nuclear balance.

One argument in favor of a more limited defensive system is that it could protect the superpowers from a "third-party" attack and from the accidental launch of one or a few missiles (Slater and Goldfischer 1986). Should one of the lesser nuclear powers or a nondeclared nuclear power (for reasons that we would

---

[31]See Glaser (1986) for a fuller statement of this argument.

obviously not consider rational) attack a state possessing a missile defense shield, the defending state could avoid or greatly limit damage.

ARMS CONTROL AND DISARMAMENT EFFORTS

The end of the cold war has dramatically changed the nuclear relationship between the United States and Russia. Although the basic logic of deterrence has carried over into the post–cold war world (and still shapes the relationship of other nuclear dyads), the emphasis on arms control has increased dramatically. In this section we want to review those efforts historically and consider the contemporary activity.

Our earlier discussion of state interest provided one reason that considerable arms control is possible: cooperation emerges most easily when interests are most compatible . While security relationships among great powers have generally had a highly zero-sum character (for instance, the conflicts between France and Germany over Alsace-Lorraine, between Britain and France over colonial empires, and between the United States and the U.S.S.R. over much of Europe), those same relationships have also had a critically important nonzero-sum element—the mutual benefit of avoiding war. When war potentially involves nuclear weapons, that mutual benefit becomes especially large.

LARGE-SCALE AND UTOPIAN APPROACHES

Of the many possible approaches to arms control, several are utopian and unrealistic. For instance, a unanimous vote of the UN General Assembly in 1960 set a goal of **general and complete disarmament**. Although the Eastern countries reiterated that proposal occasionally, they did so purely for propaganda purposes. The genie of advanced military technology is out of the bottle, and there are no global institutions to protect unarmed states. Thus states would never trust each other to really disarm, no matter how careful the inspection procedures were— there is no credible way to get there from here.

President Woodrow Wilson incorporated a similar idea for arms reduction in his set of idealistic proposals to the post–World War I peace conference. Recognizing the necessity for states to maintain forces sufficient to protect against domestic unrest, he suggested arms reduction to the lowest point consistent with domestic safety. Even police forces large enough to protect the Soviet Union or the United States against domestic unrest could be significant threats to smaller neighbors like Hungary or Grenada, however. This, too, could never attract the support of most states.

Perhaps the most "practical" of the utopian proposals involves turning over real power to a higher authority like the United Nations. In 1946 the United States put the Baruch Plan in front of the UN Atomic Energy Commission (AEC). It suggested that the AEC create an extensive inspection and control system for nuclear technology. Once such a system were in place, the United States proposed to destroy its own weapons, share atomic secrets, and rely on the AEC for control of all nuclear material, research, and explosives globally. No state was to retain any nuclear weapons capability (Riggs and Plano 1988, 155). There has been much debate concerning how serious that proposal was.

PARTIAL OR LIMITED APPROACHES

The proposals that attract serious global attention, and that in some cases lead to action, invariably involve much more limited approaches to arms control. **Qualitative limitations**, which focus on specific weapons or practices, are among the most important types of arms control (Table 5.6). As with the British proposal to the 1932 World Disarmament Conference, these often attempt to distinguish offensive and defensive weaponry, and to ban or limit the offensive ones. The movement at that time to designate chemical and biologic weaponry as offensive, and to ban it, disintegrated with the rise of Hitler and the rearmament of Germany.

TABLE 5.6
Important Qualitative Arms Control Agreements Since 1959

Year	Agreement	Provisions
1963	Limited Test Ban Treaty	Bans nuclear tests in the atmosphere, outer space, and under water
1972	Biological Weapons Convention	Bans development, production, and stockpiling of of biological weapons
1974	Threshold Test Ban Treaty	Limits underground tests of superpowers to 150 kilotons (not ratified)
1976	Peaceful Nuclear Explosions Treaty	Complements 1974 Test Ban Treaty by limiting peaceful explosions (not ratified)
1977	Environmentl Modification Convention	Prohibits weaponry which could modify the environment
1981	Inhumane Weapons Convention	Prohibits certain fragmentation bombs, mines, booby traps, etc.
1987	Intermediate-range Nuclear Force Treaty	Eliminates all missiles with ranges between 500 and 5,500 kilometers
1990	Underground Testing Verification	Adds protocol to 1974 and 1976 treaties specifying verification procedures
1992	Chemical Weapons Treaty	Multilateral agreement to cease production and eliminate stockpiles, and allow on-site inspections

Sources: Teena Karsa Mayers, *Understanding Nuclear Weapons and Arms Control*, 3rd ed. (Washington D.C.: Pergamon-Brassey's 1986), 90–91; Bruce Russett and Harvey Starr, *World Politics*, 4th ed. (New York: W. H. Freeman, 1992), 352–354.

One of the most successful qualitative limitations was the U.S.-Soviet agreement in 1987 to eliminate intermediate nuclear forces (missiles with ranges between 500 and 5,500 kilometers). The superpowers considered those missiles especially dangerous because they would greatly reduce the warning time in a strategic attack. The West became alarmed in 1977 when the Soviets deployed a new missile in this class, the SS-20. To achieve the removal of the Soviet missiles, NATO pursued a two-pronged strategy of negotiating and simultaneously deploying similar forces.[32]

In the mid-1980s a movement surfaced for restructuring Eastern and Western European forces according to a doctrine called **nonprovocative defense** (Hollins, Powers, and Sommer 1989). This concept was a direct response to the security dilemma, and the tendency of most military forces to threaten a potential opponent and engender an arms race. Looking at Swiss and Swedish force structures provides some suggestions concerning a nonprovocative approach to defense: emphasize tank traps and antitank and antiaircraft systems; build short-range fighter planes and helicopters in preference to long-range bombers; and stress civil defense systems and economic defense preparations. In 1990 top military officials of NATO and the Warsaw Pact met and jointly discussed such military doctrines.

Attempts to eliminate a particular category of weaponry sometimes depend less on the offensive-defensive categorization than on the particularly obnoxious character of the weapon. For instance, there was wide international support for the 1972 UN Convention on the Prohibition of the Development, Production, and Stockpiling of Bacteriological (Biological) and Toxin Weapons and Their Destruction, and for the 1977 UN convention banning weapons that could modify weather or affect the climate. In 1992, states completed long-term negotiations on a multilateral treaty to cease production and stockpiling of chemical weapons (a bilateral treaty in 1990 had bound the United States and U.S.S.R. to reduce stocks to 5,000 tons by 2002).

Weapon test-bans fall generally into the category of qualitative approaches. In 1963 the United States, U.S.S.R., and Great Britain negotiated the Partial Test-Ban Treaty, prohibiting atmospheric testing of nuclear weapons. That treaty held signatures of 120 states by 1987, and in the early 1990s China and France decided to sign. In 1974, a bilateral U.S.–Soviet agreement banned underground explosions of more than 150 kilotons. As with several arms control agreements, both the United States and Russia observe it, even though they have not ratified it. The UN has urged a Comprehensive Test-Ban Treaty, but the United States withdrew from discussions in 1980, expressing concerns about inspection and verification.

Quantitative limitations constitute a second limited or partial approach to arms control (Table 5.7). One of the most famous historic agreements falls into this category. Specifically, in 1922 the Washington Naval Conference restricted the construction of battleships and aircraft carriers for ten years to the following ratios: United States—5; United Kingdom—5; Japan—3; France—1.67; and Italy—1.67. The signatories extensively violated that agreement (Riggs and Plano 1988, 152).

---

[32]United States Department of State, *The INF Treaty: Questions and Answers* (February 1988).

TABLE 5.7
Important Qualitative Arms Control Agreements Since 1959

Year	Agreement	Provisions
1972	ABM Treaty (SALT I)	Limits superpower deployment of defense missile systems
1972	Interim Agreement (SALT I)	Froze superpower missile launcher numbers for 5 years
1979	SALT II Treaty	Limited superpower missile types and numbers (not ratified)
1990	Chemical Weapons Agreement	Committed superpowers to reduce chemical weapon stocks to 5,000 tons by 2002 and end production
1990	Troop levels in Central Europe	Limited U.S./Soviet forces in Central Europe to 195,000 each
1990	Conventional Armed Forces In Europe (CFE)	Limited and substantially reduced NATO and Warsaw Pact arms levels
1991	Strategic Arms Reduction Treaty (START I)	Committed U.S. and U.S.S.R. to reduce warheads to about 8,500 and 6,500 respectively
1992	Strategic Arms Reduction Treaty (START II)	Committed U.S. and former U.S.S.R. to reduce warheads by 2003 to 3,500 and 3,000 respectively

Sources: See Table 5.6

More successfully, the first Strategic Arms Limitations Talks (SALT I) led to an agreement in 1972 that obligated the United States and U.S.S.R. to restrict development of antiballistic missile (ABM) defense systems to two sites. A 1974 treaty lowered the limit to one site per country. The United States long claimed that the Soviet construction of the Krasnoyarsk radar complex violated that agreement (the Soviets admitted the violation in 1989),[33] and the Soviet Union argued that progress by the United States on the Strategic Defense Initiative (SDI) would violate the agreement. Nonetheless, the agreement has helped restrict significant ballistic defense development (as has inadequate technology).

The SALT I agreements also placed five-year interim limits on the number of strategic launchers. The SALT II treaty in 1979 placed ceilings of 2,250 on the total numbers of ICBMs, SLBMs, heavy bombers, and air-to-surface ballistic missiles (ASBMs) of both sides, with specific limits within categories as well (Box 5.1

[33]United States Department of State, *Soviet Noncompliance with Arms Control Agreements*, Special Report no. 175 (December 2, 1987).

explains nuclear weapon and arms control initials and acronyms). In addition, the SALT II treaty limited the number of warheads on each missile to ten for ICBMs and fourteen on SLBMs (failure to reach agreement to restrict warheads per missile in 1972 had lead to a MIRV race). President Carter withdrew SALT II from the U.S. ratification process in 1980 after the Soviet invasion of Afghanistan virtually assured its defeat in the Senate. Nonetheless, both sides continued to adhere for many years to the limits it established, while periodically leveling charges and countercharges of cheating.

The superpowers pursued the quantitative strategy further with the Strategic Arms Reduction Talks (START). The START Treaty, signed July 31, 1991, committed the United States and the former Soviet Union to reduce warheads to 6,000 each over seven years. In mid-1992, with START not yet ratified, the leaderships of the United States and Russia agreed further to reduce their warhead totals to 3,492 and 3,044, respectively.

Quantitative arms controls have also made headway on conventional weaponry. The Mutual and Balanced Force Reduction (MBFR) talks in Vienna sought through the 1970s and 1980s to limit nonnuclear arms and military personnel in a small area of Central Europe. The MBFR negotiations gave way to talks on Conventional Forces in Europe (CFE) among all sixteen members of NATO and seven Warsaw Pact states. The signing of the CFE Treaty in November 1990 committed members of NATO and the former Warsaw Pact to much clearer accounting and to substantial cuts in weaponry. The collapse of the Warsaw Pact and of the Soviet Union, and the shifting of tanks by Russia beyond the Urals where the arms counts would not apply to them, complicated that agreement immediately. In mid-1992 the Russians agreed to accept half, rather than three-fourths of the conventional equipment of the former Soviet Union.

Budgetary limitations are a third limited approach to arms control. The idea is to limit defense spending, but to let states determine how they will spend up to the limit. Again the concept has a long history. Russia proposed a five-year freeze in defense spending at the 1899 Hague Conference; Germany rejected the idea because it believed itself behind in that arms race.

In 1963–1965 the United States and U.S.S.R. discussed reciprocal reductions in defense spending. In 1973 the Soviet Union proposed mutual 10 percent cuts before the UN. Given the secrecy of Soviet defense spending figures, the United States properly dismissed such proposals as posturing. Specifically, the Eastern superpower refused to provide any detail on its military budget, and the total figure it long provided was about 10 percent of that calculated by Western intelligence (Sivard 1987, 54). In 1989 the U.S.S.R. finally admitted to much larger expenditures.

A fourth limited approach to arms control is **regional disarmament** or **nonmilitarization** (Table 5.8). The United States and Great Britain agreed in 1817 with the Rush-Bagot Treaty to demilitarize the Great Lakes. Although violated in the nineteenth century, that agreement now represents one of the most successful regional treaties.

TABLE 5.8
Important Arms Control Agreements Since 1959
on Regional Disarmament or Nonmilitarization

Year	Agreement	Provisions
1959	Antartic Treaty	Prohibits all military use of Antartic
1967	Outer Space Treaty	Prohibits placement of weapons in space, including on the moon
1967	Treaty of Tlateloco	Prohibits nuclear weapons in Latin America
1968	Non-Proliferation Treaty	Prohibits acquisition of nuclear weapons by non-nuclear signatories
1971	Seabed Treaty	Prohibits placement of weapons on the ocean floor

Sources: See Table 5.6

Most modern efforts have created nuclear-free zones. In 1959 the twelve countries most active on the South Pole continent signed the Antarctic Treaty, prohibiting all military use, including nuclear testing and waste disposal. Eighty-four states agreed in 1967 to the Outer Space Treaty banning orbital and moon-based nuclear weapons and denying any claims to state sovereignty in space. The Treaty of Tlatelolco in 1967 prohibits nuclear weapons in Latin America and drew ratification by twenty-two countries (Riggs and Plano 1988, 161), but three of the countries on the continent most capable of developing nuclear weapons, Argentina, Brazil, and Chile, opted not to sign it.[34] In 1968 the UN General Assembly approved the Treaty on Nonproliferation of Nuclear Weapons as a step toward restricting them from a large part of the earth's surface. Although 121 states have ratified it, the thirty-odd nonsignatories include Argentina, Brazil, India, Israel, and South Africa. Movement towards a review conference in 1995 will potentially strengthen that agreement and bring new signatories to it. The 1971 Seabed Treaty prohibits nuclear weapon placement on the ocean floor beyond the twelve-mile territorial limit of states. In 1985, eight states signed an agreement creating a South Pacific Nuclear Free Zone.

A fifth and final category of limited arms control consists of **confidence-and security-building measures** (CSBMs) (Table 5.9). Largely because of superpower recognition that their communications during the Cuban Missile Crisis were antiquated, the two countries agreed in 1963 to establish a "hotline" teletype system for maintaining constant and nearly instantaneous contact. Similar lines now link both London and Paris with Moscow. In 1971 the superpowers signed an

---

[34]Argentina and Brazil have held bilateral talks on the nuclear issue, and a 1988 pact commits them to widespread exchange of information on research and capabilities.

agreement pledging both to improve safeguards for preventing accidental use of nuclear weapons and to exchange information concerning their efforts. The Prevention of Nuclear War Agreement of 1973 requires consultation if there is danger of nuclear war. In 1986 the Stockholm Conference on Confidence and Security Building Measures and Disarmament in Europe (CDE), part of the Helsinki Agreement process, required NATO and Warsaw Pact members to undertake a variety of activities to improve communication in crises and to reduce the risk of accidental or surprise attacks. They began long-term Conventional Stability Talks (CST). In 1987 Moscow and Washington established risk reduction centers.

TABLE 5.9
Important Arms Control Agreements Since 1959
on Safety and Confidence-Building Measures

Year	Agreement	Provisions
1963	Hot Line Agreement	Maintains communication link between the United States and U.S.S.R
1971	Hot Line Modernization Agreement	Added two satellite circuits to ground cable teletype system
1971	Nuclear Accidents Agreement	Requires notification of other superpower of nuclear weapons accidents
1972	High Seas Agreement	Provides measures to prevent dangerous incidents on seas
1973	Agreement on Prevention of Nuclear War	Institutes measures to limit risk of war during crises
1975	Conference on Security and Cooperation in Europe	Requires notification of military maneuvers
1984	Hot Line Modernization Agreement	Adds facsimile transmission
1986	Confidence and Security-Building Measures and Disarmament in Europe	Establishes observers during military maneuvers
1987	Crisis Reduction Centers Agreement	Establishes communication centers in Moscow and Washington
1989	Accidental Confrontation Avoidance Agreement	Restricts provocative measures by peacetime military forces

Sources: See Table 5.6

UNILATERAL INITIATIVES: TRUE GRIT?

In addition to large-scale utopian and more partial or limited arms control proposals, a third general approach exists: unilateral initiatives. Those who advocate unilateral measures believe not only that cooperation is based on reciprocity (as those supporting limited arms control clearly also believe), but that a single actor can initiate a dynamic of reciprocity by taking several unilateral, cooperative actions. Eventually, they argue, such actions will create an atmosphere of trust and elicit reciprocity from other states.

For example, Charles Osgood (1962) proposed "graduated reciprocation in tension-reduction (GRIT)." He suggested that the United States, while maintaining nuclear weapons and a strong second-strike capability, undertake some initial unilateral steps such as destroying all B-52s or undertaking a moratorium on building bombs. The government should announce a timetable for such actions and make them verifiable. It would then encourage a Soviet response in kind, but proceeding with at least several steps before abandoning the effort. Fundamentally, the proposal aimed to set in motion a process of diffuse reciprocity in arms control.

Would such an approach work? In 1963 President Kennedy announced a "Strategy of Peace," unilaterally stopping atmospheric testing of nuclear weapons (Hardin 1982, 210). Premier Khrushchev reciprocated, and the episode led to the nuclear test ban treaty. Oswald assassinated Kennedy later that year and helped end further experiment.

In 1967, the United States temporarily placed a limit of 1,000 on ICBMs and invited the Soviets to do the same. The U.S.S.R. reached that limit and continued to build. The Soviet Union trailed the United States in other delivery-vehicle categories, notably planes and submarines, so it relied on more ICBMs to offset the American advantage. In short, the U.S. initiative played heavily to world opinion and was not fully credible. In 1985, the U.S.S.R. announced a moratorium on all nuclear tests and invited U.S. reciprocity. With extensions, the moratorium lasted until 1987, but the United States never responded in kind. Here again, however, the effort was largely propaganda. Not only was the United States behind initially, but some of its testing in the mid-1980s specifically supported an SDI research program that the Soviets wanted to stop.[35]

The demobilization that the United States undertook after the Vietnam War is another less-than-perfect example of the unilateral strategy (Figure 5.4). U.S. military spending as a percentage of GNP dropped steadily after the peak of the Vietnam War, declining dramatically from 1968–1978 (from 9.3 percent of GNP to 4.9 percent).[36] Estimated Soviet spending continued as a more stable portion of

[35]Many proponents of a freeze on testing, production, and deployment of nuclear weapons, which attracted considerable public support in the United States in the early 1980s, suggested that it be done unilaterally, illustrating again the appeal of the unilateral strategies.

[36]United States Arms Control and Disarmament Agency, *World Military Expenditures and Arms Transfers* (1979 and 1988). It is interesting to put these percentages into a broader context. At the peak of World War II, the United States, Japan, Germany, and the U.K. devoted 46, 51, 50, and 54 percent of GNP to the war, respectively (Organski and Kugler 1980, 218).

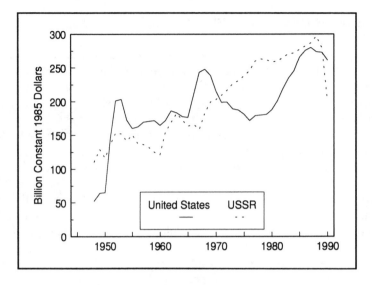

FIGURE 5.4   U.S. and Soviet Defense Spending
Sources: Assorted sources, primarily the U.S. Arms Control and Disarmament Agency, *World Military Expenditures and Arms Transfers* (Washington, D.C.: ACDA, assorted issues) and International Institute for Strategic Studies, *The Military Balance* (London: IISS, assorted issues).

their GNP, and the U.S.S.R. achieved significant leads in the numbers of nuclear missiles, in important categories of conventional weaponry such as tanks and personnel. This led to the observation by many American military leaders that "when we build, they build—when we stop, they continue building." In reality, the U.S. absolute spending level never fell significantly below that of the Soviets. Nonetheless, partly in response to the Soviet failure to reciprocate over this fairly prolonged period, the United States undertook a substantial military buildup in the 1980s.

The Soviet Union finally did announce significant unilateral cuts in late 1988, and NATO initially declared that those were necessary simply to redress the imbalance in conventional forces and would not affect NATO force levels. Many interpreted the proposed Soviet reductions as a response to domestic economic pressures, or even to the pressure generated by the U.S. military buildup rather than to an earnest desire for arms control. Yet Gorbachev continued to announce and publicize further Soviet initiatives and to call for Western response. Public opinion in the West expressed serious and growing discomfort about an absence of reciprocal response and new initiatives by their leaders (indicating the influence of democracy on interstate cooperation).

In 1989 and 1990, several Central and Eastern European countries also announced unilateral reductions in military spending, and Western states began to do the same. Public opinion clamored for more. In the early 1990s, the long-term dynamic of the East-West arms race collapsed completely. Instead of a continuing upward spiral with only limited pauses, members of NATO and the former

Warsaw Pact began to rush toward substantial conventional and nuclear arms cuts. In some cases agreements ratified the process, but in many others, unilateral initiatives appeared to drive it. It might be possible to conclude that the new downward dynamic proves the utility of tit-for-tat and GRIT strategies. It would also be possible to argue, however, that the real force behind the process was the change of governments throughout the East. The changes toward Western democratic forms and market economies encouraged the West to believe that the East sincerely desired ongoing reductions (which the state of Eastern economies compelled them to initiate) and to respond in kind. Globalists began to risk the great hope that an era of growing international community was at hand. Realists retained considerable skepticism concerning the process.

PROBLEMS OF ARMS CONTROL

Protection of state interests simply precludes many arms control efforts.[37] For instance, several potential nuclear powers believe it to be in their interest to protect the option of developing nuclear forces, and they will not sign the Non-Proliferation Treaty. Yet even when states see agreement to be in their interest, they may be stymied. A key problem in U.S.–Russian discussions has been verification. Because the Soviets were long a closed society, they rejected most U.S. verification proposals. For instance, in 1955 Eisenhower proposed an "open skies" policy to allow regular inspection flights by each superpower over military installations of the other. Although the Soviets rejected it, observation by satellites began to accomplish much of what Eisenhower had in mind. In early 1992 twenty-four countries signed the Open Skies Treaty. It allows a set number of unrestricted overflights of each member (more for large countries than small ones) with only 72 hours notice of the exact flight plan.

The openness of both sides to examination by the other has some distinct advantages. For instance, to remain within SALT II limits and still modernize their fleets, the superpowers decommission nuclear missile submarines by filling the empty missile tubes with concrete under the satellite observation of the other side. The SALT agreements also require each superpower to forgo encryption of information returned by missiles during tests, so that the other side can easily eavesdrop on the communications.

Yet electronic measures, called "national technical means," have limits, and the Soviet Union long resisted all American demands for mutual human verification of performance on arms agreements. The INF treaty of 1987 made breakthroughs concerning on-site, or so-called intrusive, inspections. These include initial inspections of all INF sites, observations of missile elimination procedures, and short-notice inspections of INF-related sites during the three-year elimination

---

[37]Jensen (1988) provides an excellent discussion of arms control efforts and problems. Kruzel (1986) shows that states are unlikely to negotiate controls on weapons systems that are not mature and fairly predictable. The uncertainty of relative advantage in young and evolving military technologies leads states to pursue them actively. This historic pattern holds out more hope for continuing East-West progress on reducing missiles than on stopping SDI.

period and for ten years thereafter (to assure that the opponent does not recon-struct the weapons).

Determination of on-site verification procedures for START proceeded simul-taneously with negotiation of a final agreement. For example, U.S. and Soviet officials undertook test inspections of bombers to establish verification methods. One proposal was to stamp each warhead with the equivalent of the bar code used on groceries to permit easy identification by the other side. The treaty allows twelve types of on-site inspections, including surprise visits to strategic weapons sites.

In 1988 the United States created an On-Site Inspection Agency (OSIA) that had conducted more than 400 INF inspections by mid-1991. Its mission expanded to verifying compliance with START and CFE agreements.

Besides verification, the most significant problem of arms control is that of comparing "apples and oranges" in force structures. For instance, both sides generally accept that the United States has higher weapon quality and Russia has greater quantity. Exactly how one balances quality against quantity in reductions is complicated. How does one compare tanks with fighter aircraft? A modern fable illustrates the problem: According to the story, the members of the animal kingdom met for a disarmament conference. The eagle called for abolition of fangs, the lion for controls on beaks and tusks, and the elephant for restrictions on the use of talons and teeth. The bear offered still another approach, the abolition of all weapons (general and complete disarmament). Instead, quar-rels should be settled by hugging.

ON STATE RATIONALITY AND CONFLICT

State interaction involves a complex combination of cooperation and conflict. We have seen that mixture in this chapter's general discussion of action-reaction strategies and in the specific history of nuclear relationships. In some instances, however, states make the decision to abandon cooperative interaction almost altogether and to go to war. This section advances and then explores three interrelated propositions with respect to that important decision. Each assumes the rationality that realists attribute to states. Realists cannot, of course, deny that sometimes states act irrationally, but irrational behavior is by definition difficult to predict.

First, states sometimes find war beneficial. When a state expects to win and when the costs of battle appear less than the fruits of victory, it should logically be prepared to fight (unless it can achieve equivalent gains simply by using threats). For instance, Iraq invaded Kuwait in 1990 because it expected relatively easy victory against a small state. Success promised Iraq a doubling of oil resources and more than $100 billion in financial assets for paying Iraq's foreign debt of roughly that same magnitude. Similarly, the United States attacked Panama in 1989 because it foresaw an easy victory and set a high priority on ending the rule of General Noriega.

Second, states will generally settle conflicts short of large-scale warfare. Very often, the probable victor of a war is apparent to both sides, and the probable loser will make concessions. Especially when the more powerful state has demonstrated the existence of its power and the determination to use it, the weaker state will find it profitable to negotiate a settlement rather than fight and then accept a potentially similar or even worse settlement. In 1962 the Soviets withdrew nuclear missiles they had placed in Cuba rather than fight a war with the United States. At that time, the nuclear capabilities of the United States vastly exceeded those of the U.S.S.R.

Third, states will sometimes fight despite having undertaken power calculations; if they do so, it is probable that both believe they will gain by fighting. In some cases both sides calculate themselves to be the stronger (Iran and Iraq may have illustrated this in 1980). In other cases, the demands of the stronger may so threaten the most basic interests of the weaker that the weaker will risk probable defeat rather than peacefully accept dictated terms (Vietnam would not accept its division). Furthermore, when the stakes of conflict are not so high for the stronger, the willingness of the lesser to do battle may eventually force the stronger to withdraw. For instance, Afghan rebels believed their entire cultural existence to be threatened by a Soviet-supported Marxist state and thus they chose to resist its imposition. The U.S.S.R. had important but smaller stakes, and the rebels raised the Soviet's costs above the benefits they could expect to gain.

EXPECTED UTILITY OF WAR

Proposition 1: War is sometimes beneficial. Force is appropriate when the benefits of using it outweigh the costs. Such a fundamentally rational decision calculus underlies the **expected utility theory** of Bueno de Mesquita (1981). Ray provides a good synopsis of that theory:

> The theory posits that leaders make three basic sets of calculations. First, they calculate their expected utility from a bilateral war, relying primarily on estimates of the probability of victory weighted by the potential payoff of a victory. Second, they calculate their expected utility from a multilateral war in which third parties join the fray on the side of the initiator, relying on estimates of the probability of victory given that aid, weighted by the probability that those third parties will in fact aid the initiator. Third, they calculate their expected utility from a multilateral war in which third parties come to the defense of the target state.... Unless the net result of all these calculations shows that the expected utility from the potential conflict for the initiator is positive, policy makers will *not*, according to Bueno de Mesquita's theory, initiate a war. (Ray 1987, 440–441)

This theory intentionally portrays states and their decision makers as cold-blooded. Although the theory does not assert that decision makers actually make such calculations formally, it argues that they behave, more often than not, as if they did. Looking at all wars between 1816 and 1974, Bueno de Mesquita finds that the initiator of war is five times more likely to have a positive expected utility than is the opponent (Bueno de Mesquita 1981, 129). The finding appears strikingly to confirm realist argument about rational state actors.

RECORD OF COERCIVE DIPLOMACY

Proposition 2: Much conflict is settled short of full-scale war in favor of the stronger side. We earlier quoted Voltaire as having supposedly said, "God is always on the side of the larger battalions."[38] Does the greater military force prevail? The Blechman and Kaplan et al. (1978) study of force without war concluded that limited force and the threat of war have been quite successful:

> In the language of coercive diplomacy, the proportions of short-term positive outcomes were exceptionally high when armed forces were used to reinforce behavior. Despite a considerable decline, positive outcomes also predominated over the longer term in these instances. When the objective was to assure that an action would be performed (for example, that the United Nations would act to restore order in the Congo in 1960), positive outcomes occurred with regard to 95 percent of the objectives after six months, and 61 percent of the objectives after three years. When the objective was to deter behavior (for example, that Cuba should not take action against the U.S. base at Guantanamo in 1960), positive outcomes occurred 85 percent of the time after six months and 67 percent of the time after three years. (Blechman and Kaplan et al. 1978, 91)

The success rate reported in the use of gunboat diplomacy was not as high but nonetheless substantial. The two superpowers succeeded with gunboat diplomacy in thirty-two cases and failed only ten times (the remainder were mixed cases). The thirty-eight–to–sixteen ratio of success to failure for other states was comparable (Mandel 1986, 64). These studies strongly suggest the truth of Voltaire's quip about battalions.[39]

FREQUENT FAILURES OF WAR INITIATORS

Proposition 3: When conflict occurs, one side has miscalculated. Large-scale use of force occurs less often than the more limited application of it, and, as noted earlier, generally indicates the failure to accomplish objectives with diplomacy or limited force. Because escalation often means that the power balance is uncertain, it should not be surprising that war often fails to accomplish the objectives of the initiator. Germany initiated large-scale hostilities in both World Wars I and II. It lost both soundly. In 1913, before the onset of World War I (see Table 4.3), the American, British, and French alliance together had a fairly striking capabilities (battalions) advantage over the German and Austrian-Hungarian combined forces.[40] In 1938, before World War II, the American, Russian, British, and French alliance overwhelmed Germany and Japan. On the basis of the power index in

---

[38]Ray (1987, 167) points out that, as with many other famous sayings, the genesis is uncertain.

[39]In contrast, however, Maoz's (1983) study of militarized disputes between 1816 and 1976 concluded that the "relative capabilities of participants are unrelated to dispute outcome," but initiators are more likely to win wars.

[40]This accounting leaves the Russians out of the successful coalition because of their early exit from the war.

Table 4.3, neither outcome should have been in serious doubt after complete involvement by all parties (the United States delayed entry into both conflicts, and the Soviets remained outside World War II until attacked by Germany). These cases indicate the considerable complexity for a state like Germany in assessing where the larger battalions actually lie. It was long uncertain that the United States would enter either war.

Let us consider some of the conflicts since World War II. The U.S.S.R. invaded Hungary in 1956, Czechoslovakia in 1968, and Afghanistan in 1979. The United States responded to the North Korean invasion of South Korea in 1950 and slid gradually into Vietnam in the early 1960s. Both superpowers have mixed records in these large-scale conflicts. In recent years the United States has picked its fights with great care. The invasions of Grenada (1983) and Panama (1989) were tremendous mismatches. The United States organized a twenty-eight–state coalition against Iraq and used the UN to assure that no significant state opposed its intervention; it then relied on airpower for twenty-six days to maximize the probability of success in a brief land war.

Lesser powers have also applied substantial force with mixed consequences. Tanzania successfully invaded Uganda in 1979 to overthrow the vicious government of Idi Amin. Vietnam invaded Cambodia in 1978 with the announced intention of ending the even more vicious rule of the Khmer Rouge; its withdrawal may eventually allow the Khmer Rouge to return. Libya invaded Chad initially in 1973 and intermittently into the 1980s to annex part of its territory; it ultimately withdrew. Other regional conflicts since World War II include those between Israel and its neighbors, between Pakistan and India, and between India and China; none of those conflicts accomplished much for the initiator. The most deadly interstate war since World War II (leaving aside the civil wars in which superpowers became involved) was the war between Iraq and Iran, which broke out in 1979 when Iraq thought that the revolutionary disruption in Iran would allow easy settlement of a long-standing territorial dispute. The cease-fire in 1988 left the territorial issues unresolved. The Iraqi invasion of Kuwait proved a major disaster for Iraq.

The record is interesting, because so many states that initiated wars failed to achieve their objectives. What is the overall quantitative record? Wang and Ray (1990) find that great powers won 58.1 percent of wars they initiated between 1495 and 1985, with greatest success in the last two centuries. Since 1815, initiators of conflict won forty-six of sixty-two interstate wars (Small and Singer 1985, 17). Sivard (1987, 28) argues, however, that the odds have moved against the initiators in the twentieth century, falling to a 39 percent chance that the initiating state will ultimately win.[41]

---

[41]Bueno de Mesquita (1981, 21–22) makes much of the success rate for initiators in arguing that the decision to begin a war is rational. This does not address the evidence that the success rate in the twentieth century may be much lower than it was previously, while wars continue to be frequent. In fact, Bueno de Mesquita's own data (adapted from the COW project) suggest that since 1913, initiators of wars have won and lost identical numbers (1981, 209). Frequent wars with a low success rate do not invalidate the basic argument that leaderships do *attempt* rational decision making, but they suggest that when wars occur, at least one set of decision makers has applied a faulty calculus of utility and probable success—it is often the initiator.

Is there basis for an argument that "times have changed?" If so, it might have important ramifications for systemic stability and peace. Two factors support the claim. First, a major reason for the success rate in the nineteenth century was the tremendous power differential between the modern industrial states and the minor states of the day. The success ratio depended on that differential, because when major powers have fought each other since 1815, initiators won only three of nine wars. Today even the power differentials between North and South have narrowed. Most recently, for instance, military spending in the North rose by a factor of 2.1 between 1960 and 1988, whereas that in the South increased 4.8 times (Sivard 1991, 50). Thus the difference in power capabilities may have become smaller than in earlier days.

Second, in the nineteenth century, warfare still involved relatively simple weapons and few troops. Today even "weak" states can field machine guns, tanks, jet aircraft, and other highly destructive weaponry. In addition they can mobilize much of their adult population to the battle. Thus war-initiating states are bound to pay a substantial cost, if their victims choose to resist. This may cause more of them (very rationally) to break off the contest than in the past.[42]

Consider, for instance, the wars in Vietnam and Afghanistan. How does one explain the withdrawal by the United States from Vietnam after the loss of 47,000 Americans in battle and without the accomplishment of its objectives? How does one explain the failure of the U.S.S.R. to accomplish its objectives in Afghanistan, directly on its own border? It admits the loss of 15,000 soldiers.[43] That seeming failure of the larger battalions to prevail is the **paradox of unrealized power** (Baldwin 1979, 163), and it has several explanations (see Ray 1987, 166-177, for a similar list).

First, apparently bilateral interactions in world politics seldom involve only two parties in reality. Both superpowers were significantly involved (through arms shipments and advising roles, if not with troops) in both the Vietnam and Afghanistan wars, even though the world considered the first a U.S. war and the second a Soviet war. These were in essence **proxy wars**—both of the superpowers used other forces to fight on their behalf and thereby avoided direct confrontation. There are, on closer examination, few real "two-party" international conflicts. In fact, a large-scale international community was actually involved in both Vietnam and Afghanistan through various types of military, economic, and humanitarian assistance. Most other countries also condemned the U.S. and Soviet interventions. Although international public opinion and UN votes come with no battalions of their own, they appear to have somewhat constrained the use of those under the control of superpowers. In sum, each superpower faced a great deal more opposition than simply local forces.

A second explanation expands on some elements of the first. In part, because the conflicts were not simple one-on-one wars, the superpowers were reticent to

---

[42]That may be especially true of democracies, of which there are greater numbers now. We shall return to that topic in the next chapter.

[43]*The World Almanac and Book of Facts 1992*, 735.

commit more than a fraction of their power potential to them. They feared escalation by the other superpower were they to do so. Additionally, in the case of the United States, internal dissension made it impossible for the government to use its power potential fully. Although Soviet public opinion presumably played little direct role in limiting Soviet force in Afghanistan, internal policy disagreements almost certainly existed within the leadership, and a fear of potential public discontent with the war may have indirectly limited the force applied.

Third, power based in one capability may not translate into power based in other capabilities. Power types are not fully **fungible** (easily convertible from one to another). Most important, the nuclear forces of the United States and U.S.S.R. were essentially useless in both conflicts.

Fourth, the stakes for Vietnam and Afghanistan were much higher than the stakes for the United States or the U.S.S.R. Threats to control of one's own territory generally bolster willpower and morale much more effectively than more abstract ideological challenges. The superpowers suffered many fewer casualties than their opponents, and in terms of population percentages, the Vietnamese and Afghan losses were dramatically greater. For example, the Vietnamese lost perhaps 2.1 million people during the U.S. involvement, and Afghanistan lost about 1.3 million before the Soviets withdrew (Sivard 1991, 24–25). The strength of will was tremendously strong in those resisting the superpowers. It appears that each superpower miscalculated the willingness of its adversary to sacrifice, and as the costs to the superpower became apparent (and rose above potential benefits) it became rational to withdraw.

If the world consisted purely of two-party interactions and if each interaction called forth the full capabilities of the two states with equal (or at least calculable) stakes, outcomes would be much more predictable, and statecraft would be a fairly pure science of power application. We could then rely on what March (1966, 54–61) calls a "basic force model." States can seldom predict, however, exactly which other states will become involved in an international issue, what their objectives will be, and what resources they will bring to bear. We need instead a "force activation model." Statecraft is much more an art than a science.

CONCLUSION

This chapter has begun to put the elements of realism (states, state interests, power, and statecraft) together into an understanding of world politics. After a review of the patterns of global conflict, it focused on the logic of interaction among a small number of states, especially on bilateral relations. That focus helped us understand security dilemmas, arms races (including nuclear ones), and selected strategies for constraining conflict or achieving cooperation (including tit-for-tat and GRIT). We need to move our attention, however, to the interaction of larger numbers of states. As the last section of this chapter indicated, even relationships that appear bilateral frequently involve many more than two actors. The next chapter shifts our attention to the interaction of larger numbers of states.

Chapter 6

DYNAMICS
OF STATE SYSTEMS

The world is a dangerous place for states. It is an environment of anarchy, in which each state holds ultimate responsibility for its own defense. Allies help, but they are unreliable. Neighboring states may promise nonaggression and even friendship, but a change in leadership and a quick flaring of old passions can convert an erstwhile friend into an invader.

Consider Turkey. Since 1700 it has fought fifteen wars (Sivard 1987, 30). As the Ottoman Empire gradually disintegrated (a process completed in 1918), Russia moved to expand its influence in the areas of weakened Ottoman control, especially in the Balkan states. Russia and Turkey fought six times.

Greece is a second traditional adversary and has battled Turkey in two wars since 1700. Greece holds most of the islands near the Turkish coast, giving rise to continued disputes over fishing and mineral rights in the areas immediately adjacent to Turkey. In addition, Turkey ruled Cyprus, which has a population that is about 80 percent Greek from 1371 to 1898. The island is now divided, and an uneasy truce prevails between Greek and Turkish populations, both supported by the mother countries (Table 6.1).

As if these traditional problems with its Russian and Greek rivals were not enough, Turkey has had to keep a wary eye on the conflicts involving Iraq and other countries on its southern border. It is linked to Syria, Iraq, and Iran in many ways, including watersheds, a resurgence of Islamic fundamentalism, and the fact that all four countries host a Kurdish minority that desires an independent homeland. In 1991 Turkey became an active member of the coalition that united against the Iraqi invasion of Kuwait. It closed its border with Iraq, but juggled delicately its interests in dampening Kurdish nationalism with the anti-Iraq coalition's interest in protecting the Kurdish population there against the central government.

Finally, it now finds itself increasingly embroiled in the affairs of the southern republics of the former Soviet Union. For example, Armenia borders Turkey and the Christian Armenians have not forgotten their genocidal expulsion from Moslem

TABLE 6.1
Conflicts Involving Turkey

Years	Identification of Conflict	Total Deaths
1730–1730	Janissaries Revolt	7,000
1806–1812	Russia vs. Turkey	45,000
1826–1826	Janissaries massacred	20,000
1828–1829	Russia vs. Turkey	191,000
1877–1878	Russia vs. Turkey	285,000
1889–1889	Cretan revolt vs. Turkey	3,000
1894–1897	Armenians vs. Turkey	40,000
1897–1897	Greece vs. Turkey over Crete	2,000
1909–1910	Massacres in Armenia	6,000
1911–1912	Italy vs. Turkey	20,000
1912–1913	First Balkan War vs. Turkey	82,000
1914–1918	World War I	1,450,000
1915–1916	Armenians deported	1,000,000
1919–1920	France vs. Turkey	40,000
1919–1922	Greece vs. Turkey	100,000
1977–1980	Terrorism; military coup 1980	5,000

Source: Ruth Leger Sivard, World Military and Social Expenditures 1991 (Washington D.C.: World Priorities, 1991), 23.

Turkey in 1915–1916 perhaps 1 million Armenians died. The conflict between Armenia and Azerbaijan over pockets of territory and population in each others' states (including a section of Azerbaijan almost bordering Turkey) has drawn Turkish concern.

To survive, and in an effort to prosper, Turkey relies on a complex mixture of the military, diplomatic, and economic initiatives—as described in the statecraft discussion in the previous two chapters. Militarily, it is an active member of NATO and strong ally of the United States. That relationship provided some assurances against Soviet aggression. The alliance does not protect Turkey from Greece, which is also a member of NATO. Because of their mutual hostility, Greece and Turkey both spend more heavily on defense than the average NATO member. In an effort to defuse tensions, the leaders of Greece and Turkey met in Switzerland in 1988 and opened direct, top-level discussions. Yet the basic areas of disagreement remain.

On the economic and diplomatic front, Turkey has applied for membership in the EC. It leads a movement to establish a free trade zone around the Black Sea. With respect to the Asian republics of the former U.S.S.R., in 1992 Turkey began broadcasting Turkish television throughout the region via satellite (on a channel formerly used by Moscow). With respect to its neighbors to the south, it has used its relatively plentiful water resources as both a carrot and a stick.

No matter how skillfully the leadership of Turkey has pursued its interests, however, the harsh reality is that Turkey is only one member of the interstate system, not a particularly powerful one, and it is buffeted by the larger patterns of the system. The end of the cold war has dramatically affected the parameters framing Turkish policy. The purpose of this chapter is to explore the structure of the world in which Turkey and other states find themselves and the interaction of that structure with the self-help efforts of states.

Methodologically, this chapter shifts our primary focus from individual states to the state system. Although we were able in the last chapter to deal with the interaction of a small number of states (usually two), it is almost impossible to simultaneously consider the interaction of closer to 200 states. Many disciplines shift approach when they move to a study of larger numbers of agents, introducing new methods of study as well as new concepts and theories. Physics has long recognized that it needs different tools to describe the interaction of many bodies than it does to study one or two. The discipline of economics divides its subject matter into microeconomics (the study of individual firms and households) and macroeconomics (the study of the entire economy). In essence, the study of world politics similarly profits from division into the study of individual or small numbers of states ("micro-world politics") and the study of the state system ("macro-world politics").[1] This chapter moves our discussion to the macro level.

Realists describe systemic structure in terms of constant anarchy but changing power distributions. What theory can they offer us concerning the implications of these characteristics for state behavior and systemic stability? To answer that question this chapter will again distinguish between two approaches to global polarity: that which sees the world in terms of power balances (whether bipolar or multipolar), and that which looks at the world through the lens of hegemonic leadership.

BALANCE OF POWER

ADVOCACY

Realists advocate conscious attention by decision makers to maintenance of the systemic balance of power as a necessary foundation for security and relatively peaceful interactions. Hans Morgenthau developed the case for dependence on balance of power through a three-step argument. First, human nature makes the struggle for power a constant across time and space. Second, only counterpower can effectively oppose power. Third, the use of counterpower will maintain a systemic balance of power, restraining aggressive power and providing a measure of peace and stability.

---

[1]This chapter does not, however, make a clean shift to macropolitics. It continues to devote much attention to the behavior of individual states. The limited number of really important actors at the systemic level makes it impossible to ignore the individual state (as macroeconomics can largely ignore the individual firm and household).

Realist statesmen have consciously followed that intellectual advice. British leaders actively pursued an interstate balance of power for generations. Winston Churchill, who guided Britain through World War II, described that pursuit as "the wonderful and unconscious tradition of British foreign policy." Former American Secretary of State Henry Kissinger similarly gave the argument his blessing: "the balance of power, a concept much maligned in American political—writing rarely used without being preceded by the pejorative 'outdated'—has in fact been the precondition of peace" (Chan 1984, 119).

Such advocates of the politics of balance of power frequently look back to the nineteenth century interlude between the Napoleonic Wars and World War I as the "golden age" of the policy. As Central Europe and the Middle East were throughout the cold war (and the former Soviet republics in Asia may be today), there were in that century two principal focal points of interstate politics at which the balance operated.

The first was Belgium, strategically located between France, the United Kingdom, and Germany. Control of that country by any of the great powers would have constituted a threat to all others. They therefore agreed in 1839 to respect the independence and neutrality of Belgium. When Germans marched through Belgium on the way to France in 1914, that violation of Belgium neutrality helped lead Britain to fight alongside France. The second focal point was in the Balkans (in the "front yard" of Turkey). The other great powers resisted Russian efforts to expand into the territory once controlled by the dying Ottoman empire. For example, the Crimean War (1854–1856) began as an effort by Britain and France (along with Turkey and Sardinia) to push the Russians back out of two Turkish vassal states. When the balance of power system finally came apart in 1914, the immediate issues centered on another Balkan state, Serbia, then an ally of Russia.

Some balance-of-power enthusiasts argue that the system was unable to control the tensions in the Balkans at that point because, instead of fluid alliance structures directed against whichever power might seek gains, two fairly rigid alliances had evolved among the great powers. Thus, instead of containing the conflict regionally and protecting the status quo, the alliances propagated the conflict throughout the system. Conversely, critics suggest that the outbreak of World War I (in which Turkey perhaps inevitably became a major battlefield) proved the essential bankruptcy of the idea that a balance-of-power system could maintain relative peace.

DEFINITION

One of the problems faced by those who prescribe a politics of **balance of power** lies in definition of it. As a static description, it means (1) any distribution of power (the balance of power is…); (2) an equal distribution (there is an equivalence of power among…); and (3) a superior position (country X holds the balance of power). As a dynamic, policy-oriented concept, it either (1) operates automatically (all states will oppose aggressive power); or (2) requires conscious attention to balance by states (Britain adopted a balancing role before World War I). Complicating the definition is the question of polarity; some authors (Kaplan 1974) and practitioners associate balance of power only with multipolar and not bipolar systems. To confuse matters further, the term is used both as concept and theory.[2]

Realists have done little to clarify the issue; Morgenthau consciously used four definitions:

> The term "balance of power" is used in this text with four different meanings:
> 1. as a policy aimed at a certain state of affairs,
> 2. as an actual state of affairs,
> 3. as an approximately equal distribution of power,
> 4. as any distribution of power. (Morgenthau 1973, 167ff.)

BALANCE OF POWER AND STATE BEHAVIOR

Realpolitik describes how individual states and leaders are supposed to behave in a balance of power:

> The elements of *Realpolitik*, exhaustively listed, are these: The ruler's, and later the state's, interest provides the spring of action; the necessities of policy arise from the unregulated competition of states; calculation based on these necessities can discover the politics that will best serve a state's interests; success is the ultimate test of policy, and success is defined as preserving and strengthening the state. (Waltz 1979, 117)

Kaplan proposed more specific rules for states in balance-of-power systems and tailored them to different system polarities. Although they fundamentally reduce to acting so as to preserve and strengthen the state, Kaplan's (1957, 23) specific rules for states in a multipolar system are:[3]

1. Act to increase capabilities but negotiate rather than fight.
2. Fight rather than pass up an opportunity to increase capabilities.
3. Stop fighting rather than eliminate an essential national actor.
4. Act to oppose any coalition or single actor that tends to assume a position of predominance with respect to the rest of the system.
5. Act to constrain actors who subscribe to supranational organizing principles.
6. Permit defeated or constrained essential actors to reenter the system as acceptable role partners, or act to bring some previously inessential actor within the essential actor classification. Treat all essential actors as acceptable role partners.

Anyone who has played board games of interstate politics, such as Risk, Diplomacy, or Axis and Allies, will recognize how the seemingly automatic adoption by players of such rules prolongs the games (the existence of the states) interminably.

---

[2]Haas (1953) and Claude (1962) elaborated various definitions.

[3]A problem with these rules is that they conjoin actions a rational state voluntarily takes (rule 1) with those the dynamics of the system impose upon states (rule 3). A rational, power-enhancing state would gladly absorb another and violate rule 3; but its former allies will oppose such a significant enhancement of power (as when the United States and Britain acted to limit Soviet expansion in Europe after World War II). For a more detailed review of problems with the rules, see Waltz (1979, 50–59).

ALLIANCES

Alliances help maintain the balance of power.[4] They allow weaker states to counter the power of stronger ones effectively. As Kaplan's rules suggest, states tend collectively to oppose threats to dominate the system. The alliances against Napoleon early in the nineteenth century, against Hitler in the mid-twentieth century, and against the Soviet Union in the cold war demonstrated that dynamics at work.

The alliance against Nazi Germany showed that ideology need not prevent the formation of interstate ties when power relations dictate them. The United States and Stalinist Russia had limited trouble in cooperating extensively after Germany invaded the Soviet Union.[5] More recently, we saw the strange combination of authoritarian Pakistan, Communist China, and a democratic United States all supporting an Islamic guerrilla movement in Afghanistan against the Soviet Union's puppet state. In power struggles, "the enemy of my enemy is my friend" (and perhaps my arms supplier).

Rational power calculations should explain not just the formation but also the size of alliances. When an alliance brings together a large portion of interstate power (significantly more than 50 percent), its members have less to gain by remaining within it. If one views the terms imposed on the vanquished as spoils (as when territory is divided or reparations are imposed), then the larger the coalition, the smaller the share any member will receive. Thus alliances should logically be large enough to win but not so large as to dilute the fruits of victory. Riker (1962) labeled the tendency for movement toward minimum size in winning coalitions the **size principle** or the **minimum winning coalition principle**.

As a corollary, when opposition power weakens, old disagreements among alliance partners will resurface, causing either dissension in the alliance or coalition breakdown. For instance, after the defeat of Nazi Germany, the United States and the Soviet Union were unable to sustain cooperation. One could argue that they began fighting between themselves over the spoils, especially those in Central Europe. One could also argue that the old ideological antipathy simply reappeared. In either case, new coalitions of more nearly comparable strength emerged around the two poles.

In the late 1980s, the Soviet threat to the West began to weaken because its economic difficulties became obvious, because it dramatically loosened its control over Eastern Europe, and because it adopted a less threatening military posture. As power theory suggests, cracks in the opposing NATO alliance became wider. In April 1989, NATO halted maneuvers because West German and Turkish participants objected to the simulated use of battlefield nuclear weapons on their territories. At the same time Germany called for East-West discussions on

---

[4]Just as the security dilemma drives each state to increase its defense spending, the fear of isolation in an anarchical interstate system pushes states into alliances (Snyder 1984).

[5]Similarly, the Nazi-Soviet pact of 1939, signed before the two states literally carved up Poland, allowed a national socialist state to cooperate with a Communist one, in spite of the intense antagonism between them.

eliminating all short-range nuclear forces. In a doctrine called **flexible response**, NATO strategy had relied since the 1960s on the threat of nuclear escalation against superior Soviet bloc conventional forces. Thus these developments posed a serious challenge to NATO.

The logic of power and the size principle do not, however, completely explain the post–World War II history of alliances. Because the United States was the larger and stronger of the two superpowers, pure power considerations should have led to a larger coalition around the Soviet Union. Explanations beyond the size principle are needed. Ideology is one—many Western states were more comfortable with the United States, despite its extensive power in the system. In addition U.S. power actually supported the development of extensive alliances through the strength of its economy, and the aid and trade it could offer.

More recently, the failure of NATO to collapse following the disbanding of the Warsaw Pact and the disintegration of the Soviet Union creates an even greater anomaly for the realist's balance of power theory. Without an apparent threat and without clear benefits to collective action, NATO's cohesion should rapidly decline. If it does not, then nonrealist theories of alliance behavior (including emphasis on the affinities of economically advanced, democratic countries) will gain considerable support.

CHANGE IN POLARITY AND ITS CONSEQUENCES

Although the military superpowers and their nuclear arsenals have dominated the global system for the last forty-five years, many observers believe that the balance of power is moving gradually from a bipolar to a multipolar character. The growing demographic, economic, and military strengths of China; the ongoing economic unification of Western Europe; and the economic rise of Japan may herald a movement toward a new multipolar system.[6] If so, it behooves us to consider how such a systemic transformation might affect world politics.

There is a long-running argument among scholars about the relative stability of bipolar and multipolar systems. Deutsch and Singer (1969) claimed that multipolar systems are more stable. They argued that **cross-cutting cleavages** in such a system can result in shifting coalitions on different issues. Thus in the five-power world that might be evolving, China, as a Communist state, might find itself opposed by the capitalistic United States, Western Europe, and Japan on some issues. The United States and Japan have a built-in propensity for disagreement on some high-technology and industrial trade issues, whereas the United States and Europe often disagree about agricultural policies. Shifting coalitions and disagreements mean that there are more potential alliance partners (and perhaps no fixed alliances), and that there is more uncertainty about power configurations and the possibility of winning in any conflict. As the last chapter discussed, states are rationally averse to entering conflicts unless there is a high probability of success.

[6]Surprisingly little theory treats reasons for systemic transformation from one polarity to another. Realists generally treat it as exogenous to their theory.

Waltz (1969; 1979, 161–193) disagrees and argues that bipolarity is more stable and less conflict prone for two reasons. First, states exhibit considerable conservatism when stakes are large. In bipolar systems, direct conflict between the two powers has often destroyed one or both (as in the Chinese and Greek state systems reviewed earlier, and as in the wars between Rome and Carthage).[7] Second, he argues that in a two-power system there is a considerable certainty about power balances that eliminates the risk of miscalculations. Both sides know who would win an overt conflict and settle differences accordingly. Research concerning the relative stability of multipolar and bipolar systems has been inconclusive.[8]

Bueno de Mesquita (1978) suggests that the real issue is certainty and uncertainty. The most dangerous times, he argues, are when polarity is changing, and power balances and alliance commitment are least certain. If true, this is not comforting, because it is now changing.

HEGEMONIC IMAGES OF THE WORLD

To this point in the chapter we have examined selected realist insights into multipolar and bipolar worlds. We have discussed, for example, the interaction of multipolar state systems and state behavior, the formation and dissolution of alliances, and the implications of change from bipolarity to multipolarity.

Insights from the balance-of-power perspective can help us make sense of the fifteen Turkish wars since 1700. In that year the Ottoman Empire was about at the end of its great power period (Waltz 1979, 162). Austria and Russia probed its weakened condition in wars of the early 1700s. In the Crimean War (1853–1956) other great powers (France and Britain) supported the much-reduced power of Turkey against further Russian efforts to benefit at its expense. By the end of the nineteenth century Turkey was essentially reduced to a lesser power and its external orientation shifted to regional power balances, especially that with Greece. After World War II it found that its interests lay in an alliance with the more geographically distant superpower, the United States.

As Chapter 4 discussed, however, another way of looking at the contemporary state system is to see the United States as a hegemonic power. If it has indeed "won the cold war," that may appear to reinforce its hegemony further. Yet Chapter 1 showed that the United States no longer has the margin of economic superiority over other states that it once did—both superpowers are exhibiting signs of decline, and Russia has simply set a much more rapid pace. Especially for those who look at the system not in terms of a political-military balance of power but in terms of economic leadership (hegemony), the period of U.S. leadership may be coming to an end. Such speculation raises at least three questions. First, what forces cause the rise and fall of hegemons? Second, what advantages might attend a stable

---

[7]Aron (1966, 139–140) argues that it is precisely this predilection for total war that makes the bipolar system more dangerous; moreover, bipolar standoffs tend to become ideological contests, inflaming passions on both sides.

[8]Midlarsky (1988) reviews the literature and supports the relative stability of the bipolar system.

leadership or hegemony? Third, are there any particular consequences for world politics of changing leadership?

RISE AND FALL OF HEGEMONS

Those who study economic leadership over the centuries note a regularity in the rise and fall of hegemons. Although British leadership lasted two centuries (the seventeenth and eighteenth), earlier hegemons, like the Dutch, remained dominant for approximately one century. Several explanations exist for the transition of hegemons.[9] We explore these in terms of their implications for U.S. systemic leadership.

Although analysts devote less attention to the rise of hegemons than to their fall, Gilpin's general theory of change in international politics (Gilpin 1981, 10–11) suggests an explanation for rise. Gilpin assumes that states are rational utility-maximizers.[10] Expansion of control over their environment (more territory, greater wealth, more prestige and influence over others) normally provides benefits (utility) and encourages that expansion. These benefits are more than psychic ("we are number one"). For instance, a hegemon gains the ability to order the global economy to its benefit. The inability of any other single state to challenge the security of the leader certainly is another important motivation.[11] Gilpin (1981, 106) concludes that a state will expand until the "marginal costs of further change are equal to or greater than the marginal benefits." When states achieve such a balance they seek to maintain it. In reality, however, they eventually decline.

First among explanations for the decline of hegemons is the cost of hegemony. Maintaining military power is expensive. Although the share of economic product that the United States devotes to defense declined significantly during the post–World War II period, it still stood at around 6.5 percent in the late 1980s. The Soviets were even more burdened by their maintenance of superpower military status, spending somewhere between 10 percent and 15 percent of their GNP on defense in the 1980s (there is wide uncertainty about both their defense spending and their GNP).

This level of spending took a toll. At the beginning of the twentieth century, the United States spent two to three times as much on education as on defense; in the late 1980s it spent 45 percent more on defense. The Pentagon used sufficient fuel in one year to power all U.S. public transit for twenty-two years (Sivard 1987, 5). In contrast, the allies and former allies of both superpowers directed lesser portions of their economic capabilities to the military. West European states typically spent between 3 percent and 4 percent of their GNP on defense. Japan has a

---

[9]For further discussion, see Gilpin (1981) and Oye (1987).

[10]The reader should clearly distinguish between the use of economic (generally cost-benefit) logic and the subject matter of its application, which need not be economics (see Radnitzky and Bernholz 1987).

[11]Modelski (1978, 227) argues generally that any monopoly creates rents, and that systemic leaders attain privileged positions in both security and economic matters.

constitutionally based commitment to limit defense forces and holds defense spending to 1 percent of GNP.

Why does the United States not only spend more than its allies on defense but also devote a larger portion of its economy to it? Members of the U.S. Congress repeatedly raise this question, noting also that much U.S. spending supposedly defends those same European allies. The principle of **exploitation of the big by the small** supplies part of the explanation (Olson and Zeckhauser 1966). Luxembourg and Iceland are both NATO countries. Luxembourg contributes only 1.3 percent of GNP to defense, and Iceland has no military at all (it provides base sites to NATO). From the viewpoint of these countries, even defense spending of 10 percent of GNP would make no real contribution to NATO, because their economies together are only 0.2 percent that of the United States. Why bankrupt themselves when they can obtain the defense of NATO anyway? Middle-sized countries, like Belgium and Denmark, which each direct about 2 percent of GNP to defense, can make the same argument, but less strongly.

The defense that NATO provides against attack is a collective good, available to all NATO members. The alliance cannot deny that good to any member, and each member thus has an incentive to obtain a free ride—to take the good but contribute as little as possible. The United States cannot make the same argument that Luxembourg or Belgium can; without the U.S. share, about two-thirds of NATO expenditures, there would be no collective defense system. Table 6.2 verifies the tendency for the largest members of NATO to spend at or above the average level (2.6 percent of GNP), and for the smallest to spend at or below the average.[12]

A second and related reason for the fall of hegemons may be the tendency to increase both public (such as defense) and private consumption as a portion of the economy, and thereby to devote less to investment (Oye 1987, 13). The United Kingdom and the United States, former and current hegemons, top the list of leading countries in the rate of consumption; Table 6.2 shows that they reinvest a smaller portion of their economies than the average NATO member. It is perhaps natural for the wealthiest to want to tap that wealth (and thereby to dissipate it). Thomas Mann described three generations of a family called the Buddenbrooks. The first generation built wealth, the second consolidated it, and the third lost control. Modelski (1978, 232) sees in the Buddenbrooks a syndrome, the **third-generation effect** (Gilpin 1981, 166), an analogy between state and individual behavior (and perhaps a reason that hegemonic leadership endures about a century).[13]

---

[12]Turkey and Greece, as discussed earlier, spend more than the average NATO member on defense, in part because of their historic regional enmities. If we remove them from the analysis, the principle of exploitation of the big by the small becomes ever clearer. Oneal and Elrod (1989) review burden sharing over time and argue that disproportionality of contributions is declining, as is U.S. hegemony, but still exists.

[13]Mancur Olson (1982) suggests the basis for a third-generation effect within states. He focuses on the gradual development within stable countries (like hegemons) of structures based on special interests that capture and constrain more dynamic political and economic agents. The demands of these structures make politics more divisive and less capable (more concerned with distribution than growth), so that gradual decline begins in economic growth.

TABLE 6.2
NATO Members and Expenditures

Country	GNP (Billion $)	Defense Expenditures (% of GNP)	Educational Expenditures (% of GNP)	Investment (% of GNP)
U.S.	$5,392	5.4	5.3	16
Germany	1,623	2.2	4.4	22
France	1,191	2.8	5.6	22
Italy	1,091	1.3	4.0	21
U.K.	975	3.7	5.1	19
Canada	570	1.7	7.3	21
Spain	491	1.8	3.2	26
Netherlands	279	2.8	7.5	21
Belgium	192	1.6	5.1	21
Denmark	131	2.0	7.9	17
Norway	106	3.3	6.7	21
Turkey	97	3.7	1.6	23
Greece	58	5.8	2.7	17
Portugal	57	1.8	4.4	32
Luxembourg	8	1.3	4.0	—
Iceland	5	0.0	4.3	—
Average	767	2.6	4.9	21
Japan	2,943	1.0	5.0	27

Sources: (GNP and Investment) World Bank, *World Development Report 1992* (New York: Oxford University Press, 1992), 222–223, 234–235; (Defense) International Institute for Strategic Studies, *The Military Balance 1991–1992* (London: IISS, 1991), 212; (Education) Ruth Leger Sivard, *World Military and Social Expenditures*, 14th ed. (Washington D.C.: World Priorities, 1991), 51–52.

Notes: GNP, investment, and defense from 1990; educational expenditures from 1987. Japan is not a member of NATO.

A third explanation, related to the first two, concerns the tax and inflation rates of leading states. Rises in both military spending and consumption in hegemonic states could lead to higher taxes and inflation, thereby choking economic vitality. Cipolla (1978, 7) notes that inflation raged in the late Roman Empire, the late Byzantine Empire, and in seventeenth-century Spain.[14]

Technology provides a fourth explanation for both the loss of leadership and the rise of new leadership. According to this argument, leadership is closely related to technological capability and often arises when some technological breakthrough (or cluster of them) provides an edge:

> For the Portuguese, their edge was associated with shipbuilding, navigation, and the Indian Ocean spice trade. The Dutch had herring, shipbuilding, textiles, and much of

[14]Gilpin (1981, 165) develops this argument further. See also Kennedy (1987).

the intra-European and European-Asian maritime commerce. The British claim was first predicated on shipbuilding, Atlantic commerce, and wool textiles. Later cotton textiles, coal, steam engines, and iron products and then railroads were at the heart of Britain's 19th century centrality in the world economy. The American rise, in its turn, was based on automobiles, steel, and petroleum. (Rasler and Thompson 1989, 5)

Once in place, however, technological leadership is vulnerable because it is less expensive to copy than it is to innovate. Other states, like Japan in the early post–World War II period, can adopt and even improve U.S. technology (and the United States often acts as if the rest of the world has little to offer it). In four studies of U.S. economic growth, estimates of the contribution of technological advance to total economic growth ranged from 44 percent to 72 percent (Press 1987, 15). If the United States has lost its edge in technological leadership, the implications for its economic growth could be substantial.

ADVANTAGES OF HEGEMONIC LEADERSHIP

The preceding discussion suggested some of the systemic advantages of hegemonic leadership, particularly the provision by hegemons of defense, technology, and other benefits to secondary powers. The **theory of hegemonic stability** pursues this line of thought (Keohane 1980, 136). The theory suggests that a combination of control and leadership by the hegemon can facilitate free trade systems; free flow of technology; agreements on environmental issues; and a generally wide range of peaceful, cooperative relations among states. Many theorists of hegemonic stability especially emphasize the collective benefits of the free markets that the British and Americans have provided for two centuries. The decline of the hegemon could mean the loss of such benefits.[15] The last half of this chapter will explore in more detail the relationship between hegemony and systemic cooperation.

The word "hegemon" does not always, however, have such a positive connotation. It can imply a domineering power, even an imperial one. Other perspectives raise the possibility that the existence of a hegemon has several negative consequences for other members of the global system. We will return later in this volume to such argument.

CHANGING OF THE GUARD

The history of transition from one hegemon to another has been a history of conflict. **Hegemonic transition theory** focuses on the reasons for the transition (extending our earlier discussion about the rise and fall of hegemons) and on the conflict engendered by the transition. The conflict arises because hegemons seldom voluntarily surrender systemic leadership; a challenging state usually forces the issue.

[15]See Kindleberger (1973). Gilpin (1975) and Krasner (1976) stress the association of the hegemon with free markets, but do not assume that all states benefit from them (Snidal 1985b).

Although leadership may be of value to the system, the hegemon also presumably benefits. As Gilpin (1981, 200) emphasizes, what is at stake is "governance of the international system." During the period of the Portuguese and Spanish empires, governance gave the right to plunder and to take tribute. In the mercantile empires of the Dutch and early British periods, it established extensive areas in which the hegemon had exclusive rights to obtain food and minerals, and to sell manufactured goods.[16] Even in free-trade eras, the hegemon has retained some exceptional privileges relative to other states. As French President de Gaulle pointed out, only the United States had the ability to spread its currency freely around the system, effectively making loans to itself. When Mexico repays its international debt, it must do so in dollars over which it has no control. When the United States repays its debt, it can do so in dollars and can, if it wishes to accept the inflationary consequences, simply issue more of them. The United States also has extensive military bases, dominant voting rights in international financial institutions, locations for its satellites in a few prime orbital positions, and other advantages of being number one.

When a challenging power wants some or all of these advantages for itself, conflict is possible. A century from now, historians may look back at World War I and World War II and describe a Germany that had surpassed Britain in economic strength, but held a decidedly secondary position in the international order. They may conclude that this tension caused the "two German wars," and that the British-German issue disappeared only when outside powers (the United States and the U.S.S.R.) decisively transformed the system from a Eurocentric one to a truly global one (which they failed to do after World War I).

Along these lines, the **power-transition theory**[17] posits that war is most likely when the balance of power is changing, and a challenging state has reduced or eliminated the power gap between it and the dominant state. The challenger normally initiates the war. A related theory is that of **status discrepancy** (Galtung 1964). If the ascribed status (prestige) of a state is below its achieved status (capabilities), that state will be dissatisfied. This theory has a psychological basis and perhaps treats states too much as if they were individuals. Nonetheless, if great powers divide systemic goods (such as colonies before World War I), and the division does not accurately reflect relative state capabilities, it is reasonable to expect that this might cause "frustration" within the leadership of a state that does not obtain its fair share. In recent years Japan has increasingly chafed at being asked to pay more of the costs for the IMF and World Bank programs without being given a larger voting share.

---

[16]Modelski (1978, 227-228) says that "Monopoly...creates rents.... In the past these benefits have revolved around greater than average security (which can be reinvested in capacity for higher organization and productivity); preferential access to, better knowledge of, and superior bargaining power in global transactions and communications (bringing additional wealth through trade and services) and a capacity to 'set the rules' in world affairs."

[17]Organski (1968); Organski and Kugler (1980). See also Midlarsky (1988), who ties the theory to the number of systemic disputes that states face at any time.

Surprisingly, the challenger does not usually win the transition war and become the new leader (Modelski 1978). Instead, the transitional war frequently weakens both the leader and challenger, and allows a third party to rise in a relatively peaceful transformation of the system after the war. That third party is often an ally of the old leader (not its challenger). For example, England was an ally of the Dutch at the end of the Netherlands' leadership period, and the United States was similarly associated with the British during the transition wars preceding U.S. leadership (Rosecrance 1987, 289). This phenomenon reminds us of the tendency for earlier state systems (Chinese, Greek, or Italian) to fall prey to outside actors after internal conflict.

The difficulty in applying hegemonic transition theory to the current period is that no obvious challenger to U.S. leadership exists. Japan's economic rise has given it an economy about one-half that of the United States. The Soviet Union appeared to pose a major challenge in the first decades of the postwar period, but Russia is now a declining military giant and an economic weakling. In fact, in the 1980s Russia's military strength relative to that of the United States slipped. Although the theory alerts us to reasons to anticipate an ongoing relative decline in U.S. relative power and to potential problems of a transition, it does not appear that a hegemonic transition is imminent. It is possible, however, that a united Europe could eventually emerge as the new systemic leader. It is now larger economically than the United States and has considerably greater military capability than Japan. The European Community is the only political unit in the postwar world that has grown geographically and that has great potential for still further expansion. Perhaps historians will one day identify the cold war as the war of transition, and a United Europe will follow in the hegemonic footsteps of the United Provinces (the Netherlands), the United Kingdom, and the United States.

THE CONTROL OF ANARCHY: INTERNATIONAL LAW

This chapter has now completed a basic review of state-system dynamics through the lenses of balance of power (bipolar and multipolar) and hegemonic leadership. Although it has emphasized conflicts and war, the discussion has also indicated considerable potential for cooperation. The remainder of this chapter focuses our attention on the cooperative efforts of states. We begin by looking at "international" (actually interstate) law. We then turn to a broader discussion of interstate cooperation and the potential for something approaching interstate public policy.

International law represents an effort by states to control some of the anarchy in the state system (it cannot eliminate the anarchy). Although globalists heavily emphasize the development of international law, realists also recognize its importance:

> It is also worth mentioning, in view of a widespread misconception in this respect, that during the four hundred years of its existence international law has in most instances been scrupulously observed. When one of its rules was violated, it was, however, not always enforced and, when action to enforce it was actually taken, it was not always effective. Yet to deny that international law exists at all as a system of binding legal rules flies in the face of all the evidence. (Morgenthau 1973, 273)

What is international law? Article 38 of the Statute of the International Court of Justice defines it as:

1. International conventions [treaties], whether general or particular, establishing rules expressly recognized by the contesting states;
2. International custom, as evidence of a general practice accepted as law;
3. The general principles of law recognized by civilized nations;
4. Subject to the provisions of Article 59, judicial decisions and the teachings of the most highly qualified publicists of the various nations, as subsidiary means for the determination of the rules of law. (Couloumbis and Wolfe 1986, 257)

This listing reflects a **positivist** view of international law, the largely realist position that law is what states make it. An earlier, more idealistic tradition called **naturalist** argued that divine law or human nature is the true source of international law and the task of legal scholars is to discover those fundamental principles. The naturalist view owes much to religious thought and the scholars of the Middle Ages, such as St. Augustine. Grotius, the "father of modern international law," built on this tradition but also began to modify it by documenting state practice. In fact, his work illustrated a confusion about the ultimate sources of law:

> He will tell us, often with regard to the same question, what is the law of nature, the law of nations, divine law, Mosaic law, the law of the Gospel, Roman law, the law of charity, the obligations of honour, or considerations of utility. But we often look in vain for a statement as to what is *the* law governing the matter. (Lauterpacht 1985, 12)

To reduce the confusion and to limit the idealistic element of international law, and thus its vulnerability to conflicting universalisms, international legal scholars at the turn of the century expounded international legal positivism (Boyle 1985, 17–19). For example, Oppenheim (1908) rejected the fundamental law of nature arguments and based international law on the customary practice of states and the agreements among them. The positivist tradition, now dominant, moves international law as a field of study away from prescription and toward description.

Domestic legal systems typically incorporate three major elements: law making, law adjudication, and law enforcement. Although the strength of the international legal system falls short of domestic ones in all three areas, the greatest failing is in enforcement. International law is decentralized law, relying on the individual or group behavior of states for much of its creation and interpretation and essentially all of its enforcement. As a result, individual state interest influences strongly the character of international law. It is for this reason that our focus here is on international law as defined by state practice.

Most of international law, largely *created* by states and for states, spells out their rights and obligations. States' rights correspond in general to their attributes (defined in Chapter 4): sovereignty (recognition by other states), territory (with boundaries), government, and population.[18] The Charter of the United Nations,

---

[18]Much of the discussion here is based on Cassese (1986). He directs our attention to the 1970 UN Declaration on Friendly Relations, for a statement of important principles.

part of international law, incorporates four elements concerning states, three that reinforce these attributes of statehood, and one that refers to states' obligations. In the words of one of its drafters:

> ...first, States are juridically equal; second,...each State enjoys the right inherent in full sovereignty; and third,...the personality of the State is respected as well as its territorial integrity and political independence.... And the fourth element [is] that the States should, under international order, comply faithfully with their international duties and obligations. (cited in Cassese 1986, 129)

Consider the parallels to a state-centric adaptation of the U.S. Declaration of Independence:

> All states are created equal in sovereignty. They are endowed with certain inalienable rights. Among these are territorial integrity, protection of their population, and the pursuit of state interest. To secure these rights law is instituted among states, deriving its obligations from the consent of the governed states. (adapted from Henkin 1991, 165)

The rest of this section considers in turn the rights of states (the protection of their sovereignty, territory, and government) and their obligations. There is also, however, a growing body of international law that seeks to protect the rights of individual humans (often against the power of their governments), and we subsequently review that as well (in Chapter 8).

RIGHTS OF STATES

States are like the animals in George Orwell's *Animal Farm*: All are equal, but some are more equal than others. Most international organizations, including the United Nations, recognize this formal equality through their one-state, one-vote decision rules. Although some organizations (like the World Bank and IMF) vary from that principle and weight voting by economic contribution and thus, effectively, by economic power, no organization weights votes by population. This fact reemphasizes that states, not human beings, are the bases of most international law.

The fundamental principle of sovereign equality underlies much of international law. It makes the granting of recognition by one state of another an important and sometimes controversial act. The United States denied the sovereign equality of the People's Republic of China (PRC) from 1949–1979 simply by refusing to recognize it, continuing instead to recognize the government on Taiwan as that of all China. The broader international community reinforced that denial of sovereignty by excluding the PRC from the United Nations until 1971.

The issue of territoriality also underlies a considerable amount of international law. Debates repeatedly surface concerning the limits of territorial waters, the rights of passage through straits, and the control over the resources of the continental shelf or other offshore extensions (such as islands) of states.

Sovereign equality and the right of states to their own government jointly produce the legal principle of nonintervention in the internal affairs of other states. International law at one level is a mutual agreement of governments to legitimize and protect their rule within their own territories. States are not to bring pressure to bear on the domestic institutions of another state, even though they might find the government repugnant. Should civil war break out, states are to refrain from intervention on the side of the rebels. In practice, however, they frequently violate this. Of 106 civil wars between 1816 and 1980, twenty-one drew overt military intervention by another country that caused at least 100 battle deaths (Small and Singer 1982, 234). Many others attracted economic or military aid. So often have more powerful states intervened in the economic, political, or social developments of the less powerful, that the nonintervention principle takes on special significance for Southern states.

In an attempt to comply with international law, states most often attempt to justify interventions that they undertake. For instance, the U.S.S.R. insisted that the legitimate government of Afghanistan invited its military involvement in 1979. In fact, the Soviets entered on request of a Communist government that their embassy had helped install in a coup during April 1978. Moreover, on entering in December 1979, Soviet special forces killed the leader who supposedly invited their involvement and put the more compliant Babral Karmal in his place (Klass 1988, 925–926). Similarly, the Soviet Union said that the Czechoslovakian government requested the very intervention in 1968 that ousted it and brought an end to the "Prague Spring."

In Vietnam, the United States maintained that South Vietnam was a separate state from North Vietnam and argued that it was assisting the South in self-defense against aggression from the North. This characterization was contradicted by both the historic evidence of Vietnamese unity and by the 1954 Geneva Accords, which were quite specific in identifying two zones of one country that were to be reunited following an election in 1956. The United States further justified its war with North Vietnam, at least the early air raids, on the basis of reprisal against Hanoi for attacking U.S. ships in the international waters of the Gulf of Tonkin. There is still a dispute as to whether the attack ever really occurred (Foster and Edington 1985, 148).[19]

OBLIGATIONS OF STATES

Another and overlapping category of international law defines the obligations of states in their dealings with each other and constitutes an effort to control anarchy. We can usefully subdivide it into three subcategories: (1) laws that treat the interactions of states during peacetime; (2) laws that seek to avoid or resolve conflict; and (3) laws that specify the rules of warfare.

[19]*The Pentagon Papers* verify that the administration was planning the air raids a half year before the attack.

PEACETIME BEHAVIOR

The status and treatment of diplomats is of great importance during both peace and war. Laws governing diplomatic interaction have a long history and high levels of compliance. The Italian city-states of the fifteenth century developed the permanent mission, or legation, and established professional corps of diplomats. As the modern European state system developed, so too did conflicts among diplomats. Coachmen were killed and duels fought over rank in the court to which they were posted (Holsti 1983, 165). The Congress of Vienna in 1815 established the ranking system with four categories that we still use: ambassadors and papal nuncios, envoys extraordinary and ministers plenipotentiary, ministers resident, and finally *chargés d'affaires*. In 1818 states agreed that within a rank, they would accord status on the basis of time in post. Thus the dean, or *doyen*, of the diplomatic corps in Washington is the ambassador from abroad who has served longest in the United States, regardless of the size and importance of the country from which he or she comes.

The **immunity of diplomats** from punishment also has a long history. The ancient Indian *Mahabharata* specifies that "The King who slays an envoy sinks into hell with all his ministers" (Holsti 1983, 166). Today law protects diplomats even against local parking tickets, a major problem for the city of New York, because United Nations diplomats flagrantly abuse their parking privileges. Should a diplomat commit any crime while abroad, the host country can declare the individual *persona non grata* and insist that he or she be withdrawn. Prosecution can only occur in the diplomat's own country. On the other side, diplomats are supposed to abide by the laws and customs of the receiving country and refrain from intervention in the affairs of that country. The norm of nonintervention is as consistently violated as that of diplomatic immunity is observed. Spying under cover of diplomatic position is quite routine, and attempts to manipulate domestic political processes are common.

During its capitalist expansion, Britain established many laws of international commerce that still apply throughout the world. For instance, international laws protect shipping from pirates and protect navigation through straits. They also specify that contracts and indebtedness are binding. The United States used this last legal principle to justify its repeated intervention in the countries of Central America early in the twentieth century, because they were not paying their debts.

International law makes treaties binding and divides them into two categories, specific and law making (Couloumbis and Wolfe 1986, 267). **Specific treaties** are most often bilateral agreements that settle specific issues and have no regional or global implications. They are part of international law for the signatories only. Multilateral conventions are **lawmaking treaties** and, as a result of United Nations action, are increasingly universal. For instance, 140 states had ratified the 1968 UN Treaty on the Non-Proliferation of Nuclear Weapons by the end of 1989 (Spector and Smith 1990, 293). In 1991, even long-time holdouts France, China, and South Africa said that they would sign. In international law such a convention cannot be binding on states that have not ratified it, but considerable pressure for compliance does build on states that do not sign lawmaking treaties with widespread support. In contrast to multilateral treaties, United Nations resolutions, even when passed overwhelmingly, are hortatory only (Cassese 1986, 192).

THE LEGALITY OF WAR

Deadly force is legal in world politics, so debate is only about *when* war is legal. Historically, scholars and practitioners placed great emphasis on the concept of **just war**. St. Augustine and other medieval churchmen or scholastics argued that war was just when fought in self-defense or to punish wrongdoers (Couloumbis and Wolfe 1986, 254). The designation of wrongdoers was a prerogative of God and the pope as his representative, but left a great deal to the interpretation of those who decided to do God's will.[20]

There are two dominant modern traditions on war as an instrument of policy. Machiavelli defined the realist tradition: The state determines when war is appropriate to its aims, when it is in accord with the *raison d'état*. Grotius sketched the globalist tradition, which denies the unrestricted right of war implied in the concept of *raison d'état* (Lauterpacht 1985, 22). Instead it restricts just war primarily to self-defense or redress of injury (punishing religious wrongdoers is not included). Kant took an extreme idealist position in his *Perpetual Peace*, published in 1775, when he argued that no war is just and called for international agreements to move toward disarmament and to eliminate the threat of war (Brown 1987, 146).

Chapter 8 will document a gradual trend in legal texts that, between 1815 and 1992, have increasingly characterized war as unacceptable. International reaction to recent wars provides further evidence of growing rejection of the just war and *raison d'état* views: There was widespread condemnation of Vietnam for its invasion of Cambodia in 1978 (despite the overthrow by that invasion of the vicious Pol Pot government). Even the Third World rejected the Soviet invasion of Afghanistan in 1979, and many of its allies did not stand behind the U.S. invasions of Grenada in 1983 and Panama in 1989. On the other hand, almost all states in the global system supported the "just war" against Iraq in 1991.

LAW OF WAR

Once war is underway, there is a large body of international law that supposedly regulates its conduct. That corpus evolved gradually through custom during the eighteenth century and with greater speed after the Congress of Vienna in 1815. The basic principle is reciprocal cooperation to limit the destructiveness of war, especially its impact on noncombatants. Examples of law regulating warfare include:

> Wars ought to be declared prior to their initiation. Combatants ought to wear distinctive uniforms so as to be differentiated from noncombatants—in other words, the wider civilian population. Damage, killing, and destruction should be

---

[20]The decision by the Ayatollah Khomeini in 1989 to offer a reward for the assassination of author Salman Rushdie, who offended Islam by publication of *The Satanic Verses*, is reminiscent of that period.

limited to what is required by "military necessity." Only military targets should be marked for bombing and destruction. Prisoners of war should not be harmed or molested, should be fed and clothed, and should be kept in good physical condition throughout their captivity. Hospital crews and Red Cross and Red Crescent vehicles should be exempted from military attacks. Museums, historic edifices, and shrines should not be bombed or destroyed. Cities declared to be open (for example, undefended) should be spared from bombing attacks. Populations in occupied territories should be properly administered and cared for. Women and children should not be raped or molested. Private property should not be looted. Private real estate should not be seized permanently by the occupying armed forces. Most of these rules have been extended to sea and air warfare. Many rules specifying permissible types of weapons have also been developed. For example, extremely painful weapons, such as poison darts, dum-dum bullets, and various nerve and asphyxiating gases, are not to be used. (Couloumbis and Wolfe 1986, 270)

The Hague conferences of 1899 and 1907 and the Geneva conference of 1949 codified such elements of the law of war. The technology of the twentieth century has rendered many of these principles immediately obsolete, however. Modern war is total war, involving full-scale mobilization of personnel, conversion of economies to war making, and use of weaponry so destructive that it simply cannot be restricted to military targets (which, in an economy geared to providing support for the military, are difficult to identify in any case).

The international community continues to struggle with these issues. For instance, a United Nations treaty in 1972 abolished biologic warfare (Riggs and Plano 1988, 171). Yet U.S. intelligence in 1988 claimed that ten countries, including the Soviet Union, pursued forbidden research. In a 1925 Geneva Protocol, the world banned the use of chemical weapons and, in an effort to make that meaningful, the UN has periodically sought to prohibit their production and stockpiling. Only in 1992 did such a treaty emerge. Nuclear weapons are the most significant threat to any moral standards in warfare. The nuclear powers have selected countervalue (economic and population) targets, not just counterforce (military) targets. Elaboration of the potential for a nuclear winter after a nuclear exchange (or at least a long "nuclear fall") makes many targeting distinctions largely irrelevant anyway (Sagan 1983).

The Nuremberg trials, convened by the victorious allies in November 1945 are the most famous attempt to enforce international law governing the initiation and pursuit of war (Chan 1984, 333–345). The allies tried twenty-two Germans for crimes against peace and humanity, and executed eleven (Göring took his own life before the allies could do it). Similar trials in Tokyo investigated twenty-eight and sentenced seven to be hanged. The arguments of defense and prosecution attorneys illustrated many of the principles of international law discussed to this point. Among the elements of the defense were appeals to the rights of states. Specifically, defense arguments included references to the principle of territoriality (which allows a government to prosecute crimes only within its own borders), local law, military necessity, and sovereign rights and immunity from the prosecution of other states. The allies countered with references to the universality of law and precedence of natural law over local law. Moreover, the allies treated the defendants as individuals rather than representatives of their states. One additional defense that they denied was that of **respondent superior**, that is, acting under orders. They ruled that the individual has the obligation to reject illegal orders.

Precedent makes law. In 1967 an international group of prominent individuals convened the Stockholm "Tribunal" to try U.S. behavior in Vietnam according to the legal standards established in the Nuremberg and Tokyo trials. Accusations against the United States included the use of the defoliant Agent Orange, napalm, and cluster bombs; the "indiscriminate" use of firepower in ways that failed to separate combatants from civilians; and the crimes of individual soldiers (murders, rapes, and so on). Those who conducted this trial had no power to enforce punishments for their claims of illegality against the United States.

In 1971, the United States itself put Lieutenant William Calley on trial for a massacre in the village of My Lai (on March 16, 1968) in which about 500 defenseless people were killed. He was convicted of the first-degree murder of twenty-two men, women, and children, and was sentenced to life imprisonment. He served three years under house arrest before his release. Many have drawn parallels between what happened in My Lai and the behavior of Germans in 1942, when they executed 1,300 Czechs in the village of Lidice after an assassination by Czech guerrillas of the German occupation force leader. A *very* important difference is that such massive reprisal was official German policy, whereas the My Lai massacre was not only unauthorized but officially condemned. Nonetheless, the light punishment in the U.S. case justifies some cynicism concerning the meaningfulness of the law of warfare.

The Nuremberg trials focused not just on warfare. They essentially put the German state on trial for massive violations of human rights in the killing of 6 million Jews and others during the Holocaust. The international community increasingly condemns actions within state borders, overriding any claims of territoriality. Examples include the global opposition to South African apartheid, to Latin-American death squads, to Soviet emigration barriers, to Serbian "ethnic cleansing," and to Chinese political repression. All of these concerns fall within the rubric of human rights, a topic to which Chapter 8 will return and which proves subversive to state control of international law.

INTERNATIONAL GOODS AND GLOBAL PUBLIC POLICY

States cooperate when it "delivers the goods"—when it promises goods or benefits greater than the costs of organizing the cooperation. Three characteristics of international goods either complicate or facilitate the efforts of states to formulate global public policy[21] and to guarantee international goods to their citizens.[22]

First, **rivalry** characterizes a good when only one individual or state can benefit from a specific unit of the good. For instance, when a state controls a piece of

---

[21]Soros (1986, 1987, 1988, and 1989) provides some of the best treatments of global public policy. His treatment grows primarily from the concept of commons, whereas the one in this chapter has deeper roots in the concepts and theory of public goods.

[22]For discussions of public goods and the problems of cooperation on them see Hardin (1982), Barry and Hardin (1982), and Taylor (1987).

territory (a good), no other state can do so. When one fishing fleet kills a herd of whales, no other can do so. We have seen that the rivalry characteristic creates zero-sum situations.[23] In contrast, however, access to radio waves or television transmissions is nonrivalrous—no one's access precludes that of anyone else (rivalry does, however, characterize the use of specific radio frequencies upon which to transmit). We might expect more cooperation when there is less rivalry.

Second, **nonexcludability** characterizes a good when it is impossible to deny access to other individuals or states. For instance, it is impossible to fence the atmosphere—air moves across borders and anyone can use it (for breathing or for disposal of pollutants). Similarly, it is difficult or impossible to restrict access to knowledge. Even high school students have been able to compile the basic knowledge involved in building an atomic bomb. In contrast, it is possible to exclude countries from the world postal system or from Antarctica. It is often said that "good fences make good neighbors." In reality, if good fences exist, they tend to reduce both cooperative and conflictual interaction (except when it becomes time to rebuild or, especially, to move the fence). When fences do not exist, interaction often intensifies, for better or for worse.

Third, **congestion** characterizes a good when the consumption of units of a good interferes with the ability of others to obtain units of it (generally when it becomes "scarce"). For instance, whales already possessed the characteristics of rivalry and nonexcludability in the eighteenth century: Consumption of a specific whale prevented consumption of it by anyone else, and yet everyone had access to them. At that time, however, there were so few who had the equipment and capability to hunt whales that there was no congestion. Currently, however, the killing of whales (in many species) limits availability to others.[24] We would expect congestion initially to increase conflict, but also potentially to increase cooperation in its resolution.

This discussion suggests that we should not always expect that cooperation and conflict in an interstate relationship will vary inversely (as one goes up, the other goes down). Often, low levels of state interaction result in limited cooperation or conflict, and high levels of interaction may lead to increased levels of either or both.

CATEGORIES OF INTERNATIONAL GOODS

Table 6.3 uses rivalry and excludability to categorize and illustrate four types of international goods: private goods, coordination goods, common property resources, and pure public goods.[25] The supply of goods in each category may or may not be congested.

[23]The term "jointness" is sometimes used instead of nonrivalry.

[24]More technically, congestion exists when the social cost of consumption is positive. Congestion interacts especially with rivalry.

[25]Samuelson (1955) stated the two characteristics of pure public goods. Weimer and Vining (1989) provide an excellent discussion of rivalry, excludability, and congestion from the perspective of domestic issues.

TABLE 6.3
Classification of International Goods

	RIVALRY	
EXCLUDABILITY	Yes	No
Yes	PRIVATE GOODS Core problem: defining property rights Examples: Alsace-Lorraine, the West Bank	COORDINATION GOODS Core problem: establishing standards Examples: international postal service; global telecommunications systems
No	COMMON PROPERTY RESOURCES Core problem: over exploitation Examples: whales, global atmosphere, geostationary orbits, radio frequency spectrum	PURE PUBLIC GOODS Core problem: underprovision Examples: knowledge to control malaria, radio/television transmissions

Private goods (in the upper left-hand cell of Table 6.3) exhibit rivalry and excludability. Territory is the best example of a private good. During the expansion of empires in the nineteenth century, Britain, France, Portugal, and Germany treated African territory as a private good. They divided it up so that they would solely benefit from individual units of it and could exclude access by others. In the early part of the century they had limited ability to exploit that continent (in part because malaria stopped them from penetrating it), and there was no congestion with respect to claims of interior territory. By the end of the century there was a great deal of congestion and much conflict about the international private good.

As this example suggests, the core problem associated with international private goods is the determination of property rights. A common solution to the problem is international agreement to privatize a good to which ownership was earlier vague or contested. The imperial powers met at the Berlin Conference of 1884–1885 and divided claims in Africa. Similarly, most countries of the world attended the Third United Nations Law of the Sea Conference between 1973 and 1982 and extended their control over ocean resources to a distance of 200 miles from their coastlines.

A second approach to property rights is to establish some form of collective control with a fairly explicit statement of privileges and obligations. For instance, the Antarctic Treaty of 1959 does not recognize previous territorial claims (or deny them) and prohibits all military activity there. Various agreements on the law of the sea guarantee free shipping on the high seas more than twelve miles offshore of states (and through key straits even when within twelve miles of shore), but these agreements also prohibit dumping of nuclear waste at sea. The global community has gone so far as to declare the seabed the collective property of humanity.

A third approach would potentially be to reduce congestion and thereby eliminate need for agreement on property rights. For instance, some argue that agreements over colonies like that in Berlin never ultimately resolved imperial disputes—it was when countries decided that the costs of colonies were greater than the benefits that the demand fell sharply and eliminated congestion.[26]

Coordination goods lie in the upper right-hand corner of Table 6.3 and exhibit nonrivalry and excludability. For instance, all countries can benefit simultaneously from international postal service (in fact, the more states that partake of the good, the greater the benefit for other states). Yet it would be possible to exclude a country (like Iraq) from any established system. International telecommunications systems have the same character.[27]

The core problem associated with provision of these goods is the establishment of initial standards and procedures (Snidal 1985). Interstate cooperation is frequently easy to obtain on these types of goods because the benefits are great, and costs are often low—interests are fundamentally harmonious. It is hardly an accident that the Universal Postal Union and the International Telegraph Union were among the very first modern international organizations.

Yet cooperation is seldom automatic. For instance, the world is now moving toward high-definition television, and there is competition among European, American, and Japanese firms to define the global specifications. The winning firm (and country) will benefit by being able initially to dominate the market for the system.

The lower left-hand corner of Table 6.3 contains international goods characterized by rivalry and nonexcludability. Because of the inability to deny access, we often call them **common property resources**. Biologic resources of the high seas, like whales or tuna, illustrate these goods. While rivalry is a fixed feature, excludability is partly a legal concept. Theoretically, we could brand whales in the same way that ranchers once branded cattle on the open range (thus legally excluding access to them by others and converting them to a private good).

Similarly, geosynchronous orbital space and the spectrum of radio frequencies have the character of common property resources. Again, although there will always be rivalry (only one satellite can efficiently use a given location), there need not always be nonexcludability. The global community could legally allocate slots and convert them into private property, even allowing purchases and sales by new owners (just as an individual can buy or sell a home).

The core problem facing states in their provision of goods in this category is overexploitation. Whaling illustrates the logic of individuals in a congested common property situation. Each whaler seeks to obtain as much of the good as

---

[26]The cost-benefit analysis of colonies changed over time—for instance, costs increased with the spread of modern weaponry, and benefits decreased with the growth of domestic markets.

[27]Weimer and Vining (1989) call these marketable public goods and provide domestic examples such as bridges, roads, and recreation areas.

possible (there is rivalry) and cannot exclude others from doing the same. Each fleet acts rationally to take additional whales each year. The individual fleet fully captures the benefits of taking more whales. The cost of doing so is smaller future harvests, and all whaling fleets share that cost. That is, the cost is largely external to the individual calculation—each fleet creates what economists call an externality for other fleets, in this case a negative one.[28]

Although the collective interest is to avoid it, individual interests in these situations often lead to overexploitation of a resource. This result has come to be known as the **Tragedy of the Commons** (Hardin 1968), in reference to the ancient tradition of a communal grazing area called a "commons" (still seen in some places).[29] As long as the population of grazing animals on the commons is small, sharing poses no problem, because the grass is an uncongested good (although rivalry already exists, because the use of a unit of grass by one precludes its use by others). As population increases and congestion develops, however, the individual interest comes into conflict with that of the group. Too many animals eventually overgraze the commons and destroy the vegetation, to the detriment of all community members.

One approach to addressing overexploitation is collectively to regulate it. The International Whaling Commission (IWC) once set global quotas for the harvest of various whale species (in essence excluding some access). Because it did not allocate these to particular countries, it created a situation like that of access to limited goods in the former Soviet Union (or to the supply of tickets for many concerts in the United States), namely a scramble to be first—a "Whale Olympics" (Soroos 1986, 278). In 1986 the IWC declared a moratorium on commercial whaling. In 1992 Norway, Iceland, and Japan announced their intention to resume, arguing that minke whales are not endangered. Theoretically the IWC could adopt the same approach that most states use domestically with deer: sell a certain number of hunting licenses, rationing them among potential hunters (by lottery or price).

Another approach, where it is physically possible, is to define legal excludability and to privatize the good. This is what the international community did with respect to oceans within 200 miles of coastlines. Still another approach is to attempt to reduce congestion. Those who seek to eliminate demand for products of whales (or for tusks or furs of endangered animals) wish to lessen the pressure on the commons.

The final quadrant of Table 6.3 includes **pure public goods**, which exhibit neither rivalry nor excludability (we call goods exhibiting either nonrivalry or nonexcludability, but not both, "impure public goods"). For example, your access to radio waves (as distinct from frequencies for broadcasting) does not preclude access by anyone else—nor is there any very effective way of denying your access. Similarly, your use

---

[28]The exploitation of a private good, like Brazil's Amazonian forests, can also cause negative externalities and "transboundary problems" (Soroos 1988, 2). In fact, many in the international community would like to redefine those forests as part of the "common heritage of humanity," or in effect as a collectively owned global good.

[29]Soroos (1989) emphasizes that commons is a legal arrangement permitting use of a public resource for private gain, while common property resources are defined by their physical characteristics that permit joint use but not division or exclusion; thus, the concepts are related, but not identical.

of knowledge does not interfere with the provision of that knowledge to anyone else, and it has been proven difficult selectively to deny access to knowledge.

This category of international goods is very small. For instance, it is traditional to cite air or the atmosphere as a pure public good. In reality, however, your use of the oxygen in a given unit of air for breathing (or polluting) precludes my effective use of the same unit. Thus although I cannot exclude you from that use, we are rivals for it. The atmosphere is actually a common property resource (which once was abundant relative to demands on it). We now recognize that use of the atmosphere for disposal of pollution from fossil fuel–burning electric plants, of CFCs, or of CO_2 interferes with the use of the atmosphere as a source of clean air for humans and wildlife, as protection against ultraviolet radiation, and as a moderator of climate.[30] As long as congestion is low, many common property resources (including whales, radio frequencies, and the atmosphere) appear much like pure public goods. When congestion increases, however, the underlying element of rivalry becomes obvious.

COLLECTIVE ACTION AND PROBLEMS OF UNDERPROVISION

Both pure and impure public goods frequently face the problem of underprovision. Although many such goods, like whales and clean air, are at least initially "natural" and simply free for the taking, others, like global satellite communication services, exist only as a result of collective action. Moreover, when "natural" goods become congested and needs for regulatory systems arise, only collective action will assure consistent access to the good. The most general problem that arises surrounding **collective action** is underprovision.[31] Especially when excludability is not an option (as with common property resources and pure public goods), states have little incentive to contribute to the costs of the collective action and the provision of the **collective good**.[32] Instead, they prefer to **free ride**, to partake of the good without contribution. There are even sometimes costs associated with the initial provision of a coordination good (with excludability) that states would prefer someone else paid. If all states decided to "let Denmark do it," there would be no collective action. More commonly, states limit their share of the contribution and the result is **underprovision**.

[30]Another way of looking at this problem is that congestion begins to create rivalry where none existed before, and it moves the good to the quadrant with problems of common property resources and overexploitation.

[31]Olson (1965) provides a classic elaboration of this argument. But scholars have recognized the conflict between individual and collective interests for a very long time. Rousseau explained it with a parable of five hunters collectively pursuing a stag. Should any of them individually break off the hunt to kill a rabbit and assure himself of sufficient food, the stag might elude the other hunters (reported in Waltz 1959). Russett and Starr (1989, 505) quote a statement of the problem by Aristotle: "What is common to the greatest number has the least care bestowed upon it. Everyone thinks chiefly of his own, hardly at all of the common interest."

[32]Some define collective goods as public goods that meet only the nonexcludability criterion (Pearce 1983, 70). Others use collective good and public good interchangeably. Russell Hardin (1982) makes the same distinction this text does and provides one of the most readable treatments of the subject.

When this problem appears within countries, the typical solution is collective coercion. For instance, travel on highways is a good that most of us would like to use without payment. If we were asked to make voluntary contributions to a national highway fund, we might kick in a few dollars, but it is unlikely that we would pay in proportion to our use. We would starve the fund for money, and it would underprovide highways. Instead, we collectively agree to tax ourselves and to force everyone to pay (with gasoline taxes payment is roughly in proportion to highway use).[33]

In the global arena, there is no central authority to administer collective coercion. Exclusion is not an option for many goods. In a **privileged group** (Olson 1965, 49–50), however, one or more members has a private incentive to provide some level of the collective good to the benefit of all.[34] Returning to our highway example, if one extremely large trucking firm existed or if a small group of firms collaborated, the firm or group might determine that its own interest lay in paying the costs of a basic national highway system and tolerating some free riding by private individuals. Although the system might still underprovide the public good, there would be some supply of it.

Privileged groups sometimes appear globally. For instance, the agreement by twenty-four countries in Montreal in 1987 to reduce CFC production and use, even in the absence of commitment by other countries, illustrates this principle. These economically advanced countries produce most of the problem, so they could assure a significant provision of the collective good of CFC reduction. In fact, a somewhat smaller subgroup, the twelve countries of the EC, subsequently decided to eliminate production totally by 2000. These leaders in the provision of the collective good do, however, worry about free riders. The production and use of CFCs in China, for example, is growing so rapidly that it could significantly offset reductions elsewhere. If so, China would become a **spoiler**, a free rider so large that it frustrates efforts by leaders in a privileged group.[35]

One of the ways in which privileged groups overcome the problem of spoilers is through side payments. **Side payments** are "exchanges among the members of a coalition to equalize any inequalities arising from their cooperation" (Luce and Raiffa 1957, 180). As an example, the richer countries will provide some CFC-replacement technology to China as a side payment to encourage Chinese cooperation on the ozone issue, and they have established a fund to assist China and other LDCs in the acquisition of this technology.

In some cases, a single country can create a privileged group. For instance, a hegemonic world leader, like the United States today or the United Kingdom of an earlier day, may be able (for private benefit reasons) to provide a collective good. In the security arena, the Pax Britannica of the nineteenth century or the Pax

---

[33] A second approach in this instance is to privatize highways by converting them to privately owned toll roads, facilitating exclusion of those not paying their share.

[34] A group in which no subgroup has such an incentive is a "latent group."

[35] Schelling (1978) discusses the size of the subgroup that can block a collective good and notes that it varies by issue. In the case of free passage through a narrow street (or narrow strait), one car (or state) can block it, so universal contribution is needed to keep it open.

Americana of the post–World War II period, long periods of unusually peaceful interstate relations, may illustrate the beneficent functioning of a hegemon. These same hegemons have also made critical contributions to the provision of free markets that benefit other states, including those that free ride by exporting into the free markets while protecting their own. We referred earlier to the identification of such benefits by the theory of hegemonic stability. It is to these two critical issues, security and trade, that we now turn this discussion of international goods.

SECURITY AND THE LOGIC OF COLLECTIVE ACTION

The characteristics of international goods—rivalry, excludability, and congestion—frequently change over time and with circumstances. For instance, we noted that both technological change and legal definition can move a good from nonexcludability to excludability (as with offshore oil resources). Perception and understanding of a good's characteristics can also change over time (for instance, an understanding of common property resource characteristics is fairly recent). Thus the association earlier of particular goods with the particular cells of Table 6.3 was a bit too tidy. So it is with security.

The classical realist portrayal of security (in a situation of anarchy) is that of a good exhibiting rivalry and nonexcludability. Rivalry exists because the effort of one state to increase its security can reduce that of others (a zero-sum situation with the classic security dilemma).[36] Nonexcludability is the rule because no state or other actor determines who has security and who does not—it is impossible to deny access to more of it by a state determined to increase its security by spending more on the military. With these characterizations, security becomes a common property resource subject to congestion and severe overexploitation.

The normal realist reaction to the security dilemma has two elements. The first is to advise states that the security system is one of self-help, and that they must guard their own security as if it were a private good. That approach is doomed to failures in providing security because the actions of individual states cannot change the nonexcludability characteristic. Arms races are a common result.

The second realist approach, represented by balance-of-power politics, is fundamentally an effort to control access to the good—to impose excludability and simultaneously to dampen rivalry.[37] Perhaps the most basic rule in a balance-of-power system is that alliances form against any actor threatening to become predominant and to use their superior power to reduce the security of other states. In essence, the rule places an upper limit on the amount of security any one state can appropriate for itself. It attempts to convert the security problem into one of coordination—a kind of standard setting with respect to security. The fundamental

---

[36]Congestion is important here. Rousseau posited a state of nature in which humans had little contact with each other, and therefore the rivalry characteristic was less important. He noted, however, that as they increased in numbers and began to come into regular contact, the competition for security grew (the kind of state of nature that Hobbes posited).

[37]Snidal (1985) describes the security issue in terms of nonrivalry and excludability.

weakness is that the costs of contributing to the provision of the collective good (setting upper limits on the power and security of any aggressive state) are high, and many states would prefer to free ride on their alliance partners. As with most collective action, underprovision plagues it.

Another strategy with respect to security problems shares much of the philosophy and many of the difficulties facing a balance-of-power system. Collective security also seeks to impose excludability and dampen rivalry, again reducing security issues to a coordination problem (see Table 6.3). Instead of ad hoc alliances against a potential hegemon, **collective security** calls for an alliance of all states against any aggressor. Again, the costs of contributing to the collective good can be high, and states will prefer to free ride.[38]

Still another strategy turns the basic balance-of-power notion on its head. Instead of protecting the system from a hegemon, the idea is to rely on the hegemon. The hegemon has a self-interest in dampening rivalry and imposing excludability on security. Although by setting the security standards of the system it favors its own interests, the hegemon also can reduce conflict over security by others. A remaining problem is that a challenger will periodically arise, and rivalry over security with the hegemon will become the central issue.

Note that all of these strategies (including balance of power) attempt to "dampen rivalry" over security as a public good. In essence, they move our conception of security from zero-sum toward nonzero-sum by suggesting that there may be ways in which to increase the total amount of security in the system. Those who characterize the realist approach as wholly zero-sum fail to recognize that the theory of balance of power effectively makes this nonzero-sum assumption (if states properly follow the coordination rules of the theory, the security of all will be enhanced).

Still another approach to security problems draws our attention even more sharply to the rivalry characteristic. In a **security community** (a group of states with expectations that they will use only peaceful means to settle disputes) there is both nonrivalry and nonexcludability with respect to security. All states recognize that they can mutually increase their security by strengthening the community, and no one is excluded from the good. Security becomes in essence a pure public good (bottom right-hand corner of Table 6.3).[39] Much of Europe increasingly appears to be a security community.

TRADE AND THE LOGIC OF COLLECTIVE ACTION

Most states want for their citizens the good of access to extensive markets. According to Western economic theory, open markets possess the characteristics of nonrivalry and nonexcludability (Snidal 1985). Specifically, there is no rivalry

---

[38]Although globalists generally support collective security, and realists attack it, the similarities with a strategy of balance of power are greater than either likes to admit. Realists might protest that balance of power calls only upon those with an immediate interest in stopping aggression to resist it—and not on those halfway around the world. The Nazi assault on Czechoslovakia, however, did not immediately threaten Britain and France. In many respects the action did threaten the interests of Canada and Australia. Boundaries of interest are hard to draw.

[39]In domestic environments, defense is a pure public good (Weimer and Vining 1989).

because all countries gain by participating in free trade, and no excludability because that would contradict the definition of the good (all have free access to the market).

In reality, however, excludability is simple physically—countries impose tariffs or simply deny access to their domestic markets. Moreover, there is a common perception by states around the world that there is rivalry. Specifically, greater access by Japan to European markets may lessen American access. Thus there is tendency for states to treat trade as a private good, excluding others from international markets and preemptively capturing external markets. At the extreme this privatization strategy would result in only intrastate markets. Short of the extreme, it might lead to rigid trade blocs, generally centered on one large country.

Thus an extensive free market is not a "natural" public good, with clear-cut characteristics of nonexcludability and nonrivalry. Instead it is a good that states must create, essentially by controlling excludability and dampening rivalry—by restricting free riding. They must overcome the problem of underprovision. How can they do that?

Once again, a hegemon can be useful. For instance, Great Britain and the United States have at times reduced rivalry over market access by opening their extensive markets to smaller powers. Perhaps as important, these hegemons exerted pressure on other states to maintain open markets themselves, thus increasing the supply of the public good. The hegemon can, however, also selectively deny access to the good. During the cold war the United States limited access, and in some cases completely excluded Communist countries from its markets.[40]

A second approach is collectively to set standards as the IMF and the GATT have done since the late 1940s. These international organizations again attempt to expand the supply of the good by maintaining open markets and dampening rivalry over them. With respect to dampening rivalry, they exert pressure on countries that have taken too much of the good (for instance, the large surplus of Japanese exports over imports) to reduce their trade surpluses.[41] With respect to controlling excludability, they make it more difficult for countries not willing to free their own markets by demanding nonexcludability within the system.[42]

LESSONS FOR GLOBAL COOPERATION

This overview of the various categories of international goods, the typical problems associated with their provision, and some common approaches or strategies for providing them suggests several general insights into the issue of interstate cooperation. Among them are the following:

[40]And a hegemon may take advantage of its position not to open markets, but to appropriate them—as Britain did in Latin America and China. Hegemons need not be benevolent providers of public goods. By dictating access to trade they effectively establish a coordination good in which they unilaterally control excludability.

[41]They also exhort deficit states to increase exports.

[42]For instance, through the reciprocity of the most-favored nation principle, to be discussed later. As with a hegemon, the control these organizations exercise over excludability moves free markets toward the status of coordination goods.

1. An extensive set of issues cry out for cooperation among states. These cross over the security, economic, and broader environmental concerns of this text.

2. These issues normally require ongoing and repetitive cooperation. At first blush it might seem that some are amenable to one-shot cooperation. For instance, once an international good is defined as a private good, it may seem only necessary to define the property rights (like those of the imperial powers in Africa or the modern states in the ocean). Unfortunately, however, property rights seldom defy attempts to redefine them.

3. An important aspect of international cooperation lies in defining and redefining the basic character of international goods. In the process, goods once seen as zero-sum in nature may be increasingly perceived as nonzero-sum (and, in fact, be provided more extensively). Much of the thrust of interstate cooperation appears to be directed at dampening rivalry (and perhaps eliminating it), creating or controlling legal excludability, or reducing congestion.

4. Collective action on international goods suffers frequently from the tendencies of states to free ride, and for goods to be either overexploited or underprovided.

5. Subgroups, including individual hegemons, may unilaterally provide collective goods. The resulting privileged groups face their own problems, however. One is that the hegemon's ability to act may decline as free riders rise to spoiler status, and a second is that challengers of hegemons tend to appear and introduce substantial conflict into the system.

PATTERNS OF GLOBAL COOPERATION

The last chapter laid out some of the strategies by which states pursue cooperation bilaterally or in small numbers. It focused on reciprocity, both specific (tit-for-tat dynamics) and diffuse (GRIT-like interaction). Now that we have better defined the types of systemic situations in which cooperation may arise, and the problems states face with respect to it, we return to the discussion of the strategies by which states organize and extend cooperation. We will see that interstate cooperation is like a body on two legs; as we proceed along the scale from bilateral tit-for-tat reciprocity on single issues to relationships involving multilateral, diffuse reciprocity on many issues, the weight of the body gradually shifts from the leg standing in self-interest to that resting in community.

REGIMES

Extended cooperation based on diffuse reciprocity, especially that involving more than two states, often requires and gives rise to more structure than is found in specific reciprocity relationships. In some cases the structure is extensive enough so that we speak of there being a regime. Although in common parlance regimes refer to domestic governments (and often to repressive ones), international **regimes** are the principles, norms, rules, and decision-making procedures that facilitate extensive reciprocity in a given issue area.[43] Regimes may or may not involve formal institutions such as international organizations. The international

---

[43]This definition builds on that of Krasner (1983, 1). An alternative definition is "institutions with explicit rules, agreed upon by governments, that pertain to particular sets of issues in international relations" (Keohane 1989, 4). At a trivial level there are principles, norms, and rules in *every* issue area. Thus the nonstandard definition of this volume requires that they facilitate extensive reciprocity before we consider them regimes.

oceans regime, although building on treaties from three UN Law of the Sea conferences, does not have a standing international organization dedicated to the regime. Nonetheless, fundamental principles, norms, and rules, such as freedom of the high seas, state rights within the twelve-mile territorial sea area, and 200-mile exclusive economic zones, guide most interstate behavior concerning the oceans. Conversely, when international organizations do exist, they help structure regimes. For instance, the WHO strongly shapes and directs the world health regime.[44]

DEVELOPMENT OF REGIMES

States develop regimes for many of the same reasons, and in much the same manner, that they structure international organizations. In general, regimes respond to a demand. It is relatively easy to establish institutions and regimes that resolve coordination problems, because the compatibility of state interests is high. As noted earlier, the Universal Postal Union was among the first international organizations of the modern state system. States benefit from the definition of mutual obligations and accounting of individual contributions that regimes provide, and they are willing to pay some start-up costs for them. Regimes, once in place, lower the cost of striking deals (transaction costs) for further cooperation, by providing negotiating forums, precedents, easier access to information, and the high probability of future cooperation for current concessions. Regimes help extend the "shadow of the future"—the anticipation that others will reciprocate cooperation.

We can also look at regimes from the supply side, focusing particularly on the behavior of a systemic hegemon. The desires of a hegemon, if one exists, strongly influence the character of the regime. In the arena of international trade, which regime theorists study actively, the Dutch commitment to mercantilism in the seventeenth century imposed a mercantilistic regime on world trade (Ruggie 1983, 198). The British and Americans subsequently opted for liberal or free-trading regimes.

The character of a regime imposed by a hegemon depends in large part on the self-interest of that hegemon.[45] British and American leaders have believed that free markets allow their economically efficient producers to capture markets globally; the Soviet Union, as a regional hegemon, used barter trade to pursue its security interests in Eastern Europe.

Yet the persistence of regimes suggests that states, even hegemons, may lose control of them once they are established. It may be possible that the rise in economic productivity among its economic competitors has made unconditional U.S. support of free trade anachronistic. In the last quarter of the nineteenth century and the first quarter of the twentieth, Britain similarly held onto a free-trade system in which it was no longer fully competitive (Cohen 1987). The Soviet

---

[44]Oran Young (1986, 107) usefully puts regimes into the category of social institutions, like marriages, markets, or electoral processes. Thinking of them in this way helps us understand how they combine institutional structures (like marriage or sales contracts) with informal, process-based patterns (cooperation, trust, and reciprocity). Coercion, too, is associated with all social institutions.

[45]We saw earlier that a hegemon may supply a public good to a privileged group but does so because of its own desire for that good.

ideological commitment to Socialist barter exchange patterns also continued long after the evidence showed them to be highly inefficient.

Krasner (1987) notes the strong element of inertia in these behaviors. That inertia may have in part a rational basis—for instance, a sensitivity to the costs of altering or abandoning a regime relative to the informational and organizational benefits it provides (Keohane 1983a). There may also, however, be a set of nonrational explanations for the persistence (in some cases even the development) of regimes, specifically the ideological (idealistic) commitments of actors to them or an unthinking acceptance of them simply because they historically served a function.[46] Although states develop regimes, regimes also shape the expectations and behavior of states.

Moreover, explanation of many regimes must move beyond the state-centric perspective of the discussion to this point. A network of scientists played a central role in directing Mediterranean states into a pollution control regime (Haas 1989). A transnational environmental community (organized by NGOs) demanded and achieved a regime limiting trade in endangered species. The United Nations Environmental Programme (UNEP) led the way to the 1987 protocol on the restriction of CFCs (Young 1989, 365). When states meet under the pressure of such nonstate actors, they frequently do not exhibit the rational, self-interested negotiating behavior expected by realists. They may instead seek fairness and equity, because they do not really know how a regime will affect their particular interests in future years (Young 1989).

SECURITY REGIMES

Jervis (1983, 174–175) lists four reasons why regimes are more difficult to establish in security than in issue areas such as economics, communications, or oceans:

1. Competitiveness is greater in security than other issue areas. There is an inherent zero-sum element to security because military power is relative rather than absolute.
2. Offensive and defensive behavior are difficult to distinguish. The development of oil stockpiles by a country will almost invariably appear defensive, whereas stockpiling bombs almost always appears threatening, and therefore offensive.
3. The stakes are higher in the security area—fundamentally they involve survival.
4. It may also be more difficult to detect cheating on agreements in the military arena (for instance, research and development programs) than in economics (where higher tariffs are obvious and even economic subsidies are usually open budget lines). Thus a concern with faithfulness to agreements arises.

Is there now a security regime for the global system? Jervis does not believe that the balance of terror based on MAD constitutes such a regime. Instead, immediate self-interest and specific reciprocity almost completely explain U.S. and Russian strategic behavior.

---

[46]Goldstein (1989) emphasizes institutional and legal inertia within the hegemon. Keohane (1988) differentiates rationalistic from reflective approaches in the study of institutions (including regimes) and emphasizes the importance of belief systems in reflective explanations.

Conversely, the signing of the INF, CFE, and START agreements in 1987, 1990, and 1991 collectively indicate important steps toward a shared adherence to principles, norms, and rules—the regularity that would characterize a security regime. Still, at this point nuclear superpower cooperation on arms control largely involves only specific reciprocity—immediate and equivalent concessions. Continued progress toward a real security regime would require a broader relationship between the major powers, including a basis for more diffuse cooperation.

COMPLEX INTERDEPENDENCE

Unidimensional security relationships do not lend themselves to the creation of regimes. Instead, extended cooperation on security, when it exists, tends to be imbedded in a broader, multifaceted pattern of cooperation—a situation in which states cooperate on multiple, overlapping issues (that is, when there is "high issue density").

A large amount of cooperation among states does not center on any single issue, but requires linkages and trade-offs across issues. Keohane and Nye sketched a pattern of interstate relationship (Table 6.4) called complex **interdependence**,[47] which is a kind of "interstate friendship."[48] Friendships normally involve extensive interaction, a wide range of mutual interests, and an absence of coercion. Keohane and Nye identify three characteristics in complex interdependence. First, multiple channels connect the societies. Not only do official diplomatic ties exist, but so too do informal ties among governmental and nongovernmental elites and a variety of relationships (for example, trade) among elements of the societies. Second, in a relationship of complex interdependence multiple issues reach the mutual agenda, and security issues do not consistently dominate. Third, the parties do not use military force in settlement of disagreements. In the U.S.–Canadian relationship, it is this pattern of complex interdependence that allows their lengthy mutual border to remain undefended. Agreements focused on only border demilitarization, in the absence of a broader cooperative relationship, would almost certainly be inadequate (as they have been with respect to the Russian-Chinese border).[49]

As the U.S.–Canada example suggests, a relationship of complex interdependence characterizes what we earlier called a **security community**—a group of states with expectations of extensive, peaceful interactions. Complex interdependence similarly ties together the twenty-four states of the Organization for Economic Cooperation and Development. Many regimes link those states, including a security regime that appears to nearly preclude military conflict among them. Existence of the security regime rests on a base of extensive cooperation, covering trade and other issues, and structured by other regimes. Trust, what we might call the "shadow of the past," characterizes security communities or zones of complex interdependence.

[47]Keohane and Nye (1977, 24–25; 1970:ix–xxix; 1987, 737–740) .

[48]For discussions of the parallels between interstate reciprocity and individual friendship see Hirsch (1976) and Krasner (1983, 3).

[49]The Rush-Bagot Convention of 1817 between the United States and Great Britain did, however, largely demilitarize the Great Lakes and was an important step in establishing peaceful conflict resolution norms in the bilateral relationship.

TABLE 6.4
Political Processes Under Conditions of Realism and Complex Interdependence

	Realism	Complex Interdependence
Goals of actors	Military security will be the dominant goal.	Goals of states will vary by issue area. Transgovernmental politics will make goals difficult to define. Transnational actors will pursue their own goals.
Instruments of state policy	Military force will be most effective, although economic and other instruments will also be used.	Power resources specific to issue areas will be most relevant. Manipulation of interdependence, international organizations, and transnational actors will be major instruments.
Agenda formation	Potential shifts in the balance of power and security threats will set the agenda in high politics and will strongly influence other agendas.	Agenda will be affected by changes in the distribution of power resources within issue areas; the status of international regimes; changes in the importance of transnational actors; linkages from other issues and politicization as a result of rising sensitivity interdependence.
Linkages of issues	Linkages will reduce differences in outcomes among issue areas and reinforce international hierarchy.	Linkages by strong states will be more difficult to make since force will be ineffective. Linkages by weak states through international organizations will erode rather than reinforce hierarchy.
Roles of international organizations	Roles are minor, limited by state power and the importance of military force.	Organizations will set agendas, induce coalition-formation, and act as arenas for political action by weak states. Ability to choose the organizational forum for an issue and to mobilize votes will be an important political resource.

Source: From *Power and Interdependence* by Robert O. Keohane and Joseph S. Nye. Copyright ©1989 by Robert O. Keohane and Joseph S. Nye. Reprinted by permission of Scott, Foresman and Company.

Is it possible that the U.S.–Russian relationship could ever take the form of complex interdependence? The period of East-West détente in the 1960s and early 1970s represented a conscious effort to move in that direction. The U.S. and the Soviet Union purposefully increased the issue density of their relationship. For instance, the grain agreement and other arrangements led to greater trade. They initiated a variety of social and cultural ties. In fact, even realists such as Henry Kissinger popularized the notion of **linkage**, and leaders sought to make deals that crossed over normal issues boundaries.[50]

Although that period of détente faded, the end of the cold war has rapidly led to a proliferation of contacts between Russia, other former Soviet republics, and the rest of the world. Those increasingly integrate the former East into the environmental and economic regimes of the West. Although many realists express serious concern about new divisions within the West (for instance, over trade issues), many globalists foresee the eventual widening of Western complex interdependence to envelope Russia and Central Europe.

Once again, rational, self-interested state behavior helps explain all levels of cooperation (bilateral reciprocity, regimes, and complex interdependence). Nonetheless, the more extensive forms of cooperation, such as trade regimes and complex interdependence, appear to take on lives of their own and begin to constrain state behavior—community emerges. The study of cooperation thus draws on and links both realist and globalist thought.[51] Seyom Brown indicates the linkage of the two traditions by redefining power in a world of complex interdependence:

> If the international power of a country is defined as the capacity to influence other countries to accede to its objectives, then in a system characterized by multiple and cross-cutting coalitions as formed around a variety of issues, the properties of power would be significantly different than in the predominantly bipolar system. In the new system, those with the most influence are likely to be those which are the most constructive participants in the widest variety of coalitions and partnerships, since such countries would have the largest supply of usable political currency—in effect, promissory notes that say: "We will support you on this issue, if you support us on that issue." (Brown 1982, 26)

Recent developments in Europe even suggest the emergence of what we might call **complex governance** in that existing region of complex interdependence. In contrast to the traditional image of states giving way to a European superstate, we may be witnessing the growth of multitiered governmental structures overlapping in complex and shifting ways. Some functions, supporting ethnic identities and communities, are devolving to local structures (see Chapter 9). Other functions, particularly in the economic arena, are moving to the European Community. The still broader Conference on Security and Cooperation in Europe increasingly contributes to governance on both security and environmental issues.

---

[50]Tollison and Willett (1979) discuss how linkages can be used to compensate actors who obtain disproportional benefits from particular issues—a kind of side payment. Thus linkages also extend the nonzero-sum character of state interaction.

[51]Keohane (1989) has adopted the label "neoliberal institutionalism," and argues that it builds on but goes beyond realism.

Various other overlapping institutions, such as the Organization for Economic Cooperation and Development and the United Nations, play important roles in still other arenas.

CONCLUSION

The last three chapters have elaborated the realist worldview. We began with a discussion of states rationally pursuing their interests via an artful use of power and the instruments of statecraft. We proceeded by considering important elements of state interaction, many of which build upon the recognition of a security dilemma. For instance, we investigated various patterns of interaction built around reciprocity. We have concluded our discussion by investigating the dynamics of interaction among large numbers of states, focusing heavily on the structuring properties of alternative systemic polarities.

In the process of investigating cooperation among large numbers of states, however, we began to see patterns of interaction that become more and more difficult to explain in terms of the self-interest of states (and impossible to explain in terms of their immediate self-interest). Although states certainly tolerate and often even encourage the development of regimes and the growth of complex interdependence, those same phenomena appear increasingly to represent a kind of global community that constrains state action. Those who extend realism in this fashion often take the label **neoliberal institutionalists** and stand somewhat uncomfortably between traditional realists and globalists.

In short, in the process of elaborating realism, we have also begun the process of criticizing it; realists have never dealt adequately with international cooperation. We also saw how fuzzy the concepts of state interest and power can be (and how weak they can be as guides to action). The next three chapters continue to point out difficulties with a simple realist worldview. Chapter 8 goes beyond criticism and puts a bit of flesh on the skeleton of a competing globalist perspective.

Chapter 7

INSIDE
THE STATE

States are dominant actors in world politics and interact in an interstate environment of anarchy. They seek to preserve and extend their power and to limit that of other states. Conflict is inevitable in this system, but balances of power limit it and hegemony may even create zones and periods of considerable cooperation. This realist worldview explains a great deal about world politics and constitutes a powerful initial basis for understanding. That it is parsimonious (simple) in its portrayal adds to its appeal.

In its pure form it is too simple, however, and even realists recognize the need to relax some of its elements. Specifically, we need to relax, and in some cases to overturn completely, four elements of the simple realist worldview. The previous chapter identified the first: immediate (sometimes even extended) self-interest fails to explain clearly significant portions of the great many cooperative interstate interactions. Second, the characterization of states as rational, unitary actors is a frequently useful fiction but stands in the way of a fuller understanding of state behavior. This chapter considers how forces inside states interact in the making of decisions and create policy that is not always rational. Third, power and security are not the only ends of international policy. Ideas or ideals, frequently centered on a definition of the appropriate scope of community and its social organization and governance, motivate the behavior of human beings including those who hold the reins of state power. Chapter 8 sketches some of those ideals and their influence on world politics. Fourth, states are not the only actors in world politics. Chapter 9 documents the growing number and strength of nonstate actors.

Many of the individual challenges to realism in these chapters are friendly amendments and extensions that realists readily accept. For example, Thucydides noted that what happened within Greek city-states influenced their external behavior. Both Machiavelli and Morgenthau, although emphasizing the primacy of power motivations, also recognized the importance of ideals concerning justice and morality. Yet when we develop the full range of amendments and extensions, they begin to transform the simple realist worldview fundamentally; idealism begins to emerge from this analysis as a broad challenge to realism.

LEVELS OF ANALYSIS

Looking at world politics from the viewpoint of individual states, and then from the perspective of the state system as a whole, helped us elaborate the realist worldview in the last three chapters. The individual state and the state system are two alternative **levels of analysis** for world politics. To better understand state behavior, however, it is useful to identify at least three additional levels of analysis that collectively constitute an intrastate perspective: the society, individuals, and the government (which generally mediates between society and individuals, on the one hand, and the external environment, on the other).[1]

Do societies differ in the extent and nature of their involvement in world affairs? How stable are such characteristics over time and what might cause them to change? What is the constellation of societal forces that helps give rise to the external orientation of a particular state?

How important are the beliefs of specific leaders? How might personalities affect foreign policy orientation? How accurate is the perception by leaders of the external environment and how can they improve it?

How do governmental structures translate pressures from society and the orientation of individual leaders into foreign policy decisions? Do democracies differ from other governments in the nature of their interstate relations?

Moving inside the state draws these questions to our attention. When we finish considering them, we will be able to return to the central issue of this chapter: the degree to which states are unitary, rational actors (and the importance of any deviations from that simplifying assumption).

Before considering each of the intrastate levels of analysis in detail, an example can convey the utility of bringing all to bear on global politics. The American occupation force drafted the post–World War II Japanese constitution of May 1947. Sometimes called the Peace Constitution, it set the stage for ongoing debates concerning defense spending and the appropriate use of Japanese military power. Article IX of that constitution states:[2]

> Aspiring sincerely to an international peace based on justice and order, the Japanese people forever renounce war as a sovereign right of the nation and the threat or use of force as a means of settling disputes.
>
> In order to accomplish the aim of the preceding paragraph, land, sea, and air forces, as well as other war potential, will never be maintained. The right of belligerency of the state will not be recognized.

[1]Singer (1961) emphasized the importance of distinguishing levels of analysis. Waltz (1959) presented a classic analysis with a focus on three levels (and, as realists are wont to do, emphasized the state system, as opposed to intrastate factors). Rosenau (1980) differentiated intrastate levels in a manner similar to the categorization used here. See also Russett and Starr (1989) for an extensive explication.

[2]Niksch (1983, 59). Smith (1987) and Frost (1987) provide the basis for this discussion of Japanese defense spending.

Interpretation of this article has changed with time. In 1950, General MacArthur, head of the occupation forces, authorized the creation of a 75,000-person Japanese National Police Reserve (McWilliams and Piotrowski 1988, 67). In 1954, the Japanese government decided that Article IX did not preclude a "minimal self-defense" and it created the Self-Defense Forces (SDF). In 1976, Japan made the decisions to increase military capabilities to allow defense against small-scale invasions, and to limit defense spending to 1 percent of GNP (that limit is *not* part of the constitution itself). In January 1987, Japan *slightly* exceeded the 1 percent limit. What determines the level of defense spending in Japan?

STATE SYSTEM

We must seek much of the answer to that question outside of the country. The United States defeated Japan in World War II and, to assure itself that Japanese militarism would not be a threat again, insisted that the constitution demilitarize Japan. After several years of direct military occupation and rule, the United States convened a multilateral peace treaty conference in San Francisco during September 1951 and succeeded in obtaining a treaty ending the war. Forty-nine states signed (the U.S.S.R., Poland, and Czechoslovakia abstained).[3]

The same day that the United States and Japan signed the peace treaty (which provided ninety days for removal of U.S. occupation forces), they also signed an agreement permitting U.S. troops to remain in assistance of Japanese defense (De Conde 1978, 333–334). Japan thereby moved under the umbrella of the defense system that the United States constructed in Asia and became a U.S. ally in the cold war. In November 1952, Vice President Nixon visited Japan and declared that the United States had made "an honest mistake" in insisting on disarmament. In March 1954, the two countries signed a mutual defense agreement that required Japan to increase spending.

Pressure from the United States for increased Japanese contribution to its own self-defense, dating especially from the Korean War, continued. The increasing strength of Soviet forces in the area, including their large naval presence at the former U.S. facility in Cam Ranh Bay (Vietnam), also provided some external incentive for greater defense efforts.

Other systemic forces have restrained Japanese spending, however. The most important may be the concerns of neighboring Asian countries such as China and Korea. They remember the Greater East Asia Economic Co-prosperity Sphere that Japan established before World War II, ostensibly to free the region from Western imperialism but used to justify brutal imperial rule by the Japanese. To increase trade with China and other neighbors after the war, Japan has felt it important to avoid raising any anxiety. In addition, the point at which American fears of

---

[3]Japan and Russia, although ending the technical state of war between them in 1956, have still not resolved claims over four Kurile Islands that the 1951 treaty ceded to the U.S.S.R. and upon which Russia still maintains troops. A U.S. Senate reservation to the 1951 treaty does not recognize Soviet sovereignty on the islands, in spite of a U.S.-Soviet agreement at Yalta in 1944 that the Soviets would obtain them after the war (De Conde 1978, 334). Japanese-Soviet discussions in 1989 failed to resolve the issue.

renewed militarism would replace American pressure for Japanese self-defense increase is not clear.

These conflicting systemic pressures have contributed to the slow pace of change in Japanese spending levels. They also explain other aspects of Japanese defense behavior. For instance, in 1990 Japan increased its contribution from 40 percent to 50 percent of the total $7.4 billion cost of supporting 62,000 American military personnel stationed at 118 installations in Japan.[4] This and various in-kind contributions placate the Americans and diminish their perception of Japan as a free rider on defense, while not explicitly increasing Japanese defense spending and therefore threatening its neighbors.

THE STATE

Japan is a geographically small, resource-poor island state. As it industrialized and its population increased, the need for raw materials and food imports rose; so, too, did its need for markets. This information is critical to understanding its prewar imperialism. Like European states before it, Japan saw the direct conquest and governance of external territories as a way of satisfying those needs. For instance, it made the island of Formosa (now Taiwan) into a food-supplying colony.[5] The Japanese need for oil, coal, and other raw materials helped lead it into additional imperialist adventures including the invasion of China in 1931 and the creation of the puppet state of Manchukuo (Manchuria).

Since World War II, the development of an export capacity, sufficiently strong to guarantee the ability to buy food and raw materials, has satisfied these same needs. The alliance with the United States has simultaneously provided Japan access to raw materials, markets for industrial exports, and some guarantee of its freedom to trade around the world. A tension exists, however, between the Japanese drive for export earnings and its alliance with the United States, which posts large trade imbalances with Japan. Japan continues to seek the strength of the alliance with as little damage to its trading position as possible. Part of its effort to maintain the alliance involves its increased contributions to American military forces. Other elements of its response to the tension are economic. In the 1980s Japan began moving significant amounts of its investment abroad (to the United States and throughout Asia)—offshore production contributes to continued wealth building but does not exacerbate the U.S. trade deficit with Japan.

SOCIETY

The Japanese society remembers the militarism that led it into World War II, the devastation of that war (including the two atomic bombs dropped on it), and the humiliation of defeat. Although periodic hints of nationalist and militarist sentiment remind the entire world how resilient former beliefs are, the bulk of the

---

[4]*The Christian Science Monitor*, November 20, 1990, 4.

[5]Although imperialism is seldom benign, and that of Japan was not, Japan redistributed land and introduced agricultural technology on Formosa that laid one of the foundations for economic prosperity in Taiwan today.

Japanese population now displays a deep pacifism. In a poll of May 1986, only 12 percent of the Japanese citizenry thought the country should increase military spending. In a 1987 poll, 55.7 percent believed that government should give domestic economic management more emphasis, but only 11.3 percent said the same about national security (Inoguchi 1989, 17–18). Even recruitment for the Self Defense Forces has sometimes been difficult.

The long-ruling Liberal Democratic party (LDP) has supported the SDF and attempts to bolster them.[6] The Japan Socialist party, the largest of the opposition parties in the late 1980s and early 1990s, has steadfastly resisted those efforts. It is probable that many Japanese link their economic success to a limitation of military spending. Americans certainly believe in such a linkage and frequently blame their own poorer economic performance on the necessity of carrying the defense burden for recalcitrant allies.

In the early 1990s, a new and quite bitter debate arose concerning the use of Japanese forces in UN-sponsored peace-keeping missions abroad. Although Japan provided generous financial support for the UN-sanctioned war against Iraq, its parliament stymied LDP efforts to send a small noncombatant "UN Peace Cooperation Corps." The LDP failed again in 1991 to pass legislation permitting units of up to 2,000 lightly armed troops to join UN missions such as that in Cambodia. Even neighbors such as South Korea and Indonesia expressed readiness, however, to accept such deployment. Moreover, opposition in public opinion polls to sending noncombatant troops abroad dropped from 78 percent in mid-1990 to 35 percent in mid-1992. Although the Japan Socialist party led an intense campaign against the measure again in 1992, the centrist Democratic Socialists and the Buddhist-minded Komeito (Clean Government) party helped the LDP pass legislation enabling such troops that year.

It is an important digression to note that Germans have similarly debated reinterpretations of their constitutional restrictions on the use of German forces abroad; they have also gradually expanded their willingness to do so. Like Japan, Germany kept its forces out of the Gulf War, arguing that its constitution forbade it. Thereafter, under the leadership of the Christian Democratic party, it sent minesweepers to the Gulf, army medics to Cambodia, and German marines to the Adriatic as part of UN efforts to monitor an embargo against Serbia. The opposition Social Democratic party strongly protested.

INDIVIDUAL

Prime Minister Nakasone (1982–1987) was right-of-center in the Liberal Democratic party and a nationalist. He had once served as defense minister and sought to propagate an image of Japan as an "unsinkable aircraft carrier." As prime minister, he actively advocated stronger security. In particular he emphasized the importance of protecting sea lanes, appealing to societal understanding of Japanese dependence on trade. His support was instrumental in the Diet's decision to

---

[6]The LDP remains a coalition of personalized factions.

exceed the 1 percent limit on defense spending for the first time (although only to 1.004 percent in 1987) and to establish the precedent for higher spending. Similarly, in 1992 Prime Minister Miyazawa put his prestige at risk in an all-out effort to pass the bill that allows Japanese troops to serve in UN missions.

It appears that Nakasone and Miyazawa, in their own evaluation of the relationship with the United States and of the strategic situation facing Japan, decided that they must lead in arguing for spending increases. In their role as primary representatives of the state, they probably weighed the external environment more heavily than did others in government. It is common that chief executives of countries visualize themselves as representing the interests of the state, and parliamentarians to a greater degree represent specific elements within society.

GOVERNMENT

The government and its decision-making process is the focal point of the various pressures from within and outside of the state. At least three factors peculiar to Japanese government have been important in decision making on defense spending. First, the existence of the Peace Constitution is a powerful factor reinforcing the societal desire to restrict spending, despite external pressure from the United States. Second, Japanese decision making traditionally lacks much of the pluralistic conflict found in Western European and North American democracies. Instead, an emphasis on consensus prevails. "To use a mischievous metaphor, the characteristic American response to a world crisis is to jump up on the table and make a speech, while the characteristic Japanese response is to crawl under the table and quietly build a consensus" (Frost 1987, 82). This contributes to a certain inertia in decision making and to a special reluctance to override the social majority opposed to higher spending. The issue of sending troops abroad evoked so much emotion in 1991 that a very uncharacteristic brawl broke out on the floor of the Diet (parliament), causing the leadership to retract the proposal. Third, among the competing groups within the government bureaucracy, the defense establishment has little clout. In their call on resources, the ministries related to economic development, such as the famous Ministry of International Trade and Industry (MITI), carry much more weight. This is, of course, a "chicken-and-egg" situation. In countries where the military is strong, they invariably also have lobbying strength.

In summary, a levels-of-analysis approach facilitates our understanding of Japanese defense spending policy and can similarly help us interpret other foreign policies. We turn now to a more detailed discussion of intrastate forces: the society, individuals, and governments.

SOCIETY AS A WHOLE

There is a long tradition in world politics of characterizing societies as a whole so as to explain aspects of state behavior. In reality, however, modern society is a dynamic aggregation of disparate elements. Thus we consider the society as a whole only in passing.

Societies vary in their level of engagement with, and character of approach to, the outside world. With respect to the level of engagement, states are generally **isolationist** or **internationalist**. With respect to the character of their approach, they may be militaristic or pacifistic. The sum of such orientations toward the external environment is the **national character**. Some observers define that character in more personalistic terms. For instance, Morgenthau made these generalizations:

> The "elementary force and persistence" of the Russians, the individual initiative and inventiveness of the Americans, the undogmatic common sense of the British, the discipline and thoroughness of the Germans are some of the qualities which will manifest themselves, for better or for worse, in all the individual and collective activities in which the members of a nation may engage. Thus the national character has given Germany and Russia an initial advantage in the struggle for power, since they could transform in peacetime a greater portion of their national resources into instruments of war. On the other hand, the reluctance of the American and British peoples to consider such a transformation, especially on a large scale and with respect to manpower, except in an obvious national emergency, has imposed a severe handicap upon American and British foreign policy. (Morgenthau 1973, 133)

An old joke says that you can differentiate the major powers of Europe on the basis of the relationship between what is permitted and what is forbidden. In Germany, what is not permitted is forbidden. In Britain, what is not forbidden is permitted. In France, what is forbidden is permitted. Finally, in Russia, what is permitted is forbidden. That we all recognize some kernel of truth and insight in such characterizations suggests that the concept of national character may have some importance. Many serious social scientists have looked for keys to the behavior of societies in their character. Weber identified the roots of European industrialization in the Protestant ethic of hard work, frugality, and achievement in this life. Perhaps the rapid economic growth of many Asian countries similarly has roots in a Confucian heritage that does not seek salvation in an afterlife but emphasizes societal contributions on earth (Palmer 1989, 332).

We should, however, be wary about sweeping societal characterizations on two grounds. First, there is a fine line between identification of societal attributes and derogation. Is a society disciplined or militaristic? Are a people pragmatic or unprincipled? Is an orientation peaceful or cowardly? Is an action one of self-defense or aggressiveness? The values and goals of the observer frequently color characterizations and make labels political tools rather than serious assessments. Second, national characters, if they are meaningful, should be slow to change. Our perception of countries seems to shift rather dramatically, however. Many believed before and during World War II that both Germany and Japan embodied expansionist militarism. Yet the peace movement in contemporary Germany ranks among the strongest in the world. Japan now appears almost isolationist (except commercially).

What about the national character of the United States? Many historians describe it as isolationist. They point, for instance, to its delayed entry into World Wars I and II, and to its post–World War I refusal to take up a leading world role (or even to join the League of Nations). Few characterize U.S. behavior since World War II as isolationist, however. It is also possible to argue that the United States was as expansionist in the nineteenth century as in the twentieth (Williams 1962). Not only did it march steadily across a continent, but when it reached the Pacific, it began to look offshore. The United States stripped Cuba and the Philippines from Spain after the 1898 Spanish-American war. Has there been a change in U.S. national character? Or those of Germany and Japan?

The Russians consider themselves a peaceful people. Many outside observers agree. Russia long exhibited a consistently expansionist character, however, gradually pushing its empire to the Pacific and into Europe under the czars, and increasing the area it dominated still further under Communist leadership. What is the Russian national character?

How about China? Long ago it built a defensive wall in the north against barbarians (rather than incorporating them into the empire), and in the fifteenth century it withdrew its great fleets (up to 317 ships) from explorations that had taken them as far as Arabia and East Africa (Boorstin 1983, 190). One explanation is that China viewed itself as the center of the world and believed that others had nothing it needed—it is fundamentally isolationist. Yet there have been periods of Chinese expansion (peoples in Tibet and Vietnam will testify to them), and they may have ended largely because of internal weakness and strife rather than by choice.[7]

In short, national character is a thin reed on which to build a study of world politics. Although it is quite probable that at any given time societies do have distinctive aggregate orientations, they may be remarkably flexible and may represent specific adaptations to a changing world. Rather than seeking further to characterize societies as a whole, let us look to the elements within them.

SOCIETAL COMPONENTS

The public, especially in modern societies, is not one but many. How can we characterize diverse public opinion on international issues? Does it have any affect on policy making? Should it have an impact? How do interest groups and parties articulate and aggregate the various opinions of individuals on foreign policy matters? Are there social groups that are dominant in the making of foreign policy? These questions frame this section. Although our focus will be largely on the United States, the same questions and generally similar answers pertain to other economically developed democracies.

PUBLIC OPINION

Three characteristics of public opinion normally catch the attention of analysts. The first is the low level of knowledge that informs public opinion;

---

[7]Traditional China nonetheless represents one of the strongest arguments that national characters are distinctive and important. Even when it sent out massive fleets, display of pride and of satisfaction with its accomplishments may have motivated China more than desire for commerce or control (Boorstin 1983: 196–193). It approached the outside world in a very different way than did the Portuguese or Spanish, and then suddenly withdrew after 1433.

the second is the volatility of opinion on many specific issues; and the third is the long-term stability of fundamental attitudinal structures. These characteristics provide a context for assessing the degree to which public opinion does and should influence policy.

LOW KNOWLEDGE LEVEL AND OPINION VOLATILITY

Polls regularly document how ignorant U.S. citizens are about science or mathematics. In similar studies, they exhibit a remarkably poor understanding of geography, history, and contemporary foreign affairs. In one poll, only 44 percent realized that the United States and the Soviet Union were allies in World War II. In 1964, only 58 percent of U.S. citizens knew that the United States was a member of the North Atlantic Treaty Organization (NATO). A surprising 38 percent believed that the Soviet Union was also a member (Ray 1987, 86).

Knowledge has improved since 1964, has it not? In 1988, three-fourths could not name a single NATO country, and 16 percent believed the Soviet Union was a member. In 1984, in the middle of extensive public debate, only 33 percent understood that the United States was giving support to the "contras" against the government in Nicaragua. In 1986, only 70 percent of Americans had heard of SALT II. A 1987 poll discovered that 25 percent of students in Dallas could not identify Mexico as the country on the southern border of the U.S. In 1989, fewer than half of American adults could locate Great Britain, France, South Africa, *or* Japan on a world map.[8] One in seven could not locate the United States.

Public opinion is also volatile.[9] In 1973, only 11 percent of Americans believed that the country was spending too little on defense. That percentage climbed to 27 percent in 1978 and soared to 56 percent in 1980. It plummeted again to 14 percent in 1985 (Schneider 1987, 43). Although changes in actual spending (decreases in the 1970s, and increases in the 1980s, as portions of the GNP) influenced the public, the spending changes were not that great. The rate from 1970 through the end of the 1980s ranged between 5.0 and 7.0 percent of GNP. Opinion volatility is not always bad. It can indicate sensitivity of the public to a rapidly changing world. It can also mean overreaction to those changes, however, and perhaps even reaction that is out of phase with the outside world (Lippmann 1955). For instance, the world faced by the United States between 1973 and 1985 had not changed that dramatically.

ATTITUDINAL STRUCTURE STABILITY

Although opinions on specific issues often change rapidly, studies repeatedly discover a large amount of underlying stability in the structure of basic attitudes and orientations (Holsti 1992). Most fundamentally (see Figure 7.1), the American public has been consistently internationalist since World War II. The trauma of the

---

[8]*The Christian Science Monitor* March 20, 1989, 13, and November 15, 1989, 18.

[9]Russett (1989) argues that public opinion on major cold-war issues stabilized in the 1950s, and that it is not volatile. Page and Shapiro (1992) recognize some instability but see the public as fundamentally rational.

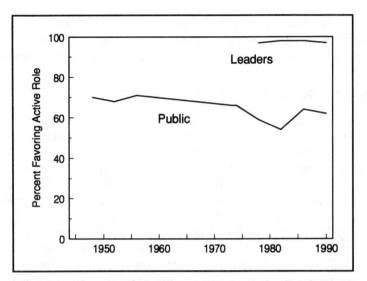

FIGURE 7.1   Percent of U.S. Citizenry Favoring Active Role in World
Source: John E. Rielly, ed., *American Public Opinion and U.S. Foreign Policy* (Chicago: The Chicago Council on Foreign Relations, 1991), 12.

Vietnam War led, however, to some retreat from that stance through the 1970s. More important, it gave rise to a differentiation among internationalists. Based on a large-scale study of foreign policy elites, Holsti and Rosenau concluded that

> The foreign policy consensus of the 1945–1965 period was shattered by the Vietnam War. The post-Vietnam period has been marked not merely by disagreements about specific applications of basic principles or details of implementation, but also by a lack of consensus on fundamental beliefs about the international system, the proper American role in it, and appropriate strategies for pursuing the national interest. (Holsti and Rosenau 1988, 31)

Wittkopf (1990, 9) suggests that Americans differentiate between cooperative internationalism (such as foreign aid or trade) and militant internationalism (such as military aid or intervention).[10] The intersection of these two dimensions of internationalism give rise to four general attitudinal orientations: **internationalists** (supportive of both kinds), **isolationists** (supportive of neither), **accomodationists** (cooperative internationalists), and **hardliners** (militant internationalists). His analysis of public opinion suggests that roughly one-fourth of all Americans fell into each category between 1974 and 1986.

Interestingly, each of the four categories draws differentially on segments of the American public. Blacks and women, for example, fall less often into the militant internationalist category. A Gallup poll in January, 1991, found that 67

[10]See also Hughes (1978, 30), who distinguished between military and nonmilitary internationalists. Holsti and Rosenau (1988) identified cold-war internationalists, post–cold-war internationalists, and semi-isolationists.

percent of men, but only 45 percent of women, supported the war to expel Iraq from Kuwait (Russett and Starr 1992, 221).

The cold war justified the militant internationalist stance. In Ronald Reagan's language, "Let's not delude ourselves. The Soviet Union underlies all of the unrest that is going on. If they weren't engaged in this game of dominoes, there wouldn't be any hot spots in the world."[11] Many have begun to wonder if the end of the cold war might give rise to another fundamental transformation in American attitudinal structures and a renewed isolationism. The trauma of Vietnam earlier gave rise to George McGovern's call in his 1972 presidential campaign to "Come Home America." Weariness with military burden and frustration with trade deficits generated similar sentiments in the early 1990s. Only time will tell what new alignment of attitudes might emerge.

For several decades American elites have been more committed than the broader public to both internationalisms (Figure 7.1 supports that). Table 7.1 presents data, however, that indicate a fairly complex pattern of leader-public attitudinal differences in the early 1990s. While leaders are more supportive of arms control and protecting the global environment, the public is more supportive of protecting American jobs (which may be an antitrade orientation), containing communism, and protecting weaker states. Apparently leaders accepted the end of the cold war more quickly than did the public and have shifted away from militant internationalism generally. It may be that in the 1990s leaders will be less supportive of militant internationalism than is the public, but remain more supportive of cooperative internationalism.[12]

TABLE 7.1
Importance of Foreign Policy Goals
Differences between Leaders and the Public (1990–1991)

Potential Goal	Leaders	Public
Preventing the spread of nuclear weapons	94%	59%
Improving the global environment	72	58
Securing adequate supplies of energy	60	61
Promoting and defending human rights in other countries	45	58
Strengthening the United Nations	39	44
Protecting the jobs of American workers	39	65
Protecting weaker nations against foreign aggression	28	57
Helping bring a democratic form of government to other nations	28	26
Containing communism	10	56

Source: John E. Rielly, *American Public Opinion and U.S. Foreign Policy 1991* (Chicago: Chicago Council on Foreign Relations 1991), 15.

---

[11]House (1980, 1), quoted in Holsti and Rosenau (1988, 31–32).

[12]The greater emphasis of the public on containing communism was already obvious in the late 1980s. (Schneider 1987, 53).

Putting together these pieces of information concerning knowledge level, opinion volatility, and stability of attitudinal structure, we can draw a general portrait of the American public (Hughes 1978, 23–24). A group called the **mass public**, constituting roughly 30 percent of the population, has limited knowledge of, or interest in, world affairs. A second segment, called the **attentive public**, and making up about 45 percent of the citizenry, has some knowledge and interest. Their attitudes have a general internal consistency and stability, but their specific opinions can change fairly quickly. The remaining 25 percent are **opinion leaders**, with considerable knowledge and interest, an ability to rapidly adapt and learn, and a willingness to communicate their understandings and beliefs to others. These individuals also, on the average, have been more internationalist in orientation.[13]

REPRESENTATION

Like the water glass that is either half-full or half-empty, depending on the perspective of the observer, the ability of the public that we have just described to guide the direction of foreign policy is either satisfactory or unsatisfactory. Yet it is difficult not to wonder, given that so much of the public is relatively uninformed about international affairs, how the public could realistically direct foreign policy. How much influence does it actually exercise? Three models of government action in response to public opinion have currency. The first, the **instructed-delegate model**, is the one in civics books, and it portrays representatives of the public as instruments for translating the desires of their constituents into policy. The second, the **responsible-party model**, recognizes divisions in the public that correspond to party preferences, and argues that policy does or should reflect the wishes of the majority party. The third, the **elitist model**, assumes that a governmental elite is better able to determine policy than the unwashed masses. In elitist phrases the eighteenth-century British Parliamentarian Edmund Burke informed his constituents that:

> I did not obey your instructions. No. I conformed to the instructions of truth and nature, and maintained your interest, against your opinions, with a constancy that became me. A representative worthy of you ought to be a person of stability. I am not to look to the flash of the day. I know you chose me, in my place, along with others, to be a pillar of the state, and not a weathercock on the top of the edifice, exalted for my levity and versatility and of no use but to indicate the shiftings of every fashionable gale. (Pearson 1965, 27)

Which of these models of representation corresponds to reality? It depends on the country, the issue, the amount of time involved, the intensity of public

---

[13]Eichenberg (1989, 224) found limited gaps between elite and public opinion in other countries. In France, Great Britain, and the Netherlands, however, elites were considerably more likely to favor increases in defense spending in 1983; elites in those countries and German elites were less likely to favor foregoing the option of using nuclear weapons first. In short, elites appeared more likely to be hardliners.

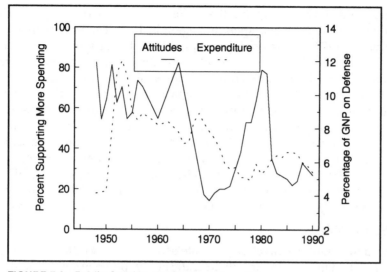

FIGURE 7.2   Public Opinion and Defense Spending
Sources: Barry B. Hughes, *The Domestic Context of American Foreign Policy* (San
Francisco: W.H. Freeman, 1978), 112; Bruce Russett and Harvey Starr, *World
Politics: The Menu for Choice,* 3rd ed. (New York: W.H. Freeman, 1989), 232;
Gallup Report, assorted issues; Arms Control and Disarmament Agency, *World
Military Expenditures and Arms Transfers* (Washington, D.C.: ACDA, assorted
editions); International Institute for Strategic Studies, *The Military Balance 1991–
92* (London: IISS, 1991), 212; John E. Rielly, *American Public Opinion and U.S.
Foreign Policy* (Chicago: The Chicago Council on Foreign Relations), 32.

sentiment (or that of elements within the public), and a variety of other factors.[14]
The public is most likely to influence policy on an international issue when there
is much time to make a decision, and when both security and economic concerns
are significant (Hughes 1978). Such issues include the size of the defense budget
and the lifting of the embargo on grain exports to the Soviet Union (imposed after
their invasion of Afghanistan in 1980).

Figure 7.2 traces public opinion in the United States on defense spending (the
percentage who favor increased spending of those with an opinion) and the size
of the defense budget as a portion of GNP. It is obvious that the relationship is not
terribly close and that the public does not control defense spending. Yet there is a
relationship. In the first two decades of the cold war (until the mid-1960s), a
majority of the public with an opinion favored *higher* defense spending. Defense
spending remained at or above 8 percent of GNP. By the peak of the Vietnam War
in the late 1960s, the public had turned against defense spending. That sharp
attitudinal shift preceded both de-escalation of the war and a subsequent decline

[14]Risse-Kappen (1991) finds differences in the influence of the public even across democracies;
in general, the domestic structures of the United States give the public greater influence than in France,
Germany, or Great Britain. Although many studies have suggested that the public has less influence on
international than on domestic issues, Benjamin and Shapiro (1983) find little difference in the United
States over the period from 1935 to 1979.

in military spending throughout the 1970s. A majority of the public became supportive of greater defense spending again in 1977. The Soviets then invaded Afghanistan in 1979, and defense spending rose in the early 1980s. Public opinion shifted against spending in the mid-1980s, and the government began to respond by the late 1980s and early 1990s (not yet fully visible in Figure 7.2).

Citizens are least likely to have an impact when decision time is short, when economic issues are relatively unimportant, and when security considerations are paramount. An example was the decision by the Bush administration to invade Panama and overthrow General Noriega. As the U.S. commitment in Panama stretched on, however, time for decision (reconsideration) increased, and the economic cost became an issue so that public support became essential. Still it is not the public as a whole that influences policies but segments of it. We must consider the mechanisms by which components of the public enter the policy process.

INTEREST GROUPS

Opinions about the direction of a state's foreign policy differ across segments of the population in all states. In a democratic polity someone must articulate these competing opinions and other actors need to aggregate them into a few coherent options for decision. Interest groups are especially active in **opinion articulation**, and political parties make a primary contribution in **opinion aggregation**.

As implied by the label, self-interest generally directs interest groups. In all democratic countries, economic interest groups are among the most influential. Their chief concerns are the ease with which they can export, and the protection that they can obtain from external competition.

As a general rule, the orientation of an economic interest group toward trade depends on whether the factor of production it represents is relatively abundant or scarce.[15] **Factors of production** are those resources used in the process of production, most notably land, labor, and capital. When a factor such as land is abundant, it will be inexpensive and activity based upon it will tend to produce goods competitive on the world market. In the United States land has always been abundant relative to other factors, whereas in Great Britain land has been relatively scarce and since early in the industrial revolution capital has been relatively abundant. In the 1800s, much British capital and many British goods flowed to the United States, and much U.S. agricultural produce went to Britain. In that century, British capitalists supported free trade, but British farmers could not compete with American ones and desired protection against free trade. In contrast, American labor and capital generally allied against free trade and American farmers supported it.

By the end of World War II, American capital was also abundant (and efficient) and U.S. policy shifted toward free trade. Although U.S. labor remained relatively scarce (and therefore expensive), the export strength of the United States quite fully employed that labor, so that it too supported free trade. Before World War II, the United States government had adopted a protectionist stance. After

[15]Rogowski (1989) presents a very readable discussion of the Stolper-Samuelson theorem and its domestic political ramifications.

World War II, it moved quickly to dismantle barriers to trade and to encourage other countries to do the same.

As long as the United States continued to export more than it imported, as it did from 1945 to 1971, interest groups based in land, labor, and capital largely continued to support free trade. In most years since 1971, however, the United States has imported more than it exported. The abundance of U.S. capital and land continues to make them competitive around the world and to seek outlets for their produce. The relative scarcity of U.S. labor makes it highly paid by global standards and therefore less competitive. Already in 1972 the American Federation of Labor and Congress of Industrial Organizations (AFL–CIO), the leading U.S. labor union organization, backed the Burke-Hartke Foreign Trade and Investment Act, which would have established quotas on all imports on a category-by-category basis and made it less profitable for multinational corporations to invest overseas (thus transferring American jobs abroad).[16]

The general principle that interests based on abundant factors will support free trade helps explain also domestic reactions to proposals for free trade agreements like that between Canada, Mexico, and the United States. American agricultural and business interests have largely supported such agreements, while American labor has opposed them. Debates over free trade agreements make clear, however, that interest groups based on the same factor of production will not always present a common front. For instance, whereas American cereal producers stand to gain from agricultural free trade with Mexico (U.S. grain land is plentiful), fresh produce growers could lose (U.S. land for winter produce is relatively scarce).

Intrafactor divisions will lead individual farmers, firms, and laborers to seek special advantage relative to their competitors. From the viewpoint of individual firms, the ideal situation would be freedom to export to open markets around the world (in fact, subsidies and credits to encourage exports), coupled with substantial barriers against access by foreign firms to the domestic market. Those owners of capital who step back and look at the "big picture," however, realize that domestic firms are unlikely to obtain access to foreign markets unless foreign firms have similar privileges.

This sets up a tension. Within the United States, individual businesses frequently press for protective trade barriers (such as quotas that set maximum import levels). Cries of the automobile industry for protection against the Japanese onslaught of the domestic car market led in the 1970s and 1980s to a "voluntary quota" set by Japan on the total number of cars its manufacturers would ship to the United States (had the quota not been observed voluntarily, Congress would almost certainly have made it compulsory). Similarly, U.S. sugar producers have succeeded in obtaining a quota on sugar imports to the United States, and U.S. textile and shoe manufacturers have their own protection. Yet American business (as represented, for example, by magazines like *Forbes* or *Business Week*, or by

---

[16]The option of profitable overseas investment reinforces American business commitment to minimal international trade and capital barriers, even in the face of intense foreign trade competition. The fear of job loss from such investment reinforces the general protectionist sentiment of labor.

organizations like the National Association of Manufacturers) tends to support free trade.[17] The U.S. shift to free trade after World War II was assisted by a movement in decision making from a congressional aggregation of individual demands for protection to an executive-branch representation of the collective interest in reciprocal access to markets.[18]

Noneconomic interest groups also adopt foreign policy stances. In the United States, more so than in ethnically homogeneous democracies, various groups that support or oppose particular foreign governments attempt to influence foreign policy. Sometimes they appear to have great success. The Committee of One Million Against the Admission of Communist China to the United Nations (the China Lobby) enrolled ninety-seven members of the House of Representatives in 1956 and seemed capable of blocking any movement toward rapprochement with mainland China. Yet by 1969 more than one-half of the American public favored admission for the PRC to the United Nations (Mueller 1973, 15–17), and in 1971 the UN did admit it. The following year Nixon visited China and began to reestablish relations.

Today the pro-Israel lobby is the most powerful of the ethnic lobbies, drawing on 6 million American Jews. In 1984 more than seventy pro-Israel political action committees (PACs) directed about $3.6 million to assorted candidates (mostly Democrats). An indication of its strength is that the United States provided nearly $3 billion in military and economic assistance to Israel in 1990. Other than Egypt (which received aid primarily because of its participation in an American-sponsored peace treaty with Israel), no other country obtained more than one-fifth that amount (see Table 4.5). An objective, realist look at the state interest of the United States would almost certainly place it on the side of the oil-producing and generally anti-Israel Moslem countries of the Middle East. The United States has repeatedly risked offending those states and jeopardizing oil exports to itself and its allies through its support for Israel. In 1973, the Arab members of OPEC directed an oil embargo against the First World because of its support for Israel. Japan and many European countries capitulated and increased their support for the Arab states in the Mideast conflict. The United States, although suffering from inadequate supplies and high prices, remained firm in its commitment to the Jewish state. During the Gulf War of 1991 the United States took special pains to prevent Israeli involvement.

The Israeli lobby is hardly all-powerful. The Reagan administration was able to push through sales to Saudi Arabia of bomb racks and missiles for F-15s, initiated by the Carter presidency, and also to sell that country Airborne Warning

[17]The differential orientations of individual firms and of business as a whole illustrate the common conflict between individual definition of self-interest and collective evaluation of interest. Individually firms would like to free ride on the system—to take advantage of the collective good of free trade, but contribute nothing to its provision.

[18]Until the early 1930s the U.S. Congress controlled the setting of tariffs directly, and special interests deluged it with lobbying for protection. Satisfying these interests led to high tariffs, culminating in the Smoot-Hawley Tariff Act of 1930 with the highest tariffs of American history. In 1934 Congress passed the Reciprocal Trade Agreements Act delegating power to the president to negotiate tariffs as a whole, a procedure that has been renewed regularly since then (Bauer, Pool, and Dexter 1972). A free trade orientation gradually emerged within U.S. policy.

and Control System (AWACS) radar planes. Lobbyists of the oil and defense industries backed the administration. Opposition was intense, however, and the Senate vote was close. The administration also needed to compensate Israel with additional aid. Moreover, Congress blocked other proposed arms sales to Arab countries during the Reagan administration.

The **pluralist model** of decision making (Dahl 1956) portrays the competition among interest groups to translate their specific interests into policy. It represents domestic and, to a lesser degree, foreign policy as a compromise outcome of interest group pressures. It has been said that a camel is a horse designed by a committee. To the degree that foreign policy similarly represents compromise among parochial interests, rather than a clear-headed pursuit of state interest, that process weakens the rational-state assumptions of realism.

POLITICAL PARTIES

Parties often draw together or aggregate the more diffuse interests within society. For instance, the Republican party in the United States aggregates many of the business interests in the country. It is thus not surprising that the Republican party was the party of protection during the early part of this century (when the mind-set of business people still focused on protecting infant industries), whereas the Democratic party, historically tied more closely to agricultural interests, supported tariffs only as a revenue raising device (Bauer, Pool, and Dexter 1972, 26). Most Republicans in Congress continued, however, to oppose the Reciprocal Trade Agreements Act for many years after World War II, even though U.S. business had become highly competitive internationally. Congressional Democrats, although by then more closely tied to labor, remained considerably more supportive of free trade. There is good reason to believe that an inertia of ideas often retards adaptation of policy orientation to changed underlying interests (Goldstein 1988; Goldstein and Lenway 1989). In the late 1960s and early 1970s, however, congressional voting positions reversed (Hughes 1978), and the parties came to more closely represent underlying economic interests.

It is difficult to make many general statements about party positions on most foreign issues (they change often and are not sharply defined). In fact, a bipartisan consensus in American foreign policy often characterized the era extending from 1948–1968 (Schneider 1987, 45). This consensus broke down, however, with the dissolution of the broader internationalist consensus within the general public. In the 1970s the Republican party generally better represented militant or cold war internationalists, and the Democrats more often captured the support of cooperative internationalists. For instance, the Republicans became the party more likely to support military spending increases, whereas the Democrats continued to give relatively greater backing to foreign aid. That differentiation persisted through the 1980s and into the 1990s.

Party differences also characterize the foreign policy debate in other Western democracies. For instance, during the 1971 debate in Britain over its entrance into the

Common Market, Conservatives were more often pro-Market and Labour members of Parliament (MPs) were more often anti-Market (Roskin 1989, 73). Some in the Labour party urged a nuclear-free Britain, eliminating U.S. and British nuclear weapons from the country, and Conservatives supported the presence of such weapons from both countries. This issue (and others) split Labour; some MPs who supported a nuclear force temporarily left Labour to establish the Social Democratic party.

In the Federal Republic of Germany, the achievement of national power by the Social Democrats (SPD) preceded a strong enunciation of *Ostpolitik*, a foreign policy directed at improving relationships with the Soviet Union and Eastern Europe. The Christian Democrats (CDU) generally took a harder line toward the East, were less willing to negotiate, and were more reluctant to accept the division between East and West Germany. In recent years the SPD, like the British Labour party, also moved toward an antinuclear position (Joffee 1985).

Across Western democracies, the parties of the right (like the U.S. Republicans, the British Conservatives, and the members of the German CDU) have been more likely to take a hard line against Communists, to support nuclear and conventional military power, and in general to act like militant internationalists or realists. Eichenberg (1989, 180) found that in Britain, France, West Germany, and the Netherlands, the parties of the right consistently supported defense spending more than did parties of the left. The parties of the left are more often inclined toward globalism or, like the Japanese Socialists, to isolationism. Politics is fluid and often seems unpredictable, however. When President Mitterrand, the candidate of the Socialists in France, took power from a more rightist party in 1981, he shifted some of the French foreign policy toward a more hard-line stance. In contrast to his (conservative) Gaullist predecessor, he spoke strongly against the Soviet invasion of Afghanistan and the suppression of Solidarity in Poland, and he favored new NATO nuclear missiles in Germany. He also generally moved France toward the Western alliance, however, proclaiming a type of cooperative internationalism (Macridis 1985). In this instance the individual character of Mitterrand was more important than the orientation of the party.

ARE SOME MORE EQUAL THAN OTHERS?

The pluralistic competition of interest groups and parties does not preclude the possibility that the power of some interests to influence policy is considerably greater than that of others. Many social critics have identified potentially advantaged or dominant interests, giving labels to them, such as the military-industrial complex or the power elite. Although emanating most often from the left, Republican President Eisenhower also raised such a possibility in his farewell address of January 17, 1961:

> Until the last of our world conflicts, the United States had no armaments industry. American makers of plowshares could, with time and as required, make swords as well. But we can no longer risk emergency improvisation of national defense. We have been compelled to create a permanent armaments industry of vast proportions.

Added to this, three-and-a-half million men and women are directly engaged in the defense establishment. We annually spend on military security alone more than the net income of all United States corporations.

Now this conjunction of an immense military establishment and a large arms industry is new in the American experience. The total influence—economic, political, even spiritual—is felt in every city, every state house, every office of the federal government....

In the councils of government, we must guard against the acquisition of unwarranted influence, whether sought or unsought, by the military-industrial complex. The potential for the disastrous rise of misplaced power exists and will persist. (Hughes 1978, 175)

Exchange of personnel and money ties together the **military-industrial complex** or **iron triangle**, the legs of which are defense contractors, the defense bureaucracy, and Congress (Adams 1988).[19] For example, $4 million moved in the 1970s and 1980s from the political action committees (PACs) of just eight leading contractors to federal election campaigns. In the 1950s more than 1,000 retired military personnel accepted jobs with defense contractors. In the 1980s this grew to about 2,000 retirees per year. President Bush's first nominee for secretary of defense, Senator John Tower, nearly moved around the entire triangle. Tower was chairman of the Senate Armed Services Committee from 1981 to 1984, and then he was the recipient of $750,000 as a consultant to defense contractors between 1985 and 1988.[20] One of the reasons the Senate refused to confirm him was its concern with these connections between government and the defense industry.

Do such linkages between government and industry affect national security policy? It is difficult to assess. A great deal of the influence wielded by contractors seeks to assure a bigger share of the pie. Although allocation of the defense budget to contractors on the basis of favoritism (and inadequate supervision of contracts) can lessen the efficiency of defense spending, the more basic question is whether iron triangle politics alters the magnitude of defense spending—the size of the whole pie. As a percentage of the GNP, U.S. defense spending (shown earlier in Figure 7.2) has decreased significantly since Eisenhower's warning. External forces and competing domestic interests appear more important than defense lobbyists in determining the level of spending. The military-industrial complex at most marginally slowed the demobilization after Vietnam, which reduced defense spending as a share of GNP by almost one-third.[21] By some estimates, the share of U.S. GNP taken by defense spending may drop from a peak of 6.1 percent in 1988 to

[19]More radical observers of capitalist political systems argue that the military-industrial complex only manifests, with respect to defense spending, the influence of a more comprehensive power elite (Mills 1956).

[20]*Newsweek*, February 6, 1989, 16.

[21]Massive lobbying does not even assure the desired piece of the pie. Between 1975 and 1977 Rockwell International spent $1.35 million in a public lobbying program for the B-1 bomber program. It called upon 114,000 employees, employees of subcontractors, and shareholders to pressure Congress (Adams 1988, 76). President Carter scrapped the program. President Reagan's subsequent revival of it grew out of that administration's concern about a "window of vulnerability," not from industry influence.

3.5 percent in 1997, eliminating nearly half of the 1.4 million jobs in armaments industries. Would a truly powerful military-industrial complex allow such a decline?

Russia has a similar internal lobby for military spending. In fact, the larger size of its military within the total economy presumably amplifies such pressures. Sometimes called the **iron eaters**, this combination of the military and heavy industry (which supports the military) constitutes a powerful force opposing dramatic reductions in defense. The ability of Russian reformers to cut military spending in the 1990s will help us assess the strength of that interest group.

Policy in democracies reflects the opinions of the general public, at least in the long run. Naturally, some domestic groups shape policy more than others. In addition, specific leaders, especially chief executives, place their particular stamps on policy. It is to the influence of individual leaders that we now turn.

INDIVIDUALS

Students of world politics, especially historians, rely heavily on **great-person theories** to explain events:

> Sigmund Freud once remarked that if a little child had the physical strength to do so, it would smash everything in its path that aroused its displeasure. The key to an understanding of Hitler's invasion of Russia is more likely found in the realm of psychology than in political science or strategic thought. Hitler was not interested in just defeating Russia; it was not even important to him to conquer and incorporate her into the grand design of his Third Reich that was to last for a thousand years. What he really yearned to do, with all the passion of his demonic nature, was to destroy Russia altogether—to crush her government, pulverize her economy, enslave her people, and eliminate her as a political entity. (Stoessinger 1985, 27)

Explanations of the external behavior of totalitarian states and of dictatorships require attention to the personality of the leadership, especially when a leader has an abnormal personality.[22] In wartime, democracies take on some of the character of dictatorships, delegating great powers to individual leaders. Thus historians describe much of World War II in terms of the behavior of Roosevelt, Churchill, Mussolini, Stalin, and Hitler. Ralph Waldo Emerson claimed that "there is properly no history, only biography" (Kegley and Wittkopf 1991, 494).

Even during war, however, and especially in democracies during peaceful times, explanations of complex events in terms of the idiosyncrasies of individuals is often a lazy substitute for the search to find deeper, longer-term, and more generalizable explanations. Consider the common references to the "Reagan defense buildup" of the American military in the 1980s (or to the "Reagan revolution" in social policy or "Reaganomics" in economics). Although such terminology is sometimes simply shorthand to label an era, it frequently

---

[22]Ray (1987) asks us to imagine a world in which Hitler had been killed in World War I. Would World War II have occurred, and if so, how might it have been different? Similarly, Hook (1943) speculates on a world without Lenin.

suggests causality. Reagan's personality, style, and beliefs certainly helped shape an era in United States history. The important question is, however, how much different would the period have been with other leaders in the presidency?

The "Reagan defense buildup" actually began under Carter, who reversed the decline in the percentage of GNP spent on defense following the Vietnam War. U.S. public opinion, as we saw earlier (see Figure 7.2), had shifted by 1977–1978 toward favoring more defense spending. Soviet military outlays had increased steadily throughout the period of relative U.S. decline, and the U.S.S.R. had aroused Western fears by invading Afghanistan and supporting new Marxist governments in Africa. Congress and the public would have exerted tremendous pressure on *any* president for a continuation of the increase that Carter began. Reagan may have personally accelerated and prolonged the buildup, but the various levels of analysis (state system, state, society, individual, and governmental) all interacted in shaping policy.

LEADERSHIP AND VISION

Our definition of statecraft earlier required that a leader have an understanding of the world and a *vision* of desirable change. According to realists, leaders should base that vision in state interest. Might there be a "higher" morality, however, perhaps based on religious values or humanistic instincts, that should guide policy? U.S. leaders have grappled with that question and have given different answers, belying any simplistic realist interpretation of actual U.S. policy.[23] Although power politics have been important to U.S. presidents, idealisms and moral visions have guided them as well.

At the end of World War I, President Woodrow Wilson's understanding of the bankruptcy of traditional power politics resonated in those who had suffered the horrors of the war. His vision of an interstate politics based in morality and conducted within the framework of the League of Nations aroused widespread excitement. He successfully imposed that vision and his will on the postwar settlement. He failed, however, to transfer that same vision to a Senate and a public that clung to an older, more isolationist image of the United States.

In the late 1930s Franklin Roosevelt understood the anachronistic character of U.S. desires to remain separate from the world economy and from the war that was beginning in Europe. By mid-1940 the Germans had sunk more than one-half of all British destroyers, but the United States remained on the sidelines. Roosevelt circumvented congressional opposition to any action that might involve the country in the war by trading, through executive order, American destroyers for British bases; he then sold the deal to the public. His worldview combined some of the moralism and aversion to traditional power politics that characterized Wilson, with a realistic recognition of the dangers posed by Nazi Germany. Roosevelt by no means fully shared, however, the more clearly realist, power politics orientation

---

[23]Stoessinger's (1979) account of eight twentieth-century American foreign policy leaders conveys their individual understandings of the world, their visions, and their abilities to shape policy and outcomes accordingly. This discussion of leaders draws on his insights.

of British Prime Minister Winston Churchill. For instance, although Churchill moved quickly to cooperate with Stalin after the German invasion of the Soviet Union, Roosevelt hesitated. After all, communism was a moral enemy, just as was fascism.

Harry S. Truman became president on April 12, 1945 after the death of Roosevelt. As a senator earlier in the war, Truman had said that "If we see that Germany is winning we ought to help Russia and if Russia is winning we ought to help Germany and that way let them kill as many as possible...." (Stoessinger 1979, 43). That was, however, not just a statement of balance-of-power politics. He held a strong moral antipathy to both fascism and communism. Although by the final days of World War II Truman had developed some belief in his ability to work with Stalin, the failure of the Soviets to withdraw their troops, as promised, from Iran after March 2, 1946 evoked the earlier moral outrage. Truman's actions thereafter indicate a combination of pragmatism and moralistic anticommunism that is difficult to disentangle. The British proved unable to maintain their traditional role in Greece and Turkey after the war. In March 1947 Truman asserted the U.S. willingness to take over that role, by enunciating the Truman Doctrine that promised support anywhere to those threatened by communism. The Marshall Plan to rebuild Europe and the formation of NATO followed during the next two remarkable years.

In the Eisenhower administration of 1953–1960, foreign policy leadership devolved to his Secretary of State, John Foster Dulles. Like Wilson, Dulles was the son of a Presbyterian minister; his moralistic anticommunism was untempered by the pragmatism of Truman. Dulles told the West German ambassador that "Bolshevism was a product of the Devil, but God would wear out the Bolsheviks in the long run" (Stoessinger 1979, 98). He repeatedly expressed a desire not simply to stop the advance of communism, but to "liberate" Eastern Europe and to "roll back" the sphere of Soviet control. He translated that vision into a worldwide chain of alliances around the Soviet Union.

The U.S.–Soviet, democracy-communism confrontation continued to dominate foreign policy during the Kennedy and Johnson administrations of the 1960s. The conflict's high point under Kennedy was the Cuban Missile Crisis in October 1962. During the Johnson presidency it was the Vietnam War. In those years the balance between moralistic and power-politics visions of the world shifted somewhat toward power politics. U.S. policy again emphasized containment of Soviet influence and a willingness to live in uneasy coexistence with communism.

The Nixon-Kissinger foreign policy team took over in 1968 and brought to the White House a new, and self-conscious, worldview and vision. Secretary of State Kissinger held a distinctly realist orientation, placing greater emphasis on power politics and less on the moralistic confrontation of the superpowers:

> Henry Kissinger thus believed that, in creating a design for world order, realism was preferable to idealism. The great American moralists, in his judgment, were failures. In the end, Woodrow Wilson proved ineffectual and John Foster Dulles turned foreign policy into a crusade that led straight into the Indochina quagmire. (Stoessinger 1979, 208)

Kissinger believed that nuclear weapons gave rise to a community of interest between the two countries, based in their need to avoid mutual destruction (Stoessinger 1976, 81). Nixon and Kissinger adopted a policy called détente, seeking to tie the two states to each other by a variety of bonds, without losing sight of the fundamental rivalry between them. Roughly the same understanding increasingly shaped Soviet perceptions and made some of their leadership willing partners in a change of relationship.

An important aspect of Kissinger's world vision centered on changing polarity:

> Military bipolarity is a source of rigidity in foreign policy....A bipolar world loses perspective for nuance; a gain for one side appears as an absolute loss for the other. Every issue seems to involve a question of survival....But the age of the superpowers is now drawing to an end. Military bipolarity has not only failed to prevent, it has actually encouraged political multipolarity. (Kissinger 1974, 56)[24]

Kissinger supported the emergence of multipolarity. On July 9, 1971, he dropped from sight in Pakistan, under the pretense of having the flu, and made a secret visit to China. He prepared the groundwork for a fundamentally changed relationship with the People's Republic of China and for a visit in May 1972 by President Nixon.

The election of Jimmy Carter in 1976 brought another highly religious man to the White House. A "born-again" Baptist, former Sunday school teacher and missionary, Carter put an ideal at the center of his foreign policy vision. Specifically, he supported human rights of individuals everywhere. That support complicated the American-Soviet relationship, placed the United States in opposition to Israel on the treatment of Palestinians and on the disposal of the occupied territories, and directed American foreign policy censure at the violation of human rights by right-wing dictatorships in the Third World, even those traditionally friendly to the United States. Some compromises with the requirements of power politics were inevitable. For instance, the administration never targeted China, a highly regimented and repressive society, for human rights action, because of its importance in the American-Soviet relationship.

The victory of Ronald Reagan in the 1980 presidential campaign brought a cold warrior to the White House. His understanding of the world returned the bipolar relationship to center stage but portrayed the United States as the weaker player. He thus sought to restore American power, especially military power, and his policies focused on defense spending increases and more active opposition to Soviet influence everywhere in the globe. This emphasis on power relationships interacted with a moralistic anticommunism. The combination led him to characterize the Soviet Union as an "evil empire" and increased his willingness to use military power. A heavy reliance on covert support to anti-Soviet forces in

---

[24]He repeated almost exactly those same words at the conclusion of his official participation in foreign affairs (1979, 67).

conflicts around the globe (especially in Afghanistan, Angola, and Nicaragua), and a periodic but highly limited use of direct American force (in Lebanon, Libya, and Grenada) were trademarks of the administration. Yet by the time he left office, the collapse of the Soviet empire was well underway and Reagan no longer saw the Soviet Union as such a dynamic, diabolic power.

The worldview of the Bush administration shifted toward a broader and more multipolar view of the world (although that view, which Bush referred to as "the vision thing," was not always clearly articulated). It devoted more attention to arms control, to trade relationships with Europe and Japan, to the Third World debt crisis, and to limiting nuclear proliferation in places such as Iraq and North Korea. The collapse of the Soviet Union, the enemy of the West for more than forty years, left a vacuum in foreign policy purpose, however, which the Bush administration had difficulty filling.

Bill Clinton rode to the White House in substantial part on promises to focus more sharply on domestic policy problems. During the campaign he provided few clues concerning any foreign policy vision, but he conveyed a generally cooperative internationalist image. The contemporary importance of foreign environmental, economic, and security issues for the United States is unlikely to allow him to separate domestic and international politics, just as it frustrated George Bush's efforts to do so.

Any discussion of the implications of leadership and vision in the determination of foreign policy would be incomplete without comment on Mikhail Sergeyvich Gorbachev.[25] Although economic weakness and social evolution explain much of Soviet behavior in the late 1980s (regardless of leadership), no one can deny that Gorbachev played an exceptional and personal role in transforming the foreign policies of the U.S.S.R. After becoming general-secretary of the Communist party in 1985, his vision of the need to retrench and focus on domestic problems, combined with a strong belief in the value of cooperation with the West, dramatically reshaped external policy. He bombarded the world with a flurry of arms control proposals containing much new flexibility (for instance, on verification). He trimmed Soviet commitment to foreign ventures around the globe including Afghanistan. He encouraged complete transformations of Eastern European political systems at the expense of local Communist leaderships. In short, he brought cooperative internationalism (and perhaps even semi-isolationism) to the leadership of the Soviet Union. Although he shifted some domestic policies radically, Russian President Boris Yeltsin left largely unchanged the foreign policy vision of Gorbachev.

PSYCHOLOGY AND FOREIGN POLICY

Our promenade down the history of American leadership (with a digression to spotlight Gorbachev) emphasized competing and shifting visions. The quota-

---

[25]Unfortunately, this limited treatment of individuals must omit discussion of other exceptional non-American leaders, such as Winston Churchill, Charles de Gaulle, Willy Brandt, and Anwar Sadat—not to mention more infamous ones like Muammar al Khadafy.

tion concerning Hitler's invasion of the Soviet Union, however, emphasized not vision but psychology.[26] Many in-depth analyses of individual leaders are largely psychological.[27] For instance, Alexander and Julette George (1964) linked Woodrow Wilson's stern and punitive upbringing and his inability to please his father to a need for self-esteem in later life. They explained his active idealism as compensation for fear of failure and rejection.

Barber (1985) suggests two categories for evaluation of personality characteristics relevant to how leaders perform in the presidency: their energy level on the job (active or passive), and their level of personal satisfaction with the job (negative or positive). For instance, active-positive presidents include Franklin Roosevelt, Truman, Kennedy, Ford, Carter, and Bush. Such individuals want results and behave flexibly to achieve them; Barber concludes that they generally handle challenges and crises well. Active-negative presidents strive to achieve and maintain power, and risk the danger of rigidly adhering to a failing policy. Barber characterizes Wilson, Hoover, Johnson, and Nixon as active-negative presidents.[28]

Another potentially useful approach to characterizing personality is specification of the degree to which a belief system is "open" or "closed." Ole Holsti (1962) did a famous study of John Foster Dulles, Eisenhower's secretary of state. Investigating the childhood of Dulles as the son of a stern Presbyterian minister, and analyzing the content of his public pronouncements, Holsti found the belief system of Dulles to be moralistic and rigid. Dulles saw the Soviet leadership and Communist party as irredeemably bad. He held what Kissinger (1962) called an "inherent bad faith" model and could seemingly view no action on the part of the Soviets as positive. Dulles interpreted even reductions in Soviet troop strength negatively—to him they indicated economic weakness and diversion of personnel to more threatening uses. Simultaneously, Dulles believed that the Soviets would perceive the United States as peaceful: "Khruschchev does not need to be convinced of our good intentions. He knows we are not aggressors and do not threaten the security of the Soviet Union" (cited in Nixon 1962, 62).

Starr (1984) did a parallel analysis of Henry Kissinger, Nixon's national security adviser and secretary of state, and found a mind-set that was more open and flexible (but with an intolerance for dissent and a taste for secrecy). Although the two foreign policy advisers undoubtedly reflected the tenors of their times, they also helped create them. Kissinger's willingness to see positive aspects of Soviet behavior helped him negotiate the SALT I treaty and to initiate a period of détente.

[26]A sociological approach to the study of leadership also has merit. Leaders around the world are overwhelmingly middle-aged and older males, better educated than the general population, and economically well-to-do. Studies of American public opinion consistently show that those with such characteristics have somewhat different attitudes than the broader population, including being distinctly more internationalist. See Hughes (1978).

[27]Kegley and Wittkopf (1979, 369-95) summarize some of this literature.

[28]Other categories of personalities include nationalists, militarists, conservatives, authoritarians, antiauthoritarians, and rigid personalities (Kegley and Wittkopf 1979, 378–379). It often proves difficult to classify presidents in such categories, which means the characteristics are not easy to define or measure.

Although psychological characterizations of personality convey useful insights, they sometimes appear subjective. We must be aware that they may tell us almost as much about the policy preferences of the analyst as about the character of the foreign policy maker.

PERCEPTION AND CRISIS

Individuals and their personalities are especially critical in periods of crisis. In crisis situations, the diversion of policy making to the highest levels, the stress induced by time pressures and threats, and the frequent inadequacy of information conspire both to force individuals to the forefront of policy making and to compel them to reach inward for help in decision making. Here again the basic realist model fails to help us adequately understand the world, because many case studies of crises are analyses of irrational behavior (Jervis 1976).

More specifically, many studies of crisis focus on the extent of misperception. For instance, social psychologist Ralph White (1985) studied the outbreak of World War I. Events proceeded quickly, at least by standards of the day, after the assassination of the Austrian Archduke Francis Ferdinand (Austro-Hungarian heir to the throne) by a militant Serbian nationalist on June 28, 1914. On July 5 Germany assured Austria of its support for firm reaction in a telegram that became known as a "blank check." The German Kaiser subsequently tried unsuccessfully to restrain Austria. On July 23 Austria presented Serbia an ultimatum with demands. Two days later Serbia accepted all but one demand, which would have required Austrian participation in police activity within Serbia so as to bring the assassin to justice. Austria thereafter severed diplomatic relations and began war preparations. Feverish diplomatic activity followed, but on August 4 the Germans invaded France, and the war quickly spread across Europe.

White analyzed the beliefs of the Austrian leadership and listed six areas of misperception and dysfunctional behavior. First, the Austrians held a diabolic enemy image, perceiving the assassins as threatening the very existence of the empire. There was, of course, some truth in that. Expecting the Russians to see the situation the same way, however, surely was self-delusion. The German Kaiser was perhaps even more subject to such enemy images. While the British were working to avert war, the Kaiser wrote on a diplomatic note:

> The net has been suddenly thrown over our head, and England sneeringly reaps the most brilliant success of her persistently prosecuted, purely *anti-German world policy,* against which we have proved ourselves helpless, while she twists the noose of our political and economic destruction out of our fidelity to Austria, as we squirm isolated in the net. (White 1985, 233)

A second perceptual problem was a virile self-image on the part of the Austrians. They feared losing great power status by not acting appropriately and strongly. They applied a strong-weak evaluation scale to their actions more strictly than a good-bad or right-wrong scale. Simultaneously, and somewhat contradictory, a third perceptual difficulty lay in maintenance of a moral self-image.Austrians viewed themselves as peace loving, civilized, and economically progressive, whereas the threatening forces exhibited opposing characteristics. A fourth misperception was that the Austrians saw the conflict as a local one and did not understand the growing concern of other powers until too late—a problem of selective attention.

A fifth difficulty was absence of empathy. The Austrians could not mentally put themselves in the place of the Serbians and see that Austrian demands appeared to be naked aggression. From the Russian viewpoint, the demands seemed a step toward annexation, like the Austrian absorption of Bosnia six years earlier, but the Austrians failed to recognize that perception as well. Sixth, and finally, the monarchy succumbed to military overconfidence. They believed that the combined Austrian-German power was adequate to deter conflict or to win it.

An important reason for listing these six points should be obvious. Throughout the cold war the danger of similar misperception by either the United States or the Soviet Union was high. Diabolic enemy images (godless communism versus imperialistic capitalism), virile and moral self-images, selective attention, absence of empathy, and military overconfidence all seemed possible categories of misperception that could, under the right circumstances, have transformed a cold war into a hot war. A British and Soviet double agent who defected from the KGB in 1985, Oleg Gordievski, reported that in 1983 there was growing fear in the Soviet Union that the United States was preparing to launch a surprise attack. Apparently the U.S. military buildup and rhetoric such as Reagan's characterization of the Soviet Union as an "evil empire" created a near panic in Soviet leadership; some believed that NATO maneuvers planned for late in the year were to be a cover for attack.[29] Although the cold war may be over, dangers of such misperception continue within U.S.–Russian, Russian-Chinese, Indian-Pakistani, and Israeli-Syrian relationships, and within many other relationships as well.

CRISIS MANAGEMENT

Recognition that crises in the past, complicated by such misperceptions, have led to devastating wars that none of the participants really wanted, coupled with realization that warfare between nuclear superpowers would create unacceptable mass destruction, have led policy makers to place great emphasis on crisis management. After the Cuban Missile Crisis, Secretary of Defense Robert McNamara declared that "Today there is no longer any such thing as military strategy; there is only crisis management" (Craig and George 1983, 205).

[29]*The Denver Post*, October 16, 1988, 19A.

The desire to balance two sometimes incompatible objectives, winning in confrontations and avoiding war, complicates **crisis management**. After the first or confrontational stage of a crisis (Snyder and Diesing 1977, 207–280), one side normally perceives its disadvantage and pursues an accommodative strategy. When neither side is accommodative, war may follow.

The first and most basic element of crisis management is to recognize that perceptions may be flawed, especially under the stress associated with crisis. The stimulus-response (SR) model views the interaction of states almost as billiard balls, the behavior of which the laws of physics can describe with considerable precision. That model (compatible with simple realism) expects a state to respond to a stimulus in a predictable fashion, like a billiard ball struck at a particular point with a specified force. That model is clearly an ideal type, however, and the same states may respond differently to external forces, depending on the configuration of social forces within it and depending on the personalities and beliefs of its leadership. In addition, because humans constitute their basic elements, states learn, both from their own experience and from that of others. We should view the state as an organism, which processes stimuli, and whose response is not completely predictable. We should thus think of interstate interaction in terms of stimulus-organism-response (SOR), not merely SR. (Holsti, North, and Brody 1968, 133)

States will often perceive the same stimulus as more threatening during a crisis than under more normal circumstances, even though the other side may not intend it to be more threatening. Therefore, to prevent an overreaction during a crisis, each side must consciously attempt to dampen their reactions.[30] More generally, Snyder and Diesing (1977) found that the receiving state accurately interpreted only four of ten messages in a crisis.

A second and related element of crisis management is recognition in advance of the need for communication channels during crises so that each state can understand what the other side wants and how it views the current situation. During the Cuban Missile Crisis of 1962, Kennedy and Khrushchev had to rely on letters sent via embassies. In an era when the speed of missiles already provided a president only twenty minutes warning of an attack, and when computer malfunctions or migrating geese could give rise to false signals, the United States and the U.S.S.R. were exchanging messages that took six hours to deliver (Ziegler 1987, 241–243). In substantial part because the Cuban Missile Crisis spotlighted the problem, the United States and U.S.S.R. established a hotline between them in June 1963. Rather than the telephone of popular belief, the hotline used teletypes (each side wants a written message for study, not some notes from a telephone conversation). Because it initially used land and sea cables, a Finnish farmer once cut the hotline with his plow. It now uses redundant satellite connection and FAX machines.

[30]Wilkenfeld, Brecher, and Hill (1989) reinforced this finding by Holsti, North, and Brody (1968).

A third contribution to crisis management is maximization of information quality. Iraq invaded Kuwait in 1990, based on grossly incorrect information about the possible U.S. response. Saddam Hussein relied perhaps too much on information from the local U.S. embassy. A good crisis manager recognizes the need for high-quality and redundant information conduits.

A fourth element is preservation of options. Sometimes defining an absolute commitment can force the other side to retreat. For instance, when the Soviets erected the Berlin Wall in 1961, any effort to knock it down would have almost certainly meant war. More often, however, it pays to start small, such as the quarantine of Iraq, which did not fully preclude U.S.–led coalition actions, such as an air strike or invasion. In addition, it can be important to preserve options, especially escape routes, for the other side, including allowing them to "save face" in any concessions they make. In the Cuban Missile Crisis, Kennedy "accepted" the proposal of Khruschchev to exchange a guarantee of noninvasion for the missile removal and was careful not to declare victory publicly. Privately, Secretary of State Dean Rusk said, when Russian ships turned back from the blockade, that "we stood eye-ball to eye-ball and the other guy just blinked"—indicating that the United States perceived the outcome as its victory.

Craig and George (1983, 206–207) list several other aspects of good crisis management that collectively are military management. These include maintaining top-level civilian control of the military, creating pauses in military actions (allowing time for response), coordinating military and diplomatic moves, and choosing military-diplomatic actions that signal a desire to negotiate rather than fight.

They drew these lessons from a study of crises including the outbreak of the Crimean War (1854) and of World War I. In an analysis of the crisis surrounding the Arab-Israel War in 1973, however, they show how difficult it is to abide by these principles. On October 6, 1973, the Egyptians and Syrians launched a coordinated, surprise attack on Israel. After initial losses, the Israelis began to take the initiative; by October 8 the Arab states appealed for Soviet help. A massive Soviet airlift of supplies began on October 10, and the United States countered with one for Israel on October 14. By October 22 Secretary of State Kissinger had negotiated a cease-fire in a trip to Moscow. Yet the Israelis continued to encircle the Egyptian Third Army. The Soviets put their forces on alert for possible airlift to the area, and General-Secretary Brezhnev suggested joint action to Nixon, while threatening unilateral action if necessary. The United States warned against unilateral initiatives and exerted increased pressure on Israel, finally obtaining compliance with the cease-fire.

Craig and George point out that the difficulty of controlling client states and the near impossibility of creating pauses in modern warfare complicates crisis management in this kind of situation. Yet they also note advantages available to decision makers in the modern era. In addition to nearly instantaneous communication among the principals and high-quality electronic intelligence from the field, Kissinger could fly quickly to Moscow and Soviet Premier Kosygin could rush to

Egypt so that the superpowers maintained face-to-face contact between them-selves and with their clients.

INDIVIDUALS IN GROUPS

This discussion of individuals has until now treated them as if single decision makers determined the direction of government, or as if groups of individuals acted much like single individuals. In reality, group dynamics can make outcomes quite different from decisions by single individuals. Some dynamics create further departures from the goal of rationality in state behavior.

The history of interstate relations is littered with bad decisions, less than ideal crisis behavior, and just plain poor management of foreign affairs. How, many have asked, could the United States ignore all the signals from the Japanese that preceded the attack on Pearl Harbor? Even more surprising, how could the invasion by Hitler catch the Soviet Union so much off guard? How could the United States have expected the invasion of Cuba at the Bay of Pigs in 1961 to succeed? How could Iraq believe it could win "the mother of all battles" against the U.S.–led coalition?

Janis (1972) attributes many such failures of policy to **groupthink**. Deci-sion-making groups frequently display much homogeneity of outlook. The age-old tendency of leaders to select advisers who agree with them ("yes men" or sycophants) reinforces this. Although new leaderships frequently accept substantial internal dissent (and consciously recognize the need for it), over time those who fit in less well are more likely to leave. A leadership faced with constant time pressures may replace dissidents with those who create less trouble. When there is no one who seriously and repeatedly questions basic assumptions, especially the outlook of the leader, decision problems arise. In fact, mutually supportive decision groups (like street gangs) are subject to many of the misperception problems that White (1985, 233–236) identified in the leadership of Austria-Hungary: an image of the enemy as diabolical (some-times also a "bunker mentality" in the decision group relative to opposition groups within the same state), a moral self-image, an inability to empathize with the other side, overconfidence, and so on. When individuals in a group reinforce each other's distorted images of the outside world, the result is groupthink, and it is potentially even more dangerous than when a single individual guides policy.

GOVERNMENT

Societal elements, individuals, and groups of decision makers all interact within the framework of government. In turning to the government, two questions are of special interest: First, how does governmental decision making bring together the various elements we have identified within the state? Second, do different types of government produce different international behavior?

DECISION MAKING

Allison (1971) articulated three models that capture most understandings of foreign policy decision making. He argued that each helps us understand that complex process, and that none individually constitutes an adequate picture. His three models are called rational actor, organizational process, and bureaucratic politics.[31]

The **rational actor model** is what civics courses teach us constitutes "good" decision making. The first step is identifying goals and objectives. The second is outlining alternatives or options. The third is assessing the potential consequences of each alternative. Finally, by evaluating the potential consequences in light of goals, an optimal choice is made.

The rational actor model assumes sufficient information to identify policy options and to assess consequences. It also often assumes a small and coherent decision unit (otherwise goals and objectives may not be clear and identifiable). In essence, it is the simple realist model. Even when we doubt that this model consistently describes how decisions are made in our own country, we tend to fall back on it in describing the decision making of other countries (especially those with closed political systems like those of dictatorships). In addition, we often believe it should be the way our own country makes decisions.

Herbert Simon (1957) argued that many preconditions of this rational actor decision-making approach, which he called **optimizing**, are not present in reality. In the real world, information is often highly limited. Time to make decisions, especially in crises, is short. Frequently, objectives are not clear even to an individual, and groups have great difficulties specifying a priority ranking. Simon suggests that most organizational decision making aims for satisfactory, not necessarily optimal, decisions, an approach he calls **satisficing**.

Allison's **organizational process model** builds on these insights. It portrays decision making as relying heavily on standard operating procedures (SOPs) and inertia. Institutions seldom discard SOPs entirely, but instead modify them incrementally in reaction to what they learned from earlier decisions and what they understand to be the unique elements of the current situation. This description of decision making is familiar in budgeting, where allocations normally change slowly.[32] The British refer to the organizational process approach as "muddling through." It assumes limited information, time, and other resources for decision making. It also suggests that decision-making bodies may be unable to give a situation their full attention, and that they may bring limited imagination and flexibility to the decision-making process.

The third description of decision making is the **bureaucratic politics model**. That model portrays the decision environment as one of groups (and individuals) in conflict. Each group may have a relatively clear set of values

---

[31]Bendor and Hammond (1989) rethink, substantially clarify, and refine these models.

[32] "Zero-based budgeting" theoretically creates budgets independent of those in previous years through rational decision making based on ultimate organizational goals.

and objectives, but priorities differ across groups. Groups often have parochial, self-interested goals—captured in the expression, "Where you stand depends on where you sit." Decisions are compromises among groups and reflect their relative strength. The bureaucratic politics model picks up at the governmental level where the pluralist model leaves off at the societal level; the major difference is that it puts more emphasis on "interest groups" within government than on those within the broader society.

Although observers of international politics regularly apply Allison's models to investigations of decision making, we should recognize that these are by no means the only models with which to organize our thinking about it. For instance, Putnam (1988) proposed what he called a "two-level game" model. Foreign policy decision makers often find themselves in two "games" at once, one internal to the country and one external. Consider, for instance, the efforts of the Cardenas administration in Mexico simultaneously to negotiate a North American Free Trade Agreement with the United States and Canada and to sell that agreement to its public. The range of outcomes that the public would accept obviously influenced the positions of the Mexican negotiators, while the range of options for agreement with the United States similarly influenced the arguments and debate within the country. It was necessary for the Cardenas administration to seek an outcome that would succeed in both arenas.

Because the image of foreign policy decision making as a two-level game treats decision makers as a unified, rational unit, it exhibits much in common with the rational actor model. Nonetheless, it opens the "black box" of the state in a fashion that also suggests similarities to the bureaucratic politics model. While we focus here on Allison's three models, you should recognize that many other descriptions of decision making could prove useful.

DIFFERENTIAL POWER OF DECISION-MAKING MODELS

The various decision-making models help in understanding a wide variety of foreign policy decisions, but there is no reason to believe that they are equally apt in all situations. The rational actor and organizational process models provide more powerful descriptions within totalitarian systems, and the bureaucratic politics model fits Western democracies better. The Soviet decision to withdraw from Afghanistan, for instance, unlike the U.S. decision to end the Vietnam War, did not reflect extensive media coverage of the war and widespread social protest (although the Soviet leadership began broader coverage of the war in support of its decision).

Within democracies, under what circumstances might the various models be most useful? In general, routine situations that have limited economic or security implications (such as the arrest of a citizen abroad or still another UN vote on sanctions against Iraq) are more likely to elicit the organizational process decision-making model. The rational actor model better suits full-scale crises, such as reaction to the invasion of South Korea by the North or the invasion by Iraq of Kuwait. The bureaucratic politics model becomes most appropriate when decision time is long and economic interests are great. Examples include the U.S. withdrawal from Vietnam, the size of the U.S. defense budget, or U.S. restrictions on Japanese auto imports. Table 7.2a and 7.2b provide additional examples of decision situations.

GOVERNMENT TYPE AND BEHAVIOR

Decision-making procedures other than rational actor throw into question the important unitary, rational behavior assumptions of realism. Instead of hard, impenetrable states interacting according to physics-like laws, other models suggest "mushy," open states with behavior that will vary according to the organization of administrative structures, the leadership personnel, and the political strength of various groups within society.

Might the behavior of states vary *systematically* with the nature of their decision-making structures? Advocates of democracy, for example, propose that democratic states are less warlike than authoritarian states because the public, which would be required to fight the war and bear the economic cost, is less tolerant of war than an elite leadership.[33] One of the very earliest idealists, Immanuel Kant, argued in his essay "Perpetual Peace" (1795) that:

> if the consent of the citizens is required in order to decide that war should be declared...nothing is more natural than that they would be very cautious in commencing such a poor game, decreeing for themselves all the calamities of war....But on the other hand, in a constitution which is not republican...war does not require of the ruler...the least pleasure of his table, the chase, his country houses, his court functions, and the like. (Garnham 1986, 283)

Conversely, democratic publics may be susceptible to waves of belligerency, sometimes stoked by the mass media. We saw, for instance, that the American public has in general been more strongly anti-Communist than its leadership. Still another counterargument to Kant is that democratic governments use warfare as a distraction from domestic turmoil and as a way of unifying their populations.[34] Marxist logic suggests that capitalist elites control what we call democracies and use warfare to obtain resources, markets, and investment opportunities.

Are democracies more peace loving? Many empirical studies suggest just the reverse. Three large-scale research projects on warfare have looked at the question. Quincy Wright concluded that:

---

[33]Farrell (1966) argued that totalitarian states are more likely to be both revisionist and prepared to take bold, high-risk action.

[34]Levy (1989) reviews the literature on scapegoating and diversionary warfare. Although empirical analyses generally fail to confirm the argument, he concludes that these analyses have inadequately tested the theory.

TABLE 7.2
A Typology of Foreign Policy Issues, with Examples

Economic Considerations Important				Economic Considerations Relatively Unimportant			
Security Issue		Nonsecurity Issue		Security Issue		Nonsecurity Issue	
Decision time long (1)	Decision time short (2)	Decision time long (3)	Decision time short (4)	Decision time long (5)	Decision time short (6)	Decision time long (7)	Decision time short (8)
Size of defense budget	Marshall Plan	Tariff structure	Chile's copper nationalization	Support Nicaraguan contras	North Korean invasion of South	Policy on West Bank uprising	UN vote to oust South Africa
Vietnam War de-escalation	Foreign oil embargo	Adherence to Law of Sea treaty	Peru's declaration of 200–mile fishing zone	Arms limitation treaty	Berlin blockade	Admission of China to UN	Arrest of American citizen abroad
Energy policy	Iraqi invasion of Kuwait	Restricting Japanese auto imports		Iranian hostage affair	Cuban Missile Crisis	Japanese contribution to U.S. troops	
SDI deployment		Eliminating CFC production			Send ships to Persian Gulf	Adherence to World Court decisions	
Common model: bureaucratic political	Common model: rational actor	Common model: bureaucratic political	Common model: rational actor	Common model: rational actor	Common model: rational actor	Common model: organizational process	Common model: organizational process

Sources: Barry B. Hughes, *The Domestic Context of American Foreign Policy* (San Francisco: W. H. Freeman, 1978), 201; some additions from Bruce Russett and Harvey Starr, *World Politics: The Menu for Choice*, 4th ed. (New York: W. H. Freeman, 1992), 226.

> Statistics can hardly be invoked to show that democracies have been less often involved in war than autocracies. France was almost as belligerent while it was a republic as while it was a monarchy or empire. Great Britain is high in the list of belligerent countries, though it has for the longest time approximated democracy in its form of government. (Wright 1965, 208)

Lewis Fry Richardson's studies of wars between 1820–1949 (1960a, 1960b) indicated that Britain alone was involved in 29.8 percent of all "deadly quarrels" (Chan 1984, 80). Similarly, Small and Singer reported that from 1816–1980 democracies were involved in 41.8 percent of all wars, although democracies have never constituted more than one-third of all states. Even more telling, democracies actually initiated 57.1 percent of all the wars involving them.[35]

There are two relationships between democracy and violence, however, that are remarkable (Rummel 1988, 6). First, *"we have not had a real war between democracies in over a century and a half, from 1816 to 1980."*[36] It is possible to list only the War of 1812 (U.K–U.S.), the American Civil War, and a few other partial or possible exceptions to the general rule for all of recorded history. Monarchies and dictatorships fight each other often (as in the two world wars). Communist countries go to war against one another (the Soviet Union against Hungary, Czechoslovakia, and China; China against Vietnam). Although the preceding statistics indicate the frequency with which democracies have battled these other forms of government (and historically taken colonies), it is almost astounding that they do not fight each other. Perhaps societal pressures preclude (or nearly preclude) democracies from substituting warfare for other mechanisms of conflict resolution, when dealing with states similarly inclined.

Second, democracies do not kill their own citizens in extensive numbers. Unlike Nazi Germany, Stalinist Russia, and a wide variety of dictatorships that attack segments of their own citizenry (consider the "disappeared" under Latin American military dictatorships), democracies do not generally so act. In fact, the "necessity" of strong action against internal groups (such as Jews, Armenians, bourgeois elements, or Communists) serves as the justification for many dictatorships. Consider two partial exceptions in the late 1980s and early 1990s to this second rule. Israel used substantial violence against the Palestinian uprising or *intifada* on the occupied West Bank. The victims of this (like the Indians killed by the United States in the nineteenth century) were never citizens, however. In addition, the numbers killed during the Palestinian uprising were not high by the standards of national oppression; an internal debate within Israel seriously questioned and restrained the application of force, and the continued access of global media to the events further reinforced a measured response. The other exception is white South Africa, which directed a substantial level of violence against its black population. Again, an internal debate over the use of deadly

---

[35]Chan (1984) concluded that when colonial wars are included, democracies participated in more than their fair share.

[36]Rummel (1983, 48); see also Rummel (1985).

force (which the outside world was able to watch and to a degree influence) restrained its intensity.[37]

ON RATIONAL, UNITARY ACTORS

The simple realist model valuably provides a parsimonious "first-cut" description of world politics and also prescribes in general terms how states "should" behave in a complex world. This chapter challenged the simple realist *description* of the world, which assumes rational, unitary actors, by looking inside the state.[38] When one does so, it is obvious that the state is far from a unitary actor. Is it possibly, however, still a rational actor?

To answer that question, we must first raise another: What is rationality? According to common definition, **rationality** requires means-end calculation such as that which characterizes the rational actor decision model: "behavior involving a choice of the best *means* available for achieving a given *end*" (Harsanyi 1986, 83). There are three reasons to question whether foreign policy decision making relies regularly on such means-end calculation. First, information for means-end calculation is frequently limited. Second, the actual decision process often seems to omit or even preclude such calculation. Third, many outcomes of decisions prove unhappy ones. Let us consider each point.[39]

The information for a sophisticated means-end calculation is seldom available. For example, we have seen how difficult it is to assess the capabilities of various states and how states sometimes conceal or misrepresent intentions. How calculating could even an absolute dictatorship be when such basic information for linking actions to probable consequences is absent or highly inconsistent? Consider again the consequences to Iraq after its invasion of Kuwait. Nonetheless, information limitations do not preclude rationality within those limits—a **bounded rationality** (Simon 1957).

Our review of decision process, however, suggests that decision makers do not always use even limited information in a means-end calculation. Groups, not individuals, make most decisions. When decision-making groups contain individual members urging rational pursuit of very different goals, it is not at all clear that the outcome of the process will be optimal for the state. Sometimes the group decision-making process clearly diverges from any acceptable definition of rationality. For instance, the groupthink decision process

---

[37]It is also interesting that among democracies, only South Africa, Israel, and the United States maintain legal capital punishment (and Israel has only used it against the Nazi war criminal, Adolf Eichman). Almost all nondemocractic governments rely upon it.

[38]It is worth noting that although realism has been the dominant worldview among students of world politics, writers on the foreign policy of individual states, who generally look within the state for explanations of behavior, do not draw as heavily on it.

[39]Some additional work focuses on the subjectivity of understanding and suggests that interpretation of information will vary so much across individuals that responses to identical stimuli would also vary radically, even if preferences were identical. See Carbonell (1981).

that led to the invasion of Cuba at the Bay of Pigs was simply irrational—only psychology, not means-end calculation, can explain it.[40]

It might appear that organizational process decision making, relying on standard operating procedures, is as irrational as groupthink because it fails to embody a means-end calculation. Standard operating procedures could be highly rational, however, because they put in motion tried-and-true responses. Similarly, allowing a policy decision to be the outcome of a process of competition among social groups and elements of the bureaucracy, resulting in a kind of influence-weighted compromise, might on first glance appear irrational. Perhaps, however, determination of the state interest, a concept important to realists but often too vague to be meaningful, comes in part from just such competition. Nonetheless, reconciling either organizational process or bureaucratic politics decision making with means-end rationality requires that we relax our conceptualization of rationality considerably.[41] Table 7.3 indicates how far the actual decision process normally differs from the rational means-end calculation ideal.

The degree to which rationality in foreign policy decision making is bounded becomes even clearer when we look at outcomes. Consider that supremely important decision, the initiation of war. Austria-Hungary destroyed its empire by initiating World War I. The invasion of Iran by Iraq proved disastrous, but Iraq subsequently invited further defeat by invading Kuwait. The fact that initiators of wars since 1913 have been as likely to lose as to win suggests that decisions to go to war are frequently mistakes. Thus even if leaders employed means-end calculations in making the decisions, the calculations were faulty.

Finally, there are at least two reasons that means-end rationality, even when states achieve desired outcomes, may produce "nonrational" results. First, the time horizons of decision makers may be relatively short, and they may sacrifice longer-term benefits for short-term gain. Second, individually rational action may lead to collectively unsatisfactory results.[42] For instance, decisions to raise tariffs in the 1930s successfully protected states against imports but spread a mutually destructive global depression. Decisions to release increasing volumes of CO_2 into the global atmosphere provide economic advantage but are changing the global climate. The individual state decision making that sometimes leads to such collective failures may properly follow a means-end calculation process.

Where does this leave us? We still have some reason to believe that many decision makers (like the decision committee established during the Cuban Missile

[40]Some would argue that it was the execution of the invasion, not the decision to undertake it that was irrational—the point is unchanged.

[41]Simon's (1985, 294) "procedural rationality"; that is, the "methods of choice that are as effective as its [the decision-making organism's] decision-making and problem-solving means permit" appears closer to reality than a means-end rationality. March (1986) elaborates a series of "rationalities" that take into account limitations of the process; they include limited rationality, contextual rationality, game rationality, process rationality, and adaptive rationality.

[42]Harsanyi (1986) suggests that a general theory of rational behavior would include utility theory (and expected-utility theory), game theory (considering the interaction of rational actors), and ethics (focusing on the collective action dilemma).

TABLE 7.3
Decision Making: Rational Ideal and Common Practice

Task	Rational Ideal	Common Practice
Goal setting	Identification of "state needs," interests, and priorities	"State interests" are the object of competing claims; goals are established through political struggle
Information gathering	Thorough, rapid, accurate gathering, interpreting, and reporting	Always incomplete; system susceptible to overload; delays and distortions in reporting; biases and ambiguities in interpretation
Option formulation	Comprehensive search for options; tallying of probable costs and benefits of each	Limited search for options; comparisons are made in general terms according to predispositions rather than according to cost-benefit items
Choice among options	Selection of option most likely to provide optimal ratio of gains to costs	Choices made in accordance with prevailing mind-sets, influenced by "groupthink" and political considerations

Sources: John P. Lovell, *The Challenge of American Foreign Policy* (New York: Macmillan, 1985), 27, 32.

Crisis) strive to make decision making as nearly rational as possible—to apply a bounded rationality—and that outcomes are on average better when they do so. Thus the simple realist characterization is a helpful one. It is incomplete, however. Extension of the simple realist model to consider the flaws that inadequate information, misperception, group interaction, and collective-action logic frequently introduce to decision making moves us toward a better understanding of world politics.

Attention in this chapter to the assumption of means-end rationality by unitary actors has highlighted a weakness of the realist model. We have seen that states are far from unitary and that their calculus often falls short of what rational decision making demands. Attention to the definition of ends may do realism even greater damage, however. More than a struggle for security motivates people. Religious and secular ideals, many surrounding the definition and organization of community, arouse both passions and actions. We consider next the importance of ideals.

Chapter 8

IDEAS
AND
COMMUNITIES

The Middle East is perhaps the most dangerous spot in the world. Domestic and international political turmoil are intense, and the region that cradled many ancient civilizations birthed the first major war of the post–cold war era (that of UN-sanctioned forces against Iraq).

A power politics perspective helps us understand the Middle East. Five states in the region (Saudi Arabia, Kuwait, Iran, Iraq, and Abu Dhabi) report proven oil reserves surpassing 60 percent of the world total (British Petroleum 1992, 2). Historically, Britain, France, and Germany extended their influence into this region to assure themselves a share of those energy resources. After World War II, the United States became the primary external actor, seeking to continue the flow of oil to its allies and itself. For instance, it sent naval forces to the Persian Gulf during the Iran-Iraq War (1980–1988) to protect oil tankers. Many in the U.S. justified the 1991 war against Iraq after its takeover of Kuwait as the protection of the oil flow from the region by denying Iraq control of too large a portion of the oil reserves; a successful incorporation of Kuwait into Iraq would have doubled Iraqi reserves to nearly 20 percent of the world total. Although it supported the war against Iraq, the former Soviet Union tradition-ally had an interest in weakening the hold of the West on the region, and it supported states, like Libya and Iraq, that wished to break ties with the United States or Europe. Russia could someday again play that same role.

Some states in the region have played the great powers against each other in efforts to assert their own independence. For instance, Egypt resisted early postwar pressures from the United States and Britain to enlist in anti-Soviet alliances, and in 1955 it turned to Czechoslovakia for arms. The United States responded by canceling its support of the project to build the Aswan Dam. The Egyptians then nationalized the Suez Canal. The British, French, and Israelis reacted in October 1956 with an invasion of Egypt. Although the United States condemned the invasion, the rift between Egypt and the West remained, and Egypt subsequently turned to the Soviets for support in building the dam. In 1972 (after completion of the project) the Egyptians complained of inadequate Soviet support, threw their Soviet advisers out, and turned back toward the United States. Egypt effectively used the most important source of power it had—the desire of both superpowers to deny its allegiance to the other and to limit conflict in the Mideast.

It is, however, impossible to understand the Middle East through the lens of power politics alone. How, for instance, do we explain the series of wars (1948, 1956, 1967, and 1973) between Israel and its neighbors? Explanation requires understanding that Israel is a Jewish state, newly formed in 1948, in a region dominated by Moslem peoples. Even while dispersed throughout the world in what is called the Diaspora, many Jews retained a sense of community, and the Holocaust of World War II greatly reinforced it. The Arabs who lived in what is now Israel (there were only 60,000 Jews there in 1920 but 600,000 Arabs) also had a community identity (Boyd 1987, 114). They fought the international declaration in 1948 of the Jewish state called Israel (by which time there were 600,000 Jews and 1.1 million Arabs in Palestine) and enlisted neighboring Moslem states in their cause. Power has been important in creating and sustaining Israel, but the conflict is fundamentally one of competing religions and nationalisms.

Community identities and ideals also unite many peoples throughout the Middle East. For example, the predominantly Arabic inhabitants of the region share a culture and identity. Between 1958 and 1961 Egypt and Syria actually merged to create the United Arab Republic (UAR), abolishing national citizenship and labeling themselves simply Arabs. Even after the failure of the UAR, the idea of Arab community persisted. In 1963 Egypt (officially the Arab Republic of Egypt), Syria (the Syrian Arab Republic), and Iraq held discussions on recreating another United Arab Republic.

In 1945 regional states formed the Arab League, which had twenty-one members in 1992. The league has sponsored a common market, an Arab development bank, an Arab press, and many other cooperative projects (Plano and Olton 1988, 324). The separate peace treaty that Egypt signed with Israel at Camp David, Maryland, in 1978 dealt a serious blow to Arab unity (the league suspended Egypt until 1989). Nonetheless, a 1980 survey of people in Arab countries found that "eight out of ten respondents believed that the Arabs belonged to a single nation, and that they were culturally distinctive" (Dawisha 1986, 10). In 1991 the Iraqi army briefly captured the Saudi town of Khafji. Someone telephoned the town's hotel and the Iraqi soldier who answered declared, "I am for the Arabs, for Arabism.... See you in Jerusalem." Ironically, even in a war pitting Arab states against one another, the ideals of pan-Arabism and Islam motivated soldiers (*The Economist*, February 16, 1991, 11).

Most of the Middle East is also Moslem, and the Middle East is the fount of Islam. Although a shared religion reinforces the common Arabic identity, Islam is sometimes also divisive. It has two main and competing sects, Sunni and Shiite. Iran is predominantly Shiite Moslem. Iraq's population is 60 percent Shiite and 35 percent Sunni, but the Sunnis control the government. Desire to overthrow the

Sunni government of Iraq underlay the Iranian refusal to break off its war with Iraq, even after it pushed Iraq out of Iranian-claimed territory.

Why does Syria remain dedicated to destroying the state of Israel? Why has the Islamic Republic of Iran displayed such strong antipathy toward the United States? Why did the Egyptian leadership's signature on a peace treaty with Israel put it at odds with many of its own population? Religious and nationalist idealisms help explain these and other aspects of politics in the Middle East.

When we re-focus our attention outside of the Middle East, we also see that considerations other than power and security motivate states and peoples around the world. It is difficult to explain the intensity of conflict between the United States and the Soviet Union during the cold war unless one looks at ideological commitment. Although power relationships were one reason for the split between the Soviet Union and China in the late 1950s and early 1960s—China resented its subordinate position—we can understand neither that conflict nor the tentative rapprochement in the late 1980s without considering the strength of attachment by state leaderships to competing versions of Communist doctrine.

Turning to a completely different issue, why do Norway, the Netherlands, Sweden, and Denmark give such high levels of foreign aid? Each of those countries donates more than the 0.7 percent of GNP that Southern states request (Norway provides more than 1 percent). The Scandinavian countries have no former colonies with which they seek to maintain strong commercial ties (as does France with similarly high aid levels). They have no bases or troops overseas and no alliance structures to maintain. In addition to official aid from their governments, the people of Norway and Sweden give approximately an additional 0.1 percent of GNP as voluntary aid. This behavior is almost impossible to explain unless one looks to a sense of global or human community as a motivating force.

The remainder of this chapter considers the impact on world affairs of a variety of ideas or ideals concerning community: nationalism, religious idealism, universalism, and globalism. Some may think it strange simultaneously to consider nationalism (which underlay the racism of Nazi Germany and its murdering of many millions), religious community (which can variously be a source of peace or war), and universalism (which includes both the democratic impulse of globalism and the socialist ideal of Marxism). Attention to the specifics of identity and governance ideals can help us better understand the similarities and differences among these idealisms.

IDENTITY AND GOVERNANCE IDEALS

All idealisms, whether they motivate peaceful or violent actions, share an interest in specifying the community: Who is included, who is excluded, and how the community is organized socially and politically. Table 8.1 roughly sketches the relationship between identity and governance ideals, on the one hand, and types of idealism, on the other. **Identity ideals** can be either narrow, excluding as well as including individuals, or universal, reaching out to all of humanity. Although it dramatically oversimplifies, **governance ideals** tend to divide into those that call for decentralized, individual-oriented government (an orientation we characterize as "liberal") and those that call for more hierarchical, centralized governance.

TABLE 8.1 **A Typology of Idealisms/Communitarianisms**			
	Governance Ideals		
Identity Ideals	*Liberal,* *Decentralized*	*None* *Unclear,*	*Hierarchical,* *Centralized*
Narrow (Exclusive)		Nationalism	
Mixed		Religious Idealism	
Universal	Globalism (Western Idealism)		Communism

The roots of nationalism are in identity ideals and those ideals have a narrow character, distinguishing sharply between those who are included and those who are excluded. You are either German, Welsh, Russian, Armenian, or Serbian—or you are not. Nationalists attach themselves to a wide variety of governance ideals. When they find themselves struggling against powerful state forces, they frequently take hope in the governance ideals of the opposition. Thus many African nationalistic wars against European colonialism initially looked to the hierarchical forms of communism, and many Eastern European countries and former Soviet republics eagerly embraced the liberal democracy of Western Europe.

Religious idealists belong near the ambiguous center of Table 8.1 (and can be found in all corners of it). Although religions often define fairly distinct borders between those who belong to the community and those who do not, those borders seldom rigidly exclude those outside of them. In fact, many religions actively proselytize and convert outsiders in order to extend the perceived benefits of the community to them. Similarly, religions take differential positions on governance ideals. For instance, while Catholics have traditionally organized their own governance very hierarchically, many Protestant sects have adopted quite democratic and decentralized governance structures.

Marxism has always been universal, focusing its attention on humanity as a whole and excluding no one from its definition of the global community. What we call the "Communist" variation of Marxism installed highly centralized political and economic systems throughout the countries where it captured power.

There exists also a Western liberal idealism, similarly universalistic in its attention to humanity as a whole and in its belief that certain governance forms will ultimately best serve all humans. In contrast to communism, however, the governance ideals of Western idealism are liberal democratic. This book has adopted globalism as the label for that Western idealism.

Each of these idealisms has had profound implications for world politics. The rest of this chapter investigates the impact of each of them in turn. With the end of the cold war it has recently been argued, however, that Western liberal idealism has emerged victorious in the long-term struggle among ideologies (Fukuyama 1989). The last portions of this chapter therefore devote special attention to globalist thought.

NATIONS AND NATIONALISM

The emergence in Europe of modern states, geographic units with relatively fixed territories and an independent government, interacted with the growth of nationalism. As the new states took shape, the appeal of political and religious universality declined, and peoples ceased looking outside the local environment for artistic and social standards (including the use of Latin for literature). Local languages arose (furthered by Gutenberg's movable-type printing invention in 1436–1437), and the collective identity of those within the developing states increased. That is, nationalism grew. **Nationalism** is just such a sense of collective identity or "we feeling," and a **nation** is a group of people bound together by nationalism.

Sets of shared characteristics, such as language, literature, culture, race, or religion generally reinforce collective identity. They do so in large part because they facilitate communication—it is no accident that "commun" serves as a root for both community and communication. Intensive interaction and contacts among the members of a population facilitate translation of shared qualities and understandings into nationalism.

Once in place, the intense "we feelings" of nationalism frequently engender two kinds of political activity. The first is an effort to capture or create a state. A state reinforces the collective identity and empowers the nation. **Self-determination** has been the rallying cry under which nations, including the Palestinians, have sought to create states. Natural extensions of this state building include the desire to bring into the state parts of the nation not yet within it—**irredentism**. German irredentism before World War II was a primary cause of the war (there were Germans in Czechoslovakia and elsewhere, not just in Germany). Self-determination and irredentism share the goal of identifying the state with the nation.

A second category of nationalistic political activity follows from the desire to be self-contained (Rourke 1986, 77). Specifically, the creation of "we feelings" sometimes gives rise to a sense of superiority and to "they feelings"—the identification of out-groups. When the bases of nationalism lie in common "race" or religion, intense nationalism sometimes becomes linked with racism and militant fundamentalism. Racism can lead to efforts to conquer and subordinate, or even exterminate, inferior groups.

GROWTH OF MODERN NATIONALISM

The French Revolution and the French revolutionary and Napoleonic wars (1789–1815) define an important period in the growth of modern nationalism, comparable with the Thirty Years War in the growth of the state. In an earlier era, Louis XIV (1643–1715) made his famous and egotistical pronouncement *L'État, c'est moi* ("I am the state"), differentiating the state from the people. During the French revolution, however, the larger population effectively captured the state. In 1789, the Declaration of the Rights of Man and Citizen decisively rejected the position of Louis XIV: "Sovereignty resides essentially in the nation; no body of men, no individual, can exercise authority that does not emanate expressly from it" (Rejai and Enloe 1981, 39). We can see one impact of this capturing of the French state by the French nation in the character of the military. Before the revolution, armies tended to be relatively small and to recruit mercenaries or those with a personal loyalty to the king:

> Foreign units of the French army were composed typically of Swiss Guards, and Irish units were also used when the French could recruit them. Scottish regiments were regularly found in the services of Holland. The French Army before the Revolution was half-composed of men who were not French; and the army of Frederick William I was one-third foreign. (Rosecrance 1963, 20)

In 1791 the French instituted mass conscription, the *levée en masse*, to protect and extend abroad the popular gains of the revolution. Those citizen armies went abroad for the greater glory of the French nation, not the French king. Napoleon's large armies helped accelerate the emergence of nationalism outside of France by making other states require the support of similarly popular armies.[1]

Nationalism spread throughout Europe in the nineteenth century. The European revolutions of 1830 and 1848 reflected nationalistic passions (as well as commercial and aristocratic class antagonisms) and were advance warnings of the threat to the multinational Austrian Empire. Before about 1800, state building most often preceded the creation of nations within Europe, but increasingly thereafter nationalism began to redefine states. The formation of a German state (in 1871, with the success of Prussia in the war against France) and an Italian state (roughly 1861, with the coronation of Victor Emmanuel II) followed the growth of nationalist fervor rather than preceded it. This pattern has continued through to the current day as the Irish, Hungarians, Jews, Palestinians, Kurds, Croats, Tamils, and many others have acquired, or sought to acquire, control of their own state.

---

[1]The nationalism of the French Revolution also had an important philosophical basis in the thought of Jean Jacques Rousseau (Macridis 1986, 252–253). He emphasized the importance of community bonds and the existence of the "general will." O'Brien (1988, 2) argues that nationalism arose simultaneously in France and Germany: "Cultural nationalism as ideology begins in Germany with Herder; post-Christian political nationalism begins in France with Rousseau."

Although nationalism became a strong state-building force within Europe, in the rest of the world many new states resulted from reactions against colonialism rather than from nationalism. The process in the Third World has often had more in common with the sixteenth- and seventeenth-century developments that created early European states like France and Britain than with the nineteenth-century emergence of Italy and Germany. One reason for the contemporary weakness and instability of many Third World countries is their need simultaneously to build a modern state and to create a real nation. The processes of state and nation building are often violent:

> War in the second half of the twentieth century has become an artifact of ethnic, religious, and language nationalism, and not infrequently, of tribalism. It is the manifestation of the birth of a global international system, the membership of which remains contested in some areas of the world. A high proportion of the wars and violence of the era have been perhaps less wars of national liberation than wars of national formation. They have had everything to do with the creation of states, and relatively little to do with the traditional causes of conflict in the European-centered states system, such as gaining territories, imperialism, balances of power, dynastic ambition, and the like. (Holsti 1986, 370)

Some writers use the term **nation-state** interchangeably with "country" or "state." The label implicitly recognizes the importance of states for the nation-building process and of nations for the state-building process. To the degree that it implies a coincidence between nations and states, however, it is often misleading. A study of 132 states found only twelve to be ethnically homogeneous. In twenty-five additional states a core nationality accounted for 90 percent or more of the total population.[2] At the other extreme, the largest ethnic group in thirty-nine states constituted less than 50 percent of the population, and fifty-three states contained five or more significant ethnic groups. Under these circumstances it is surprising that scholars of world politics, after making clear and important distinctions between states and nations, continue to use the term "nation-state" synonymously with country.

NATIONALISM AND WORLD POLITICS

There are nations (not just states) in the world that lack homogeneity of ethnic origin. The Swiss, with four languages (French, German, Italian, and Romansch), and the Americans, with multiple racial groupings and great diversity in country origins, are hardly homogeneous. Yet the Swiss all call themselves Swiss—the 72 percent who speak a German dialect and the 28 percent who do not. In the United States, it seldom takes more than one generation before the primary identification is American, not Russian, Mexican, Haitian, or Vietnamese.

---

[2]Jorgenson-Dahl (1975, 653–654). Nielsson and Jones (1988, 1) argue that "only 30 of the world's 165 states would meet the test of near congruence between the members of a nation and the inhabitants of a state." See also Nietschmann (1987).

In a great many cases, however, diversity of ethnic origin, with associated language, religious, and cultural differences, precludes the identification of the entire population in a state with a single nation. When the self-identification of a minority ethnic group is intense enough, that people often constitutes a nation wanting its own state. Some or many Basques in Spain; Sikhs in India; Kurds in Iran, Iraq, and Turkey; Dinkas in the Sudan; French-speakers in Canada; Scots in the United Kingdom; and Catholics in Northern Ireland do not consider themselves to be part of the nation dominating their state and do not want to be part of the state as it is currently constituted. These conflicts almost invariably spill over from one state to the larger state system.

Failure of national and state borders to coincide has caused much of the greatest suffering in the twentieth century, including that in World Wars I and II. The catalyst of World War I was the assassination in Sarajevo of the Archduke Francis Ferdinand, heir to the Austro-Hungarian throne. The reactive material into which that catalyst was thrown, however, consisted of a state incorporating various nationalities in addition to the Austrian and Hungarian: Serbian (national "brothers" of the assassin), Czech, Polish, Romanian, and so on. At the end of World War I, Woodrow Wilson presented his famous Fourteen Points to structure the peace settlement. He included the national self-determination principle in an attempt to defuse the problem of nationalism.

Wilson's effort left the world far short of his goal. Consider German nationalism and World War II. Hitler's Germany justified its irredentist aggression before World War II as a necessary expansion of the German state borders so as to include the entire German nation. Germans, it said, lived also in Austria, Czechoslovakia, and Poland, and wished to be part of the German state. A general acceptance by other states of the self-determination principle partly rationalized and even explained their failure to resist naked aggression. The Nazis also justified their "Final Solution" for the Jews in terms of the purity of the nation (or race).[3]

The ideology of fascism glorifies the nation and the collective will. The entire nation replaces individuals or classes as the fundamental social unit of importance. A powerful state is the political manifestation of the successful nation. In the words of World War II Italian dictator Benito Mussolini:

> The State, as conceived of and as created by Fascism, is a spiritual and moral fact in itself, since its political, judicial, and economic organization of the nation is a concrete thing; and such an organization must be in its origins and development a manifestation of the spirit. The State is the guarantor of security both internal and external, but it is also the custodian and transmitter of the spirit of the people, as it has grown up through the centuries in language, in customs, and in faith. And the State is not only a living reality of the present, it is also linked with the past and above all with the future, and thus transcending the brief limits of individual life, it represents the immanent spirit of the nation. (Ingersoll and Matthews 1986, 231)

---

[3]Although the death of perhaps 6 million Jews and others in the Holocaust is best known, other genocides are well documented. These include the deaths of about 1 million Armenians in Turkey at the turn of the century, of as many as 3 million in Kampuchea in the 1970s (Sivard 1987, 30; Harff and Gurr 1988, 364), and of unknown numbers of Kurds in Iraq and Dinkas in the Sudan during the 1980s.

World War II no more successfully extinguished the fires of nationalism than had World War I. On the contrary, the Holocaust reinforced a sense of nationality among many Jews and intensified pressures for a corresponding state. Resistance of Arab Palestinians to the creation of the Jewish state of Israel, and the eventual displacement of more than 2 million Palestinians from traditional homelands (in the British mandate of Palestine) now fuels Palestinian nationalism. The PLO actually declared a Palestinian state in 1988, despite its inability to control the territory of the West Bank. The Mideast wars in 1948, 1956, 1973, 1978, and 1982 all had their roots in the competing claims of various nations to the areas occupied by the states of Israel, Jordan, and Lebanon. Failure to resolve the mismatch in borders of states and nations will inevitably make the region a continued bed of war, terrorism, and anarchy.

THE MODERN NATION SYSTEM

Nations pose some difficulties for the neat model of realists—states interacting with other states in a constant struggle for power and security. On one hand, nations reinforce states when the boundaries coincide; the loyalty and commitment of nations to their own states constitutes a source of power. On the other hand, nations can undercut and even destroy states in a manner that makes the nations global "actors" in their own right. As Connor Cruise O'Brien (1988) characterized nationalism, "the stuff is like fire; you need it to warm you, but it can destroy you if it gets out of control."

Writers often inappropriately use the term international system as a synonym for interstate system (so regularly that this book fails fully to break the convention).[4] When we think about it more carefully, however, there really does exist an **international system**, with nations as constituent elements rather than states. Failures of state and nation borders to coincide exist around the world.

Nietschmann (1987) estimated that there exist approximately 5,000 distinct "communities" in the current world of fewer than 200 states. Nielsson and Jones (1988) suggest that 575 ethnic groups could support potentially distinct political entities. We have already suggested that international conflict in the international system may be more pervasive than interstate conflict in the interstate system, and much conflict is at the intersection of the two systems (nationalism-based civil wars in states). Using a more inclusive definition than we have before of war, Nietschmann argues that eighty-six of 120 wars in the late 1980s pitted indigenous nations against states. He speaks of that very messy conflict as an undeclared "World War III." Sometimes the nations have formed alliances of convenience with oppositions to the state, based within the dominant nation but motivated by a universalistic ideology (for example, native Americans in South America with Communist groups).

---

[4]Interestingly, Kenneth Waltz's (1979) realist *Theory of International Politics* contains no index entries to nations or nationalism (he uses nation as a synonym for country).

We will explore in somewhat more detail four instances of failure of nation and state borders to coincide and of the conflict that incongruity causes: the former U.S.S.R., the former Yugoslavia, the Middle East, and the continent of Africa.

The Soviet Union was the last of the large European multinational empires. The others that divided much of the world among themselves in 1914, the Austro-Hungarian, the Ottoman, and the less formally integrated world empires of the British and French, fell apart in the face of divisive nationalism. The reforms of General-Secretary Gorbachev brought into the open the desires of many Estonians, Latvians, Tartars, Georgians, Armenians, and other nationalities for their own states.

Approximately 100 ethnic groups make their home within the former Soviet Union. Table 8.2 shows the population size and ethnic composition of the fifteen states that emerged from the U.S.S.R. Russia clearly dominates demographically and also covers 76 percent of the land area of the former country. The Ukraine is the second largest new state.

TABLE 8.2
New States of the Former Soviet Union (1990)

State	Population (Millions)	Native Population (Percent)	Russian Population (Percent)
Russia	148.0	82	82
Ukraine	51.8	73	22
Uzbekistan	20.3	71	8
Kazakstan	16.7	40	38
Belarus	10.3	78	13
Azerbaijan	7.1	83	6
Georgia	5.5	70	6
Tajikistan	5.2	62	8
Moldova	4.4	64	13
Kyrgyzstan	4.4	52	21
Lithuania	3.7	80	9
Turkmenistan	3.6	72	9
Armenia	3.3	93	2
Latvia	2.7	52	34
Estonia	1.6	62	30

Source: Central Intelligence Agency, *The Republics of the Former Soviet Union and the Baltic States: An Overview* (Washington, D.C.: CIA, 1992).

Table 8.2 makes obvious the nationalistic divisions that tore apart the former U.S.S.R. Only about half of its total population was Russian, and other ethnic groups were growing more rapidly (some Russians said, "They are winning in the bedroom"). Even the Ukrainians were never totally reliant partners for the Russians. Many Ukrainians and Byelorussians welcomed the Germans as liberators during the invasion in World War II, until they experienced the brutality of the Nazis.

Desire for full independence from the Soviet Union rather than greater autonomy or a redrawing of republic borders was especially strong in the Baltic republics of Estonia, Latvia, and Lithuania.[5] Having complex histories of independence and subordination, these three peoples became independent in 1918 when the Bolshevik Revolution in Russia weakened the grip of the empire. The U.S.S.R. forcibly reincorporated them in 1940 after a pact between Hitler and Stalin (the United States never recognized their loss of independence). With *glasnost* in the Soviet Union, new nationalist organizations flowered in each of the Baltic republics. In 1989 Lithuania and Latvia passed laws moving the republics toward economic sovereignty. In 1991 the republics received independence, and thus began the dissolution of the Soviet Union.

Table 8.2 also makes obvious the continuing problems of the newly independent states. Only in Russia, Azerbaijan, Lithuania, and Armenia do the native populations reach 80 percent of the total. In the former Soviet Union as a whole, 75 million people reside outside of their original republics and one of eight marriages is mixed.[6] Even in those states a variety of nationality groups protest in support of greater autonomy or outright independence (as Armenians do in Azerbaijan, Russians do in Lithuania, and the Tartars do in Russia). Short of a forceful reintegration of part or of all of the old Soviet Union, the region will likely experience seccessionist and irredentist conflicts indefinitely. Among the most dangerous such issues, because of the size and power of the states involved, are those that divide Russia and the Ukraine. For instance, in 1959 Khrushchev transferred the Crimea to the Ukraine, but the population of this strategically important peninsula remains 70 percent Russian.

Religious differences reinforce some ethnic divisions. Many of the non-Russian populations are historically Moslem (and many of those share a common Turkish identity). For example, strife has pitted Christian Armenians against Shiite Azerbaijanis. Armenians in a region of the Azerbaijan Republic called Nagorno-Karabakh have demanded that the borders be redrawn to place them in the Republic of Armenia. War erupted over this dispute in 1990.

Yugoslavia's disintegration proved even more traumatic than that of the U.S.S.R. The former state consisted of six republics: Serbia, Montenegro, Croatia, Slovenia, Bosnia-Herzegovina, and Macedonia. In 1991–1992 the last four of these declared their independence and other states soon recognized all but Macedonia (Greece protested that new state's use of the name "Macedonia"). Slovenia, the most ethnically homogeneous of the group, won its independence with a spirited military campaign. Croatia, with a Serbian minority of less than 10 percent, fought an extensive civil war in which Serbian forces consolidated their grip on a considerable portion of the new state's territory. Ethnically complex Bosnia (formerly 44

[5]It is more widespread, however. In April 1989 at least sixteen people died when soldiers attacked large crowds in Georgia, led by nationalists demanding independence.

[6]Pushkov (1992, 151). Large-scale migrations are, however, rapidly changing ethnic balances. Between 1985 and 1992, 800,000 people left Uzbekistan, leaving the new state primarily in the hands of Uzbeks (*The Economist*, August 8, 1992, 29).

percent Muslim, 31 percent Serb, and 19 percent Croat) broke down in especially vicious civil war, marked by Serbian expansion over 70 percent of the territory and an "ethnic cleansing" of large areas to rid them of non-Serbian peoples. Religion again reinforced national divisions. Whereas Serbs are predominantly Eastern Orthodox, Croats accept Roman Catholicism. Slavic Muslim populations in Bosnia frequently became the victims of both.

We have already referred to a third region of ongoing troubles rooted in nationalism and religion. Table 8.3 provides data that indicate the depth of the remaining problem. It shows where the 5.6 million Palestinians resided in 1991. Since the formation of Israel, Jordan has become a largely Palestinian state (they may ultimately dominate it). Although Palestinians lived throughout the Middle East even before the formation of Israel and prior to the 1973 Arab-Israeli War in which Israel occupied the West Bank and Gaza Strip, many in the Palestinian diaspora wish to return and most desire a Palestinian state in what is now greater Israel. On the other side, there were 4.3 million Jews in Israel in 1991, and the country sought to absorb a large influx of Jews from the former U.S.S.R.; the Israeli population was growing rapidly and already had a density of 606 per square mile, (compared with 268 in more fertile France). In 1987 riots in Gaza initiated the *intifada* or the Palestinian general uprising, pitting the two claims for land against each other. Despite the initiation of direct negotiations between Israel and the Palestinians in 1992, the roots of the conflict run very deep.

TABLE 8.3
Location of Palestinian Refugees

Location	Number
Jordan	1,700,000
West Bank	1,100,000
Israel	690,000
Gaza Strip	620,000
Lebanon	330,000
Syria	300,000
Kuwait	100,000
Other Gulf States	293,000
Other Arab States	102,000
Other	175,000
TOTAL	5,560,000

Source: Institute for Palestinian Studies, as reported in *The Christian Science Monitor*, October 28, 1991, 11.

No area in the world can match the nationality problems of Africa. Colonial escapades of the Europeans drew state borders during the late nineteenth century with almost total disregard for national or tribal boundaries. In the Berlin Conference of

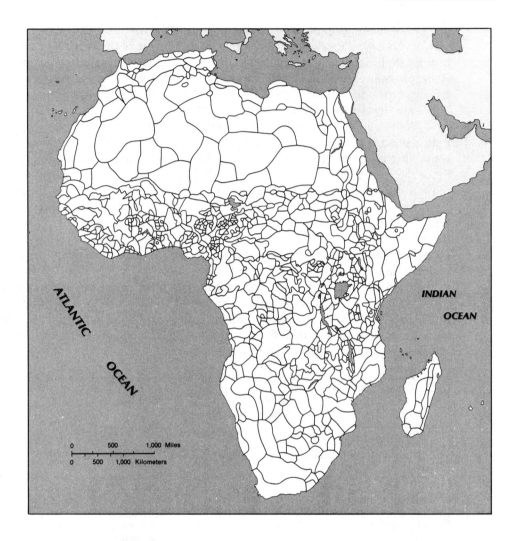

FIGURE 8.1 Ethnic Groups of Africa
Source: Martin Ira Glassner and Harm J. de Blij, *Systematic Political Geography*, 4th ed. (New York: John Wiley and Sons, 1989), 532.

1884–1885 imperialists made adjustments to those borders simply with pen and ruler on a map of the continent. In a continent with many tribal groupings, this created multinational states and arbitrarily split nations by state boundaries. Only four sub-Saharan countries (Lesotho, Somalia, Cape Verde, and the Comoros Islands) are composed of single national groups. One might, therefore, expect Somalia to avoid ethnic conflict of the type that rent it in 1992, but regional and clan-based antagonisms divide it deeply. Other African countries contain as many as 126 tribes (Tanzania) and seldom encompass fewer than three or four. Figure 8.1 shows the ethnic boundaries on the continent—it looks little like the political map of Africa (refer to the front of this volume). Resultant ethnic strife in Africa helps explain the poor economic and political development performance of many states on the continent.

African nationality problems become interstate affairs in two principal ways. First, many refugees cross state borders. Second, civil wars in the Sudan, Chad, Ethiopia, and elsewhere, many of which pit national and religious groupings against one another, have regularly drawn participation by non-African states, including the superpowers. Linkages to interstate politics are unlikely to disappear in the near future.

We could also have focused on unsatisfied nationalisms in India, China, Romania, or Kurdistan. The continuing and perhaps even increasing nationalism of the contemporary world, coupled with growing pressures in many arenas for interstate cooperation led Lincoln Bloomfield to label ours the "Age of Nationalism Without Autonomy" (1988, 14).

RELIGION AND WORLD POLITICS

The history of world politics cannot be told without interweaving in it the history of religion.[7] For instance, both military conflict between Christianity and Islam and their fruitful exchange of ideas frame much of European and Middle Eastern history since A.D. 622, the first year of the Islamic calendar. Within a century of its founding Islam had swept through Spain and to within 100 miles of Paris, until Charles Martel's victory in the Battle of Tours arrested its northward progress. At the other end of the Mediterranean, Moslem forces laid siege in 716 to Constantinople, then the capitol of the Byzantine Empire. They failed, but the city fell to Islam seven centuries later.

This Islamic onslaught helped reverse the decentralization that had characterized Europe since the end of the Roman Empire. The Catholic church took a leading role in reestablishing broader political-social order. It organized the first crusade in 1097–1100 to "recover" Jerusalem; the crusaders established the Latin Kingdom of Jerusalem and maintained it until 1187. By 1250 Christian forces had pushed Islam out of all Spain except Granada. Thereafter a give-and-take situation characterized military relations between the two religions. In 1529 the Ottoman Empire reached the gates of Vienna. Even in 1878 much of the Balkans remained under its control. Most Albanians today are Moslem.

Christianity (like Islam) suffered internal schisms that frequently erupted into warfare. In 1517 the Augustinian friar Martin Luther posted his Ninety-five Theses against indulgences on the door of the Wittenburg castle church. Thus began a revolution (the Reformation), challenging established church institutions, especially their control over doctrine and the conditions of salvation. John Calvin (1509–1564) further articulated the challenge. The Thirty Years War (1618–1648)

---

[7]O'Brien (1988, 3) traces the linkages between nationalism and religion, going back to the Hebrew Bible in which "God chose a particular people and promised them a particular land."

had many interacting and overlapping causes: power struggles among leaders, personal loyalties and feuds, and even emerging nationalisms. The settlement of the war, however, with the Peace of Westphalia recognized the primacy of religion:

> And as for the original cause of the war, religion, the delegates agreed merely to reestablish the principle laid down at the Peace of Augsburg in the previous century: each prince would determine the religion of his people now, even if he was a Calvinist. As a result the Hapsburgs drove all Protestants from their land, and many of the Lutherans and Calvinist princes compelled their Catholic subjects to choose between conversion and emigration. (Garraty and Gay 1981, 590)

The interaction of subsequent European imperialism and religion was also close. Although the superior technology and power of the Europeans would almost certainly have driven them abroad and to conquest regardless of religion, the cross and sword supported each other.

> Missionaries appear to have only indirectly imperial aims, but the conversion of souls in tribal societies often rested upon imperial protection and had imperial consequences. A Gikuyu proverb from East Africa reflects the relationship: "One White Man gets you down on your knees in prayer, while the other steals your land." Christianity appeared to many African tribes the ritual aspect of imperialism. (Doyle 1986, 170)

In contrast to Latin America and Africa, widespread conversion failed in much of Asia, largely because of the stronger political systems (and more numerous peoples) that the Europeans found there:

> Japan's first contact with Europeans had occurred in 1542, when Portuguese merchants visited its shores.... However, the most important aspect of Western culture introduced was surely the Christian religion. By late in the sixteenth century the number of Japanese Christians may have been as high as 150,000. Whole domains of western Japan were converted when their daimyos became Christians.... From the time of Hidyoshi [1582–1598], however, a reaction set in. Japanese rulers...began to suspect that European missionary activity might be a prelude to political conquest by the Spanish king [as they knew it had been in the Philippines]. (Garraty and Gay 1981, 637)

The modern era appears to be characterized by a somewhat greater tolerance of alternative religions. There are many important exceptions, however. Despite the best efforts of Mohandas Gandhi, he could not bridge the gaps between the Moslems and Hindus in India. When independence from Britain came in 1947, the colony split into predominantly Hindu India and predominantly Moslem Pakistan. Approximately 800,000 people died in the conflict accompanying partition and the resettlement of peoples across the new borders (Sivard 1988, 30).

The religious conflicts within India did not cease with partition. That country has a population that is 83 percent Hindu, 11 percent Moslem, 3 percent Christian,

2 percent Sikh, and 1 percent assorted other religions. One major problem currently is in the Sikh community. Some nationalists seek to establish the new state of Khalistan, the "land of the pure." In 1984 an Indian army raid on the Golden Temple, the holiest shrine of Sikhs and a center for militant struggle, resulted in about 1,000 deaths. Four months later, Sikhs in her own body guard assassinated Indian Prime Minister Indira Gandhi. A second problem for India is in Kashmir, which still has a Moslem majority and which is split between India and Pakistan. They fought over it in 1965, and fighting flared on the Indian side again in 1990 (Table 8.4).

TABLE 8.4
World Religions

	Africa	Asia	Europe	Latin America
Christian	48.0%	8.1%	82.6%	93.5%
Muslim	40.8	2.0	2.5	0.3
Non-religious	0.3	22.1	10.5	3.7
Hindus	0.2	22.5	0.1	0.3
Other	10.7	45.3	4.1	2.2
Total	100.0%	100.0%	100.0%	100.0%
	North America	Oceania	Former USSR	World Total
Christian	85.4%	83.1%	37.3%	33.3%
Muslim	2.0	0.4	13.4	17.7
Non-religious	8.0	12.1	29.1	16.4
Hindus	0.5	1.3	0.0	13.3
Other	4.1	2.3	20.2	19.3
Total	100.0%	100.0%	100.0%	100.0%

Source: The World Almanac 1992, p. 725.

The ancient Christian-Moslem opposition continues in some areas.[8] One reason for the continued mutual antipathy of Greece and Turkey, and an obstruction facing Turkish efforts to draw closer to Europe and the Common Market, is the fact that Turkey is 98 percent Moslem (Greece is 97 percent Greek Orthodox). In Africa, Christian minorities in the Moslem states of Egypt and Nigeria are periodically restive. In the Sudan, an effort by the majority Moslem population to impose Islamic law, the *sharia*, on the entire country initiated a civil war in the southern portion of the country, where animist and Christian minorities live.

[8]More generally, Moslem peoples struggle to maintain a cultural and religious self-identity in the face of a universalistic Western culture (Gordon 1989).

Some fear that a new and widescale Christian-Islamic conflict will fill the "vacuum" left by the end of the cold war. A radical Egyptian monthly agrees:

> The secondary conflict between socialist and capitalist systems has ended and everyone is released for the essential conflict with Islam.... The meaning of this is that Muslims must be aware and alert and prepared (*The Economist*, August 1, 1992, 34).

Religious divisions within Christianity and Islam also continue to fuel domestic and periodic interstate conflicts (seldom does a conflict that reaches the stage of a civil war remain completely free from the involvement of other states). Within Christianity, a civil war between Protestants and Catholics in Northern Ireland has continued since the early 1970s. It has roots in the partition of Ireland into the independent Republic of Ireland (Catholic) in the south and British Northern Ireland. (Before partition Britain had long controlled, or at least sought to control, all of Ireland.) Protestants constitute two-thirds of the population in the six counties of Ulster making up Northern Ireland (three counties of Ulster are now part of the Irish republic), and they wish to maintain affiliation with Britain. It is remarkable that Ireland and the United Kingdom have been able to maintain peaceful relations, even cooperative ones, with the passions of this conflict raging. Perhaps it illustrates the ability of democratic states to limit conflict among themselves. In 1985 the Anglo-Irish Agreement granted the Irish Republic a role in Northern Ireland and committed the British to protect the rights of both Protestants and Catholics, and to prevent discrimination. It reinforced the principle of majority consent for any changes in the status of Northern Ireland.

Another kind of intrareligious conflict, primarily domestic rather than international, has emerged in recent years. It is difficult to label, but generally pits forces of populism, social reform, and religious fundamentalism against established elites. For example, in 1981 Moslem fanatics assassinated President Anwar Sadat of Egypt, because they opposed his dealing with Israel and the secular character of the Egyptian state that Sadat promoted. The broader fundamentalist and populist movement is not always violent. In Egypt members have also sought to provide basic community services. By 1987 they had established 3,000 medical clinics and 6,000 schools.

Within Christianity the **liberation theory** of Latin America is a somewhat equivalent phenomenon. After the Vatican II Council of 1962–1965 gave greater autonomy to local bishops on social and economic issues, a Catholic social activism emerged at local levels (Macridis 1986). "Base communities," formed around local parishes to serve community religious, economic, and social needs, are one manifestation of this. They organize collective self-help efforts among the poor and seek broader social system change on behalf of the disadvantaged. In Brazil the movement mushroomed in the 1980s to 100,000 Christian base communities with 3 million members (Durning 1989, 10). In both the Middle East and Latin America, these religious movements, which often have interstate linkages and outside support, are responding to needs that the states and societies have failed to meet, especially among the poor.

It would be possible to list and discuss many more examples of the interaction of religion and domestic or world politics. Consider the growth of fundamentalist parties within Israel and the refusal of many within them to negotiate about the establishment of a Palestinian state on the West Bank (which they call Judea and Samaria). Or consider the additional animosity between the United States and the former U.S.S.R. engendered by the sentiment of many in the United States, including some in leadership, who felt that the battle was between Christianity and godless communism. Let us turn our attention now to ideologies.

UNIVERSALISM

Religion is sometimes a nationalistic force that seeks to define the boundaries of the community and to establish control within those boundaries (as with the Sikhs in India), sometimes a universal philosophy (consider the Christian missionaries), and still at other times a call for community reform (as in the case of liberation theology). In this section we focus specifically on universal philosophies, and although religious movements sometimes are universalistic, the universalisms of greatest importance today are secular, political **ideologies**.[9]

> A political ideology is a system of beliefs that explains and justifies a preferred political order, either existing or proposed, and offers a strategy (institutions, processes, programs) for its attainment.[10]

We should distinguish ideologies from philosophies. "'Philosophy' means literally love of wisdom" (Macridis 1986, 3). The theories of philosophy help us understand, whereas the strategies and goals of ideology propel us into action. Unfortunately, the distinction is not always so clear in practice. What constitutes a philosophy for one person, such as socialism, may be a call to arms for another. The distinction becomes blurred because ideologies invariably draw on philosophies for understandings of human nature, the relationship between the individual and the group, and the proper character of political authority.

Realists agree on the inappropriateness of basing the application of power on universalism—whether religious or secular:

> The Wars of Religion have shown that the attempt to impose one's own religion as the only true one upon the rest of the world is as futile as it is costly. A century of almost unprecedented bloodshed, devastation, and barbarization was needed to convince the contestants that the two religions could live together in mutual toleration. The two political religions of our time have taken the place of the two great

[9]We should not ignore economic ideologies. Goldstein (1988, 1989) argues that U.S. commitment to free trade in manufactures represents the victory in the 1930s of one competing set of ideas, now enshrined in institutional structure and law.

[10]Herbert Waltzer's definition cited in Foster and Edington (1985, 34); see also Macridis (1986, 2–4). Hagopian (1988) makes another definitional distinction, between ideologies and ideals. He argues that democracy, socialism, and nationalism are ideals, not ideologies, and that specific ideologies (such as anarchism, communism, and liberalism) interpret them in different ways.

Christian denominations of the sixteenth and seventeenth centuries. Will the political religions of our time need the lesson of the Thirty Years' War, or will they rid themselves in time of the universalistic aspirations that inevitably issue in inconclusive war? (Morgenthau 1973, 542)

That is a prescriptive, not a descriptive statement—*in reality*, the commitment to universalistic idealisms underlies a considerable portion of interstate behavior, and realists often unjustifiably ignore that reality.

HISTORIC UNIVERSALISM

Religions have often taken on the character of universalistic ideologies. Islam and Christianity were both aggressive belief systems during the many periods of Islamic expansion, the Christian crusades, the religious wars in Europe, and the imperial epochs.

One of the early secular ideologies was that of the French Revolution. Although that revolution was in part nationalistic and therefore exclusively French, it was also universalistic. It offered the promise to peoples throughout Europe that governments could be ruled by the people rather than by sovereigns, that social justice could be an aim of government, and that the rationalist ideals of the Enlightenment could guide the application of law. Napoleon's armies initially went abroad to defend the revolution against the efforts by the Prussians and Austrians to take advantage of French weakness during the unrest. They used propaganda decrees, however, to assure foreign peoples that France stood behind their efforts to overthrow monarchies (Garraty and Gay 1981, 769). Although Napoleon often installed monarchies in client states (relying heavily on his own relatives), he also brought the Napoleonic legal code and the revolutionary ideals of liberty, equality, and fraternity. The French Revolution thus gave rise to a secular and universalistic ideology that posed a grave threat to the monarchies of Europe.

In general, peace will not be easily found in a world with a revolutionary, expansionist, universalistic power, whether that power is Republican France in a world of monarchies, the Marxist U.S.S.R. in a world of capitalist states, or Islamic Iran in a world dominated by Christian states.

MODERN UNIVERSALISM: SOVIET THREAT AND U.S. RESPONSE

After World War II a debate raged concerning the degree to which the U.S.S.R. was a traditional state and the extent to which an expansionist, universalistic Marxism dominated it. The correct characterization was critical, because it determined whether a sphere of influence could satisfy it, or whether only a world remade in its image would sate it.

For example, at the end of World War II the Soviet armies that had defeated the Germans remained in much of Eastern and Central Europe as occupying forces. They supported the installation of Communist regimes with leaderships thoroughly subservient to Moscow. The West faced the question of whether these were the actions of a traditional state or were the manifestation of aggressive universalism.

The interpretation of Soviet behavior as that of a traditional state rested primarily on the relative absence of natural boundaries to Russia and the constant struggles that an exposed position has caused (well before the arrival of the Communists and Marxist philosophy). Russia reacted to its vulnerable position by creating buffers around it, either by incorporating other peoples into the empire or by establishing client states. According to this view, the Soviet expansion into Eastern Europe after World War II was not significantly different, merely reflecting the lesson of the Nazi invasion that even more extensive buffers were necessary.

The universalistic interpretation of Soviet behavior gained support in the interwar period. Lenin wrote that "As long as capitalism and socialism exist, we cannot live in peace: in the end, one or the other will triumph—a funeral dirge will be sung either over the Soviet Republic or over world capitalism" (Schlesinger 1967, 47). In 1919 the Soviet Union founded the Third International—the Comintern—to coordinate and control the Communist parties around the world from headquarters in Moscow (Macridis 1986, 132–134). Initially thirty-five parties joined, and the total climbed to near sixty by 1939 and the outbreak of World War II. Lenin subjected all members to twenty-one conditions. These included: all Communist parties in the world supported the U.S.S.R., all accepted "democratic centralism," all rejected pacifists and pacifism, all undertook to aid revolutionary movements of the colonial peoples, and all were to establish underground organizations and be ready for illegal activities.

These Communist parties accepted dramatic changes of policy under direction from Moscow. In 1928 the Soviet Union declared socialist parties to be the primary enemies of communism and forbade cooperation with them (Macridis 1986, 134). In 1935, however, Moscow ordered acceptance of Socialist parties and other democratic parties in "popular front" alliances against the hated Nazis. Then in 1939, the U.S.S.R. reversed course again and signed a "nonaggression" pact with Nazi Germany.

Following World War II, the Soviets established in 1947 the Communist Information Bureau (Cominform) to organize control over the Communist countries and parties of Europe. The nine members were the U.S.S.R., Yugoslavia, Bulgaria, Romania, Hungary, Poland, Czechoslovakia, France, and Italy. Its organization was based on assumptions that

> (a) war with "imperialism"—notably the United States—was inevitable; (b) the Soviet Union—the fatherland of revolution—was being encircled by the "imperialists"; and (c) all Communist parties should continue by all possible means to defend the Soviet Union. (Macridis 1986, 135)

As in religions, schisms and heresies began to develop within communism. Albania did not join Cominform. Moscow expelled Yugoslavia in 1948 because President Tito defied Soviet supremacy. Stalin died in 1953, and the Cominform dissolved in 1956.

Under the leadership of Nikita Khrushchev the Soviets tried again for some sort of global Marxist unity through a conference of eighty-one Communist parties in December 1960. Although they held the meetings secretly, details of substantial conflicts emerged. The Chinese accused Khrushchev of revisionism in his condemnation of Stalin. Various European Communist parties, in coming to the defense of Khrushchev, carried revisionism even further by "updating" Lenin's thought, rejecting the notion of the "dictatorship of proletariat," and suggesting reconciliation with Social Democrats (Crankshaw 1978).

The Chinese leadership later harshly criticized the general-secretary for backing down in the face of the American "paper tiger" during the Cuban Missile Crisis (Stoessinger 1986, 55). Militarized border disputes actually erupted in 1963 between the two powers in Sinkiang and Mongolia. In 1964, the Chinese exploded their first nuclear bomb, announcing a capability that sealed their independence from the Soviets.

Various domestic and foreign policy failures, including the break with China and the withdrawal of missiles from Cuba, led the party leadership to depose Khrushchev and install Leonid Brezhnev in 1964. The Brezhnev leadership orchestrated the invasion of Czechoslovakia in 1968 and the overthrow of the Czech reformist regime. It simultaneously announced the Brezhnev Doctrine, which declared the right of the U.S.S.R. to eliminate threats to "socialism" in any state. Although such action could be consistent with a spheres-of-influence orientation, that leadership also increased military and other aid to Egypt, Syria, Vietnam, Algeria, Angola, Somalia, and Ethiopia. In 1979 the Soviet Union invaded Afghanistan. A substantial domestic arms buildup had continued throughout the 1970s, despite parity with, and even superiority to, the United States in many categories of weaponry. Many in the West interpreted these actions to be those of an aggressive universalism.

Brezhnev died in 1982, and brief periods of leadership by Yuri Andropov and Konstantin Chernenko followed. Neither had time, energy, nor perhaps inclination to reorient Soviet politics substantially. In 1985, however, the party selected Mikhail Gorbachev as general-secretary. He held many summit meetings with U.S. presidents Reagan and Bush. He greatly accelerated negotiations on arms control (see Chapter 6) and signed an Intermediate Nuclear Forces (INF) treaty with President Reagan in 1987, eliminating an entire class of nuclear weapons. He initiated selected unilateral troop and tank withdrawals from Eastern Europe, and began to reduce domestic arms spending. His leadership withdrew all forces from Afghanistan and scaled back various foreign commitments, including those in Africa. The Soviet Union dissolved in 1991.[11] Not surprisingly, the relative strength of the traditional power image has increased dramatically.

Some in the West revised their portrait of the Soviets well before the reforms of the 1980s and the collapse of the union. By 1967 Arthur Schlesinger was able to document a revisionist school of historians who were rewriting history about the origins of the cold war. He contrasted two interpretations:

[11]Those few who retain the latter image can point out that Lenin's New Economic Policy in 1920 ushered in an era of greatly improved relations with the West, denationalization of industry, and even articles in *Pravda* celebrating Soviet millionaires (Stoessinger 1986, 45). It obviously did not last.

The orthodox American view, as originally set forth by the American government and as reaffirmed until recently by most American scholars, has been that the Cold War was the brave and essential response of free men to communist aggression....Thoughtful observers (a phrase meant to exclude those who speak in Dullese about the unlimited evil of godless, atheistic, militant communism) concluded that classical Russian imperialism and Pan-Slavism, compounded after 1917 by Leninist messianism, confronted the West at the end of the Second World War with an inexorable drive for domination.

The revisionist thesis is very different. In its extreme form, it is that, after the death of Franklin Roosevelt and the end of the Second World War, the United States deliberately abandoned the wartime policy of collaboration and, exhilarated by the possession of the atomic bomb, undertook a course of aggression of its own designed to expel all Russian influence from Eastern Europe and to establish democratic-capitalist states on the very border to the Soviet Union. (Schlesinger 1967, 23–25)

Schlesinger's analysis forces us to consider as well the nature of the U.S. approach to the world after World War II. Were Americans universalistic? Roosevelt's thinking explicitly contrasted the traditional "sphere-of-influence" view of security with a Wilsonian commitment to universal international organization. Roosevelt had been a member of Wilson's subcabinet and had campaigned for the League of Nations. He, and even more his secretary of state, Cordell Hull, rejected a postwar world redivided into spheres of influence. Moreover, a universalistic outlook was widespread in the United States: Other advisers, much of public opinion, and even many opposition Republicans (for instance, John Foster Dulles, who was to become Eisenhower's secretary of state) thought that the United States must struggle against British and Soviet desires for a return to spheres of influence. They thought that the United States should be involved in decisions throughout the world. There were some sphere-of-influence proponents in the United States, most notably the famous diplomat George Kennan, ambassador to the U.S.S.R. and developer of the **containment** doctrine. He argued that the United States should leave the Soviets alone in their sphere but deny them any possibility of expansion. In time, he argued, internal changes would make the country a more hospitable international partner.[12] It is easy to see how the Soviets could have interpreted the system of alliances all along their borders not as containment but as instruments of universalistic aggression.

In the West it is now common to claim that "the cold war is over, and we won." A globalist idealism, with its image of interstate cooperation within a framework of institutions such as the United Nations, has gained renewed strength. The Nobel Prize Committee even honored the United Nations Peace Keeping Forces with the Nobel Peace Prize in 1988. From one viewpoint, this resurgent idealism is a triumph of reason and humanity.[13] From another, it is perhaps a premature declaration of victory by a Western democratic and capitalist universalism.

[12]In 1989, he argued that the United States needs to turn its primary attention from the Soviet Union to two critical problems: the control of nuclear weapons and the global environment (Kennan 1989).

[13]Francis Fukuyama (1989) went so far as to ask whether humanity has reached "the end of history." He argued that the victory of Western liberalism has ended the historic clash of universalistic ideals.

IDEALIST CHALLENGES TO REALISM

Idealisms pose individual and collective challenges to realism at a wide variety of levels. Whereas realism draws our attention to states as the only really important global actors, idealisms insist that a variety of communities are more fundamentally central to human interests and that states exist in large part to serve those communities (sometimes serving them very poorly or even disrupting them). Whereas realists draw our attention to state interests in security, involving the maintenance and enhancement of power, idealists refocus our primary attention on issues of group identity with associated inclusion and exclusion, and on the proper organization of the community. Realists tell us that states rationally pursue their security interests. Idealists make clear that depending upon the ideals that motivate state leaderships, those leaderships may pursue dramatically different definitions of interests and do so in manners that other potential or actual leaderships, pursuing other interests, will not always label rational.

In short, attention to idealisms can lead us to see the simple model of realism itself as a prescriptive "ideal," rather than the realistic description of the world it presents itself to be. A focus on idealisms does not, however, offer a comparably simple model in place of the realist one. Instead, it offers a much fuzzier image of world politics as the interaction of overlapping and discrete, of complementary and competitive ideals and the communities they define.

The remainder of this chapter considers two aspects of world politics in which idealisms either augment or challenge the realist model. First, we look at selected efforts of various idealisms to capture or fundamentally alter the territory or government of states. Second, we investigate mechanisms by which community development may move political organization beyond the state.

TO CAPTURE OR CREATE A STATE: TERRORISM

In Chapter 4 we briefly reported one historic view of how states come into being, namely, through the processes of guaranteeing some security to their citizens (and charging for it), a process that frequently required war making to consolidate territory. That description drew our attention to the search for security, but ignored any relationship between state building and community. In that model, leadership or governance changes reflect primarily the superior ability to deliver security.

It may be true that historic state building preceded community formation. In the modern era, however, the creation of states, the redefinition of borders, and changes in governance seem more often to reflect the pressures of various idealisms. One manifestation of this, as we have already discussed, is the fact that most modern wars are civil wars. Another is the prevalence of terrorism.[14]

Terrorism is not just a modern phenomenon. In the years A.D. 6–135, Jewish nationalists, calling themselves Zealots, maintained a terrorist campaign against the Romans then ruling Palestine, and against their Greek and Jewish collaborators. After a Zealot uprising in A.D. 6, the Romans crucified 2,000 Jews (Schlagheck 1988,

[14]Kegley (1990) explores the characteristics, causes, and control of terrorism.

16). Zealots used violence, especially assassination, to disrupt Roman rule. Targets were unpredictable, but generally public so that word and fear would spread. One technique was to use small daggers against Roman officials in crowds. After such an attack the terrorists would then disappear into the crush. The Romans took increasingly strong measures to stamp out the decentralized movements, finally deciding after A.D. 135 to expel all Jews from Palestine. That created the scattered community of Jews in exile, the Diaspora, which sought for two millennia to return to its homeland.

The techniques of **terrorism** are similar today, and definitions of it generally list several characteristics. Violence, especially against humans, is key. Forty-eight percent of terrorist attacks in 1988 were bombings, and 28 percent were arson—in both cases the target is often human life, and the victims are indiscriminate (U.S. State Department 1989, viii). Publicity is necessary. Terrorism becomes a kind of theater, in which the need for media attention and the global spotlight is great. Should the media or public become inattentive or jaded, the level of violence must escalate. Unpredictability is important, as are symbolic targets for the violence. Terrorists seek to engender fear and reaction, especially overreaction, by their opponents. They want adherents to flock to their cause—they wish to sharply define community boundaries and to bring within them those who remain ambivalent.

Terrorism is the weapon of the weak idealist against strong states and their governments. Nationalists undertake a large portion of international terrorism. In terms of our earthquake analogy, terrorism often reflects a pent-up and growing nationalism for which the state fails to provide any release. Among others, the most important national groups with terrorist factions today are Palestinians, Sikhs, Basques (in Spain and France), and Armenians (originally concentrated in Turkey but now dispersed in still another diaspora). In the case of the Irish Republican Army (IRA) in Northern Ireland, nationalist and religious motivations interact. Sometimes the motivation for terrorism is primarily religious, for instance that of the Shiite groups operating loosely under the guidance of Iran—including the Islamic *Jihad* (*Hizbollah*), which in 1983 killed 241 American marines and 56 French marines in a suicidal attack in Beirut with bomb-loaded truck. Still other terrorist groups have ideological motivations. These have included the Baader-Meinhof Gang (or Red Army Faction) and the Red Brigades, both leftist organizations operating primarily in Germany and Italy.

Through the 1980s, the trends in terrorism were disturbing. In 1968, 124 incidents occurred globally, but in 1988 the total reached 672 (Figure 8.2). The focal point for nearly half of the incidents in recent years has been the Middle East. Western Europe is the second most seriously afflicted region, followed by Latin America and Asia. Despite the reality that publics in Europe and the United States view the trend with alarm, terrorism caused only 8,009 deaths between 1968 and 1991. Although this is not an unimportant total, by comparison, 21,000 Americans died from home accidents in 1990 alone, and 46,300 died in automobile accidents. Moreover, the 1990s began with a dip in terrorism—the PLO renounced it and the former Communist states quit supporting it.

Some states have supported terrorists in a manner analogous to the superpower use of proxy forces. The United States has at one time or another identified

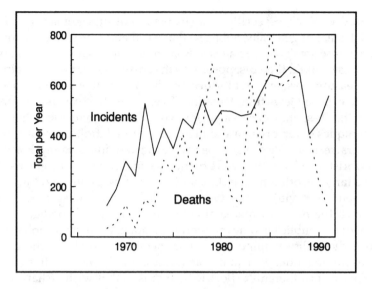

FIGURE 8.2 Global Terrorist Episodes and Deaths
Source: Data courtesy of the U.S. Department of State, Office of the
Ambassador at Large for Counterterrorism, 1992.

Libya, Syria, Iran, and Cuba as countries that supported terrorists with financial contributions, training, and even leadership. Several Communist Eastern
European countries also gave support. Terrorist-supporting countries are too
weak to directly confront the United States or major European powers (except
on their own soil, as in the Iranian hostage crisis), making covert support for
terrorism abroad a seemingly viable alternative. The great powers have difficulty retaliating because the terrorist group, rather than the state sponsor,
normally claims responsibility. In one exception, the United States bombed
Libya in April 1986, following a terrorist bombing of a West Berlin discotheque
for which President Reagan said there was "irrefutable" proof of Libyan planning and assistance in its execution.

Lesser powers have long argued that some use of force against them by the
great powers is, in essence, **state terrorism**. For instance, in the absence of a
declaration of war, the United States mined the harbors of Nicaragua in 1984. The
International Court of Justice declared the action illegal. Because terrorism is
sometimes defined in terms of the use of illegitimate or illegal force, the accusation
that such covert military action by great powers is state terrorism carries weight.
In such examples, too, force is in essence an instrument selected from weakness.
Covert behavior indicates an unwillingness to accept the brunt of domestic or
international public criticism that would result from overt force.

Nearly all of these examples of violence, even those performed in the name
of the state, can be attributed to some kind of idealism. This discussion should not
end, however, by leaving the impression that all idealism is bad. Even hard-core

realists often have their favorites; one person's terrorist is another's freedom fighter or patriot. Instead, we should conclude by noting once again that a simple model of power politics at the state level is inadequate to a full understanding of world politics.

BEYOND THE STATE? GLOBAL COMMUNITY BUILDING

Terrorism may change the borders or governance of one or more states. It constitutes an important aspect of world politics that lies outside of the basic realist understanding. Nonetheless, it does not threaten the existence of the state system or its central importance in world politics, and thus it is possible to augment realism with an understanding of this phenomenon of nationalist, religious, and even universalist idealisms.

In contrast, the ultimate vision of globalists is the creation of a global community capable of restraining state action and ensuring peace. Many globalists have argued that a process akin to nation building might proceed at the global level and precede any substantial development of global institutions. The formation of both Germany and Italy, which had come to think of themselves as nations before the development of governmental structures, provides something of a precedent for a global "nation-building" dynamic.

What were the forces that created nations historically? Among other factors was the development of common languages, aided in turn by advances in printing and the spread of literacy. Before the thirteenth century, the Fancien dialect, which came to be the root of modern French, was spoken only in a relatively small area around Paris (Deutsch 1966, 43). The invention by Guttenberg of movable-type printing in 1436–1437 facilitated the adoption of selected dialects by broader populations; it would have been almost impossible to accommodate the wide variety of European dialects with individual hand-written languages. Deutsch more generally emphasized the importance of communication capabilities in nation building. Such capabilities may or may not require a common language, but do require common concepts, shared experiences, and an essentially similar culture.

Is there potentially a comparable process occurring globally (or through-out much of it)? Many point to the infatuation of young people around the world with Coca-Cola, blue jeans, and rock music, to increasingly extensive tourism, to the global sharing of movies and television, and even to the spread of English into the role of a common language, as evidence of an incipient (and perhaps insipid) global culture. The rapidity with which global contacts are exploding is remarkable. For instance, international telephone traffic was about 3.5 billion minutes in 1985 and reached 19 billion in 1991. Global culture, however, would consist of a great deal more than a veneer of pop culture; it would require similar attitudes toward a wide range of social and political institutions. Contacts like North-South tourism often create tensions among people rather than good feeling and understanding. For the latter to be the case, evidence suggests that contacts must be on the basis of relative equality, and benefits must be mutual (Russett and Starr 1985, 423).[15]

Although extensive community building on a global scale is at best a remote prospect, it is not unrealistic to argue that something of the kind is going on now at a regional level. Karl Deutsch defined a **security community** as an international region in which one can identify the development of "institutions and practices strong enough and widespread enough to assure, for a 'long' time, dependable expectations of 'peaceful change' among its population" (Deutsch and others 1957, 2).[16] Canada and the United States constitute such a security community and have not felt the need in nearly a century to defend the long border between them. More generally, the Organization for Economic Cooperation and Development has come to be such a security community. Organized in September 1961 to promote economic and social welfare, it now has twenty-four member countries: most of the states of Western Europe, plus Australia, Canada, Japan, New Zealand, and the United States. There has not been a single war among organization members since 1945.

The existence of a common external threat to these countries from the Soviet Union and its allies certainly *helps* explain their peacefulness.[17] Chapter 7 proposed the most convincing explanation, however—namely, that democracies are not inclined to fight one another—a rule that characterizes the last 200 years, not just the last forty-five. Sharing stable democratic governments may provide a basis for communication and require considerable societal and cultural similarity. Although the citizens of France and Germany have certainly not forgotten the long series of brutal wars in which they and their ancestors fought, they now appear to share the "dependable expectations" for peaceful resolution of differences that are the basis for a security community.

GLOBAL GOVERNANCE NORMS: THE SPREAD OF DEMOCRACY

Given the potential importance of this factor, it is useful to review the progress of democracy globally:

> What could reasonably be called a democratic political system at the national level of government first appeared in the United States in the early nineteenth century. During the following century democratic regimes gradually emerged in northern and western Europe, in the British dominions, and in a few countries in Latin America. This trend, which Alexis de Tocqueville had foreseen in 1835 and which James Bryce documented in 1920, appeared to be irreversible if not necessarily universal. (Huntington 1985, 255)

Nonetheless, following World War I, the war to make the world "safe for democracy," democracies fell during the 1920s and 1930s in Germany, Italy, Austria, Poland, the Baltic states, Spain, Portugal, Greece, Argentina, Brazil, and Japan. It took World War II to restore it to many of those countries, and to set the stage for its

---

[15]Some idealistic schemes suggest purposefully spreading shared values and attitudes. Falk (1975) proposes raising the global population consciousness that humanity cannot maintain security and other values in the existing state-centric world and that drastic change is needed. Mobilizing mass pressure upon elites to build global institutions is to follow.

[16]For a review of concepts and theory see Puchala (1981).

[17]Russett and Starr (1985, 416-437) review several alternative and partial explanations.

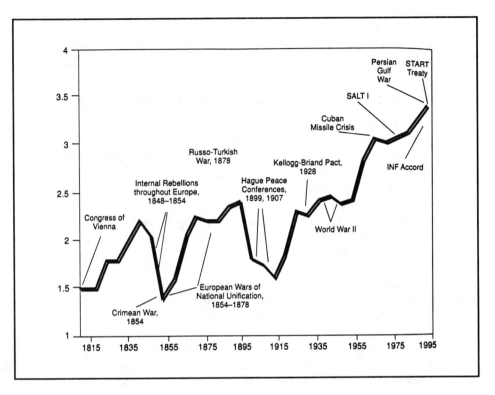

FIGURE 8.3   Legal Prohibition of War, 1815–1988
Source: Based on The Transnational Rules Indicators Project (TRIP), as described in Charles W. Kegley, Jr., and Gregory A. Raymond, *When Trust Breaks Down* (Columbia, S.C.: University of South Carolina Press, 1990). Courtesy of Charles W. Kegley, Jr., and Gregory A. Raymond.

extension to the new countries of India and Israel. Between the early 1950s and the 1980s, there was relative stability in the numbers of humans living under democracy, with movement both into and out of the category. In the 1980s, a substantial transformation of Latin American countries (including Argentina, Brazil, and Chile) from military rule to democratic rule held out the hope that democracy was achieving a new plateau. So, too, did the dramatic transformations of Communist regimes toward multiparty democracies in Eastern Europe. Yet debt, slow economic growth, and related crises in those countries could reverse many gains. For instance, in 1992 a coup by the president eliminated democracy in Peru.

There is other evidence that there is a growing community of opposition to war, especially among the Organization for Economic Development and Cooperation (OECD) countries.[18] One study of international legal texts from 1815 until 1992

[18]Although the emphasis here has been on the potential contribution of mutual democracy to pacific behavior, the OECD example of a security community suggests that the key factor could be extensive trade. Domke (1988), without focusing on democracy-democracy interaction, finds that political openness does not by itself contribute to peaceful orientation, but that extent of trade does; the two variables together become more powerful than trade alone.

evaluated the permissibility of war, creating an index that ranged from 1.0 (war is generally legal) to 4.0 (war is generally illegal) (Figure 8.3). Although there have been many periods of regressive shift toward the acceptance of war, the clear trend has moved against war. In 1992 the index value had climbed to about 3.3.

GLOBAL IDENTITY NORMS: PROTECTION OF HUMAN RIGHTS

Along with the global spread of democracy and the accompanying emergence of security communities in which the probability of interstate violence seems very low, there has been a spread in the attention to individual human rights. The international human rights regime has evolved slowly, but generally in the direction of what most would consider moral progress. Consider, for instance, slavery. Philosophers from Aristotle through John Locke (1632–1704), one of the fathers of modern liberal thought, justified enslaving other human beings (Ray 1988, 1). Great Britain, however, prohibited the slave trade in 1807 and ended slavery in territories under its control in 1833. The Civil War of the United States ended slavery in 1865, and Brazil abolished it in 1888. Almost certainly, economic advance and ongoing social mobilization have contributed to the greater acceptance of the dignity of the individual, to the abolition of slavery (enshrined in a 1926 interstate convention), and to progress on other human rights issues.[19]

Perhaps the most popular human rights issue of the twentieth century has been the right to self-determination of peoples. Defined in many league and UN documents, resolutions, and declarations, it affirms the right of nations to control their own destinies within their own states. The central thrust of efforts to establish and enforce this principle has been aimed at dismantlement of colonial empires.

When we think of human rights, however, we more often focus on the rights of the individual. What are **human rights**? The most powerful international statement was that of the Universal Declaration of Human Rights in 1948. The declaration is comprehensive, and besides reiterating the illegality of slavery and the right to a nationality, includes a right to privacy; a right to emigrate from and return to one's country; protection against arbitrary arrest; a right to impartial trial; a right to ownership of property; freedom of thought, conscience, and religion; freedom of opinion and expression; freedom of peaceful assembly and association; a right to education; a right to leisure; and a right to an adequate standard of living. Various UN covenants and conventions during the last forty years have spelled out many of these rights and freedoms.

Many Western states have been especially uncomfortable with the inclusion of various economic entitlements (such as a right to leisure and an adequate standard of living) with political rights and freedoms. It is partly for this reason that U.S. ratification of these measures has been slow. The United States did not even ratify the Genocide Convention (formulated by the UN in 1948) until 1986, and it has failed to ratify most other international human rights conventions (Table 8.5).

[19]Press reports regularly remind us that slavery may be illegal globally, but remains a reality. By one estimate there are 100,000 slaves in Mauritania (*Newsweek*, May 4, 1992, 32).

TABLE 8.5
U.N. Human Rights Conventions

Convention (grouped by subject)	Year Opened for Ratification	Year Entered Into Force	Number of Ratifications, Accessions, Acceptances (April 1986)
General Human Rights			
International Covenant on Civil and Political Rights	1966	1976	78
Optional Protocol to the International Covenant on Civil and Political Rights	1966	1976	31
International Covenant on Economic, Social and Cultural Rights	1966	1976	80
Racial Discrimination			
International Convention on the Elimination of All Forms of Racial Discrimination	1965	1969	122
International Convention on the Suppression and Punishment of the Crime of Apartheid	1973	1976	70
International Convention against Apartheid in Sports	1985	—	—
Rights of Women			
Convention on the Political Rights of Women	1952	1954	88
Convention on the Nationality of Married Women	1957	1958	55
Convention on Consent to Marriage, Minimum Age for Marriage and Registration of Marriages	1962	1964	39
Convention on the Elimination of All Forms of Discrimination against Women	1979	1981	72
Slavery and Related Matters			
Slavery Convention of 1926, as amended in 1953	1953	1955	77
Protocol Amending the 1926 Slavery Convention	1953	1955	50
Supplementary Convention on the Abolition of Slavery the Slave Trade, and Institutions and Practices Similar to Slavery	1956	1957	101
Convention for the Suppression of the Traffic in Persons and the Exploitation of the Prostitution of Others	1949	1951	49
Refugees and Stateless Persons			
Convention Relating to the Status of Refugees	1951	1954	95
Protocol Relating to the Status of Refugees	1966	1967	96
Convention Relating to the Status of Stateless Persons	1954	1960	30
Convention on the Reduction of Statelessness	1961	1975	11
Other			
Convention on the Prevention and Punishment of the Crime of Genocide	1948	1951	92
Convention on the International Right of Correction	1952	1962	11
Convention on the Non-Applicability of Statutory Limitations to War Crimes and Crimes against Humanity	1968	1970	24
Convention against Torture and Other Cruel, Inhuman or Degrading Treatment or Punishment	1984	—	—

Source: Robert E. Riggs and Jack C. Plano, *The United Nations* (Chicago: The Dorsey Press, 1989), 245. Reprinted by permission of Brooks/Cole Publishing Company Pacific Grove, CA 93950.

Data: "Human Rights International Instruments: Signatures, Ratifications, Accessions, etc., 1 September, 1983," U.N. Document ST/HR/4/Rev. 5; Richard B. Lillich, ed., *International Human Rights Instruments* (Buffalo, N.Y.: William S. Hein, 1985); and *Department of State Bulletin* 84–86, nos. 2087–2110 (June 1984–June 1986).

The East-West conflict also politicized human rights issues. Western states proceeded cautiously in endorsing multilateral human rights measures because they believed the East viewed them as propaganda instruments, to be ignored internally, whereas Communist states simultaneously trumpeted any violations in the more open West. For example, the U.S.S.R. and other socialist states consistently and actively supported the self-determination principle, in part because they could use it to embarrass and harass the colonial powers of the Western world. Ironically, however, that principle undercuts any multinational state in which national subgroups struggle for autonomy, and the Soviet Union has proved to be this principle's victim. With respect to political and social rights of the individual, it has been the West, rather than the former U.S.S.R., that has led the movement toward identification and acceptance of the basic principles of human rights. Although Communist states did not hesitate to use issues of individual human rights for criticism of governments in South Africa, Chile, or Israel, they found themselves increasingly on the defensive concerning enforcement of individual human rights.

The signing by thirty-five countries in 1975 of the Final Act of the Conference on Security and Cooperation in Europe, better known as the Helsinki Agreement, intensified the pressure on the East. Although that agreement committed the West to accept the boundaries created by World War II (the territorial issue again), it also bound the Eastern signatories to respect human rights and fundamental freedoms. The Final Act contained agreements in three groupings or "baskets" (Riggs and Plano 1988, 172):

1. Security, including confidence-building measures.
2. Economics, science, technology, and the environment.
3. Human rights, culture, and information exchange.

Signatories agreed to regular review conferences to extend the process.

Each of the review conferences (the second in Madrid from 1980–1983 and the third in Vienna from 1986–1989) proved embarrassing for the East, as the Western states detailed Communist human rights violations.[20] Citizen groups formed in Eastern Europe to monitor the observance of human rights and to assist the West in drawing attention to violations: Helsinki Watch in Moscow and Charter 77 in Czechoslovakia. Although Communist states had long harassed, jailed, and exiled members for their activities, the groups maintained ties with Western media and continued to be outspoken. In justifying their suppression of the human rights groups and their poor records on human rights, the Communist countries fell back on the state-centric legal principles of the sovereign equality of states and the noninterference in the domestic affairs of other states. But the status of these human rights groups improved greatly in 1989 and 1990. The West even agreed to hold a human rights review conference in Moscow in 1991.

Several international organizations form the backbone of the evolving human rights regime. These include Amnesty International, Human Rights Watch,

---

[20]The United States Department of State prepares semiannual reviews on the performance of the Eastern states on issues in each of the first three baskets. See, for example, *Implementation of Helsinki Final Act*, Special Report No. 182 (October 1, 1988–March 31, 1989).

the International Commission of Jurists, the International League for Human Rights, the International Federation for Human Rights, and the World Council of Churches (Riggs and Plano 1988, 247). They work actively with the media to draw global attention to violations such as political arrests, instances of torture, and the activities of death squads. Amnesty International, formed in London in 1961, is probably the best known, and it received the 1977 Nobel Peace Prize. Human Rights Watch, established in 1978, is an umbrella organization for national groups like Helsinki Watch. Although such organizations hold no true enforcement power, there is little doubt that they have influenced governments. Unfortunately, violations of human rights remain pervasive. For instance, in its review of global human rights for 1987, Amnesty International claimed that eighty-two countries tortured or mistreated prisoners, and that eighty-five states held prisoners of conscience (Amnesty International 1988).

The strength of the global human rights movement nonetheless supports the globalist contention that a global community is developing:

> Carried to its logical extreme, the doctrine of human rights and duties under international law is subversive of the whole principle that mankind should be organized as a society of sovereign states. For, if the rights of each man can be asserted on the world political stage over and against the claims of his state...then the position of the state...has been subject to challenge....(Bull 1977, 152)

Were the author of that paragraph to rewrite it today, he would almost certainly change "mankind" to "humanity" and "each man" to "each human." The developing global community also increasingly seeks equal status for women and men.

CONCLUSION

The preceding chapter directed a relatively narrow and simultaneously quite friendly challenge to realism. While leaving intact the argument that states are the dominant actors in world politics, it questioned how unitary they can be, and how rationally they can behave in the light of domestic elements (a broad public, interest groups, and leaders with competing visions) that understand state interest in very different ways and strive to take the foreign policy of the country in very different directions. By considering alternative visions of leaders and by speculating on whether the behavior of democracies is systematically different than nondemocracies, however, it opened a crack for a wedge that mounts a much broader attack on realism.

This chapter used that wedge—the concepts of ideals and community. It sketched a very different map of the world than that of the state system, namely a complex global community system of nations, religious groupings, and ideological affinities. It described a very different basis for world politics than that of state interaction in the search for security, namely, struggles for identity and autonomy coupled with battles over the character of governance. In essence, however, the chapter has not so much rejected realism as supplemented it. We can begin to see the world as a complex interaction between state and community systems.

In that interaction we might even catch a glimpse of a theory of world politics in which changes in community systems drive changes in systems of political institutions. The breakdown of the community of Catholicism preceded the dissolution of the Holy Roman Empire and the formation of the modern state system (which, in turn, helped create a new community system of nations). National identities have dramatically transformed that state system since the end of the twentieth century. Because Gurr and Scarritt (1989) can identify 261 "numerically significant" nonsovereign peoples whose rights are at risk in current states, that transformation appears not yet complete. At the same time, apparently increasing acceptance around the world of some basic principles of identity (all humans are equal and have inherently equal rights) and of governance (democratic systems serve humans especially well) suggests possible growth of global community with new pressures for change in fundamental political institutions.

Ideas are powerful.[21] Identifications with communities and choices of approach to their governance motivate individuals to great efforts on behalf of those communities and approaches. They lead to attacks on the territorial definition of individual states, on the governance structures of those states, on the acceptability of immediately self-centered state behavior, and even on the legitimacy of the state system itself. Realists may, in turn, question the legitimacy of such motivations and the rationality of actions based on them, but they should not doubt the power of them. Ideas do have consequences.

---

[21]The contributors to Reich (1990) explore how community attachment to ideas can often explain U.S. political behavior better than can theories based on self-interest.

Chapter 9

REGIONAL AND GLOBAL INSTITUTION BUILDING

Simplified models help us understand complex phenomena. The basic realist portrayal of world politics (states acting rationally so as to maintain and enhance their security in the interstate system) helps us comprehend the constant jockeying for position by states in an environment of anarchy. States do not always behave as rational, unitary actors, however. Their behavior is shaped by an array of intrastate forces, including the personalities of leaders, the pressure of key social groups, and the character of the foreign policy decision process. Nor does maintenance and enhancement of security motivate all interstate behavior. Both leaders and followers pursue a variety of ideals. The last two chapters drew our attention to those inadequacies of the simple realist model. This chapter focuses on still another, the fact that states are not the only autonomous actors in world politics.

Important nonstate actors include individuals, groups, corporations, and international organizations. For instance, many individuals not playing official leadership roles have influenced the flow of international events. Bishop Desmond Tutu won the 1984 Nobel Peace Prize for his work in South Africa against apartheid, and he became a figure to which states around the world looked when evaluating appropriate sanctions against South Africa. After his release from prison in 1990, Nelson Mandela increasingly moved into that role. Near the top of anyone's list of internationally important individuals would be Mohandas Gandhi (the Mahatma or Great Soul), who energized the nonviolent struggle for Indian independence from Great Britain (successful in 1947).

This chapter focuses only on one category of nonstate actor, however, the international organization (like the United Nations). There has been a tremendous growth in such regional and global institutions. What are the reasons for such growth? Have international organizations begun to limit or even control the behavior of states? Those are the principal questions that frame this chapter. First, however, what is an international organization?

INTERNATIONAL ORGANIZATIONS

An **international organization** (IO) is a "formal arrangement transcending national boundaries that provides for the establishment of institutional machinery to facilitate cooperation among members in security, economic, social, or related fields" (Plano and Olton 1988, 416). IOs differ from each other on three dimensions: the building blocks of the institutions, their geographic scope, and their functions.

One class of IOs, **intergovernmental organizations** (IGOs), builds on states and their governments (Table 9.1). The United Nations, the World Bank, and NATO are IGOs. In contrast, **international nongovernmental organizations** (INGOs or NGOs) draw on individuals or associations for their membership. For instance, Amnesty International, Greenpeace, and the International Red Cross are INGOs. Both IGOs and INGOs have regularly scheduled meetings of representatives from their membership base (whether states, individuals, or associations) and a permanent secretariat. Although this book does not, some volumes argue that multinational corporations (MNCs), such as Exxon, General Motors, or Nestlé, are also INGOs.[1]

TABLE 9.1
A Classification of Intergovernmental Organizations (IGOs)

	Multiple Purpose	*Functional*
Universal	United Nations	United Nations Development Program International Civil Aviation Organization World Health Organization
Regional	Organization of American States Association of Southeast Asian Nations European Community Arab League	Asian Development Bank North Atlantic Treaty Organization Organization of Petroleum Exporting Companies

Universal IOs draw members from around the world. The United Nations and the Catholic church are essentially universal, although even these institutions fail to represent some parts of the world. **Regional IOs**, like NATO, seek only to draw on a limited geographic area.

The last major division of IOs differentiates among them by scope of function. **Multiple-purpose IOs**, like the United Nations, address a combination of security,

---

[1]Jacobson (1984) suggests that these should be a separate category, transnational organizations, because hierarchically structured bureaucracies organize the institutions. The distinction is fuzzy, however, since General Motors has elements of democratic structures (such as shareholder meetings), and Amnesty International has an influential international bureaucracy.

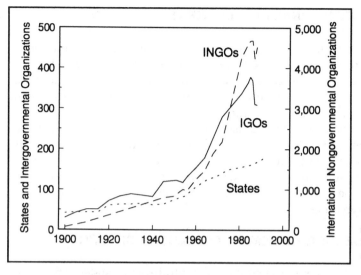

FIGURE 9.1 **International Actors**
Sources: Courtesy of J. David Singer and the Correlates of War Project: Union of International Organizations (UAI), *Yearbook of International Organizations* (Brussels: UAI, assorted years).

economic, environmental, or other needs of their members. **Functional IOs**, however, serve only specific functions. For instance, Amnesty International focuses on the treatment of individual civil rights by states, and the World Health Organization obviously emphasizes health.

Although the prevalence of international organizations is a recent phenomenon in world politics, there are many historic prototypes. For instance, the Delian League linked Greek city-states for all but twenty-six years between 478 and 338 B.C. Although sometimes little more than a tool of Athenian power, it was at other times a genuine military alliance. Another example is the Hanseatic League, which facilitated trade among North German towns between the eleventh and seventeenth centuries (Jacobson 1984, 8–9). A number of still-existing Catholic organizations can trace their origins to the early Middle Ages. For instance, the Canons Regular of Saint Augustine dates to about A.D. 400, and the Benedictine Confederation was established in 529 (Union of International Associations 1985, R1637).

Perhaps the first modern IO was the Central Commission for the Navigation of the Rhine, created at the Congress of Vienna to facilitate free navigation through the various political jurisdictions along the Rhine. In the count of Wallace and Singer (1970), there were forty-nine IGOs and more than 170 INGOs by 1914. IGOs require sovereign states (or largely autonomous units like the towns of the Hanseatic League) as bases, and therefore growth in their numbers accompanied that of the modern state system. In recent years, however, that numerical growth seems to have taken on a life of its own. By the early 1990s, there were nearly 400 IGOs and in excess of 4,600 INGOs (Figure 9.1).[2]

[2]These are not easy to count with precision, because definitions vary. The source of most totals is the *Yearbook of International Organizations*, Union of International Associations, Brussels. If IOs created by other IOs are included (a development that has gained momentum since the 1960s), the totals more than double. Bursts in the creation rate of these organizations occurred at the end of both world wars (Wallace and Singer 1970; see Jacobson 1984, 37).

UNDERSTANDINGS OF INSTITUTIONAL DEVELOPMENT

Regional and global institutional structures may evolve either because they serve needs for the states that allow and even encourage them to develop or because they serve the needs of the citizens of those states better than do the states themselves. In the former case, the new institutions pose little threat to states; in the latter case they may fundamentally threaten them.

This section investigates three dynamics underlying regional and global institutional development: collective security, federalism, and functionalism. The first is largely compatible with state control of the process; the second and third suggest movements beyond the state. We will then return to a consideration of the United Nations and the European Community, evaluating their development in light of these three dynamics.

DAMPENING THE SECURITY DILEMMA: COLLECTIVE SECURITY

Collective security accepts the continued central role of states. The minor challenge it poses to realism lies in prescriptively pushing states beyond passive acceptance of global anarchy and reliance on self-help toward collective efforts to control anarchy.

The theory of collective security builds on an analysis of the security problem. Improved defensive military capability almost invariably raises offensive potential simultaneously. Thus when states attempt to guarantee their own security, they lessen the security of other states. We have more than once identified this collective predicament of states as the **security dilemma**. We have noted before that the security dilemma underlies arms races. When State A spends and builds in a defensive reaction to earlier gains in military capability by State B, State B feels compelled to react.

In essence each state is internalizing, or capturing for itself, the entire benefit of higher arms spending, while externalizing much of the cost of that spending. This suggests that a resolution of the dilemma requires somehow reducing, if possible even eliminating, the costs to other states of one's own military spending. How can that be done? Making the additional capability as clearly defensive as possible reduces costs for other states. Between 1988 and 1991 states of the former Warsaw Pact moved toward acceptance of the NATO argument that tanks are more clearly offensive than antitank weaponry; the Conventional Forces in Europe (CFE) treaty greatly reduced tank numbers, especially in the East.

No pattern of spending, no matter how nonprovocative, actually eliminates all costs to other states. An effective collective security agreement, however, could do so. A **collective security** arrangement theoretically guarantees that all states will act to restrain and punish any aggressor in the interstate system. If such an agreement were credible, State A would believe that the forces from three of the States B, C, D, and E would come to its defense in case of aggression from any one of them, thus making accretion of military strength in those states quite nonthreatening. Woodrow Wilson proposed such a system during World War I:

> There must now be, not a balance of power, not one powerful group of nations set off against another, but a single overwhelming group of nations who shall be the trustee of the peace of the world. (cited in Jacobson 1984, 143)

A collective security arrangement looks inward to punish wayward members of the state system (Riggs and Plano 1988, 124–125). Alliances, like NATO, sometimes call themselves collective security organizations to obtain the respectability that the term conveys. They are, however, outward-looking **collective defense** organizations, not collective security arrangements.[3]

The first global effort to create a collective security organization was the League of Nations in 1919. Article 16 of the League Covenant provided that boycotts and embargoes would be applied to aggressor states and authorized the council to recommend the use of collective force by member states should that be deemed necessary.

The machinery of the League of Nations did assist in preventing the escalation to warfare of border disputes between Albania and Yugoslavia in 1921, and between Greece and Bulgaria in 1925 (Brown 1987, 157). It failed in several other important cases, however. The League repudiated Japan's establishment of a puppet government in Manchuria in 1931, but Japan withdrew from the League rather than from Manchuria and suffered no sanctions. In 1933 an Italian bombardment of the Greek island of Corfu failed to elicit League punishment. In 1935 the council declared Italy's invasion of Ethiopia illegal. For the first time in history, most countries of the world embargoed arms and "strategic materials" to an aggressor. Fifty-two countries participated, and the action quickly reduced Italian trade by nearly 50 percent (Riggs and Plano 1988, 10). The embargo, however, was porous and exempted oil, so it did not significantly weaken the Italians. By this time the French and the British were more interested in building a coalition against Nazi Germany, and the League withdrew sanctions after eight months. The full-scale Japanese invasion of China in 1937–1938 elicited practically no League response.

There are several reasons for the failure of collective security to work during this period. One was the failure of the United States to join the League and associate its power with the principle. A second was the complete unacceptability of the World War I settlement to Germany, one of the key global powers. That settlement took substantial territory from Germany (in both the

---

[3]Morgenthau (1963, 126) made this distinction by providing two definitions of collective security. He said that "Collective security as an abstract principle of utopian politics requires that all nations come to the aid of a victim of aggression by resisting the aggressor with all means necessary to frustrate his aims.... Collective security as a concrete principle of realist policy is the age-old maxim, 'Hang together or hang separately,' in modern dress."

east and the west), required heavy economic reparations, and dictated restrictions on the German military (including the demilitarization of territory west of the Rhine). It made German economic recovery nearly impossible and interacted with the Great Depression of the 1930s in contributing to the economic and political upheavals within that country.

The presence in the interstate system of a powerful **revisionist** state will make it difficult to apply collective security principles.[4] Before World War II the world simultaneously faced three such states: Germany, Italy, and Japan. After World War II the Soviet Union and its allies became the revisionist states that greatly complicated application of collective security.

It is possible that the world is never long free of powerful revisionist states. If true, that calls collective security into question generally.[5] Realists have drawn that conclusion for years and consider collective security hopelessly "idealistic," a delusion of globalists about the strength of global community. On the other hand, even if collective security proves lacking for action against aggressive great powers, it may succeed in controlling smaller ones. In 1991 the United Nations acted against the Iraqi invasion of Kuwait under the banner of collective security. Later in this chapter we return to the history and prospects for collective security among the United Nations.

BEYOND THE STATE?

Collective security does not fundamentally challenge the state system. Instead it brings into question the assumption of inherent anarchy in that system. Is it possible that there could develop an international institutional structure that will in some significant way supplant the state? That certainly is a favorite globalist theme. For instance, tapestries hung in the Palais des Nations (of the old League of Nations) in Geneva portray human beings moving progressively into larger, more comprehensive communities, beginning with the family and continuing through the tribe, the city-state, and the nation. This portrayal implies the existence of an underlying process that could ultimately culminate in a global society with global institutions (Jacobson 1984, 14). Although there is no near-term threat to the state's power in world politics, we can still reasonably wonder if there is an important long-term process under way.

One approach to addressing this issue is to ask what forces underlay the historic movement from smaller feudal units to states, and then to consider whether these same forces operate to supplant states. Technological advance played an important part in the earlier transition. We return in Chapter 16 to a

---

[4]Lamy (1988) emphasizes the importance of what he calls "system transformers."

[5]Using a computer simulation model, Cusack (1989) argues, however, that even when only a limited number of states adopt collective security orientations externally (rather than using power for systemic balancing or self-aggrandisement), they not only stabilize the system, but increase their own security.

more detailed consideration of the impact that technology has on world politics. Here consider briefly the implications of just two military technologies: gunpowder and nuclear weapons.

Gunpowder was available in China by the ninth century and entered Europe in the fourteenth century.[6] Herz (1957) argued that the European development of cannon made the small feudal units of medieval Europe, generally centered on a fort or castle, indefensible. In doing so it changed the logic of security, putting a premium on larger geographic territories. The development of the superior artillery took some time, and there is a debate concerning whether the principal impetus was in the fifteenth century (Bean 1973), or during the sixteenth and seventeenth (Tilly 1985, 177-178).[7] The fact that the conquest of Constantinople by the Turks in 1453 was greatly aided by the use of artillery supports the earlier dating of the significance of gunpowder (Quester 1977, 47). In any case these developments coincided generally with the rise of the modern state system in Europe.

Herz further argued that the introduction of nuclear weapons and intercontinental delivery systems in the late twentieth century has put in jeopardy even the largest states. By analogy he suggested that the inability of states to defend themselves would undercut the state system.[8]

Economic factors also help explain the rise of the modern state system. These include the demand for larger markets and for more extensive access to raw materials than feudal systems could easily accommodate. Changes in trading (such as shipping) and production technology created some of the pressures for more extensive economic units that gave rise to states. These forces remain active and help explain the shift of preeminence in the global system from smaller European states to continental powers like the United States, the Soviet Union, and China. In fact, no state, even the physically largest, can any longer satisfy the economic desires of its citizenry from within its own borders. Extensive interstate flows of goods, capital, and technology are now essential.

The importance of military and economic technological change lead many to conclude that the state simply cannot maintain its position as the dominant, in fact practically the only important, actor in world politics. If that assessment is correct, what might be the dynamics of movement toward suprastate actors? Let us consider two possible dynamics: federalism and functionalism.

---

[6]Van Creveld (1989) says that the Chinese designed primitive grenades with bamboo tubes in the twelfth century. The technology of metal guns appeared in various places, including the Moslem world and Europe, by the early fourteenth century, initially only in handguns and cannon (rifles came later).

[7]Tilly (1985) notes the military technology argument but places less weight on it, arguing that artillery technology came so late that it reinforced the state-building process, rather than drove it. Holmes (1988, 77-79) provides useful data supporting the Herz thesis.

[8]In a subsequent reconsideration of his argument, however, Herz (1969) took the view that the state as an institution serves a number of other needs for human beings, such as manifesting a territorial imperative of the nation, which will give it longevity.

FEDERALISM

Many globalists look at the predicament of humankind, the inability of states to guarantee the security of their citizens except through a balance of terror that may ultimately be disastrous, and conclude that the only viable alternative is **federalism**—a contract among states giving over sovereignty to a supranational government. Following the same logic that led Hobbes to call for a social contract between citizens and a central government (the "Leviathan"), these idealists call for a voluntary global federalism.[9]

They can even point to historic precedent for abrogating sovereignty to deal better with threat. The United States was formed by colonies willing to overlook very different and frequently strong religious associations in order to achieve and maintain independence from England. Switzerland represents a union among peoples with different religious, cultural, and even linguistic backgrounds, established in part to protect their mutual neutrality in European wars. Federalists argue that the threat now is the destruction of humanity in any future war. It gives new meaning to an old German proverb, "If thou wilt not my brother be, I'll smash thy skull most certainly" (Deutsch 1974, 181).

Plans for world federation have a remarkably long history. Philosophers generally produce them, because statesmen consider them unrealistically utopian.[10] Perhaps the first truly global government plan came from a French monk, Emeric Crucé, who presented in 1623 a proposal called *Le Nouveau Cynée* (Brown 1987, 116). Crucé suggested a council of ambassadors, with representatives from the European states, Turkey, Persia, India, China, and the kingdoms in Africa, as well as representatives of the Pope and of the Jews. Majorities would prevail in votes of the council, a structure of voluntary negotiation and arbitration with a world court would settle disputes, and the council would have available a military to enforce decisions, if needed. The Crucé plan was remarkable in its anticipation of features of the first actual global international organizations of the twentieth century.

Most other early plans considered only Europe. In 1712 another Frenchman, Abbé de Saint-Pierre, proposed a European Union with representation from twenty-four states. Three-fourths majority votes would permit treaties and territorial changes, and mediation and arbitration procedures would facilitate dispute resolution. When all else failed, the combined forces of the union would punish outlaw states. The plan of Saint-Pierre is interesting because it drew the attention of Jean-Jacques Rousseau, who labeled it "an absurd dream," arguing that sovereigns would never accept such constraints on their authority or on their use of warfare. Rousseau's arguments prevailed in practice, and the search for security turned convincingly to reliance on diplomacy and the balance of power.

---

[9]Riker (1964, 11) defined federalism as "a bargain between prospective national leaders and officials of constituent governments for the purpose of aggregating territory, the better to lay taxes and raise armies."

[10]For reviews of many plans, see Jacobson (1984, 21-29) and Brown (1987, 111–123).

World Wars I and II revived interest in global federalism. The Union of European Federalists, the Association to Unite the Democracies, and the World Federalist Association continue to support world (or at least regional) government.[11] Federalist plans still gain few adherents for two reasons. First, even those observers who deem the end state desirable often feel that there is "no way to get there from here." Second, many question whether such a world would, in fact, be a happy one. Although federalist plans have invariably called for majority voting of some type, that principle by itself does not guarantee "good" decision making. Most of the world has never lived in a democratic society and therefore has little concept of the need to protect minorities from the power of the majority, and little understanding of the difficulty of so doing. In a world federation, for example, the poor majority would almost certainly call for significant income redistribution. That might be a happy world for the global South but would not excite many living in the North. In light of these two problems, federalism poses a weak challenge to realism. Many globalists who find themselves uncomfortable with the state system of realism turn elsewhere, especially to functionalism.

FUNCTIONALISM

Federalists argue that "the worst way to cross a chasm is by little steps."[12] In essence functionalists propose exactly such an incremental strategy for bridging the chasms separating states. Rather than describing their strategy as one of "little steps," however, they would be more likely to describe it as one of throwing increasing numbers of rope bridges across the chasm rather than trying to put a superhighway bridge in place immediately.

The individual rope bridges of functionalists consist of functionally specific international organizations, each satisfying a common need of the member states that the organizations link. Functionalists argue that the number of these organizations will increase naturally with advances in international transportation and communication technology and with resultant growth in international trade and other transactions. Because these organizations are ultimately rooted in technological advance, and because they represent technical solutions to limited problems, functionalists sometimes refer to these organizations as **technical**. Early examples of such organizations were the Universal Postal Union (1874), the International Telecommunications Organization (1875), and the International Office of Weights and Measures (1875).[13]

Functionalism avoids direct confrontation with the security issues of high politics. Instead the proliferation of functional international organizations is supposed ultimately to ensnare states within patterns of cooperation and raise

---

[11]Two Harvard Law School professors, Clark and Sohn (1960), presented a new proposal in *World Peace through World Law*. In the brave new nuclear world, their plan recognized that a strengthened United Nations might even require nuclear weapons to enforce the peace.

[12]Streit (1961); cited in Nye (1971, 50).

[13]Idealists began to elaborate functionalist theory early in this century as such institutions emerged and international conferences increased in number (see Baldwin 1907). The first theoretical statement with a large impact was by Mitrany (1966; originally 1943).

significantly the stakes of any conflict that disrupts interstate ties. In David Mitrany's words:

> Every activity organized in that way would be a layer of peaceful life, and a sufficient addition of them would create increasingly wide strata of peace—not the forbidding peace of an alliance, but one that would suffuse the world with a fertile mingling of common endeavor and achievement (Mitrany 1966, 70).

One criticism of the functionalist approach to bridging the chasms between states is that it might result in many "rope bridges" but never produce a usable "highway bridge". That is, functionalism may need a strategy that will ultimately move the process from the narrowly technical to the broadly political. In 1950 French Foreign Minister Robert Schuman stepped forward with a plan to unify the coal and steel markets of Europe that was intended to illustrate in practice, not just in theory, how that leap from the technical to the political, from low politics to high politics, could be made.

Based on the philosophical and practical work of Jean Monnet, the Schuman Plan was a conscious attempt to move toward the federalist goal, using a functionalist logic called **spillover**—a splashing of integration from one arena to another. Functionalists argue that international coordination and cooperation in one arena or sector actually creates or intensifies problems resulting from failure to coordinate in other sectors and will give rise to pressures to extend cooperation. This "expansive logic of sector integration," once under way, need not be restricted to strictly economic or technical arenas of state interaction, but can lead to spillover into the very heart of politics. This continuing process is one of gradual **integration** of the states involved in it.

Consider a simple example of the process of spillover. When European countries eliminated tariffs on manufactured goods crossing their borders, many trucks began to transport goods among them. Given border-crossing restrictions, however, such increased transport volume overloaded customs stations and led to long delays and high shipping costs. The manufacturers and truckers exerted political pressure for the elimination or simplification of border-crossing procedures, thus extending integration.

The partially automatic process of spillover may help states that initiate it move up a **scale of economic integration**, consisting roughly of five stages (Belassa 1961). A group of states that eliminate tariffs and border restrictions among them is called a **free-trade area** and has reached the first stage. At that point there will be growing pressure to coordinate the tariffs of the member countries with respect to outside states, otherwise all goods from the outside would tend to flow into the organization through the member state with the lowest external tariffs (complex "rules of origin" can partly stanch such flow). When states eliminate tariffs among them and establish a common external tariff, they have created a **customs union**.

With reductions in intercountry barriers to goods, markets will grow and manufacturers will seek to establish production centers in other countries more easily. They will want to buy foreign companies or to build new facilities to be closer to their expanded markets. They will press to move capital and personnel more easily across state borders. A customs union that also allows free flow of labor and finance within it constitutes a **common market**. It is because the European countries of the Shuman Plan established this goal for themselves that we often refer to them as the Common Market.

Should enough individuals begin to live parts of their lives in different member states of the common market, as a result of expanded interstate corporate operations, pressures will grow on the governments for coordination of retirement benefits and other social programs. With increased movements of goods, capital, and labor, it will become increasingly difficult for individual states to pursue policies dealing with inflation, interest rates, or unemployment. Pressure will develop to coordinate such policies. When a common market harmonizes economic policies, it becomes an **economic union**. A single currency would then replace those of individual states.

If Europe were to reach this level (it is at present nearer to a common market than an economic union) what might happen next? All of these pressures for increased coordination and cooperation will strain central institutional capabilities and require extensions and additions. As the central economic institutions become more powerful they will be able to dispense greater benefits and impose greater costs. The benefits will contribute to the building of loyalties to the structures, and the costs will shift domestic political activities toward them. At some point, central economic institutions become dominant over those of the state, and an economic union evolves into the fifth stage, total **economic integration**.

The higher stages of the economic integration process increasingly involve elements that everyone would characterize as highly political and near to the core of state interests (for instance, control over money, taxing, and spending). It would still require a step of considerable size to move from economic integration to **political integration**. That last big step would require the transference of the "locus of sovereignty" from states to the central institutional structures. That is, the states would no longer be the dominant decision-making elements, delegating authority to the common institutions; instead the central institutions would permit the residual state governments to maintain certain functions. Perhaps most important, a central military would replace the state militaries. When we consider that last step, the arguments of realists about the distinction between high and low politics resurface.

How might spillover occur between economic and political integration? For instance, European armament and aerospace manufacturers might recognize the economies of scale associated with sales to several member governments and also understand that larger-scale production gives them greater competitive capability relative to U.S. producers. On projects that require extensive research and more capital than the firms can easily access, the corporations may pressure multiple governments to cooperate in supporting large-scale joint research and development projects. With much overlap in weaponry and many common military interests, the states could begin to experiment with greater military coordination. Desire may even arise among the peoples of the member states to exert more direct control, through a parliament, over both the economic and political-military elements of the process rather than to leave matters in the hands of existing state governments. Functionalists point out that much of this has, in fact, already happened in Europe.

This description of a process by which spillover could lead to ever higher levels of integration suggests that some of the steps up the scale, especially the last leaps to political integration, are quite large. **Neofunctionalists** argue that the process can never be as gradual and automatic as early functionalists argued and that it will require elites, motivated perhaps by federalist ideals or personal glory, to periodically push the process forward.[14]

The Schuman Plan of 1950, not a spillover process, led to the creation of the European Coal and Steel Community (ECSC) in 1952. Moreover, the ECSC did not simply lower tariffs to set in motion the idealized process described earlier. Although lower tariffs on coal and steel were part of the effort, so too were the establishment of a unified labor market and an institutional structure called the High Authority. Members assigned that organization the power to deal directly with individuals and some power to tax, borrow, and lend (Nye 1971, 39). A fundamentally idealist desire by many European political leaders to move toward union initiated the integration process and continues to nurture it.

Europe, as we will see in more detailed discussion later, has moved quite steadily up the ladder of economic integration. Going back to our analogy of the chasm, a solid bridge has been constructed. In reviewing this globalist logic, however, a realist could reasonably argue that the initial goal of a solid bridge across a chasm was an inadequate one—true political integration, if the goal is a superstate, is not a matter of building bridges but of filling in the chasm. Moreover, realists argue that the ties among states constructed by the functional process can lead to conflict as well as to cooperation:

> Closer interdependence means closeness of contact and raises the prospect of at least occasional conflict. The fiercest civil wars and the bloodiest international ones have been fought within areas populated by highly similar people whose affairs had become quite closely knit together. (Waltz 1982, 81)

Nonetheless, Domke (1988, 151) found systematic empirical evidence that participation in limited membership organizations is associated with lower likelihood of involvement in wars. The functionalist web of interstate ties appears to constrain state behavior.

---

[14]Scholars differ in identifying the distinctions between functionalists and neofunctionalists. Riggs and Mykletun (1979) suggest: "As contrasted with functionalism, neo-functionalism is more self-consciously rooted in social science theory, more concerned with the detailed elaboration of explanatory variables, including political variables, and more systematic in explaining the process by which economic cooperation spills over into the political sphere." A key to the distinction is the greater attention by neofunctionalists to political logic.

UNITED NATIONS

The remainder of this chapter focuses on two international organizations (or perhaps more correctly, families of organizations): the United Nations (UN) and the European Community (EC). The UN is the premier global institution and the EC is by far the most developed regional institution. In addition to considering the background and structure of these two bodies, we wish to treat them as laboratories for investigation of the arguments of realists and globalists. To what degree do they provide support for those competing understandings of world politics?

The United Nations (Figure 9.2) has deep roots in collective security theory. It also, however, has a strong functionalist basis, building on the technical organizations that constituted one of the real successes of the League of Nations.

Although it had earlier rejected involvement in the League, the United States took an active role in the development of the United Nations. The United States and its allies wrote the Charter in San Francisco during the spring of 1945, before the conclusion of World War II, and New York hosts most of the organization. There are six central institutional components:

1. The General Assembly, the central organ, sets the budget, selects the secretary-general, and designates the nonpermanent members of the Security Council. Each state has one vote. "Important questions" (defined by the charter to include peace and security recommendations) require two-thirds majority in order to be resolved, whereas simple majorities resolve other issues. The League of Nations required unanimity on many votes (Riggs and Plano 1988, 32). The General Assembly theoretically supervises a variety of functional agencies such as the United Nations Children's Fund (UNICEF), the UN Development Program (UNDP), and the UN Environmental Program (UNEP). In reality, many of these bodies maintain separate governing structures and rely heavily on contributions outside of the UN budget assessments, thus securing for themselves virtual autonomy.

2. The Security Council is a second legislative organ and its structure represents a conscious effort to learn from the failures of the League. The five permanent members of the council are the United States, Russia, Great Britain, China, and France (which coincidentally became the five declared nuclear powers of the 1970s and 1980s). Ten nonpermanent members with staggered terms, selected by the General Assembly, join these great powers on the council. The permanent members have vetoes on substantive matters, an arrangement that recognizes, as League institutions did not, that no action can be taken against a great power. Unlike the League, which allowed each member to decide on economic or other sanctions against aggressor states independently, the Charter gives the Security Council the power both to identify an aggressor state and to direct a military force or sanctions against it. To provide such a military force, the charter theoretically obligates all members to make armed forces available to a Military Staff Committee. In reality, the UN has fielded only ad hoc military forces, under the direct control of the Security Council rather than of the committee (Brown 1987, 158–159).

3. The Secretariat is the executive institution. At its head sits a secretary-general, charged with bringing appropriate issues to the UN institutions. The bureaucracy of the Secretariat, among many other duties, maintains an extensive global data base, of no mean importance to anyone who wishes to understand the state of the world.

4. The judicial institution is the International Court of Justice, also known as the World Court. The Security Council and General Assembly elect the fifteen justices, who serve staggered, nine-year terms. The court supposedly has compulsory jurisdiction over some classes of cases, and it issues binding decisions. But several states have attached reservation clauses to their acceptance of that jurisdiction. For example, in 1946 the United States attached the Connally

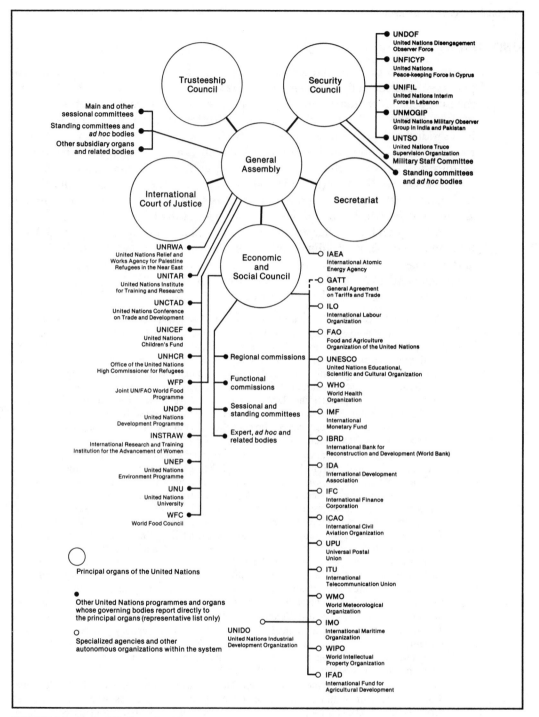

FIGURE 9.2   United Nations System

Source: Robert E. Riggs and Jack C. Plano, *The United Nations* (Chicago: The Dorsey Press, 1989), 30. Reprinted by permission of Brooks/Cole Publishing Company, Pacific Grove, CA 93950.

Amendment that, at its discretion, reserves jurisdiction to its domestic courts (Plano and Olton 1988, 270). It used this reservation in the 1980s to reject the right of the World Court to rule on Nicaraguan claims against the United States, including the mining of Nicaraguan harbors.

5. The Economic and Social Council (ECOSOC) coordinates sixteen affiliated functional organizations (called specialized agencies) with varying amounts of autonomy. These include the Universal Postal Union (UPO), the World Health Organization (WHO), the International Monetary Fund (IMF), the International Labor Organization (ILO), the Food and Agriculture Organization (FAO), and the UN Educational, Scientific, and Cultural Organization (UNESCO). ECOSOC also oversees the activities of five regional (by continent) economic commissions and has consultative arrangements with about 750 nongovernmental organizations (Riggs and Plano 1988, 62).

6. The Trusteeship Council deals with the remnants of colonial empires and is an anachronism. At the end of both world wars, colonies were taken from the losers and given to the winners "in trust," with the expectation that the trustees would move them toward self-governance. These colonies, and those of the victorious states, have now almost all achieved independence. In 1963, a UN report listed sixty-four colonies, mandates (the League equivalent of trusteeships), and trust territories. In 1985 this list had dwindled to eighteen, almost all of which were small islands. The biggest remaining problem area was Namibia (South-West Africa), which is a former League mandate to South Africa and which that country refused to release for UN trusteeship. Namibia held its first independent (UN-sponsored) elections in 1989 and gained independence in 1990. In 1991 only one Trust Territory (the Republic of Palau, administered by the United States) remained.

Two major trends significantly changed the UN organization between 1945 and the early 1990s. First, membership expanded from fifty-one states initially to 179 in 1992. UN members finally allowed the People's Republic of China to take its seat (replacing the government on Taiwan) in 1971, giving representation to one-fifth of humanity. Now only a handful of states remain outside. Switzerland chooses nonmembership in protection of a strict definition of its neutrality. The Palestine Liberation Organization (PLO) has observer status.

The second trend over much of that period was a shift from voting dominance by majorities centered on the United States to those that most often opposed it. From 1946–1950, 75 percent of roll calls agreed with the United States and only 34 percent supported the Soviet Union (Figure 9.3). From 1981 through 1985, the majority included the United States only 14 percent of the time but represented the Soviet position on 79 percent of all votes (Riggs and Plano 1988, 86). The transformation was quite steady, with the U.S. loss of majority position occurring in the early and mid-1960s. The United States formerly complained about the obstructionist use of the veto by the Soviet Union. From 1945–1955, the U.S.S.R. used seventy-seven vetoes in the Security Council, and the United States used none at all. From 1976–1986, the United States vetoed forty-six measures, whereas the Soviets said "nyet" to only seven (Riggs and Plano 1988, 77).

What underlay these two related trends? Until 1955 the United States and the Soviet Union blocked most of the membership applications supported by each other, slowing membership growth and protecting the U.S. majority. In the thaw of superpower relations that followed Stalin's death, a package deal in 1955 allowed sixteen states to enter. Thereafter membership became virtually open, and

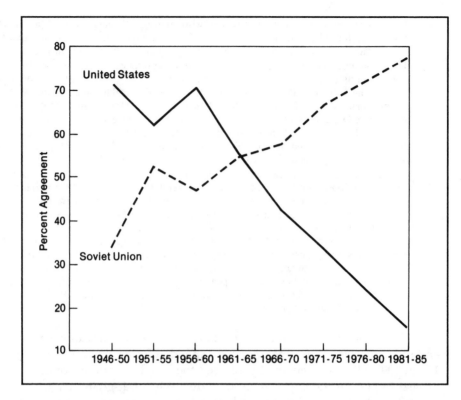

FIGURE 9.3   U.S. and Soviet Union Percentage Agreement with the UN Majority
Source: Robert E. Riggs and Jack C. Plano, *The United Nations* (Chicago: The Dorsey Press, 1989), 87. Reprinted by permission of Brooks/Cole Publishing Company, Pacific Grove, CA 93950.

with continuing decolonization large numbers of African countries entered. Many LDCs vote consistently against the United States and the former colonial powers of Western Europe. Even the Latin American countries, on which the United States once counted heavily, shifted to frequent opposition with the movement of their attention from the cold war to autonomy and development questions.

The ongoing financial crisis of the United Nations has its basis in the periodic unwillingness of great powers to pay their assessments in the face of what they consider unacceptable votes. UN assessments are based on GDPs, and the seven largest members pay 70 percent of the total. Although the U.S. assessment has dropped to 25 percent, voluntary contributions to various programs bring its share of total UN operations to about 50 percent (Riggs and Plano 1988, 48–50). Two-thirds of the members, enough to pass an anti-American measure, pay a total of only 2 percent (Ray 1987, 373). The Reagan administration withheld U.S. dues in 1987 and 1988. Bush, a former U.S. ambassador to the United Nations, resumed payment, but in 1992 the United States owed approximately $740 million (for regular and special assessments).

The end of the cold war and the breakup of the Soviet Union accelerated the first long-term trend (expansion of membership) and greatly disrupted the second (decreasing U.S. influence). With respect to membership, both North and South Korea joined in 1991, as did Estonia, Latvia, Lithuania, and two Oceanic micro-states. In 1992, additional former republics of the Soviet Union joined (as did San Marino), pushing membership to 179. Russia took over the seat of the former U.S.S.R.

At the same time, however, the coalition of anti-American and often anti-Western votes largely collapsed. On a wide variety of issues, including the sanctions imposed by the UN on Iraq after its invasion of Kuwait (1991) and on Libya for its failure to turn over two suspected terrorist bombers of a jetliner (1992), Russia and members of its former empire began to vote with the United States. In fact, while the UN could agree to impose sanctions only twice between 1945 and 1990, it imposed them four times in 1991 and early 1992 alone. Similarly, in its first forty years, the UN undertook a total of thirteen peace-keeping missions. By mid-1992 the UN was running eleven missions simultaneously, with a total of about 50,000 soldiers (more than four times the number at the end of 1991).

The UN itself divides its efforts on behalf of peace into four categories: peace enforcing (collective security), peace keeping (policing cease-fires), peace making (diplomacy), and peace building (addressing the roots of conflict through functionalist programs). We consider each in turn.

COLLECTIVE SECURITY (PEACE ENFORCING)

How has the United Nations done in enforcing the peace? The League of Nations' inability to impose sanctions on great power aggression tore it apart. The veto system of the United Nations, by recognizing the unreality of collective action opposed by one or more great powers, has preserved institutional integrity—no state has withdrawn as Japan did. That same system, however, greatly limits the UN's ability to act.

During the cold war, the UN supported only one collective security action. When the Korean War erupted in 1950, the U.S.S.R. was boycotting the Security Council in protest of its failure to seat the People's Republic of China (which took control of the mainland in 1949). The United States pushed through a resolution committing the United Nations to support South Korea. When the Soviet Union returned, it could block further action but not reverse that already taken. Even the Korean War did not illustrate collective security in the full sense of the theory. Only twenty-two of sixty member states offered forces to the United Nations command, and the United States and South Korea together supplied more than 90 percent of total personnel. The world understood the United Command to be a euphemism for U.S. command (Riggs and Plano 1988, 130).[15]

---

[15]In an attempt to protect the UN's ability to implement collective security measures in the face of great power vetoes, the United States secured General Assembly passage in 1950 of the Uniting for Peace Resolution. That asserted Assembly responsibility for recommending action should the Security Council be unable to act (that is, should it be blocked by veto). This measure has been unable to resolve the dilemma.

At the end of the cold war, the United Nations undertook a second collective security action. In August, 1990, the Security Council voted fourteen to zero to demand Iraq's withdrawal from Kuwait. Following eleven intervening resolutions, the council set a deadline of January 15, 1991 for withdrawal, after which it authorized Kuwait's allies "to use all necessary means." On January 17, the United States led a twenty-eight–state force into attacks on Iraq. Again, however, the United States provided the bulk of personnel and equipment. It is not at all clear that the action established a clear model for collective security actions to follow the cold war.

During the cold war even economic sanctions did not secure widespread observance. Between 1948 and 1955 a nonmandatory embargo on arms shipments to Israel and the Arab States of the Mideast was but partially successful, and was ignored thereafter. Since 1963 members have also frequently violated a similar voluntary embargo on arms sales to South Africa; the embargo was made mandatory in 1977 (Riggs and Plano 1988, 132–33).

PEACE KEEPING

The problems associated with collective security include (1) the inability to apply sanctions to great powers or over their strong opposition, (2) the difficulty of identifying aggressor states in many conflicts, and (3) the unwillingness of states to commit extensive resources. UN **peace-keeping** efforts have evolved to live within these significant constraints—they do not confront great powers, they often do not identify an aggressor, and the level of resource involvement is low. This often means placing small peace-keeping forces or observer missions between combatants who are ready to cease hostilities and can use some noncoercive help in doing so (although at times the UN mission is more active than that suggests). The United Nations personnel use force only in self-defense.

The UN supplied such a mission in 1947–1949 on the northern border of Greece to monitor external support for leftist guerrillas. In 1949, the UN put a military observer group in India and Pakistan; in 1992 there were still forty observers there.

The UN first fielded larger peace-keeping military forces in 1956 during the Suez War. A United Nations Emergency Force (UNEF) took control of the area around Egypt's Suez Canal, so as to facilitate the withdrawal of British, French, and Israeli forces. Both the United States and the U.S.S.R. supported it and jointly condemned the invasion. Other peace-keeping forces have played roles in West New Guinea (West Irian), Cyprus, and the Middle East (UNEF II). The force in Cyprus not only separated the Greek and Turkish communities, but adjudicated local disputes and assisted in maintenance of local order. In 1989 the UN Transition Assistance Group (UNTAG), a force of 4,650, moved into Namibia to enforce a separation of South African and South-West Africa People's Organization (SWAPO) military forces.

Still larger forces, backed by the full support of the great powers, begin to blur the line between peace keeping and collective security (peace enforcing). Both superpowers supported the early stages of an operation by a force in the Congo during 1960–1964 that was large enough, with 20,000 troops from twenty-nine countries, to attempt active conflict termination rather than the simple separation of weary belligerents. The forces backed an anti-Soviet faction in the struggle for control of the Congo, however, and the joint sponsorship disintegrated. The Soviet Union and France, among others, refused to pay, and the expensive mission precipitated a UN financial crisis. Unpopular peace-keeping missions subsequently created other financial crises for the organization. That history must serve as a warning whenever the UN moves toward more expensive and potentially unsuccessful or even divisive peace-keeping missions.

At the end of the cold war the United Nations had ongoing peace-keeping missions in Jerusalem (dating from 1948), India-Pakistan (1949), Cyprus (1964), the Golan Heights (1974), and Southern Lebanon (1978). In 1991 and 1992 the United Nations sent military personnel additionally to El Salvador, the Western Sahara, Angola, Iraq-Kuwait, Cambodia, the former Yugoslavia, and Somalia. The Cambodian presence of 22,000 made it the largest UN military undertaking ever. In a total of thirty-two active conflicts underway around the world in early 1992, the UN was involved in eight, while foreign states participated significantly in only six.

Between 1948 and 1989 the United Nations organized a total of seven peace-keeping forces and six military observer missions, involving a total of 400,000 soldiers and costing $3.5 billion (Harrelson 1989, 257). In 1991–1992 the number of missions grew to twelve running simultaneously. Peace-keeping expenses reached $600 million in 1991 alone. The efforts in Cambodia and Yugoslavia further dramatically increased annual costs—the Cambodian effort in 1992 cost $1.9 billion. Although such figures remain a small portion of global military spending, the rate of increase was dramatic.

DIPLOMACY (PEACE MAKING)

The use of large- or small-scale force is not the only method by which the United Nations contributes to global conflict resolution, and by which we should judge its efforts. Article 33, Paragraph 1, of the Charter lists other procedures:

> The parties to any dispute, the continuance of which is likely to endanger the maintenance of international peace and security, shall, first of all, seek a solution by negotiation, enquiry, mediation, conciliation, arbitration, judicial settlement, resort to regional agencies or arrangements, or other peaceful means of their choice. (Riggs and Plano 1988, 186).

The United Nations assists parties to disputes in many of the preceding ways. Haas (1986) studied 319 international disputes involving violence between July 1945 and September 1984.[16] Of those, 137 attracted the attention and involvement of the UN. Haas's conclusion is that

[16]He built on earlier work of Haas, Butterworth, and Nye (1972).

> The impact of the UN on moderating international conflict has been marginal, but not absent. Abatement of disputes, without settling or isolating them is the UN's major contribution. Its ability to stop hostilities is confined to Arab-Israel and Cypriot confrontation and to certain cases of decolonization. (Haas 1986, 55)

Statistics from the International Court of Justice actually suggest that reliance on international organization for assistance in dispute settlement was declining prior to the end of the cold war. States voluntarily filed thirty-four cases with it between 1947 and 1960, whereas they placed only nineteen before the court between 1960 and 1986 (Riggs and Plano 1988, 194).

Negative assessments appear premature. Changes in Soviet foreign leadership and foreign policy of the late 1980s began to allow the UN to play a more positive role. For example, in 1988 the UN played a role in helping resolve long-term, cold war–related problems in Angola. In 1990 the great powers of the Security Council moved toward agreement on UN-supervised elections in Cambodia, where China, the U.S.S.R., and the United States had long supported opposing factions. Now that the cold war has ended, the UN may be able to play a useful role in decreasing the numbers of conflicts that involve the newly independent and nonaligned countries of the Third World—as it did at the end of the conflict between Iran and Iraq.

What might be the categories of constantly reoccuring issues (meta-issues) of the 1990s and early twenty-first century? In addition to interstate Third World conflicts, they could include the self-determination of peoples within existing states. The 1992 UN peace-keeping efforts in Cyprus, the Western Sahara, India-Pakistan, Jerusalem, and Yugoslavia all involved issues of self-determination.

A realist could read this assessment of the role of the United Nations in collective security, peace keeping, and diplomacy as confirmation of the principles that (1) any UN ability to resolve conflict simply reflects a delegation of power from states, and that (2) the UN will resolve no conflict unless the great powers want it to do so. In reality, success or failure is terribly difficult to measure, because we never have a control case; that is, we never know what might have happened had the UN not existed or not become involved. Empirically, the realist assessment of UN impotence is as difficult to evaluate as the globalist view that the UN has made an important difference.

FUNCTIONALISM (PEACE BUILDING)

Evaluation of performance on questions of low politics provides more definitive evidence for an important role of the United Nations and other IOs. The total number of international organizations and nongovernmental organizations (more than 5,000) has exploded during the twentieth century (see Figure 9.1). States and citizens apparently believe that those institutions often serve functions and provide collective goods in a manner that would be impossible without a global institutional structure.

Many of these IOs serve economic functions. Three international organizations that are officially specialized agencies of the UN (under the coordination of ECOSOC), but that in reality maintain complete independence of action, provide much of the structure within which international trade, aid, and capital flows occur. They are the General Agreement on Tariffs and Trade (GATT), the International Bank for Reconstruction and Development (IBRD or the World Bank), and the International Monetary Fund (IMF). World commerce would certainly occur with or without these organizations. Moreover, as Chapter 13 details, the Third World often criticizes all three. Yet there is no doubt that the functioning of these IOs has facilitated the dramatic trade and economic growth of the postwar era.

Some of the world's first functional and least controversial organizations are now part of the UN family. These include the Universal Postal Union, founded in 1874, and the International Telecommunication Union, established in 1875. Smooth functioning of global communications (mail and telecommunications) and transportation (of people and of goods) requires such IOs.

Many other organizations have laudable records. For instance, the World Health Organization (WHO) directed a campaign against malaria that eliminated it from much of Asia and the Americas and from all of Europe. The campaign unfortunately did not succeed in Africa. Even more remarkable, WHO successfully eradicated smallpox from the world (except for samples in two laboratories). In 1974, WHO initiated the Expanded Program on Immunization (EPI) with the goal of vaccinating all children globally by 1990 against diphtheria, measles, whooping cough, poliomyelitis, tetanus, and tuberculosis. Programs of WHO for the year 2000 are even more ambitious (Riggs and Plano 1988, 254).

These economic, technical, and health organizations provide collective goods at remarkably low cost. The provision of some of these collective goods fundamentally requires IOs and universal involvement. For instance, the campaign to eliminate smallpox could have failed if even a single country declined to participate.

Some functional elements of the UN are, however, controversial.[17] For instance, the International Labor Organization (ILO) seeks to establish and secure acceptance of an International Labor Code. That code consisted, by 1985, of 160 conventions and 170 recommendations covering hours, wages, and other working conditions. The United States withdrew from the ILO between 1977 and 1980 in protest, however, concerning what it saw to be neglect of violations in the Second World and excessive attention to conditions in selected countries, including Israel (Riggs and Plano 1988, 250). Similarly, the United States withdrew in 1985 from the United Nations Educational, Scientific, and Cultural Organization (UNESCO) because (in part) of demands from many in the Third World for a **new international information order**. LDCs charged that advanced states control the international news media (including all the major news services) and cover events in the Third World through biased eyes, when they cover them at all. The United

---

[17]In the mid-1980s the United Nations disaster-relief organization (UNDRO) spent more on air-conditioning than on sending staff to disaster zones (*The Economist*, December 2, 1989), 23.

States and other developed countries feared that the requested changes by LDCs would shift control of the media from private hands to governments and thereby invite censorship. In 1989 UNESCO abandoned positions that deviated from support for the free flow of information.

The functional benefits of the UN do not always require an ongoing institutional framework; sometimes special conferences provide them. For example, the United Nations Law of the Sea Conferences (UNCLOS) in 1958, 1960, and 1973–1982 developed international policy on use of the oceans. The centuries-old convention that gave states control of the ocean for three miles from their shores supposedly had roots in the inability of countries (using cannon) to defend a greater distance. As weaponry developed, and as the ability of states to exploit the economic resources (oil, minerals, and fish) of the oceans grew, pressure rose for state control of greater areas. UNCLOS sessions resolved the conflicting desires of various countries (including those of land-locked states). Those meetings established the principles of twelve-mile territorial seas (with guaranteed passage through navigable straits even within the twelve-mile limit) and of 200-mile Exclusive Economic Zones (EEZs), within which the bordering states have sole rights to fishing and minerals. The treaty of 1982 also called for an International Sea-Bed Authority to approve and tax mining beyond 200-mile EEZs. The United States is one of the few states with the technology for such deep-ocean mining and objected to such international oversight. Its refusal to ratify the treaty placed it in limbo. Nonetheless, the principles established by these conferences became the new international law (the United States officially accepted the twelve-mile limit in 1988).

Again, a realist can correctly point out that states allow the functionalist process to proceed, inside or outside of international organizations, only within fairly strict limits. The ability of the United States to bring pressure on UNESCO (its leadership and policies changed after U.S. withdrawal) or to ignore the widespread acceptance of the International Sea-Bed Authority indicate that ultimate power still rests with the great powers. The extent of cooperation and compromise in the provision of these collective goods is still impressive, however. A globalist can reasonably suggest that functional institutions set in motion processes and engender cooperation that states can no longer truly control.

THE EUROPEAN COMMUNITY

While the United Nations has close and explicit ties to both collective security and functionalism, the founders of the European Community had federalist aspirations but chose primarily functionalist means. Three organizations make up the European Communities (EC), now increasingly (and in this volume) identified as the European Community. The Schuman Plan of 1950 led to the establishment in 1952 of the European Coal and Steel Community (ECSC) and the movement toward a common market in the key coal and steel economic sectors. The Treaty of Rome in 1957 brought two additional associations into being during 1958. The purpose of the European Atomic Energy Commission (Euratom) is to coordinate the common development of nuclear energy including the sharing of research, investment capital, and specialists in that sector. The most famous element of the triad is the European Economic Community (EEC), better known as the Common Market, because it set the creation of such a market as its goal. The structures of the three institutions merged into the EC in 1967.

BACKGROUND

Four permanent institutions support the EC: an executive organ (the Commission), a legislative body (the Parliament), a judicial organ (the Court of Justice), and a body representing the member states (the Council of Ministers).[18] The Commission initiates policy and seeks to advance community interests. Its commissioners represent the twelve member countries and select a Commission president from their number. Thousands of "Eurocrats" serve the Commission.

In 1962, a European Parliament replaced the Common Assembly, established initially for the ECSC. Since 1979 Europeans have elected representatives directly to the EC Parliament, replacing the selection of them by the various state parliaments. This legislative arm of the EC, however, plays a secondary role to the Commission and in fact controls only about 5 percent of the EC budget (although it can reject the budget as a whole). The Court of Justice is the judicial branch and resolves disputes for all three organizations. Individuals, as well as states, can bring cases before it. The court may rule national law invalid because of conflict with community law.

One representative of each government, usually the Foreign Minister but variable by issue, sits on the Council of Ministers, which has a rotating presidency. The council must approve the policymaking of the commission. Although the Treaty of Rome foresaw majority voting after 1966, the French blocked that change in 1965, and all important matters still require unanimity. Although the Commission's strength has grown quite steadily, the Council of Ministers and periodic special summits still give member governments the ultimate control.

Those who urged the creation of European institutions have always had their eyes on high politics. In May 1952, the six original members of the ECSC signed a Treaty for a European Defense Community (Curtis 1965, 17–19). It was to establish a common armed forces with a common budget. The six states also held discussions on a full European Political Community, and proposed a treaty in March 1953. Both memories of two world wars among the member states and the new perception of Soviet threat in the early cold war years motivated this "fast-track" approach to a united Europe. The process came to an end in August 1954 when the French Parliament refused to ratify the European Defense Community treaty, in part because of the refusal of Britain to participate.

The failure of the fundamentally federalist approach to integration of Europe disappointed proponents of integration, and they then fell back on the procedures of functionalism, buttressed by the periodic "big pushes" by elites that characterize

[18]Overturf (1986) and Daltrop (1986).

neofunctionalism. The Treaty of Rome committed the original member states in 1967 to establish a customs union (with no internal tariffs plus common external tariffs) by January 1, 1970. They did so eighteen months early. It also committed them to develop a Common Agricultural Policy (CAP), which they elaborated during the 1960s (Jacobson 1984, 253). The attempt to coordinate individual state policy in this particularly difficult sector has been, at best, a mixed success. The EC has often developed joint policies on the basis of the **lowest common denominator principle**, extending subsidies or benefits obtained by farmers in one country to those of other countries. This has led to a highly subsidized agricultural sector, producing surpluses that have come to rival those of U.S. farmers and absorbing (in 1992) about 53 percent of the total EC budget.

Throughout much of the 1970s and early 1980s the functionalist process continued slowly. In 1979, the European Monetary System (EMS) came into existence linking nine European currencies to each other in a "snake." The wiggles of the snake are fairly narrow bands within which the relative values may vary. A European Currency Unit (ECU) came to serve as a unit of account for many EC transactions. Then, in 1986, community leaders took another large step up the integration ladder by adopting the Single European Act, an amendment to the 1957 Treaty of Rome. The goal was a true common market by 1992, and the EC largely achieved it.[19] The Single Act required removal of remaining trade restrictions in four categories: goods (primarily nontariff barriers, such as the quality requirements that kept almost all foreign beer out of Germany), services (such as barriers to the opening of bank branches across borders), the movement of labor (such as country-specific professional requirements for doctors and lawyers), and capital movement (such as exchange controls limiting interstate capital flows). Economic gains from improved efficiency as a result of the Single Act will be substantial (Cecchini 1988). Non-European states, including Japan and the United States, fear that in the process of eliminating remaining internal barriers, external ones will arise, creating a "Fortress Europe." Skirmishing over that prospect began in 1988, when the United States retaliated against exclusion from the EC of U.S. beef from cattle that had been fed hormones (Europeans claimed that the hormones posed a human health hazard).

In late 1991, leaders of member states agreed via the Maastricht Treaty to still another set of substantial amendments to the Treaty of Rome. The 250 pages of the accord specified movements toward a joint currency and a single central bank (steps in that direction began in the late 1980s). The treaty also set a goal of joint foreign and security policy, and it targeted a common defense policy. The Maastrict Treaty is officially a "Treaty on European Union." But many Europeans began to have second thoughts; the Danes rejected Maastricht in a referendum in 1992. Moreover, a series of currency devaulations disrupted the EMS in the same year. The Treaty of Rome itself, as well as the Single Act and the Maastricht Treaty, have

[19]Although 1992 became a magic number in Europe, many Americans seemed unaware of its significance (or believed that it was thoughtful of Europe to help them celebrate the five hundredth anniversary of the discovery of America).

established, however, the precedent of the periodic "big steps" that neofunctionalists claim are necessary to keep the integration process moving. The EC scheduled another treaty revision conference for 1996.

As the EC gradually and irregularly moved up the scale of economic integration, it also expanded geographically. The original six members of the EC organizations were Belgium, the Netherlands, and Luxembourg (known collectively as BENELUX),[20] France, Italy, and West Germany. Britain applied for membership in 1961, as did Denmark, Ireland, and Norway in 1961–1962 (Feld 1976, 68–70). De Gaulle's France vetoed U.K. membership in 1963 and again in 1967, claiming that the "special relationship" of the British with the United States made their application a "trojan horse."

Nonetheless, the EC accepted Britain, Denmark, and Ireland in 1973. Greece gained membership in 1981, and Spain and Portugal entered in 1986, doubling the initial number of states. The addition of the last three members caused special problems because they are poor, relative to other member states. The GNP per capita of all twelve states in 1990 varied from $4,890 in Portugal to $28,770 in Luxembourg. This new southern tier of states is competitive with the north in neither industry nor agriculture. Greek fears of further competition for its relatively inefficient farmers forced the EC to provide $1.4 billion in aid to Greece before it would approve the admission of Spain and Portugal.

The excitement generated by the new momentum of the EC attracted many other countries. Turkey applied for membership, but the EC postponed the candidacy of it and all other prospects until after 1992. In 1992 Austria, Cyprus, Finland, Malta, Sweden, and Switzerland also stood in the queue. Czechoslovakia, Hungary, and Poland signed trade pacts with the EC and would like to move toward membership.

FEDERALISM OR EUROPE "À LA CARTE"

Many who study or participate in the process of European integration continue to target the federalist goal of an integrated European state. Periodic summits of EC leaders call for political union and the Maastricht Treaty promised to move sharply toward it.

Yet something else seems to be evolving in Europe, a much more complex form of governance. Some portray it as a Europe of concentric circles, in which the innermost countries have proceeded furthest toward political integration, and the extent of integration drops as the circles become larger. For instance, with respect to border control, an eight-member subgroup of the twelve EC countries has agreed to create a passport-free zone. Others suggest that such an image is too tidy, and that the circles of integration overlap, depending on the issue area. This last image carries labels such as **variable geometry,** or Europe à la carte.

---

[20]The BENELUX countries had agreed to establish a customs union among themselves already in 1944, and brought it into operation in 1948.

In economics there is one set of concentric circles. At its core are the twelve members of the EC. They are joined in the next circle by the members of the European Free Trade Association (EFTA), formed in 1959 and composed in the early 1990s of Austria, Iceland, Finland, Norway, Sweden, and Switzerland. In 1993, the EC and EFTA established a European Economic Area, applying many of the Single Act requirements to the EFTA states. The next circle is the Organization of Economic Cooperation and Development (OECD), which adds non-European members.

In security there is another set of circles, overlapping those in economics, and not particularly neat themselves. At the center perhaps is the Franco-German joint military corps of 35,000. Somewhat broader is the Western European Union, established in 1955 with the aim of creating a unified European military. It enrolls all EC members except Greece, Denmark, and Ireland, but has failed to develop any significant institutional structure. NATO has a broader membership and also greater power. The Conference on Security and Cooperation in Europe (CSCE) adds still additional countries.

We could identify still another set of partly concentric and partly overlapping circles with respect to environmental issues. For instance, countries bordering on both the Baltic and Mediterranean Seas have their own groupings.

Complicating further the image of evolving governance, substantial pressures for breaking states into smaller units have intensified rather than disappeared. Belgium adopted a federal constitution in 1979 providing considerable autonomy to Flanders, Wallonia, and French-speaking Brussels. A Basque regional government took power in 1980. In the 1980s France granted Corsica its own assembly, and Spain allowed the Catalans, Andalucia, and Galicia to redevelop regional institutions. The list goes on and on.

Some of the nationality groups of Europe have advocated an inter*national* approach to European governance in which they, rather than traditional states, would be the basic units. A Bureau of Unrepresented Nations has, in contradiction of its name, represented them in Brussels since 1977. In 1985, 112 states, regions, and autonomous communities created the Assembly of European Regions and it grew to 179 members in 1992.

These national groups have often joined with states in supporting the principle of **subsidiarity** in European governance. That principle calls for governmental functions to be pushed down to the lowest level at which they can efficiently be performed.

This complexity of institutional development suggests that it might be better to look at the European Community not as the embryo of a superstate or a supernation, but as one organ in the embryo of an altogether new form of human governance, one that we might call **complex governance**. It is a form of governance remarkably compatible with functionalist expectations. At this point, however, traditional states remain very much in charge of the process. Only about 1.2 percent of the GNP of the EC flowed in 1992 to EC institutions, compared to the 40 percent that state governments took.

OTHER REGIONAL ECONOMIC ORGANIZATIONS

Many other regional economic organizations have come into existence during the postwar world, but none has had the success of the EC. We have already discussed the European Free Trade Association and its progressive absorption by the EC. In 1949 the Communist countries of Eastern Europe established the Council for Mutual Economic Assistance (CMEA or Comecon). Comecon coordinated joint development and cooperative use of economic infrastructure. In 1990 this institution came under severe pressure as many of its members reorganized their economies toward free markets, and as several members (including the Soviet Union) indicated a desire to move toward trade denominated in Western currencies. The organization disbanded in June 1991.

Other regional organizations have also had difficult histories. In 1961 Kenya, Uganda, and Tanzania established the East African Common Services Organization (EASCO), which became the East African Community in 1967, but collapsed in 1977. The reign of terror by Idi Amin in Uganda, the socialism of Tanzania, and the disproportionate benefits reaped by Kenya collectively undercut the organization.

Indonesia, Malaysia, the Philippines, Singapore, and Thailand created the Association of South East Asian Nations (ASEAN) in 1967 (Brunei joined in 1984). Although primarily economic and relatively successful, the organization also considers issues of joint political importance, such as the Vietnamese invasion of Kampuchea.

The Americas have spawned the greatest number of regional organizations. The Latin American Free Trade Association (LAFTA) lasted from 1960 to 1980. Eleven countries of the region sought to eliminate tariffs blocking the flow of goods among them. In 1980 they replaced LAFTA with the Latin American Integration Association (LAIA), which recognized the wide differences in economic development within Latin America and called on the most developed countries (Argentina, Brazil, and Mexico) to make the greatest reductions in tariffs. In 1969 a subgroup of LAFTA (Bolivia, Colombia, Ecuador, Peru, and Venezuela) established the Andean Common Market in an effort to accelerate progress. These countries, too, have recognized the problem created by different development levels and give special treatment to the poorest members. In 1973 countries of the Caribbean region began attempting to establish a customs union under the auspices of Caribbean Community and Common Market (Caricom). It repeatedly failed to agree on common external tariffs.

In 1988 the United States and Canada agreed to establish a free trade area and in 1992 they negotiated with Mexico to extend it. In 1991, Argentina, Brazil, Paraguay, and Uruguay joined in the Southern Common Market, or Mercosur, to accelerate tariff reduction; they set a 1994 deadline to eliminate all tariffs. In 1990 the United States announced an Enterprise for the Americas Initiative, proposing a hemispheric system of free trade areas (Saborio 1992, 3). If pursued actively, that could be the most important U.S. program in the region since the Alliance for Progress in the 1960s.

Two special problems plague all regional economic organizations, especially those that involve countries of the Third World. First, differences in levels of development prove troublesome. Instead of economic well-being spreading to less developed countries and equalizing incomes within an organization, resources (such as capital and skilled labor) often concentrate in more advanced areas and the disparities intensify. That is, **backwash effects** (the concentration) prove stronger than **spread effects** (Myrdal 1957). This is similar to the concentration of industries like steel, automobiles, film making and microcomputers in particular American cities before the longer-term dispersal of them (still by no means complete in any of these industries). Even the European Community has had to take extraordinary steps to assure that poorer regions, like southern Italy, benefit from integration. Second, especially among LDCs, exports are frequently competitive (being similar or identical raw materials) rather than complementary, so that the possibility of expanding trade within a group of LDCs is limited. This led ASEAN to agree with the EC in 1980 to further trade between the organizations rather than to seek to increase trade within ASEAN significantly.

A NEW WORLD ORDER?

The changes in the United Nations and the European Community in the early 1990s are so substantial and so rapid that it is difficult to keep up with them, much less to forecast where they might be leading those institutions and their member states. Together the changes, especially the seeming ability of Russia and the United States to work together in the post–cold war world, have generated something close to euphoria among many globalists. Do these developments indeed indicate a triumph of globalism and complex interdependence over a state-centric order?

The new initiatives and new institutional developments are so substantial that even traditional state leaders such as former U.S. President Bush have spoken regularly of a **new world order**. There are many reasons, however, to call for cautiousness in perceptions of fundamental change. First, when state leaders talk of a new world order, they almost invariably mean a new distribution of global power, not a supplanting of the state role by interstate institutions. They expect balances of power and polarities to remain the basic ordering structures of international (read "interstate") politics.

Second, and most important, realist images of the world do have a very long historic record upon which to draw, and that record suggests that the anarchy of the state system will invariably give rise to interstate conflicts. The period of euphoria about peace in the 1920s is only the most recent potential analogy to the current period. The League of Nations came into existence in January 1920, with twenty-four members, growing to forty-eight by the end of the year (DeConde 1978, 91). Although it did not join the League, peace movements in the United States were booming and a large disarmament contingent forced an initially reluctant U.S. administration to negotiate naval force limitations with other powers (naval forces were in essence the strategic weapons of the day). U.S. cooperation with the League and involvement in interstate agreements on arms control continued to grow throughout the decade, culminating in the 1928 Pact of Paris (Kellogg-Briand Pact), committing its fifteen signatories (all great powers except Russia) to renounce war and to settle disputes by "pacific means" (DeConde 1978, 96). Forty-six states had ratified the agreement by mid-1929. A World Disarmament Conference convened in 1932 and again in early 1934. Even those who do not know the details of world politics through the 1930s know that they rapidly deteriorated.

CONCLUSION

This chapter should not end on a note of great skepticism about a new world order with globalist elements. The fact remains that the United Nations is today stronger than any global organization of states has ever been. In addition, the European Community is a unique arrangement among states in which they have already and voluntarily given over considerable elements of economic sovereignty to a central body. Potential members clamor at the gate. Global communication and transportation systems have undoubtedly created more global community than has ever existed among humans. The cold war is over and Western liberal idealism, with its emphasis on democracy and human rights, has declared victory. All is well with the world?

Chapter 10

CONTINUITY
AND CHANGE
IN POLITICAL BEHAVIOR

This chapter returns explicitly to the theme of continuity and change in world politics and provides a review and consolidation of the argument so far. Chapter 2 introduced two organizing devices that shape the presentation in this book. The first is division of the subject matter into three components: international political behavior (the concern of Chapters 3 to 10), the global political economy, and the world political ecology or broader environment. Two primary worldviews organize thought within each subject matter (as realism and idealism have structured our discussion of political behavior). The second organizing device is a hierarchy of understanding: Worldviews selectively rely on theoretical perspectives; theories, in turn, draw predominantly on a particular set of concepts; any given set of concepts directs our attention to a specialized body of factual information.

We now introduce a third organizing device for understanding world politics, namely a categorization of approaches to describing change. There are three possible characterizations of dynamics in the interstate system.[1] The first portrays the system as exhibiting stability within fairly narrow limits. For instance, realism sketches an interstate system that maintains stability through the balance of power. That is not to say that the system is unchanging over time; actor numbers, relative power, and the technology of military and nonmilitary interaction evolve. Yet in this image the base structure remains intact and patterns of behavior vary little during long periods.

A second characterization emphasizes cyclical change, possibly with a regular cyclical period. Some structural realists (or neorealists) draw a cyclical portrait of world politics by describing the rise and fall of systemic hegemons. The third characterization points to trends or progressive change that could over time fundamentally alter the character of the system. Here we see the stamp of idealists.[2]

[1]Rosecrance (1987) lists the same dynamics, and focuses on the cyclical.

[2]A fourth possible pattern of change is abrupt and significant system transformation (see Holsti, Siverson 1980). Many transformations, however, such as the breakdown of a universalistic system, are better portrayed as phases of a cyclical pattern; others, such as the emergence of nuclear weapons, might be better seen as the reaching of a threshold in a process of progressive change. Although we must be alert for system transformations, the three categories of change appear to incorporate most or all of them.

Table 10.1 summarizes the interaction of the three organizing devices: subject matter, levels of understanding, and characterization of change. Across the top are the types of change. On the side, are the dominant subject matters. In the body of the table are two levels of understanding—namely, worldviews and, in *italics*, related theories (the reader could add concepts from Table 3.1 and from the text of the preceding chapters). The rest of this chapter clarifies and elaborates Table 10.1.

TABLE 10.1
Realism, Extensions, and Challengers

	Characterization of Change		
Dominant Subject Matter	*Stability (and Unpatterned Change)*	*Cycles*	*Progressive Change*
Political	Realism *Balance of power; coalition behavior; statecraft* *Intrastate analysis (friendly challenge to realism)*	Structural realism *Rise and decline of hegemony or leadership; hegemonic stability; hegemonic transition*	Globalism *Functionalism; collective security; regime theory; federalism; international legal order proposals*
Economic	Mercantilism *Convertability of power and wealth*		
Broader Environment	Geopolitics *Contribution of technology and resources to power; imperialism*		
	Predominantly zero-sum logic		Nonzero-sum logic

REALISM

The emphasis of realists is on continuity and stability. Continuity and stability in a system indicate that the system is in **equilibrium** or balance; constant interaction and mutual cancellation of opposing powers creates a balance of power and gives rise to equilibrium. For the realist, the substructure forces and trends documented in Chapter 1 give rise to shocks that rattle the superstructure, but cause no fundamental change in it. Demographic, economic, technological, and environmental change may alter the power of states over time, and give rise to conflict, but the state system will adjust.

Morton Kaplan, who identified and labeled six possible polarities of the interstate system (balance of power, loose bipolar, tight bipolar, universal, hierarchical and unit veto), characterized these as "six states of equilibrium of one ultrastable international system" (1957, 21). He identified rules of behavior that states normally follow within these equilibrium states, and that will guarantee the continuing equilibrium of the system. The rules of Kaplan (see Chapter 5) transform self-serving political behavior of states into a stable international system that provides a certain amount of security for states.

The emergence of equilibrium from individual state action is comparable to the working of the invisible hand in economics, which translates the self-serving economic behavior of individuals and firms into an economic system that improves efficiency of production and distribution, and that provides increasing volumes of goods and services. Unlike the invisible hand of economics, which provides progressively greater volumes of goods, the invisible hand of realist power politics can at best provide security most of the time and is subject to repeated failure. There is no promise in power politics of increasing security over time as there is of increasing welfare within economics.

Another realist, Kenneth Waltz, extensively developed the realist worldview in his *Theory of International Politics* (1979). He, too, emphasizes stability:

> The texture of international politics remains highly constant, patterns recur, and events repeat themselves endlessly. The relations that prevail internationally seldom shift rapidly in type or in quality. They are marked instead by dismaying persistence, a persistence that one must expect so long as none of the competing units is able to convert the anarchic international realm into a hierarchic one. (1979, 66)

Waltz is perhaps even more sanguine than Kaplan about systemic stability.[3] Kaplan thinks that some conscious attention to his rules and avoidance of universalistic urges is required, whereas Waltz rejects the notion that states follow any system-serving rules and argues that self-serving action within the balance-of-power structure will automatically (through coalitions) constrain even universalistic powers.

Many realists, particularly traditional, historically oriented ones, emphasize the importance of statecraft. Statecraft, the artful choice and application of diplomatic, economic, and military tools available to the state, aids in the pursuit of state interest. States must work at maintaining and enhancing their power and will thereby preserve the systemic equilibrium. Attention to statecraft suggests, however, a less deterministic view of state behavior than does an exclusive focus on the dynamics of power balances. In a friendly challenge to realism (but a poten-

---

[3]Like Kaplan, Waltz stresses the importance for state behavior of system polarity but fails to identify any rules by which system polarities might change. In a discussion of system transformation, Waltz does tautologically note that eliminating states in a multipolar world can transform the system into a tripolar or bipolar world, but he does not generalize about the transformation process (Waltz 1979, 199). Ruggie (1983) details his failure to treat any dimensions or determinants of change.

tially damaging one), some analysts go still further and look inside the state at a broad array of policy determinants—from interest groups to political parties to the personalities of leadership.

Although the roots of realism may be solidly in high politics (predominant emphasis on the political system) and in theories of stability and continuity, the branches of the worldview have spread widely. Some of those branches extend the scope of realist understandings into economic and broader environmental subsystems. Others, in more recent formulations, carry realist thought into an analysis of cycles in the world political economy. We consider each of these two directions of growth in turn.

THE REACH OF REALISM BEYOND POLITICS

Mercantilism (which we will elaborate in Chapter 11) extends realism into the realm of economics.[4] Mercantilists recognize that economic well-being provides the longer-term underpinnings of state power, and that the application of state power can secure wealth. Thus mercantilists hold that wealth and power are both proper ends of policy and are largely interchangeable (Viner 1958).

Geopolitics refers to a similar two-way linkage between power and the broader environment. It sees the bases of state power and many of the objects of power struggles in that environment. Morgenthau (1973) detailed the contribution of resource bases, broadly defined in terms of population, food, and raw materials, to power. Some geopoliticians have even given a dynamic character to their theory by considering how technological change might alter the military advantage of particular states (for instance, land versus sea powers).

The broader environment does not simply provide resources for the eternal international political struggle, it also motivates it. Theorists of imperialism (for example, Hobson and Lenin) have long argued that capitalist countries require markets and resources, and that the requirement motivates expansion and conflict. Others suggest that all countries, regardless of economic system, face similar incentives for expansion.[5] Waltz (1979) generalized the argument in discussing the motivation of the state to external expansion by the "three surpluses": people, goods, and capital.

REALISM AND CYCLES IN WORLD HISTORY

Although the state system exhibits long-term stability, polarity of the system varies, and there appears to be some regularity in that variation (see Chapter 4). At the end of his review of international politics in the Chou Dynasty, the Greek city-state system, Renaissance Italy, and the modern state system, Holsti argues that

> These categories of international systems emphasize the recurrence of various power structures and interactions patterns in different historical contexts.... Each of the historical examples at some stage became transformed from the diffuse type to either

[4]On the association of mercantilism with realism see, for example, Choucri (1980, 112–115).
[5]See, for instance, the Choucri and North (1974) theory of lateral pressure.

the diffuse-bloc, multipolar, or polar type. Diverse conditions might be responsible for this phenomenon, but the trend is unmistakable. No system originally comprising a large number of roughly equal units, with power diffused among them, retained that structure for a very long period, and the usual direction of development was toward a polar structure.

Even polar structures were not very stable. Starting with the anti-French coalition between the eighteenth and nineteenth centuries, polar structures have developed into diffuse structures, only to turn into polar or multipolar structures again. (Holsti 1983, 91)

Realists devote surprisingly little attention to the discovery of patterns in polarity transformation and explanations for it. Presumably, among the reasons for the failing are the limited number of historic state systems, the incompleteness of information about them, and the differences (such as military technology) among them.

Instead of theorizing about polarity transformations, much recent thought (within structural realism) has focused on the modern state system and cycles of hegemony (or leadership) within that particular state system.[6] Three issues hold central place in theory surrounding hegemony: What explains the rise and fall of hegemons? What are the implications for system management of the existence of a hegemon or of its decline? How does the rise and fall of hegemons interact with international conflict?

Modelski (1978) and other observers of system leadership see not only a regularity in patterns of hegemonic rise and fall, but also a constancy in period.[7] Specifically, Modelski argues that the modern system has experienced five cycles of about 100 years. The systemic leader (Modelski avoids the word "hegemon") has been, in turn, Portugal, the United Provinces of the Netherlands, Great Britain (two centuries), and now the United States. In terms of the forces of Chapter 1, the change in hegemon is tied primarily to economic structural change.

Chapter 6 sketched the evolving theory concerning the rise and decline of systemic leaders, focusing on the implications for the contemporary leadership of the United States. Theorists propose several explanations for hegemonic fall (with implications for hegemonic rise): the costs of hegemony (including military expense), the shift of hegemonic expenditures from investment to consumption (the third-generation effect), the rise of taxes and inflation (linked to the first two explanations), and the change of technological leadership in the world system.

Chapter 6 also outlined the theory of hegemonic stability, which explains some of the benefits that a hegemon may bring to the interstate system, including the development of trade regimes. British and American leadership have in turn supported free-trade regimes. Whether the liberal regime will persist as U.S.

---

[6]Again it is important to stress that there is more to neorealism than attention to the international political economy and cycles within it. For instance, a greater attention to both scientific method and social theory (especially structural) distinguishes it from classical realism. See Chapter 3 for an elaboration of those distinctions. Nor do only neorealists draw attention to long cycles.

[7]Thompson (1988, 44–45) stresses that a "global society" perspective informs much of Modelski's work.

leadership declines is obviously of considerable interest and is one question on which our upcoming discussion of political economy will focus.

Major international conflicts marked the transitions among previous system leaders and the theory of hegemonic transition attempts to explain those wars. Fundamentally, both leader and challenger seek to attain the benefits accorded by hegemonic status. Underlying power realities, driven again by the forces described in Chapter 1, have frequently changed much more than the status of the major actors (and their benefit share) before the outbreak of the conflict. Ironically, wars of transition often result in the relative fall of both leader and challenger, and the rise of a third state.

IDEALISMS

Challenges to realism arise with respect to almost all of the elements of that perspective: the definition of states as rational, unitary actors; the predominant emphasis of realists on security and power rather than on other ideals concerning the definition and character of the human community; the almost exclusive emphasis on states and resultant inattention to important nonstate actors; and the focus on conflict rather than on the extensiveness of international cooperation.

Neither these challenges individually, nor the set of them collectively, fundamentally undercut the importance of the realist perspective. In fact, most realists modify the basic worldview sufficiently to mollify many of the challengers. In particular, realists recognize the validity of suggestions that states cannot always be understood as unitary, rational actors. Realists readily admit that such a characterization is a prescriptive ideal for statecraft rather than a consistent reality. Chapter 7 presented that first, "friendly" challenge.[8] Instead of presenting the ideal of statecraft, that chapter looked at how policy actually is made. Societal elements, the personalities and idiosyncrasies of individuals in leadership positions, and even governmental structures significantly affect the policies of states toward each other.

The descriptive insights into state behavior gained through a levels-of-analysis orientation do not invalidate the realist image of balance of power in international politics. The insights do, however, raise questions about the predictability of state behavior and the achievability of largely conflict-free equilibria. In the same way that realists chide challengers for developing "ideal" international structures that look useful theoretically but that "in reality" do not work to dampen conflict, idealists can point to a realist model of rational state behavior as an "ideal" that is too frequently far from "reality." Idealists can argue that even a few leaders who incorrectly calculate power balances or who misperceive the intentions of other states will consistently disrupt the supposed equilibrium of the state system.

Nonetheless, it is the other challenges, those that draw our attention to ideals other than power and security, to nonstate actors, and to extensive global cooperation, that begin to elaborate an alternative, idealistic view of world politics. Although there are many idealisms, including various nationalisms and

---

[8]It is "friendly" because those who look inside the state still fundamentally accept a state-centric view.

universalisms, all of which call into question the motivational assumptions of realism, the idealism that attracted most of our attention is globalism—an elaboration of the potential for, and benefits of, a more peaceful, global community.

With respect to the substructure forces of Chapter 1, globalists argue that increasing damage to the global environment (as a result of population growth and spreading industrialization) and rapid jumps in the lethality of weaponry create incentives for global community building, and that ongoing social mobilization provides a source of energy for the process.

Globalists reject the search for security solely through the supposedly self-stabilizing elements of an anarchic global state system. In place of the realist's invisible hand, the challengers propose collective, cooperative action. Seyom Brown (1987) reviews three categories of collective action that globalists often favor.[9] The first is arms control directed at "making military balances less likely to provoke war" and limiting war destructiveness should it occur (Brown 1987, 173). Brown endorses specific measures, including negotiated reductions in armaments, confidence-building measures (such as the hotline) and even limited unilateral measures (such as restraint in the development of counterforce weaponry).

Arms control is consistent with realist thought. Most agreements are clearly self-serving efforts and involve only specific reciprocity. For a realist, state action to maintain reasonable balances in military strength and to avoid spending unnecessarily on armaments (which would strain resources and threaten continued economic growth) are inherently in the state's rational self-interest. Morgenthau wrote that[10]

> an unlimited nuclear arms race does not only endanger peace, as do all arms races; but it is also irrational because the unlimited accumulation of nuclear weapons, in contrast to that of conventional ones, adds nothing to military security once a certain measure of destructive power has been achieved. (Morgenthau 1973, 404)

Brown's second category of cooperation contains efforts to reduce the role of war. In this category he lists "international law, diplomatic accommodation and restraint, collective security institutions, and special measures to settle disputes and resolve conflicts" (Brown 1987, 141). Again, with the general exception of collective security institutions, this category of action includes much that realists would find to be rational and self-interested state behavior. In fact, Brown lists nine rules of diplomacy proposed by Morgenthau within the category of diplomatic accommodation and restraint. Brown also lists, however, several efforts in this category, including the Kellogg-Briand Pact, the Covenant of the League of Nations, and the Charter of the United Nations, that Morgenthau argued to be "of doubtful efficacy (that is, they are frequently violated), and sometimes even of doubtful validity (that is, they are often not enforced in case of violation)" (Morgenthau 1973, 273).

---

[9]This presentation reverses the order in which Brown discusses them.

[10]It is obvious that Morgenthau, despite his preeminence in twentieth century realist thought, cannot speak for all realists. Nonetheless, his thought usefully illustrates the differences between many realists and the challenging worldviews.

More generally, Brown includes development and enhancement of institutions within this category. Although he emphasizes security organizations, we should in addition reiterate the functionalist and neofunctionalist emphasis on development of IGOs and INGOs as actors that can increasingly constrain state behavior within webs of cooperative interactions. Further, we could add the development of interlocking regimes, which link issues and expand time horizons of cooperative endeavors, helping create patterns of complex interdependence and governance.[11]

Brown's third category of cooperative action contains efforts to purge war from the world. It is here that we find the most utopian proposals and those most certain to generate hostile reactions from realists (and even from many globalists). Brown subdivides this category into proposals based on the "political-constitutional restructuring of world society" and those based on the "reeducation and moral-psychological reform of human beings" (Brown 1987, 115). The first subcategory includes federalist proposals.[12] Within the second subcategory lie the pacifist teachings of various philosophers, including Thoreau and Gandhi.

In embracing some or all such proposals, globalists stress the nonzero-sum nature of many issues in international politics.[13] For instance, globalists argue that population, food, the environment, and natural resources present problems that often only collective action can solve, and solutions will provide benefits for all parties in excess of the costs. For globalists, however, no issue is as important as the modern security dilemma. Although individual state attempts to achieve security could fail in the past, miscalculation could never result in the near total destruction of the citizenry. Now that the penalty for failure is so great, both individual humans and states have a strong stake in collective action.

Perhaps most fundamentally, the globalist challengers perceive a pattern of progressive change in international politics. Since the beginning of the modern state system, agreements have regularly, and to a considerable extent cumulatively, enhanced the corpus of international law and added to the strength of international organization. Although Brown (1987, 223) observes how disturbing it is that most advance has occurred only at the end of major global wars, that only adds to the urgency of the task in the nuclear age.

---

[11]Regime and complex interdependence theory really lies at the intersection of neorealism and globalism; Keohane and Nye (1989) see their work as an effort of synthesis. Nonetheless, in framing the poles of theory that they seek to synthesize, they present complex interdependence as a strong ideal type in contrast to realism (see Table 9.2).

[12]For instance, those of Clark and Sohn (1960), and of the World Order Models Project (WOMP) led by Richard Falk (1975), who proposes institutional growth based on mass mobilization.

[13]Realists portray states as "status maximizers," who measure their performance in terms of others (Mishan 1982; Young 1986, 118). For instance, power and rank are intimately related. For globalists, states are "utility maximizers," who look to their own gains or losses, not to their relative performance. The difference in perspective can determine whether the same situation (for instance, an agreement on technological cooperation) is zero-sum or nonzero-sum.

CONCLUSION

Simplified realist and globalist perspectives are frequently in direct conflict. Truth often lies between simple images. World politics can only be understood as a mixture of behavior by state and nonstate actors (both narrowly self-serving and ideal motivated) with respect to issues that are sometimes zero-sum but frequently nonzero-sum. Power and security strongly motivate states, but other values and ideals interact in complex ways to drive actor behavior. The line between high and low politics is often quite clear, but the complexity of international linkages blurs it in other instances. The task for the student of world politics is to draw on both worldviews and to create a mental synthesis of them. Because the utility of the viewpoints will continue to change as the world does (and because the relative validity of the views is subject to ongoing study), your synthesis should be open and flexible.

Chapter 11

LIBERALISM, MERCANTILISM, AND STRUCTURALISM

Do the following have anything to do with world politics: the size and growth rate of the world's economy, the distribution of economic well-being across countries, and global patterns of trade? Yes, they do. To this point, however, we have devoted little attention to the world economy, focusing instead on the international politics of conflict and cooperation. This chapter, introducing Part Two of the volume, broadens our perspective to a consideration of the interaction between world politics and economics—to the global **political economy**. Three worldviews, liberalism (a relative of globalism), mercantilism (an extension of realism), and structuralism, organize most thought about the global political economy.

LIBERALISM

The terms **liberal** and **liberalism** will confuse many readers unless we immediately discuss that possible confusion. In European politics, and in academic or intellectual writing around the world, a liberal is one who favors limited governmental intervention in the economy. Most European countries have a liberal party with exactly that platform. In the contemporary political discourse of the United States, however, a liberal is one who often favors considerable governmental intervention, both in efforts to manage the economy and in the use of economic resources on behalf of less privileged members of society. Stated in this way, the European and American liberals appear to be near opposites.

We adopt the European or academic usage here for reasons that will become clearer during the subsequent discussion of international trade (liberals support "liberal" or "free" trade). At times we will use the expression **classical liberal** to designate the European liberal, because this definition of liberal goes back about 200 years. When we need to refer to the liberal position in the modern American sense, we will always label it **modern liberal** (in European usage these are "social democrats," not liberals).

How did the terminology become so confusing? First, classical liberal thought shaped the traditionally limited relationship between government and the economy in the United States. Thus those in the United States who wish to conserve American traditions (often called "conservatives") seek, in fact, to preserve classical liberalism. They may, of course, also desire to conserve or preserve various social or religious traditions that have little to do with classical liberalism. Second, the modern American liberal, while not always uncritically supportive of domestic and international freedom of commerce, continues to maintain some elements of thought fundamental to the classical liberal position. In particular, the classical liberal emphasized protection of the rights of individuals in society. Modern liberals continue to do so when they support free speech on unpopular positions, equal civil rights for those of all races, sexes, or religions, and even socially provided educational and economic opportunities for those born into low economic and social stations.[1]

Although (classical) liberals emphasize the importance of maintaining a separation between politics and economics, they simultaneously believe that the nature of the economic system affects the political system. Many liberals argue that a freely functioning economy generates a wide range of competing economic and social entities that translate their interests into political and social competition. That is, liberal economies create political **pluralism**. Producers, distributors, consumers, employees, financial institutions, and other economic actors have interests that set them in conflict with each other, within and across these categories. Like James Madison, who stressed the importance of balancing power among institutions to prevent tyranny, these liberals argue that the power balances within a pluralistic society are fundamental to political freedom. Friedrich Hayek and Milton Friedman made exactly that kind of argument in their books on *The Road to Serfdom* (1944) and *Capitalism and Freedom* (1962), which argued that political democracy is only possible in capitalist societies. Robert Samuelson suggests three problems that capitalism presents for authoritarian political systems:

1. Market economies require dispersed decision making—a direct threat to central political control.
2. Market economies create political grievances that have no outlet in authoritarian regimes.
3. [Market economies make it] impossible to stay isolated from the rest of the world—which means becoming infected with democratic ideas. (*Newsweek*, June 12, 1989, 46)

The Central European and Soviet revolutions of 1989–1992 suggest more generally that all modern economies generate pluralistic pressures and that market economies simply intensify them.

At the end of World War II many liberals in the U.S. government were convinced that a highly integrated but simultaneously pluralistic global economy, based on freely

[1]Hayek (1963, xi, xii) made clear the continuity between classical and modern liberals, and their joint disagreement with social conservatism, when he wrote, "A conservative movement, by its very nature, is bound to be a defender of established privilege and to lean on the power of government for the protection of privilege. The essence of the liberal position, however, is the denial of all privilege, if privilege is understood in its proper and original meaning of the state granting and protecting rights to some which are not available on equal terms to others."

functioning markets, was fundamental to the support of democracy and to the maintenance of long-term peace. Franklin Roosevelt's secretary of state, Cordell Hull, was an especially enthusiastic proponent of such views. This logic explains the relationship between liberalism and globalism. As Victor Hugo said, "Markets, open to trade, and minds, open to ideas, will become the sole battlefields."

CONCEPTS

Table 11.1 summarizes the conceptual and theoretical elements of the classical liberal and structuralist worldviews, and serves as a reference for the discussion of this chapter. Emphasis on the individual is central to the definition of the liberal worldview. Liberalism developed as a challenge to the feudal order of the late Middle Ages (Ingersoll and Matthews 1986). In that order, the individual had a diminished role, greatly limited by religious, secular, and economic authorities (joined in the form of the feudal aristocracy). For instance, salvation required the assistance of the church and its personnel. Martin Luther (1483–1546) helped set in motion the forces that generated liberalism by arguing that the relationship between an individual and God was personal. He rejected the claim that only the church's representatives could interpret the scriptures. Similarly, Francis Bacon (1561–1626) and René Descartes (1596–1650) placed the individual at the heart of a new search for knowledge about the universe (rather than accepting that knowledge from ancient authority). Descartes made this revised role of the individual clear in the famous statement at the foundation of his philosophic enterprise: "I think, therefore I am."

Chapter 3 earlier credited Thomas Hobbes (1588–1679) for his role in the development of the realist worldview. His political analysis also contributed significantly to the development of liberalism. He began by defining human nature and the patterns of interaction that individuals would develop in the absence of government. Although this analysis led him to an illiberal conclusion, namely the requirement for a social contract giving over power to a strong central government, his thoughtful consideration of the relationship between individuals and their government was an important building block for others.

John Locke (1632–1704) was one of those others, and historians often regard him as the founder of liberal democratic thought. Basing his argument on a belief that God created humankind, he concluded that humans have certain natural rights, including self-preservation of one's own person. He extrapolated those rights into the right to sell one's own labor and to own additional property, justifying a capitalist society. He also made a strong case that the government should not interfere with the exercise of these rights. Many others, including Jeremy Bentham, John Stuart Mill, and James Madison, gradually created a body of politically liberal thought based on universal suffrage and social institutions with limited power.

In the economic realm, Adam Smith (1723–1790) provided the classic statement of liberalism in his *Inquiry into the Nature and Causes of the Wealth of Nations*, originally published in 1776. He argued that it was human nature to "truck, barter, and exchange" and that individuals act rationally to pursue their self-interests in trade. He began the discussion of exchange, involving employers

TABLE 11.1
Political Economy Worldviews

Worldview Name(s)	Liberalism; pluralism	Structuralism; Marxism; world systems theory; dependency theory
Central Concepts: Agents/Structures	Individuals; firms–households; markets	Classes (domestic and international); world system (core and periphery)
Values of Agents	Profits; utility	Position; share
Central Concepts: Bases of Interaction	Mutually beneficial exchanges	Class relationships (hierarchy and domination)
Theories: Systematic Dynamic Descriptions	Growth: capital accumulation growth of trade: comparative advantage; division of labor modernization: stages of growth; structural transformation	Capital accumulation; imperialism; cycles of expansion; dependence; dual economy development
Theories: Typical Forecasts	Continued growth; progressive spread of income	Continued crises; system transformation
Values of Worldview Proponents	Efficiency; growth	Equality; growth
Typical Prescriptions	Laissez faire; solution of market failure problems	Revolution in the center; autarky or self-reliance

and suppliers of goods (firms) on the one hand, and consumers and suppliers of labor (households) on the other, that occupies the economics based on classical liberal thought to this day.[2]

[2]Chapters 7 and 8 challenged two assumptions of the realist worldview: that states are unitary, rational actors; and that security is the exclusive value pursued by humans in collectivities. Analogously, Etzioni (1988; see also Levine 1988) questions whether individual human beings always behave "rationally" and only pursue their self-interest. He presents a paradigm (worldview) in opposition to liberalism that focuses on humans in social collectivities or communities and on motivations other than self-interest. For instance, he points out that "Many people forgo 'free rides' out of a sense of public duty and commitment to fairness; refuse welfare because it violates their dignity; choose to cooperate as their solution to the Prisoner's Dilemma, and so on." (Etzioni 1988, 22).

Individuals (or their firm and household aggregates) come together in **markets** for **mutually beneficial exchange**. Firms seek to maximize profits, and households seek to maximize income and the utility of consumption based on it. If they act freely and in their rational self-interest, no party will enter into any exchange unless it benefits the party. One of the most famous contemporary classical liberals is Milton Friedman, who has described this mutually beneficial exchange process:

> In its simplest form a [free private enterprise exchange economy] consists of a number of independent households.... Since the household always has the alternative of producing directly for itself, it need not enter into any exchange unless it benefits from it. Hence, no exchange will take place unless both parties do benefit from it.... So long as effective freedom of exchange is maintained the central feature of the market organization of economic activity is that it prevents one person from interfering with another in respect of most of his activities. The consumer is protected from coercion by the seller because of the presence of other sellers with whom he can deal. The seller is protected from coercion by the consumer because of other consumers to whom he can sell. (Friedman 1962, 13–14).

THEORY

Liberals identify three forces that operate within market economies and that give rise to economic growth and increased welfare. The first important force underlying growth in liberal economic theory is reinvestment by producers of a portion of their profits (earnings minus expenses) in such a way as to increase production efficiency, volume, and future profit. That is, they accumulate capital. Physical capital, largely production machinery and the buildings housing it, is a key factor of production, and therefore growth in the economy requires such **capital accumulation**.

The second force is special advantage in the production process. Adam Smith recognized that producers have differential access to raw materials, capital, technology, labor, or other inputs to the production process. They therefore advantageously specialize in the production of that which they can produce most efficiently and trade for that which they cannot so easily produce. If I am a good tailor (and already have a sewing machine) and you are a good vintner (and have a vineyard in the Napa valley), it hardly makes sense for me to grow my own grapes or for you to make your own clothing. I should make clothing, you should produce wine, and we should "truck and barter" our products. We each have an **absolute advantage** in the production of some good.

We can easily extend this example into international trade. Consider the international positions of England and Portugal. Assume initially that both countries produce only cloth and wine, and do not trade (Table 11.2). Assume further that, using all of their resources, both England and Portugal can produce 50 units of each product. Thus acting individually, the two countries could each deliver 50 units of cloth and 50 units of wine to their populations. If, however, the cost of cloth production in England were lower than the cost in Portugal and if England were to specialize in cloth, it might produce 120 units; similar cost advantage and specialization might also allow

Portugal to produce 120 units of wine. These results of specialization reflect hypothetical absolute advantages of the two countries (Portugal can more easily produce wine than England, because of its climate). If they were to so specialize and then trade half of their production with one another, their populations would obtain 60 units of each product rather than 50 units. Obviously this trade is beneficial.

TABLE 11.2 The Advantage of Trade						
No Trade						
	Production		Trade		Consumption	
	Cloth	Wine	Cloth	Wine	Cloth	Wine
England	50	50	0	0	50	50
Portugal	50	50	0	0	50	50
Specialization and Trade						
	Production		Trade		Consumption	
	Cloth	Wine	Cloth	Wine	Cloth	Wine
England	120	0	-60	+60	60	60
Portugal	0	120	+60	-60	60	60

David Ricardo (1772–1823) recognized that in some cases one potential trading partner might have an absolute advantage in all production. Imagine that you own both the sewing machine and the vineyard. Is trade with me still desirable? It is, because your **comparative advantage** may be greater in wine than in cloth (there is no way I can produce grapes without land, but my needle and thread allow me to produce clothing). Therefore we should still trade your grapes or wine for my cloth. Ricardo extended these insights into an understanding of the mutual beneficiality of international trade, even if England could produce both wine and cloth more efficiently than Portugal (or if the United States could produce both autos and wheat more efficiently than Mexico).[3]

A third important force for growth is **division of labor** in the production process.[4] In Adam Smith's famous example of the pin factory, he argued that individuals producing entire pins could not produce as many each day as when they specialize—one drawing out thin wire, another cutting it, another producing pin heads, and so on. Today we can see division of labor at work both within

[3]It is only necessary that the ratio of costs for the products be different in the trading countries, thereby establishing comparative advantage.

[4]See Caporaso (1987) for an excellent elaboration of the concept and some applications to the modern international political economy.

factories and across country borders. For instance, factories around the world produce parts for the Ford Escort.

The individual capitalist's self-interest in acquiring wealth drives these three growth processes. All lead to greater wealth and well-being for the society as a whole. Liberal political-economic theory has built steadily on the base provided to it by Smith and many others of his period. A perspective labeled "neoclassical" gradually led to the theory of market operations. It identified how prices rise and fall with scarcity, and thereby bring supply and demand into equilibrium.[5] Most economic theory and research in the United States and other developed market economies remains generally within this elaborated liberal worldview.

In addition to its primary emphasis on domestic economic development in developed economies, liberal political economic theory has also turned its attention to the problems of economic development in the South, to **modernization**. Can the LDCs transform themselves into more developed countries? Liberals believe that they can. In general, liberals see the experience of developed, market-oriented countries as a model for the development of additional countries. One early portrayal sees the development process as consisting of several **stages of growth** (Rostow 1971b). Although the exact experience of every country differs, and countries can benefit from those that trod the road earlier, liberals suggest that all countries will initially undergo development in a limited portion of their economy and in a restricted geographic area. Increases in the rate of investment initiate the limited growth and further increases subsequently fuel the spread of it. Creation of physical infrastructure, such as transportation, communication, and power systems, will be another important part of the development process.

Some liberal critics of the stages-of-growth portrayal argue that increased investment is a necessary but insufficient condition for growth. Significant **structural transformations** must also occur throughout the economy, including a shift from primary goods production to manufactures, an increase in literacy, and often greater ties to the world economy (Chenery 1979). In the 1980s and 1990s liberals also frequently have argued that LDCs need to free their economies from heavy state intervention as a prerequisite of economic growth.[6]

Liberals have also worked to develop understandings of how the processes of economic growth interact with those of distribution. Simon Kuznets presented one such theoretical perspective (Kuznets 1966, 217; 1984). He argued that in the early stages of industrialization, income inequality increases. One reason is that industrialization, and the benefits it confers, begins selectively, assisting perhaps one region of a country. It initially does not help the masses of people employed

---

[5]More recently, John Maynard Keynes (1883–1946), working to explain the Great Depression of the 1930s, specified how the drive for capital accumulation can lead to an emphasis on savings that diminishes effective demand and thereby gives rise to a disequilibrium between production capacity and demand. Hicks and others have worked to integrate the analysis of Keynes with neoclassical thought (to create a neoclassical synthesis) by understanding the importance of rigid wages and the liquidity trap (Pearce 1983, 236).

[6]Todaro (1989) reviews the evolution of development theory including liberal and competing perspectives.

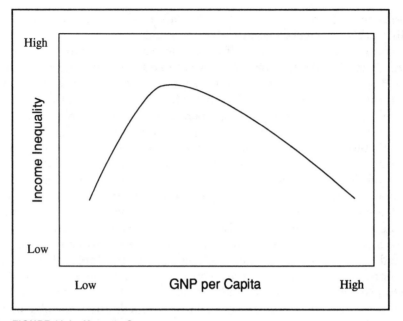

FIGURE 11.1 Kuznets Curve

in traditional agriculture. Further, it historically benefits the capitalists considerably more than the workers, given large surpluses of labor and the low wages workers are therefore willing to accept. Over time and with continued industrialization, the income distribution begins to improve again. For instance, industrialization spreads throughout the country and draws in people even from the most backward sectors and geographic areas. This is the **spread effect**. As industrial employment grows and labor becomes scarcer, wages rise (as is happening in South Korea and Taiwan now). Kuznets stresses also the growing role of government in transferring income within the more economically developed countries. Evidence on the Kuznets theory is mixed and it is hotly debated.[7] Figure 11.1 presents what has come to be known as the **Kuznets curve**.

Kuznets developed his theory of income distribution and its improvement with continued growth to explain what happens within countries. The same logic might help explain, however, why global income distribution worsened dramatically in the decades following the beginning of the industrial revolution, and such logic may hold out hope that, with time and international spread of industrialization, global income inequalities will lessen.

VALUES AND PRESCRIPTIONS

The topic of distribution creates difficulties for liberal theorists, in part because the core values of liberals are growth and **efficiency** (maximum produc-

[7]Loehr and Powelson (1977). Limited longitudinal data exist to test it, and the cross-sectional test, although generally supportive of the theory, is not fully satisfactory. For a most extensive analysis, see Adelman (1986). For a comparative test of several theories of distribution, see Chan (1989).

tion possible with given resources), looked at for the society as a whole.[8] The classical liberal perspective continues to be that distributional issues are largely beyond the scope of economics and are a matter for social decision making and politics. Liberals are more likely to emphasize **equity** (impartiality and fairness) than **equality** (identical income or wealth shares). Classical liberals often argue that an emphasis on efficiency and growth best serves the interests of all, because it will help create a growing pie rather than focus attention on how to divide it differently.

Prescriptively, support for restraint of government has especially deep roots in liberalism. As Adam Smith helped develop liberal thought 200 years ago, he was reacting against what he saw to be stultifying governmental control of the economy. He was, in essence, a spokesman for the growing commercial or middle class and its desire for a freewheeling capitalism against the remnants of the aristocratic and feudal perspective. As we might say today, he wanted to "get the government off the backs of efficient producers and traders." The liberal prescription of **laissez faire** (French for "let do") calls for precisely that. Although Smith recognized an appropriate role of government, for instance in national defense, he called for sharp circumscription of its role elsewhere.

Over the years liberals have identified several other areas in which government activity may be appropriate, often in reaction to **market failures**. For example, pollution represents a market failure, because decisions about production do not consider the costs pollution imposes on society. Some economic sectors, like electricity distribution, are natural monopolies—another market failure. Economic activity in these fields requires such great capital investment that, when one firm is in place, it can manipulate prices so as to reap high profits and simultaneously prevent entry of other firms.[9] Such market failures call out for collective societal action through government. In addition, society may deem it valuable that government redress income or wealth inequalities.

Liberals express great differences of opinion with respect to the extent of appropriate governmental intervention in the face of market failures and persistent income inequalities. McKinlay and Little (1986, 45) refer to those liberals who seek considerable governmental action as "compensatory liberals." In this terminology we again can see the connection between what we have termed "classical liberals" and the "modern American liberals." Although some modern liberals in the United States give short shrift to the market, many do believe

---

[8]The search by liberals for a Pareto optimum, a state of the economy in which the situation exists where no one can improve his or her condition without hurting the position of at least one individual, actually reinforces the difficulties liberals have with distributional questions and with any policy intervention into the economy. Practically no policy will avoid damage to the interests of someone (for instance, redistributional policies will invariably injure those from whom society takes income or wealth). Welfare economics recognizes this and turns to the "potential Pareto" or Kaldor-Hicks criterion, "which specifies that a course of action is a correct one if potential gainers could compensate potential losers and retain a net benefit" (Bobrow and Dryzek 1987, 34). Although the potential Pareto criterion for policy action sanctions nearly any activity that increases the overall economic pie, it still will not support action that merely redistributes the slices of that pie.

[9]More precisely, a natural monopoly exists when fixed costs are so high relative to variable costs that average cost declines over the entire range of demand (Weimer and Vining 1989, 61).

that individuals acting in their self-interests within markets are fundamentally important to economic efficiency and social well-being. They also believe, however, that government should be active in the face of market failures and persistent social inequalities.

MERCANTILISM

Mercantilism is a second political-economy worldview. It extends the concepts and theories of realism (see Figure 3.1) into economics.[10] For mercantilism, as for realism, states are central actors and operate in an anarchical state system. They use power in the pursuit of security. In its extension to economic concerns, mercantilism elevates wealth to central conceptual status along with power and security:[11]

> I believe that practically all mercantilists, whatever the period, country, or status of the particular individual, would have subscribed to all of the following propositions: (1) wealth is an absolutely essential means to power, whether for security or for aggression; (2) power is essential or valuable as a means to the acquisition or retention of wealth; (3) wealth and power are each proper ultimate ends of national policy; (4) there is long-run harmony between these ends, although in particular circumstances it may be necessary for a time to make economic sacrifices in the interest of military security and therefore also of long-run prosperity. (Viner 1958, 286; quoted in Gilpin 1987, 32)

The philosophy of mercantilism grew up with the modern state and state system, and it dominated political-economic thought during the sixteenth and seventeenth centuries. It had consequences for both domestic and international policy. Domestically it led to state support for the manufacturing sector and the exports of it (which could secure bullion). For instance, a leading French mercantilist, Jean Baptiste Colbert (1619–1683), with the ear of the king, used subsidies and tariff protection to encourage industry, while simultaneously building a large navy in support of commerce and colonization.

Externally, mercantilism required the development and protection of markets. For instance, the British Navigation Act of 1651 forbade importation of many goods unless carried in British ships. Subsequent acts required, for example, that all goods shipped to the American colonies go through British ports. Parliament did not repeal these acts until 1849.

The linkages between classic mercantilism and imperialism are apparent. The typical colonizing country demanded that the colonies trade only with them. The colonizer dictated insofar as possible what the colonies could trade and at what prices. It used various mechanisms to extract the maximum economic benefit from exchanges with the colonies. The British colonies on the Atlantic coast of North America faced less onerous and complete control than did the Spanish colonies in South America, but still resented the restrictions on their trade and the taxes (such

---

[10]Not all realists follow the path paved by their concepts into mercantilist economics. As Chapter 2 emphasized, many draw a sharp boundary between international politics and economics, adopting liberal thought in international economics.

[11]Wealth, like power, even takes on the character of both means and end.

as that on tea) imposed by Britain. Before World War II, both Nazi Germany and militaristic Japan adhered to variants of imperialist theory that led them to demand economic control of regions (such as Eastern Europe and Manchuria) that they believed necessary to sustain the economic and political power of the state.[12]

In the postcolonial era, we speak frequently of **neomercantilism**. States no longer value bullion so highly, but they still value wealth, for instance in the form of large stocks of dollars, yen, and marks. Many of the modern methods for increasing state wealth are little changed from earlier years: subsidies to select industries, tariffs, and assorted nontariff barriers to trade, so as to favor exports over imports. Box 11.1 elaborates.

BOX 11.1   Mercantilism and Neomercantilism

Classical mercantilism emphasized acquisition and retention of bullion as a store of wealth for the state. States could obtain bullion by maintaining trade surpluses with other countries, by plundering, and through exploitative relationships with colonies.

Today we more often view gold and silver as sterile and maintain wealth in the form of productive investments such as factories. "**Neomercantilism** is a trade policy whereby a state seeks to maintain a balance-of-trade surplus and to promote domestic production and employment by reducing imports, stimulating home production and promoting exports" (Blake and Walters 1987, 18).

Certain instruments of neomercantilism may target the domestic economy, and only incidentally and even unintentionally improve the international position of firms:

1. Development of infrastructure. More efficient transportation facilities assist exporting firms.
2. General assistance to industries. Support for research and development, subsidies, and the provision of financing for firms provide advantages in both local and international markets.

Other measures clearly assist domestic firms in global competition, and states may adopt them specifically for that reason:

1. Tariffs (taxes on imports).
2. **Non-tariff trade barriers (NTBs)**. These include quotas, which limit the imports of a particular good. The United States continues to limit sugar imports and long restricted oil imports. Orderly marketing arrangements (OMAs) do the same, but are more often bilateral. States sometimes purposefully adopt health standards, like those that the EC uses to exclude some American beef, as trade barriers. Japan has relied on bottlenecks at borders, such as inspection requirements and inadequate numbers of custom agents, to limit some imports. In addition, Japan has historically restricted bidding on many governmental contracts to domestic firms. Such NTBs are a considerably greater barrier to trade than tariffs.
3. Maintenance of an undervalued currency. Many NICs keep the price of their currencies low in order to make their goods inexpensive abroad and to make foreign goods expensive at home.

---

[12]Although mercantilism can give rise to imperialism, not all imperialism flows from mercantilism. Waltz (1979) writes of the three surpluses: people, goods, and capital. Choucri and North (1974), in their elaboration of the theory of lateral pressure, focus on the demand for land, food, and raw materials.

Neomercantilism, like realism, views the world in zero-sum terms, and its manifestations therefore give rise to conflict among states. The primary source of tension between the United States and Japan today lies in U.S. claims that the Japanese protect their domestic economy while pursuing advantages abroad in a self-centered effort to improve their own economic condition at the expense of others.

STRUCTURALISM

A third political-economic worldview is the **structuralist**.[13] Structuralist thought generally rejects both the individual and the state as the appropriate basic unit of analysis. Two principal units of analysis emerge instead: the **class**, and the global political economy, or **world system**, as a whole. (Actually, structuralist thought often points to interacting sets of structures based on class, race, and gender differences—we limit our attention here to class.) Structuralist thought, although always rooted in these concepts, has undergone considerable transformation as the world it describes has changed. This discussion briefly sketches structuralist thought, from Marxism, through theories of imperialism (including Lenin's thought), to contemporary structuralist theory.[14]

MARXIST CONCEPTUAL ROOTS

Many structuralists root their thought in Marxism. And for Marxists, the class is the fundamental unit of analysis (Milbrand 1977). Even those structuralists who emphasize the global system as a whole, often, like Karl Marx (1818–1883), see the whole as an interaction of classes. He wrote:

> The proletariat and wealth are opposites. As such they form a whole. They are both products of the world of private property. The whole question is what position each of these two elements occupies within the opposition. (as cited in Tucker 1978, 133)

Marx saw national and international politics, past, present, and future (until the establishment of the "dictatorship of the proletariat" and the "withering of the state"), in terms of class structures and the interactions of classes within the whole political economy.

For Marx, history was a study of the ownership of the means of production and the opposition that property set up between the owners—whether they be slave holders, feudal aristocrats in control of the land, or capitalists—and all others. These economic divisions condition political and social relationships, even values,

---

[13]Another possible label, "radical" (Hughes 1985; Blake and Walters 1987), carries a great deal of baggage. McKinley and Little (1986) use "socialist" to identify approximately the same worldview (see also Holsti 1985 and "neo-Marxist"). Viotti and Kauppi (1987) struggle with the terminological difficulty and choose "globalist," because they correctly argue that the worldview incorporates Marxists and non-Marxists. Yet globalist better fits the challengers of realism (see Maghroori and Ramberg 1982), than it does the challengers of liberalism. We join Banks (1984, 1985) in adopting "structuralist."

[14]Shannon (1989) focuses on the world-system perspective, but provides a readable overview of the linkages among these bodies of thought.

morality, and religion. More specifically, the dominant economic class controls important institutions, including the state and the church, and uses them to reinforce its position within society.

The system or mode of production changes over time. Marx identified Asiatic (primitive communist, tribal societies), ancient (slave societies of Egypt, Greece, Rome), feudal, and capitalist. Different "forces of production" (fundamentally the technology of the era and resources available to the society) characterize each system. So do different "relations of production," the relationships among people in the production process.

Marx argued that the relationships among people (class relations) change slowly, whereas the forces of production (and the technology underlying them) are quite dynamic. Sometimes the class relationships impede change in the forces of production, creating tensions or contradictions (much as we have stressed that tensions often build between the substructural forces of world politics and the superstructures). In the face of tensions, class antagonisms harden, setting the stage for a revolution that will usher in a new mode of production. For instance, in the modern or capitalist era, Marx argued that the concentration of wealth in the hands of capitalists and the impoverishment of laborers frustrate the ability of the new production techniques to satisfy the needs of all and would eventually lead to such a revolution.

That Marxist view of class relationships, and of hierarchy and domination in the political economy, differs sharply from the liberal view of economic interactions. Liberals portray individuals interacting in their self-interest, but doing so in a mutually beneficial milieu of market exchanges. Interactions are win-win or nonzero-sum; all can benefit. In Marxist analysis, however, the gains of one class generally come at the expense of another. The classes seek to maintain or enhance their position in the relationship and therefore their share of economic product.[15] The game is win-lose or zero-sum. The world of structuralists is, in this sense, a harsher one than that of liberals and more akin to that of mercantilists.

Yet, Marx did not doubt the strength of the forces for technological progress and welfare improvement that capitalism and capital accumulation set in motion. He deplored, however, the neglect of distributional issues and the implicit acceptance of low wages, maximum profits, and uncaring social policies. He wanted to build communism on the technological and productive dynamism of capitalism, but to eliminate scarcity. In this sense, the world of the Marxists was ultimately to be "kinder and gentler" than that of many early liberals.

Marx foresaw the spread of capitalism around the globe and approved of it as a progressive force in societies dominated by more primitive modes of production and by feudal class relations. He also foresaw the inability of many capitalists to compete and a growing concentration of capital in a few hands. He further anticipated increasing impoverishment of the masses during the intense struggle

[15]According to Marxists the working class does not always, however, see through the self-serving, mutual-benefit arguments of capitalist economists and recognize their class status and interests. It is frequently necessary to raise their class consciousness.

for existence and dominance among capitalists. In the long run, only those capitalists who were most effective in squeezing wage costs would survive. Ultimately this would lead to an uprising of workers against capitalists.

IMPERIALISM

In the early 1900s, the Marxist forecasts of the spread of capitalism and the concentration of capital appeared to be unfolding. On the latter point, large firms with a global reach were emerging, and they were absorbing smaller ones or driving them to bankruptcy.[16] The conditions of workers in many industrial countries, however, improved rather than deteriorated—a trend that contradicted the Marxist supposition of increasingly antagonistic class relations, and a development not likely to lead to revolution against capitalism. Those who wanted to build on Marxist theory thus needed to explain this phenomenon and why it was to be only temporary.

John Hobson (1858–1940) provided the basis of an explanation. He argued, as Marx had, that the concentration of income and wealth in the hands of a few, and the removal of income and consumption power from the workers, set up a situation of surplus production. He saw the principal outlet for this surplus in **imperialism**. Although Hobson believed that a better solution would be redistribution of income, what he saw around him, when he published *Imperialism* in 1902, was a use of government by capitalists to promote foreign interests and to export surplus labor and capital to more backward societies. Such imperialism, he argued, relieved the society of these surpluses, both through their export and by wasting them on the associated militarism.

Lenin picked up many of the arguments of Hobson in his own study of *Imperialism, the Highest Stage of Capitalism*, published in 1916. He quoted Cecil Rhodes, the British industrialist, namesake of Rhodesia (now Zambia and Zimbabwe), and patron of Rhodes scholarships:

> I was in the East End of London [a working-class quarter] yesterday and attended a meeting of the unemployed. I listened to the wild speeches, which were just a cry for "bread! bread!" and on my way home I pondered over the scene and I became more than ever convinced of the importance of imperialism.... My cherished idea is a solution for the social problem, for example, in order to save the 40,000,000 inhabitants of the United Kingdom from a bloody civil war, we colonial statesmen must acquire new lands to settle the surplus population, and to provide new markets for the goods produced in the factories and mines. The Empire, as I have always said, is a bread and butter question. If you want to avoid civil war, you must become imperialists.[17]

Lenin linked such imperialism firmly to capitalism and saw it as the factor that explained the relatively good condition of workers in the more advanced capitalist states, in contradiction of the Marxist expectation that their condition

---

[16]Marxists today continue to point to mergers and bankruptcy of firms as indicative of this process of emerging monopoly capital.

[17]Reported in Ingersoll and Matthews (1986, 169). Parts of this chapter draw upon their discussion.

should deteriorate. As the world became divided among capitalist states, so that outlets for the surpluses became scarce, he foresaw an inevitable clash among the imperialist states (like that of World War I, which erupted in 1914). In short, imperialism could prolong the era of capitalism but not save it.

The truth of Lenin's link between capitalism and imperialism is a matter of heated debate. Waltz (1979, 24–27) argues that noncapitalist powers such as Rome and Athens also relied on imperialism for various reasons. Thus capitalism is unnecessary for imperialism (unless imperialism is trivially defined to be capitalist expansion). He also points out that at the turn of the century England had about half of its capital invested outside of colonies, especially in the United States, implying that imperialism was not necessary for the disposal of surpluses by capitalist states. Nonetheless, Lenin's argument still draws support from some Marxists.

CONTEMPORARY STRUCTURALISTS

Lenin foresaw the nearly immediate end of capitalism in the clash of imperialisms around him. That did not happen, and imperialism, to the degree that it exists today, is very different in form from that of the early twentieth century. Thus structuralist theory again faced the necessity of adaptation.

An important recent development that offers assistance in that enterprise is **world systems theory**. Although generally eschewing the Marxist label, and in fact often attacking contemporary Marxist thought, the world system theorists adopt much of the basic conceptual framework of Marxists.[18] André Gunder Frank describes world systems theory in terms of classes and an economic whole:

> This approach, which recognizes the exploitative class basis of past and present development, seeks to offer a historical perspective and an analytical approach to the examination of the past, present, and future development of the whole world within a *single modern world system*. (Frank 1983, 28)

World system theorists argue that capitalistic development has proceeded in **cycles of expansion** rather than in the sudden surge that Lenin described. They see long waves of expansion and stagnation, or even contraction, beginning with the birth of the capitalist world system in feudal Europe (Wallerstein 1976 and 1980). These cycles have gradually expanded the scope of the capitalist world system from a small initial area to a global domain. Lenin wrote near the peak of one expansion cycle.

Whatever the geographic scope of the capitalist world system, world system theorists see within it a **core** of states and economies that dominate the system and a **periphery** of subordinate economies. They also identify a semiperiphery of countries such as Argentina at the turn of the century (it fell back to the periphery) and the newly industrialized countries today. In fact, most world system theorists essentially portray what is essentially an international class structure, in which the development of the more advanced countries has occurred at the expense of the

[18]Holsti (1985) labels them neo-Marxist.

less developed. Frank calls it the "development of underdevelopment." This is an important and sharp contrast to the thought of Marx, who saw the spread of capitalism to the less developed countries as a progressive force promising the same advantages in those countries that it had given Europe.

This new understanding of the world economy helps structuralists address two issues. The first is the submergence of conflict among the economically developed countries, the states that Lenin believed would inevitably fight over access to the developing world. World systems theorists see continuing competition among those countries, but they also see shared interests, as members of the core collectively gain from the inexpensive labor, cheap resources, and large markets of the periphery, and from the investment profits generated there.[19] Second, the world systems perspective helps explain the *persistence* of the great gap between the North (core) and South (periphery). Third, the orientation explains why global crises of the capitalist system, such as that at the time of World War I, do not inevitably result in the triumph of socialism over capitalism. World systems theory, although expecting continuing crises and an eventual transformation of the world capitalist system to a socialist one, does not attempt to identify which cycle and which crisis period will give rise to the **system transformation**.[20]

The global economic downturn that began in the 1970s reinforced structuralist belief in periodic capitalist crises and drew the attention of many academics in the First World to the structuralist worldview. The failure of global inequalities to narrow has also supported structuralism. In addition, the relative inattention of liberal theorists to the long-term and to analysis of systemic change increased the attractiveness of world systems theory and the treatment it provides of long-term change. The theory also attracts those who believe the boundary line fixed by liberals between the economy and the political system to be artificial.

Another and complementary modern variant of structuralist theory is **dependency theory**, often called *dependencia* theory because many of its developers were Spanish-speaking Latin Americans. Dependency theory does not generally share the long-term horizon of world systems theorists. Instead, it focuses on the contemporary relationship of core and periphery states, and the asymmetrical **dependence** that the latter have on the former (or the penetration of the latter by the former).

Dependency theorists question the mutual beneficiality of trade that liberal theorists associate with the logic of absolute and comparative advantage. They suggest instead that power relationships, historically those between metropole

---

[19]Hymer (1987) and many other postwar Marxists now emphasize the development of an international capitalist class rather than discrete and antagonist national capitalisms.

[20]Many who work within the world-systems framework exhibit much greater complexity and flexibility of thought than this simplified exposition suggests. Cox (1987) begins by specifying twelve different modes of production in the late twentieth century and sketching correspondingly complicated class relations. He suggests an autonomous role for the state in the determination of production relations and in the structuring of the world order. He shares with other world system theorists, however, the belief that the world political economy entered a period of crisis in the 1970s, and that it will give rise to significant restructuring of the social order.

(the colonizing country) and colony, but even today between rich and poor, influence the terms of trade or exchange so that poorer and weaker countries frequently obtain lesser benefit from trade. Table 11.3 shows a second hypothetical trade relationship between England and Portugal (compare it with Table 11.2), positing the same ability of the two countries to increase cloth and wine production through specialization. Instead of assuming that the countries will exchange wine and cloth unit for unit, however, Table 11.3 calculates the effect of exchanging seven units of wine for five units of cloth. Although the English benefit greatly from the trade, the Portuguese do no better than they would without it. What rate of exchange for the two products will occur in reality? There is ongoing dispute between the two worldviews. In the terms of Chapter 6, trade relationships are those of strategic interaction in which the division of benefits is uncertain—there is a compatibility of interests but not an identity.[21]

TABLE 11.3
An Illustration of Unequal Trade

No Trade

	Production		Trade		Consumption	
	Cloth	Wine	Cloth	Wine	Cloth	Wine
England	50	50	0	0	50	50
Portugal	50	50	0	0	50	50

Specialization and Trade

	Production		Trade		Consumption	
	Cloth	Wine	Cloth	Wine	Cloth	Wine
England	120	0	-50	+70	70	70
Portugal	0	120	+50	-70	50	50

Dependency theory also claims that interaction with developed countries of the core distorts the domestic economies and social-political systems of LDCs in various ways. Limited portions of the developing country come into contact with the core and are linked to its economy. This creates a **dual economy** within the developing country—one part superficially modern, international, and wealthy; one part traditional, domestic, and poor (Galtung 1964). Although liberals also foresee the growth of a dual economy (in fact, the argument of Kuznets builds on it), dependency theorists characterize the growth of a "modern" sector of the

[21]Liberals argue that the law of reciprocal demand determines division of benefits (the post–trade exchange rate). Structuralists argue that the division has more political basis; for instance, the law of first exchange suggests that imperial power may establish unfair trade prices in an initial exchange and thereby set long-term precedent, sometimes reinforced by continuing political interference.

developing country's economy as negative, rather than as the leading edge of widespread modernization. Outside interests control it directly or through the holding of debt and develop it only to exploit the poorly paid labor or inexpensive raw materials of the periphery. In addition, the "modern" sector's existence establishes a propensity to social and political instability. Some in the internationally linked portion of the economy develop close relationships with the core; they may seek and obtain support from the core in their effort to maintain a privileged position in their domestic economy. They constitute in essence an instrument of the core in the periphery.

Although an economic association with the core brings great benefits to a select few, it may significantly harm many in the dependent economy. For example, the technology that the firms of the core bring to the periphery is often capital intensive and labor saving, because of its development in capital-rich core countries. That technology can intensify unemployment and income inequalities in the periphery. In addition, landowners may redirect agricultural land once used for domestic food production to the production of nonfood crops for export (such as coffee, cocoa, or tea) or to food crops grown specifically for export (such as oranges, bananas, or palm oil). In Central America, for example, owners devote much land to grazing cattle for beef export. Local incomes often prove inadequate to create a strong indigenous food market.

Like world system theorists, dependency theorists argue that the existence of already developed capitalist countries creates a context for the expansion of capitalism to additional countries that places those additional countries at great political and economic disadvantage.

VALUES AND PRESCRIPTIONS

The values of those espousing the more modern structuralist theories remain largely unchanged from earlier Marxism. Marxists, like liberals, emphasize growth. They place much greater emphasis on equality, however, than do liberals.

How can greater equality be obtained? Historically, Marxists have splintered when it came to supporting various prescriptions (even more bitterly than they did with regard to analysis). Marxists of the right (revisionists) argued early in this century that the existence of extensive suffrage and fairly open political institutions in Europe made revolutionary action no longer necessary. Those of the left, like Lenin or Rosa Luxemburg, put much emphasis on continuing class antagonism and on the necessity of violent revolution.

Similar important divisions characterize modern structuralist thought. World systems theory and dependency theory are primarily analytical perspectives. The writing of many theorists conveys an impression of inevitability in the movement to socialism. In contrast, Marxism is an ideology and remains more action oriented.[22] Some Marxists continue to believe that until capitalist institu-

[22]This is reminiscent of the distinction within idealism between analytically inclined globalists, and action-oriented nationalists or universalists.

tions are overthrown in the core, neither the developed countries nor those developing will break out of dependency relationships. They point to the actions that core countries, especially the United States, have taken or supported against Marxist governments, such as in Cuba, Chile, and Nicaragua, as evidence of the near impossibility of transformation in the periphery alone.

Other structuralists have found a model of self-reliance or autarky (economic independence) attractive. China, from the establishment of a Communist government in 1949 until its reentry into the global economy in the early 1980s, provided an example of such self-reliance. But the admission of economic problems in that country greatly lessened the attractiveness of autarky. The movement of nearly all of Central and Eastern Europe toward free markets has also dramatically undercut the appeal of central planning as a prescription. Structuralists are in considerable disarray.

The next two chapters develop liberal, mercantilist, and structuralist worldviews in more detail. They do so while exploring two contemporary international political-economic issues: the rise and maintenance of extensive and generally open international markets, and the persistence of a large economic gap between the North and South.

Chapter 12

THE RISE
AND MAINTENANCE
OF A GLOBAL ECONOMY

Universities separate the study of international politics and international economics, normally placing the two subject matters into different disciplines (political science and economics). This implies that the world of international power and national interest is somehow separate from the world of trade and finance. The real world does not maintain such a clean distinction.

THE HALTING GROWTH OF FREE TRADE

The power of Athens and later of Rome structured and protected extensive long-distance trading relationships. Trade, and the military ability of the two cities to extract economic resources from their allies and empires, supported the comparatively elegant and rich lifestyles of the imperial centers.[1] The collapse of Athenian power reduced trade in the Aegean; the fall of the Roman Empire preceded a restructuring of Europe into feudal units, which were largely self-contained political-economic systems with limited need for trade.

The rebirth of extensive trade coincided with the birth of the modern state system. In fact, the history of the modern state system could hardly be more entwined with the history of the modern world economy. In 1500 Venice was the hub of an extensive early world political economy, dominating shipping throughout the Mediterranean, to Britain and Scandinavia via the Atlantic Ocean, and to Asia on overland and land-sea routes. Genoa and Antwerp subsequently challenged or supplanted the Venetians as the scope of European commerce continued to grow.[2] Spain and Portugal established extensive colonial empires but were less able to capture and hold dominant positions in the European-centered world economy.

[1] Doyle (1986) emphasizes the transnational, commercial character of both Athenian and Roman empires. In fact, he argues that empires require such elements.

[2] Braudel (1979) and Wallerstein (1976 and 1980) detail the expansion of the world economy. Although the dates and interpretations they provide of transitions in leadership differ somewhat, the general logic of capitalist and trade expansion they describe is comparable.

Many factors, including the expansion of the Ottoman Empire, contributed to the relative decline of Venice and of southern Europe more generally. By 1650, Amsterdam and the United Provinces (now the Netherlands) had emerged as the clear center of an ever more extensive capitalist world economy. In 1700, only 40 percent of the population in the Netherlands was engaged in agriculture, and the per capita income was about 50 percent higher than that of England, its nearest rival (Maddison 1982, 14 and 29). The scope of trade and political penetration had become global (Magellan's expedition circumnavigated the world in 1522).

At the peak of its power, the Netherlands dominated the oceans with superior ships and many of them. In 1670 the Dutch owned more ship tonnage than England, France, Portugal, Spain, and the Germanies combined (Wallerstein 1980, 46). Their great naval superiority would seemingly have allowed them to dominate in free economic competition. In addition, Hugo Grotius, the Dutch jurist considered the father of international law, argued in the early 1600s that the seas of the world should be open to all. Yet instead of adopting the free-trade orientation of liberalism, the Dutch actively pursued mercantilist policies; that is, they sought to exclude others from principal roles in international trade and from their markets.

> The seventeenth-century world was still a place with limited markets, in which the success of trading countries depended on beggar-your-neighbor practices. Thus the Netherlands blockaded Antwerp's access to the sea from 1585 to 1795, taking over its entrepôt trade and textile industry. Its successful struggle with Portugal was similarly responsible for Dutch monopolies in trade with large parts of Asia and Latin America. It should be noted that the bulk of Dutch trade (probably three-quarters) was of an entrepôt character, involving transhipment and warehousing in Amsterdam. (Maddison 1982, 32).

England admired the Dutch success but chafed under it. For example, the efficient Dutch fleets could fish off England and deliver product to the English market at less cost than local fisherman. Although the English had played a key role in defeating Spanish naval power in their battle with the Armada in 1588, thus setting the stage for Dutch naval dominance, England remained an inferior commercial center.

England was larger than the Netherlands, with a more extensive internal market, partially protected by the English channel. It copied much of the Dutch technology and many of its policies, including a self-serving mercantilism. Most important, the industrial revolution began in Britain in the late 1700s and the early 1800s. With the British rise on the global stage, merchant capitalism (involving trade and transhipment) gave way to industrial capitalism (tied to efficient production).

As England moved into global leadership, the competition for dominance of Europe and the world economy was increasingly between the French and the English. From the days of Colbert, the controller general of finances in France near the end of the seventeenth century, the French monarchy used its resources to build the domestic economy through mercantilist policies (including subsidies, tariff protection, and the regulation of manufactured product quality). Colbert acted also to break down trade barriers within France and to construct shipyards, harbors, and a large navy. The English followed similar policies.

Yet the outcome of the English and French competition was still in doubt in 1783 at the signing of the Treaty of Paris (or Treaty of Versailles), when Great Britain (England, Scotland, and Wales were united in 1707) acknowledged the independence of the United States, and when the European conflict involving France, Spain, and Britain ended. At that time the GNP of France was about double that of Great Britain, and its population was three times as great (Braudel 1979, 384). France won that war but lost the subsequent peace. Although the industrial revolution and naval growth proceeded fairly steadily in Britain, revolution and the Napoleonic Wars greatly disrupted France.

Between 1820 and 1850, after approximately a century in a leading position, Britain moved from international policies based on mercantilism to those based on free trade. One of the most famous actions was the repeal in 1846 of the corn laws. In the early nineteenth century both consumers and manufacturers increasingly objected to the restrictions on low-cost grain imports (called "corn" imports in Britain), and eventually succeeded in having the barriers dropped.[3] The government also eliminated prohibitions on the export of machinery and the emigration of skilled labor. It had earlier feared that such export would aid foreigners in competition with Britain.

The reasons for the movement of Britain from mercantilism to free trade remain relevant in debates on trade today.[4] The increasing competitiveness of the British economy played a key role. Advocates of free trade argued that foreigners, even using British machinery, could not compete, because technology was advancing so rapidly that by the time they obtained it, the machinery would be outdated. Thus Britain could sell both the machinery and the products of it. The domestic shift of power from the landed aristocracy to the growing industrial bourgeois also supported free trade (as discussed in Chapter 7). The former benefitted from high food prices, whereas the latter wanted low prices for their own consumption and for that of workers. Similarly, many in the bourgeois wanted inexpensive raw materials and thus desired an absence of barriers to their import. Other analysts argue that the reasons for movement to free trade were ideological, that the theoretical arguments of liberals like Adam Smith convinced increasing numbers of Britons. Liberals believed that the British economy would be more productive and innovative when subjected to international competition, as would economies throughout the world. It is likely that all of these explanations are partially true and interactive.

Although support for free trade grew throughout the global economy, often under British pressure, the United States did not join in opening its economy. The United States used tariffs in the nineteenth century to protect the growth of domestic industry, while simultaneously promoting exports.

---

[3]Already by 1361 England had laws prohibiting the export of grain in order to maintain cheap and adequate domestic supplies. It also periodically controlled imports, including enacting the corn law in 1815 to avoid agricultural depression after the Napoleonic Wars.

[4]Kindleberger (1987) reviews the primary arguments.

While pursuing protectionist policies, the U.S. economy became increasingly important in the world. In 1870 Britain accounted for 24 percent of world trade compared with 8.8 percent for the United States (Lake 1987, 151). By 1900, the British share of world trade had dropped to 17.5 percent and the U.S. share had risen to 10.2 percent (in 1929 the U.S. share exceeded the British). Other countries, faced with a growing American challenge, moved toward restricting their markets. The United States, although continuing to protect its domestic market, began to argue in support of liberal policies abroad. For instance, when the British limited commercial access of other powers in China, the United States issued the Open Door notes in 1899, calling for nondiscriminatory access. The United States increasingly offered reciprocity, that is, access to its markets in exchange for maintenance of access to those of others. In terms of the concepts defined in Chapter 5, the United States moved toward specific reciprocity—it would cooperate when a clear and immediate quid pro quo was forthcoming.

Yet with the coming of the Great Depression, the United States did not stand behind its emerging liberal principles. Instead, the Smoot-Hawley Act of 1930 raised tariffs on all imports to 19 percent (on dutiable industrial goods to 60 percent). Other states reacted with similar sharp increases. In fact, some critics argue that U.S. policy turned the early stages of the Great Depression into a downward spiral in global trade that greatly deepened and prolonged it.[5] Only in 1934, after the collapse of world trade, did the United States become active in support of free trade. The Reciprocal Trade Agreements Act of that year encouraged the president to negotiate with other countries for reciprocal access to each other's markets and for lower tariffs. The act was part of Secretary of State Cordell Hull's liberal and globalist vision (Spero 1981, 76).

This new direction set the stage for post–World War II global leadership by the United States on behalf of liberal policies. It is to that era that we turn now. As we do so, we should carry two lessons from this historic review with us. First, although liberals prescribe a world of markets in which state intervention is highly limited, the reality has been and remains a world of markets in which state intervention is substantial and important. Second, there has historically been a single country that has, depending on one's perspective, either led or dominated the world economy and thereby established the character of the global economic system. When we survey the period of U.S. leadership in the next section, we should consider whether or not that leadership remains strong and capable.

LIBERALISM ASCENDANT: BRETTON WOODS SYSTEM

At the end of World War II, the European and Asian economies on both sides of the conflict were in ruins. The United States, the only great power that escaped attack and bombing, emerged stronger than before the war. In the earliest postwar days, the United States produced nearly one-half of the goods and services of the

[5]Global trade (imports of seventy-five countries) fell steadily from $2,998 million in January 1929 to $932 million in January 1933 (Kindleberger 1973, 172).

world. Those goods, and U.S. dollars with which to buy them, were in tremendous demand. The United States entered the new era in a position of dominance within the world economy and, in contrast to its withdrawal from responsibility in the 1920s and 1930s, it actively offered leadership.

Even before the war ended, in July 1944, the United States hosted representatives of forty-four countries in Bretton Woods, New Hampshire, for a discussion of the postwar economy. Collaborating with England, the country that had dominated the world economy for about two centuries, the Americans presented a plan for international public management of the global economy. The participating states accepted that plan, and the resultant structures and policies became known as the **Bretton Woods system**.

INSTITUTIONS OF BRETTON WOODS

Proceeding from a predominantly liberal outlook, the industrialized countries identified three principal international economic needs of the new era: stable exchange rates, international assistance to war-damaged economies, and low tariffs. Bretton Woods gave responsibility for meeting the first two needs to two new institutions: the International Monetary Fund (IMF) and the International Bank for Reconstruction and Development (IBRD), better known as the World Bank. It took until 1947 to establish a third institution, the General Agreement on Tariffs and Trade (GATT), with the charge of pursuing low tariffs. Both the IMF and the World Bank have headquarters in Washington, D.C. Voting in each depends on capital contributions, and the United States has had a weight reflecting the relative size of its economy. In brief, the United States is first among equals. GATT has less institutional structure and is primarily a framework within which states conduct international trade negotiations.

The IMF and GATT were reactions to the collapse of world trade in the 1930s. Faced with trade imbalances at that time, countries had raised tariffs to exclude foreign goods and had devalued their currencies (lowered values relative to other currencies) to make their export goods more competitive abroad. They thus used both restraint of imports and promotion of exports to keep domestic producers busier and employment higher. When many countries simultaneously pursued the same neomercantilist policies, however, the result was widespread constraint of imports and therefore reduction in global trade. (Box 12.1 explains some of the basic concepts of international trade and finance.) As in other collective action dilemmas, the pursuit of individually rational policies created a collectively irrational result.

The IMF encouraged stable exchange rates in two ways. First, no state could change the value of its currency without approval from the IMF (this is no longer the case, as we shall discuss later). Second, the IMF offers short-term financing for countries with trade deficits. Each member country contributes to the financing of the IMF and initially draws against its own contribution when in need. As countries draw on greater shares of their own contribution, and especially when they draw beyond it, the IMF poses increasingly strict requirements, referred to as **conditionality**, on the borrower. The IMF is *not* a foreign aid institution.

BOX 12.1 Concepts from Trade and International Finance

This and subsequent chapters assume knowledge of some terminology concerning international trade and finance. Many of the terms center on the exchange rate of currencies, and we therefore begin by defining it.

EXCHANGE RATE

The exchange rate between two currencies is the number of units of one currency (for example, German marks) that it takes to buy a single unit of another (for example, the U.S. dollar) in the global market place. When the central banks of two states guarantee that the rate does not vary from day to day, the exchange rate is **fixed**. When governments allow the rate to vary with supply and demand, the rate is **floating**.

DEVALUATION

Downward change in the exchange rate of one country relative to the value of the currencies of its trading partners. States often purposefully devalue their currency. An example explains the policy. If it costs two German marks (DM 2) to buy one U.S. dollar ($1), and $1 will buy a hamburger, a German can buy a hamburger with DM 2. It may also cost DM 2 (and therefore $1) to buy a bratwurst. If the German government wanted to discourage the purchase of hamburgers (which we will assume are imported from the United States), and encourage the purchase of German bratwurst, it could devalue the mark so that it cost DM 3 to buy $1. Germans would then find that it cost them DM 3 to buy a hamburger but still only DM 2 to buy a bratwurst. Americans would find that it cost $1 to buy a hamburger but only $0.67 to buy a bratwurst. Both Americans and Germans would likely buy more bratwurst and fewer hamburgers.

REVALUATION

Upward change in the nominal value of the currency of one country relative to the value of the currencies of its trading partners.

BALANCE OF TRADE

The value of exports from a country minus the cost of imports. The balance is **favorable** when exports exceed imports (reflecting mercantilist preferences for such a situation). The balance of trade is part of the balance of payments.

BALANCE OF PAYMENTS

International credits minus international debits. Credits include exports, earnings from tourists, profits from foreign investment, foreign aid receipts, and inflow of long-term capital investment. Debits include imports, tourist spending abroad, interest payments on foreign debt, foreign aid donations, and outflow of long-term investment. The balance is favorable when credits exceed debits. The market revalues floating currencies normally in response to favorable balances and devalues them in response to unfavorable balances.

Britain initially drew more heavily on the IMF than any other country and faced IMF conditionality in the mid-1960s and late 1970s. By the late 1970s and early 1980s, however, because of their debt crisis, LDCs drew nearly all IMF credits.

GATT pursues free trade generally, and reduced tariffs and nontariff barriers to trade specifically, through periodic rounds of multilateral negotiation. Members initiated the Uruguay round in 1986 (the first meeting of it was in Montevideo, Uruguay). GATT members grant each other **most-favored nation (MFN)** status, which means that they extend to all GATT members (and others with MFN status) the lowest tariff rates given to any state. They make some exceptions, including preferential tariffs (lower than MFN tariffs) on selected goods from LDCs. Members are supposed to negotiate all exceptions, within the GATT framework. Outside of GATT, countries often put different tariff rates on the same good, depending on its source. For instance, the United States charges higher duties on goods coming from Albania (not a GATT member) than on goods coming from France.

The MFN principle is a good example of diffuse reciprocity (see Chapter 5 on cooperation strategies). States open markets, and in some cases accept considerable economic costs by doing so, in the expectation that in the long run, the actions of other states will compensate them by doing the same.

The World Bank directed its initial efforts toward the countries of war-torn Europe. It is a lending institution, making loans on careful economic criteria and boasting a good record of loan repayment. Over the years it has shifted attention from the reconstruction of Europe to the development of the Third World. In 1956 participating states created the International Finance Corporation as an affiliate of the Bank with the aim of supporting private companies in LDCs (Riggs and Plano 1988, 319). Reacting to criticism by recipients that loan terms were too demanding, the international community created still another affiliate in 1960, the International Development Association (IDA). The IDA makes "soft" loans, without interest and with easy repayment conditions.[6] The IBRD and IDA together approved loans totaling about $22.7 billion in 1991 (UNDP 1992, 51).

The First World controls the IMF, GATT, and the World Bank. Many Third World countries have felt alienated from the Bretton Woods system (although most are members), arguing that it ill serves their interests; they have proposed, as we shall see in the next chapter, an alternative set of international economic institutions. The United States pressed the Soviet Union to join the new Bretton Woods institutions in the late 1940s, but that country chose to remain outside of them. During the cold war the U.S.S.R. also kept most the states of Eastern Europe from joining. By the end of 1992 nearly all of these states and the former republics of the U.S.S.R. had joined the IMF and World Bank.

How successful have the Bretton Woods organizations been? Many give them considerable credit for that fact that world trade expanded from $77 billion in 1953 to $3,311 billion in 1990. Figure 12.1 shows that trade expansion has been considerably more rapid than economic growth. In 1952 industrial countries as a whole exported goods equivalent to 9.1 percent of their GNP. By 1990 they exported 23 percent of GNP.[7]

---

[6] A convention established the Multilateral Investment Guarantee Agency (MIGA) as the fourth member of the World Bank Group in 1989.

[7] Thompson and Krasner (1989) point out, however, that world exports as a portion of GNP did not surpass the levels preceding World War I until the 1970s. Foreign investment as a portion of the GNP of developed countries is still only a small fraction of the rate in 1900. We should not overemphasize the economic interdependence of the world relative to earlier eras.

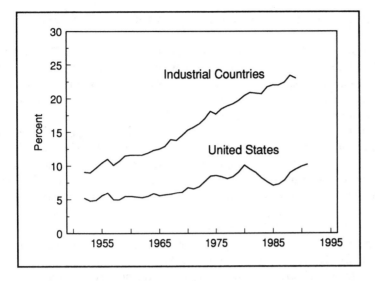

FIGURE 12.1 Exports as Portion of GNP
Sources: Courtesy of the Office for Development Research and Policy Analysis of the United Nations Secretariat, July 12, 1985. International Monetary Fund, *International Financial Statistics Yearbook* (Washington, D.C.: IMF, assorted years).

The United States, because it has such a large domestic market, is not as closely tied to the world economy as other industrial countries. Yet its exports grew from 5.2 percent to 10 percent of GNP in the same period. William Brock, former U.S. trade representative, offered these statistics concerning the importance to the United States of trade:

> Twenty-three percent of what we manufacture and 40 percent of all that we grow on the farm now goes for export. We grow more acreage in the country for sale to Japan than there are acres in Japan! Eighty percent of the new manufacturing jobs created in this country in the last five years were created in those industries which were involved in international trade. (Kegley and Wittkopf 1985, 168)

CHANGE AND EROSION

Already by 1947 the system, as originally conceived, proved inadequate.[8] Because of the weakness of other economies (substantial food and energy shortages still plagued much of Europe), the demand for U.S. goods was great, and the U.S. trade surplus was huge and growing. The United States held 70 percent of the world's monetary gold supply, making it impossible for most countries to buy those American goods with gold. They needed dollars and the embryonic international institutions could not provide enough of them. These realities forced the United States to take a more unilateral role in managing the world economy from

[8]This section draws upon the discussions of Spero (1981, 36–70), and Blake and Walters (1987, 62–89).

1947–1960, principally by supplying dollars and thus the wherewithal to buy American goods.

Between 1948–1952 the United States provided sixteen Western European countries with $17 billion through the European Recovery Program, known as the Marshall Plan. The United States spent billions more abroad by stationing its troops in the growing defense system. The American government even encouraged some protectionist policies and devaluation of currencies in the recovering countries.

The outflow of dollars helped set in motion the European and Japanese economic miracles of the 1950s. As the rest of the world recovered and began to be competitive in the world market, however, the hemorrhage of currency from the United States became a problem rather than a boon. By 1959 the dollars held abroad had risen to $19.4 billion and the gold remaining in the country, at the official exchange rate of $35 per ounce, had a value of $19.5 billion (down from $24.4 billion in 1948). The United States had in essence committed all of its gold abroad. (Figure 12.2 shows the dissipation of the U.S. gold value supply and the growth in U.S. foreign debt.) Throughout the 1960s the outflow of dollars continued, and a large "overhang" of dollars developed. The government encouraged allies like Germany to hold the dollars rather than to request gold, as the Bretton Woods system guaranteed they could. President de Gaulle of France argued that this ability of the United States to print money to pursue its interests abroad was an "exorbitant privilege" not available to other countries, and he insisted on delivery of gold. International speculators increasingly did the same.

Although many countries continued to support dollars by holding them, rather than demanding gold, the international community simultaneously made efforts to substitute other forms of international liquidity (currency needed in transactions) for the dollar. After much negotiation, IMF members decided in 1970 to issue Special Drawing Rights (SDRs), a kind of international currency backed by the assets of the IMF.

The IMF action was too late to save the dollar, however. By 1971 U.S. foreign liabilities exceeded the value of its gold by more than five to one. In that same year, the United States imported more goods than it exported for the first time in the twentieth century. Until then, it had spent dollars on foreign aid, military bases, and foreign investments, but its exports had been strong. The total payments deficit or dollar outflow in 1971 reached $10.6 billion, however. In August 1971 the Nixon administration decided without consultation abroad that it would no longer convert dollars to gold, and that it would impose a 10 percent surcharge on all imports. It also insisted on a 10 percent revaluation (upward price change) of the Japanese and German currencies. These actions did not resolve the crisis of confidence in the dollar, and in 1973 the United States again devalued the dollar by 10 percent and left its future value in the hands of the international market. Henceforth the dollar's value was to float, depending on supply and demand forces. Other countries quickly followed that move.

The movement to floating exchange rates introduced another problem into the international financial system, exchange rate instability. Many economists

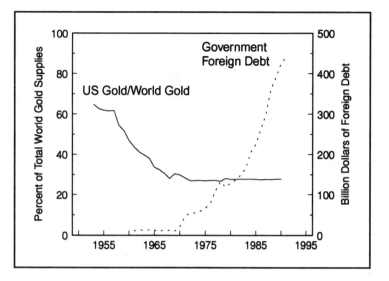

FIGURE 12.2   U. S. International Financial Position
Sources: International Monetary Fund, *International Financial Statistics Year-book* (Washington, D.C.: IMF, assorted years).

argued that floating rates would be self-regulating. Should an economy develop a negative balance of payments (defined in Box 12.1), the net outflow of currency from that country would create a surplus of it in the international currency markets and depress its value. The market-driven devaluation would lower the prices of the country's goods abroad and increase exports, while raising domestic prices of foreign goods and dampening imports. These changes in trade would bring the financial accounting of the country back into balance. After some initial adjustments to compensate for existing distortions in exchange rates under the old system, and after participants in the modified system learned the new rules of the game, liberals expected exchange rates to be quite stable.

In reality, movements of 50 percent in the value of a currency relative to other currencies have occurred in the space of a year or two, often to be quickly reversed in following years. For instance, the value of the Japanese yen rose 28 percent relative to the dollar between 1977 and 1978, only to lose much of that gain in the next four years. Initially central banks maintained a "hands off" policy with respect to these free-market fluctuations. In recent years, however, they have pursued coordinated and covert strategies to provide a more orderly currency market. Because corporations and private parties can move tens and even hundreds of billions of dollars between currencies in hours, potentially swamping the resources of central banks, instability is likely to remain a feature of the market (Figure 12.3).

When the United States initially allowed its currency to float in 1973, it expected the market to devalue it and to bring U.S. external accounts back into balance. As expected, the dollar fell nearly 20 percent by 1978 relative to the currencies of its trade partners, and the U.S. accounts did improve. In the 1980s,

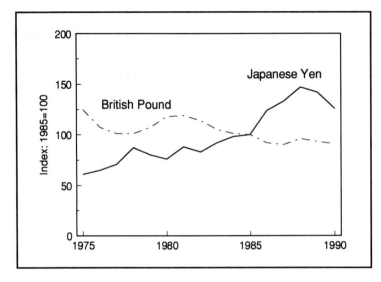

FIGURE 12.3   Effective Exchange Rate (Nominal)
Source: International Monetary Fund, *International Financial Statistics Year-book 1991* (Washington, D.C.: IMF, 1991, 460–61, 746–47).

however, various forces drove up the dollar's value, and by 1984 it stood 30 percent above the 1973 level (Blake and Walters 1987, 72). Demand for the dollar was strong for at least two reasons: the strengthening U.S. economy at a time when many European economies were stagnating (thus making investments in the United States, including those in the stock market, attractive), and the international debt problem and the financial insecurities that it generated (many in debt-ridden LDCs looked to dollars as a safe haven from their own depreciating currencies). Although the United States ran increasingly large trade deficits, and thus exported dollars to pay the deficits, the dollar demand was so strong that its value remained high until late in the 1980s.

Many designate the 1971–1973 period as the end of the Bretton Woods system and label the current system "post–Bretton Woods." Two major breaks with the earlier system separate the eras: the unilateral actions by the United States, in an international economic order supposedly based on cooperation within international institutions; and the abrogation of the concept of fixed exchange rates with a linkage to gold. The IMF, World Bank, and GATT remain in place, however, as do widespread international commitments to free and orderly trade. Thus it might be better to label the current system "modified Bretton Woods." The modified system for managing the global political economy faces a number of difficult challenges.

CHALLENGES FACING THE GLOBAL POLITICAL ECONOMY

Five difficult issues face the contemporary political economy and all attempts to manage it: (1) the perennial appeal of mercantilist trade behavior, (2) the rapid growth of transboundary financial flows, (3) the need to reintegrate the economies of Central and Eastern Europe, (4) a shift of global economic power away from the United States, and (5) the continued poverty of a large portion of the world. The rest of this chapter surveys the first four of these, and the next chapter explores the fifth in more depth.

TRADE: THE SHADOW OF MERCANTILISM

Perhaps the most fundamental ongoing challenge to the modified Bretton Woods System is neomercantilism. Although the philosophy of liberalism and the theoretical commitment to open international markets is widespread, the mercantilist belief persists that governments can improve the international economic performance of their country through selective intervention in the economy.

BASES OF NEOMERCANTILISM

There are at least two reasons for persistence of mercantilism. First, governments routinely intervene in their domestic economies. Even the British and Americans, historically committed to liberal principles, favor certain industries over others through tax benefits, research and development subsidies, infrastructure development, loans, and occasionally direct public ownership. In fact, many international trade issues grow out of what governments see as purely domestic activities. For instance, developed countries provide various forms of support to their agricultural sectors, intending to ease the pain in farm households as that sector declines within the overall economy. A direct result of these policies, such as price supports, is agricultural surplus. The domestic policy has international consequences when, in their efforts to dispose of the surpluses, governments give food away internationally or sell it at reduced rates. Although ardent liberals decry almost all such interventions, whether or not they have an international impact (they suggest letting the market work to reward strong producers and eliminate weak ones), governments are unwilling to follow such advice fully.

The second reason mercantilism persists in the international environment is that it appears successful. The Japanese government has worked closely with Japanese industry throughout the postwar period. It has helped with acquisition of technology and finance and with penetration of foreign markets. At the same time it has acquiesced in or reinforced various barriers to imports, the most effective of which have not been tariffs, but rather quotas, customs procedures, standards requirements, exclusionary domestic distribution networks, government procurement policies, and others. It also maintained an undervalued yen on foreign exchange markets for many years.[9] Liberal theory strongly supports the argument that deviations from free trade internationally lessen the overall efficiency of the system and create welfare losses in the aggregate. It does not, however, preclude an individual country from taking advantage of a liberal economic order to strengthen its own relative position, and Japan appears to have accomplished that.

[9]Even after exchange rates began to float, restrictions on access to Japanese financial markets limited demand for the yen (necessary to buy Japanese financial instruments) and thus helped protect a low yen price.

To understand how an individual actor can gain at the expense of others, consider a domestic economy. Should one firm gain a monopoly position within an industry, it can benefit greatly by raising prices above those found in a competitive market. Should competitors appear with lower prices, its economic strength may be great enough to drive the upstarts out of business. It was for these reasons that the United States government broke up John D. Rockefeller's Standard Oil, and that it continues to apply antitrust policies. Imagine the potential power of such a firm if the government were to support it with research and development funds, and with direct subsidies.[10] With enough skill a government could selectively choose industries in which it could give its own firms not only dominant positions in the domestic market but highly competitive ones abroad. Leading technologies internationally are high-profit ones. Japanese neomercantilism has consciously targeted such industries (ship-building, automobiles, and electronic goods earlier, and, most recently, aerospace) and shifted its support with changing technology.[11]

THE CHALLENGE OF NEOMERCANTILISM

Although liberals see international economics as nonzero-sum, mercantilists view it as zero-sum. Instead of focusing on the vast multitude of transactions among firms and households that result in increased system efficiency, production, and welfare, the mercantilist focuses on the transactions among states implied by their balances of trade. Every billion dollars of Japanese trade surplus must be offset by a billion-dollar trade deficit in other countries. The production of goods that generates a billion-dollar surplus employs many Japanese workers; were there no Japanese surplus, the same industries could potentially employ a comparable number in other countries. The belief that other countries (especially Japan) are taking jobs away from locals has led to a surge of protectionist sentiment in the United States and to trade barriers in Europe.

Many who express concern about large trade imbalances are not mercantilists but rather liberals who want "a level playing field." That is, they want all countries to play by the same free-trade rules (Kline 1985, 208). They recognize the benefits that free trade can bring in the aggregate for the world economy and the inefficient absurdity of suggesting that each country should make all of its own goods so as to maximize employment. They believe that countries that pursue liberal policies, however, cannot allow mercantilist countries to take advantage of them. In 1984, the United States decided that other countries supported their steel industries and dumped their surpluses on the U.S. market. U.S. production had declined from 137 million tons in 1937 to just 77 million tons in 1983. Congress therefore approved a quota system restricting imports to 20 percent of the U.S. market. Congress subsequently moved to give the administration special powers to retaliate against countries that restrict access to American goods. Even more, the Omnibus Trade

---

[10]The nuclear energy industry had such a position in the United States for many years. When environmental activism forced a reduction in governmental assistance, the industry floundered.

[11]Although this discussion singles out Japan, all countries pursue some mercantilist policies. And many economists attribute Japanese economic success less to such policies than to factors such as a high savings rate and a capable work force.

and Competitiveness Act of 1988 *required* the U.S. Trade Representative (under the "Super 301" provision) to take retaliatory action to open foreign markets to U.S. goods. Other members almost unanimously viewed this unilateral measure as a violation of GATT. In 1989, the United States named Japan, Brazil, and India under the provision. The United States and Japan held negotiations called the Structural Impediments Initiative to defuse the issue.

In a sense, these trade policies attempt to combine specific and diffuse reciprocity. They communicate the message that when other countries repeatedly take advantage of cooperative actions by the United States, and fail to deliver on their long-term obligations under diffuse reciprocity, the U.S. government will move to a specific reciprocity relationship with these countries. The danger some liberals see is that these **countermercantilist policies,** such as denying access to American markets for Japanese semiconductors in response to Japanese restrictions on American computers, might lead to trade wars that significantly restrict all markets. The line between countermercantilist and snowballing protectionist policies is thin.

The problem is again one of collective action. It is possible to take advantage of the collective good of free trade (unimpeded access to markets around the world), while not contributing significantly to the provision of the good.[12] If countries can obtain individual gains at the expense of others in a liberal international system, they are free riders. A few small free riders in an international system with a strong leader may pose no problem. As noted earlier, the United States actually encouraged Europe and Japan to adopt some mercantilistic practices when it dominated the system and almost unilaterally provided open markets. Should the free riders become numerous, however, or the size of any one become large compared with the main provider of the collective good, then they become spoilers.[13] Spoilers hold the negative power of being able to disrupt the system and destroy the provision of collective goods. In contrast, supporters are countries like Great Britain that are not systemic leaders but make important contributions to the collective good provision.

It is the danger of spoilers that worries many liberals today. The threat comes from three quarters. The first is Japan. In 1991 Japan ran a $45 billion trade surplus with the United States (down from nearly $60 billion in 1987). Japan appears to be opening its internal financial and goods markets and moving from many earlier mercantilist policies (Box 12.2). Access to its markets in wood products, medical equipment, telecommunications, and beef and citrus has improved. Nonetheless, the large trade surpluses of Japan still pose a serious threat to the system. A Harris poll in 1989 found that 68 percent of Americans felt that the economic threat from Japan was greater than the military threat from the U.S.S.R. In the United States these surpluses give rise not only to "Japan bashing," but to doubts concerning the value of liberal trade policies more generally.

[12]Chapter 6 discussed how free trade is by no means a pure public good and how both rivalry and excludability appear in its provision.

[13]Lake (1987) develops the categories of free riders, spoilers, supporters, and hegemonic leaders. He defines spoilers as middle-sized or large low-productivity states. This text focuses on size and policy, not productivity.

BOX 12.2   Is Japan Mercantilist?

Japanese tariffs are low, even by GATT member standards. Japan uses decreasing numbers of implicit nontariff barriers to trade. Its currency has appreciated sharply, making imported goods less expensive. Yet it continues to run large surpluses with the United States and some other trading partners.

Why? One explanation is that Japanese businesses benefit from superior access to finance (the high Japanese savings rate); a well-trained, motivated and socially cohesive labor force; and internationally aggressive marketing. A second explanation is that Japan does not have open domestic markets like those of the United States, and that, even in the absence of easily recognizable neomercantilist barriers, its markets are largely impenetrable. Observers call Japan a "network state" or a "developmental state," referring to the close relationships among public institutions and private firms. Family, university, regional, corporate, and other social ties create personal relationships, trust, and reciprocal obligations that set up nearly insurmountable barriers to equal treatment of outsiders.

There is undoubtedly some truth in both explanations. The difficulty is knowing which set of factors is stronger and how rapidly the Japanese networks may be opening to foreigners (see Krasner 1987b).

The NICs, following in the footsteps of Japan, are achieving rapid economic growth through promotion of exports and pose the second threat. Generally they rely on various neomercantilist policies, including undervalued exchange rates, to achieve rapid export growth. As other countries, including large ones like Brazil and India, examine the success of such policies enviously, a danger arises of too many free riders or ones that are too large. Trade surpluses of Taiwan and South Korea, vis-à-vis the United States and other trading partners, rose sharply in the 1980s and contributed further to American protectionist sentiment.

Some see an incipient third danger in the movement of Europe toward economic integration, especially in the accelerated push for a Common Market by 1992. They fear a "Fortress Europe," in which states practice free trade internally but raise barriers externally. In 1992 a dispute between the United States and the EC arose over agricultural trade, perhaps foreshadowing growing difficulties. In retaliation against EC failure to reduce agricultural subsidies to its satisfaction, the United States announced large hikes in tariffs on EC white wine and cheese.

TRADING BLOCS OR GLOBAL FREE TRADE?

The 1992 episode differed little from previous spats among the trading partners concerning pasta, wine, ham, beef, and other goods, one of which was called the "chicken wars." The fear, however, is that completion of the Common Market will create a fundamentally more protectionist Europe, and that the world may be splitting into giant trade blocs, substantially closing their markets to each other. In the global economic collapse of the 1930s, countries retreated into such trading blocs. The movement toward free trade between Canada and the United States beginning in

1989 (adding Mexico in 1992) suggests a second potential regional trade bloc. Closer Japanese ties with East Asian neighbors could be the seed of a third.[14] Figure 12.4 presents some basic data on these three potential trade blocs.

Yet the historic and philosophic commitment to free trade in both Europe and North America is great enough that existing regional associations will not automatically lead to strong trade blocs. It would probably require a significant global economic downturn, with substantial and growing unemployment to entice Western countries away from the liberal worldview and into policies of regional mercantilism. At the same time that some movement toward trading blocs became especially obvious, 108 countries continued to pursue discussions concerning freer global trade in the context of the Uruguay Round of GATT. That round, the seventh since the formation of GATT, made considerable progress on issues such as global protection of intellectual property rights and freedom of trade in services. The primary issue that caused it to stretch on much longer than initially anticipated was a demand by a number of agricultural exporting countries, led by the United States, for rapid and deep cuts in agricultural subsidies that the European Community had resisted.

Experts debate the degree to which global trade agreements and regional free-trade areas (FTAs) compete with or complement each other. Provisions of GATT actually allow regional FTAs, so long as they do not raise external trade barriers. Some analysts portray regional arrangements as stepping stones to progress at the global level. Others see them as the precursors of localized blocs that will, in fact, raise barriers to each other. The debate promises to be a prolonged and important one.

Still another issue arose in the early 1990s to complicate trade discussions on both free-trade areas and the global system. Environmentalists began to watch both the North American Free Trade Agreement (NAFTA) and GATT discussions closely, with an eye to obtaining trade agreements that protect the environment. The Sierra Club opposed NAFTA, arguing that Mexico does not adequately enforce environmental protection. Other environmentalists criticize GATT because it prevents a state from refusing to import a product for environmental reasons (that would be a nontariff barrier to trade). For instance, GATT struck down a U.S. ban on Mexican tuna, implemented because Mexican fleets used techniques that imperiled dolphins (porpoises).

FINANCE: THE SURGE OF CAPITAL FLOWS

The founders of Bretton Woods established institutions to deal with the trade-system problems of the 1930s (especially protectionism and competitive devaluations). In recent years, however, transboundary financial flows have increased even more rapidly than trade. Increases in capital flows initially undercut the fixed exchange-rate system and recent surges now lie at the root of several

[14]Formalization of any Asian trade grouping is unlikely because it would revive memories of the Greater East Asia Co-prosperity Sphere that Japan imposed on its neighbors prior to World War II. Economic ties are increasing rapidly, however. In 1988 Japan gave $7.6 billion aid within Asia (compared to $500 million from the United States). Japanese imports from the Asian countries grew 68.6 percent between 1986 and 1988, and Japanese investment in those countries approximately tripled (*Business Week*, April 10, 1989, 42–45). The yen is becoming the dominant regional currency.

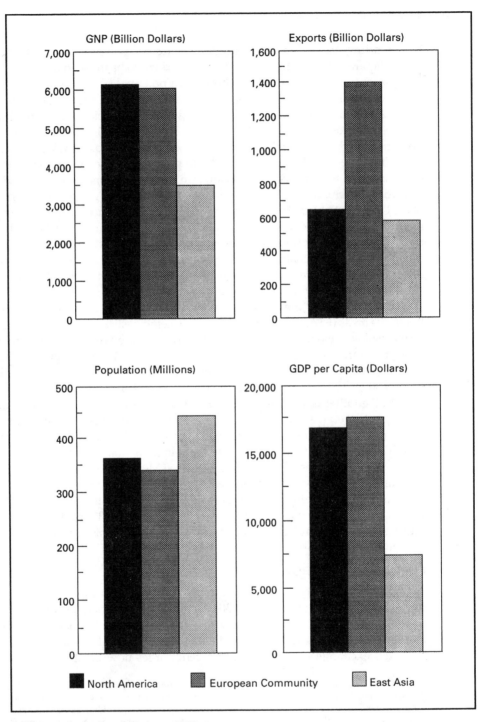

FIGURE 12.4 Regional Markets, 1990

Sources: World Bank, *World Development Report 1992,* (Washington, D.C.: World Bank 1992, 218–19, 222–23, 244–45).

problems in the current system, including the instability of exchange rates. Whereas at one time most capital flows responded to the need to finance trade, in the contemporary environment the flows have become a very powerful force that affects exchange rates and therefore trade. What was once the tail now wags the dog.

International financial flows take several forms. When investors buy partial or total ownership in companies abroad with the intention of participating in the management of those firms, it constitutes **foreign direct investment (FDI)**. When investors buy shares of stock in companies on a stock exchange without such an intention to manage, it constitutes equity investment. **Portfolio investment** includes equity investment and other paper instruments such as treasury bills. Although much portfolio investment seeks a long-term gain from the companies or governments toward which it flows, a substantial portion of international financial flows are short-term speculation on changes in the value of exchange rates.

Worldwide direct investment *stocks* (that is, total amount in place) rose from $67 billion in 1960 to $1,500 billion in 1989 (CTC 1988 and 1991). Annual direct investment *flows* (that is, the amount moving across borders in a given year) grew from $22 billion in 1975 to $196 in 1989. During the 1980s FDI grew especially fast. Between 1980 and 1990, the global economy grew at an average rate of 2.8 percent annually. Like earlier decades, world trade grew more rapidly, posting 4.1 percent annual increases. In sharp contrast, foreign direct investment flows rose at a 13.9 percent pace (CTC 1991, 75).

Foreign equity investment has grown even more rapidly (at an annual rate of 28 percent). It increased twentyfold after 1979 to an annual level of $1,500 billion in 1991 (*The Economist*, January 11, 1992, 98). By 1991 one of three stock trades in Europe and one of five in the United States involved a foreign stock or foreign buyer.

Figure 12.5 captures still another aspect of international financial flows by reporting foreign bank deposits (by financial institutions other than monetary authorities). These surpassed the annual volume of international trade in the late 1970s. By 1990 foreign bank deposits in industrial countries as a whole were twice the size of exports.[15]

Consider also what Peter Drucker writes about the Eurodollar market (borrowing and lending dollars outside of the United States), which scarcely existed in the 1960s:

> The London Eurodollar market, in which the world's financial institutions borrow from and lend to each other, turns over $300 billion each working day, or $75 trillion a year, a volume at least 25 times that of world trade. (Drucker 1986, 782)

Long-term capital flows such as foreign direct investment can substantially restructure the world's economy. For instance, they potentially convey an ability to compete in the world economy to the recipient country by allowing them to build factories, to fill them with advanced equipment, and to orient production

---

[15]Foreign deposits are a stock, but trade is a flow; thus the two series are not truly comparable. Nonetheless, comparison of foreign deposits with GNP (also a flow) allows us to see relative growth.

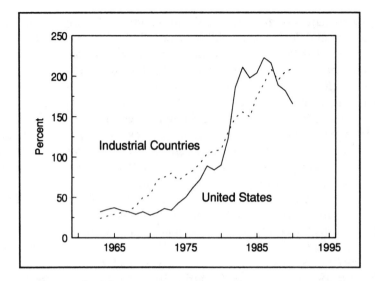

FIGURE 12.5   Foreign Bank Deposits as Percentage of Exports
Source: International Monetary Fund, *International Financial Statistics Yearbook 1991* (Washington, D.C.: IMF, 1991, 73, 102, 121).

toward world markets. Chapter 13 returns to the implications for developing countries of access to such investment.

At the same time, vast increases of international liquidity (short-notice spending power) account for much of the instability in the international currency market and for the rapid and dramatic changes in exchange rates that we saw earlier.[16] U.S. dollars, German marks, Swiss francs, and other currencies managed by banks outside of the currencies' home countries (collectively known as foreign exchange) grew from $45 billion in 1970 to $666 billion in 1988 (IMF 1989b). Although the global stock market crash of October 1987 resulted primarily from movements of liquid assets within domestic economies (and transmission of anxiety across countries), it suggested the potentially disruptive effect of large-scale and rapid international financial flows. This is a vulnerability that the original Bretton Woods system (when central banks, not private companies, dominated international finance) did not share.

REINTEGRATION OF CENTRAL AND EASTERN EUROPEAN ECONOMIES

First World states that have benefitted from four decades of increasingly free trade (and nearly two centuries of relatively free trade) pose the neomercantilist challenge to liberalism. Companies shifting massive volumes of capital around the world at high speed present some additional difficulties for economic management. Yet both First World states and multinational companies retain considerable commitment to maintaining the liberal international economic regime that has served them well. In contrast, the Second World refused after World War II to

---

[16]In late 1989 daily foreign exchange market volumes averaged about $500 billion, compared with U.S. intervention of $11.9 billion. States can no longer control exchange rates.

participate at all in the liberal international economic order. The United States sought U.S.S.R. involvement in the Bretton Woods system and even considered postwar recovery loans to it (Spero 1981, 289).[17] The Soviet Union declined. Before World War II Eastern Europe traded predominantly with Western Europe, whereas after World War II the Soviet bloc turned inward. Stalin chose isolation from the liberal trade and finance system of the West and began competition with it. In his words:

> The disintegration of the single, all-embracing world market must be regarded as the most important economic sequel of the Second World War and of its economic consequences....China and European people's democracies broke away from the capitalist system and, together with the Soviet Union, formed a united and powerful socialist camp confronting the camp of capitalism. (Spero 1981, 290)

In 1949 the Soviet Union created the COMECON in response to the development of the Bretton Woods institutions in the West and to the Marshall Plan.[18] It was to assist the Communist states of Eastern Europe with their development in isolation from the West. These countries established trade in prices and amounts that governments set and that therefore often did not reflect the liberal principle of comparative advantage in markets.

Although the isolation of the COMECON countries from the Western system was by choice, Western policies reinforced it. The United States led the establishment in 1949 among its allies of the Coordinating Committee (COCOM), which specified lists of items to be embargoed from trade with the Soviet Union and its allies. The lists of strategic goods contained primarily military and high-technology items. The export restrictions imposed by COCOM further limited East-West trade.

The United States also denied MFN trade status to much of the East. In 1972, during the détente period, the United States and U.S.S.R. moved toward a commercial accord that would have conferred MFN status on the Soviet Union and provided Export-Import Bank credits (Spero 1981, 316). Congress added the Jackson-Vanik amendment to the bill and linked trade concessions to freer emigration from the Soviet Union. Congress also placed ceilings and limitations on the credits. The entire deal broke down at the end of 1974, when the Soviets refused to accept what they considered interference in their domestic affairs.

Even now that there is strong desire on both sides for reintegration of Eastern and Central Europe into the liberal world economy, those states find it difficult to make the transition. To understand the difficulty of freer trade for the Eastern economies, consider an example. The former Soviet Union set food and energy prices low, relative to the world market, as a concession to the domestic consumer. Now that Russia wants to reintegrate its economy into the world market, it needs to move such prices toward those found throughout the world. Otherwise, as it opens its borders, those subsidized goods will flow out rapidly and domestic

---

[17]The U.S.S.R. applied for GATT membership in 1986 (it was rebuffed) and has expressed interest in the IMF and World Bank. The United States opposed Soviet entry in the late 1980s.

[18]COMECON expelled Albania when it supported China in the Sino-Soviet split. Mongolia, Cuba, and Vietnam joined the Eastern European members.

supply will be inadequate. Several-fold increases in the prices of such basic goods can, however, devastate those with little opportunity to increase low incomes (especially retired workers) and those whose apartment-heating systems routinely waste much energy.

Poland initiated this painful process in 1989–1990 by adopting the "shock" approach—suddenly opening its borders to trade and freeing domestic markets from central control. It no longer subsidized the purchase of food or energy. Other countries in the region have moved more gingerly. Russia acted in 1991–1992 to decontrol most food prices.

Another difficulty for the Eastern countries is the privatization of property. Determining ownership of land and firms has been a challenge. In some cases, such as Bulgaria, governments have returned land to those from whom it was nationalized several decades earlier. States have distributed shares of stock in industry through sales and even lotteries. Hungary was the first to establish a rudimentary stock exchange, encouraging Western ownership, and even allowing firms to go bankrupt if they cannot compete. Other countries have followed at various speeds.

It remains unclear how far or fast internal reforms will proceed and thus how fast reintegration can occur. The continued implementation of reforms has led to considerable unemployment and inflation.[19] Many in those societies already complain about the increasing inequality of income and living standards, as new entrepreneurs amass wealth. The Soviet Union was committed to socialist ideals of equality and protection of the downtrodden for more than seventy years, and many of its former citizens are willing to sacrifice considerable economic efficiency in continued pursuit of those ideals. Many, including those in oversized government bureaucracies, attained economic security within the centrally planned system and also resist its dismantlement.

There are signs that reintegration is occurring. Czechoslovakia questioned the continued existence of COMECON in 1990, and it collapsed in 1991. Increasingly, the trade of the East is oriented toward the West rather than directed internally. Hungary even began to run surpluses in its trade balance with the West in 1990–1992. For the most part, however, the economies remain fragile and continue to seek external help. Gorbachev and then Yeltsin attended meetings of the Group of 7 asking for aid packages. The West has gradually created a pattern of assistance that ties loans and aid to continued reforms, essentially the standard conditionality of the IMF. The West also established the European Bank for Reconstruction and Development (EBRD), along the lines of the World Bank, as an instrument of its integration effort.

For many years the centrally planned economies, under the dominance of the Soviet Union, chose the radical strategy of withdrawal from the world economy and pursuit of economic autarky (independence). That strategy is now in

---

[19]The reforms create unemployment, because inefficient firms falter; they cause inflation, because countries have eliminated state subsidies for underpriced goods, have devalued their currencies to encourage exports (raising the price of imports and shipping some domestic production abroad), and have tried to cushion the blow of unemployment and higher prices by printing more money.

disrepute. The Soviet and Central European economies were largely stagnant for more than a decade before the central planning system collapsed. Life expectancy in the U.S.S.R. actually decreased in the 1980s. In contrast, the West experienced one of the longest periods of economic expansion in history during the 1980s. In light of these performance differentials, the central-planning experiment now holds much less attraction than it once did. That is true also in the Third World, where many countries once saw central planning and economic independence as a respectable model. We will move to a discussion of the position of the Third World in the global political economy in Chapter 13.

GLOBAL POWER SHIFT

The global political economy faces issues of protectionism in trade, volatility in financial flows, and the reintegration of Eastern and Central Europe into the world economy. That is a large agenda. In addition, however, there is a critical question concerning leadership. Whereas once the United States unilaterally managed the institutions of Bretton Woods, there is increasingly a triad of important powers: the United States, the European Community, and Japan.

A shift of power within the institutions of Bretton Woods has become noticeable. At the 1988 IMF meetings in Berlin, the financial strength of Japan thrust it onto center stage and it has stayed there. The movement of the United States from the position of the world's largest creditor to that of the world's largest debtor, with continuing large trade and payments deficits, sharply limits the leverage the United States can now exert within the global financial system.

All three of the primary issues from the Uruguay Round (agriculture, trade in services, and intellectual property) are of special interest to the United States and indicate the important role it continues to play in the management of world trade. Yet the difficulties of reaching any agreement in that round suggest again the declining American influence over global trade.

Japan's active involvement on trade issues is essential to the maintenance and especially to the extension of the liberal order of Bretton Woods. Six rounds of GATT negotiations prior to the Uruguay Round brought the level of tariffs on dutiable industrial goods down to an average of only 2.9 percent for Japan, 4.3 percent for the United States, and 4.7 percent for ten major European countries. The primary barriers to trade within the First World are no longer tariffs. Instead, they are nontariff barriers, which are perhaps now 10 times as restrictive as tariffs (Walters and Blake 1992, 37). Because these are much more difficult to identify and measure, they have been much more resistant to GATT efforts. There is little question that such nontariff barriers remain stronger in Japan than in most developed countries.

Similarly, Japan and Europe have become critical players in the international financial system and in efforts to rebuild and reintegrate the East. Japan's annual foreign direct investment moved from one-tenth of that originating in the United States in 1980 to two-thirds more than that from the United States in 1989 (CTC

1991, 33). The stock of direct investment controlled by countries from the EC grew to equal that originating in the United States in 1988. Japan and the EC supported most of the U.S. expenditures in the war against Iraq in 1991. Russia looks to them for assistance in rebuilding its energy and raw materials industries and for advanced technology, although the dispute over the Kuriles prevented Japan from entering actively into early Western programs for Russia. Similarly, no solution of the Third World's debt crisis can work without the full participation of the EC and Japan.

At the same time that it has lost ability to unilaterally accomplish its objectives, the United States resists transfer of its dominant Bretton Woods power to Japan or other countries. Votes in the World Bank and IMF are proportional to capital contributions and the United States holds about 20 percent of the vote in each. To maintain that position in the World Bank, it has promoted the creation of "special" facilities that increase the relative contributions of other states without increasing their voting shares (Feinberg and Goldstein 1988, 7–2). In 1988 Japan provided 23 percent of new capital (compared with 9 percent from the United States) but cast only 6.5 percent of votes (World Bank 1988b, 55 and 169). Moreover, the United States had provided only 58 percent of its basic IMF quota in 1988, and therefore only 10.9 percent of the total IMF currency holdings, while retaining 19.1 percent of voting shares (IMF 1988, 156 and 178). In 1989 the IMF annual meeting increased Japanese voting share so as to move it into second rank, at the expense of Britain and France. It began to maneuver to have a Japanese citizen in the position of managing director. The imbalance between contribution and voting privilege will become a greater issue as the gap grows between the U.S. desire to lead (control) the system and its financial ability to contribute to the system.

Diminished U.S. leadership capability in international trade and finance raises issues that Chapter 6 identified with the theory of hegemonic stability. Specifically, can a collective international grouping, rather than a dominant state, provide leadership on trade, finance, reintegration, and development issues? It is the central question of the 1990s for the global political economy.

Chapter 13

A WORLD DIVIDED

Liberalism is the dominant political-economic worldview in the developed world, countries that account for about two-thirds of the world economy. Those same states contain only 15 percent of the world's population, however. Much of the rest of humanity lives in countries that sometimes officially question whether liberalism is in their interest, and they frequently adopt domestic and international policies that deviate sharply from practices prescribed by liberalism. This chapter looks in particular at the LDCs. For the most part they have remained actively involved in the world economy, but they often maintain an uneasy relationship with it. That unease has a historic basis in colonialism.

IMPERIALISM AND DECOLONIZATION

Two waves of empire building preceded World War I. In the sixteenth and seventeenth centuries, Portuguese, Spanish, Dutch, English, and French explorers claimed newly discovered territories in Asia and in the Americas. Processes of looting, religious conversion, trading, and settlement followed, with the balance depending on the wealth, population, and political strength of the societies encountered (Doyle 1986). The spread of empire suffered some important but partial reverses: the United States declared its independence in 1776, and the Latin American countries broke away from Spain and Portugal in the early 1800s, especially 1807–1825.

The second wave, focused on Africa, crested at the end of the nineteenth century.[1] The "Scramble for Africa" resulted in formal division of Africa into colonies by the European powers at the Berlin West Africa Conference of 1884–1885. Only Ethiopia, Liberia, and South Africa remained formally independent in

[1]Counting former colonies, Headrick (1981, 3) traces the expansion of imperialism: "In the year 1800 Europeans occupied or controlled thirty-five percent of the land surface of the world; by 1878 this figure had risen to sixty-seven percent, and by 1914 over eighty-four percent of the world's land area was European-dominated."

1914. Many explanations for this wave of imperialism have focused on the dynamics of capitalist expansion. The arguments of Hobson and Lenin are best known (see Chapter 11). They argued that the need for outlets for surplus capital and goods, and the need for raw material inputs forced the European capitalist countries to acquire colonies. The competitive character of the process can also support a more traditional realist interpretation, however. The acquisition of colonies may have preemptively denied possible advantage to other states and offered a second-best alternative to advantages on the continent.[2] Whatever the reasons, European empires stretched across most of the globe by the end of the 1800s.

In 1900 the British dominated the largest empire by a considerable margin. It covered one-fifth of the world's land surface and incorporated about a fourth of the world's population (Kegley and Wittkopf 1985, 77). The French Empire ranked second in size. This global scope of imperialism changed little during the first half of the twentieth century, although the victors relieved Germany of its limited colonies at the end of World War I. Imperialism was violent and oppressive. When Gandhi was asked what he thought about Western civilization, he replied that "it would be nice."

Colonialism unraveled fairly quickly at the end of World War II, and the British, who had the most, lost the most. India, the crown jewel of the empire, gained its independence in 1947. India had been a wealthy colony and the key to maintenance of much of the rest of the empire (Doyle 1986, 236). Palestine, Sri Lanka, and Burma quickly followed India out of the empire. A nationalist government under Gamal Abdel Nasser took power in Egypt during 1952 and grabbed independence. The most troublesome colonies were those that had substantial European settler populations, such as Malawi, Kenya, and Rhodesia. In these areas the fight for independence ultimately became a struggle of native populations with the settlers, rather than with Britain.

The French became involved in two substantial colonial wars that delayed independence for some of its colonies. The first began in Vietnam in 1945, when a nationalist movement that had fought the Japanese occupation declared independence—the French fought to recapture the colony, not abandoning the effort until 1954. The second began in Algeria during 1954; a large European settler population and the French attitude that Algeria was an integral part of the republic, not simply a colony, greatly complicated the eight-year war.

The remnants of Dutch, Belgium, and Portuguese empire gradually fell away as well. The decolonization process in Africa was most dramatic because the continent had only three independent states in 1945 but counted fifty-two in 1970.

There are now about 110 states that fall into the Third World or LDC category, most of which are former colonies. They vary dramatically in per capita income, economic and political structure, culture, the residual impact of colonialism, and prospects. Illustrating one extreme, when Belgium rather precipitously left the

---

[2]In a reference to a suggestion that African countries would substitute for the loss of Alsace-Lorraine to Germany in the Franco-Prussian War, Paul Déroulède, member of the French Assembly, exclaimed that "I have lost two children, and you offer me twenty domestic servants" (Doyle 1986, 310).

Congo (now Zaire) in 1960, there were fewer than a dozen locals with university degrees (Papp 1988, 326). Large-scale racial violence broke out immediately, and internal conflict flares repeatedly. Despite extremely rich mineral resources, the per capita GNP in 1990 was still only $220. At another extreme is Taiwan, a former Japanese colony, now dominated by a Chinese population that fled to the island after the Communists captured the mainland in 1949. It boasts a highly competitive industrial economy and a per capita GNP in 1990 of $7,380.

Liberals expected that, after independence, Third World countries would follow in the economic and political development footsteps of the First World (they would modernize) and would catch up with the North. Liberals foresaw economic progress, including industrialization, and the development of pluralist societies with democratic institutions. Certainly, they recognized that the widely varying conditions of LDCs would mean that the process could take much longer in some countries than in others, and that it might advance in fits and starts. W. W. Rostow articulated the economic elements of this perspective and argued that all societies pass through stages of economic growth that have a largely unvarying logic across countries and over time:

> It is possible to identify all societies, in their economic dimensions, as lying within one of five categories: the traditional society, the preconditions for take-off, the take-off, the drive to maturity, and the age of high mass consumption....These states are not merely descriptive. They are not merely a way of generalizing certain factual observations about the sequence of development of modern societies. They have an inner logic and continuity. They have an analytic bone-structure, rooted in a dynamic theory of production. (Rostow 1971b, 4 and 12–13)

Although few expected political development to so smoothly follow a pattern of stages,[3] there was a strong belief that the political experience of the West was a road map for the newly independent states as well:

> The "progress" promised by the enlightenment—the spread of knowledge, the development of technology, the attainment of higher standards of material welfare, the emergence of lawful, humane, and liberal polities, and the perfection of the human spirit—now beckoned the third world, newly freed from colonialism and exploitation, and straining against its own parochialisms. The challenging question confronting the scholars of the 1950s and 1960s was how these new and developing nations would find their way into the modern world....Some thought...that all good things go together, that science, technology, industry, and democracy were part of a seamless web.... (Almond 1987, 439)

Although Almond wrote this in the past tense, the fact is that more than a few scholars, and many First World citizens and leaders, continue to believe that, despite setbacks, the Third World will follow the lead of the industrialized, democratic countries, and that LDCs will close the economic and political gaps between them and the North.

[3]See, however, Black (1966) and Organski (1965).

NORTH-SOUTH GAP

It is the economic gap that draws the most attention. Little or no economic gap between North and South existed at the beginning of the industrial revolution. One estimate places the per capita GNP in Western Europe in 1800 at $212, whereas that in what we now call the Third World was $200 (Braudel 1979, 534).[4] The gap, however, opened steadily thereafter:

> By 1850 the ratio between incomes in the industrializing societies and those in the rest of the world was perhaps 2 to 1. In 1950 it had opened further, to about 10 to 1, in 1960 to nearly 15 to 1. If trends of the past decade continue, it may reach 30 to 1 by the end of the century. (Brown 1972, 42)

In fact, however, the trend documented by Brown did not continue after 1960. Figure 13.1 shows the ratio of per capita GNP in the First and Third Worlds since then. Using slightly different categories than Brown did, the figure shows that despite some intervening fluctuation, the 1988 ratio remained near nineteen to one. Has the gap thus stabilized, and is it perhaps even on the verge of declining? That is a matter of great dispute.

Some structuralists reject this measure and argue that the gap is still increasing steadily. Instead of looking at the ratio of income, they focus on the absolute gap between conditions in the North and South. In 1960 a $6,160 per capita GNP difference existed between the $6,520 in the North and $360 in the South. By 1988

FIGURE 13.1   North-South Gap: Ratio of Per Capita Incomes
Source: Ruth Legar Sivard, *World Military and Social Expenditures 1991*, 14th ed. (Washington, D.C.: World Priorities, 1991), 9.

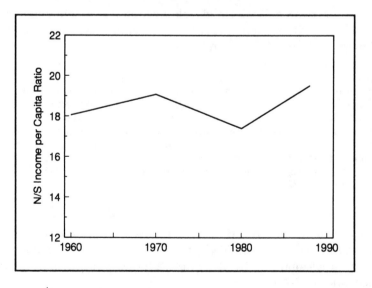

[4]Stavrianos (1981, 38) claims that the per capita income gap between First and Third Worlds was already three to one in 1500 and five to one in 1850. He provides no source.

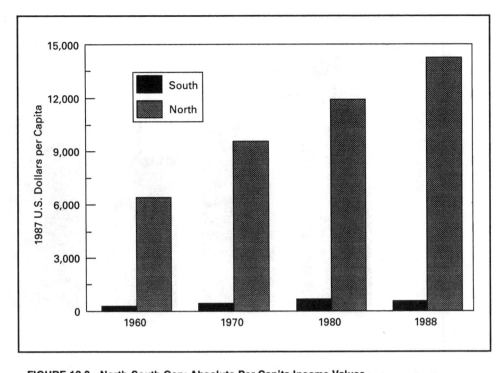

FIGURE 13.2   North-South Gap: Absolute Per Capita Income Values
Source: Ruth Legar Sivard, *World Military and Social Expenditures 1991*, 14th ed. (Washington, D.C.: World Priorities, 1991), 9.

a $13,280 gap separated GNP per capita of $14,000 in the North from $720 in the South (Sivard 1991, 50). By this measure the gap doubled between 1960 and 1988 (Figure 13.2)

There is, in fact, a ratio measure that suggests even greater growth in global income disparity. The U.N. Development Programme (1992, 34) calculated the incomes of the richest and poorest 20 percent shares of humanity between 1960 and 1989. They found that the ratio began at 30 to 1 and grew to 59 to 1 (again about a doubling).

Some liberals suggest still another way of looking at the gap (Simon 1981). Income may be less important than what it does for our quality of life, and an excellent first measure of quality is length. Figure 13.3 shows that the average life expectancy in the South has been steadily closing on that in the North since 1960—the gap fell from 22 years to 11 years.

Which measure is most appropriate? If your income is one-tenth that of your neighbor and you both succeed in doubling your income, should you focus on the fact that your income is still only one-tenth that of your neighbor, that the neighbor increased his or her income ten times as much as you did, or that there are some absolute benefits of your much-improved diet and quality of life? There is no inherently correct answer—it depends on your perspective.

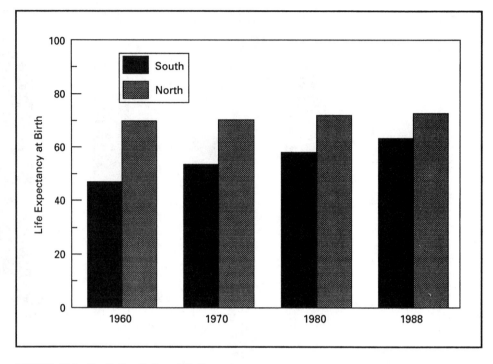

FIGURE 13.3   North-South Gap: Life Expectancy
Source: Ruth Legar Sivard, *World Military and Sicial Expenditures 1991*, 14th ed. (Washington, D.C.: World Priorities, 1991), 9.

THE STRUCTURALIST PERSPECTIVE

The failure of the North-South gap to close decisively, and the evidence on many measures that it continues to widen, has for some observers discredited the liberal-pluralist theories of economic development and given support to alternative and popular perspectives, rooted in the structuralist's class-oriented view. The starting point for structuralists is to cease looking at the world as individual states (or economies) and to begin looking at it as a single economic system. When England and France developed industrial economies and democratic institutions, they did so as independent states with a high level of control over domestic economies. As discussed in the last chapter, they used various mercantilist mechanisms to initiate their economic development before subsequently adopting liberal policies from positions of economic strength.[5] Although Dutch incomes were once twice those of England, that advantage did not translate into significant political-economic penetration and control of England. The country in second-place remained in charge of its own economy.

[5]"Bismark insisted that free trade was the weapon of the dominant economy anxious to prevent others from following its path" (Kindleberger 1973, 303).

In contrast, structuralists argue, LDCs today exist in a world in which they face actors much more politically, militarily, and economically powerful than themselves—actors that do strongly influence their political economies. There are three concrete structural manifestations of this relationship that we should consider explicitly.[6] The first is the existence of an international division of labor, a highly integrated global economy in which countries tend to specialize with respect to production. Second, the advanced countries have established international institutions (those of Bretton Woods) and regimes in international policy that LDCs cannot ignore. Third, powerful multinational corporations (MNCs) have evolved and, whether they are instruments of the developed countries or independent actors in their own right, have great influence in LDCs. When Britain industrialized, or when states such as France and the United States followed, none of these three structural characteristics of the global economy existed, except in rudimentary form. Today the LDCs must cope with all of them. In much of the rest of this chapter, we consider the implications of each characteristic in turn.

GLOBAL DIVISION OF LABOR

Although it is less true year by year, the economies of low and middle income LDCs depend heavily on the export of primary commodities (raw materials, both agricultural and mineral). Such products account for 47–48 percent of their combined exports, whereas manufactures contribute 52–53 percent (World Bank 1991, 234). Figure 13.4 shows that the exports of large numbers of African countries are more than 90 percent commodities. The more developed economies as a group depend on manufactured goods for the bulk of their export earnings (80 percent). The disadvantages of the LDC position in the global division of labor include:

1. *Dependence for export earnings on a few export products.* More than 50 percent of the export earnings of many countries came in 1987 from just one or two products (Figure 13.4): for example, Zambia (copper); Ethiopia (coffee); Chad (cotton); Niger (uranium); Botswana (diamonds); Mauritania (iron ore and fish); and Bolivia (natural gas and tin).[7] Most OPEC countries earn more than 75 percent of their foreign exchange from oil.

Prices of raw materials are notoriously unstable. Although prices of manufactured goods might fluctuate 5 to 10 percent from one year to the next, it is not uncommon for commodity prices to double, triple, or fall by similar amounts. Imagine a government attempting to build roads, an electric grid, schools, and hospitals when the bases of its revenues fluctuate so dramatically. Once they initiate projects, it is difficult to stop them, so in bad years governments turn to foreign borrowing to offset revenue declines. American farmers, for whom the U.S. government has long sought to stabilize similarly dramatic price fluctuations, can attest to

[6]Susan Strange (1988) draws attention to four global structures: production, finance, knowledge, and security. This discussion focuses on the first three, and we return subsequently to security.

[7]IMF (1988b). Actually experts guess that the official statistics for Bolivia are incorrect, and that it obtains over 50 percent of its foreign earnings from cocoa leaf products.

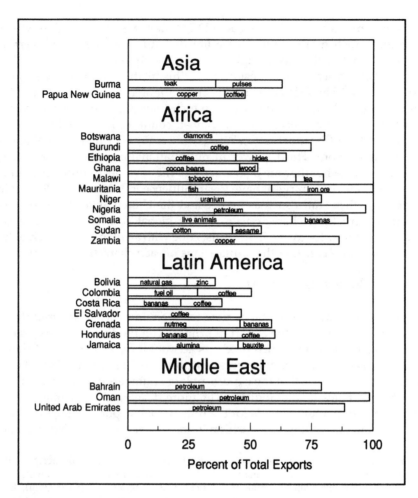

FIGURE 13.4   Developing Countries with Heavy Dependence on Primary Commodities
Source: International Monetary Fund, *International Monetary Statistics 1991* (Washington, D.C.: IMF, 1991).

the ease with which one mistakenly comes to believe that the good years are normal, and to the trap of making spending plans based on revenues during those years.

2. *Dependence on restricted export markets (and import sources).* Although this is less common than in colonial times, when the imperial power required that it be the colony's only trading partner, there is still a tendency for LDCs, reinforced by the dominant presence of a few MNCs, to rely on limited export markets and import sources and therefore to lose some of the advantage of competitive international trade. For instance, French corporations often maintain a predominant position in the former French colonies of Africa. When these MNCs operate in several countries, but each country works primarily with one firm (in an industry), the MNCs have the greater bargaining power.

A particularly striking example of dependence on limited numbers of commodities and limited export markets could be Bolivia. It has been estimated that 50 percent of its exports are coca, ultimately bound for the United States. That relationship, replicated on a lesser scale in other LDCs, has led to substantial U.S. pressure on the Bolivian political-economic system.

> 3. *Declining terms of trade.* The **terms of trade** is the trade-weighted ratio of export and import prices; that is, it is the ratio of the prices of goods a country sells (considering how much of each good it markets) to the prices of goods it buys. If a developing country is dependent on primary good exports and the price of that good in world markets decline, while prices of manufactured imports remain stable, the terms of trade for the LDC are deteriorating. It must export more and more of its primary good to buy the same manufactured imports.

Raul Prebisch presented an argument, widely accepted by structuralist critics of liberalism, that deterioration in the terms of trade is the long-term fate of LDCs. There are several reasons. For example, as global incomes rise, people spend higher portions of total income on manufactured goods and services, and smaller portions on primary products (causing demand and prices to weaken). To understand this, think of an individual. At a low level of income, the individual will spend most available funds on food (primary products). As individual income rises, more and more will be spent on manufactured goods (cars and stereos) and services (doctors and professors). Technological advance that allows manufactured products to use less material input in total and to substitute increasing amounts of synthetic materials[8] reinforces the tendency for raw material demand to weaken. Consider only one dramatic example: the downsizing of computers from room-filling behemoths based on vacuum tubes to desk-top marvels using silicon chips. For this reason, the use of steel per dollar of GNP in developed countries dropped by about 50 percent from 1970 to 1988 (World Bank 1991b, 21).

The evidence concerning trends in the terms of trade is mixed, and it both supports and contradicts the Prebisch thesis. If one cynically wished to seek support for the thesis, it would be best to look at change in the terms of trade since about 1952 (when the Korean War had forced raw material prices up sharply) and to focus on non-oil commodities (oil is now more expensive than in 1952 and dominates global commodity trade). If one wished to reject the thesis, a different starting point for the analysis, say 1948 or 1960, and the inclusion of petroleum would help make the case (Figure 13.5). Our inability to evaluate and measure quality changes over time also greatly complicates the analysis of evidence. Although a ton of copper today is no different from that of fifty years ago, automobiles and machine tools, although perhaps not priced so much higher in real terms, are much superior to those produced a half century ago . Even committed scholars often begin with an attachment to one worldview or another and are not immune to selective perception of mixed evidence.

[8]The analysis of Mikesell (1988) supports both the income and technology arguments. Grilli and Yang (1988, 34) calculate that nonfuel commodity prices fell 40 percent relative to manufactures between 1900 and 1986, although quality improvements in manufactures account for an uncertain part of that.

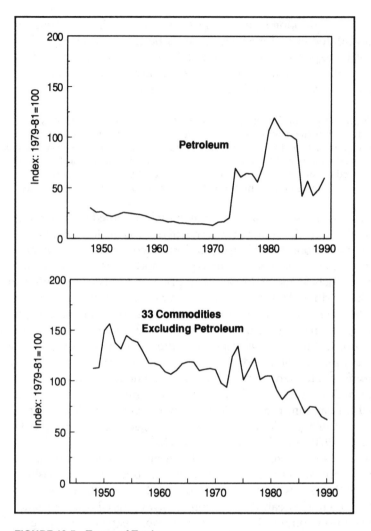

FIGURE 13.5   Terms of Trade
Sources: World Bank, *Commodity Trade and Price Trends 1987/88* (Baltimore: Johns Hopkins University Press, 1988), 46; British Petroleum, BP Statistical Review of World Energy (London: British Petroleum, 1992), 12; World Bank, *Global Economic Prospects and the Developing Countries* (Washington: D.C.: World Bank, 1991), 46.

The international division of labor is, of course, not static. In 1965 only 28 percent of the merchandise exports of low-and middle-income LDCs were manufactures, whereas in 1990 the figure was 51 percent. A continuing shift of manufacturing to LDCs will eliminate some of the disadvantages of reliance on primary goods (including price instability). Yet it is not the most technologically advanced manufactures, with the highest profit margins, that move to LDCs. According to Vernon's (1987) **product cycle theory**, manufacturing moves South only when competition has squeezed profits and when lower-cost production is needed. If this is true, and there is considerable supportive evidence, LDCs remain at a competitive disadvantage in the global division of labor.

POLITICAL-ECONOMIC INSTITUTIONS AND REGIMES

Colonialism is all but dead in today's world, and formal control by the countries of the North over the polities or economies of the South has evaporated. The ratio of Northern and Southern per capita incomes is about nineteen to one, however, and the ratio of military power may be even greater. Although direct rule through formal colonialism is gone, high levels of influence remain through the exercise of political and economic power including that of institutions and regimes dominated by the North. Some refer to the modern pattern as **neocolonialism**. The earlier review of the liberal economic order (in Chapter 12) emphasized how that order structures trade and financial relationships among developed states. Let us look now at the way it shapes the trade and financial relationships between Northern and Southern states. In particular we will focus on the trade issue of tariffs and on the financial issue of debt.

TRADE AND TARIFFS

Tariffs illustrate how structuralists argue that the international political structure can work against LDCs. Tariffs served two important functions in the development of most industrial economies. First, they provided state revenues. New governments could relatively easily collect them at borders. Effective income tax mechanisms are much more complicated, are phenomena of the twentieth century even in developed countries, and are still not widespread in LDCs (countries as advanced as Italy continue to have difficulty enforcing income tax collection). In 1990 various taxes on trade still accounted for about 30 percent of low-income LDC government revenues as compared with 2 percent of revenues in industrial countries.[9] Second, they protect **infant industries** (newly established and not always efficient and competitive firms) against external competition. France used tariffs for both purposes in its early development. Nor did the United States pursue laissez faire economic policies in its early push for development:

> In evaluating early American economic development, it should be recognized that there was *a great deal of government intervention and even public investment in the economy so as to develop industry and commerce*.... The most important federal measures directly supporting economic growth took the form of investment in the Bank of the United States and, more important, protective tariffs to encourage domestic industry against products manufactured in England. (Lipset 1963, 48)

In fact, every country that industrialized successfully after Britain in the nineteenth century used tariffs to protect infant industry (Doyle 1986, 264).

[9]Personal income taxes raised only 10–20 percent of government revenues in typical low-income countries versus 30–60 percent in developed states (World Bank 1992, 240). Tariffs were the largest single source of revenue in LDCs, followed by sales taxes and business taxes. Social security taxes raise the most in MDCs, followed by personal and sales taxes.

The existence of politically and economically powerful developed countries has made it difficult for developing countries to use tariffs for these two purposes. The more developed countries now insist on low tariff levels if LDCs want reciprocal access to their markets.[10] The pressure of firms for access to LDC markets has made it difficult for more developed country (MDC) governments to respect the infant industry argument. The industrialized countries have regularly sought to break down any barriers by LDCs to their exports.[11]

LDCs reasonably argue that they are denied the benefits of protective tariffs that currently industrialized countries once reaped. The central principle of the GATT-based tariff system, reciprocity, works against LDCs:

> The bargaining principle of reciprocity underlying all tariff reduction negotiations is another characteristic of GATT long criticized by less developed countries. Poor states...argue that reciprocity is equitable when applied to negotiations among states at approximately the same stage of economic development, but in negotiations between industrialized and less developed states, reciprocity...is a call for equal competition among fundamentally unequal economic units. (Blake and Walters 1987, 35)

Furthermore, MDCs do not always apply the principle of reciprocity fairly. At the same time that they pressure LDCs to forgo the benefits of protective tariffs on more advanced manufactured goods from infant industries, the MDCs frequently place unusually high tariffs on the less advanced goods that LDCs already produce competitively. Although the rounds of GATT negotiations have greatly reduced average tariffs, "the manufactured and semimanufactured products of particular export interest to less developed countries (such as textiles and semiprocessed metal or wood products) typically face tariff levels of two to four times this average" (Blake and Walters 1987, 34). In 1974 LDCs had become competitive in artificial fibers and wool, and the North pushed the Multi-Fiber Arrangement (MFA) through GATT, allocating LDC market shares. In 1990 a World Bank report concluded that Bangladesh could export 50 percent more textiles without the MFA. Behind this phenomenon is the fact that the industries in which LDCs are competitive tend to be older industries, generally in decline within the advanced capitalist countries. Unemployment in those industries in the MDCs leads to pressures within the developed countries for support and protection. In the industrialized states, the lobbyists of LDCs seldom carry the clout of those from the declining domestic textile or shoe industries.[12]

[10]Historically, MDCs also sometimes directly confiscated LDC tariff revenues. When the U.S. marines repeatedly entered Central American countries in the early nineteenth century, a common rationale was to ensure the efficient collection of tariffs for repayment of foreign indebtedness. Thus it removed the principal revenue collection mechanism from the hands of the local government.

[11]Emmanuel (1972) did a classic study of how free trade can lead to very unequal benefits for the trading partners and how international pressures to eliminate protective tariffs can weaken the position of LDCs.

[12]LDCs do not, however, normally face significant tariffs on exports of raw materials to countries that need those materials and have no local producers to protect. The system thus encourages them to remain exporters of raw materials.

Liberals recognize some validity in the LDC claims concerning lack of fairness in the system. In particular, they agree that more advanced countries *should* adopt tariff structures consistent with free trade and not discriminate against the products of developing countries.[13]

Bowing to the pressure of the LDC argument, industrial states agreed in the early 1970s to a Generalized System of Preferences (GSP). In a departure from the principle of reciprocity, economically advanced countries have now eliminated all duties on some categories of imports from LDCs, especially on manufactures and semimanufactures. As countries develop they "graduate" and lose these preferences. In 1988 the United States imported goods worth $18.4 billion under this program, 19 percent of all its imports from non-oil exporting LDCs (Walters and Blake 1992, 49). Along lines similar to the GSP, the EC agreed through the Lomé Convention to allow some goods of forty-six African, Caribbean, and Pacific states (at first mostly former colonies of the members, and then later expanded in number) preferential access (Spero 1990, 214). Individual developed countries, however, exclude many key goods from these programs or limit their import by quota. For example, the United States exempted from the GSP two manufactures of great importance to many LDCs, shoes and textiles.

FINANCE AND DEBT

Financial help from abroad supported the development of many countries over the last 200 years. British capital built railroads, other infrastructure, and industry in the United States during the nineteenth century. The British invested directly and through debt instruments issued by the U.S. government. In 1870, the U.S. public debt, partially held abroad, was substantial: $2.4 billion or $61 per capita. It declined steadily (to $12 per capita in 1910) before ballooning in response to the two world wars (World Almanac 1988, 96). Despite substantial public debt in the early twentieth century, the private sector became so strong that the United States transformed itself from a net international debtor into the world's largest creditor.

Liberal development theorists argue that this kind of progression is natural: a reliance on foreign capital to build an industrial base and then a use of that base to export, to retire foreign debt, and eventually to invest abroad. One obvious flaw emerges in this portrait, when examined from a structuralist viewpoint: Not all countries can ultimately become creditor states (for every credit there must be a debit), and it may be extremely difficult for many LDCs to retire debt in a highly competitive, widely industrialized world.

The issue of debt became especially important after the global oil shocks of 1973–1974 and 1979–1980. Most LDCs depend heavily on imported oil and in those years world oil prices rose dramatically. To finance oil imports and to maintain economic growth in this period, they borrowed heavily from abroad. Credit was inexpensive during the 1970s, because the oil-exporting countries had large sur-

---

[13]This might remind us of the realist argument that states *should* act rationally in interstate politics. Both liberal and realist prescriptions often ignore the reality of intrastate politics and decision making.

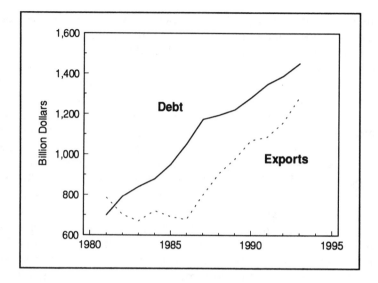

FIGURE 13.6   LDC Debt and Exports
Source: International Monetary Fund, *World Economic Outlook* (Washington, D.C.: IMF, 1989), 186; International Monetary Fund, *World Economic Outlook* (Washington, D.C.: IMF, 1992), 171, 176.
Note: LDCs exclude Eastern Europe and former U.S.S.R.

pluses of cash. They recycled those surpluses to the global financial community through the burgeoning Eurocurrency markets. Funds were so readily available that LDCs also borrowed for new investment projects and even consumer goods. In the past LDCs had borrowed primarily from governments or international organizations, whereas they turned in this period to the private banks holding the Eurocurrency resources.

Problems arose for LDCs in the early 1980s for three reasons. First, in a war against inflation, waged by the more developed countries, global real interest rates rose. This made the debt burden more onerous. Second, the level of debt outstanding began to frighten private financial institutions, which then frequently refused to loan additional funds. In the late 1970s several countries had begun to borrow simply to meet the interest and principal payments on their earlier loans. Third, the global economy weakened, and therefore markets for the exports of the LDCs contracted. Markets exhibited the normal instability of prices for primary goods; commodity prices fell sharply. Thus the export earnings of LDCs failed to grow as projected and as needed to repay indebtedness (Figure 13.6).

In 1981, before the widespread recognition of a debt crisis, LDC debt had reached $750 billion, and payments on it absorbed 16 percent of all LDC export earnings. Because of the inability of many countries to meet those payments, debt grew to nearly $1.3 trillion by 1989, and payments began to require nearly 20 percent of the export earnings of LDCs (IMF 1989, 186). Although the absolute dollar value of the debt is highly concentrated in Latin America, the debt burdens many LDCs. For instance, many African countries have little debt in absolute terms, but their weak economies face severe repayment problems. Table 13.1 shows the debt levels for ten major debtors, together accounting for about 45 percent of the total. Just three Latin American countries, Brazil, Mexico, and Argentina, are responsible for 25 percent of the problem.

	Total Debt (Billion Dollars)		Debt Service/Exports (Percent)	
	1980	1990	1980	1990
Brazil	70.2	116.2	63.1	20.8
Mexico	57.5	98.8	49.5	27.8
Argentina	27.2	61.1	37.3	34.1
Korea	29.8	34.0	19.7	10.7
Indonesia	20.9	67.9	13.8	30.9
Venezuela	29.6	33.3	27.2	20.7
Philippines	17.5	30.5	26.6	21.2
Chile	12.1	19.1	43.1	25.9
Yugoslavia	18.5	20.7	20.8	13.7
Nigeria	8.9	36.1	4.2	20.3
Total	292.1	517.7	30.5	22.6

TABLE 13.1
Selected LDC Debtors

Sources: John W. Sewell, Stuart K. Tucker, and contributors, *Growth, Exports, and Jobs in a Changing World Economy: Agenda 1988* (New Brunswick, N.J.: Transaction Books, 1988), 233; World Bank, *World Development Report 1989* (New York: Oxford University Press, 1989), 204–209; World Bank, *World Development Report 1992* (New York: Oxford University Press, 1992), 258–59, 164–65.

The first real evidence that the debt problem had become a debt crisis appeared in Mexico in 1982. Ironically, that country had not borrowed to finance oil imports, the commonest pattern. Instead, major oil discoveries in the 1970s led it to borrow in anticipation of earnings and to develop the oil resources more rapidly. Oil prices peaked in 1981 and began to decline sharply thereafter, creating a severe predicament for Mexico. In the summer of 1982, the U.S. government cobbled together a package worth $8 billion to save Mexico from default on principal and interest payments (Feinberg 1985, 55).

Once banks came to perceive a debt crisis, *private* capital flow to the South collapsed, and the situation became even worse. Annual net private flows to LDCs exceeded $50 billion in 1981 but fell to about $8 billion in 1985. Between 1983 and 1988 commercial banks removed capital from LDCs (a total of $13.2 billion during 1983–1986), by receiving more in interest and principal repayments than they offered in new loans (Sewell, Tucker, and others 1988, 228–230). The bankers and private investors have acted in their individual self-interests, denying additional credit at the first real sign of borrower weakness. That behavior has not always been in their collective interest, because it helps create defaults by hard-pressed borrowers. Sub-Saharan Africa and Latin America have the greatest debt problems—in 1992 cumulative debt was 100 percent and 50 percent of GNP, respectively (UN Development Programme 1992, 45).

Because the World Bank is a lending, not an aid-giving institution, it cannot resolve the debt crisis. In fact, repayments to the Bank from seventeen highly indebted, middle-income countries in 1988 exceeded new loans by $1.3 billion (World Bank 1988b, 34). Although it loaned a total of $14.8 billion to all LDCs in 1988, the net transfers (funds loaned after repayment of old debt) were only $0.7 billion, and net transfers turned negative in 1991.

Similarly, the IMF is not a development or general lending institution.[14] It did increase transfers to the Third World sharply in 1982 and 1983 as the debt crisis unfolded, but resource constraints led to a subsequent retreat (despite a doubling of its resources by member states in the mid-1980s). By 1986 it, too, was removing more capital from LDCs than it provided to them. Specifically, it received $7.9 billion more than it loaned in 1987.[15] Figure 13.7 shows the net transfer to LDCs of the World Bank, the IMF, and all lending sources combined (including private capital). Combined transfers have been negative since 1984, and the drain reached $35 billion in 1988.

The IMF assists more indirectly with resolution of debt problems by organizing refinancings of LDC private debt. It brings the lending banks into consortia to extend the repayment periods, to lessen the interest burden, and now and then even to offer additional capital to prime the dry economic pumps of the borrowers. To make any relaxation of loan payment terms more palatable to lenders, it imposes, as it does with its own loans, conditions on the borrowers in the new agreements. This **conditionality** draws on liberal theory and requires the LDCs to reduce government spending and deficits and to eliminate impediments to trade. Frequently, for instance, the IMF calls on LDC governments to rid themselves of money-losing, state-owned industry, to reduce subsidies and welfare expenditures, and to devalue local currencies to make exports more attractive. As liberals would say, it is necessary to "get the prices right"—to let the market work.

The domestic consequences in LDCs of acting to meet these conditions have been severe. They include increased unemployment (as governments pare bureaucracies and state-owned industries), decreased support systems for the poorest in society (as they cut health, education, and welfare programs), and increased consumer prices (as they devalue currencies to make imports more expensive and to raise exports). The GNPs per capita in Africa and Latin America actually declined in the "lost decade" of the 1980s by annual averages of 1.7 and 0.4 percent, respectively.[16] From the point of

---

[14]The Brandt Commission report (1983, 96) suggests the need for a third international financial institution, a World Development Fund, to circumvent these limitations of the existing ones.

[15]In 1987 net transfers of the Inter-American Development Bank also turned negative.

[16]UN(1992, 37). Compare that with an increase of 2.2 percent per year for the industrial countries during the same period.

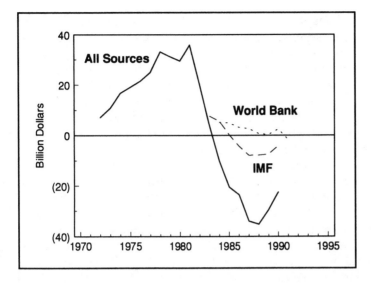

FIGURE 13.7   Net Lending to All Developing Countries
Source: United Nations Development Programme, *Human Development Report 1992* (New York: Oxford University Press, 1992), 50–51.

view of citizens in LDCs, these results of conditionality make the international institutions, especially the IMF, part of the problem rather than of the solution. The IMF is now extremely unpopular in many LDCs. President Mubarak of Egypt called it the "International Misery Fund."

Even when successful in increasing exports and cutting imports, these policies have not really lowered Third World debt, which grew from $650 billion in 1980 to $1,400 billion in 1992.[17] Some LDCs began to take the matter into their own hands and abrogated the original terms of the loans. Brazil suspended principal payments on its private debt in 1987, and Venezuela did the same in 1989. Some voices, including that of Cuba's Fidel Castro, called for the creation of a debtor cartel, which would use the combined bargaining power of debtors, all threatening to default simultaneously, to obtain satisfactory restructuring of terms.

The more-developed countries have moved gradually, and without clear direction, to address the problem. In addition to whatever humanitarian impulse motivates them, they seek to balance two self-interested objectives: (1) avoidance of default, which would damage their private financial institutions, and (2) reinitialization of growth in the Third World, so that it can again become a market for their export-oriented industries.

[17]Brazil managed to transform a trade deficit in 1981 into a $11.1 billion trade surplus in 1987; Mexico eliminated a $3.6 billion deficit in 1981 and created an $8.4 billion surplus in 1987 (IDB 1989, 113). These surpluses, achieved at great domestic cost, provided the capability to pay interest charges on the debt, but not to repay principal. To add insult to injury, the United States, facing its own trade deficits, began to accuse Brazil in the late 1980s of unfair trade practices and to ask for constraint on some categories of exports.

What solutions to the LDC debt crisis are possible? One idea is to swap forgiveness of loans for equity in the same state-owned industries that the IMF says should be privatized in any case. Such debt-equity swaps have had limited success. Environmentalists even propose trading reduction of debt for new policies to protect the Brazilian rain forests and other environmental assets.

In reality, only the governments and institutions of developed states can resolve the problems. In 1989, U.S. Treasury Secretary Brady proposed that the IMF and World Bank lead a plan by which private banks would forgive some indebtedness in exchange for guarantees on remaining loans. The first agreement under that plan reduced the Mexican commercial debt burden by about 20 percent. The Brady Plan subsequently helped Costa Rica, the Philippines, Uruguay, and Venezuela reduce debt levels. Latin American debt stabilized in the late 1980s and early 1990s at $400–450 billion. In 1990, the U.S. forgave all the economic-assistance debt (about $735 million) of twelve African countries. Although economic growth in Latin American turned positive in the early 1990s, severe financial problems remained on both continents.

As a final note in discussion of the debt crisis, serious indebtedness is not restricted to the Third World. Several countries in the Second World also borrowed heavily in the 1970s, near the end of the détente era, and they, too, have yet to extricate themselves. The debts of Poland, Hungary, and Yugoslavia in 1990 reached $39 billion, $18 billion, and $13 billion, respectively (World Bank 1992, 259). In 1992 the external debt of the former Soviet Union was $74 billion, of which 80 percent fell to Russia. This burden is damaging domestic economies in the East as well.[18]

MULTINATIONAL CORPORATIONS

We have now discussed two elements of the global structure in which rich and poor countries interact: the global division of labor, and the existence of interstate political-economic institutions that First World countries and their philosophies dominate. **Multinational corporations (MNCs)**, sometimes called **transnational corporations (TNCs)**, constitute a third element. Broadly defining a multinational as a corporation that controls assets in two or more countries, we count over 10,000 such entities (Walters and Blake 1992, 108).[19] The foreign assets of multinational corporations constitute direct investment as opposed to portfolio investment in paper instruments. Chapter 12 discussed the dramatic increases in such investment in recent years.

Where does foreign direct investment (FDI) come from? The U.S. share of total stocks is decreasing steadily, falling from 47 percent in 1960, to 35 percent in 1985, and to 31 percent in 1988. Nonetheless, the United States still controls the most foreign investment, followed by Britain with 16 percent. The Japanese share of foreign direct investment grew from 0.7 percent in 1960 to 9.8 percent in 1988, putting them in third place.

---

[18]In 1989 the Polish government and Solidarity (the trade union and political organization) agreed to issue a joint appeal for relief of debt, which had grown to $37.9 billion. Rumania paid off its external debt in 1989 after several years of extreme austerity, imposed by one of the world's most repressive governments.

[19]Papp (1988, 80) says 7,500, and estimates are uncertain. UN negotiations on a code of conduct for MNCs bogged down for much of the 1980s on the issue of definition.

Where does FDI go? Table 13.2 shows that more than three-fourths of global investment finds its way from developed countries to other developed countries. For most of the World War II period, the principal targets of foreign investment were Canada and Western Europe (flows from the United States). The United States rapidly came to be the primary host country in recent years, however, receiving 40 percent of world flows in the early 1980s. By 1988 companies based in other countries had invested $329 billion in the United States, compared to $239 billion in all of the EC and $10 billion in Japan (UNCTC 1991, 32). During 1985–1989 an average of $46 billion found its way to the United States each year. Latin America hosts more foreign direct investment than other LDCs, but the greatest growth in is Asia.[20]

TABLE 13.2 Sources and Hosts of Direct Foreign Investment Stocks			
Sources	*1960*	*1985*	*1988–1989*
United States	47.1%	35.1%	30.5%
United Kingdom	18.3	14.7	16.2
Japan	0.7	11.7	9.8
Germany	1.2	8.4	9.1
Switzerland	3.4	6.4	
Netherlands	10.3	6.1	6.8
Canada	3.7	5.1	
France	6.1	3.0	5.1
Other	9.2	9.5	22.6
Total	100.0%	100.0%	100.0%
Total (Billions)	$67.0	$713.5	$1,500
Hosts	*1975*	*1985*	*1988–1989*
United States	11.2%	29.0%	27.0%
Western Europe	40.8	28.9	
Other Developed Countries	23.1	17.1	51.7
Latin America	12.0	12.6	9.4
Asia	5.3	7.8	9.3
Africa	6.7	3.5	2.5
Japan	0.6	1.0	
Other	0.9	1.0	0.1
Total	100.0%	100.0%	100.0%
Total (Billions)	$246.8	$637.2	

Source: United Nations Centre on Transnational Corporations, *Transnational Corporations in World Development: Trends and Prospects* (New York: United Nations Centre on Transnational Corporations, 1988), 24–25; World Bank, *Global Economic Prospects and the Developing Countries* (Washington D.C.: World Bank, 1991), 12.

Notes: The discrepancy between total source and host values for 1985 indicates measurement problems. The data in 1988–1989 are only partially compatible.

[20]Between 1975 and 1985, FDI constituted about 16 percent of total capital flows to LDCs and about 3 percent of total investment (United Nations Centre on Transnational Corporations 1988, 139).

In the 1980s, an important shift of FDI from developing to developed countries took place. In the 1980–1984 period, 25.2 percent of global flows went to the LDCs, but in 1988–1989, only 16.9 percent did (UNCTC 1991, 11). Moreover, in the 1980s ten relatively rapidly growing LDCs received three-fourths of the total flows. Although LDCs frequently complain about the pernicious impact of foreign capital for reasons we discuss later, some observers say that "the only thing worse than being exploited by capitalists is not being exploited by them."

To what sectors does FDI flow? Historically, much FDI was in the primary sectors (petroleum, minerals, and agriculture). Foreign investment in minerals and agriculture, however, dropped from 33 percent of the U.S. total in 1897 to about 10 percent in 1970 (Krasner 1978, A-2 and A-3). Host countries nationalized most foreign investment in petroleum during the 1970s. Most FDI has flowed into manufacturing since World War II.

Reflecting the transformation of the developed countries into postindustrial economies, however, FDI now increasingly appears in the service sector. Fifty percent of the world stock of FDI, and 55–60 percent of annual flows, were in services in the mid-1980s (UNCTC 1991, 15). Banking, other finance, and trade-related services account for most of the FDI. The United States and Japan are the clear leaders in this global movement toward the internationalization of services. Table 13.3 shows the home of the top ten firms in major service industries.[21]

ECONOMIC IMPACT OF MULTINATIONAL CORPORATIONS

In the 1980s, the 600 largest industrial MNCs accounted for between one-fifth and one-fourth of the global production of goods. MNCs largely control global trade; for example, they direct 80 percent to 90 percent of American and British exports.

More-developed countries voice concerns about the power of the corporations and the character of the deals that their governments, or their domestic firms, are able to strike with the MNCs. In Germany in 1974, foreign firms owned 33 percent of the capital in chemicals and 51 percent of that in electrical machinery, two of the most important sectors in the German economy (Blake and Walters 1987, 106). In 1971, Ford Motor Company considered closing its British operations and the British government had minimal control over the decision. The developed countries also worry that their own multinationals may be exporting capital, technology, and jobs to the detriment of the home economy. Measurement of net job destruction and creation from the activities of MNCs is so complicated that it is not clear whether the United States and other developed countries gain or lose employment because of their dealings.

LDCs face MNCs from positions of even less power and with equally uncertain assessments of their net impact. Although there is no question that

[21] Almost all of the largest service firms are now transnationalized. On the average, however, service MNCs based in the United States are only about half as transnationalized as manufacturing MNCs. Altogether, about 3 percent of U.S. corporate assets are invested abroad. Companies in some other countries are much more transnationalized (especially in smaller, developed countries). The figures for West Germany and Britain in the mid 1980s were 7 and 31 percent, respectively (United Nations Centre on Transnational Corporations 1988, 26).

TABLE 13.3
Home Countries of Major Service Firms

Industry	Number Of Firms Among Largest Ten			Global Assets of Top Ten (Billion Dollars)
	U.S.	Japan	Other(Country)	
Banking	1	7	2 (France)	3,258.7
Securities and finance	9	1	0	462.7
Insurance	5	4	1 (Germany)	526.2
Trading	10	0	0	175.5
Retailing	9	0	1 (Germany)	116.4
Accounting	8	0	2 (Netherlands)	13.7 (income)
Advertising	7	2	1 (U.K.)	6.2 (revenue)
Construction	4	5	1 (France)	66.3
Publishing	5	0	5 (Assorted)	29.0
Transportation	6	2	2 (Germany, France)	201.4
Airlines	6	1	3 (Assorted)	34.6
Hotels	8	0	2 (U.K., Germany)	15.1 (sales)
Fast Food	10	0	0	33.5 (sales)

Source: United Nations Centre on Transnational Corporations *Transnational Corporations in World Development: Trends and Prospects* (New York: UNCTC, 1988), Annex Tables B.1–B.17.

MNCs bring the benefits of technology, managerial skills, and access to markets, they are hardly LDC-controlled agents of development. Whether they are agents of international capitalism, tools of the states from which they originate, servants of their stockholders, autonomous units acting on behalf of management, or some combination of these, there can be little doubt that their masters exist outside of the LDCs in which they operate.[22] The economic size of the larger corporations is comparable with that of the LDCs. General Motors, Royal Dutch Shell, Exxon, and Ford had annual sales in 1991 larger than the GNPs of Iran, Turkey, Argentina, and Yugoslavia, respectively (Table 13.4).

Structuralists point out that Britain, France, the United States, and Germany did not face such powerful external economic actors when they developed. MNCs have often imposed unfavorable economic terms on LDCs. Until the mid-1960s, the major oil companies coordinated a scheme in which they served all of West Africa by ship with oil products in rotation. Each company charged for products as if they purchased them in Caribbean ports and shipped from there, regardless of actual origin and cost. Only when the countries of West Africa began to refine their own oil could they break free of this system (Odell 1986, 171). Similarly, until World War II companies charged India for oil as if they shipped it from the Gulf of Mexico, when in fact they had obtained it from the Persian Gulf or the Dutch East Indies, closer to India.

[22]Krasner (1978) produced one of the most serious studies of the relationship between MNCs, economic interests, and states.

TABLE 13.4
The World's 100 Largest Economic Units (1990–1991)—Billion Dollars

1.	United States	5,392	51. *Philip Morris*	48
2.	Japan	2,943	52. Venezuela	48
3.	Russia	1,625	53. *Fiat*	47
4.	Germany	1,623	54. *Volkswagen*	46
5.	France	1,191	55. *Siemens*	45
6.	Italy	1,091	56. Czechoslovakia	44
7.	United Kingdom	975	57. Phillipines	44
8.	Canada	570	58. *Samsung Group*	44
9.	Spain	491	59. New Zealand	43
10.	Brazil	414	60. Ireland	43
11.	China	365	61. *Nissan*	43
12.	Australia	296	62. Malaysia	42
13.	Netherlands	279	63. Algeria	42
14.	India	255	64. *Unilever*	41
15.	Mexico	238	65. *ENI*	41
16.	South Korea	236	66. Colombia	41
17.	Sweden	228	67. *Du Pont*	38
18.	Switzerland	225	68. *Texaco*	38
19.	Belgium	192	69. Peru	37
20.	Austria	157	70. *Chevron*	37
21.	Taiwan	151	71. *ELF Aquitaine*	36
22.	Finland	137	72. Pakistan	36
23.	Denmark	131	73. *Nestlé*	36
24.	*General Motors*	123	74. Iraq	35
25.	Iran	116	75. Nigeria	35
26.	Indonesia	107	76. Romania	35
27.	Norway	106	77. Singapore	35
28.	*Royal Dutch*	104	78. *Toshiba*	33
29.	*Exxon*	103	79. Egypt	33
30.	Turkey	97	80. Hungary	33
31.	Argentina	93	81. *Honda Motor*	31
32.	South Africa	91	82. *Philips*	30
33.	*Ford*	89	83. *Renault*	29
34.	Yugoslavia	82	84. *Chrysler*	29
35.	Saudi Arabia	81	85. *Boeing*	29
36.	Thailand	80	86. *ABB Asea Brown*	29
37.	*Toyota*	78	87. *Hoechst*	28
38.	*IBM*	65	88. *Peugeot*	28
39.	*IRI*	64	89. *Alcatel Alsthom*	28
40.	Poland	64	90. *BASF*	28
41.	*General Electric*	60	91. *UAE*	28
42.	Hong Kong	60	92. Chile	28
43.	*British Petroleum*	58	93. *Procter & Gamble*	27
44.	Greece	58	94. *NEC*	27
45.	*Daimler-Benz*	57	95. *Sony*	27
46.	Portugal	57	96. *AMOCO*	26
47.	*Mobil*	57	97. *Bayer*	26
48.	*Hitachi*	56	98. *Daewoo*	25
49.	Israel	53	99. *TOTAL*	25
50.	*Matsushita Elec*	49	100. Morocco	25

Sources: Fortune (July 27, 1992), p. 179; World Bank, *World Development Report* (New York: Oxford University Press, 1992), pp. 222–223; U.S. Central Intelligence Agency, *The World Factbook 1991* (Washington, D.C.: U.S. Government Printing Office, 1991).
Notes: Figures for corporations are annual sales; those for countries are GNP.

Is it any wonder that LDCs today feel that the MNCs still take advantage of them economically, even if it is more difficult to prove? For instance, increasing amounts of world trade consists of sales across state borders but between units of the same corporation.[23] In such internal corporation transactions, the companies have nearly complete control over **transfer pricing** (the prices one division of a corporation charges another division for a product). Critics frequently accuse them of setting transfer prices to avoid taxation or limitations on the repatriation of large profits from LDCs. In the 1980s, MNCs exported timber from a Pacific island country (unnamed), using "third-country invoicing" to avoid all local corporate income taxes. That is, the MNCs priced timber exports low from the country of origin, "sold" them at considerably higher prices in paper transactions in a country that charges little or no tax, and then delivered timber to market at the higher price (United Nations Centre on Transnational Corporations 1988, 94–95).[24]

One reason LDCs desire the presence of multinational corporations is to obtain investment capital from the companies. Many studies indicate, however, that MNCs obtain large portions of their capital in the host country:[25] Similarly, in 1990, the U.S. Internal Revenue Service reported that more than half of the 37,000 foreign firms doing business in the U.S. paid no taxes—on gross sales of over $550 billion they reported net tax losses. Analysts cited transfer pricing as the reason.

> Financing of foreign investment is done largely with host country, not foreign capital. For example, between 1958 and 1968, U.S. manufacturing subsidies in Latin America obtained 80 percent of all financing locally, through either borrowing or subsidiary earnings. (Spero 1981, 228)

Through repatriation of profits back to the home country, MNCs actually set up net capital transfers from South to North (dos Santos 1984, 95; Parenti 1989, 13). Table 13.5 reports UN figures on the net inflow of FDI to LDCs, and on the net outflow of profits from LDCs during the 1975–1985 decade. It appears that corporations took about $85 billion more from LDCs than they provided to them during that period.[26] Although some data also suggest that MNCs make unusually high profits in the LDCs,[27] recent analysis puts rates of return in more- and less-developed countries in the late 1980s at 17 and 12 percent, respectively (UNDP 1992, 53). Those figures are consistent with a shift of investment flows to more developed countries.

[23]In 1981–1985 about 30 percent of U.S., Japanese, and U.K. exports were intrafirm transfers (United Nations Centre on Transnational Corporations, 1988, 92).

[24]One study found that pharmaceutical imports into Colombia were overpriced by $3 billion (Spero 1981, 229). One MNC imported the hormone progesterone into Mexico in 1972 at a price 22 times higher than that at which another MNC exported it (Gereffi 1985, 91).

[25]Even economically advanced countries have had the same concern about the MNCs. In the 1960s, U.S. corporations staked out major positions in European countries. Jean-Jacques Servan-Schreiber published a book in France in 1968 called *The American Challenge*, in which he lamented that the French and other Europeans were in effect paying U.S. corporations to buy those of Europe.

[26]The roughly two-to-one ratio of outflows to inflows was also the case in 1970–1971 (United Nations Centre on Transnational Corporations 1985, 27 and 30).

[27]According to a calculation in the mid-1970s, the average return on U.S. investment in developed countries was 12.1 percent, but that on the book value of investment in developing countries was 25.8 percent (Spero 1981, 228).

TABLE 13.5
Net Flows to LDCs of FDI and FDI Profits, Annual Averages (Million Dollars)

Net Inflows of FDI	1975–1980	1981–1985
Southern Europe	133	180
Africa	735	1,602
Latin America	3,804	4,907
Western Asia	476	185
Other Asia and Oceania	1,890	4,410
Total LDCs	7,038	11,282
Net Outflows of Profits	1975–1980	1981–1985
Southern Europe	39	38
Africa	3,323	4,090
Latin America	3,670	5,679
Western Asia	4,057	6,514
Other Asia and Oceania	3,118	5,869
Total LDCs	14,208	22,189

Source: United Nations Centre on Transnational Corporations, *Transnational Corporations in World Development: Trends and Prospects* (New York: UNCTC, 1988), Annex Tables A.1–A.4.

Reverse capital flows and high profits do not necessarily mean, however, that MNCs financially harm LDCs. The value of the technology, management skills, and production that LDCs gain could be much more than the net cost of capital. It is nearly impossible to assess the positive economic impact of MNCs on LDC production levels, but one can reasonably ask if many LDCs would have *any* modern manufacturing without MNCs.

Capital is but one factor of production. Two others are labor and technology, and LDCs feel disadvantaged with respect to them as well. Labor does not flow freely across the borders of countries, because states restrict immigration. The developed countries allow some immigration, however, particularly that of skilled professionals. This sets up a **brain drain**, in which many of the most educated individuals from the South move North. MNCs play a role in this as employers. In 1986, 75 percent of all immigrants from LDCs to the United States were skilled workers (UNDP 1992, 56). If a conservative value of $5,000 were placed on the education of each, that movement would constitute a gross annual subsidy of $2.5 billion from the South to the United States. Nearly one-half of the graduates of Philippine medical schools leave the country, and 80 percent of the Chinese from Taiwan who study in the United States fail to return home (Blake and Walters 1987, 158).[28]

[28]The electronics industry of Taiwan has benefitted greatly, however, from the return of entrepreneurial citizens who gained both education and corporate experience in the United States.

Todaro suggests that the domination of world science by the North distorts the priorities of Southern scientists in a manner that constitutes an even more damaging "internal" brain drain:

> For example, one constantly finds developing nations with numerous doctors specializing in heart diseases while preventive tropical medicine is considered to be a second-rate specialty. Architects are concerned with the design of national monuments and modern public buildings, while low-cost housing, schools, and clinics remain an area of remote concern. Engineers and scientists concentrate on the newest and most modern electronic equipment while simple machine tools, hand- or animal-operated farm equipment, basic sanitation and water-purifying systems, and labor-intensive mechanical processes are relegated to the attention of "foreign experts." (Todaro 1989, 353)

The other side of the brain-drain argument is that remittances of workers back to families in the LDCs contributes substantially to the country of emigration. In cases such as Turkey, Egypt, Portugal, Pakistan, and Morocco, remittances can exceed 5 percent of GNP. One study found that Mexican migrants send back more than twice what they can make at home (UNDP 1992, 56). The conventional wisdom of structuralists has therefore shifted from seeking solely to avoid the brain drain of the educated to arguing also in favor of freer immigration for the less skilled.

Technology, like capital, is a production factor that LDCs hope to attain from multinationals; its pursuit is the most important reason they court FDI. LDCs have three primary complaints in this area. First, they believe that MNCs charge too much for existing technology. Reasonable cost for technology is extremely difficult to determine. Second, they argue that MNCs maintain the research and development function in the home countries, and thus retard LDC efforts to develop their own innovation capabilities. Third, and most important, however, they complain about the size of technology flows to LDCs; as FDI shifted North in the 1980s, so did capital flows. Whereas the trade in capital goods (machinery carrying technology) grew among industrial countries at 10.2 percent annually in the 1980s, North-South trade grew at only a 1.5 percent rate (UNDP 1992, 66).

When countries do purchase technology from abroad rather than developing it locally, additional problems can arise, related to the character of the imported manufacturing technology. First, industrial countries that are rich in capital but poor in labor often do not develop **appropriate technology** for LDCs that are poor in capital and rich in labor. Second, high-technology machinery often requires expensive imports to support it. Third, the imports may abort the gestation of embryonic local research and development capabilities, because the local efforts cannot compete. Great debates rage over what technology is appropriate and how LDCs can encourage its inflow.

POWER OF MULTINATIONAL CORPORATIONS

LDCs sometimes believe that they are relatively powerless compared with MNCs. Although both sides may gain, bargaining from a position of weakness often means obtaining an unequal bargain. Individuals in economically advanced countries can certainly understand this concern with unequal benefits. Who has not felt, in negotiations with a bank, insurance company, law firm, or employer, that his or her position was so weak that the powerful institution dictated unfair terms? Moreover, such noninternational transactions occur in an environment with collectively established legal constraints on the behavior of institutions, whereas international economic transactions occur in an environment of near anarchy.

Even governments in more-developed countries often question their ability to deal successfully with MNCs. States and cities within the United States often find themselves in bidding wars over the location of MNC plants. For instance, in 1991 United Airlines negotiated for a prolonged period with Denver, Indianapolis, and other cities over the building of a maintenance facility. In the competition, the governments repeatedly provided concessions that reduced the net benefits to them while increasing the benefits to the corporation. The competition among LDCs is equally fierce.

In contrast, liberal theorists view multinational corporations as positive agents of economic development in LDCs. Although recognizing that monopolistic practices are possible, they argue that the forces of competition in an increasingly global and competitive economy act to restrain inappropriate practices and to increase the bargaining power of LDCs. Moreover, host countries increasingly impose strict performance requirements on MNCs; they have moved up a "learning curve" in their dealings with them.

Raymond Vernon's concept of the **obsolescing bargain** can help us better understand bargaining positions—and the love-hate relationship between companies and countries. When MNCs first approach Third World countries (or, for that matter, First World countries), the states often actively pursue the MNC and the benefits it can bring (as do various U.S. states or localities). A courtship by multiple potential hosts allows the MNC to strike a favorable bargain. Countries may offer land, tax benefits, and favorable treatment under national laws. Once a corporation has invested its capital, however, power shifts to the host country. The country can hold the ultimate threat of nationalization over the company's corporate head, and short of that it can bring to bear the entire legal system it controls (including health and safety standards, environmental controls, and labor regulations). The government may request increased taxes, greater local ownership, higher levels of exports, or other concessions of interest to it.

There are many examples of the success that LDCs increasingly have in dealing with MNCs, both during the initial investment-decision stage and as the bargain obsolesces. For instance, Brazil, Argentina, and Colombia do not allow MNCs to repatriate profits freely; Brazil insists that none can leave in the first two years after an investment, and that thereafter only 5 percent of total profits can be sent out of the country (Papp 1988, 84). In 1985 Mexico traded access to its markets for an IBM research and development facility on semiconductor technology (Blake and Walters 1987, 157). Many argue reasonably that as the economic strength and managerial skill level of individual LDCs increase, the countries will gain larger shares of the mutual benefits that liberals tell us are part of all MNC-LDC transactions.

The concern of structuralists with MNCs extends beyond their economic roles, however, to their political ones. MNCs have interfered in the politics of states and have also attempted, sometimes with apparent success, to involve their home states on their behalf. There is as much debate over the political power of MNCs abroad as over their economic influence:

> *Dependencia* writers have tended to assert that multinational firms have solid local political alliances and great local political influence, with the margin for autonomous domestic policy action extremely thin. International business writers, in contrast, tend to argue that foreign companies are continuously buffeted by hostile local forces, discriminated against on a regular basis, and left to operate almost totally without domestic political clout. (Moran 1985, 15)

Specific examples of interference frequently involve bribery. United Brands has been accused of bribing local officials in Guatemala (Blake and Walters 1987, 108) and Honduras (Spero 1981, 240). A U.S. congressional inquiry found that 100 MNCs had made improper foreign payments totaling more than $100 million (Kegley and Wittkopf 1989, 170). Some executives even defend bribery by arguing that it is a normal way of doing business in LDCs.

The most notorious example of MNC political interference was in Chile. International Telephone and Telegraph Company (ITT), a U.S.–based MNC, worked actively to avoid the election of Salvador Allende, Socialist party leader, to the presidency in late 1970, because it feared nationalization (Krasner 1978, 303). It put $350,000 into the coffers of his conservative opponent. It also approached the CIA before and after the election with offers to support action against him. The U.S. government did undertake covert activity both to prevent the election and to foment the 1973 coup that overthrew and assassinated Allende. This example is, however, quite unique and should not imply that MNCs consistently behave in such a manner. Moreover, it appears that the U.S. government took action independently of pressure from ITT.

The rise of MNCs in the postwar period has been so dramatic that some perceive them as a growing international political force, eventually strong enough to undercut the sovereignty not only of LDCs but of economically developed states (Vernon 1971). States will become so economically interdependent, and MNCs so free to shift capital and production, according to this argument, that the corporations will dictate terms to states and prevent any state action (perhaps including conflict) that would harm MNC interests. Some globalists believe that MNCs join NGOs and IGOs in creating a web of ties that bind states together. Other analysts respond, however, that even LDCs deal more and more successfully with MNCs, as their new state apparatuses develop, and that states need fear no sovereignty loss. (Gilpin 1975b reviews the contrasting arguments.)

Is there any evidence on the changing relative strength of MNCs and states? Figure 13.8 summarizes the relative economic size of the two categories of actors, building on several tables, such as Table 13.4. It traces over time the ratio of GNPs of states in the top 100 global actors to sales of MNCs in that set. It displays the

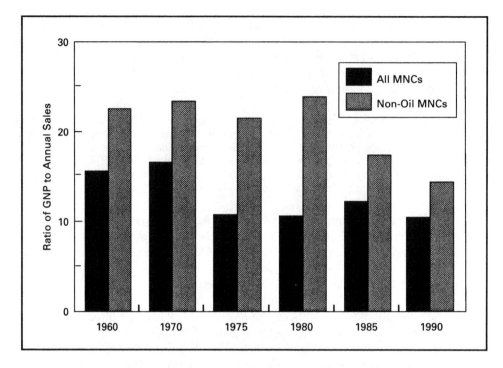

FIGURE 13.8   Relative Size of States and MNCs in Largest 100 Global Economic Acts
Source: Assorted tables, for example Table 13.4.

ratios for all MNCs and for non-oil MNCs separately, because the oil shocks of the 1970s greatly increased sales of MNCs in the energy industry and might distort the analysis. Both measures suggest that the size advantage of states may have declined slightly since 1960. If MNCs are becoming a serious economic challenge to states on the basis of size, however, it is happening slowly.[29]

Since 1982 negotiations have proceeded within a UN framework on an extensive code of conduct governing the relationship between MNCs and states. In addition to regularizing relationships on issues such as technology transfer, environmental protection, labor relations, and dispute settlement,[30] code provisions explicitly recognize the sovereignty of the state and its control over the activities of MNCs operating within its borders. For instance, the provisions note the permanent sovereignty of the state over natural resources, economic activities, and wealth; recognize the right of nationalization and expropriation (subject to nondiscrimination and appropriate compensation), and proscribe all political

[29]Clairmonte and Cavanagh (1982, 149, 152 and 155) indicate that between 1960 and 1980 the top 200 MNCs increased their revenues as a percentage of global GDP from 18 to 29 percent. Figure 13.8 suggests that the temporary growth of energy-producing MNCs explains their finding.

[30]Dispute settlement is important. An agreement to use the International Chamber of Commerce to arbitrate contract disputes facilitated the contract between France and Walt Disney Company to build a Disneyland near Paris.

activities by MNCs, including specifically corrupt practices such as bribery (United Nations Centre on Transnational Corporations 1988, 354–357). Although relative economic power may strongly influence state-MNC relationships in practice, the legal superiority of states is clear.

COMBINED IMPACT OF STRUCTURES

The existence of an international division of labor, well-established international political-economic institutions dominated by developed countries, and powerful MNCs jointly support the structuralist contention that we must look at the world political economy as a whole, and that paths of development blazed by industrial countries may be irrelevant to contemporary LDCs. Structuralists argue that global economic relations occur not between equal actors, but between a **core** (rich, powerful countries) and a **periphery** (poor, often powerless countries). Such economic relations, they propose, are unbalanced and result in unequal benefits from transactions.

In addition, structuralists claim, relationships with the international economy create and reinforce internal divisions *within* Third World countries. For instance, MNCs initially concentrated investment in LDCs on primary products. Foreign investments often established large mining complexes or plantations. Frequently these imported high percentages of the goods needed by the complex, including home-country foodstuffs, clothing, and household goods for the foreign managers as well as equipment for production. These practices established **enclave economies**, effectively distinct from the domestic one. The main connections with the local community were to obtain low-cost, unskilled labor and to maintain political relationships with local leadership so as to reduce any threat to the investment.

The enclave economy pattern helps explain the history of heavy influence by corporations in domestic affairs. American films still unfairly and even maliciously portray Central American states as "banana republics." That label arose in a period when strong external corporation presence and political interference interacted with weak domestic political institutions to help produce frequent coups and government changes. The banana-exporting United Fruit Company (now United Brands) was a major actor.[31]

Manufacturing MNCs bring another set of problems to LDCs. They often contribute to the creation of a **dual economy**. The modern portion of it, dominated by external firms, is relatively high technology, capital intensive, and closely tied to the world economy. The traditional portion of the dual economy includes agriculture and small local industry and handicrafts. The connections between the

---

[31] Although local governments have taken over most large mineral production facilities in LDCs, the enclave economy pattern still exists. The model helps explain, for example, why the international oil industry could continue to expand within Angola throughout the 1980s, even in the face of a Marxist government and a civil war. The location of oil development is distant from both the war and the government, in an enclave, so that war does not threaten the industry and the industry does not threaten the government.

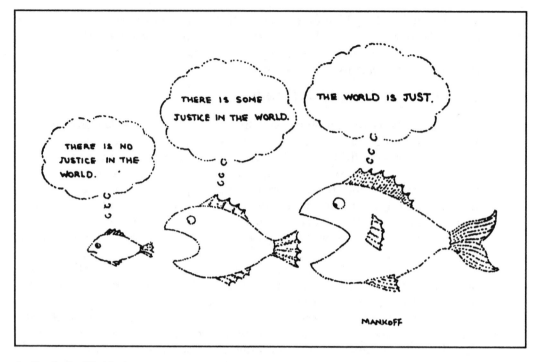

Justice in the World
Drawing by Mankoff; © 1981 The New Yorker Magazine, Inc.

two components are minimal. Two separate labor forces exist with great skill and income differences.

The dual economy constitutes a source of social cleavage and instability. Galtung (1964) argued that within both core and periphery countries, there is a division between a center social group and a peripheral social group. In the core countries the division is not intense, because high levels of employment and income, coupled with open political institutions, ameliorate social tensions. In the periphery, the income inequalities are much greater (Table 13.6), unemployment and underemployment is pervasive, and political institutions are frequently not very open; they may be controlled by traditional landed aristocracies, the new bourgeoisie, the military, or a rotation among these elites. Internationally oriented elites in LDCs may actually have an interest in maintaining divisions within the society rather than closing them. They may live well because of the supply of inexpensive labor, foodstuffs, and raw materials on which they can draw.

A strong version of these arguments posits that not only do global trade and financial linkages combine to retard economic and political development in the LDCs, they actively "de-develop" the Third World. They undercut indigenous industry and technological advance and they create internal divisions that social and political institutions cannot reconcile, and that in turn produce debilitating instability.

TABLE 13.6					
Income Distribution, Most Recent Year					
	Percent of Income Received by the			Percent of Income Received by the	
	Lowest 20 Percent	Highest 10 Percent		Lowest 20 Percent	Highest 10 Percent
Latin America			*Africa*		
El Salvador	5.5	29.5	Kenya	2.6	45.8
Peru	4.4	35.8	Zambia	3.4	46.4
Costa Rica	3.3	38.8	Côte d'Ivoire	5.0	36.3
Brazil	2.4	46.2	Ghana	7.1	28.5
Mexico	2.9	40.6	Botswana	2.5	42.8
Panama	2.0	44.2			
Argentina	4.4	35.2	Average	4.1	40.0
Venezuela	4.7	34.2			
Guatemala	9.8	25.4			
Colombia	4.0	37.1			
Average	4.3	36.7			
Asia			*Selected Developed Countries*		
Bangladesh	10.0	23.2	Spain	6.9	23.5
India	8.1	26.7	New Zealand	5.1	28.7
Sri Lanka	4.8	43.0	Italy	6.8	25.3
Indonesia	8.8	26.5	Great Britain	5.8	23.3
Philippines	9.9	32.1	France	6.3	25.5
Thailand	5.6	34.1	Germany	6.8	21.2
Malaysia	4.6	34.8	Japan	8.7	22.4
South Korea	5.7	27.5	Sweden	8.0	20.8
Hong Kong	5.4	31.3	Canada	5.7	24.1
Pakistan	7.8	31.3	United States	4.7	25.0
			Switzerland	5.2	29.8
Average	7.1	31.1			
			Average	6.4	24.5

Source: World Bank, *World Development Report 1989* (New York: Oxford University Press, 1989), 222–223; World Bank, *World Development Report 1992* (New York: Oxford University Press, 1992), 276–277.

In contrast, liberals suggest that inequality is a natural element of the development process and is transitory (see the Kuznets curve discussion in Chapter 11). The existence of a dual economy proves that modernization is beginning and will eventually transform the remainder of the traditional economy. The theoretical debate is complicated by the existence of some developing countries like Brazil, in which structuralists can point to extensive and persistent inequality, alongside other developing countries like South Korea and Taiwan, which also maintain close ties to the world economy and yet boast quite egalitarian income distributions. This phenomenon leads some to reject the relevance of either liberal or structuralist arguments about the implications of contemporary ties to the world economy and to emphasize cultural and historic issues (Harrison 1985). The Portuguese colonized Brazil and established massive plantation agriculture with its inherent inequalities between landowners and laborers. The Japanese colonized Taiwan and encouraged smaller and more nearly equal landowners to produce food crops. Those historic and cultural legacies may explain political and economic performance better than does contemporary interaction with the IMF or MNCs.

We should complete this review of structuralist arguments with the presentation of one final line of thought. It appears increasingly that the liberal global political economy, with its ideology of laissez faire policies domestically and internationally, the strength of its global institutions, and the power of a global division of labor and of multinational firms, may be "internationalizing" the state apparatus in LDCs (Cox 1987). That is, the governments in those countries have often moved from being agents that support local development processes, and which buffer them against the outside world (as it has long been the case in France, became so in Japan, and now is in Taiwan), to ones that seek to adapt the local political economies to the demands of the global one. As a result, rapid reduction in government size and lowering of trade barriers characterized most LDCs in the 1980s and in the early 1990s. It will be interesting to watch the consequences of this transformation.

COLD WAR STRUCTURALISM

Structuralist arguments draw our attention to the negative consequences for the South of North-South power and development differentials. To this point, however, we have treated the North as a whole, ignoring the divisions within it. A variation of structuralism, which we can call **cold war structuralism**, focuses on the implications for the South of the dominant Northern cleavage after World War II, the division between East and West. A Swahili proverb summarizes those implications: "When two elephants fight, the grass gets trampled" (Shepherd 1987, 1). After the breakdown of their World War II alliance, the superpowers moved rapidly to organize as much of the world as possible around them. LDCs quickly became objects of their interest and instruments of their power.

The NATO (1949) and Warsaw Pact (1955) groupings drew the more developed countries of Europe around the superpowers. The American alliance system quickly expanded around the world, however, and drew in LDCs. In 1947 the Inter-American Treaty of Reciprocal Assistance, signed in Rio de Janeiro, committed twenty-one Western Hemisphere states to mutual defense. The same states formed the Organization of American States (OAS) in 1948, an entity that continues to react to external aggression and to settle internal disputes. In 1962 and 1965 the OAS invoked its provision for collective defense against left-leaning governments in Cuba and the Dominican Republic. The United States orchestrated the actions.[32]

In 1954 the Southeast Asia Collective Defense Treaty bound Australia, Great Britain, France, New Zealand, Pakistan, the Philippines, Thailand, and the United States to mutual defense, and in 1955 the same countries established the Southeast Asia Treaty Organization (SEATO). In 1955, a U.S. initiative led to the Central Treaty Organization among Great Britain, Iran, Iraq (until 1959), Pakistan, and Turkey.[33]

The Soviet Union never established a global alliance structure similar to that which implemented the U.S. containment policy (see Chapter 7). Yet it had Southern allies and client states, including China (in the 1950s) and North Korea. Those Soviet clients were the focal point of the first major East-West war. In June 1950 Communist North Korean forces invaded the non-Communist South, converting the cold war into a hot one. The United States led an alliance of seventeen non-Communist powers under the banner of the United Nations against the aggressors.

For many years thereafter, subsequent East-West battles in the South took place with less overt violence, frequently through covert action. In 1953 the United States helped a new Shah capture the throne of Iran, ousting a popularly elected, leftist government. In 1954 the United States supported the overthrow of a leftist Guatemalan government. Neither the United States nor the Soviet Union cheerfully watched changes of government within their spheres of influence that appeared to give the other superpower an edge.

Cuba was long a focal point for East-West tension. After the victory of Castro in Cuba in 1959, relations with the United States soured and the Soviet Union backed the new Communist government. In reaction, the United States sponsored a disastrous invasion attempt by exile forces at Cuba's Bay of Pigs in 1961. The Soviets then attempted in 1962 to use Cuba as a platform for nuclear missiles, and the United States successfully forced the Soviets to cease construction of the installations during the Cuban Missile Crisis.

Asia became the major battlefield once again, however. Simmering involvement by the United States in the Vietnamese civil war during the early 1960s escalated in 1964 to bombing attacks on the Communist North, where there were Soviet advisers. American troop commitment built rapidly to a peak in 1968 of about 500,000 (more than 56,000 Americans died there). The final Americans withdrew in April 1975.

Between 1974 and 1979 the Soviets became especially aggressive in the Third World (Saivetz and Woodby 1985). The Soviets sponsored a Cuban intervention in

---

[32]The organization failed to follow U.S. leadership in similar fashion when called upon with respect to Grenada (1983) and Nicaragua (during the 1980s). The organization also declined to react in the war between Britain and Argentina over the Falklands (Malvinas) in 1982.

[33]Although SEATO dissolved in 1977, the treaty of 1954 remains officially active. Pakistan withdrew from Central Treaty Organization (CENTO) in 1979, and the Iranian revolution of that year removed its focal point and killed the alliance.

the Angolan civil war in October 1975; when withdrawal finally began in 1989, there were 50,000 Cuban soldiers there. In 1979 another Cuban force went to Ethiopia as a Soviet proxy. In December 1979 the Soviets invaded Afghanistan. The involvement of about 115,000 troops lasted nearly a decade and culminated in a retreat nearly as ignominious as that of the United States from Vietnam.

Superpower interventions continued around the world through the 1980s. In 1983 a U.S. invasion overthrew the Cuban-oriented government of the tiny Caribbean island of Grenada. A running battle between the United States and Libya (a Soviet friend) continued throughout the decade, including a surprise bombing attack on suspected terrorist support facilities there in 1986 and the downing of two Libyan fighters in the Mediterranean in 1989. Throughout the decade the United States maintained publicly observable "covert" support for the Contras in Nicaragua, and the Soviets supplied the Sandinista regime. In 1989 the United States invaded Panama.

The preceding list only scratches the surface of overt and covert intervention by the United States and the Soviet Union in the affairs of other countries. Another important arena in which they sparred was that of weapons support for client states. Early in the cold war they provided gifts and sold inexpensive equipment that was obsolete in the superpower arsenals. The United States supported Yugoslavian resistance to Soviet pressure in that way. In the 1980s they sold highly sophisticated military technology at high prices. In that decade the two superpowers accounted for about 60 percent of total global arms sales, and their NATO and Warsaw Pact allies provided most of the rest. (Third World suppliers like Israel, South Korea, and Brazil are becoming important, however.) The United States was the world's largest supplier until the late 1970s, but the Soviet Union subsequently took over that place of honor. In the 1980s, arms sales (Figure 13.9) constituted nearly 20 percent of total Soviet exports (compared with less than 5 percent for the United States), making armaments an important source of foreign earnings (US ACDA 1991).

Conflicts would certainly have occurred in the Third World even without superpower intervention. Their involvement initiated many, however, and militarily intensified most:

> The core powers have supplied the means for Arabs and Israelis to fight three wars, for Somalia to attack Ethiopia, and for Iraq and Iran to wage a major war. Pakistan and India have fought each other four times with heavy weapons provided by the dominant powers. (Shepherd 1987, 4)

In the late 1980s some cooperation began to appear between the United States and the Soviet Union in resolving Third World conflicts, especially in the Mideast and in southern Africa. The Soviet Union began a major withdrawal from its global outposts even before its collapse.

There always was, however, another side to the involvement of the superpowers in the South. Although they engaged in proxy wars and provided the arms for many conflicts, they also sought to dampen conflict within their spheres of influence and even to prevent confrontations at their intersection. For example,

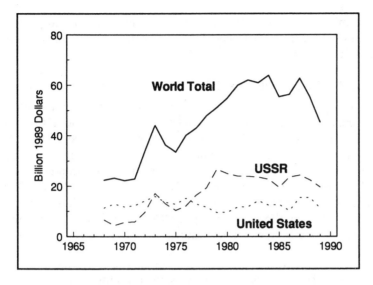

FIGURE 13.9 Arms Sales
Source: United States Arms Control and Disarmament Agency, *World Military Expenditures and Arms Transfers, 1968–1977*(Washington, D.C.: US ACDA, 1979), 113, 147, 151; United States Arms Control and Disarmament Agency, *World Military Expenditures and Arms Transfers, 1988* (Washington, D.C.: US ACDA, 1989), 69, 103, 104; United States Arms Control and Disarmament Agency, *World Military Expenditures and Arms Transfers, 1990* (Washington, D.C.: US ACDA, 1991), 89, 123, 127.

after the Korean War the peninsula remained quiet. While arming the parties of the Middle East, the superpowers also often used their influence to prevent or stop conflict. In addition, the cold war motivated the superpowers to provide substantial development aid to LDCs. Cuba, for instance, benefited greatly from Soviet aid.

The important question for the 1990s is how the end of the cold war will affect Northern participation in the creation and dampening of conflict in the South and in development efforts. There are many possible forecasts. Many realists would anticipate at most a brief respite in competition among great powers for the resources (including markets) of the South. Some of that competition will inevitably lead to military conflict; the oil resources of the Middle East will likely remain a focal point. Globalists would hope for, but not necessarily forecast, collective efforts by the North to reduce causes of Southern conflict and to improve the delivery of development assistance. On this issue structuralists are likely to agree with realists: Historically, the elephants have badly trampled the grass throughout the Third World; they are unlikely to develop better manners.

STRATEGIES FOR COPING

Southern countries must somehow cope in the world they face, and the strategy they adopt will depend on their perception of that world. Three dominant strategies exist: withdrawal, reform, and participation. Structuralists have sometimes supported the first strategy; reform attracts attention from both selected structuralists and liberals; and many liberals strongly recommend participation. That pairing of systemic perspective with preferred strategy is far too simplistic, but it suggests the inevitable linkage between description and analysis, on the one hand, and policy prescription, on the other.[34]

WITHDRAWAL AND SELF-RELIANCE

When developed countries hammered together the Bretton Woods institutions, the Havana Charter for an International Trade Organization (ITO) contained early proposals for a postwar trade system. At the insistence of the LDCs, it incorporated provisions to relax the conditions of free trade. It would have allowed, under some circumstances, import controls, regional preference systems, and commodity agreements (Spero 1981, 184). That system died for lack of U.S. support, and the GATT structure became instead the framework for international trade. GATT did not allow the flexibility for LDCs provided in the ITO, imposing instead the same free trade rules on all countries:

> Recognizing these biases, many underdeveloped countries chose not to join GATT or to participate in the international trade negotiations sponsored by GATT.... During the first postwar decade, the trade policy followed by many Southern states was an inward-looking policy of industrialization through import substitution. (Spero 1981, 185)

Import substitution is a policy of producing domestically as much as possible of that which a country traditionally imported. Many LDCs, especially in Latin America, maintained their high prewar tariffs or added additional barriers to imports so as to encourage local industry in a wide variety of sectors. In addition, import substitution required government support for the infant industries through subsidies and other policies (sometimes through direct ownership).

Some countries carried the strategy to real extremes and literally withdrew from the world political economy. China largely cut itself off from the world economy and Albania fully did so, withdrawing from both East and West. Burma withdrew politically and considerably scaled back economic contacts. Cuba sought to withdraw from the entangling economic relationships it had with the West (including wide-scale foreign ownership of land and capital assets), but found that it needed to turn to the Soviet Union for a sugar market and for supplies of oil and other needs.

By the late 1980s most countries had concluded that import substitution was not working (or that they had sheltered the nascent industries long enough). The strategy had often led to high-cost, inefficient domestic production, relatively little of which could be exported. Most countries have gradually abandoned or weakened import substitution. In a study of thirty LDCs, the World Bank (1992b, 13) found that on a scale of trade openness ranging from 1 to 5, they had moved from 1.1 in 1978 to 2.5 in 1988.

[34]Ruggie (1983b) identifies the same three strategies by different names and similarly associates them with political orientations.

The Communist countries had attempted a collective withdrawal from the liberal world economy but reversed this policy in the 1980s. Even China, with its huge resource base and internal market, and with the official maintenance of communism, concluded that it needed to reestablish economic ties with the outside world.

Countries adopting the withdrawal strategy today are more likely to frame it in terms of maximizing **self-reliance** while maintaining involvement in the world economy. That is, they see relationships with the powerful economies of the West as inevitable, and even beneficial, but they seek, insofar as possible, to approach transactions with them on their own terms and to obtain a greater share of the benefits.

Nationalization of foreign-owned assets is sometimes part of the self-reliance vision. At one time a large portion of the investments by MNCs in the Third World were in petroleum, mining, and plantation agriculture. In 1914, for example, 13 percent of U.S. direct foreign investment was in petroleum, 27 percent in mining, and 13 percent in agriculture (Krasner 1978, 355–357). LDCs have now nationalized most of these investments; takeovers of petroleum assets in the 1970s by the oil-producing countries largely completed the process. Western governments did not always accept that process gracefully, particularly because radical regimes often directed it. Several postwar U.S. foreign interventions, including those in Iran (1953), Guatemala (1954), and Chile (1971–1973), attempted to retard nationalization or to control the terms of it.

Another important element of many self-reliance strategies is a focus on **basic human needs** (food, shelter, clothing, and education) of the poor and attention to income distribution. Structuralists argue that waiting for the benefits of growth to "trickle down" is unacceptable (and may never happen). Mahbub ul Haq of Pakistan puts it succinctly: "We were taught to take care of our GNP as this will take care of poverty. Let us reverse this and take care of poverty as this will take care of the GNP" (Todaro 1989, 144). Structuralists reject both the necessity and desirability of allowing income distribution to worsen substantially in the early phases of growth, as the Kuznets curve implies is inevitable.[35]

It requires redistribution of assets, such as land, to improve distribution substantially. Even the U.S.-sponsored Alliance for Progress with Latin America urged such measures in the 1960s. The difficulty is that those who hold assets most often also hold political power and naturally resist loss of their property. This reality is what leads many structuralists to propose collective, even revolutionary action in the struggle against the owners of land and capital. Although that collective struggle often occurs within LDCs, it can also occur between South and North. That is our next topic.

COLLECTIVE STRUCTURAL REFORM

Southern countries have worked steadily to reform the liberal, Northern-dominated system and to maximize their collective leverage within it. These efforts predate independence of much of the Third World from the colonial empires. In

---

[35]Todaro (1989, 143–181) reviews alternative theories and empirical studies concerning the relationship between economic growth and income distribution.

1927 a Congress of Oppressed Nationalities in Brussels brought together 175 delegates representing thirty-seven territories and countries (Woodby and Cottam 1988, 30). This conference, and Pan-Asian, Pan-African, and Pan-Arab movements during the same period, sought to develop a Southern coalition in support of independence movements. The independent states in Africa and Asia were, however, too few in number and too powerless to be successful. Latin-American countries, independent since the early 1800s, did not play strong supportive roles.

After World War II, India hosted Afro-Asian conferences (1947 and 1949). Other meetings followed in Egypt and Ceylon (now Sri Lanka). At the top of the agenda in each meeting were collective protests of efforts by the European powers to reestablish their colonial empires after the disruption caused by the war.

By the early 1950s superpower pressure on LDCs to enlist on one side or the other of the cold war was sufficiently great that it became a central issue. In 1955 leaders of twenty-seven states met in Bandung, Indonesia. From the Bandung Conference emerged the Nonaligned Movement (NAM) under the leadership of Tito from Yugoslavia and Nehru from India. It represented a collective effort to resist the superpower pressure. The NAM held its first formal summit in Belgrade in 1961 and has met approximately every third year since then, including a session in Zimbabwe in 1986 which 101 countries attended.

In truth, the NAM was never free of the very East-West tensions against which it sought to provide a united front. The movement proved unable to condemn the American war in Vietnam or the Soviet invasion of Czechoslovakia, because friends of the respective superpowers opposed condemnation. The United States and other Western countries noted that in 1979 it met in Cuba, a close Soviet ally. It granted North Korea membership, but refused it to South Korea and the Philippines on the basis of their associations with the United States (including U.S. military bases in each). Yet we should put these Western accusations that the NAM leaned toward the East into the context of the earlier discussion of cold war structuralism. In the postwar period the primary focus of the Soviet Union (as indicated by overt interventions) was on its uncertain periphery in Eastern Europe, whereas the United States and the former colonial powers exhibited greater activism in the Third World. Although the Soviet Union made progress in extension of its influence into the South (playing important roles in Egypt, Indonesia, Algeria, Syria, India, Cuba, Vietnam, Laos, Nicaragua, Angola, Ethiopia, and many other countries at one time or another), many Third World countries never perceived that progress as a threat, at least not a threat comparable with that of domination by the United States and the West.

The Afro-Asian movement and decolonization fed each other during the early postwar period. Colonial empires that had grown up during a period of nearly four centuries collapsed totally in four decades. Eighteen African countries became independent in 1960 alone. Two developments logically followed the proliferation of independent Third World states.

First, the United Nations gradually became a preferred focus for Southern collective efforts. In 1945 membership was fifty-one states, and only a handful were Afro-Asian. That total grew to seventy-six in 1955 and 100 in 1960, with most of the new entrants from the Third World (Riggs and Plano 1988, 59). By 1961 most of the 104 members were Afro-Asian, and an additional twenty were from Latin America (in 1989, 124 of 159 members represented the Third World).

Second, the focus of Afro-Asian interests and activities shifted to postcolonial (structuralists might say neocolonial) economic relationships with the North. In contrast to its earlier disengagement, Latin America shared an interest in these economic issues and took an active role in collective Third World efforts to reshape the Bretton Woods system that the First World had put in place.[36]

Thus it is hardly a coincidence that the new Third World majority established two organizations at the United Nations to represent them, and that the organizations quickly focused on economic interests. Both the Group of 77 (G-77), with more than 125 members by the late 1980s, and the United Nations Conference on Trade and Development (UNCTAD) date from 1964. G-77 operates as a caucusing group on anticolonialism, human rights, and arms control issues, as well as economic concerns.

UNCTAD I in 1964 was a forum for the G-77 to propose a new international trade organization that would supersede GATT. The West resisted demands for such an organization and, as a compromise, UNCTAD itself became a permanent institution with meetings approximately every four years. In addition the South began at UNCTAD I to urge a Generalized System of Preferences (GSP) that would allow access to Northern markets through low tariffs, while permitting the South to protect their infant industries. The South reiterated the GSP proposal without success at UNCTAD II in 1968. UNCTAD III integrated discussions on international trade, finance, and development issues. Again in 1972 the North resisted any systemic change (Table 13.7).

TABLE 13.7
Sessions of the Nonaligned Movement and UNCTAD

Nonaligned Movement Meetings		UNCTAD Meetings	
1961	Belgrade, Yugoslavia	1964	Geneva, Switzerland
1964	Cairo, Egypt	1968	New Delhi, India
1970	Lusaka, Zambia	1972	Santiago, Chile
1973	Algiers, Algeria	1976	Nairobi, Kenya
1976	Colombo, Sri Lanka	1979	Manila, Philippines
1979	Havana, Cuba	1983	Belgrade, Yugoslavia
1982	New Delhi, India	1987	Geneva, Switzerland
1986	Harare, Zimbabwe	1992	Cartegeña, Colombia
1989	Belgrade, Yugoslavia		
1992	Jakarta, Indonesia		

Source: Jack C. Plano, The International Relations Dictionary, 4th ed. (Santa Barbara: ABC-CLIO, 1988), 22; Charles W. Kegley, Jr. and Eugene R. Wittkopf, World Politics, 3rd ed. (New York: St. Martin's Press, 1989), 226–227; A. Singham, "Outside the Fort: Summit in Belgrade", The Nation 249 (October 2, 1989), 1337; Liu Chu, "NAM is Full of Vigour," Beijing Review 35, no. 23 (June 8, 1992), 16–17; UN, "Spirit and Commitment of Cartegena: Results of UNCTAD VIII", UN Chronicle 29, no. 2 (June 1, 1992), 67–70.

[36]Internal dissension racked the Afro-Asian movement in the 1960s and it withered.

At a nonaligned summit in Algiers in 1973, the Southern leaders called for a **New International Economic Order (NIEO)**. Frustrated by Northern inaction, and emboldened by the OPEC cartel's success in raising oil prices, the Third World subsequently pushed through UN General Assembly resolutions titled "Declaration on the Establishment of a New International Economic Order" and "Program of Action on the Establishment of the New International Economic Order" (Woodby and Cottam 1988, 106). The elements of the NIEO include the following proposals, gradually elaborated in later UNCTAD meetings and other forums (Blake and Walters 1987, 82, 194–195):

1. Creation of an Integrated Program for Commodities (IPC), focused on eighteen primary agricultural and mineral commodities that together constitute 75 percent of LDC commodity exports. This proposal suggests stockpiling ten of the eighteen, and using a Common Fund to finance the international stocks, which would accumulate in periods of oversupply and be sold into the market during periods of scarcity.
2. Change in the allocation to countries of Special Drawing Rights by the IMF. That is now done in proportion to the IMF quotas, thus restricting the LDC share to about 30 percent (Blake and Walters 1987, 82). The South argues for allocation related to development need.
3. Easier access to IMF credits, with lower interest rates and less conditionality.
4. Provision of foreign assistance equivalent to 0.7 percent of First World GNPs.
5. Extension and liberalization of the Generalized System of Preferences.
6. Development of a program for debt relief.
7. Enhancement of Southern research and development capabilities and of technology transfer mechanisms.
8. International regulation of MNCs to control some of the most negative impacts on the Third World.

First World response was lukewarm. LDCs differed sharply with respect to how aggressively they wish to pursue confrontation to achieve the NIEO. The North is unlikely to ever address the proposals as a whole, but the ideas frame the contemporary North-South dialogue.

Not all approaches to collective action have been global. The Andean Common Market consists of Colombia, Peru, Venezuela, Bolivia, and Ecuador. They established rules for foreign investment, prohibiting it in some sectors, "including banking, insurance, broadcasting, publishing, and internal transportation" (Blake and Walters 1987, 135). The countries restricted the share of foreign ownership in other sectors, the repatriation of profits, and payments for imported technology. They adopted a united approach to limit the ability of MNCs to shift investments among these similar economies and to play one against another.

OPEC appeared in the 1970s to offer LDCs still another model for collective action vis-à-vis the North. In 1973–1974 the OPEC countries seemed to bring about a quadrupling in the price of oil and an even more dramatic increase in revenues, simply by holding a small percentage of this necessary commodity off the market after the 1973 Mideast war. In a show of Southern solidarity, OPEC members attempted to translate their success into an increase in the more general bargaining power of the South. They insisted on a North-South conference, which took place in Paris in 1975–1977, calling itself the Council on International Economic Cooperation (CIEC). The meetings discussed many of the NIEO proposals but accomplished little. Although the North pledged to meet the aid target, 0.7 percent of GNP, and accepted the principle of a Common Fund for commodity price support, implementation did not follow.

A producer **cartel** is a group of states (or firms) that operates in concert to restrain production in an attempt to raise market prices and increase profits. Other producer cartels gained renewed interest in the glow of OPEC success and the boom of commodity prices during the 1970s.[37] These include the Intergovernmental Council of Copper Exporting States (CIPEC), made up of four countries that dominate the world's copper trade: Zambia, Chile, Peru and Zaire.[38] The apparent success of almost all such organizations, including that of OPEC, evaporated in the global commodity-price downturn of the early and mid-1980s. At one level, the LDCs were simply relearning a lesson about their position in the world division of labor—commodity prices are unstable. The boom-and-bust cycle of the 1970s and 1980s initially fooled many into thinking that this particular boom was a new phenomenon and would continue indefinitely. Among the reasons for the misperception was the size of the upswing, the fact that OPEC countries appeared to have precipitated it and appeared to be able to control it, and the extensive expectation in the 1970s of a long-term scarcity in raw materials (Meadows, and others 1972).

Instead of the boom being the harbinger of a new era, the boom-and-bust cycle ultimately reinforced the arguments made by liberals concerning the power of market responses to foil price-manipulation efforts.[39] The momentum that collective action by the South appeared to have in the 1970s dissipated almost completely in the 1980s. The fall of producer prices, the renewed attention to cold war issues in the North, and the great internal weakness of Southern countries strapped by external debt sapped the vitality of collective action and reform pressures in the South. One additional factor shaped the climate of North-South relations in the 1980s—the great economic success of the handful of Southern countries known as the NICs. We turn next to the strategy pursued by them.

---

[37]Fried (1976) provides a very useful analysis of the commodity boom of 1972–1974 and of world commodity trade.

[38]In 1975 those four countries accounted for 65 percent of world primary copper exports. Similarly, in 1974 seven countries controlling 63 percent of world production created the International Bauxite Association (IBA). Bauxite is the raw material for aluminum. And also in 1974 seven Latin American countries accounting for two-thirds of the world's banana exports established the Union of Exporting Countries. Other producer organizations that exist or have existed include the Association of Iron Ore Exporting Countries, a sulfur organization initially based on four American firms but more recently encompassing producer states, and groups of countries with dominant positions in mercury, natural rubber, and coffee production (Mikdashi 1976).

[39]As liberals point out, long-term elasticities of demand and supply for all raw materials, even oil, are substantial. Decreases in demand and increases in supply have undercut large numbers of previous efforts by would-be cartels to sustain higher prices. Chapter 17 elaborates that point.

THE LIBERAL REBUTTAL: GROWTH-ENHANCING STRUCTURALISM

Liberals recognize that global structures now exist, and that they influence development prospects of LDCs. Liberals argue, however, that current global structures promote and facilitate development:

> Today we would expect the process [of economic development] to go much more rapidly in many of the developing nations, the central reason for this being the existence of the gap between the developed and the developing that many deplore as the source and cause of underdevelopment. (Kahn, Brown, and Martel 1976, 34)

There are three principal subthemes in this argument.[40] First, technology is less expensive and less time-consuming to adapt than to develop. The LDCs today have 200 years of industrial revolution technology on which to draw. For example, the rapid rise of the Japanese economy came during a period when Japan was a technology importer and adapter, not an innovator.

Second, capital is more widely available today than ever before. Just as British capital helped develop the United States, American and Japanese capital bring modern technology (generally through the vehicle of the MNCs) to the entire world. The transformation from predominantly agricultural to largely industrial economies is occurring at a remarkable pace in LDCs, as a result of Northern technology and capital (review Figure 1.6). In the LDCs as a whole, the share of industry in GNP was already 31 percent in 1965 and rose to 36 percent in 1990 (World Bank 1992, 222). Agriculture declined from 30 percent of the total to 20 percent.

The third theme is the existence of markets in the more advanced countries. What good, liberals ask, were vast African deposits of cobalt, copper, or uranium until the establishment of global industrial markets? The prospects for economic development in Zaire or Zambia may not be great today, but are they not better now that there is a market for their resources? Would resource-poor countries like Taiwan and South Korea have been able to make incredibly rapid progress and become industrial powerhouses without Western markets?

Although per capita economic stagnation in Africa since 1970 and in Latin America during the 1980s weakens the liberal argument, per capita GNP advanced throughout the South as rapidly in the 1950s and 1960s as it ever had in the developed countries. In much of Asia during the 1980s, growth in per capita income outstripped any ever achieved in the North. Overall the GNP of the North grew by a factor of 2.7 between 1960–1988; that in the South rose by a factor of 3.8 (Sivard 1991, 50). Only the high population growth rate in the South held Southern per capita gains to approximately the same level as those in the North. The bottom line for liberals: The per capita GNP of Southern countries today is higher than it has ever been, and it is growing, neither of which would be true without the spread of the industrial revolution from North to South.

Foreign aid is another potential advantage that the South obtains by virtue of its position in the international system structure. The impact of foreign aid has

---

[40]Gershenkron (1962) writes of the "advantages of backwardness."

WittyWorld's prize went to Igor Varchenko for this cartoon

FIGURE 13–10 Drawing by Igor Varchenke. Reprinted by permission of Witty World International Cartoon.

proved surprisingly difficult to evaluate,[41] however, and many liberals are as skeptical about aid as structuralists, who argue that aid is used to control LDCs, not to develop them. Although these extreme orientations reach the same conclusion, an intermediate position favors aid and believes that it does assist growth. Willy Brandt, former Social Democratic Chancellor of West Germany, established a commission of similarly minded individuals to study the problem of the North-South gap. Among their conclusions was the following:

> The most urgent need is for the programme of large-scale transfer of funds from North to South to be stepped up substantially from year to year during the final two decades of this century. Such an effort effectively directed towards the solution of the major problems discussed in this Report will benefit the South and turn back the rising tide of poverty; it would also provide important benefits to the North. (Brandt Commission 1980, 237)

In summary, liberals believe the existence of economically advanced countries to be on balance of clear advantage to the South. The availability of Northern technology, capital, and markets give the South opportunities, they argue, for more rapid economic progress than was ever possible in the North.

THE LIBERAL PRESCRIPTION: PARTICIPATION

This analysis of the liberal perspective makes their recommendation for economic strategy of the South clear: LDCs should participate actively in the world economy to seize the benefits it offers. They should be open to the import of technology and capital and they should actively pursue global markets.

During the 1970s and 1980s, the most successful economies in the Third World combined high rates of growth, substantial industrialization, and heavy reliance on the export of their new industrial production. This combination generally characterizes the **Newly Industrialized Countries (NICs)**. Like many other country categorizations, this one is fuzzy. Even the name is uncertain, since many prefer newly industrializing countries to indicate a process under way, or newly industrialized economies (NIEs) to stress that the phenomenon is economic. Definition is often by example and the countries cited include Hong Kong, Singapore, South Korea, Taiwan, Brazil, Chile, and Mexico (Walters and Blake 1992, 190). The first four are known collectively as the Four Tigers or Four Dragons (or as the Gang of Four) and appear on all lists of NICs. Another source adds Portugal, Spain, and Yugoslavia (Spero 1981, 204). The OECD adds Argentina and Greece (Todaro 1989, 15).

Let us arbitrarily require, as an entrance criterion for the set of NICs, that manufacturing be at least 20 percent of the economy.[42] This criterion would actually exclude Australia and Denmark from industrialized status, even though the World Bank traditionally classified them industrialized (in 1990 the Bank began

---

[41]Bremer and Hughes (1990) review the literature and undertake an analysis of the conditions under which aid can improve economic performance. See also Cassen (1986).

[42]The reason for using manufacturing to define NICs, rather than industrial production, is that the latter includes mining, construction, electricity, gas and water, as well as manufacturing. Fifty-eight percent of the GNP of Botswana is industry (because of mining), but that country is not a NIC.

to use the terminology "high-income" instead of "industrial"). In fact, only 17 percent of the U.S. economy came from manufacturing in 1989, down from 28 percent in 1965. The 20 percent criterion is a substantial hurdle. Even the two developed countries most dependent on manufacturing, Germany and Japan, derived only 31 percent and 29 percent of their GNP from manufacturing in 1990, respectively. Applying this criterion to countries that supply adequate data to the World Bank,[43] and that the bank does not consider high income, a list of twenty-one NICs or potential NICs emerges (see Table 13.8). Rapidly approaching the 20 percent level are India, Pakistan, El Salvador, and a number of other countries. Interestingly, Singapore and Hong Kong have in reality graduated: they are clearly now in the high-income category. Moreover, the share of manufacturing in Hong Kong's economy has dropped from 22 percent in 1987 to 18 percent in 1990; although it continues to appear on most lists of NICs, it is increasingly a postindustrial or service economy (Spain is similarly now a high-income country with manufacturing at the 18 percent level.)

There are two reasons for this extended definitional discussion. First, although NIC is a widely used concept, it is a vague one. Second, the extensive list of potential candidates for NIC status, in combination with the many economies that are rapidly approaching the 20 percent level, indicate again the spread of industrialization around the world. Many countries are now, or soon will be, newly industrialized, and it is no longer appropriate to see the Third World only as "drawers of water and hewers of wood."

Some observers pare the listing of NICs by implicitly or explicitly applying additional criteria (not clearly relevant to being "industrialized"), including rapid rates of economic growth and high dependence on exports. Setting a minimum standard of at least 5 percent annual growth in GNP during both the 1970s and 1980s would pare the list of NICs in Table 13.8 to seven: China, Indonesia, Thailand, Turkey, Mauritius, South Korea, and Taiwan (again ignoring Singapore and Hong Kong). Zimbabwe, the Philippines, Ecuador, Paraguay, Peru, Columbia, Mexico, Brazil, and Hungary met the growth criterion in the 1970s, but did not do at all well in the 1980s.

Many observers also list the use of exports to facilitate industrial expansion as a feature of NICs:

> they have all placed great emphasis on outward-oriented growth policies as a means of promoting rapid industrialization. Their policies typically include special tax incentives to local and foreign investors (especially for production of exportable goods); duty-free entry of imports (raw materials, intermediate goods, machinery) necessary for producing goods to be exported; currency devaluations to maintain a competitive position for national production in world markets; income policies designed to keep wages low; and maintenance of an hospitable environment for direct foreign investment. (Blake and Walters 1987, 172)

Requiring export of at least 20 percent of GNP to indicate an outward economic orientation is not unreasonable.

---

[43]Taiwan joins this list on the basis of additional data, because it is an important NIC.

	TABLE 13.8 NICs and Candidate NICs, 1990				
	GNP Per Capita (Dollars)	Percent Manufacturing	Annual GNP Growth 1965–80	1980–90	Exports as Percent of GNP
China	370	38	6.8	9.5	18
Zambia	420	43	2.0	0.8	32
Indonesia	570	20	7.0	5.5	26
Zimbabwe	640	26	5.0	2.9	32
Philippines	730	25	5.7	0.9	28
Ecuador	980	23	8.8	2.0	31
Paraguay	1,110	23	7.0	2.5	34
Peru	1,160	27	3.9	-0.3	11
Colombia	1,260	21	5.7	3.7	20
Thailand	1,420	26	7.3	7.6	38
Jamaica	1,500	20	1.4	1.6	59
Turkey	1,630	24	6.2	5.1	19
Mauritus	2,250	24	5.2	6.0	67
Mexico	2,490	23	6.5	1.0	16
South Africa	2,530	26	3.7	1.3	26
Venezuela	2,560	20	3.7	1.0	39
Uruguay	2,560	28	2.4	0.3	27
Brazil	2,680	26	9.0	2.7	7
Hungary	2,780	27	5.7	1.3	33
Korea	5,400	31	9.9	9.7	32
Taiwan	7,380	39	9.7	6.5	45
High-Income NICs:					
Singapore	11,160	29	10.0	6.4	190
Hong Kong	14,490	18	8.6	7.1	137

Sources: World Bank, World Development Report 1992 (New York: Oxford University Press, 1992), 222–223, 234–235; Republic of China, Taiwan Statistical Data Book 1988, 1–2; Central Intelligence Agency, The World Factbook 1991 (Washington, D.C.: CIA), 350.

Only five low- and middle-income countries in Table 13.8 meet all three criteria: 20 percent of the GNP in manufacturing, consistent GNP growth of 5 percent or more, and exports of at least 20 percent of GNP. Those are Indonesia, Thailand, Mauritius,[44] South Korea, and Taiwan; we should add Turkey because it exported 19 percent of its GNP in 1990, but historically has exported more than 20 percent. Brazil, frequently placed in the NIC category, exported only 7 percent of its GNP in 1990, depending instead on a large internal market for much of its growth.

[44]Mauritius is an island the size of Rhode Island in the Indian Ocean and has only 1 million inhabitants. It remains heavily dependent on sugar exports and perhaps for that reason does not generally appear on lists of NICs.

Although manufacturing no longer plays the role in Hong Kong it once did (the city-state increasingly relies on its Chinese hinterland for workshops), it is easy to see why the Four Dragons, sometimes also called the New Japans or the Little Japans, show up consistently on all lists of NICs. Because their incomes top the list in Table 13.8, they appear to exemplify the benefits of active export participation in the world economy; liberals trumpet their successes.

There are at least two problems, however, with placing such great weight on these four cases and suggesting that other countries should emulate their strategy. First, these countries have not consistently adopted liberal policies, and with the exception of the British Crown Colony of Hong Kong, exhibit a generally neomercantilist orientation. For example, they have maintained undervalued currencies so as to make their exports inexpensive to other countries. In the late 1980s this contributed to large export surpluses, and the United States pressured Taiwan and South Korea, with some success, to raise the values of their currencies. In addition a substantial role for the state is the general rule in these countries. For instance, Korean government spending and planning played a critical role in its rapid industrial growth. Singapore is notorious for strong government direction of the economy.

The second problem is their size. The Four Dragons together have a population about one-half that of Brazil. Their collective economy is only one-fourth larger than that of Brazil and only one-sixth as large as that of Japan. The attention they obtain is thus disproportional to their role in the global system. Yet the United States and Europe have voiced serious concern about their export strength and trade surpluses. Were a few countries the size of Brazil, China, or India to emulate their attention to trade seriously, the effect on the global economy could be highly disruptive. It is possible that only relatively small countries, and, even then, perhaps only a few of them, can reasonably pursue such an aggressive international strategy.

Fortunately, the progress of many other LDCs in both manufacturing and economic growth, even if less dramatic than that of the Four Dragons, indicates that successful participation in the world economy may not require intense promotion of exports. Turkey maintains fairly steady economic progress, and although open to the world economy, it does not promote exports fervently. The Latin-American countries that experts regularly listed as NICs in the 1970s also participate actively in the world economy, without relying on large export surpluses to drive their growth.

It is remarkable how skewed the world distribution of income is (see Table 13.9) and how few countries have broken free of the cluster of those that remain mired in poverty. Only four of the twenty-three NICs listed in Table 13.8 can boast GNPs per capita higher than $3,000. Whether any strategy or combination of them can help many Third World countries to close the North-South gap is still an unresolved question.

CONCLUSION

This chapter illustrated how all of the worldviews discussed to this point bring their intellectual arsenals to bear on the issues of North-South relations. We gave

TABLE 13.9
The Global Distribution of Income, 1990

GNP/Capita (Dollars)	Population in Millions (Number of Countries)	GNP/Capita (Dollars)	Population in Millions (Number of Countries)
0– 999	3,223 (54)	9,000– 9,999	4 (1)
1,000–1,999	283 (16)	10,000–10,999	5 (1)
2,000–2,999	481 (20)	11,000–11,999	9 (2)
3,000–3,999	41 (4)	12,000–12,999	3 (1)
4,000–4,999	10 (1)	13,000–13,999	0 (0)
5,000–5,999	53 (2)	14,000–14,999	0 (0)
6,000–6,999	0 (0)	15,000–15,999	10 (1)
7,000–7,999	41 (4)	16,000–	747 (17)
8,000–8,999	0 (0)		

Source: World Bank, *World Development Report 1990* (New York: Oxford University Press, 1992), 218–219.

most attention to structuralism, because we had not previously elaborated it in depth, and because many in the South see their relationship with the North to be one of dominance and subordination—a continuation of patterns established under colonialism. Although we emphasized class relations, we could also have focused on race- or gender-based structures. Yet we saw also that liberalism, in its attention to remarkable long-term economic growth and structural transformation in the South, particularly on the part of NICs, provides a useful perspective. It offers a much more optimistic image of recent history and holds out real hope that the North-South gap will begin to narrow.

Alert readers also saw the shadows of realism and idealism throughout this chapter. Realism, looking at North-South relations through a state-centric lens, drew our attention to a cold war variant of structuralism and to the mercantilism of both Northern states and many NICs. Even globalism appeared implicitly in our discussion of the growth of global institutions and transactions centered on trade and finance. Many globalists direct our attention to multinational corporations, not as structuralist instruments of rich against poor, but as actors that increasingly constrain states and integrate the world.

Although all of the perspectives thus provide some insights, one question probably building in your mind is how to judge the relative accuracy and contribution of the competing worldviews. One approach is to focus on the accuracy of their predictions. We began this chapter by discussing understandings and predictions about the evolution of the North-South gap, and we ended it by looking at forecasts that a substantial class of Southern countries, the NICs, might move from one side of the divide to the other. Liberals and structuralists vary considerably in their expectations for the future of the world political economy, and in the next chapter we turn again to the question of change.

Appendix

INTERACTION OF WORLDVIEW AND METHODOLOGY

Realists focus on states and the interstate system, liberals on markets and participants within them. Realists and liberals recognize the historic existence of many interstate systems and markets. Scientists working within realist and liberal worldviews can search for patterns across the agents on which they focus, and across space and time with respect to the systems within which they interact. For instance, in their search for rules governing states, realists can compare the contemporary international behavior of India, the United States, and Croatia, and can further look at the historical behavior of Athens or Prussia. They can compare the ancient Chinese state system with that of the ancient Greeks, with that of eighteenth-century Europe, and with that which exists today.

The methodology that most often characterizes science within the realist and liberal worldviews is **positivism**. Scientists adopting positivist methods seek to put like phenomena into conceptual categories (for instance, Armenians, Palestinians, and Kurds are all nations) and attempt to generalize about relationships among concepts (for instance, nations not in control of states frequently pursue such control through various violent and nonviolent actions). This method requires multiple objects in multiple categories.

Another view of the world, often (but by no means always) found in the thought of idealists and structuralists, is that humans learn and society evolves in ways that make them unique across space and time. For instance, many structuralists argue that there is only one world political economy (or world system), that it has unfolded over a long period, and that there has never been anything truly comparable in the past (Wallerstein 1976). If there is only one world system to examine, how can one search for generalizations and understanding? Methodology becomes more historical and holistic. It seeks to understand the dynamics of systemic evolution as an integrated phenomenon. Rules of repetition become less important than observations and insights.

Idealists face a similar problem of uniqueness when they look at the development of ideas and their interaction with community. Consider how the concept of human rights has evolved over time as humans gradually proscribed slavery and torture (by no means fully eliminated) and as we began to believe that a certain level of material well-being (minimally, for instance an access to food) is the right of all. Many idealists and structuralists turn to an examination of language (our definition of concepts like human rights, sovereignty, or power) in an attempt to understand both the world around us and the way in which the evolution of language and ideas contributes to that world (Ball 1988;

Der Derian and Shapiro 1989).[45] Because the methodology of positivism has links to the modern, scientific world (and worldview), they call for **postmodernism** in methodology.

Critical theory provides one methodological orientation that we can contrast with positivism.[46] Critical theory, attractive to many structuralists, takes positivism to task on two grounds in particular. First, critical theorists argue that positivists mistake a time and culture-bound image of the world for an objective understanding of it. This book illustrates the point. Each worldview has adherents who have difficulty seeing the world from other perspectives. Their location of birth (for instance, the First or Third World), their status within society, and the time in which they live all conspire to provide the perspective from which they mentally organize the world. For instance, the choice one makes of "basic" concepts will reflect one's experiences.

> It is important to suggest...that both the motivations and the basic conceptual frameworks which the student brings to his study arise out of the total life experience of the investigator: before he breaks apart "reality" for "scientific" analysis and experiment, he must have some vague notion or hunch of what that reality is in terms of its wholes and some impression of the relations of its parts to its wholes and to one another....
>
> Thus all knowledge is "tainted" by personal participation at all levels. We cannot even begin to know and to understand without shaping that which is known. (Sibley 1967, 55 and 56)

More strongly, theory will not only reflect one's experience, but support one's interests. Robert Cox has said that theory is always for someone for some purpose.

Positivists counter that there is still but one truth, even if some see only parts of it. They have difficulty understanding how their reproducible (by others with different worldviews) search for patterns across time and space is more likely to lead to imposition of a particular and limited perspective on reality than is an approach that reaches deep inside oneself for analysis of particular instances. They believe that knowledge obtained through observations and insights from single instances is not reproducible—that two scholars studying the same world system historically (or linguistically) and holistically are likely to arrive at very different understandings of it.

Second, critical theorists claim that positivists deny (or at least downplay) conscious human involvement in history and control of it, and that they therefore adopt a social conservatism. Positivists seek to understand society, not to change it:

[45]Keohane (1986) calls this methodological approach "reflective."

[46]It is very difficult to generalize about structuralist methodology, within which there is much methodological heterogeneity (George and Campbell 1990). Some even readily adopt positivist methods (for example, Chase-Dunn 1979). The early successors of Marx preferred dialectical materialism. The critical theorists of the Frankfurt school (founded 1923) rejected it as a form of positivism, however. The attention here to critical theory reflects its substantial impact on neo-Marxists.

> Positivist consciousness objectifies the social as well as the natural world....The social world is reified: socially created rules, conventions and regularities are comprehended as "natural," "the ways things have been and always will be." Social facts are given the status of natural facts. Historical laws are given the same status as natural laws. But these concepts of social life are inadequate to their object(s). Men and women are of nature but make history....[Laws of history] change and can be changed. (Held 1980, 168)

Although some structuralists similarly place themselves outside of society and seek only to understand it, many others want to act on it. Contrast the liberals who describe the regular and beneficent operation of the world economy, and who approve of it, with structuralists who see instead an unjust and repressive class structure that inspires them to advocate change. Critical theorists want to bridge the gaps between philosophy, social observation, and social action.

This brief synopsis cannot do justice to the incredibly complex debate between positivists and their critics. An understanding of the depth of dispute between liberals and structuralists, however, requires realization that it often goes beyond facts, concepts, theories, and even values. It extends also to **epistemology,** to questions of how we study the world and how we understand.

Chapter 14

CONTINUITY AND CHANGE IN POLITICAL-ECONOMIC THOUGHT

How do liberals, mercantilists, and structuralists treat change? This chapter focuses on that question, simultaneously reviewing the theoretical argument of the last three chapters. Table 14.1 summarizes the discussion.

LIBERALISM

Those early economists, such as Adam Smith, who initially formulated the classical liberal worldview, emphasized accumulation of capital, plus continued division of labor and specialization, as directed by comparative advantage in production. They identified these processes as the engines of *progressive* economic growth.

They recognized, however, that population growth interacted with economic growth. Significant debates centered on the degree to which economic growth could outstrip that of population and allow net improvement in the condition of the citizenry. We must remember that Smith and his contemporaries were writing early in the industrial revolution, and that workers then often faced miserable conditions. The literature of Charles Dickens tells us how miserable they were. Many political economists believed that the forces of production growth would lift living conditions only temporarily, and that population growth would literally eat up the gains. Thomas Malthus was best known for his pessimism, but even Smith suggested such a long-term result:

> In a country fully peopled in proportion to what either its territory could maintain or its stock employ, the competition for employment would necessarily be so great as to reduce the wages of labour to what was barely sufficient to keep up the number of labourers. (Smith 1910, 138)

Analysts labeled such a dismal outcome the "iron law of wages"—wages will inevitably fall to the subsistence level. Only later did many thinkers become convinced that production growth, driven by improving technology, could indefinitely exceed population growth and improve living conditions for the average worker.

TABLE 14.1 Liberalism, Extensions, and Challengers			
	Characterization of Change		
Dominant Subject Matter	Stability (and Unpatterned Change)	Cycles	Progressive Change
Political			Pluralism Neofunctionalism
Economic	Mercantilism-neomercantilism	Liberalism (neoclassical)	Liberalism
	Convertability of power and wealth	Economic cycles	Capital accumulation; stages of growth; structural transformation
	Dependency	World systems theory	Marxism
	Dependence; dual economy development	Cycles of expansion	Capital accumulation; imperialism; system transformation
Broader Environment			
	Predominantly zero-sum logic		Nonzero-sum logic

Speculation about the interaction of economic and population growth was not an idle philosophic debate. If one believed, as Malthus did, that human beings inevitably reproduce to the limits of the food supply, there was little reason for attempting to improve the conditions of the working class. Those who opposed social reforms on behalf of the poor could and did use such arguments throughout the nineteenth century. Karl Marx, who believed strongly in the power of capitalism to produce more goods and services, indignantly rejected that logic:

> The hatred of the English working class against Malthus—the "mountebank-parson" as Cobbett rudely calls him—is therefore entirely justified. The people were right here in sensing instinctively that they were confronted not with a *man of science* but with a *bought advocate*, a pleader on behalf of their enemies, a shameless sycophant of the ruling classes. (cited in Pavitt 1973, 143)

After nearly two centuries in which global economic growth has exceeded that of population, most liberals also believe that economic growth is winning the race with population and can continue to lead (an issue that we will take up again in the next chapter). Most liberals now view economic growth as a progressive force, capable of continually improving welfare for increasing portions of humanity. The forces of comparative advantage, division of labor, and capital accumulation work to drive that progressive growth. Theories about stages of economic growth, and structural transformations of the economy outline its operation. Therefore Table 14.1 places liberal theories in the column emphasizing progressive change.

In the last century the analysis of economics, and therefore of liberalism, has increasingly taken long-term growth for granted and focused on the more immediate workings of the economy. Economists have developed a theory of demand to accompany the earlier dominant emphasis on production and have tied together their understandings of demand and supply in neoclassical theories of equilibrium in which the rise and fall of prices play a critical role.[1] In addition, economists give considerable attention to the cycles that manifest themselves regularly in all countries. These include the four-year business cycle, the seven-year Juglar cycle, the twenty-year Kuznets cycle, and the much disputed fifty-year Kondratieff cycle (Maddison 1982, 64–65). In short, neoclassical economics, although built on a theoretical base of liberalism that emphasizes progressive change, devotes much attention to cycles.

THE REACH OF LIBERALISM BEYOND ECONOMICS

The sharp focus of liberalism on economics limits the implications of liberal thought for politics or the broader environment. Nonetheless, some liberals venture suggestions about the impact of progressive economic growth on political change. Many believe that increasing international economic ties, especially trade, will contribute to international political harmony. For instance, the U.S. secretary of state at the end of World War II, Cordell Hull, argued forcefully in favor of a liberal international order as a means of linking countries through trade and financial ties and thereby making war less likely. The core of the argument is that as economic ties improve welfare (through mutually beneficial transactions), the cost of severing those ties increasingly exceeds any possible benefit of interstate conflict.[2] Saburo Okita, the former president of the Japan Economic Research Center, agrees:

[1]Neoclassical economics elaborates these theories of demand and equilibrium and builds upon the work of Marshall, Pareto, Walras, and many others. "While classical economics was concerned with long run developments of economies as a whole, and in particular the relationship between the distribution of the economic surplus and the pattern of development, neo-classical value theory became essentially a theory of the allocation of scarce resources in a static economy" (Pearce 1983, 308).

[2]Rosecrance (1986) contrasted "trading states" like Japan with states focused on traditional political-military and territorial concerns such as the former U.S.S.R., and argued that the world is on a cusp between futures dominated by one or the other. The extent of international conflict will depend on direction of movement from that cusp.

> We are living in a century when such military action is no longer viable. To build up military power just to protect overseas private property is rather absurd in terms of cost-benefit calculations. The best course for the Government in case of nationalization or seizure of overseas private Japanese assets is to compensate Japanese investors directly in Japan rather than to spend very large amounts of money to build up military strength. (Gilpin 1979, 356)

There is empirical evidence for beliefs that free trade and peace are linked. Domke investigated the relationship of democracy, trade, and membership in international organizations with war involvement. The strongest relationship he found was with trade: "governments of nations that are more involved in foreign trade are less likely to make decisions for war."[3]

Pluralism, the peaceful interaction and competition of multiple interests, implicitly links economics and politics in those arguments. Pluralism and liberalism have much in common, in particular the focus on rational self-serving behavior of many actors. Both liberalism and pluralism portray a process involving differences in individual objectives, but also bargaining, compromise, and mutually beneficial solutions. Liberals frequently anticipate that free enterprise economies will support the development of democracy (domestic pluralism) and that democratic states in turn will build a pluralistic, peaceful interstate system. Many liberals adopt a fundamentally globalist perspective and foresee a strengthening of global community and institutions in which pluralism can flourish.[4] As an example, the dramatically increased trade ties within the EC, and more generally among the Organization for Economic Cooperation and Development countries, does appear to have fostered a pattern of interdependence that makes intense conflict less probable and that facilitates cooperation. A pluralistic security community has emerged.

Neither liberals nor pluralists, however, fully develop the linkage between markets and intergovernmental cooperation. Liberals do not clearly specify mechanisms by which increased trade and other economic interactions might lead to increased intergovernmental cooperation (or at least decreased intergovernmental conflict). In reality, one trade partner frequently perceives trade as unequal and unfair (as is seen between the United States and Japan), so that increased economic ties can damage political relationships. Similarly, one partner may fear that trade is creating a dependence on a stronger economy or that increased trade has somehow distorted its economy. Liberals, while asserting the mutual beneficiality of trade, do not generally respond to the reality that trading partners sometimes question whether they receive any benefits, and that they regularly question the division of the benefits. In the early 1990s analyses emerged indicating that

---

[3]Domke (1988, 137). In an analysis of interstate relations between 1976 and 1980, Rummel (1983, 67) concluded that to add economic freedom to civil liberties and political rights is to reduce significantly the level of violence for a state overall .

[4]It may at first glance seem anomalous that Hayek (1966), the pure classical liberal, calls for a pluralistic international political order within a federal system (building initially on the community of interests between the United States and Western Europe). He rails against Carr and the realists. Yet Table 14.1 helps clarify the logical connections of Hayek's political and economic thought.

although both the United States and Japan benefitted from their bilateral trade, Japan obtained the greater relative benefit. Realists, with their attention to relative gain, wave a red flag in such a situation.

One explicit mechanism by which markets might influence and constrain governments is the effort by MNCs to protect the economic interests they have in free trade and financial flows. MNCs may pressure governments to resist any actions, including military hostilities, that would disrupt their transnational activities. Vernon (1971) raised the possibility that continuing growth in MNC strength might put "sovereignty at bay." One stolid liberal and globalist elaborated the argument:

> In an important sense, the fundamental problem of the future is the conflict between the political forces of nationalism and the economic forces pressing for world integration. This conflict currently appears as one between the national government and the international corporation, in which the balance of power at least superficially appears to lie on the side of the national government. But in the longer run economic forces are likely to predominate over political, and may indeed come to do so before the end of the decade. Ultimately, a world federal government will appear as the only rational method for coping with the world's economic problems. (Harry Johnson, cited by Gilpin 1979, 355)

Is the corporation supplanting the state? Figure 13.8 showed that their growth in economic size has been comparable since 1970. There is some anecdotal evidence of MNC constraints on states, however. For example, the Western industrialized countries proved unable to protect the dollar's value in the early 1970s, when MNCs moved substantial capital to gold and other currencies in anticipation of dollar devaluation. Still, increases in international capital flows and investment, like those in trade, can contribute to interstate conflict, as well as to cooperation. French, American, and Canadian concerns with extensive foreign ownership surface regularly; in LDCs, where foreign presences normally constitute a much larger portion of the domestic economy than in advanced countries, MNCs almost certainly aggravate political relations with other states rather than improve them.

Neofunctionalist theory and the spillover process provide an alternative explanation of the linkage between growing economic activity and increased political cooperation. Specifically, increases in international economic activity in one arena (for example, in trade volumes) lead to pressures on the political system for changes in regulation or coordination in other arenas (for example, in international capital flows). When states coordinate policy in the new arenas, perhaps by strengthening international institutions or regimes, further expansion of economic activity and interdependence may occur and lead to additional political pressures.

We have been considering the relatively underdeveloped extension of liberalism into the theory of interstate politics. Liberals also make only limited connections—in fact, typically draw a relatively sharp boundary—between the economy and the broader environment. For instance, they typically identify many environmental impacts of economic activity, such as pollution, as externalities. An

externality is an effect of production or consumption that is outside the cost-benefit analysis of individual producers or consumers. Moving across the boundary between economics and the environment in the other direction, liberals frequently treat raw materials, fundamentally important to the functioning of economies, as being little different from manufactured goods, and they devote limited attention to the possible exhaustion of nonrenewable resources. Similarly, technological advance, although it contributes much to the progressive character of liberal theory (along with capital accumulation), remains exogenous to the basic theoretical structure. We will turn to economy-environment linkages in Part Three of this book.

THE NEOMERCANTILIST CHALLENGE

Realists argue that states, not economic actors like MNCs, continue to play the key roles in world politics. States give their individual economic and political objectives priority over that of global economic efficiency. They compete with other states for markets, investment outlets, and sources of raw materials. In particular, they seek maximum economic growth and full employment of their citizenry. These objectives lead them to stimulate technological advance through support for research and development, and through the direction of governmental spending to domestic industry. The objectives also cause them to expand their external market shares and to protect their domestic markets, relying on various tariff and nontariff mechanisms to promote exports and restrict imports. Because states achieve gains with respect to many of these policies only at the expense of other countries, they correctly perceive their neomercantilist competition as zero-sum.

Like the mercantilists of old, neomercantilists believe that economic wealth can buy power (military, political, and economic) and that power can be converted, through the appropriate policies, to wealth. The Achilles' heel of all mercantilist thought is that the competition of states over the size of their slices may reduce the total size of the pie. In fact, there is no real theory of growth or progress associated with mercantilism. It is for this reason that liberals prescribe squelching the debate over slice size and devoting our efforts to baking a larger pie. Nonetheless, neomercantilists pose a serious real-world challenge to liberals.

THE STRUCTURALIST CHALLENGE

All the structuralist challenges to the basic liberal view share one feature: They emphasize the connections between, even inseparability of, the economic and political systems. Although for structuralists the center of attention remains economics, structural change in politics is far more than an idealistic afterthought.

In fact, Marx's thought synthesized understandings of politics, economics, and the broader environment (especially technology). He found the basic motive forces of change in the economic production process, both in its nature (rooted in the technology of production) and in its organization (notably the ownership of the means of production). Social and political institutions are superstructures, growing out of the nature and organization of production. For instance, modern manufacturing technology requires capital and in the West a capitalist class controls that means of production. That class has developed institutions by which it also dominates society and government. Before capitalism bloomed in Europe, production was based on land; a feudal aristocratic elite both owned the land and dominated broader social and political relationships.

The capital accumulation logic of liberals retains a central place in Marxism (at least in describing the capitalist epoch); Marxists identify technological advance as a second progressive force (with an even broader historic span). Thus Marxism shares, and in some ways more fully develops, the liberal belief in progressive change. It is thus not surprising that Marxists also foresee the kind of positive global political developments that pluralists identify. In the *Communist Manifesto*, Marx and Engels sound almost like liberal globalists:[5]

> National differences and antagonisms between peoples are daily more and more vanishing, owing to the development of the bourgeoise, to freedom of commerce, to the world market to uniformity in the mode of production and in the conditions of life corresponding thereto.
>
> The supremacy of the proletariat will cause them to vanish still faster. United action, of the leading civilized countries at least, is one of the first conditions for the emancipation of the proletariat.
>
> In proportion as the exploitation of one individual by another is put to an end, the exploitation of one nation by another will also be put to an end. In proportion as the antagonism between classes within the nation vanishes, the antagonism of one nation to another will also come to an end. (Feuer 1959, 26)

Major differences obviously separate the liberal and Marxist worldviews. Liberals emphasize the mutually beneficial bargains of economic exchange and the spread of well-being throughout society. Marxists point to the ability of those with economic, social, and political power to expropriate the bulk of the benefits in economic transactions (including those generated by the employment bargain). Furthermore, according to Marxists, competition among capitalists concentrates capital within the capitalist class. Impoverishment of the workers in the same society that steadily increases its productive capacity creates serious tensions or contradictions. The inability of workers to purchase that which they produce is clearly one of them. Although such problems may be overcome for a time by measures such as exporting the capital and goods surpluses, there are limits to such remedies. Ultimately the tensions will become so great that they will lead to a transformation of the society—a socialist revolution in which the workers take control of the means of production.

World systems theory is a variant of the Marxist challenge to liberalism that elaborates the development of capitalism in Europe and its global expansion. It

---

[5]In his development of a theory of imperialism, however, Lenin elaborated a much more realistlike image of interstate politics, in which the struggle among capitalist countries for markets, investment opportunities, and resources would intensify steadily.

divides the world into the more powerful, economically advanced states of the core (or center) and the weaker states of the periphery. Although it retains the expectation of an ultimate transformation of capitalism to socialism, it focuses primarily on cycles of capitalist expansion and on the changing leadership (hegemony) of the capitalist state system core throughout the expansion process.[6]

> [World systems theory] constitutes a large-scale and long-term framework for the study of selected systemic structures, cycles and secular trends. Three central processes are stressed, the historic development of a core–periphery division of labor, the episodic rise and fall of hegemonic powers, and the gradual geographic expansion, coupled with the periodic growth and stagnation, of the world economy. (Thompson 1983, 11)

World systems theorists explain the cycles of capitalist expansion and the rise and fall of hegemonic powers in terms that sound much like the explanations of neorealist theorists of hegemonic stability (presented in Chapter 6). For example, the dynamics of hegemonic decline lie in

> the high overhead costs of hegemony, the diffusion of capital, and the strong probability of relative improvements in the economic capabilities of rival core states. The cyclical decline of hegemonic control, in turn, is given responsibility for ushering in a period of power diffusion, increased freedom of maneuver for the core states, and increased exploitation of the periphery—all compounded by a phase of general economic contraction or stagnation. Attempts to restructure the world market in each core actor's interest lead to acute competition and conflict, and eventually, world war between the core powers. (Thompson 1983, 12–13)[7]

Dependency theory provides still another variation of the structuralist challenge to the liberal view. Marxism presents the broadest historical sweep, spanning major epochs and great system transformations, and world systems theory narrows the focus primarily to the emergence and cyclical development of capitalism, whereas dependency theory further focuses the structuralist worldview on the relationship between First and Third World countries in the contemporary era. Dependency theory takes as a backdrop the hierarchical relationship between core and peripheral states (the dynamics of which world systems theory explores) and investigates the implications of that relationship, and the ways in which it reinforces itself or mutates.[8]

---

[6]Clearly the approach suggests progressive change as well as cycles (just as earlier Marxism posits cycles in addition to progressive change). Thus world systems theory fits somewhat uncomfortably into the middle column of Table 14.1.

[7]To make the impact of economic contraction or stagnation on the periphery more concrete, consider how this description might fit the period of the 1970s and 1980s, in which the decline of U.S. control over the global economy (in part because of the heavy costs that of leadership) was associated with diffusion of economic and military power throughout the core (notably to Europe and Japan), with the debt crisis of the Third World, and with slower global economic growth than in the 1960s.

[8]Thus Sylvan and others (1983, 80) develop a formal model of dependency, about which they say, "The model deals only with the processes stemming from external penetration and, unlike theories of imperialism, makes no statements about the causes of penetration."

Dependency theory identifies and investigates several consequences of the unequal relationship between core and periphery states. An important one is the existence of a **comprador class**, which receives its rewards and seeks its support from external actors. This local elite in many LDCs depends on and serves the interests of the multinational corporations, the bilateral and multilateral aid agencies, and other manifestations of the Northern elites. It is a two-way relationship in which the local elite receives economic rewards and political support in an implicit exchange for a perpetuation of the existing, exploitative economic order. The existence of a comprador class, and of deep political-economic divisions within LDCs, grows from the development of enclave or dual economies, in which only a portion of the LDC population enters the modern economy, while the rest remains a vast, disorganized army of inexpensive labor.

Like mercantilism, dependency theory draws our attention to the convertability of economic and political-military power and to the zero-sum character of power relationships. Some dependency theorists (and world system theorists) argue that the hierarchical relationships are so strongly structured, and that the core countries and LDC elites so greatly benefit from them, that there is no serious prospect for change in the relationship or for Southern economic development.

Some difficult questions face all variants of structuralism. How can they explain the steadily improving living conditions of those in the North? For that matter, does not considerable and rapid progress in average incomes, life expectancy, literacy, and nutrition in much of the South (especially in states intensely involved in the world economy) call into doubt the argument that global economic relationships are exploitative?

Like liberalism, structuralism has little to say about the broader environment. Although Marx believed technological advance to be a driving force behind economic change, he devoted limited attention to technologies (and certainly did not foresee those that underlie the postindustrial revolution). Structuralists seldom analyze issues of raw material exhaustion and pollution (and the Marxist leaderships of Central and Eastern Europe all but ignored the issues). We need to turn now, away from political-economic perspectives, and to those that give the broader environment a more prominent place in world politics.

Chapter 15

MODERNISM
AND ECOHOLISM

Do the size and growth rate of the world's population, the amounts and distribution of various energy resources, the quality of the earth's air, or the sophistication of industrial technology affect world politics? Of course they do. Some of the perspectives discussed already, such as the geopolitical school, briefly diverted our attention from considerations of international politics and economics to aspects of the broader global environment. For adherents to **political ecology** worldviews, the environment constitutes far more than a diversion—it is the core subject matter.

This chapter initiates Part Three of the book. Part Two extended our attention beyond interstate politics to the global political economy. Now we widen our horizons still further to the biologic and physical environment. This chapter introduces the primary worldviews of political ecology, and the next two elaborate the manner in which those views interact with understandings of world politics. The two worldviews of this discussion hold less inherent "political" content than do the others we have examined—but they interact with the earlier worldviews in important ways, adding essential flesh to understandings of world politics.

MODERNISM

Modernism emphasizes accumulated human progress in mastering the broader environment—in shaping and controlling it so as to improve human well-being, generation after generation. Technological advance is so important to this worldview that some refer to its adherents as "technological enthusiasts." Americans indicate the influence of this view in their thought by emphasizing "American know-how" and by the popular philosophy of "can do," even in the face of seemingly insurmountable obstacles. Although Europeans sometimes voice a wry amusement at such optimism, the entire "modern" world shares a comparable attachment to technology.

SKETCH OF THE WORLDVIEW

Table 15.1 summarizes the modernist and ecoholist worldviews, specify-ing concepts, theories, values, and prescriptions (it inevitably oversimplifies the complexity and variation of the worldviews). At the core of the modernist worldview are humans in search of knowledge. Teilhard de Chardin coined the term "noosphere" (**knowosphere** is a better spelling) to refer to the accumu-lated body of knowledge on which humans draw and to which they add with time (Boulding 1981, 109). Humans use knowledge to control their environ-ment. The environment is both adversary and resource; human ingenuity overcomes the obstacles it presents (for instance, disease) and uses the bounty it provides. Life expectancy and material comfort measure success in the effort. By these measures, as we shall see in the next chapter, humanity has been very successful indeed.

TABLE 15.1
Political Ecology Worldviews

Worldview Name(s)	Modernism; technological enthusiasm	Ecoholism; neotraditionalism
Central Concepts: Agents/Structures	Innovators; accumulated knowledge or "knowosphere"	Species; ecosystems
Values of Agents	Knowledge	Survival; propagation
Central Concepts: Bases of Interaction	Control of environment	Carrying capacity; delays
Theories: Systematic Dynamic Description	Knowledge accumulation (virtuous cycle); acceleration of progress; technological innovation	Tragedy of the commons; externality creation; free-rider behavior
Theories: Typical Forecasts	Progressive control of environment	Overshoot and collapse
Value of Worldview Proponents	Progress	Sustainabilty; quality of life
Typical Prescriptions	Laissez innover (see text); support research and development	Control population; minimize economic throughput; control technology

Knowledge is for modernists what capital is for liberals or power for realists. It is both a means and an end. It is at the center of a **virtuous cycle** or **positive feedback loop**. That is, just as states apply power to obtain more power, and entrepreneurs reinvest capital to yield additional capital, scientists and engineers utilize knowledge in the search for greater knowledge. The famous investment advisor John Templeton illustrated this view in an interview with *Forbes* magazine:

> The world is now spending about $1 billion each business day on scientific research. Half of all the scientists who ever lived are alive today....Two centuries ago 85% of the world's people were needed just to produce enough food. Now, in America, fewer than 4% are producing food, yet they produce such a surplus that they don't know what to do with it. That's going on in other nations, too....Our studies indicate that the [world's] standard of living is going to quadruple again in the next 40 years, instead of the next 70 years. We are living in the most glorious period of world history. We are looking ahead toward an extraordinary period of long-range prosperity. (*Forbes*, January 25, 1988, 81)

Templeton's forecast of accelerating progress in satisfying human needs and wants follows logically from the theoretical perspective that technological advance "snowballs." He, like most humans, values such progress highly.

When modernists qualify their optimistic portrayals, they most often point to the dangers of "mismanagement,"[1] in particular to interference with the process of technological advance. Again there is a parallel with earlier worldview debates. Realists accept (or see) few restrictions on the rights of states to act in the world, while their globalist critics believe that transnational actors and human rights law can or should limit state action. Liberals accept few restrictions by government on the rights of producers and consumers to interact in markets, and they codify that principle as laissez faire. Their critics frequently call for much greater government intervention on behalf of disadvantaged classes. Similarly, modernists prescribe **laissez innover** (McDermott 1972, 155), the freedom to innovate. Modernists do not, however, *proscribe* all government action with respect to technology; in fact, they *prescribe* strong societal support for research and development. Critics claim that certain technologies, such as the genetic engineering of new microorganisms, may hold great dangers and society should carefully oversee them.

Are there international political ramifications of a focus on technological advance? Consider these. First, the world of many modernists is predominantly nonzero-sum. All of humanity can benefit from a vast variety of technologies. Humans can share knowledge without losing it. Second, human interaction within and between states depends specifically on our communications and transportation technologies. As those technologies progress, they inherently alter, and many modernists would argue improve, the nature of human interaction. Modernists are unlikely to consider some less positive implications of technological advance. For instance, and third, although technology has a nonzero-sum character in the long run, it creates inequalities in the short run. The most obvious examples of the

---

[1]Kahn and others (1976) used the term and extended it also to the misuse of technology—for instance, nuclear war.

dangers of uneven advance lie in military technology. Fourth, technology advances unevenly across time. Accelerations or decelerations in technological change may affect economic growth and that, in turn, may influence international politics. Fifth, certain military technologies may alter the balance between offensive and defensive capabilities. When offensive weaponry has an advantage, it may strengthen incentives to expand territory. In the next chapter we explore these five issues.

IMPORTANT CONTRIBUTIONS TO MODERNIST THOUGHT

Modern science emphasizes concepts or categories (which group like phenomenon) and theoretical structures (which explore the relationships among concepts). Aristotelian science (of the ancient Greek Golden Age) also emphasized categorization, but often stressed identification of hierarchies and distinctions among categories rather than connections or relationships. At the center of the search for knowledge in Aristotelian science lay the desire to place things into categories, and to elaborate the attributes of things and categories. It used the syllogism extensively to do that. For instance:

All living creatures are mortal.

Humans are living creatures.

Therefore, humans are mortal.

Such science has a limited ability to identify points at which humans can intervene. Its intent is to describe nature as it exists or as God created it (the science of the church in the Middle Ages built on the Aristotelian approach). Modern science, although retaining emphasis on categorization, devotes a great deal more attention to linkages among concepts, to causality. For instance, raising the temperature of a liquid can convert it into a gas and cause its volume to expand. An understanding of causal linkages among the concepts of temperature, liquid, and gas creates the possibility of human intervention in the causal process and practical use of knowledge. Converting water to steam can drive a piston and a rod attached to it, thus creating a steam engine. When scientific knowledge is causal, it can be the basis for **technology**—knowledge adapted to human purposes.[2]

Near the beginning of the seventeenth century, science in Europe became more active in searching for explanations and dynamics and in adapting these to human purposes. Francis Bacon (1561–1626) helped develop the philosophy of this new science. He explicitly attacked the passive classificatory orientation of the old science:

Human knowledge and human power meet in one; for where the cause is not known the effect cannot be produced....The logic now in use serves rather to fix

[2]Actually, Heron of Alexandria, who lived near the time of Aristotle, understood the principles of steam and created a number of mechanical and pneumatic contrivances. Thus the discussion exaggerates the distinction between the basic science of the two periods. Nonetheless, the fact that Heron's work did not lead to a steam engine in his era reinforces the argument here with respect to application of knowledge.

and give stability to the errors which have their foundation in commonly received notions than to help the search for truth. It does more harm than good. (cited in Hampshire 1956, 24)

Instead of the syllogistic methods, Bacon suggested an experimental science involving active search for new information and truths. Bacon even stressed the importance of "rejections and exclusions," a fundamental component of modern scientific method, in which the search for instances to disprove theories is constant. Those theories that have withstood attempts to contradict them are those to which we continue to adhere. Contradiction, if it occurs, intensifies the search for new or revised theory.

Others who contributed to this transformation of thought included Galileo, Hobbes, Descartes, Pascal, Spinoza, Leibniz, and Newton. They and their contemporaries initiated a scientific revolution and laid the foundations for the industrial revolution. Their Age of Reason ushered in the modern science and set the stage for the modernist belief system centered on knowledge accumulation, progress, and the use of knowledge. Bacon himself wrote *New Atlantis*, a utopian novel about an island on which a giant laboratory assured technological progress and the comfort of inhabitants.[3] Jeffrey Hart described the period:

> Sometime during the fifteenth century, the great and glorious project of modernity was launched in earnest. To put it briefly: whereas ancient Greek and Roman culture, with their extension [sic] and modification in medieval Christian culture, sought to understand the world and live according to that understanding, the modern project sought not to understand the world in its totality but to control it and use it. (Hart 1988, 3)

The scientific advances of the seventeenth century built the foundations of Enlightenment thought in the seventeenth and eighteenth centuries. Faith in humanity's ability to master the environment gave rise to faith in humanity's ability to structure superior societies, both domestic and international. Hume, Locke, Rousseau, Voltaire, and many others contributed their varied and often contradictory ideas to this effort; Diderot encouraged and cataloged their thought.

ECOHOLISM

Labels carry connotations or implications that can prejudice us favorably or unfavorably. The challengers to modernism are sometimes called "pessimists" or "ecopessimists." Those labels implicitly convey a negative connotation, because most of us prefer optimists to pessimists—optimists are more fun to have around.

[3]Most of the "Age of Reason" scholars remained profoundly religious and sought to use their new scholarly methods on behalf of their God. Descartes even felt it possible to use logic to prove the existence of God. Yet conflict periodically arose between the dynamics of cause and effect identified by the scientists and the world of the earlier logic, with fixed categories supposedly established by a creator. For instance, Charles Darwin (1809–1882) came gradually to replace the static conceptualization of individually created and categorized plants and animals with a dynamic theory of evolution and flux, which explained the rise of new categories. He drew the wrath of many in the clergy and the debate he initiated continues today (Appleman 1977).

Hence, those friendly to perspectives that challenge modernism suggest alternative terminology. Grant (1982) proposes "Jeremiads" and contrasts them with "Cornucopians." Pirages (1983, 1989) prefers "inclusionist" (one who stresses the position of humans within the environment) and juxtaposes that view with the "exclusionist" (one who places humans outside of, and in control of, their environment). Haas (1990, 66) proposed **ecoholist**, emphasizing like Pirages the attention of the perspective to ecological wholeness. We adopt that term here. We sometimes interchangeably use **neotraditionalist** (Hughes 1985), because the explicit challenge to modernism of that term recalls the attitudes concerning the intimate and interdependent relationship of humans and their environment that characterized more traditional (premodern) societies.

CHALLENGERS IN BRIEF

The ecoholist or neotraditionalist begins with the concept of ecosystem. An **ecosystem** "is essentially a biotic community in interaction with its physical environment" (Dasmann and others 1973, 29). For the ecoholist, human beings are a part of that ecosystem, not above nor beyond it. Humans, like other species in the ecosystem, seek to survive and to propagate—to preserve and to increase their numbers. No portion of the system can indefinitely expand without damaging the system and therefore itself, however. A **carrying capacity** limit defines how large a species population can become before it overuses the resources available in the ecosystem. In reference to a species within the ecosystem that grows without respect for such bounds and thereby destroys its host, some ecoholists suggest the analogy of a cancer within a human body.

Another important concept is that of **delays**. There are often significant time lags between an action that affects the environment and any noticeable impact. Movement of a pesticide like DDT through the food chain is an example. Water and air systems take DDT applied on farm land to the ocean; it subsequently moves into plankton, into the fish that eat those organisms, and eventually into human fatty tissue. Because of the slow speed at which it moves through the physical environment and up the food chain, the concentration in fish and humans will increase for many years after discontinuation of DDT use (Meadows and others 1972, 89–94).

Ecoholists combine the concepts of carrying capacity and delay into a theory of **overshoot and collapse** behavior. A limited ecosystem, like that on an island, helps us provide a simple example. If a predator population, such as wolves, grows too large on an island, it will eventually exceed the carrying capacity limit defined by its prey, such as the rabbit population. It may continue to grow for some time beyond that limit (the period of overshoot), while it decimates the prey. That is, there will be a delay between the time when the predator population begins to reduce the prey and the time when the prey becomes so scarce that the predator can no longer survive. At some point the wolf population will collapse to the level that a much reduced rabbit population can sustain, and the cycle is complete. In many biologic systems another cycle will begin as the prey population rebuilds.

The ecoholist points to the collapse of the Central American Mayan civilization (possibly from damage to land fertility through overexpansion of maize cultivation), and to collapses of other agricultural-based civilizations, as evidence that human beings have not been historically immune to the logic of ecosystems. Has modern technology changed the rules? Not according to the ecoholist. Instead, it temporarily relaxes ecosystem limits and leads us to overshoot them further without immediate consequences.

Many of the theories of ecoholists focus specifically on the pattern of human interaction with the ecosystem. Several of these build on the concept of commons (common property resource problems) and the tension between individual action and collective interest (you might wish to review the discussion of Chapter 6, although the next two paragraphs quickly summarize some of it).

In the classic **tragedy of the commons**, each farmer individually decides to graze additional animals on a common field, and the resultant overgrazing destroys the vegetation and the ability of all farmers to make a living. Why does this happen, when it is so obvious that all farmers would benefit by limiting the number of animals to the carrying capacity of the land? One reason is that the individual farmer captures all of the benefit of the extra animal but externalizes much of the cost to other farmers. Although our individual behavior often damages the ecosystem, others will eventually bear many or all of the costs of damage. For example, those who cut the Amazonian rain forests to create homesteads for themselves reap the rewards individually, but may harm the global environment and negatively affect all of humanity.

No individual can solve the problem. For instance, a factory owner who restricts emissions, to protect the air or water, will pay all costs individually. The improvement in environmental quality, although marginally benefiting the factory owner, will be a positive externality that all others in society capture. That reality will encourage factory owners to urge other owners to reduce emissions, for the good of humanity and the ecosystem, but avoid doing it themselves. Everyone would prefer to obtain benefits, without paying costs, to a free ride.

Achievement of an acceptable quality of life, **sustainable** within carrying capacity limits over the long-term, ranks high among the values of the ecoholist. Many adherents of this worldview question the necessity or desirability of constantly expanding consumption. Many also define progress in terms of spiritual or intellectual achievement, rather than in material terms.

Foremost among prescriptions of most ecoholists is population control. Should humans not act to limit their own numbers, the ecosystem will do it for them. In addition, they argue that we can manufacture and consume goods with much less pressure on resources and much less generation of waste than we currently accept. That is, for a given level of production and consumption, we should minimize **economic throughput** (Daly 1980). A more limited number of ecoholists also favor restrictions on technological development, especially in areas such as genetic engineering, where the technology may alter and perhaps damage the ecosystem—or simply exacerbate the overshoot phenomenon (Rifkin 1984).

Ecoholists disagree concerning the implementation of these prescriptions (on the direct political implications of their thought). Some favor voluntary individual action, informed by the knowledge that large-scale efforts are necessary. The Hunger Project mobilizes millions internationally, asking each to make a contribution to eliminating world hunger based on their own definition of the problem and their own capacity for action. Other ecoholists argue that the inherent individual tendency to ignore externalities (as a smoker does in a room of nonsmokers) and the tendency to free ride ("let George clean it up") means that only collective action, using coercion to enforce it, will succeed.

This debate extends to international policy issues. Will states act individually to limit damage to the global environment from acid rain, the greenhouse effect, or the depletion of atmospheric ozone? Can they agree to act in the numbers necessary, with the knowledge that other states may free ride on their sacrifices? Do such problems inherently require stronger global institutions, possessing instruments for policy enforcement? These are the issues of Chapter 17.

IMPORTANT CONTRIBUTIONS TO ECOHOLIST THOUGHT

Traditional hunting and gathering or agricultural societies observed the limits on human population at close range. They experienced periodic famines and developed great respect for their environment.[4] These traditional peoples often perceived a harmony between themselves and their environment. A letter that Chief Seattle of the Suquamish tribe purportedly wrote to President Pierce in 1855 illustrates the view well:

> The great Chief in Washington sends words that he wishes to buy land....How can you buy or sell the sky—the warmth of the land? The idea is strange to us. Yet we do not own the freshness of the air or the sparkle of the water. How can you buy them from us? We will decide in our time. Every part of this earth is sacred to my people. Every shining pine needle, every sandy shore, every mist in the dark woods, every clearing and humming insect is holy in the memory and experience of my people.
>
> We know that the white man does not understand our ways. One portion of the land is the same to him as the next, for he is a stranger who comes in the night and takes from the land whatever he needs. The earth is not his brother, but his enemy, and when he has conquered it, he moves on. He leaves his fathers' graves, and his children's birthright is forgotten. The sight of your cities pains the eyes of the redman. But perhaps it is because the redman is a savage and does not understand.[5]

The belief that an environmental carrying capacity limited humans was dominant until recently. In fifteenth-century Italy, Niccolò Machiavelli defined the cost of reaching those limits:

---

[4]Harris (1977) argues that the neolithic revolution and the beginning of fixed agriculture, far from indicating human progress vis-à-vis the environment, was a necessary response to increased population density and overhunting. He cites evidence that nutritional standards and physical health deteriorated considerably in the new agricultural societies, relative to those of stone-age peoples.

[5]Apparently, Ted Perry, a film writer and professor embellished Chief Seattle's words in an environmental film (*Denver Post*, April 22, 1992). Read the quotation as poetry, not necessarily history.

> When countries become overpopulated and there is no longer any room for all the inhabitants to live, nor any other place for them to go, these being likewise all fully occupied—and when human cunning and wickedness have gone as far as they can go—then of necessity the world must relieve itself of this excess of population...; so that mankind, having been chastised and reduced in numbers, may become better able to live with more convenience. (Machiavelli 1940, 298).

Even in a period and society becoming increasingly permeated by modernist thought, Thomas Malthus (1766–1834) reiterated and elaborated this thesis. Based on his famous argument that population grows geometrically (what we would call exponentially), while food supply increases only arithmetically (linearly), he initially concluded that only war, famine, and disease maintained the balance between humans and their environment. In a later edition of *An Essay on the Principle of Population*, he signaled the ecoholist emphasis on population control by introducing "moral restraint" as a fourth mechanism for checking population (Box 15.1).

The subsequent century and a half appeared to repudiate his conclusions as human population globally increased more than fourfold from that of Malthus's time and average diets simultaneously improved. Malthusian argument resurfaced in the last half of the twentieth century, however, as global population growth rates reached historic highs. In the early 1970s the Club of Rome widely publicized the results of an analysis based on a computer simulation of global development (see also Meadows and others 1992). That study, released immediately before a two-year period of drought and famine in Northern Africa and parts of South Asia, became the focal point for an intense debate. It argued that

> If the present growth trends in world population, industrialization, pollution, food production, and resource depletion continue unchanged, the limits to growth on this planet will be reached sometime within the next one hundred years. The most probable result will be a rather sudden and uncontrollable decline in both population and industrial capacity. (Meadows and others 1972, 23)

In the 1970s and 1980s ecoholism spilled over into politics very directly. Environmentalist movements appeared in most developed countries and gave rise to "green" parties. By 1992 "green" parties were formally organized in 50 countries. Concern for the environment even proved a powerful unifying force for groups opposing Communist leaderships in Eastern Europe. It appears probable that the extent of commitment to environmental protection will become a long-term political dimension in most developed countries, adding to historic religious and economic divisions.

Internationally, environmentally committed NGOs, like Greenpeace and the World Resources Institute, gained membership rapidly, carrying a new set of issues to global forums. In 1989 UN Secretary-General Javier Pérez de Cúeller declared that "It is generally agreed that the environment has moved to the top of the world's political agenda."

BOX 15.1   ALTERNATIVE GROWTH PATTERNS

Linear growth occurs when equal increments are added year after year. The graph shows growth of 0.2 units each year for 20 years

Exponential growth occurs with a constant percentage change each year to an increasing base. The graph shows growth by 10 percent each year (an initial increment of 0.1 units). Population and economic growth have been **super-exponential** in the last two hundred years, because the percentage growth rates of each has increased over time. Positive feedback processes (both vicious and virtuous cycles) are exponential.

When exponential growth bumps up against limits, slows, and stops, it is **saturating exponential growth.** Demographers expect human population to follow this pattern as we move into the twentieth century.

When exponential growth exceeds sustainable levels, it creates an **overshoot and collapse.** Many environmental growth patterns take this form.

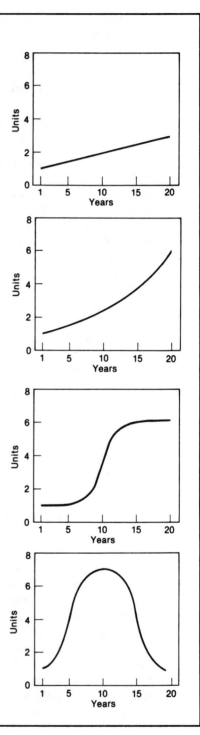

Both modernist and ecoholist analyses have always interacted with political argument. Malthus used his theory about the inevitability of poverty and distress to argue against public programs to relieve it. Members of the Club of Rome used the modern computer analysis to argue in favor of population control, environmental protection, and slower economic growth.

In the mid-1970s, President Carter commissioned a report on these global issues that generally reinforced his own ecoholist perspective. It began with this paragraph:

> If present trends continue, the world in 2000 will be more crowded, more polluted, less stable ecologically, and more vulnerable to disruption than the world we live in now. Serious stresses involving population, resources, and environment are clearly visible ahead. Despite greater material output, the world's people will be poorer in many ways than they are today. (Council on Environmental Quality 1981, 1)

Carter favored increased international cooperation to address these issues. The authors actually delivered the report in the early days of the Reagan administration. Reagan's beliefs were considerably closer to the modernist perspective, and he shelved the report and its recommendations. Instead, that administration embraced a technological optimism, illustrated by the appeal of the SDI or "Star Wars" program, and by its weakening of the U.S. Environmental Protection Agency. The Bush administration's cool attitude to the Earth Summit of 1992 in Rio expressed a similar preference for market forces and technological solutions, relative to collective environmental action. In a reversal of direction, Clinton chose an environmentalist as his vice president.

Popular attachment to the two perspectives varies over time and depends on the circumstances of the day. In general, international crises in the environment or in resource availability (as in the mid-1970s) strengthen the ecoholist perspective, whereas periods free of immediate crisis reinforce the modernist view. Because we can expect continued alternation between such conditions, regardless of any dominant long-term trend, the relative popularity of the two worldviews is likely also to rise and wane cyclically. Let us now consider each perspective in more detail.

Chapter 16

TECHNOLOGICAL
ADVANCE
AND HUMAN INTERACTION

Technology directly affects the way in which humans and states interact with one another. For example, we no longer need be within stone-throwing range to hurt each other—we can do it from the far side of the world. More indirectly, most of the global megatrends that Chapter 1 identified were tied to technological advance and those megatrends clearly affect human interaction. Given the tremendous importance of technology, it is surprising that our theoretical understanding of the relationship between technology and human interaction is very weak.

Modernists predict continued technological advance and tend to be very positive about its implications for human interaction. Our understanding of other worldviews allows us to go further, but makes us less uniformly optimistic. This chapter will consider five specific propositions about the implications of technological advance. The globalist perspective helps provide the first two.

First, much technological advance is essentially nonzero-sum—individuals and states can very often assist one another without cost to themselves. Therefore, *long-term technological advance is a basis for international cooperation*. Second, *many technologies increase and potentially improve the interaction of states and transnational actors*. These include communications and transportation technology. The realist perspective leads us into the remaining three propositions. Third, despite the nonzero-sum nature of technological change in the long-run, interim leads in certain technologies create inequalities. Thus *in the short-term technology can be a basis for conflict*. Fourth, technology advances unevenly over time as well as across states. *The cyclical character of its progress may affect interstate relations*. Fifth, some specific technologies, particularly military ones, can make conflict more likely. In particular, *certain technologies favor offensive military action*. This chapter considers each of these propositions in turn.

PROPOSITION 1: HUMAN PROGRESS AND COOPERATION

A large variety of measures suggest continuing or even accelerating improvement in the human condition. Life expectancy is an important summary indicator of how well humans do in nutrition, health care, environmental quality, and social interaction. In the England of 1800 it was only thirty-two years; in the Great Britain of 1992 it reached seventy-six years. In the developing world of the early 1950s it was forty-three years; by 1992 Third World parents could expect their children to live an average of sixty-two years. Unimpeded global spread of medical technology explains much of the increase.

Chapter 1 documented a long-term increase in global food production per capita (with the exception of Africa). Famines, once common and inevitable in all societies, now occur rarely and appear to be preventable anomalies. Support from the U.S.–based Rockefeller Foundation helped initiate the green revolution in Mexico in the 1950s. It spread quickly around the world with assistance from other foundations, international organizations and national governments. No questions of national advantage delayed the dissemination of the new knowledge.

Average global income levels have also climbed as the world industrialized. In 1800 the per capita GNP in West Europe was $940, and that of the Third World

Life Expectancy
Source: Reprinted with permission by John Jonik.

"You figure it. Everything we eat is 100% natural
yet our life expectancy is only 31 years."

was $883 (in 1990 dollars).[1] Although the average per capita GNP of the developing countries only grew to $1,096 in 1990, and that of the developed countries climbed to $19,590, both groups did advance.

Energy available for human industrial activity further illustrates the rapid pace of progress. Watt's steam engine generated 40 horsepower in 1800, a dramatic improvement upon the 5.5 horsepower of Newcomen's steam engine in 1712 and on water mills and windmills of that era (3 to 14 horsepower). A modern, large-scale electric power plant, either coal-fired or nuclear, delivers 1.5 million horsepower, however (Cook 1976, 29).

No one country could unilaterally have accomplished the progress made globally on these four indicators in the last 200 years (Figure 16.1). Modernists who are also globalists point out that the spread of agricultural, industrial, and health technology around the world made possible this collective global success (that the spread is incomplete explains many of the great inequalities still existing globally). Do not individuals from around the world who are better fed, clothed, housed, and educated increase their own contributions to technological advance and thus our collective well-being? Impoverished and hungry Russians and Japanese might not threaten our military security, but they would also make limited contributions to global fusion or electronic technology. Richer and better-fed Indians might compete with us in world markets, but they would also push back technological frontiers and improve our own lives in ways we could never anticipate.

Technology moves via various mechanisms, and at different speeds, around the world. Today a new technology, whether beneficial or not, will affect the entire globe within a few decades. The diffusion speeds appear to be rising. Although most technology still moves among industrialized countries or from North to South, a small but increasing flow moves from South to North.[2] Mastery of industrial technology around the world explains this incipient reverse flow. In 1950, the North produced 78 percent of world steel, whereas that figure fell to 55 percent in 1980 (Robinson 1988, 31). Even the Northern share of automobile production fell from 96 percent to 82 percent during that period. In the 1980s exports of manufactures from LDCs grew by 7.6 percent annually; exports from more developed countries grew by 4.5 percent each year.

Northern governments transfer some technology to the South through public programs, such as the U.S. Agency for International Development, the U.S. Peace Corps, the Swiss Institute for Intermediate Technology, the British Colombo Plan, and the Economic Development Fund of the EC (Robinson 1988, 61–62). Public agencies heavily target agricultural and medical technology.

[1]Braudel (1979, 534) provides figures of $213 and $200 in 1960 prices; consumer prices increased by a factor of 4.4 between 1960 and 1990. Contemporary numbers come from the World Bank (1992). The low-income countries in 1990 had a per capita GNP of only $350.

[2]See "Exports of Technology by Newly-Industrialized Countries," a special issue of *World Development*, (May–June 1984).

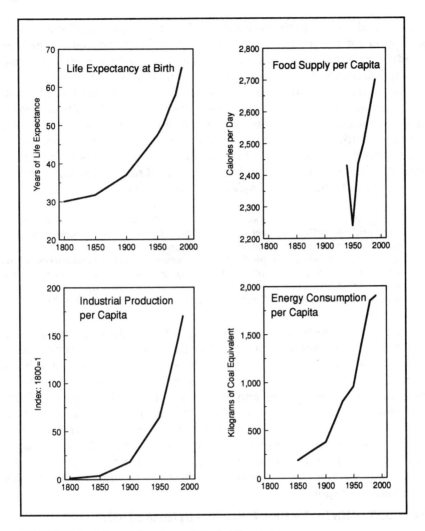

FIGURE 16.1   A Broad Spectrum of Global Progress

The world's corporations control most industrial technology, however, and therefore organize most interstate technology transfer. The global recognition of patents regulates the pattern of transfer. Innovators register patents within a state and thereby create a monopoly on rights to the patented innovation. This allows the inventor to capture the benefits of invention for that period. Without patent protection, the invention would immediately be a public good, and this would encourage free riding rather than innovation. The United States and Canada, for example, provide protection of patents for seventeen years.[3] International agree-

[3]Many LDCs provide fewer years protection (as few as five) and desire a global agreement on shorter periods so as to encourage faster transfer (Rao 1989).

ments extend patent protection abroad. Ninety countries adhere to the Paris Convention for the International Protection of Property Rights (1883) and its amendments.[4] Under that convention, issuance of a patent in one country normally bars application elsewhere and reinforces the monopoly (Robinson 1988, 139).

The individual, corporate, or state entity controlling the patent can use the technology abroad (one basic reason for the existence of multinational corporations) or license it to others. There are obvious incentives to exploit the technology during the period of patent protection and to establish a dominant market presence before the protection ends. This system facilitates rapid domestic development and international transfer of new technology. The specific mechanisms of **technology transfer** include the following:

> the supply of information and knowledge (publications, personnel, technical assistance, and so forth); the licensing for a fee of production processes or advanced techniques; the sale of machinery and equipment embodying sophisticated technology; the sale of advanced production processes, as in the construction of turnkey plants (factories that are bought and sold as complete units, ready to operate as soon as they are completed); and the transfer of related management and marketing systems, as well as technical personnel. (Holzman and Portes 1978, 81)

Pirating also exists on a wide scale and further hastens the international flow of technology. Most pirating consists of violation of consumer-good trademarks; imitation goods then flood global markets. Pirates also steal patented technologies, however, such as those in microprocessors at the core of personal computers. Large corporations use their patent and trademark registration rights to fight such infringement, but they face serious difficulties in enforcement abroad; small corporations have little chance to protect their technology. The Uruguay Round of GATT devoted special attention to this problem. In general, the movement of the global economy into the "information age" should increasingly refocus GATT attention on legal and illegal transfers of technology around the world rather than on the transfers of goods.

PROPOSITION 2: TECHNOLOGIES OF HUMAN INTERACTION

Human interaction requires transportation and communication. Although the word "revolution" is overused, no other word can adequately describe nineteenth- and twentieth-century developments in these arenas. A trip around the world in 1800 required several years by sailing ship. Jet aircraft can now circle the earth in one day and an orbiting spacecraft can do it in ninety minutes. Before the invention of the telegraph in 1840, nearly all messages traveled with human beings so that communication speeds were the same as those found in transportation. Today communications satellites transmit information between any two points in the globe almost instantaneously.

---

[4]In 1988 the United States finally ratified the Berne Convention for the Protection of Literary and Artistic Works, dating from 1885. That action will help the U.S. Copyright Office protect software, films, and other intellectual property against growing piracy.

As Seyom Brown (1988, 174–178) argues, states erect the real barriers to the movement of people and messages now: passport and customs requirements, overflight and landing restrictions, the jamming of broadcasts, the selection of nonstandard communications systems, and other conscious or unconscious actions that disrupt the constantly growing demand to use the available technology. The Communist governments of Eastern Europe and the Soviet Union most purposefully restricted what have come internationally to be considered two basic human rights: access to information and freedom of movement. The United States, in part because of its influence over international electronic media and partly because of its open society, has consistently supported Article 19 of the Universal Declaration of Human Rights, affirming the right "to receive and impart information and ideas through any media regardless of frontiers."

International telephone traffic illustrates the pace of change in global communication volume (Figure 16.2). The world now has nearly 100 telephone lines for each 1000 people. The cost of a three-minute call from New York to London dropped (in real terms) from $244.65 in 1930 to $31.58 in 1970, and to $3.32 in 1990 (World Bank 1992b, 34).

In 1950, 1 million calls connected the United States with other countries; by 1975 this had grown to 75 million, and it rose to about 250 million in the mid-1980s (Dizard 1985, 148–172). Global communications have been growing 10 percent to 15 percent annually.[5] The Intelsat network facilitates this explosion. Intelsat put its first communication satellite in orbit in 1964; by 1992 the system offered thirteen satellites, each with 120,000 telephone circuits and thirty-two TV channels. Voting in Intelsat depends on state share in the system's use and expenses. The United States initiated the system and in 1965 held 60 percent of the votes. By the mid-1980s this had dropped under 25 percent. Satellites have finally eliminated the barriers to direct communications among LDCs. Mail among Third World countries, and later electronic communications, had passed for centuries through gateway cities in the more-developed countries.

Global movement of people and goods has grown less rapidly than communications, but considerably faster than population. For instance, world tourism rose from a total of 25 million arrivals in 1950 to 429 million in 1990.[6] Its growth has averaged 4.9 percent, nearly triple that of world population, since 1970. In 1987 it was the world's largest industry, employing 6.3 percent of the global workforce. Figure 16.3 conveys the pace of growth in international sea and air transport (about two-thirds of all international personal travel is tourism).

Globalists argue (see Chapter 8) that increasing international transaction volume fosters growth of "global community." For instance, during the 1980s the

---

[5]We should not underestimate the communications capabilities of earlier eras. By 1880, undersea telegraph cables (mostly British) connected Europe with North and South America, South Africa, India, and even Australia (Headrick 1981, 161).

[6]Data courtesy of the World Tourism Organization, Madrid. That organization forecasts 637 million arrivals in 2000.

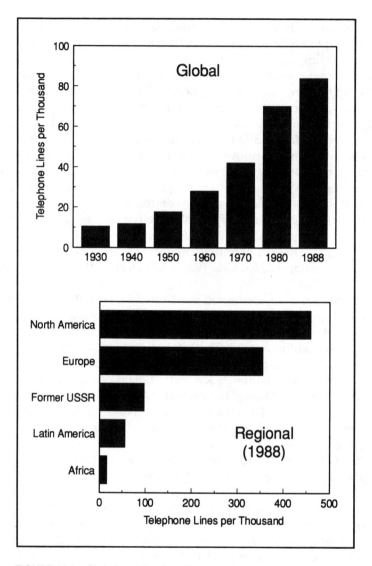

FIGURE 16.2 Global and Regional Telephones
Source: AT&T, *The World's Telephones: A Statistical Compilation as of January 1, 1982* (Morris Plains, N.J.: AT&T, 1982); *AT&T, The World Telephones* (Whippany, N.J.: AT&T, 1989).

spotlight of media attention on human rights violations in countries like Chile, South Africa, and the Soviet Union connected the victims with the global community and led to pressure on the governments (not always successfully but steadily) to undertake reforms. The communications media also regularly portrays hunger and malnutrition in Africa to the rest of the world. Just as humanity now collectively rejects human sacrifice and slavery, we appear to be moving toward collec-

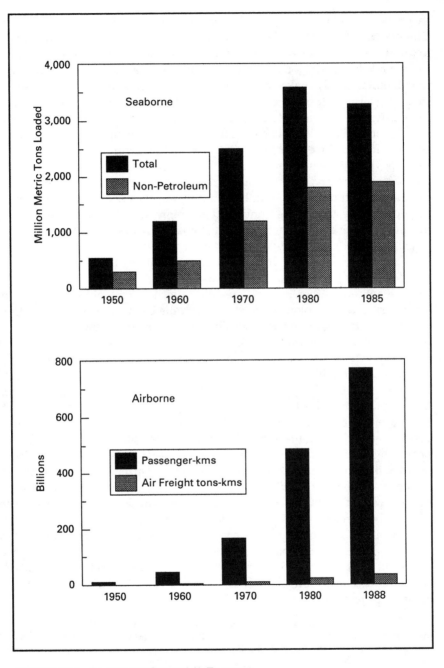

FIGURE 16.3 International Sea and Air Transport
Source: United Nations, *Statistical Yearbook*, (New York: United Nations), (1985), 1047;
(1977), 591; (1966), 459. *ICAO Bulletin*, (Nov. 1988), Vol. 43, No. 11, 12; (May 1972),
Vol. 27, No. 27, 18; (May 1959), Vol. 14, No. 2, 56.

tive condemnation of political violence and starvation.[7] In June 1989, when the Chinese army brutally crushed the democracy movement, color film took the story to international news networks and ignited a global storm of protest.

While building global community, modern transportation and communication simultaneously make contemporary states permeable and increase **penetration** by external actors (Rosenau 1966). In a dramatic example, a German, Mathias Rust, penetrated Soviet air defenses in 1987 and landed his small private plane on Red Square.[8] Yet societies can cut off transport much easier than they can restrict communication. For example, under the Shah, Iran controlled the electronic media, as do governments in many states. The Ayatollah Khomeini, an Iranian exile in Paris, developed and strengthened a network of support, in part, by distributing cassette tapes throughout Iran. In addition, opponents can sometimes turn communications systems once controlled by repressive regimes against them. For instance, the revolutionary regime in Romania in 1989 seized and initially governed from the Bucharest television station.

Similarly, one of the main information sources for millions of Chinese in pro-democracy protests during 1989 was Voice of America radio transmissions. The Chinese authorities therefore resumed electronic jamming of them for the first time since they restored diplomatic relations with the United States in 1979.[9] They were unable or unwilling to cut telephone linkages, however, and the daily volume of calls between the United States and China rose from 10,000 to 30,000 during the protests.

Although Eastern countries long attempted to restrict the import of video cassettes, they fought a losing battle against a medium so easily copied. Similarly, the simple exchange of floppy disks full of data and text undercut the restrictions that Communist countries had placed for years on the import and distribution of literature, information, and ideas—restrictions that included highly limited access to paper copying machines. International telephone networks also increase permeability of societies, despite state restrictions. The commercial necessity of being tied into the global network has provided average citizens the technology to contact their peers around the world. Civil rights or political dissidents can maintain communication with activists, media, and organizations outside the borders of their country.

In the summer of 1990 an American foundation distributed in Central Europe what it called "Democracy Kits," each containing a copier, a computer, and a fax machine. If it had been possible to add a radio, a television, and an international airline ticket to the kit, it would truly have symbolized the increased interconnectedness of people globally and their capabilities for collective self-defense against oppression.

[7]Communications and transportation technology also, however, have dark sides. For instance, totalitarian governments have relied on communication networks to manipulate opinion and beliefs and to enforce control. It appears increasingly difficult, however, for any government to monopolize communications channels.

[8]Perhaps 18,000 illegal flights enter the United States each year, many bringing illegal drugs (*The Christian Science Monitor*, March 23, 1989, 1).

[9]North Korea has taken a more direct approach to restricting communications from the outside: It prohibits most individual ownership of radios and provides one-channel "speakers" for homes.

PROPOSITION 3: COMPETITION FOR SHORT-TERM ADVANTAGE

Technology development may in the long-run be a nonzero-sum matter for a humanity divided into more than 180 separate states. Medical, transportation, communications, and production technologies developed anywhere on the globe eventually come into use everywhere in the world. In the short and mid-runs, however, realists point out that all of these technologies confer to particular states advantages that translate into relative power. At the end of the seventeenth century, England and France established the Royal Society for the Advancement of Science and the Académie Francaise, respectively, simultaneously demonstrating and solidifying their leadership in the emerging state system (Strange 1988, 121). The contemporary attempt by the United States government in GATT to protect the technological advantage of its firms is no historic anomaly—it recognizes that advantage as a contribution to state strength. Military technologies even more clearly affect relative state power. Thus individual countries seek to develop a wide variety of technologies, especially those with military application, before their acquisition by other states, and act to maintain their monopoly as long as possible. The struggle for relative advantage gives rise to considerable interstate rivalry.

COMPETITION OVER MILITARY TECHNOLOGIES

The U.S. Export Control Act of 1949 was an explicit attempt to limit interstate technology flows, particularly those with any military implications. It allowed the president to prohibit categories of exports to the communist countries. After passage, the United States immediately set up the Coordinating Committee on Multilateral Export Control (COCOM) to coordinate Western policy on trade with the East.[10] COCOM prepared a list of embargoed items. The Mutual Defense Assistance Control Act of 1951 further authorized the president to eliminate aid to any country providing strategic goods to the Soviet Union or Eastern Europe, thus giving the United States a stick with which to secure adherence to COCOM guidelines (Spero 1981, 294–296). These measures nearly shut down East-West trade at the peak of the cold war. The Export Administration Acts of 1969 and 1979 updated and replaced the Export Control Act (MacDonald 1986).

The West eased restrictions during the détente of the late 1960s and early 1970s, but the invasion of Afghanistan by the U.S.S.R. in 1979 led to tightening of export and technology policy. For instance, in 1977 the Carter administration had encouraged Western Europe to increase imports of oil and gas from the U.S.S.R. so as to diversify supply sources, but in late 1979 the same administration suspended licenses for exports of oil and gas exploration and production equipment to the Soviet Union. In 1982 the Reagan administration entered into an acrimonious and unsuccessful effort to prevent European companies from selling to the Soviets oil and gas equipment that incorporated American technology.

[10]Membership includes all NATO states except Iceland; Japan also participates and Australia joined in 1989. It has a secretariat in Paris.

The other principal multilateral effort to control military technology flows centers on nuclear proliferation. Even during the cold war, the Western nuclear states managed to cooperate with the Soviet Union to limit primarily North-South flows of technology. Already before the 1968 signing of the Treaty on the Non-Proliferation of Nuclear Weapons, states established the International Atomic Energy Agency (IAEA) in Vienna to monitor the flow of nuclear materials. In 1974 most nuclear states (including both superpowers) established a "trigger list" of equipment that they would export only if importers agreed to IAEA safeguards, restricting their use to peaceful atomic programs. In 1987 major Western states created the Missile Technology Control Regime to limit the proliferation of delivery vehicles. Russia subsequently accepted its provisions.

Three problems frustrate any effort to deny technology to specific states. The first involves collective goods and free riders once again. All members of the NATO alliance long benefited from a militarily weaker Eastern opposition and such weakness thus constituted a collective good for the alliance. Yet each individually could benefit by expanding trade ties with the East, and thus the incentive existed to cheat on the collective policy. Cheating did not take the form of blatant shipments of military goods to the Soviet Union and its allies, but rather of trading in categories that were in the large gray area between goods that have only economic character and those that carry military implications. Consider, for example, the ambiguity of technology for a truck factory or oil refinery. With respect to efforts to control nuclear proliferation, such items are called "dual use" technology, and include supercomputers and vacuum pumps.

A second problem is that technology, although less fungible than commodities like oil or wheat, is still sometimes difficult to identify by origin. Thus technology that the Iraqi nuclear program obtained from the West has often been nearly untraceable. This has encouraged cheating on the nonproliferation of nuclear weapons regime.

Finally, would-be proliferators of this technology to the Third World, like the Soviets and their Warsaw Pact allies, have circumvented restrictions with an extensive network for economic and military technology espionage, using diplomatic missions, exchange students, and other personnel. One estimate was that more than half of the eighty Soviet intelligence officers expelled from industrial democracies in 1983 were collecting strategic technology (Schneider 1984, 69). In an early post–World War II success, the Soviets obtained secrets that helped them build their own nuclear bomb. Countries seeking nuclear capability have also actively sought individuals or firms in the West who would break the laws and ship prohibited goods. For example, Pakistan used a number of West German firms in the late 1980s to obtain an extensive range of prohibited nuclear technologies (Spector 1990, 34–35).

COMPETITION OVER INDUSTRIAL TECHNOLOGIES

It is not only the issue of military technology that has realist overtones; there is a definite character of **technological mercantilism** to the competition for technological advantage within the West. Japan, although beginning the post–World War II era in a position of inferiority, now sets the pace for the technical competition.

An important tool of Japan is cooperation between government and industry. The Ministry of International Trade and Industry (MITI) targets technologies of the future, stimulates research and development, and helps secure financing for Japanese industry.[11] For example, the Japanese government and forty-five corporations were at work in 1988 within a consortium on superconductor technology, even though scientists expect few significant applications before the end of the century. Japan has also protected its domestic markets against high-technology imports such as supercomputers, while encouraging export growth in the same industries.[12]

Europeans recognize that their individual states cannot compete with the United States or Japan. One facet of their response has been a series of collective efforts under the auspices of the EC. The Framework Program defined joint effort and priorities from 1987 to 1991 (Van Deelen 1988, 27). Joint programs include research on energy, health, the environment, information and telecommunications, and raw materials. The largest focused program is European Strategic Program for Research and Development in Information Technology (ESPRIT). Other important cooperative efforts are Research and Development in Advanced Communications Technology (RACE), Basic Research in Industrial Technology for Europe (BRITE), and Joint European Submicron Silicon program (JESSI). The European High Technology Programme (EUREKA) even reaches beyond the European Community and draws on the expertise of six other West European states. Interindustry consortia supplement governmental efforts. The EC provides one-third of the funds to consortiums in various projects (300 by 1989). For instance, the three corporate electronic giants of Europe (Siemens, Philips, and the Franco-Italian Group, SGS-Thompson) established a research consortium to develop the next generation of computer chips.

Supplementing such precompetitive, EC-wide research cooperation, many high technology projects in Europe lead to joint production activity. The French-British Concorde project is among the best known. More commercially successful is the five-country Airbus project (Kirchner 1988, 17f). The same countries and firms developed and produce the Ariane rockets for satellite launching and are the core of the ESP (European Space Programme), which is working toward a space shuttle and space station.

The success of the Japanese and European models for government support to advanced technology industries has initiated a debate concerning industrial policy and government-industry cooperation in the United States. In reality the U.S. government has already taken several steps toward an industrial policy that will strengthen the international competitive strength of its companies. For instance, in 1984 Congress revised antitrust laws to facilitate joint research by U.S. corporations. By 1990 more than 125 cooperatives had formed.

[11]Chandler (1987) argues that MITI has even facilitated circumvention of COCOM controls, like those bypassed in the Toshiba case.

[12]For example, the Japanese patent office delayed action on a material called "Metglas" for twelve years while the clock was running on the limited time its American inventing company could exercise exclusive control. Similar examples abound (*Business Week*, October 1, 1990, 32).

Semiconductor technology is of special interest (and at special risk of falling to Japanese leadership); in 1986 the U.S. government encouraged the establishment of Sematech, a consortium of U.S. electronics companies engaged in joint research.[13] The Pentagon provided part of the funding. In 1989 a group of manufacturers announced U.S. Memories, Inc., a joint venture to manufacture advanced chips. Its collapse in 1990 triggered renewed American introspection with respect to its competitive position.

The government has sponsored new engineering and scientific research centers on U.S. campuses, while also lowering the barriers between governmental research centers and companies able to commercialize their discoveries. In addition, the U.S. government now seeks more vigorously to protect the existing technological advantage of domestic corporations. For example, in 1983 it prosecuted Hitachi for stealing secrets from IBM (MacDonald 1986, 53–54). U.S. trade legislation in 1988 also took unilateral action to protect American firms by requiring the U.S. Trade Representative to provide a list of countries that "inadequately protect American goods from counterfeiting or infringement."[14] Failure to improve protection will invoke automatic sanctions after six months.

In 1989 a bitter debate erupted in the United States over proposed cooperation between General Dynamics and Mitsubishi on the development of a fighter plane called the FSX. The proposal was to provide the Japanese with the technology for the General Dynamics F-16, on which the FSX was to be based, in exchange for advanced Japanese technology to be incorporated into the new plane. The allies were to share production. Proponents pointed out that the Japanese Defense Agency's research and development institute called in 1985 for Japan to build such a plane alone, potentially taking from the United States one of the last clear areas of its technological advantage.[15] Opponents claimed that the deal would help them do exactly that. The corporations signed the contract in 1990.

Not all search for technology is competitive. In 1991, the EC, Japan, the United States, and Russia agreed to cooperate on a nuclear fusion research project using magnetic confinement. Because it would cost about $1 billion to design and $4 billion to build, such an experimental facility increasingly exceeds the capabilities of individual states. Nonetheless, in a world where technology has become ever more central to economic performance, we can expect to see continued conflict over the control of it.

[13]In an interesting illustration of balance of power and coalition theory, the EC's JESSI and U.S.'s Sematech projects, both seeking to regain technological leadership in chipmaking, have discussed cooperation against the Japanese who held about 80 percent of the world market for dynamic random-access memory chips in 1989. Similarly, IBM joined in 1990 with Siemens AG of Germany to develop chips in competition with Japan.

[14]*Business Week* May 22, 1989, 86.

[15]Papathanasis and Vasillopulos (1988, 19) argue that "Pioneers of technological change, including the U.S., benefit when their technology becomes the world standard—even if they 'give it away.'...What is most important is protection of one's technological leadership [because it forestalls] the emergence of alternative, and possibly superior technologies. Competitors are transformed into functional subsidiaries." Although the dispute did not derail cooperation on the project, it caused the Japanese military to intensify pressure for minimizing technological dependence on the United States.

PROPOSITION 4: LONG WAVES OF TECHNOLOGICAL ADVANCE AND CONFLICT

While globalists may argue that technological advance will ultimately diffuse throughout the world and help all of humanity, the last section indicated that a problem lies in the geographic unevenness of that advance. States who obtain technologies early have an advantage. In addition, technological advance does not necessarily proceed uniformly over time. Many economists have noted what they call **Kondratieff** (or Kondratiev) **cycles** of approximately fifty to sixty years in the world economy. These take their name from the Russian economist who identified them in the 1920s. Joseph Schumpeter proposed an explanation for these **long waves** in 1939. Schumpeter made distinctions among **invention** (identifiable technical change), **innovation** (the "introduction of new products, techniques and systems into the economy" [Freeman 1988, 38]), and **diffusion** (the widespread use of the new products in ways that clearly affect the growth of productivity and of the economy). For example, James Watt patented his invention of a steam engine in 1769. A stream of innovation used the engine to power textile production machinery, milling processes, and transportation systems (the first steamship was demonstrated on the Potomac in 1787). Diffusion took longer. In transportation applications, a ship powered only by steam finally crossed the Atlantic in 1838, initiating the large-scale replacement of sailing ships by steamships.

According to Schumpeter there have been repeated "gales of creative destruction" in which new invention clusters led to accelerated periods of innovation and diffusion and thus to economic upswings. Observers have identified four:[16] (1) the early stages of the industrial revolution (beginning in the 1780s), led by innovation in cotton textiles, iron, and the steam engine; (2) the railroad era (after about 1842); (3) what Simon Kuznets (1940, 261) called the mercantilist Kondratieff wave (after about 1898 and including the *belle epoque* before World War I), dominated by electricity and chemical technologies, and by better and cheaper steel; and (4) the post–World War II wave (beginning in the late 1940s), characterized by the automobile and an inexpensive, oil-based energy system.

The theory argues that after the initial invention, surge of innovation, and associated economic growth, a period of diminishing productivity improvements and slower growth follows. Although the technologies (as inventions) for a new upswing are often available throughout the downturn, they initially contribute little to productivity. In fact, recognition of their potential contributions may even retard investment and contribute to slowing economic growth or stagnation. Peter Drucker (1969, 24) notes that an inventor brought forward the first practical electrical generator in 1856 and that entrepreneurs established nearly all contemporary electric-apparatus companies before 1879. In that year Edison invented the electric light bulb and initiated the modern electric industry. That critical product and others like it facilitated diffusion and finally set in motion a new Kondratieff upswing at the end of the nineteenth century.

[16]See Goldstein (1988, 32), Freeman (1988, 54), and Hughes (1985, 79). Goldstein (1988) traced the cycles back to 1495. Students of the cycles admit that they become less clear-cut prior to the industrial revolution.

Computers have been available (as inventions) since the late 1940s. Drucker argued in 1969 that the computer-based innovations needed to set off another cycle of diffusion and an economic upswing would be information-systems capable of delivering knowledge cheaply and nearly universally. The development of microelectronics in the 1960s, microcomputers in the early 1980s, and extensive electronic networks in the late 1980s and 1990s, may constitute such critical innovations. If so, the recent period of global Kondratieff downturn, dating from the early 1970s,[17] may be nearing its end. Interestingly, we still tend to measure productivity in terms of steel produced or energy consumed (measures appropriate to the third and fourth long waves). We may need measurements in terms of bits of information[18] available and efficiently organized.

We must emphasize, however, that evidence for the very existence of Kondratieff cycles is unclear. We also lack theoretical understanding. In addition to Schumpeter's innovation theory (actually more of a dynamic description), explanations include (1) the life cycle of capital investment, and thus a tendency for waves of investment and overinvestment, (2) periodic swings in the availability of food and raw materials, like those related to energy transitions, (3) changing rates of profit in the world economy and periodic crises of capitalism, and (4) a cycle in international conflict behavior (Bruckmann 1983, 6–9; Goldstein 1988, 21–39). Although various explanations somewhat overlap and converge, the confusion within the theory-building effort has caused highly regarded economists like Kindleberger and Samuelson to refer to the cycles as "astrology" and "science fiction."[19] Most disconcerting for Kondratieff theorists is difficulty in clearly identifying and dating the economic cycles they attempt to explain. The cycles actually appear more clearly in price data than in production patterns (Figure 16.4).[20]

The potential relationship of the technological-economic cycles to international conflict behavior obviously interests us here. Some scholars note a moderately strong association between intensified conflict and the upswing phase of the cycle (Imbert 1956; Thompson and Zuk 1982). Why would that be? The upswing could benefit some states more than others and thus change the interstate power balance, or it could cause an intensified struggle for resources (Chapter 5 discussed both as potential sources of conflict). Goldstein generally accepts the

[17]In the 1960s the world economy grew 5 percent annually; in the decade after 1973 growth averaged 2.7 percent. Baily and Chakrabarti (1988) explored the failure of rapidly proliferating computers to improve white-collar productivity in the 1980s.

[18]More likely it will be terabytes (trillions of characters).

[19]*Forbes*, November 9, 1981, 166; Goldstein (1988, 21).

[20]Maddison (1982, 80–83) noted the anomaly of relative inattention to GNP or production data by long wave theorists. In addition, he replicated the economic data presented by Mandel (1975). Mandel reported world economic growth of 2.2 percent for the second downswing (1870–1890) and 3.7 percent for the third upswing (1891–1913). Maddison says that better data indicate rates of 3.4 percent and 3.8 percent, respectively—hardly dramatic differences. On the other hand, Maddison (1982, 44) computes a drop in annual GDP per capita growth for sixteen industrial countries from 3.8 percent between 1950 and 1973 to 2.0 percent between 1973 and 1979. Maddison places more confidence in ad hoc explanations, such as the breakdown of the Bretton Woods system, than in long cycles.

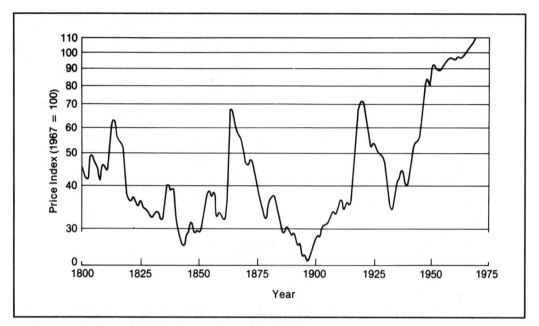

FIGURE 16.4   Kondratieff Cycles in U.S. Price Data
Source: Joshua S. Goldstein, *Long Waves: Prosperity and War in the Modern Age* (New Haven: Yale University Press, 1988), 35.
Note: The price data are derived by combining two time series for wholesale prices, one from 1800 to 1890 (series E52) and one from 1890 to 1970 (series E23). Data from U.S. Department of Commerce, Bureau of the Census, *Historical Statistics* (1975 ed.).

upswing argument, and warns that should a new upswing start about 1995, the greatest danger of substantial conflict would be in the first twenty-five years of the next century.

Other scholars direct our attention to the potential relationship between the roughly century-long waves of hegemonic domination and the Kondratieff cycle of about half that length. They divide a hegemonic century into two waves. During the first upswing the hegemonic power is ascending, whereas during the second upswing the mature power is approaching decline. Hopkins and Wallerstein (1982) argue that acute conflict is most likely during the first upswing (ascending hegemony) and the second downswing (declining hegemony).

We do best in conclusion to be cautious: Technological advance *may* occur in long waves that *may* affect both economic performance and interstate conflict propensity; although these are important research questions, the evidence is mixed.

PROPOSITION 5: MILITARY TECHNOLOGY AND OFFENSIVE ADVANTAGE

Earlier chapters (see especially Chapters 1 and 5) reviewed the progress that humans have made in explosive power, chemical and biologic weaponry, and the ability to deliver these weapons anywhere in the world. That process has bound humanity together as surely as have advanced communications and transportation technology. Do continuing advances in military technology, however, make interstate conflict more or less likely? There is no easy answer to that important question. Part of the answer may lie in the degree to which new technologies favor defense or offense.

One of the recurring themes of military technology throughout history has been the relative advantage of defensive and offensive systems. For instance, the invention of the machine gun gave a substantial advantage to the defense. Massive waves of men during World War I, even following large-scale heavy artillery attacks, could not often dislodge those in the trenches armed with machine guns—hundreds of thousands died in such attempts. One of the important miscalculations that led to World War I was the belief preceding it (based in part on Bismark's earlier success against France) that modern military technology gave great advantage to the offensive, and that "it will all be over before you know it." The German Schlieffen plan mapped a war strategy involving quick mobilization and transport by railroad of soldiers, and the Kaiser counted on rapid victory in the West so that forces could be shifted East, before the less industrialized Russians mobilized fully.

An invention near the end of World War I, the tank (first used on the Somme in September 1916), really did shift advantage to the offense. It became a dominant weapon in World War II and allowed Nazi Germany to achieve remarkable success in a technique called *Blitzkrieg*, combining the use of tanks to penetrate defensive lines with the drop of paratroopers behind them. Offensive tank assaults by Warsaw Pact forces in Europe long remained a primary concern of NATO planners, and it is the reason they feared the massive numerical superiority of Soviet tank forces.

Recently there has been ongoing debate as to whether the conventional advantage lies with improved and heavily armored tanks or with sophisticated antitank weaponry. The Iran-Iraq war ended in a stalemate, in part because of the successful antitank tactics of the Iraqis. Both Vietnam and Afghanistan conflicts, especially the latter, illustrate also how the new antiaircraft missiles (like the Stinger) can protect otherwise inferior forces against helicopters and even bombing aircraft. Similarly, the war between the British and the Argentines over the Falklands (Malvinas) proved that relatively inexpensive, electronically guided missiles could destroy very much more expensive and heavily armed warships. All of this suggests a relative advantage for the defense in modern conventional weaponry (Barnaby 1986).

Reviews of military history (Quester 1977; McNeill 1982) support a conclusion that defensive superiority helps maintain the political status quo (and relatively quiet interstate relations), but periods of offensive superiority more often coincide with attempts by some actors to overthrow the status quo. Jervis (1978) builds his analysis of this issue on the security dilemma and emphasizes not just defensive or offensive advantage, but also ability to clearly differentiate defensive and offensive forces. Table 16.1 indicates four "worlds," based on the intersection of these two variables.

TABLE 16.1
Military Technology and Systemic Stability:
The Interaction of Military Advantage and Clarity of Force Posture

	Offense has the Advantage	*Defense has the Advantage*
Security Dilemma: Offensive Posture not Distinguishable from Defensive One	Doubly dangerous	Security requirements may be compatible
	For example, Nuclear forces with first-strike capabilities only	For example, Unrecognized reality of situation before World War I (trench and machine gun warfare)
	For example, Situation believed to exist before World War I	
No Security Dilemma: Offensive Posture Distinguishable from Defensive One	Status-quo states can follow different policy from aggressors— warning given by force posture	Doubly stable
	For example, Contemporary conventional force balance in Europe if tanks have advantage	For example, Contemporary conventional force balance in Europe if antitank weaponry has the advantage

Source: Based on Robert Jervis, "Cooperation Under the Security Dilemma," *World Politics* 20, no. 2 (January, 1978): 211.

The distinction between offense and defense quickly weakens, however, when large-scale explosive devices (even tactical nuclear weapons) are used. NATO strategy in defense against a Soviet tank-led invasion included nuclear attacks behind the lines of the opposition. In a nuclear conflict the issue of defense versus offense interacts with the existence of first- and second-strike capabilities (a topic that Chapter 5 explored) and becomes exceedingly complex. As the debate concerning the SDI has shown, it is difficult to characterize a weapon system related to nuclear war as either defensive or offensive. Quester (1977, 211) argues that the basic question instead should be, Does the technology favor caution or preemption? Today, the uncertainties are sufficiently great, and the dangers so large, that it seems to favor caution.

FUTURE TECHNOLOGICAL DEVELOPMENTS

Advances in communications and transportation shrink and integrate the world. Like other technologies with a nonzero-sum character, such as agricultural and medical change, they seem on the whole to call forth and facilitate international cooperation and integration. It is thus not surprising that many modernists are also globalists and foresee an inevitable strengthening of global community and institutions (see, for instance, Drucker 1969).

Military technology also shrinks and integrates the world. All states must now attend to the military capabilities and intentions of many other states scattered around the globe. It is less clear, however, whether this force will develop global community and institutions, or whether it will reinforce states in their unilateral efforts to provide security.[21] As we have seen, technological advantage can also be the object of interstate competition. Thus some modernists are realists rather than globalists and foresee an indefinite continuation of interstate rivalry.

Although the political implications of technological advance are thus mixed and uncertain, they obviously depend significantly on the exact nature of technological developments. It is therefore useful to speculate on near-term technological change. What are some of the technologies in which we can expect to see progress, and what might be their impact?

Unfortunately, both technological advance and its impact remain unpredictable. In World War II, scientists invented DDT to protect soldiers against insects—no one then thought of using it on crops and contributing to the great postwar advances in food production. Similarly, a forecast in the late 1940s concluded that the world market for computers in the year 2000 would be 1,000 at most (Drucker 1986b, 214–216). Both DDT and computers reshaped the post–World War II world. Despite the inevitability of such surprises, we will risk brief speculation on some possible technological advances and their consequences.

Although we cannot with certainty identify which complex of technologies will lead the next Kondratieff upturn (should such waves actually exist), the combination of microelectronics and communications stands out as the leading candidate. Even many who reject the Kondratieff cycle regard these technologies as having taken us to the edge of a new economic era, the Information Age—an era that will perhaps bring changes as profound as those of the industrial revolution.

MICROELECTRONICS

In 1946 scientists unveiled the first electronic computer, ENIAC, built around 18,000 vacuum tubes. Researchers invented the transistor in 1947, and it eventually replaced vacuum tubes in nearly all applications. Integrated circuitry, combining many transistors on a single chip, emerged in 1959; the Japanese call these integrated circuits the "rice of the information age." Intel developed the microproces-

---

[21]The second possibility was, of course, the image of the unit-veto world that Chapter 5 described.

sor, basically a computer on a chip, in 1971. Widely distributed computers came of age with the desktop or personal computer in the early 1980s. The workstation of the late 1980s brought massive computing power under the control of individuals for the first time. The number of computers in the world climbed from 2 million in 1980 to perhaps 91.9 million in 1990 (Organization for Economic Cooperation and Development 1988c, 16). The speed of invention and product innovation in the microelectronics industry has not slackened.

The output of the global electronics complex grew more than 13 percent annually from 1965–1985. In 1985 the output of that industry equaled that of the world automobile industry (about 4 percent to 5 percent of world product) and exceeded that of the world steel industry (Castells and Tyson 1988, 57). If the last long economic wave were based on the automobile and inexpensive oil, as suggested earlier, then this signals the changing of the guard. The range of applications for microelectronics continues to grow. For instance, use of robotics in manufacturing appears to be in its early stages.

We remain uncertain about the international implications of these developments, but they promise to be quite dramatic. Consider their impact on the East-West relationship and the breakdown of communism. Slowing economic growth in the Soviet Union and Eastern Europe became noticeable in the 1960s. Among many other reasons for the slowing, those countries lagged in the development and use of new electronic technology. The Soviet Union actually abolished the computer division of its Academy of Sciences in 1962, and the Soviet government long seemed as concerned about the potential dangers that distributed computing posed for social control as with the economic benefits of the technology.

Their decision in the late 1960s and early 1970s to pursue détente with the West and to seek Western technology through trade had many bases, but perception of a linkage between technological weakness and growth difficulties was important. The resulting technological infusion may have helped somewhat, but it was limited (for reasons described earlier). It also began to be obvious that the highly centralized political-economic system of the Communist countries was reasonably effective in taking standardized industrial production technology and reproducing it on a large-scale, but the system did not quickly and smoothly diffuse new technology. Moreover, electronic technology in the West allowed smaller-scale, more flexible manufacturing, something that Soviet centralized planning could not efficiently oversee and which therefore threatened it.

Continued economic stagnation (relative to earlier rapid growth)[22] increased pressures not only to develop or import the technology but to adopt a decentralized political-economic system better suited to its diffusion and effective use. Although many other factors were at work, this helps us understand the Gorbachev emphasis in the 1980s on "restructuring," or *perestroika*.[23] Changes

---

[22]Although official Soviet data put annual GNP growth between 1980 and 1988 at 3 percent to 4 percent, CIA estimates set it at 1 percent to 1.5 percent (*Newsweek*, March 13, 1989, 29).

[23]In a speech during November 1989, Gorbachev explained his reforms in terms of the need to catch up to the West technologically.

necessary to accomplish the restructuring affect the entire Soviet social system and its relationship with the outside world. That restructuring, once begun, proved impossible to control and the Communist system collapsed.

Many Central and Eastern European countries also eagerly adopted microelectronic technology in part because they faced labor shortages, and the modern manufacturing systems based on electronics save labor as well as improve quality. In sharp contrast, nearly all Southern countries have considerable labor surpluses. They thus look at microelectronics with ambivalence. On the one hand, they often cannot be competitive internationally without it; on the other, it displaces labor. For instance, the introduction of robotics into the Japanese automobile industry made it impossible in 1980 for the South Koreans, with a wage rate of $1 per hour, to be competitive, even though the Japanese rate was $7 per hour (Castells and Tyson 1988, 70). The Koreans had to adopt the robotic techniques themselves. The diversification and dynamism of NIC economies, such as South Korea and Taiwan, mean that other sectors can absorb the displaced labor. For many LDCs, however, the technologies intensify unemployment problems.

COMMUNICATIONS

The communications revolution combines innovation in transmission media, such as satellites in geostationary orbit 22,300 miles above the equator, with computer equipment, such as that which can oversee the simultaneous laser transmission of many separate communications through the same glass fiber.

Although communications technology already allows near-instantaneous contact around the world, the introduction of the rapidly improving equipment is far from complete, and the full impact will be felt for decades. It is difficult to even measure the progress of that implementation. One indication of its speed is that between 1985 and 1991 the number of minutes of international phone traffic expanded from about 3.5 billion to an 18.8 billion. Because increasing portions of such traffic are devoted to rapid transfers of large volumes of data, rather than to slower voice communications, the growth in international information flows is even more rapid.

In the 1960s, IBM began construction of a global network for electronic mail (messages sent at high data transfer speeds), which connected 145 countries by 1989. In 1987 it carried 3 trillion characters of information solely among IBM employees, and IBM allows network use by others.[24] The proliferation of such networks and of connections among them creates an entirely new set of state security concerns. In 1989, the West German government arrested several spies working for East Germany who had apparently spent years searching through international research and defense electronic networks.

---

[24]European national telephone companies (state-owned) long restricted flexibility in data communication relative to what U.S. citizens take for granted. European recognition that they lagged behind not just the United States, but some of the NICs, strengthened their resolve that government barriers fall by 1992.

The day has not yet arrived when the average citizen in Russia, China, or Latin America can pick up a telephone and call nearly anyone in the world without restrictions, much less transmit significant volumes of data to that person. Nonetheless, satellite dishes on rooftops throughout Latin America now receive cable television stations from North America (often without payment). An excellent satellite telephone system ties together Indonesian islands, and Indian villagers can obtain national television broadcasts on at least a single community-owned set. Moreover, Chinese citizens continue to listen to radio broadcasts from the Voice of America, the British Broadcasting Corporation, and other Western sources, despite prohibitions. Domestic and international social mobilization, one of the most important forces underlying change in world politics, depends in part on these new technologies and their advance promises to be steady.

OTHER TECHNOLOGIES OF IMPORTANCE

American Indians and Australian Aborigines can attest to the international impact of transportation and have reason to wish that long-distance sailing had never been developed. More recently and less dramatically, technological change in transportation affected Egypt. Most Persian Gulf oil en route to Europe flowed through its Suez canal until the development of the supertanker, incapable of using the canal and traveling instead around Africa's Cape of Good Hope. That new system, encouraged by interim closure of the canal in the 1950s, cost Egypt very substantial canal revenues. Transportation technologies have not evolved as dramatically in recent years as those in communications. Whereas the cost of a trans-Atlantic phone call dropped by a factor of 10 between 1970 and 1990, air transport costs decreased only by 60 percent, and ocean cargo costs were stable. Nonetheless, we can expect some further progress in transportation.

High temperature superconductivity is a technology that could usher in unpredictable changes in global relations. Japanese, American, and European scientists spent perhaps $320 million in 1988 on this new technology in both cooperative and competitive search for scientific breakthroughs and commercial applications. Improved electric power transmission over long distances is one possible application. Already the United States imports electricity from Canada, and one can imagine much more extensive interstate networks. Another feasible application is faster and less expensive rail transport, using magnetically levitated trains, potentially increasing rail competition with airlines in the market connecting countries.

Biogenetic engineering could potentially be the basis for a second "green revolution," which would have dramatic international consequences. The field is very new: Researchers cloned the first gene in 1973; entrepreneurs established Genentech, the first company in the field, in 1976; and scientists did not express the first plant gene in another plant species until 1983 (Office of Technology Assessment 1986, 362). Imparting to grains such as wheat or rice the ability to fix nitrogen from the air, rather than requiring nitrogen fertilizers, might be one breakthrough in a second revolution. Improved resistance to drought could be another. The industry may ultimately build such advances on what have been called "designer genes." Such developments could greatly increase food production and economic prospects in currently food deficient countries of the Third World. Conversely, countries reliant on agricultural exports, such as the United States, Canada, Australia, Argentina, and increasingly the EC, could lose markets.[25] Perhaps the most exciting single effort in this field is the Human Genome Project, assigned the task of determining the function of all 50,000–100,000 human genes. Early in the twenty-first century it will lead to treatment for many genetic diseases; it could also lead some states into genetic engineering experiments.

The biogenetic field already has begun to raise issues of international law. The major question concerns the responsibility of states for the negative consequences outside their borders of new organisms that they might release into the environment. The Trail Smelter case of 1941 established the principle of such state responsibility (Wiegele 1990, 99).

Energy technology has an important influence on both military and economic relations among states. New solar technologies, or breakthroughs in nuclear fusion, would certainly affect world politics, differentially benefiting various states. The emergence of an oil-based global economy after World War I illustrates the international importance of energy. The United Kingdom, with fairly plentiful coal supplies but little known oil, somewhat reluctantly converted its navy to a more efficient oil-fired fleet. The United States and the U.S.S.R. were able to do so with more enthusiasm, given their status as the two dominant world oil producers. Through its decision, Britain effectively made a long-term commitment to involvement in the Middle East. Germany and France recognized the same realities, which led to intense competition among the European powers for position in the region. After World War II the United States, although then still self-sufficient in oil, picked up the commitment to the Middle East, in part to guarantee supplies for its new allies and to deny them to its new adversaries.

Oil-trade volume now exceeds, by a considerable margin, world trade in any other category (see Figure 16.3) and the Middle East retains its pivotal position. Although the percentage contribution of oil and natural gas to the total energy budget of the world is now diminishing, great power rivalry over vast stretches of oil-rich desert real estate is unlikely to disappear in the near future.

CONCLUSION

Technologies now spread quickly around the globe; advancing microelectronic and communication techniques will further accelerate that diffusion. In the last 200 years many new technologies have greatly improved collective human well-being, including our life expectancies. Much technological advance promises still greater well-being for the average person, and perhaps even the narrowing of

[25]Other observers (consider their structuralist orientation) suggest that the West might be able to adapt to new conditions the agricultural crops that the Third World now exports (such as coffee), and thereby undercut Southern export earnings.

gaps between rich and poor. Expectations of such developments are at the heart of the modernist worldview.

Advances in communication, transportation, and military technologies have integrated the world and made states more permeable. Transnational interactions, with potential for both good and harm, have intensified. Many modernists are also globalists and argue that advance in these technologies may now be bringing us to a cusp between old and new interstate political relationships. To them, new military capabilities make the old state-centric, power politics relationships and behavior patterns unsustainable, at the same time that communication and transportation developments make possible new transnational relationships.

But in the short- and mid-run, the historic state struggle for relative position continues, even concerning technologies that ultimately hold the promise of global benefits. Because of the decline of U.S. leadership, and especially if the global economic downturn of the 1970s and 1980s persists, those struggles may well intensify. Once again, the realist worldview can also help us make sense of the world. In general, modernists fail to develop fully the mixed political ramifications of their technological optimism.[26] This chapter began that elaboration.

---

[26]The attention by Naisbett (1982), for example, to the impact of technology on social and political systems, seldom goes beyond foreseeing "electronic democracy," the need for "high touch" to balance "high tech," or other extrapolations of the microelectronic and communications revolutions. Most often, technological optimism translates uncritically into economic and political optimism.

Chapter 17

ENVIRONMENTAL CONSTRAINTS

In 1970 international relations textbooks referred to the broader environment of politics only incidentally or in geopolitical discussions of the interaction between resources, power, and conflict.[1] The greenhouse effect was essentially unknown, as were ozone holes in the Antarctic and acid rain. By 1980 many textbooks began to recognize the importance of these issues and of arguments concerning population pressure on the ecosystem; the macroenvironment (population, food, energy, and pollution) became a standard topic in texts.

In 1980 world politics textbooks referred to the microenvironment (bacteria and viruses) only historically, for example by noting the Bubonic Plague, which killed one-third to one-half of all Europeans between 1347 and 1350 (Heise 1988, 20). The growing plague of acquired immunodeficiency syndrome (AIDS) in the 1980s and 1990s brought human attention back to the microenvironment. Although its primary focus is the macroenvironment, this chapter begins by considering briefly how an epidemic like AIDS can influence world politics.

MICROENVIRONMENT

William McNeill (1976) traced the long-term relationship between disease and human social development in his classic book, *Plagues and Peoples*. Between 1300–1700 Europe experienced a series of major plagues as it gradually established regular contact with the rest of the world and imported its diseases. By 1700 Europe had largely "domesticated" epidemic diseases from around the world and European population began a major and steady expansion (McNeill 1976, 224–225). Having adapted to many diseases also increased the edge of the Europeans over other populations to which they carried a lethal combination of illnesses. McNeill

---

[1]The textbook of Sprout and Sprout (1971) broke this pattern. They argued that although the study of "high politics" and war dominated international politics, a no less lethal danger was "worldwide catastrophe through progressive disorganization and destruction of the ecology of the earth" (1971, v). Pirages (1978) provided another extensive early treatment.

points out that the Spanish conquest of Mexico, pitting 600 men under Cortez against the Aztec Empire, benefited from superior military technology and the local alliances that Cortez formed. The Spanish also brought smallpox to the New World, however, and it ravaged the Aztec Empire during the conquest. More generally, Old World diseases help explain the precipitous collapse of both New World populations and their civilizations.

Their own diseases, especially malaria, long protected the Africans; malaria once killed about one-half of all Europeans attempting to penetrate the interior. The manufacture of quinine after 1820, and its widespread use by 1850, finally opened Africa to the Europeans (Headrick 1981).

The impact of disease on human relations is not necessarily a thing of the past. As late as World War I, a global influenza epidemic (1917–1918) killed 20 million or more, helped by the large troop movements of the war and the weakened condition of many peoples. McNeill concludes:

> Even without mutation, it is always possible that some hitherto obscure parasitic organism may escape its accustomed ecological niche and expose the dense human populations that have become so conspicuous a feature of the earth to some fresh and perchance devastating mortality....Infectious disease which antedated the emergence of humankind will last as long as humanity itself, and will surely remain, as it has been hitherto, one of the fundamental parameters and determinants of human history. (McNeill 1976, 289–291)

Does AIDS, recognized only in 1981, perhaps constitute a modern version of the plagues that historically altered the course of human events? Experts estimate that about 2 million cases of AIDS had developed globally through 1992 (about 200,000 in the United States), and the WHO guessed that more than 10 million people carried the virus by 1992 (more than 1 million in the United States).[2] The rate of human immunodeficiency virus (HIV) spread is uncertain. In the early 1990s the number of infections in some parts of Africa and Asia doubled about every eighteen months. Extrapolations by WHO suggested that HIV will infect 40 million humans by 2000. Because AIDS in the developed world has been most heavily concentrated in certain populations, especially among male homosexuals and intravenous drug users, there appear natural obstacles to rapid spread. Moreover, behavioral practices in these populations are changing. On the other hand, more than one-third of all those infected globally are now women. Thus all forecasts must be treated with some skepticism.

Incidence is lower in Eastern Europe and in much of Asia than in Western Europe or Latin America.[3] AIDS incidence in Africa is especially high, and although precise statistics do not exist, about one-half of cases worldwide may be on that continent. Those in developing countries are in especially great danger because other sexually transmitted diseases such as chlamydia, syphilis, and gonorrhea are more prevalent; genital sores from untreated diseases facilitate the

[2]Population Reference Bureau, *Population Today* 17, no. 2 (February 1989), 4.

[3]Medical practices in Romania before the revolution left behind a large-scale problem among children, however.

spread of HIV. Because of this mode of transmission, AIDS is predominantly a heterosexual disease in the Caribbean and sub-Saharan Africa. Two frightening estimates are that 1 million of the 8.5 million people in Malawi could be dead of AIDS before 2000, as could 10 percent of the 10 million people in Zimbabwe. The rate of infection is growing even more rapidly in South Africa's population of 42 million.

To put the worldwide AIDS epidemic in context, 5 million children die *every year* from diarrhea (or 50 million in a decade from that single cause), cigarette smoke–related disease claims perhaps 2.5 million people annually, and 1 million die from malaria in Africa alone. The economic impact of AIDS is, however, relatively greater per death, because 90 percent of those who die are between twenty and forty-nine years of age (and thus are economically productive), and because the costs of treatment during the prolonged illness induced by AIDS is high. One study suggests that the total economic cost to just seven countries in Africa by 1990 was $980 million. AIDS patients occupy 25 percent of all hospital beds in some central African hospitals (Heise 1989, 130).

How might the continued spread of AIDS affect interstate politics? One hypothesis is that it could give rise to a substantial program of global cooperation:

> But with farseeing leadership, this great human disaster could lead to rescue and interim management by some international consortium in the name of humanity. As more countries need help, this management could become a sort of new Marshall Plan, a stepping stone to a new global order....In the next few years, the challenge of coping with AIDS at all levels could give the world a new sense of planet-wide interdependence and responsibility for human survival and for the future. (Platt 1987, 45)

That idealistic image of global response has often run aground on the shoals of individual state interest. In fact, the epidemic has to date affected world politics in a somewhat different way. Selected countries, like the Central European states that managed to avoid high incidence of the disease, look with increasing suspicion at those who might bring it from the outside. Many countries screen foreigners or put some AIDS-related restrictions on their travel.[4] In 1988 Cuba became the only country in the world to mandate human immunodeficiency virus testing of all citizens. It consigned all carriers to an isolated camp, raising international concerns of human rights violations.

States, not the global community, have organized most responses to the epidemic. Individual country programs of AIDS research offer global benefit, should they be successful. The French and U.S. medical efforts, which led to identification of the virus in 1983, and the many national research teams around the world, all make essential contributions to the control of AIDS. Communication of results among these teams is very rapid—regular global conferences help. Individual country costs of the disease are sufficiently great to justify high levels of individual state expenditure, the results of which are a global collective good

---

[4]Heisse (1989, 122); the United States denies entrance to those infected.

(in the terms of Chapter 6, the group of states served by a potential treatment for AIDS is privileged). In addition drug companies undertake their own research in the hopes of being able to capture, through patent protection, at least some of the public good that an AIDS vaccine would produce.

The logic of collective action, which resurfaces repeatedly in global affairs, suggests, however, that there is little incentive for many countries to make substantial individual contributions to AIDS research. Why should a small LDC spend a significant fraction of its governmental budget on AIDS research, when that expenditure might do no more than allow its scientists to keep up with the larger research programs of the United States or France? Thus a few large, developed countries with high incidence of AIDS undertake a disproportionate amount of AIDS research. The U.S. sponsors more than half of the basic research (Foreign Policy Association 1992, 76).

The collective international effort is important but not extensive. The WHO program in 1989 proposed a $95 million budget and a staff of 222 (Heise 1989, 126). In contrast, in 1991 the U.S. National Institute of Health spent $805 million and the Center for Disease Control budgeted $427 million—in fact, the United States also contributed 27 percent of the WHO budget in 1990. WHO has encouraged the establishment of national AIDS committees in more than 150 states, forty-eight of which developed three- to five-year plans for slowing the epidemic. Most of those focused on integration of AIDS education with family planning information, not on research.

The AIDS epidemic has had a major psychological effect globally, perhaps out of proportion to its physical impact. Just as the civil war in Yugoslavia taught Europeans born after World War II that the suffering of war was not simply something in the history books, and just as the LDC economic problems of the 1980s taught those born after the Great Depression that economic disasters are still possible, the AIDS epidemic is teaching all humanity that it has not yet banished plague from the world.[5] A resurgence of cholera in Latin America in the early 1990s reinforced the lesson. That recognition of human vulnerability in the face of the physical and biologic environment increasingly extends also to the macroenvironment, the subject to which we now turn.

POPULATION PRESSURES

More than any other single issue, ecoholists or neotraditionalists draw our attention to the rapid growth of the world's population. In conjunction with increased economic activity per capita, the size of that population places stress on the environment in two principal ways. First, the population demands increasing volumes of inputs from the environment; food, energy, and other raw materials are the most important. Second, the increasing economic activities of growing

[5]It is important to refer again to the modernist perspective and to rapid human progress. For instance, a federally funded project in the United States will spend perhaps $3 billion over fifteen years to identify all 3 billion bases of the human genetic structure. In addition to the obvious contribution this will make to progress against 3,000 inherited diseases, it will support unpredictable advances against bacteriological and viral infections.

population produce outputs that affect the environment; soil erosion, deforestation, and air and water pollution illustrate these outputs. In the rest of this chapter we look in turn at the growth of global population and then at its input requirements and output effects.

Chapter 1 identified the demographic transition as one of the most important contemporary global forces. That discussion made several points with respect to the growth of population:

1. Declining mortality caused an acceleration of population growth in Europe during the 1800s, and in the Third World since 1945. Fertility decreases have come more slowly.
2. The acceleration of global population growth rates reached a peak about 1970 (2 percent each year), and growth rates have declined somewhat since then. We can expect increasing annual increments to world population until about the end of the century, despite slowing percentage growth rates.
3. Population growth rates are much higher in the global South than in the North, and that will remain true for many decades. Some Northern countries even have declining populations and pronatalist policies.
4. Rapid population growth increases the size of the dependent population under fifteen, whereas slow population growth increases the size of the dependent population that is retirement age.

COMPETING PERSPECTIVES

A die-hard realist reaction to demographic trends might emphasize the growing share of global population located in the South and the contribution such population should eventually make to Southern power. Realists would also note how larger populations could affect the definition of state interests, especially if they force states to look externally for necessary food and resources. Will not some countries with powerful military forces use their power rather than risk slipping into economic or political chaos internally? For example, Iraq has one of the very highest annual rates of natural population growth in the world, nearly 4 percent.

Those approaching world population issues from the perspectives of political economy draw our attention to economic aspects. Both liberals and structuralists point to the strong relationship between income level and family size. In a somewhat rare show of agreement, both argue that individuals *desire* larger families when children provide net economic benefits, through contributions to family income or support of parents in old age. These net benefits diminish as family incomes rise and children are more likely to require financial support for education than to augment income. Moreover, as societal incomes increase, governmental programs begin to replace children in providing disability and old-age insurance. Liberals draw our attention more to national averages and individual cost-benefit logic, whereas structuralists point specifically to the plight of the poor and to the social structures that reinforce poverty. Yet both recognize much truth in the slogan that "development is the best contraceptive."

The ecoholist focuses on the environmental burden of population. Lester Brown (1987) argues that a significant portion of the Third World may be caught in a demographic trap. The rapid population growth in those countries places unsustainable demands on their food, resources, and environmental systems; they are destroying their support systems and their economic prospects. Rather than moving to higher incomes and lower birth rates, they may experience deterioration of incomes and higher death rates. That is, they may regress to the pretransition situation of traditional peoples, achieving a balance between birth and death rates only because both are high. In short, the **demographic trap** is a vicious cycle of high population growth, environmental damage, economic failures, and high population growth again. Many ecoholists are also globalists, and argue that both moral obligation and self-interest should engender collective assistance to the poorest countries.

In our discussion of AIDS we have already discussed one of the major global policy issues tied directly to population, namely health. The global community has been very important in helping LDCs raise average life expectancy from forty-eight in 1960 to sixty-three in 1992. For instance, in 1980 only 20 percent of the world's children received vaccinations against six common childhood diseases. The WHO's Expanded Program on Immunization raised that to 80 percent in 1991. We direct our attention here, however, to two other population-based issues: immigration and population control.

MIGRATION AND REFUGEES

On a day-to-day basis, population issues intrude on international politics primarily through the migration of people among countries. Population pressures and inadequate economic opportunities (even food scarcity such as that in nineteenth-century Ireland) *pushed* out of Europe most of the Europeans who emigrated in the 1800s and early 1900s; war and social unrest drove many others from home. The wealth of the New World *pulled* many to the Americas.

Although at one time most of the Americas and considerable portions of Africa were open to immigrants, in the 1990s there remain only three principal recipients: the United States, Canada, and Australia. Between 1820 and 1988 the United States accepted a total of 54.4 million migrants from around the world (76 percent from Europe and Canada).[6] In the 1980s the United States restricted normal immigration to 270,000 each year. Special provisions for various groups (such as Vietnamese "boat people"), however, raised actual influx to between 500,000 and 600,000 in most years of the decade. A new law in 1990 raised levels to 700,000 in the early 1990s; illegal immigration could increase the number to 1 million. Whereas in 1965 Europeans made up 90 percent of the legal total, by 1985 non-European regions contributed 90 percent.

In the early 1990s migration to Western Europe from the former communist countries became a major issue. In 1990, 1.3 million emigres from that region moved West. In 1992 Germany faced an influx that threatened to reach 500,000 (its constitution assured asylum seekers consideration); the inflow set off nationalistic rioting around refugee camps. Ironically, during the cold war the West encouraged the East to open its borders. Now the West wants the floodgates at least partially closed.

[6]*World Almanac*,1990, 560. The fact that Europe was able to rid itself of about 50 million people between 1846 and 1930 (Strange 1988, 68) certainly made its demographic transition easier—LDCs have no comparable relief valve today.

For much of the rest of the world, the issue is not legal or illegal migration but refugees—displaced peoples who at least initially hope to return one day to their own homeland. The number of such people climbed from 1.5 million in 1951 to over 18 million in 1990. Perhaps another 16 million live abroad as illegal aliens, and civil war and ecological disruption displace 15 million more within their own countries.[7] Table 17.1 shows the countries that contribute or accept more than 50,000 identified refugees.

TABLE 17.1
International Refugees and Asylum Seekers
(December 31, 1991)

Principal Countries of Origin	Numbers	Principal Countries of Asylum	Numbers
Afghanistan	6,600,800	Pakistan	3,594,000
Palestinians	2,525,000	Iran	3,150,000
Mozambique	1,483,500	Jordan	960,200
Ethiopia/Eritrea	752,400	Malawi	950,000
Somalia	717,600	Sudan	717,200
Liberia	661,700	Guinea	566,000
Angola	443,200	Ethiopia	534,000
Cambodia	392,700	Gaza Strip	528,700
Iraq	217,500	Thailand	512,700
Sri Lanka	210,000	Zaire	482,300
Burundi	208,500	West Bank	430,100
Rwanda	203,900	India	402,600
Sudan	202,500	Lebanon	314,200
Sierra Leone	181,000	Syria	293,900
Western Sahara	165,000	Germany	256,100
Vietnam	122,650	Tanzania	251,100
Yugoslavia	120,000	Côte d'Ivoire	240,000
China (Tibet)	114,000	Algeria	204,000
Burma	112,000	South Africa	201,000
Zaire	66,700	Zimbabwe	198,500
Mauritania	66,000	Uganda	165,450
Bangladesh	65,000	Zambia	140,500
Laos	63,200	Djibouti	120,000
Mali	53,000	Kenya	107,500
Iran	50,000	Burundi	107,000
		United States	68,800
		Hong Kong	60,000
		Senegal	53,100

Sources: U.S. Committee for Refugees, *World Refugee Survey 1992* (Washington, D.C.: U.S. Committee for Refugees, 1992), 32–34.

[7]Courtesy of the Office of the United Nations High Commissioner for Refugees and the U.S. Committee for Refugees (1989).

During 1988–1992 the largest single creator of refugees was the civil war in Afghanistan. Nationalism explains the circumstances of additional large numbers of those uprooted from their homes (such as the Palestinians and various peoples of the former Yugoslavia): They may be attracted to another country because their national group is dominant there, or what is more likely, a dominant national group that no longer wants them present may push them from their homeland. In many other refugee situations, such as Mozambique and Ethiopia, environmental pressure is the primary factor. Even when civil war or nationalism is the apparent cause (as in Haiti), population and resource pressures may fuel those fires.[8]

Although the office of the UNHCR coordinates some of the global refugee relief effort (for instance, for Palestinians), most refugees rely on the generosity of neighboring or otherwise interested states (such as the German efforts on behalf of former Yugoslavs). A few countries, including Iran, Jordan, Germany, Algeria, and Zimbabwe, have accepted especially large numbers of refugees for permanent resettlement, relative to their own populations. On the whole, however, as pressures to resettle refugees and immigrants have grown, willingness to accept them has declined.

POPULATION CONTROL EFFORTS

Fertility control is a second important international population issue. What policy responses have governments and the international community developed in reaction to rapid global population growth? Many individual states have acted. India established perhaps the longest running family planning program in the world in 1952. By 1982 approximately fifty-three developing countries made at least a weak effort to limit population growth.[9] Surprisingly, nearly as many LDCs still had very weak programs or none at all. It is interesting that the list of eleven LDCs with the most active programs included primarily NICs (see Table 17.2 and compare it with Table 13.8).[10] Commitment to family planning programs continues to grow, however. In 1976 only one-third of African governments thought fertility was too high—in 1989, this figure was two-thirds (although only one-half had programs to reduce fertility).

Success of family planning programs is not simple to measure, but there is little question that global contraceptive use has increased.[11] The portion of married couples in Latin America using contraception grew from under 20 percent in 1960 to nearly 80 percent in 1990; in Africa the rate went from 10 percent to 20 percent (World Resources Institute 1992, 77). Nonetheless, the World Fertility Survey of the United Nations, probably the largest international survey ever undertaken, found that the unmet demand for contraception in much of the Third World remains very

[8]Jacobson (1989) places the number of environmental refugees at 10 million.

[9]World Resources Institute (1988, 23). Programs differ so dramatically, from focusing on the health of the mother and child to applying tremendous pressure for family size limitation, that counting family planning programs becomes difficult (Hughes 1985, 197–198; Harf and Trout 1986, 190).

[10]Although the overlap could mean that population control efforts improve economic performance, it may mean that strong states can implement both effective economic programs and population control.

[11]Multicountry (cross-sectional) analyses indicate success for family planning programs (Bogue 1980; Lapham and Maudlin 1984).

TABLE 17.2
Contraceptive Prevalence and Availability

Country	Percentage of Married Couples Using Any Method	Country	Percentage of Married Couples Using Any Method
High Use		*Low Use*	
South Korea	77	Egypt	37
Mauritius	75	Morocco	36
Singapore	74	Algeria	36
China	71	Togo	34
Costa Rica	70	Botswana	33
Cuba	70	Bangladesh	31
Thailand	68	Grenada	31
Brazil	66	Guyana	31
Colombia	66	Bolivia	30
Turkey	63	Jordan	27
Sri Lanka	62	Kenya	27
		Nicaragua	27
		Guatemala	23
Moderate Use		Swaziland	20
Panama	*58*	Syria	20
St. Vincent	58	Iraq	15
Jamaica	55	Nepal	14
Mexico	53	Ghana	13
Antigua	53	Senegal	11
Trinidad/Tobago	53	Rwanda	10
Ecuador	53	Haiti	10
Lebanon	53	Sudan	9
Vietnam	53	Benin	9
Malaysia	51	Burundi	9
Tunisia	50	Pakistan	8
Paraguay	49	Malawi	7
Venezuela	48	Liberia	6
South Africa	48	Mali	5
Barbados	48	Lesotho	5
Indonesia	47	Nigeria	5
Peru	46	Uganda	5
Philippines	44	Côte d'Ivoire	3
Zimbabwe	43	Afghanistan	2
St. Lucia	43	Cameroon	2
India	43	Mauritania	1
Honduras	41	Yemen	1

Source: World Resources Institute, *World Resources 1992–93* (New York: Oxford University Press, 1992), 256–257.

high, implying a potential for even greater success with more active programs. For instance, if prospective parents avoided all undesired pregnancies in South Korea, Nepal, Pakistan, Sri Lanka, Guyana, Jamaica, Mexico, and Peru, annual population growth would drop by about one-third (population growth rates would drop by more than 1.0 percent).[12]

Northern states have increasingly supported family planning programs of LDCs. The United States took a position early, when President Johnson made support for LDC programs an important component of the overall foreign aid effort in 1965. It provided about two-thirds of the total international effort between 1965 and 1975 and still accounted for 45 percent in 1991. Many other states followed that lead.

Because of divisions in perspective on the population issue, the international community reacted more slowly than individual states. In 1967 the United Nations established its Fund for Population Activities (UNFPA). The United Nations also sponsored two World Population Conferences. A split characterized the meeting in Bucharest of 136 countries and numerous NGOs in 1974. More-developed countries stressed the urgency of attention to population control in the South. Some states in the South protested that Northern pressures for population control were an extension of colonialism, and a few even labeled it a form of genocide.

The 1984 UN conference in Mexico City differed dramatically. Most of the South had shifted in the interim to the viewpoint that population growth severely threatened their development prospects. China, which had taken an anti-North position in 1974, and which had thereafter adopted a one-child-per-family policy, exemplified the change. In essence, the ecoholist view had come to influence the South strongly. The eighth of twenty-two points in the final declaration of the conference indicates the new thinking:

> In the past decade, population issues have been increasingly recognized as a funda-
> mental element in development planning. To be realistic, development policies, plans
> and programmes must reflect the inextricable links between population, resources,
> environment and development. Priority should be given to action programmes
> integrating all essential population and development factors, taking fully into account
> the need for rational utilization of natural resources and protection of the physical
> environment and preventing its further deterioration. (Harf and Trout 1986, 195)

Ironically, the leading early supporter of Southern family planning, the United States, changed its position in 1984. Under the influence of classical liberal philosophy, and reflecting the Reagan administration's opposition to abortion, the U.S. delegation declined to support active family planning efforts (legal abortion is an element of population control programs in many countries). Instead, the United States argued that adoption of market-oriented economic policies would stimulate growth and thereby smaller family size. It also substantially reduced bilateral and multilateral economic support for family planning programs in the 1980s and ceased it altogether for countries using abortion. For example, the

---

[12]Lightbourne and Singh (1982, 46–47). On the other hand, in 1988 three countries in the developed world (Hungary, West Germany, and Denmark) experienced negative population growth and many others, especially in Eastern and Western Europe, are very near population stability. At least eight developed countries have programs in place to encourage population growth (Harf and Trout 1986, 191).

United States eliminated all of its funding for the UNFPA in 1985 and for subsequent years because of the organization's support for the Chinese family planning effort, which reportedly has applied coercion in abortion decisions.

RESOURCE SCARCITIES: FOOD

Which has been growing faster in the last forty years, world population or world food supply? The discussion of food in Chapter 1 gave you the basis for an intelligent answer to that question:

1. For the world as a whole, food production has grown faster than population in the postwar period. Per capita increases slowed substantially in the late 1980s.
2. This has often led to large surpluses and difficulties in disposal of those surpluses in many of the more-developed countries of the world, especially in Canada, Australia, the United States, and Western Europe.
3. Averages conceal much, and in Africa, especially in the countries of the Sahel, food production (up 40 percent between 1970 and 1991) has fallen short of population growth, causing starvation and increasing dependence on food from the outside world. A few other countries around the world face the same adverse trends. Similarly, within many countries, even the relatively prosperous states of Latin America, significant hunger persists.

These characteristics of the world food situation may suggest what seems a straightforward "solution" to world food problems. Given surpluses of food in the West and shortages in Africa, it is only necessary to transfer the food surpluses to where they are needed. Yet this book continually emphasizes that there are multiple sides to every issue; it is no different with respect to food.

COMPETING PERSPECTIVES ON GLOBAL FOOD SUPPLY

Not everyone believes that the world has a continuing ability to support the growing global population, even with such transfers of surplus food. Many ecoholists argue that the human population is running up against the carrying capacity of its environment. Lester Brown calculates that level to be 6 billion people, a limit the earth will reach shortly before the year 2000.[13]

Brown argues that the global trend of increasing food per capita is unsustainable, because it is destroying the environmental base for food production. Historically, bringing additional land under cultivation provided most of the per capita increase in food production; the opening in the nineteenth century of the agricultural potential of the American Midwest illustrated that process. More recently, expanded cultivation has used marginal land, often better suited for grazing or forest. Much newly cultivated soil has little long-term productivity. The soil under the Amazonian rain forests of Brazil, for example, is of considerably lower quality than that of most temperate regions. When exposed directly to tropical rains, water runoff easily removes (leaches) its limited nutrients.

[13]Brown (1981, 145). In contrast, Kahn, Brown, and Martel (1976) foresee no difficulty providing 15 billion people diets comparable to those of Americans today, using advanced agricultural technology.

The continuing process of agricultural land expansion creates two problems. First, it destroys forests and grasslands, important biologic resources. **Deforestation** (Table 17.3) has reduced global forest area to one-fifth of world land area (from perhaps one-fourth early in the century), and it will reduce it further to one-sixth by 2000; the Philippines have lost 2.4 acres of hardwood forests every

TABLE 17.3
Deforestation, Worst Cases of the 1980s

Regions and Countries	Forest Area (thousand hectares)	Annual Deforestation (thousand hectares)	Percent per year
Africa			
Algeria	1,777	40	2.3
Cote d'Ivoire	9,834	510	5.2
Guinea-Bissau	2,105	57	2.7
Liberia	2,040	46	2.3
Malawi	4,271	150	3.5
Mauritania	554	13	2.4
Niger	2,550	67	2.6
Nigeria	14,750	400	2.7
Zaire	177,590	370	0.2
Latin America			
Costa Rica	1,798	65	3.6
Guatemala	4,452	90	2.0
Honduras	3,997	90	2.3
Mexico	48,350	615	1.3
Nicaragua	4,496	121	2.7
Argentina	44,500	1,550	3.5
Brazil	514,480	2,323	0.5
Colombia	51,700	890	1.7
Ecuador	14,730	340	2.3
Paraguay	19,710	212	1.1
Peru	70,640	270	0.4
Venezuela	33,870	245	0.7
Asia			
Indonesia	116,895	620	0.5
Malaysia	20,996	255	1.2
Nepal	2,236	84	4.0
Sri Lanka	1,659	58	3.5
Thailand	15,675	379	2.4

Source: World Resources Institute, *World Resources 1988–89* (New York: Basic Books, 1988), 286–87; World Resources Institute, *World Resources 1992–1993* (New York: Oxford University Press, 1992, 286–287).

minute during the last fifty years.[14] A study by the UN Food and Agriculture Organization in 1991 reported that the global rate of deforestation had increased by 50 percent over a decade earlier. Second, the process degrades marginal land, and this land may after a time not even be suitable for its original use. In 1991 the UN Environment Programme reported moderate to extreme degradation on 11 percent of the earth's vegetated surface—an area equal to India and China combined (Table 17.4). Some of the land becomes desert after initial vegetation is removed. Every year **desertification** claims an area twice the size of Belgium (Postel 1989, 21).[15] In addition we appear to be mistreating even our high-quality agricultural land, by practices that allow substantial soil erosion. Citing U.S. Department of Agriculture sources, Brown estimates soil loss in the United States at 2 billion tons annually, twice the amount newly formed, and equivalent to 781,000 acres of cropland (Brown 1981, 18). Another estimate puts net loss of soil in the formerly very fertile Ethiopian highlands at 1 billion tons each year.

Between 1950 and 1976 world land devoted to cereals expanded from 590 to 720 million hectares, by 22 percent (Brown 1988b, 123). Between 1976 and 1988, it remained quite stable, in part because of these physical limits. In fact, cultivated land *per capita* is declining steadily. Growth in food production now comes overwhelmingly from increased productivity per unit of land rather than from cultivation

TABLE 17.4 Human-Induced Soil Degradation 1945 to Late 1980s		
	Total Degraded Area (million hectares)	*Degraded Area as a Percentage of all Vegetated Land*
World	1,964.4	17
Light Degradation	749.0	6
Moderate Degradation	910.5	8
Strong Degradation	295.7	3
Extreme Degradation	9.3	0
Africa	494.2	22
North and Central America	158.1	8
South America	243.4	14
Asia	748.0	20
Europe	218.9	23
Oceania	102.9	13

Source: World Resources Institute, *World Resources 1992–93* (New York: Basic Books, 1992), 290.

[14]Council on Environmental Quality (1981, 318–319). Such estimates are crude. So, too, is the guess that 0.6 percent of tropical rain forest is being cleared annually (World Resources Institute 1988, 71).

[15]Or does it? In 1991 studies using satellite measurement indicated that the Sahara expands and contracts much more each year than believed; between 1984 and 1990 the net change was a contraction (*Science News*, July 20, 1991, 38).

of more land. Even with some expansion of cultivation into marginal areas, the global average of 0.28 hectares of cropland per capita will drop to about 0.17 hectares in 2025.

Productivity increases require inputs, two of the most important being water and energy. In 1900 the world irrigated 40 million hectares; by 1989 the figure reached 236 million, and most of the increase has occurred since 1950. Much water used in agriculture, however, comes from unsustainable sources. In the United States, irrigated areas are now declining because farmers are depleting the aquifers that earlier sustained them, especially the Ogallala aquifer of the Great Plains. Irrigated area fell 7 percent from 1978 to 1988 (Brown 1989, 50). Similarly, the energy input to high-productivity agriculture may be unsustainable, because it draws on limited fossil fuels. Tractors and fertilizer manufacture use the most, although irrigation pumps require a substantial amount. Finally, much irrigation has led to salination of the land; perhaps one-fourth of the world's irrigated land is becoming too salty.

Water issues spill over into interstate politics; conflicts in the Middle East are among the most serious. In 1990 Turkey shut off the flow of the Euphrates to fill the Ataturk Dam. Doing so brought protests from two downstream countries, Syria and Iraq. Syria and Iraq nearly went to war in 1975 over the waters of that river. Israel, Jordan, and Syria continue to argue about the Jordan River, which supplies most of Israel's water. Future conflict between the Sudan and Egypt concerning the Nile is also quite possible. Obviously each of these disputes over water is also a potential basis for improved cooperation; the Mideast peace talks have raised water issues.

Those who fall generally into the modernist category reject such pessimism. Farmers have planted the high-yielding varieties of green revolution rice and wheat on less than one-third of grain-producing land globally, and on only 1 percent of such land in Africa (Wolf 1988, 139). Although green revolution techniques have also improved potential yields for other crops, like those more commonly grown in Africa (such as millet and sorghum), actual productivity on a considerable portion of the world's land is little changed since early in the century. Thus the potential for productivity growth appears great, simply with the adaptation of improved techniques already available. In addition, satellite sensors have detected substantial, perhaps massive groundwater beneath Egypt's Western Desert.

The Washington-based Consultative Group on International Agricultural Research (CGIAR) funds a network of thirteen international research centers (Table 17.5) that strive continually to push back the current technological limits.[16] But the next surge in agricultural productivity could owe much to the private sector. Biotechnologies, based on the development of recombinant DNA techniques in 1973, may promise food crops that need less chemical fertilizer and are more resistant to drought, soil salinity, and insects. In 1988 the U.S. Patent and Trademark Office issued the first patent in the world for a genetically altered animal (World Resources Institute 1988, 64). Genetically engineered farm animals should appear within a few years. By 1988 Monsanto had already invested $100 million in biotechnologies, and many other corporations were at work (Wolf 1988, 153).

[16]In 1989 CGIAR had a budget of $200 million, provided by forty-two donors.

TABLE 17.5
International Agricultural Research Centers

Year	Center and Location	Focus
1960	International Rice Research Institute (Philippines)	Improved rice varieties; germplasm collection bank
1966	International Maize and Wheat Improvement Center (Mexico)	Maize, wheat, barley, and triticale
1966	International Center of Tropical Agriculture (Colombia)	Beans, cassava, rice, and beef in the tropics of the Western hemisphere
1967	International Institute of Tropical Agriculture (Nigeria)	Cowpea, yam, cocoyam, sweet potato, cassava, rice, maize, beans, among others
1971	International Potato Center (Peru)	Potatoes in the Andes and lower tropics
1971	West Africa Development Association (Liberia)	Rice in West Africa
1972	International Crops Research Institute for the Semi-Arid Tropics (India)	Improved quantity and reliability of food production in the semi-arid tropics
1974	International Board for Plant Genetic Resources (Italy)	International network of genetic-resource (germplasm) centers
1974	International Food Policy Research Institute (U.S.)	Governmental and international agency intervention in national, regional and global food problems
1974	International Laboratory for Research on Animal Disease (Kenya)	Trypanosomiasis (transmitted by the tsetse fly) and theileriosis (transmitted by ticks)
1974	International Livestock Centre for Africa (Ethiopia)	Improved livestock production and marketing systems
1977	International Center for Agricultural Research in the Dry Areas (Syria)	Rain-fed agriculture in arid and semiarid regions in North Africa and West Asia
1980	International Service for National Agricultural Research (Netherlands)	National agricultural research systems

Source: World Resource Institute, *World Resources 1988–89* (New York: Basic Books, 1988), 55.

COMPETING PERSPECTIVES ON FOOD DISTRIBUTION

Let us assume away for the moment the potential problems of unsustainability in global food production and the possible unattainability of necessary future production gains and focus directly on the distributional issue. Let us at least temporarily accept Griffin's (1987, 17) view that "there is no world food problem, but there is a problem of hunger in the world."[17] Maldistribution of food itself, of income to purchase food, and of land and resources to produce food, all potentially contribute to the hunger problem. Let us begin with the distribution of food itself. Are global hunger problems easily resolved by food transfers?

The two categories of transfers are gifts (food aid) and sales (trade). Food gifts are a long-standing approach to the food distribution problem. In 1954 the U.S. Congress passed P.L. 480, better known as the Food for Peace Act. This seemed to be the perfect solution to the asymmetrical problems of food surpluses in the United States and shortages in countries such as India. In 1960 the United States gave away in this program, or sold on concessional terms, 27 percent of what it exported (Lewis and Kallab 1983, 236).

Such largesse subsequently decreased substantially, however, for two reasons. First, the U.S. surpluses nearly disappeared in the early 1970s when crop failures in Africa, Asia, and the Soviet Union combined to create a trade demand sufficient to absorb them. Second, those taking a look at the economic impact on recipient countries of long-term food aid, whether liberal or structuralist, began to argue that the assistance depressed local food prices and therefore the profits of local farmers. This economic disincentive to production retarded growth in indigenous supplies and thus perpetuated the very food shortages the aid was supposed to resolve.[18]

Whatever the reason, international food transfers increasingly consist of trade rather than aid. In the early post–World War II period there was little world grain trade (grain trade is the most important food trade) (Table 17.6). In 1950 the United States and Canada exported grain to Western Europe, continuing a pattern established a century earlier. Very little grain trade existed globally outside of this bilateral linkage.

In the 1960s and 1970s Asia became a significant importer, as did Africa in the 1970s and 1980s. The Soviet Union and Eastern Europe avoided importing in the period between the Soviet collectivization of agriculture (the 1930s) and the early 1970s, primarily by belt tightening.[19] For internal political reasons, and reflecting the more relaxed atmosphere of the détente period, Soviet shortages in

---

[17]Hopkins and Puchala (1978), Hayami and Ruttan (1985), and Hollist and Tullist (1987) present competing political economy approaches to global food issues.

[18]Maxwell and Singer (1979) provide a good review of the impact of food aid given in different ways. See Bauer and Yamey (1984) for a presentation of the liberal argument that foreign assistance supports state intervention.

[19]Soviet leader Khrushchev did strike a deal with the West for grain imports in 1964, but it was not as substantial as those of the 1970s. The large purchase of cereals in 1972 initiated a longer-term trade exchange.

TABLE 17.6
Annual World Grain Trade (Billion Metric Tons)

	1934-38	1950	1960	1970	1980	1988
North America	5	23	42	54	131	119
Latin America	2	1	(1)	4	(10)	(11)
Western Europe	(10)	(22)	(25)	(22)	(16)	22
Eastern Europe/U.S.S.R.	1	0	1	(1)	(46)	(27)
Africa	0	0	(5)	(4)	(15)	(28)
Asia	(1)	(6)	(19)	(37)	(63)	(89)
Oceania	3	3	6	8	19	14

Sources: Barry B. Hughes, *World Futures* (Baltimore, Md.: Johns Hopkins University, 1985), 133; Lester R. Brown, "Reexamining the World Food Prospect", in *State of the World 1989*, ed. Lester R. Brown (New York: W. W. Norton, 1989), 45.

Note: Parentheses indicate imports.

the early 1970s led to a substantial movement into the world market. North American and Australian exports rose to meet the increased trade demand. The green revolution technologies and the policies of the EC (see the discussion of the EC in Chapter 8) transformed Western Europe from a significant net importer to a substantial exporter.

The dramatically changed pattern of world grain trade in the 1970s and 1980s had international political repercussions. Some realists and cold war hardliners began to see the control of food exports as a source of international power. Proposals surfaced in the 1970s to use food exports to the Middle East as a bargaining tool for obtaining oil at favorable prices—*food for crude*. The logic of power politics prevailed when the Soviets invaded Afghanistan in 1979. One of the first retaliatory actions of the Carter administration was to limit grain shipments to the Soviet Union to the lowest level permitted under the grain treaty between the superpowers. The effectiveness of such embargoes, discussed in Chapter 4, is not generally very high, and that proved true in this instance.[20]

Two problems arise from food trade. The first is the political leverage it may provide exporters. The second is that many LDCs cannot afford imports over a long period. Thus most discussion on distributional issues inevitably returns to proposals for facilitating increased production in regions such as Africa. Why is production in many parts of the world inadequate to meet local needs?

Liberals draw our attention to inappropriate state intervention, particularly the tendency of Third World governments to mandate food prices below

[20]In contrast to the seeming inefficiency of international embargoes, domestic efforts to deny food to local populations have been much more successful. In the 1980s both the Ethiopian and Sudanese governments successfully denied grain trade and grain aid to regional populations that rejected central authority. Even in these instances, however, the international aid community was able to provide some relief to the northern portions of Ethiopia, and in 1988–1989 the United States and other donors airlifted food to the southern half of the Sudan, against the will of the government.

those that a naturally functioning market would establish.[21] The reasons Third World governments set low food prices range from the humanitarian to the selfish. The humanitarian impulse comes from a recognition that many of their people would be less well nourished, or even starve, should they allow prices to rise. Even this logic can be self-serving, because LDC governments seek to placate the urban dwellers of the capital and other major cities so as to defuse political instability. Whatever the motivation, low prices are literally counterproductive.

Government intervention in the market similarly aggravates the persistent food surpluses of the advanced capitalist states. Efficient production has created surpluses, depressed prices, and lowered farm incomes. Among the new economic policies growing out of the Great Depression period were farm price supports, which required the government to pay farmers the difference between market prices and a floor price. In Europe the political compromises necessary to secure French participation in the EC resulted in a Common Agricultural Policy with especially strong protection for farmers. In both the United States and the EC the subsidies to farmers allow them to remain on the farm and encourage them to overproduce. Japan's commitment to its farmers is even greater. In the 1980s Japanese government direct or indirect subsidies provided more than 60 percent of the gross receipts of farmers, about twice that in the EC or the United States (World Resources Institute 1992, 105).

The clear relationship between government policy and either underproduction or overproduction suggests a seemingly straightforward way out of the problem—allow prices to rise in regions with food shortages. That is not simple, however. When the Egyptian government tried to raise subsidized prices in 1977, large riots ensued, and the government officials retreated.

One cannot discuss the distribution of food without discussing the distribution of income. If the citizens of Niger had higher incomes, there would be no food problems there. The structuralist perspective carries the argument one step further, however, arguing that the problem is not limited to income distribution but extends to the distribution of land (the key production factor). Large landowners are much more likely to use their land for nonfood crops targeted to the export market. Colonial processes in much of the world concentrated considerable land in a few hands, and current political economic structures often maintain those concentrations.[22] Table 17.7 shows countries around the world with nonegalitarian land distributions.[23] One can imagine the problems in Kenya, for instance, where

[21]D. Gale Johnson (1978, 275) indicates the size of the gap between local and world food prices that government policies can create; between 1968 and 1972 Indian farmers received $91 to $136 per ton of rice, but imported rice cost $175.

[22]In 1975 more than one-half the agricultural land in fifteen African and Latin American countries was devoted to export crops rather than food production. In another fifteen countries more than one-third of the land produced coffee, cotton, sugar, cocoa, bananas, tea, rubber, and other export crops (Christensen 1978, 186).

[23]The countries in Table 17.7 report at least 10 percent of land held in both holdings of less than five hectares and holdings of more than fifty hectares. Unequal land holdings could represent an appropriate response to variable land quality within some countries.

TABLE 17.7
Land Distribution, Worst Cases of 1980

Regions and Countries	Agricultural Area: Distribution by Size of Holdings (Percentage)		
	Less Than 5 Hectares	Between 5 and 50 Hectares	More Than 50 Hectares
Africa			
Algeria	14	63	23
Kenya	47	13	40
Liberia	36	35	29
Zaire	60	5	35
Zambia	34	19	47
Regional Average	60	26	15
Latin America			
Dominican Republic	13	30	57
El Salvador	20	31	57
Guatemala	13	24	63
Jamaica	28	17	55
Suriname	28	28	45
Regional Average	13	20	68
Middle East and Asia			
Cyprus	31	53	16
Israel	14	14	71
Jordan	19	53	28
Philippines	51	37	12
Saudi Arabia	10	32	58
Turkey	20	68	12
Regional Average	41	42	17
Western Europe			
Italy	16	39	45
Norway	16	55	29
Portugal	20	24	56
Regional Average	8	56	36
North America			
Regional Average	0	5	95

Source: World Resources Institute, *World Resources 1988–89* (New York: Basic Books, 1988), 276–277.

the land is split primarily between very small and quite large landholdings, with few midsized properties. The worst regional pattern is that of Latin America, in which two-thirds of the land is in holdings greater than fifty hectares, but where most farmers are on small and midsized holdings. That

pattern is a remnant of colonialization, and remains a source of great political and social instability.

GLOBAL ATTENTION TO FOOD PROBLEMS

What role can the international community play in ameliorating world food problems? A global food regime now exists to limit food shortages. We have already noted the network of thirteen research institutions under the sponsorship of the CGIAR. A cooperative effort of the Rockefeller Foundation and the Mexican government in 1941 successfully developed new wheat varieties that could triple traditional yields (with fertilizer, pesticides, and sufficient water). That led in 1960 to the founding of the first permanent center, the International Rice Research Institute in the Philippines. CGIAR itself came into being in 1971 and is an informal association of governments, IOs, and foundations that supports the centers (World Resources Institute 1988, 55).

The founders of the UN in 1945 established the United Nations Food and Agriculture Organization (FAO). It provides information and technical assistance to member states. In 1963 and 1970, the FAO sponsored World Food congresses (Riggs and Plano 1988, 63). The most famous of FAO meetings was the World Food Conference in 1974, organized in response to the global food crisis of 1972–1974. At that time the global community established the Global Information and Early Warning System (GIEWS) in an effort to reduce the risk of extensive, unanticipated food shortages. It also established the World Food Council to maintain attention to world food problems. It also set up an International Fund for Agricultural Development (IFAD), which began operations in 1977 with an initial capitalization of $1 billion and the charge of assisting the poorest LDCs (Hopkins and Puchala 1978, 31). In 1992 the UN's World Food Programme had a budget of $3 billion and handled over 25 percent of the world's food aid. It emphasizes using food to support development projects rather than simply providing aid.

In the 1970s the World Bank shifted its priorities toward food. Before 1958 only 8 percent of its total lending supported agriculture and rural development, whereas that rate increased to 32 percent by 1981 (World Bank 1981, 13). Because of LDC debt and other priorities, however, World Bank lending to agriculture fell to about 20 percent of its total disbursements in the late 1980s.

The technical assistance and relief NGOs are also important forces in efforts to increase production and consumption where it is most urgently needed. These include Oxfam, the International Red Cross, and Care. Increasingly, such organizations have turned their attention to long-term initiatives for increasing food production capability rather than reacting only to the problems of immediate food scarcity. In addition, a growing global mass movement supports a wide variety of solutions to world hunger, crossing over worldview differences. The global Hunger Project exemplifies that movement (Hunger Project 1985). In the

United States a related group, Results, lobbies actively on domestic food legislation with an eye to ending world hunger.[24]

Despite the effort by all of these IGOs and NGOs, periodic regional food shortages still appear. For instance, in 1992, famine put two-fifths of Somalia's population of 5 million at risk. By one estimate, at least 300,000 died in 1992. One frequent proposal for dealing with food shortages is to maintain a global grain reserve. Calculations of the amount of grain needed to assure that 95 percent of all shortages could be met suggest quite modest costs for such a scheme—about $0.5 billion each year. To put that figure in context, U.S. citizens spend $10 billion annually on admissions to movies and theaters. Why then is the proposal not implemented? First, producers in the grain exporting countries effectively maintain adequate reserves now—the problem has always been distribution, not total food stores. Second, there would probably be considerable difficulties administering it on a public rather than a private basis. For instance, acquisition rules for food buffer stocks in the EC and the United States have almost always led to surpluses larger than desired.

The crux of the problem is not storing food, but getting it to those who need it. In 1992 the UN finally had to send troops to Somalia in order to help distribute food aid, and the United States had to restore order and to begin simply flooding the region with food. Often by the time the global community becomes aware of a problem and decides to act, the situation has become severe.

RESOURCE SCARCITIES: RAW MATERIALS

A variety of raw materials support the world's economy in the same fundamental way that food supports the world's population. Chromium, cobalt, gold, manganese, nickel, petroleum, platinum, silver, tin, and tungsten are among the raw materials for which the world depends on a handful of major producers. For instance, Zaire, South Africa, Canada, and Malaysia have provided at some time since 1970 more than 40 percent of the world's total production of cobalt, gold, nickel, and tin, respectively.

Are there dangers in the concentration of mineral production in the hands of a few states? South Africa is a major producer and exporter of several key commodities, including chromium, diamonds, gold, manganese, and platinum. The difficulties associated with transferring political power to the black majority in that country raise concern about civil disorder, and even suggest the possibility of an anti-Western government that might intentionally use mineral export restraints as a weapon. Unintentional disruption of supplies during prolonged civil unrest is a

---

[24]Discussion of the regime that seeks to end world hunger would be incomplete without mention also of transnational, nongovernmental actors. The five great international grain trading houses, Cargill, Continental, Bunge, Louis Dreyfus, and André, draw much attention (Morgan 1979). It may appear that these companies control the global grain system and hold the key to solving food problems. It is true that they control international distribution of grain and are very important forces in making grain a fungible commodity. They do not, however, affect production or consumption levels in any fundamental way.

serious possibility. South Africa is unlikely under any government to consciously withhold raw materials from the world market, however. A revolutionary interval and new social pressures from a black majority would actually
increase the need for revenues from mineral sales. Many states, like the United
States, hold stockpiles of strategic materials to carry them through such disruptions, whatever the reason.

We should not ignore the damage that disruption of mineral exports, especially from countries like South Africa or Russia, could do to the world's economy.
The metallic mineral and precious stone trade are remarkably small compared with
the world trade in petroleum, however (Table 17.8). Copper is the largest nonenergy
raw material in global trade value, but the value of global copper trade is less than
3 percent that of oil. Moreover, the world economy is much more vulnerable to
shortages in energy. Although energy constitutes only 5 percent to 10 percent of the
GNP of most countries, without energy the economies would absolutely grind to a
halt. Thus we focus our attention here on the *master resource*, energy.

TABLE 17.8
World Commodity Export Concentration, 1982–1984 Average

Commodity	World Market Billion $	Major LDC Exporters (Percent Of World Market)		
Petroleum	240.5	Saudi Arabia (17.9)	Mexico (5.7)	Iraq (5.7)
Sugar	10.7	Cuba (43.8)	Brazil (5.3)	Thailand (3.3)
Coffee	9.9	Brazil (21.9)	Colombia (16.2)	Mexico (4.6)
Copper	7.5	Chile (22.9)	Zambia (11.9)	Zaire (7.5)
Timber	16.4	Malaysia (12.0)	Indonesia (3.3)	Philippines (1.6)
Iron ore	6.9	Brazil (23.9)	India (5.9)	Liberia (4.1)
Rubber	3.1	Malaysia (45.6)	Indonesia (25.7)	Thailand (15.7)
Cotton	6.6	Egypt (6.7)	Pakistan (3.6)	Sudan (3.4)
Rice	3.9	Thailand (25.6)	Pakistan (9.6)	China (7.0)
Tobacco	4.3	Brazil (10.8)	Turkey (6.2)	Greece (4.4)
Maize	9.7	Argentina (7.3)	Thailand (4.0)	Yugoslavia (1.4)
Tin	2.1	Malaysia (28.7)	Indonesia (15.1)	Thailand (12.4)
Cocoa	2.3	Ivory Coast (26.9)	Ghana (14.3)	Nigeria (11.7)
Tea	2.2	India (23.8)	Sri Lanka (19.6)	China (12.6)
Palm oil	2.1	Malaysia (69.4)	Indonesia (5.7)	Papua New Guinea (2.0)
Beef	7.5	Argentina (4.2)	Brazil (2.7)	Uruguay (2.3)
Bananas	1.4	Costa Rica (16.6)	Honduras (15.1)	Colombia (11.5)
Wheat and meslin	16.7	Argentina (6.2)	Greece (0.8)	Turkey (0.4)
Phosphate rock	1.7	Morocco (32.0)	Jordan (9.2)	Tunisia (5.1)

Source: World Bank, *Commodity Trade and Price Trends 1987–88* (Baltimore, Md.: Johns Hopkins University Press, 1988),
8–19; United Nations, *Energy Statistics Yearbook 1986*, Table 15.

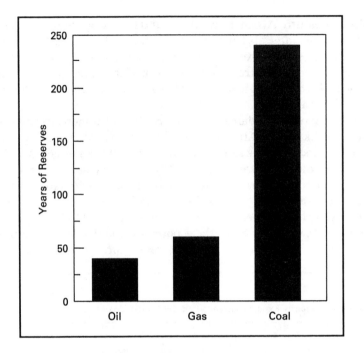

**FIGURE 17.1   Lifetime of World Energy Reserves at Current Pro-
duction Rates**
Source: British Petroleum, *BP Statistical Review of World Energy* (London: British Petroleum, 1992), 36.

   Three general descriptive statements can summarize the discussion of global
energy trends in Chapter 1:

1. The world is in no imminent danger of running out of energy. World coal supplies alone are
    sufficient to carry a growing world economy easily through the twenty-first century (Figure
    17.1).
2. The fossil supplies of conventional oil and natural gas are, however, more limited.[25] Although
    the world has not yet produced and consumed even 50 percent of the amounts that are readily
    accessible, it appears probable that peak global production will occur early in the next century
    and that the contribution of oil and natural gas to our total energy budget will generally continue
    the decline initiated in the 1970s. That is, we have entered a transition from an energy system
    dominated by conventional oil and gas to one in which those fuels play a less central role.
3. Oil and natural gas are unevenly distributed around the world. Although in 1990 OPEC
    countries produced only 38 percent of the non-Communist world's oil, they held 87 percent
    of the known reserves (British Petroleum 1992). Moreover, just five OPEC countries (Kuwait,
    Saudi Arabia, United Arab Emirates, Iraq, and Iran) contain within their borders 63 percent of
    global reserves.

[25]The emphasis throughout this discussion on **conventional oil** and **gas** is intentional. Unconventional supplies, like those in tar sands or oil shale, could considerably prolong the contribution of
petroleum to world energy. The costs, technology requirements, and global distribution of unconventional supplies are, however, so different from conventional sources that they are essentially different
energy forms.

COMPETING PERSPECTIVES ON ENERGY

The international power politics orientation of the realists serves us especially well in understanding the world energy situation. The global oil industry initially grew with the two superpowers to be, and both the United States and the Soviet Union claimed the site of the first oil well (Odell 1983, 50). Even in the early 1990s, the former Soviet Union and the United States produced more than other states, including Saudi Arabia. In addition to supplying its own needs, Russia exports significant amounts of oil and natural gas to both the former Soviet republics and to the rest of Europe.

The other great powers of the early twentieth century were hardly oblivious to the rise of oil and, given their limited domestic supplies, to the need for external sources. Britain created the Anglo-Persian Oil Company in 1913 to finance exploration in modern-day Iran. Great Britain, France, and the United States competed actively to secure oil concessions throughout the Middle East. Few better examples of geopolitics exist than the scramble for control of the region's resources, resolved at least temporarily in 1935 by an agreement among the external powers.[26] The United Kingdom retained a dominant position in the Mideast until the end of World War II, at which time the United States moved into a clearly preeminent role.

The major oil companies long reinforced the U.S. position in the global oil system. For many years after World War II, the seven major oil companies or "seven sisters" dominated Middle Eastern production and global oil distribution. Those corporations all rank among the largest in the world (see Table 13.4): Exxon, Mobil, and Chevron (all scions of the original Rockefeller Standard Oil monopoly, which the U.S. government dismantled in 1911), Gulf and Texaco (two additional U.S.-based corporations), British Petroleum (descendant of Anglo-Persian), and Royal Dutch/Shell (a Dutch-British corporation). Until the early 1970s the oil companies not only helped assure access by the United States and its allies to low-cost Middle Eastern oil, but returned healthy profits to the U.S. shareholders.

Most LDCs with oil initially had little power and little alternative to accepting the terms that the advanced states and the big oil companies offered. Mexico was the world's second largest oil producer in 1921, but the control of its industry by British and U.S. companies stoked a nationalistic desire to expropriate their assets. Unrest resulted in the patrol of U.S. naval vessels off the Gulf of Mexico. According to the U.S. secretary of state, this was to keep the Mexicans "between a dangerous and exaggerated apprehension and a proper degree of wholesome fear" (Engler 1961, 194). Mexico nonetheless expropriated the oil in 1938, and the majors virtually excluded Mexican oil from world markets for many years thereafter. The companies shifted their emphasis to Venezuela, which by 1946 became the world's second largest producer, behind the United States. It, too, sought control over its own resources, although it did not succeed fully until the 1970s.

---

[26]As the great powers had earlier essentially carved Africa into pieces of private property, they did the same in the 1930s with Middle Eastern oil. In both cases legal exclusion resolved the problems of what had earlier been treated as a common property resource.

The biggest battle over control of oil came in the Middle East and was postponed until the world had become very dependent on petroleum. Several LDCs formed OPEC in 1960 in an effort to stem a downward slide in world oil prices. Yet control over the level of oil production within OPEC countries remained in the hands of the oil companies. Power shifted in the 1970s. Libya held a relatively enviable position among the OPEC countries. It had a small population and rapid growth in production and revenues, as a result of activity by twenty-one oil companies including some outside of the powerful seven-sisters group. Libya used divide-and-conquer tactics against the oil companies, first exerting maximum pressure on Occidental Petroleum, which had a substantial exposure in the country and relatively little oil elsewhere (Bill and Stookey 1975, 112–116). It nationalized the companies between 1970 and 1973. Iran also acted during this period to obtain greater control.

These events took place in an international oil market that was tightening as U.S. imports rose sharply in the early 1970s (see Figure 17.2).[27] In October 1973, war erupted between Israel and its Arab neighbors. The anger of Arab oil-exporting countries toward supporters of Israel rose simultaneously with the power those countries felt relative to the world oil market. They instituted an oil embargo against the United States and the Netherlands for their continued support of Israel (several other industrialized, oil-importing countries accepted demands for a policy realignment and avoided OPEC wrath).

The embargo was not successful in depriving only those two countries of supplies, because oil, like grain, is a fungible commodity. The 10 percent export restriction imposed by the Arab oil-exporting countries, however, did cause a four- to fivefold increase in global oil prices within a year. This event was the **first oil shock**. It convinced the OPEC countries that they had a tool available with which to increase their oil revenues dramatically and to achieve other ends, such as support for the Palestinians in their conflict with Israel.

Joining realists in this emphasis on the use of international power, structuralists saw in these events the possibility for the exercise of Southern power relative to the global North. They urged the formation of other producer cartels and the exercise of that power, not simply for the limited economic end of additional revenues but for broader reform of the international political-economic order. As Mazrui (1988, 134) urged, "There is a crying need for other producer cartels, no matter how weak in the short run." Chapter 13 discussed the generally unsuccessful attempt by the South to use this newly discovered power.

Near the end of the 1980s, Iran was the second largest OPEC oil producer and exporter, following Saudi Arabia. The revolution in Iran during 1978–1979 sharply restricted production. This initiated the **second oil shock**, or major increase, in world oil prices (Figure 17.3), roughly another doubling. The Iran-Iraq War began in 1980, further restraining Iranian production and additionally lowering that of Iraq.

[27]Although the United States became a net importer of oil in 1947, oil imports long remained low. In fact quotas established in 1959, in the name of national security, put an upper limit on U.S. imports. In retrospect some critically call this the drain-America-first policy. In any case, U.S. oil production peaked about 1970; the country initially loosened the quotas and in early 1973 abolished them (Davis 1978, 81). These developments moved the United States actively into the world oil market at a critical time.

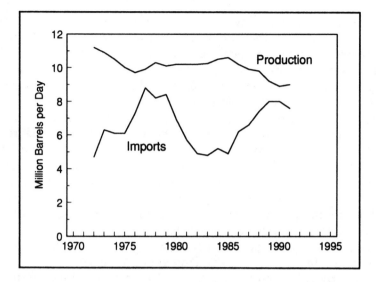

FIGURE 17.2   U.S. Oil Production and Imports
Source: Independent Petroleum Association of America, "United States Petroleum Statistics," February, 1992, Tables 7 and 9.

FIGURE 17.3   World Oil Prices
Sources: World Bank, Commodity Trade and Price Trends, 1987–88 (Baltimore: Johns Hopkins University, 1988), 80; British Petroleum, *BP Statistical Reveiw of World Energy* (London: British Petroleum, 1992), 12.

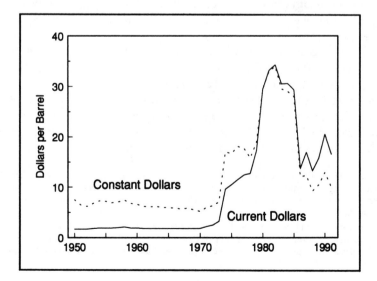

The response of liberals to the two oil shocks was to analyze the economic basis for such increases in oil prices. They compared the new oil prices with the long-term costs of alternative energy sources such as coal, nuclear power, or solar energy. They concluded that the oil prices were too high to be sustained, because they would elicit new oil supplies (like those in the North Sea or in the Alaskan North Slope) and encourage development of alternative energy sources. Eventually global energy surpluses would force down oil prices. Important to understanding the liberal analysis is the concept of **elasticity**, the responsiveness of demand and supply levels to price changes. When the price of energy rises, market forces increase the supply of energy and decrease the demand for it. If these reactions are minor, then the price elasticities of supply and demand are low; if significant increases in supply and decreases in demand develop, the elasticities are high.[28] For a cartel to successfully maintain higher prices and thus profits, elasticities (reactivity of supply and demand) must be low; liberal energy experts argued that they were not low.

It took longer than many liberals expected, and the greater response to higher price proved unexpectedly to be in demand rather than in supply, but oil surpluses appeared in the early 1980s, and oil price then fell. In fact, the price of crude oil by 1986 (after adjusting for inflation) was only about twice that preceding the oil shock in 1973 (see Figure 17.3). Oil producers such as Mexico, which had built spending plans around expectations of continued high or even increasing prices, did not anticipate the rapid decrease. This **third oil shock** created adjustment problems for oil-exporting countries (including Mexico) as great as those that the first two shocks posed for oil-importing countries.

Ecoholists interpreted the first and second oil shocks as indicators of physically limited world oil supplies and the beginning of a transition away from an oil-based global energy system. Many exaggerated the shocks by arguing that the world had entered an **energy crisis**, a prolonged period of energy shortages. Discrediting of the exaggeration has unjustly drawn attention away from the potential significance of energy transition onset.[29] Among likely consequences of an ongoing energy transition will be continued volatility in world energy markets. When the world moved from coal to oil and natural gas, the substitute energy forms were higher quality, cleaner, and more easily transported—they were also widely available and relatively inexpensive. There is no clearly superior energy form toward which the world can now move. Thus additional oil shocks appear likely. The embargo and war against Iraq in 1991–1992 caused a small shock. Note again in Figure 17.2 the sharply increased U.S. dependence on imported oil and thus vulnerability to shocks in the early 1990s.

[28]Specifically, the supply-and-demand elasticities are the percentage responses of supply and demand, relative to the percentage change in price. A greater than 1 percent change in supply or demand in response to a 1 percent change in price indicates an "elastic" commodity, and a less than 1 percent change means that it is "inelastic."

[29]Global oil production per capita peaked in 1973 (Brown 1981, 73). Total global oil production peaked in 1979 (British Petroleum 1989). Neither of those peaks had been exceeded by 1990, and it is very possible that production per capita will never again reach the 1973 level (just over five barrels per capita).

As the transition continues, the strategic importance of the Mideast will wax and wane with the need for its oil. In the early stages, political and economic relationships with the states of that region will remain critical, as they have been in the last two decades. In the longer term (perhaps twenty to forty years), Mideast oil will cease to be so dominant a portion of the world's energy budget, and the importance of the region should similarly decline.

ENERGY POLICY ISSUES

Most global actors view food availability as fundamentally nonzero-sum. More food can be produced globally, and world welfare can be improved. We therefore were able to talk about collective international responses to food problems, a food regime, directed by organizations like the FAO, the Hunger Project, and the research network of CGIAR. Because of surpluses, the First World also sees food as a "low-politics" issue, not bearing directly on national security. Energy issues have a more nearly zero-sum character and little collective global attention to them has emerged; the rule instead has been competitive responses.[30] First World countries perceive energy as a "high-politics" issue, directly related to national security. In 1977 President Carter went before the public to talk about the energy situation:

> Tonight I want to have an unpleasant talk with you about a problem unprecedented in our history. With the exception of war, this is the greatest challenge our country will face in our lifetimes.... This effort will be the "moral equivalent of war." (*Congressional Quarterly*, 1979, 1)

Importers as a group seek security of supply and low prices. Importers also compete with each other in efforts to attain that security. Exporters collectively want control over supply and high prices. Yet exporters compete with one another for larger shares in the world market. Let us consider some of the individual and collective policy responses generated by these conflicting interests.

In response to OPEC and the first oil shock, seventeen importers formed an organization known as the International Energy Agency (IEA) in 1974. IEA membership largely replicates that of the OECD. France declined to enter; it sought to deal individually and directly with oil producers rather than to confront them collectively. The IEA countries agreed to share information concerning energy and jointly to facilitate technological advances to decrease dependence on imported oil. They further agreed to share oil supplies should another embargo or inadvertent supply disruption limit them. In reality, members expect little from the IEA in an emergency but hope that it can facilitate the longer-term transition.

Importing countries have more effectively acted individually to secure energy supplies. The immediate response of the U.S. government to the first oil shock in 1973 was to declare Project Independence and set a goal of zero imports by 1980.

---

[30]This assumes a focus on the short term; in the longer run, issues such as energy research and development can be nonzero-sum.

That proved totally unrealistic. Subsequently, the United States acted more rationally, by establishing a strategic petroleum reserve to store oil when plentiful (it used releases from that reserve to calm world markets during the embargo against Iraq in 1991). Most importers have created some type of stockpile. In addition importing countries rely on taxes, subsidies, and regulation to reduce their dependence on external supplies. Moreover, they seek special relationships with oil exporters.

The Carter administration also sought to reduce the probability of the kind of conflict that triggered the first oil shock. To this end it pursued an active process of facilitating reconciliation between the Middle Eastern antagonists, including sponsorship of the Camp David Accords in 1978, which settled territorial issues between Egypt and Israel. A comprehensive peace treaty between those two states followed in 1979.

The United States additionally brought its military might to bear on the issue. Although the government resisted calls during the shocks of the 1970s for direct action in the Persian Gulf to secure supplies, it never fully precluded the possibility. In fact, the potential need for the capability to intervene and secure oil supplies, reinforced by the impotence felt by the United States during the Iranian hostage episode, led it to develop a special Rapid Deployment Force (Hastedt 1988, 298). Moreover, in 1980 the United States stated the Carter Doctrine, namely, that "an attempt by an outside force to gain control of the Persian Gulf region will be regarded as an assault on the vital interests of America and such an assault will be repelled by any means necessary, including military force" (Kegley and Wittkopf 1985, 335).

The Reagan administration reiterated the Carter doctrine, verbally and in practice. In 1987 that administration introduced naval forces into the Persian Gulf to protect Kuwaiti and other tankers (some were allowed to fly the U.S. flag) against the attacks of Iran or Iraq in the pursuit of their wartime objectives. Although they sent some mine sweepers, other NATO members participated only modestly in the military effort to assure the flow of oil through the Persian Gulf and the narrow Straits of Hormuz. Because more of that oil flows to Europe than to the United States, this puzzled U.S. citizens. One explanation is that Europeans are less inclined to rely on military measures than are Americans—they frequently perceive less threat, and they more often seek diplomatic and multilateral mechanisms. A second is that they could easily free ride on the leadership of the United States in providing a collective good, the continued flow of oil.

In 1991, the UN coalition officially sanctioned Iraq for its invasion of another sovereign power. Many argued that the real reason was that a successful incorporation of Kuwait would double Iraqi oil reserves to nearly one-fifth of the global total. The failure of the UN in 1992 to apply military measures against Serbia when it supported Serbian aggression in Bosnia seemed to reinforce that interpretation.

The interest of Russia in the oil of the Middle East is a matter of considerable debate. It remains not only self-sufficient in petroleum but an exporter of oil. Nonetheless, Russia might in some circumstances wish to disrupt the flow from the Persian Gulf to the West. More immediately, oil production in Russia faces the same decline that U.S. production entered in 1970. Production fell in 1984–1985 for the first time in forty years, resumed its climb in 1986–1988 only at great investment cost, and then fell sharply in 1989–1992. Even if they have no need for Middle Eastern oil for many years, they will continue to have an interest in its ultimate availability.

Exporters may appear on the surface to have more common interest and perspective than importers. The formation of OPEC and the simultaneous efforts of the oil-producing countries in the early 1970s to gain control over their own oil supplies suggested the strength of that common interest. So did their agreement to support collectively major increases in oil prices during the first two oil shocks. Below that surface, however, lie substantial elements of competition. Once again we see a battle between self-interest and collective interest. OPEC countries all benefit from high oil prices—those prices are a collective good that they each translate into higher revenues. They capture the benefits of those prices, however, whether or not they contribute to maintaining them. Thus there is a natural inclination to cheat on the cartel or to free ride. Many OPEC producers, especially countries such as Indonesia and Nigeria, with large, poor populations and nearly desperate needs for immediate additional revenues, regularly exceed the production quotas set for them in OPEC meetings.

A few OPEC countries like Saudi Arabia, Kuwait, and the United Arab Emirates have less urgent need for revenues and traditionally reduce production (Figure 17.4), even below their quotas, to support higher prices. The existence of such members is a boon for a cartel—one reason for the weakness of the Intergovernmental Council of Copper-Exporting States is the absence of countries with capital surpluses in that copper cartel. The weak world oil market of the 1980s, and the continued cheating by large numbers of OPEC members, gradually resulted in financial problems even for the economically stronger producers, however. In the late 1980s Saudi Arabia sought to restore price discipline by increasing production, flooding the market, driving down prices, and then dictating a return to quota observance as the price for renewed export constraint. Leadership in cartels, like leadership in the global market economy, is not always easy.

Throughout the period since energy problems came to the top of the global agenda in 1973, there have been periodic calls for a global approach to production and pricing, involving cooperation between exporters and importers. In an environment of high-politics competition, within consumer and producer country groupings and between those categories of countries, significant collective global action appears unlikely.

ECOSYSTEM VULNERABILITY

This chapter has focused until now on the extractive demands that human systems place on their environments, notably through their requirements for food and energy. We move now from input to output issues—to the impact that human activities have on the broader biologic system and on such natural systems as

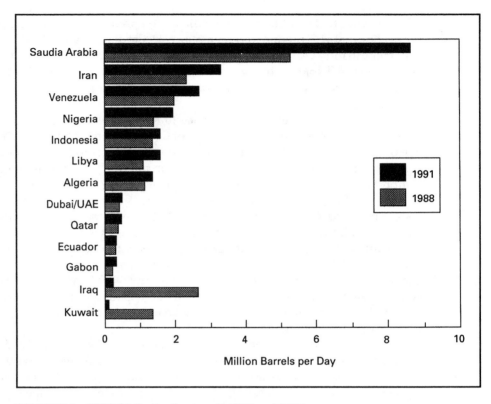

FIGURE 17.4   OPEC Oil Production Levels (1988 and 1991)
Source: British Petroleum, *BP Statistical Review of World Energy* (London: British Petroleum, 1992), 5.

climate. Chapter 1 already summarized many of these impacts (such as creation of ozone holes in the atmosphere and the greenhouse effect) our purpose here is to analyze global reactions to them.

COMPETING PERSPECTIVES AND INATTENTION TO THE ENVIRONMENT

Modernists generally downplay environmental problems by making two types of arguments. First, much human activity actually improves the environment. Extermination of smallpox from the earth and progress against other diseases illustrates this. So, too, does the draining of swamps, the control of irritating or dangerous insects, and the extinction or relegation to zoos of larger human predators. The steady increase in human life expectancy indicates the progress that humanity has made in improving its environment. Second, even when human activity damages the environment, such as air pollution in cities or water pollution on a regional basis, identification of the problem normally leads to its amelioration. Air quality in many British and American cities and water quality throughout much of the two countries has improved quite steadily since the early 1970s. Modernists argue that once economic progress satisfies the most urgent human needs for food and shelter in LDCs, those countries, too, will turn their attention to the environmental damage that they now accept willingly as the price for advancement.

Realists divert little attention from issues of high politics to environmental concerns such as the greenhouse effect and ozone depletion. Although the realist view may have little to say prescriptively about addressing environmental problems, it is once again helpful in describing the actual approach states take to regional and global environmental issues. The world is one of states coexisting in an anarchic system. How will states in such a system behave on environmental issues? First, they will pursue individually rational strategies despite collective consequences. Second, they will act to shift the burden of dealing with the problems to other states, insofar as their power position allows them to do so. Let Denmark do it.

Like realists, neither liberals nor structuralists focus more than marginally on the environment. For liberals, environmental damage from economic activities is an externality explicitly outside their cost-benefit calculations for individual producers or consumers; many do, however, point approvingly to policy instruments such as effluent taxes, which force firms to consider pollution a cost of business (internalize its cost), and thereby providing incentives to restrict it. Structuralists are likely to stress that the rich and powerful exploit the poor and weak by transferring polluting industries to them and even by exporting the pollutants. That is unlikely to change, they argue, unless wealth and power are better distributed.

AN ILLUSTRATION: TOXIC WASTE

Although none of these perspectives place high priority on environmental issues, they collectively help us understand global approaches (or the lack of them) to the issues. Consider, for instance, global hazardous waste disposal. A realist's understanding of states (and corporations) acting from rational self-interest explains much behavior on the issue. Nonetheless, in 1989 a global convention on hazardous waste movement opened for signing by states, and it has begun to manage interstate flows.

In the first national survey of toxic waste generation and disposal, the U.S. Environmental Protection Agency estimated that the United States generated 22.5 billion pounds of hazardous substances in 1987. Table 17.9 shows where most of that went. Other developed countries produce comparable volumes from rubber, plastic, textile, chemical, refining, and metal industries. First World firms have increasingly faced difficulties and great expense in disposing of such wastes domestically. Only a few countries, notably Japan, West Germany, Canada, and the United Kingdom, have developed capabilities for processing wastes at home (in some cases even accepting them from other countries).[31]

---

[31]See Norris (1982, 71); also "The Global Poison Trade," *Newsweek*, November 7, 1988, 66–68. Pearson (1987) focuses on the role of MNCs.

TABLE 17.9
Toxic Waste Disposal in the United States, 1987

Disposal Location	Billion Pounds
Air	2.7
Streams, surface water	9.7
Wells	3.2
Landfills	2.7
Waste facilities	2.6
Other	1.6
Total	22.5

Source: Environmental Protection Agency, as reported in the Denver Post, April 13, 1989, 2A.

High profits lure many shady operators to the disposal business and have led to several scandals, in which firms sought to, or actually did dispose of their wastes in LDCs, especially in smaller Caribbean and African countries. Among the targets were Haiti, Antigua, the Bahamas, Sierra Leone, Equatorial Guinea, and Guinea-Bissau.[32] A Norwegian firm delivered 15,000 tons of "new materials for bricks" to Guinea. It proved to be toxic incinerator ash from Philadelphia. As a rule poorer states do not have adequate treatment capability and often possess inaccurate or inadequate information about the risks. Yet the enticements for LDCs can be great. A Swiss firm offered Guinea-Bissau $600 million over five years to accept wastes, more than the country's foreign debt and thirty-five times its annual export earnings. In a good example of liberal cost-benefit logic carried to an extreme, one World Bank economist suggested in 1992 that low-income countries should accept such waste dumps.

Such shifting of externalities from the rich to the poor countries cannot occur without at least implicit state complicity through failure to regulate the disposal cycle. Adverse publicity has, however, forced waste-exporting states toward stronger controls. Italy, tarred by a 1988 scheme that transported radioactive nuclear waste to Nigeria (with the help of corrupt Nigerian port officials), banned further toxic waste shipments to the Third World. The EC now requires clear labeling and has some export restrictions, although operators seeking large profits continue to circumvent them. In March 1989 a UN treaty on toxic-waste exports bound 100 states to regulate them so as to stop clandestine commerce.[33] Forty members of the Organization of African Unity refused to sign the treaty, calling for an outright ban on waste exports to Africa.

[32]Waste disposal in larger LDCs such as Mexico, Nigeria, and Turkey has also created scandals in those countries.

[33]A related issue is that developed countries continue to ship some hazardous substances to LDCs that they have banned domestically. The United States prohibited all but emergency uses of DDT in 1973 (Norris 1982, 21). Yet it exported DDT to twenty-one countries during 1980.

In 1991 all African countries except South Africa signed the Bamako Convention banning such trade. Greenpeace discovered in that year that some exporters had then targeted Central and Latin America. Those countries have in turn tightened controls on imports.

States also have proven relatively inattentive to movements by air and water of their pollutants across borders. Canada long accused the United States of significantly damaging its lakes and forests by failure to control acid rain sources. A study by a highly politicized U.S. government group concluded in 1987 that there was little evidence for a significant acid rain impact on lakes and streams in the Northeast United States (and by implication in eastern Canada). Canada's environment minister labeled the report "voodoo science."[34] The United States subsequently moved to address the problem.

Nor is there often much that can be done even when states admit responsibility. It is difficult to apply the legal precedent of state responsibility established by the Trail Smelter case in 1941. For example, radioactive material, released from the Soviet nuclear plant at Chernobyl in April, 1986, spread around the world and measurably affected plants and animals in Central Europe and Scandinavia. Public outcry forced the U.S.S.R. to acknowledge the disaster, somewhat belatedly, but it is unlikely that any financial claims can be pressed against Russia. Lives were lost in the episode, but the European victims will die only over time and without clearly drawn connections to the accident.[35] Similarly the last atmospheric test of a nuclear weapon was by China in 1980. Yet one study predicted 430,000 cancer deaths by 2070 from more than three decades of testing.

The fact that U.S. industry "disposes" of more than one-half of all toxic wastes by dumping them into the air or water (see Table 17.9) indicates that even developed countries have only begun to deal domestically with the problem. It is therefore not surprising that global environmental efforts lag.

INTERNATIONAL POLICY APPROACHES

Although traditional realism can help us understand the origins of many global environmental problems, it does not take us very far toward solutions. We need to turn again (as in Chapter 6) to a consideration of cooperative action, drawing on the insights of neorealists and globalists.

As the scale of interstate movement of pollutants rises, states have come to see the need for collective action. European states fully realize that they can no longer individually protect their major water drainages (like the Rhine and Danube), their bordering seas (the Baltic and Mediterranean), or their air. In dealing with global problems such as ozone depletion and the greenhouse effect, individual states completely lose their ability to control the issues and policy approaches.

[34]"Discounting the Threat of Acid Rain," *Science News*, September 26, 1987.

[35]The toxic chemical release from the Union Carbide plant in Bhopal, India, in December 1984 was very different in that India was able to seek and obtain damages from a specific company concerning a specific incident with clearly identifiable loss of life (Gladwin 1987).

Clean water and air are collective goods, and the problems of providing them are problems of the commons. Unlike food and energy, which states can largely secure for themselves, there is no alternative to collective action with respect to the ecosystem. Recognizing that a clean environment is a collective good helps us understand why it is so difficult to secure—because of free-rider problems, collective goods are normally underprovided. How then can humanity approach problems of the global commons? Four approaches to dealing with the tension between individual action and collective interest have surfaced again and again in this volume: voluntarism, leadership, privatization, and collective regulation.

Voluntarism, although naturally limited in a world strongly influenced by the self-interested behavior of states and economic actors, still has a role to play. **Voluntarism** often involves individuals, rather than states, and reflects a growing sense of global community. Like the strategy of GRIT, it involves unilateral action with the hope that others will eventually reciprocate. For instance, an organization called the Programme for Belize began in 1988 to solicit funds from around the world to "endow" a tropical forest area in Belize, that is, to provide sufficient funds that the zone could remain intact indefinitely. Similarly, private organizations helped Bolivia retire some of its international debt in exchange for protecting a forest area. We should not underestimate the importance of rising global consciousness on environmental issues and the contributions individuals are willing to make on behalf of the global community. Nevertheless, the voluntaristic approach by itself is inadequate.

The United States has provided **leadership** in security and economic arenas since 1945, although its capacity for doing so has gradually declined. Leadership on environmental issues may be more difficult. For example, should the United States dramatically scale back use of fossil fuels in attempts to decrease CO_2 emissions (it alone produces 25 percent of the problem), it would capture only a share of the benefit of its action. Much would accrue to the remaining 95 percent of the world's population, which would be very happy to have the United States alone carry the burden of slowing the greenhouse effect.

It may be possible for Europe and the United States, or for the Organization for Economic Cooperation and Development, to provide collective global environmental leadership. Twenty-two such countries agreed in Montreal in 1987 to reduce production of CFCs (Figure 17.5) by 50 percent before 2000 (in London in 1990 a larger group agreed to a complete phaseout by 2000). Leadership by example alone, however, will often be inadequate. China wishes to increase its production of CFCs tenfold by the year 2000 to allow its citizens to have inexpensive food refrigeration.[36] Environmental leadership will thus require side payments (see Chapter 6) to countries like China that could otherwise spoil the effort to provide collective goods. The signatories of the 1991 agreement established a $240 million fund to help Third World countries phase out CFCs.

---

[36]Although China produces only 2 percent of CFCs globally, its production is growing at 20 percent annually; although refrigerator production increased 133 times from 1981 to 1988, there were still only 7.4 million units for a population of over 1 billion (*The Christian Science Monitor*, March 23, 1989, 1–2).

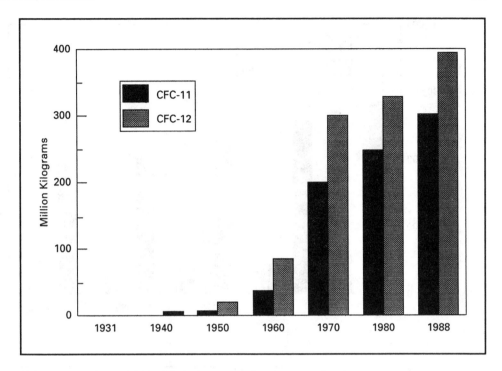

FIGURE 17.5   Annual Global Emissions of CFCs
Source: Council on Environmental Quality, 21st Annual Report (Washington, D.C.: Council on Environmental Quality, 1991), 319.

Europe alone may lead on some issues. In 1991, the EC Commission proposed a "carbon tax," a tax on the emission of carbon from the burning of fossil fuels. Many argue that such taxes will provide environmental benefits greater than the economic costs to the country that introduces them. If so, a self-motivated leadership could emerge on greenhouse gas emissions.

International action on acid rain (Figure 17.6) has been difficult to obtain because fossil fuel–burning electric plants release the chemicals that produce it, including nitrogen and sulfur oxides. Technology to reduce the emissions exists, and U.S. legislation calls for such reductions, but the cost is high. In 1988 twenty-four countries agreed in Sophia, Bulgaria, to freeze nitrogen oxide emissions at current levels by 1995. For most of the 1980s, the United States did not actively support international agreements on the issue because the Reagan administration claimed that research was incomplete. This was ironic, considering the scope and cost of efforts simultaneously taken within the United States. The United States may eventually become a leader in collective action to control acid rain. Because control of emissions is expensive, large LDCs, such as India and China, and industrialized countries facing severe economic difficulties, such as those of Eastern Europe, are again likely to free ride on the global effort.

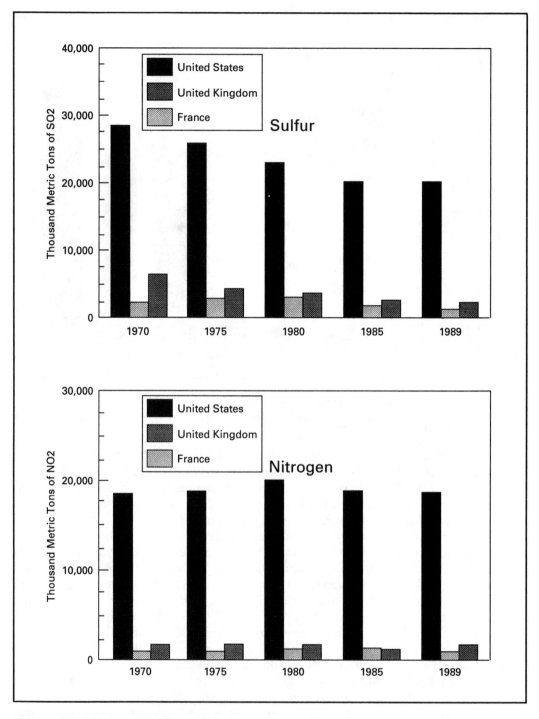

FIGURE 17.6 Sulfur and Nitrogen Emissions
Source: World Resources Institute, *World Resources 1992–93* (New York: Oxford University Press, 1992), 361.

Leadership with side payments could also help protect resources in which the global community has an interest but that exist within the boundaries of individual states (transboundary problems). In October 1988 Brazilian President José Sarney pronounced himself firmly against further destruction of the Amazonian rain forests. The value of that region as a safety valve for the economically deprived and politically disaffected of Brazil, however, makes such declarations difficult to translate into policy. Brazil suggests that if the international community believes protection of the Amazon to be so important, the world should not require Brazil to pay all the costs. Other states could contribute. In 1990 Japan announced a $6 million payment to Malaysia through the International Tropical Timber Organization (ITTO) to help it slow deforestation.

Privatization is a third approach to problems of the environment. In the case of the ocean commons of the earth, the establishment of Exclusive Economic Zones (EEZs) by the United Nations Conference on Law of the Sea III (UNCLOS III) extended control by states over ocean resources 200 nautical miles from their shores. That action transfers to state jurisdiction about 40 percent of the ocean area, containing 90 percent of the harvestable biologic resources and all known commercial energy resources (Soroos 1986, 273). Moreover, it gives more than 50 percent of the newly "fenced" area to only thirteen states (Soroos 1986, 290). It leaves little beyond currently unattainable mineral resources in the remaining commons. The action does, however, solve a common property resource problem: It provides incentives for each state to manage the fish catch within their zones so as to maintain yields in the long run.

For some, this example may seem to provide an attractive approach to other environmental problems. Does privatization offer a general model? No, for two reasons. First, EEZs do not even resolve all of the commons problems of oceans, because that over which the states theoretically have control actually moves across state jurisdictions (physical excludability is not possible, thereby precluding effective legal excludability). Many fish, such as tuna, do not spend their lives only in the EEZ of Peru. Similarly, pollution drifts easily with ocean currents. Problems of movement are still greater in the atmosphere, and that common property resource cannot be privatized. Second, it would be difficult to specify private property rights in most remaining commons. It is nearly inconceivable that states could agree on divisions of the Antarctic, the deep ocean bottom, or space.

Instead states turn to **collective regulation**. The Antarctic Treaty of 1959 prohibits all territorial claims and bans nuclear explosions or dumping of radioactive wastes (Riggs and Plano 1988, 160). Only the United States initially withheld approval of a 1991 treaty with a fifty-five-year ban on mining in the Antarctic. UN resolutions specify that the use of space is "only for the betterment of mankind." Such collective regulation must be the central approach to many environmental issues.

A regime that organizes cooperation on a broad range of environmental issues, relying on a mixture of these four approaches to cooperation, is slowly emerging. Table 17.10 lists some of the primary global conventions that constitute the backbone of the regime. In an important early step, the United Nations held a

Conference on the Human Environment in Stockholm during 1972.[37] That conference symbolized for the first time global attention to the environment. It also created UNEP, with headquarters in Nairobi, Kenya. Most UNEP activities involve information gathering and environmental monitoring including a Global Environment Monitoring System (GEMS) and an International Register of Potentially Toxic Chemicals (IRPTC). UNEP undertakes some project funding, principally education, training, and technical assistance (UNEP 1979).

TABLE 17.10
Principal Global Environmental Conventions

Wildlife and Habitat	Atmosphere
Antarctic (1959 and 1980)	Nuclear Test Ban (1963)
Wetlands (1971)	Ozone Layer(1985)
World Heritage (1972)	CFC Control (1987)
Endangered Species (1973)	Climate Change (1992)
Migratory Species (1979)	
Biological Diversity (1992)	Hazardous Waste
	Biological and Toxin Weapons (1972)
Oceans	Nuclear Accident Notification (1986)
Ocean Dumping (1972)	Nuclear Accident Assistance (1986)
Ship Pollution (1978)	Hazardous Waste Movement (1989)
Law of the Sea (1982)	

Source: World Resources Institute, *World Resources 1992–93* (New York: Oxford University Press, 1992), 358–361.

The 1972 Ocean Dumping Convention and the 1973 Endangered Species Convention further strengthen the international regime. Despite its privatizing of the ocean commons, the international effort to structure a modern law of the sea contributes to environmental regime building. UNCLOS I began in 1958, UNCLOS II in 1960, and UNCLOS III in 1974 (Swing 1976, 529–531). The last forum met twelve times before closing in 1982 (Soroos 1988, 346). The United States backed away from the agreements of UNCLOS III because they would require it to submit to an international agency controlling disposition of deep sea mineral resources; the United States is a leader in technology for exploiting such resources and might be able privately to capture that remaining portion of the global oceans commons. Instead of signing the UNCLOS III treaty, it sponsored a minitreaty among those countries with the technological capabilities to exploit the resources.

The most difficult global environmental problem to control, and unfortunately perhaps the most important, is increase in atmospheric CO_2 and resultant intensification of the greenhouse effect. Because any burning of fossil fuels produces CO_2 (burning oxidizes carbon), only reductions in fossil fuel use can constrain production of the gas that scientists believe accounts for about one-half of

[37]A UN conference on Environment and Development was held in 1992.

the greenhouse effect. Environmentalists have called for just such action, but it appears unlikely in the foreseeable future.[38] The economic costs of limiting fossil fuel use would be very large. Moreover, nuclear power, the energy source most likely to be substituted for carbon-based energy, has its own environmental hazards. Instead of leadership toward action, in 1989 the United States, Japan, and the Soviet Union blocked multilateral endorsement of a timetable to reduce CO_2 emissions. In 1990 the Bush administration concluded that scientific evidence on the greenhouse effect was inadequate to justify expensive action.

Attempts to reach agreement on reducing greenhouse emissions were high on the agenda at the United Nations Conference on Environment and Development (UNCED) or the "Earth Summit" in Rio in 1992. Like the Stockholm Conference of twenty years earlier, it was an ambitious effort to reach agreement on many environment issues—in fact, with 118 heads of state attending, it was the largest summit meeting ever held. The United States resisted efforts to set mandatory reductions in greenhouse gases in spite of support from almost all other states.[39] Nonetheless, two new global conventions, one on climate change and the other on biological diversity, were opened to signature. The forum also established the Sustainable Development Commission with the responsibility of monitoring adherence to other environmental agreements. It will draw on evidence gathered by NGOs (representatives at Rio from about 13,000 NGOs staged their own parallel meetings) and rely heavily on the pressure of public opinion, as does the UN Human Rights Commission.

Another important characteristic of the Earth Summit was the very explicit and strong linkage between the environment and development. The South argued that it needed help (side payments again) if it were to implement stronger environmental protection, including curbs on deforestation. The large package it requested did not materialize.

Although states remain in charge, a global regime is developing, with norms and values enforced by elements of the global conscience such as Greenpeace, and with budding institutional structures like UNEP to facilitate agreement on collective action. If a state finds any individual global action too costly (relative to immediate benefits), it may not participate. Yet considerable pressure on states from NGOs and public opinion does often seem to make a difference.

CONCLUSION

Several global forces interact to create increasing turbulence in the environment of world politics: rapid population growth, the ongoing energy transition, the global spread of industrial technology, and the increasing scope of biologic and physical

---

[38]"Toronto Climate Conference Calls for Sharp Cuts in Carbon Dioxide Emissions," *Climate Alert*, 1, no. 3 (Fall 1988), 1.

[39]One U.S. delegate to a preparatory conference told the delegation from Bangladesh about climate change: "This is not a disaster, it is merely a change.... The area won't have disappeared, it will just be under water. Where you now have cows, you will have fish." (Hunger Project 1991, 1).

environmental damage from human systems. Environmental issues, such as famine in Africa, oil shocks, and the greenhouse effect, appear regularly on the front pages of our daily newspapers and have become focal points of international attention.

It is impossible to understand fully those issues without bringing to bear all of the worldviews presented in this book. Consider, for instance, famine in Africa. Ecoholists draw to our attention the long-term change in rainfall patterns that explains the drought and crop failures (Weisbund and Raloff 1985). They suggest that human activities, such as those that cause deforestation and desertification, have helped cause that climate change. Modernists inform us about the technological efforts to solve food problems including those at the four CGIAR centers in Africa (in Nigeria, Kenya, Ethiopia, and Liberia).

Liberals contribute an understanding of how governmental decisions to set prices for consumers below market levels can lessen incentives for local farmers (Eicher 1982). They also explain how agricultural policies in the United States and Europe, which create surpluses there, distort the world market and further weaken incentives for African producers. Structuralists clarify the historic connections between colonialism, plantation agriculture, and a contemporary emphasis on nonfood export crops at the expense of food production.

Idealists explain that nationalist and religious passions, such as those that divide the Sudan into the Islamic north and the Christian and animist south, rise in response to food shortages and contribute additionally to them (Vestal 1985). Globalists document the international effort to satisfy immediate food needs and to assist in raising local long-term agricultural potential. Realists (and structuralists) see the difficulties that interstate power politics, especially the superpower rivalry, have created for local actors. For instance, outside powers fueled the civil wars in Ethiopia and Somalia.

All of the issues in this chapter require a multiplicity of perspectives for a reasonably full understanding. You should now have the tools to undertake more complete analyses than many found in brief, journalistic accounts.

Chapter 18

CONTINUITY
AND CHANGE
IN POLITICAL ECOLOGY

Although modernism and ecoholism have limited inherent political content, they are important to an understanding of world politics. They organize thought about a set of broader contextual issues that have become increasingly important in both domestic and international politics. They also provide important interpretations of the forces of global change that Chapter 1 identified as establishing a foundation for changing global politics. This chapter explicitly examines the way in which these two worldviews treat change.

MODERNISM

The concept of progress stands at the core of modernist thought. Modernists measure progress in terms of the human condition. For instance, Simon (1981) stresses the importance of nearly monotonic increases in life expectancy in the West during the last two centuries and around the world since World War II. Herman Kahn (1976, 1979) heavily emphasized GNP per capita. Additional and related economic indicators include productivity (the quantity of goods produced by a worker per hour) and consumer purchasing power. For instance, annual American productivity gains averaged 2.3 percent during the 100 years between 1890–1992.[1] The cost of wheat in the United States relative to average wages fell by a factor of about twenty between 1800 and 1980 (Simon 1981, 75).

Technological advance is the driving force of such progress. Modernists have, however, no particularly good theory of technological advance. It is a kind of *deus ex machina*[2] that has been on the stage for such a long time that we never think to

---

[1] Maddison (1982, 37) reports 2.3 percent until 1979, and the IMF (1992, 115) reports 2.4 percent between 1980 and 1992.

[2] Classical Greek and Roman plays sometimes introduced a god by way of stage machinery, in order to direct a certain course of events arbitrarily.

ask where it came from or doubt its future contributions. General efforts to understand the march of technology fall into two categories (Ayres 1969, 29). One school holds that technology has its own, largely uncontrollable and unpredictable dynamics. Major inventions, such as the plow, the stirrup, or the transistor, may have been "inevitable" in a broad sense, but their timing was far from predictable. The other school sees a relationship between invention and the social, military, and economic needs of the time. In this view, humans control technological advance to a degree. The Manhattan project to build an atomic bomb during World War II and the National Aeronautics and Space Administration project to put a human on the moon during the 1960s illustrate how decisions to develop a technology can lead to its attainment.

When modernists extend their attention beyond the broader environmental issues (technology and the biologic-physical environment), they normally maintain the perspective of progressive change (Table 18.1). Because both liberals and Marxists also share a belief in progress, either worldview is compatible with modernism. Postwar leaders in both the East and West were believers in the benefits of technological progress. In the former Soviet Union, strong commitment to nuclear power, relative inattention to environmental issues (there were other accidents besides the one at Chernobyl), and strong support for basic research might indicate an even deeper attachment to the modernist perspective than in the West.

TABLE 18.1
Modernism, Extensions, and Challengers

	Characterization of Change		
Dominant Subject Matter	Stability (and Unpatterned Change)	Cycles	Progressive Change
Political			Globalism
			Neofunctionalism
Economic			Liberalism-Marxism
			Capital accumulation
Broader Environment		Ecoholism-Neotraditionalism	Modernism
		Tragedy of commons; overshoot and collapse	Technology advance
	Predominantly zero-sum logic		Nonzero-sum logic

Anticipating progressive change in political behavior as well, many modernists are globalists. Some believe that by banishing material want and substituting abundance, modern technology progressively eliminates the major causes of war and creates a more peaceful world. H. G. Wells sketched just such a world in *Things to Come* (1936). Others stress that advance in communications and transportation technologies create a shrinking world that allows the development of global community and institutions:

> This growing interdependence may be confidently projected into the future, in the absence of strong government action to retard the process, because it is based on the technological advances in transportation and communication which increase both the speed and the reliability of moving goods, funds, persons, information, and ideas across national boundaries—in short, the same forces that are producing the much-touted shrinking world, in terms of both economic and psychological distance. (Cooper 1987, 21)

Many optimistic Western modernists are pluralists who see a positive, two-way interaction between democratic institutions and new technologies. Three popular futurists, Peter Drucker (1969), Alvin Toffler (1970, 1980),[3] and John Naisbitt (1982; Naisbitt and Aburdene 1990) fall into this category. All place heavy emphasis on advances in electronics and applications in computing and communication. Naisbitt (1982) identifies ten "megatrends" related to these and other high-technology advances, four of which have a decidedly pluralist cast: (1) a "bottom-up" society (an increasing movement of ideas from the local level to the national one), (2) a "participatory" rather than "representative" democracy, (3) self-help rather than institutional help, and (4) informal communications networks rather than chain-of-command forms.

Most modernists, however, devote remarkably little attention to the implications of technological advance for domestic or international politics, and there is sometimes a kind of political naïveté and wishful thinking in the approach of those who do. In contrast, another modernist and liberal, Herman Kahn (1976), saw no inherent problems in obtaining what humanity wants and needs from the environment, but felt strongly that both domestic mismanagement and international conflict were serious threats to actually doing so. He was, in fact, a realist who believed that nuclear military technology could lead not to global community but to nuclear war.

In addition to focusing on the power of modern weaponry in the hands of states unconstrained by superior force, there are at least two potential linkages between modernist thought and realism. First, the competition among states for technological advantage may be increasing with their growing state sponsorship of technological advance. Second, some neorealists seeking an explanation of hegemonic transition (discussed in Chapter 5) have adopted the long-wave theory of technological change to help explain the rise of new hegemons. For instance,

---

[3]Toffler (1980) notes that in his youth he was a Marxist; his adult orientation is that of a liberal, again indicating the ease with which a modernist can adopt either political-economy stance.

Gilpin (1987, 109) wrote:

> The clustering of technological innovation in time and space helps explain both the uneven growth among nations and the rise and decline of hegemonic powers....Periods of slowing rates of growth appear to be associated with the shift from one set of leading industrial sectors and centers of economic growth to another and with the transition from one hegemonic leader to the next. (Gilpin 1987, 109)

The loss of technological edge by the United States, and the weakening of its global leadership, may usher in a dangerous period.

ECOHOLISM

Ecoholists or neotraditionalists share with modernists a perception that important change is occurring in the broader context of world politics. They see that change not in technological advance, however, but in environmental deterioration and resource depletion. In addition to proliferation of local pollution problems, they point to the global scope of environmental damage from atmospheric ozone depletion, increased atmospheric CO_2, and the international movement of the pollutants causing acid rain. Unlike modernists, ecoholists anticipate problems rather than progress.

Theoretically, ecoholists rely heavily on a systems perspective with some parallels to those of neorealists and neoclassical liberals. All describe equilibrium-seeking processes. For neorealists the equilibrium is one of power balance among competing political units, and for liberals it is between supply and demand in markets, whereas for ecoholists the equilibrium is between human systems (population and economic) and their biologic and physical environment. Some neorealists believe that, within the interstate environment, selected states grow in power, become dominant in the system, overextend themselves, and decline relative to more dynamic powers. Neoclassical liberals often describe processes in which producers overinvest or overproduce, build capacity or inventories too high, and then must substantially retrench. Ecoholists believe that, within the ecosystem, some species increase in numbers, overextend themselves, and then decline. That is, they see a repeated dynamic of overshoot and collapse.[4] In the case of the human population on earth, both growing population size and rising economic requirements per capita place increasing pressures on fixed amounts of topsoil, raw materials, and environmental renewal capacity.

One of the key mechanisms underlying overshoot is the clash between individual and collective interests. Popularized by Hardin (1968) as the tragedy of the commons, the argument is that the rational self-interest of individuals leads them to increase their exploitation of a public good. When all individuals make the same calculation, however, their actions become self-defeating. In this book we

---

[4]This is exactly the behavior of the World 3 computer simulation model described and popularized in *The Limits to Growth* (Meadows and others 1972, 1974).

have discussed the clash between individual and collective logic across a wide range of examples, including states erecting barriers to imports despite believing in free trade; countries within OPEC cheating on other members of the cartel by producing above their quotas; states wanting to harvest a disproportionate share of the whale population of the oceans; and humans jointly polluting the global atmosphere. The same individual desire to capture private benefits and externalize costs lies also at the heart of the security dilemma: States seek to increase their security by building their military capabilities, even when it threatens the security of others.

Although no one can deny that life expectancies and GNPs have increased globally over the last two centuries, many ecoholists are skeptical that humanity can extend, or even maintain, such improvements. They note that many other civilizations similarly expanded their exploitation of the environment in the past, only to overshoot and subsequently collapse. Lester Brown draws our attention to the fate of the Mayans and to scholarship that suggests that the Central American civilization ran up against ecological limits before its still mysterious collapse:[5]

> Using the latest techniques of paleo-ecological research, scientists determined that the number of Mayans in the lowlands of Guatemala had expanded continuously over 17 centuries, beginning about the time of Homeric Greece in 800 B.C. Doubling on the average of every 408 years, the population by A.D. 900 had reached five million with a density comparable to that of the most agriculturally intensive societies of today....Within decades, the population fell to less than one-tenth of what it had been....As population pressure increased, soil erosion gradually accelerated. The topsoil was being washed into the area's lakes, draining the cropland of its productivity and one of the world's early civilizations of its sustenance. (Brown 1981, 3–4)

The extension of ecoholist thought into economics and politics builds on this analysis of the human predicament. Ecoholists emphasize three possible approaches to reconciling private and collective interests in the long term and postponing, if not avoiding, disaster. The first, when physically possible, is to privatize the commons. For instance, society can divide shared grazing land among the farmers, forcing each to internalize the consequences of decisions to add grazing animals, because it will damage the farmer's own vegetation. This

---

[5]Students of the rise and fall of civilizations disagree markedly about the reasons for their fall. In contrast to Brown's understanding, Toynbee (1972, 141) emphasized the loss of technological or creative impetus. Rostow's explanation combines neotraditionalist and neorealist (hegemonic stability theory) elements:

> Although we know less than we would wish to know about population movements in ancient empires, the mechanism of technological constraint appears to be more complex than a simple shortage of food in the face of an expanding population: the devastations of war and the attractions of the city pull men off the land; the limits of agricultural technology prevent full and productive employment in the cities, throwing welfare burdens on the state which become increasingly burdensome in the face of simultaneous and enlarging claims of security policy; the struggle for Eisenstadt's "free economic resources" leads to levels of taxation so high that they accelerate rather than stem the tide. (Rostow 1971, 52)

approach has many proponents among ecoholists who are also liberals, because it relies on private property ownership and the market (see Portney 1982).[6] For instance, a society will be less likely to deforest mountainsides when it enforces private rights to tree lots than when it collectively uses the forest as a source of fuel wood. As we saw in Chapter 17, however, this approach has little applicability to most global commons, because they cannot be easily divided—the 200-mile EEZs are an exception.

Many ecoholists argue that a second possible approach is to convince farmers who externalize the negative consequences of their grazing decisions about the error in their ways. If farmers voluntarily cease expanding the scope of their activities, they will not collectively bump against the environmental limits. Similarly, when an overly large human population is the problem, society can teach prospective parents to consider the social implications of additional children rather than simply the personal ones. This approach appeals to ecoholists who have a globalist, or more generally idealistic, orientation. Those partial to other approaches might argue that appeals to social responsibility are politically naïve; yet adherents can point to success stories, such as changed attitudes about littering and recycling that, even in the absence of significant penalties and enforcement, have had a substantial impact in many countries. Even in issue areas with much greater personal costs for voluntary individual sacrifice to the common good, such as restricting family size, it is possible that changes in attitudes about the relationship of humans and the environment has altered behavior in economically advanced countries.

A third approach involves collective coercion. It is possible for the farmers to decide collectively on the maximum total herd size and to assign individual herd sizes to their membership. Similarly, society can dictate maximum air pollution allowed per automobile or factory. Internationally, states can assign whaling quotas, ban CFCs, and license use of the deep oceans. Hardin emphasizes this approach, suggesting its extension even to collective decisions about the number of births. Hardin argues that allowing individuals to decide whether or not to restrict family size results in those with less social consciousness outbreeding those with more (free riding again). The collective-coercion approach generally appeals to realists, who are frequently pessimistic about voluntaristic human behavior and who emphasize the functioning of power relationships in society. It is reminiscent of the argument by Hobbes that the society that seeks public order must turn over power to the Leviathan. To the extent that society can voluntarily agree on collective coercion and periodically review it, the approach also appeals to many globalists (Mendlovitz 1975; Falk 1975).

Because there is no collectively coercive international order now in place, ecoholists with a realist bent tend to be rather pessimistic about prospects for

---

[6]One can also argue that emphasis on markets undercuts collective approaches. Encouragement and even exaltation of individualistic, self-serving behavior may destroy the social glue provided in earlier societies by clan or religion. Polanyi (1944) saw this problem at the heart of the social upheavals which gave rise to fascism. See also Hirsch (1976) and Bell (1976).

reaching an equilibrium with the environment. Moreover, they believe that environmental problems will often translate into interstate conflict—what Pirages (1983, 251) calls **ecoconflict**.[7] In conflicts over resources, such as water in the Middle East, global inequalities could worsen:

> In any situation of growing scarcity, some international actors will have a relative advantage in control of capital, technology, or special access to depleting resources. They can be expected to use that leverage for further economic advantage, as did the OPEC countries and some multinational energy corporations....It is chimerical to expect that advantaged states in a situation of worsening ecological scarcity will accept [proposals] for a "global compact" and a "world tax system" to close the gap between rich and poor nations. (Gurr 1985, 59)

CONCLUSION

This book has gradually expanded the scope of our subject matter and the range of perspectives we can bring to bear on that material. Realists restrict their attention largely to interstate high politics. Idealists direct us to ideas and communities including the nation and global community. It would be impossible to understand recent events in Central Europe and the former Soviet Union without both realist and idealist insights. Liberals tell us to look at markets, and structuralists point us to class structures. In combination with realist and idealist perspectives they make the evolution of the Bretton Woods system and of North-South relations intelligible to us. Finally, modernists and ecoholists focus our attention on technology and the environment. Together with all earlier perspectives, they help us make sense of global food, energy, and environmental issues.

We have now completed a wide-ranging discussion of global politics. In the process, however, we have continually added to the complexity of argument. The next chapter addresses the confusion that such complexity can cause.

---

[7]Choucri and North's (1975) "lateral pressure" was often a type of ecoconflict.

Chapter 19

ALTERNATIVE FUTURES: THE CLASH OF PERSPECTIVES

This book has now presented six views of the world in some detail. There is only one world, however. Are you confused? Do you have trouble falling asleep at night because you cannot decide if you are a realist or a globalist, a liberal, structuralist, modernist, or ecoholist? Probably not. The issue actually is a serious one, however, because your interpretation of world developments will influence how you vote, what organizations you join or support financially, and how you deal with individuals in other countries when you travel or work abroad. We all want to have as much self-knowledge as possible, and developing and understanding our own worldviews is an important part of that. How can you create order from possible confusion? How can you put the perspectives together?

PUTTING THE PERSPECTIVES TOGETHER

Worldviews structure thought. They focus attention on particular sets of issues; they direct adherents to a limited set of concepts and theories; they emphasize selected values. Table 19.1 combines Tables 10.1, 14.1, and 18.1 to summarize the various worldviews and theories that this book presents. Use it to review the wide variety of perspectives on world politics that we have discussed.

Once we understand the worldview(s) of a newspaper columnist or world leader, we can often anticipate how he or she will approach a new policy issue. In the 1980s, both American President Ronald Reagan and British Prime Minister Margaret Thatcher drew heavily on realist and (classical) liberal understandings of the world and therefore found themselves often in agreement with one another—for instance, on the need to build strong security systems and to revitalize the liberal trading order. Reagan's predecessor, Jimmy Carter, drew in addition on globalist and structuralist perspectives. For instance, his emphasis on human rights grew out of a belief in an emerging global community, based on the rights of individuals, and his sensitivity to the Third World implicitly recognized the existence of global structures.

TABLE 19.1
Summary of Worldviews and Theories

	Characterization of Change		
Dominant Subject Matter	Stability (and Unpatterned Change)	Cycles	Progressive Change
Political	Realism	Neorealism	Globalism Pluralism
	Balance of power; coalition behavior; statecraft	Rise and decline of hegemony or leadership; hegemonic stability; hegemonic transition	Functionalism; neofunctionalism; collective security; regime theory; federalism; international legal order proposals
	Intrastate analysis (friendly challenge to realism)		
Economic	Mercantilism- neomercantilism	Liberalism (neoclassical)	Liberalism
	Convertibility of power and wealth	Economic cycles	Capital accumulation; stages of growth; structural transformation
	Dependency	World systems theory	Marxism
	Dependence; dual economy development	Cycles of expansion	Capital accumulation; imperialism; system transformation
Broader Environment	Geopolitics	Ecoholism- neotraditionalism	Modernism
	Impact of technology and resources on power; imperialism	Tragedy of commons; overshoot and collapse	Technology advance
	Predominantly zero-sum logic		Nonzero-sum logic

National leaders and analysts of world politics use worldviews in one of three very different ways. Some people follow the model of the child given a hammer for Christmas—he or she hammers everything in sight. The intellectual version of the "law of the hammer" involves forming an extremely strong attachment to a single worldview, using it to understand as much as possible, and deciding that what the worldview cannot explain must be unimportant. We call such people "ideologues." Popular newspaper columnists often have a heavy anchor in one worldview.

The second approach is adoption of a combination of worldviews. Analogous to selecting food from categories on a menu (appetizers, entrées, and desserts), it is possible to adopt one perspective on political behavior, another on political economy, and a third on the broader political ecology. Table 19.1 helps us understand why some combinations arise more often than others. Modernists frequently are liberals and globalists, because all three perspectives share a belief in progressive history. Someone interested in the analysis of hegemonic cycles in world politics may turn to both world systems theory and neorealist theory; despite the different conceptual groundings of the approaches, they both emphasize a cyclical understanding. Realists, mercantilists, and geopoliticians share an attention to zero-sum aspects of world politics and to continuity in international relations.

There are tensions inherent in any combination of worldviews. For instance, in recent years the realist, liberal, and modernist worldviews have been dominant in the United States. An individual whose thought integrated these three perspectives would need to struggle with some important questions. Specifically, rapid advance in communication and transportation technologies (which the modernist anticipates), and increased capital, technology, and goods flows (the result of forces that the liberal sees as operative) inevitably intensify and complicate interactions across state borders. Do not these interactions, and the agents involved in them, at some point begin to undercut the traditional freedom of action and therefore sovereignty of the state (central to the realist perspective)? In thinking about a combination of worldviews, imagine the child at Christmas again, given a large pipe wrench, a small screwdriver, and a pair of plastic pliers. The tools complement each other, but crudely.

The third intellectual approach sees some value in each of the worldviews (see Banks 1985). The world is one of states, of actual and incipient communities, of markets, of enduring and self-reinforcing economic structures, of ecosystems and of technological progress. There is no reason that theory concerning each of these elements should not be important to a complete understanding. Unfortunately, the synthetic approach can lead to analysis and action paralysis, symptoms of the disease, "on-the-other-hand it is." A child who receives a complete adult's toolbox for Christmas may initially have little idea when to use the various hammers, screwdrivers, or wrenches, and may give up the whole enterprise in frustration.

The analogy suggests that the trick is learning to know when to reach for one tool or for a combination, and when others are appropriate. If the subject matter is nuclear strategy, realism helps us understand it, but when it is nationalism, realist thought is of remarkably little use, and idealism offers some insight. If the subject matter is international organizations, globalism helps put Amnesty International into a proper context, whereas liberalism and structuralism provide a much better basis for comprehension of multinational corporations.

It is thus possible to imagine a more comprehensive understanding of world politics in which the worldviews of this volume complement each other rather than compete. In fact, this book has attempted to begin mapping the issues for which various worldviews contribute the most understanding.

A second step might be a more formal attempt to synthesize the views (Burton 1990). For example, Abraham Maslow (1970) argued that all humans have a hierarchy of needs: physiological (such as a need for food), safety, belongingness and love, cognitive (the desire to know or understand), aesthetic (the craving for beauty), esteem (a need for recognition and status), and self-actualization (the fulfillment of ones own potential). He suggested that humans require at least minimal satisfaction of more basic needs before they can move on to higher level ones. It is possible to see connections between such needs and the values that we have associated with worldviews, for instance between the security motivation underlying realism and Maslow's safety need, or between the identity and autonomy values of idealisms and Maslow's need for belongingness and love. Clearly humans create states, build communities, participate in markets, become bound into hierarchical structures, pursue knowledge, and struggle to survive and propagate because such activities fulfill needs. If some needs were more basic than others, it might help us identify priorities among such activities.

Others have questioned, however, whether there is such a universal hierarchy of needs and values. Remember that many humans have unnecessarily starved or subjected themselves to the dangers of war in the name of nationalism and religion, or even for recognition and status. The idea of a single synthesis of worldviews is attractive, but it may also be remote. Worldviews and the understandings and values on which they stand may sometimes complement each other, but frequently they sharply contradict each other. For instance, realists and idealists fundamentally disagree about the extent and importance of global community, liberals and structuralists are at loggerheads on the implications of the North for Southern economic development, and modernists and ecoholists stand apart on the long-term ability of the growing global population to feed itself. There is room for compromise and intermediate positions on many issues, but not for wholehearted commitment to all worldviews.

Every individual needs to develop his or her own understanding of the world, and that requires using worldviews (and associated theories and concepts) singly or in combination. Without worldviews, world affairs would seemingly consist only of random events, and knowledge would be simply a kind of trivia expertise. The worldviews presented here, variations of them, or perhaps others not within the conception of this author, are fundamental to understanding world politics.

COMPETING PERSPECTIVES AND THE FUTURE

If you remain uncertain about your worldview, you are not alone. All but doctrinaire ideologues generally maintain an open and complex worldview, subject to both extension and change. If there were one obviously correct worldview or combination of them, we could theoretically put that knowledge together with an understanding of the forces that Chapter 1 identified and present a picture of the future evolution of the global system. To illustrate the impossibility of that, and to help you further assess your own worldview, the rest of this chapter will present six scenarios of the future.

Many of the students reading this book will be near retirement age in the year 2035. We have every reason to believe that the changes coming before then will hold comparable drama with those since 1945. What should we expect? Let us make the simplifying and hopeful assumption that between now and then the world will avoid a nuclear war involving the great powers. What might happen in a world free from superpower war? Each of these six hypothetical futures *exaggerates* the understandings of a particular worldview. Events will likely prove much in these scenarios false by the time this volume reaches your hands—some may also appear prescient.[1]

BUSINESS AS USUAL FOR STATES

This world of 2035 is much more nearly multipolar than bipolar. During the last three decades the United States and Russia have continued their long decline in relative power. Problems have been particularly severe for Russia, because of its ongoing political instability and the border tensions with the Ukraine and China. Although it lost control of Central Europe in the 1990s, it eventually used repressive force to maintain its own territorial integrity and to recentralize its political system. Its military might remain great, but its economic progress has been slow relative to that of many Western and Southern states.

The EC completed the establishment of a common market in 1992. Several member countries dashed high hopes of movement toward economic union when, led by Denmark and Britain, they refused to cede control of monetary and fiscal policy instruments. Spillover to even more highly politicized issues, such as the joint military force proposed by the BENELUX countries, never materialized. The European integration process appears to be at a dead end, incapable of going beyond trade and selected environmental issues.

Nuclear proliferation in the Middle East has continued, and now Iraq, Libya, Egypt, Israel, and Iran have declared or undeclared nuclear forces and delivery vehicles putting other Middle Eastern countries (and in Israel's case, most of the world) within strike range. Development of nuclear strike doctrine was turbulent

---

[1]Scholars of international politics seldom use their theories to speculate about the longer-term future. Thompson (1988) reviews a limited number of exceptions.

in the tense 2000–2010 period because the restricted geographic area made nuclear weapons in the Middle East into mutually destructive "doomsday machines." The Israeli acknowledgement and then mobilization of its nuclear weapons during its conflict with Syria in 2003 nearly plunged the region into nuclear war. An uneasy relative stability now exists in the Middle East.

India and Pakistan are also substantial nuclear powers, with missile-launching submarine capabilities like those of Israel, Egypt, and Iran. More generally, the global proliferation of nuclear capabilities, chemical and biologic weapons, and missile systems has created an extensive unit-veto system. The complexity of monitoring the capabilities of other states, when so many have devastating potential, has become extraordinarily great. Competition for satellite orbital locations, to facilitate both electronic espionage and to maintain communications with surface vessels and submarines, caused several major interstate disputes in the last two decades.

The trade wars at the turn of the century did not surprise many. Continued Japanese trade surpluses, coupled with growing surpluses in the NICs, intensified protectionist pressures around the world. Increased use of those surpluses to buy real estate and industrial facilities in the United States and Europe brought the issue to a crisis point. The U.S. Congress fired the first shot by passing legislation that required the bilateral trade deficit with Japan to be completely phased out in five years, using a combination of tariffs and quotas to assure that result. The Japanese stock market collapsed, and the national economy contracted sharply, reducing its imports, triggering even sharper cutbacks in U.S. purchases from Japan, and setting in motion a downward trade spiral. World financial markets were in turmoil as Japanese and NIC capital sought to find safe havens. Third World countries added to global financial problems by repudiating their debts. Disruption spread around the world, and it took nearly eight years before global growth began to recover.

Part of the Japanese package of fiscal measures to restart its economic engine was a sharp increase in its defense spending. The immediate impetus was its desire to support governments (and markets) in Malaysia and Indonesia against domestic disruption brought on by economic collapse. The United States, which had earlier pressed for such action in light of renewed military competition with Russia, quickly reversed its position and urged restraint.

After several years of global depression and increased international tension, the United States, Japan, the NICs, and the EC succeeded in creating a new economic order that gradually initiated a new round of reduction in protectionist barriers. Global economic growth resumed.

Although states often do find bases for limited cooperation, the world remains one of anarchy and struggle for relative position. The historically great scholars of world politics, such as Thucydides, Machiavelli, and Morgenthau, would have little difficulty understanding the world of today. It may be a more dangerous place than ever, but the rules that guide its dynamics remain largely unchanged.

LOCAL AND GLOBAL COMMUNITY BUILDING

It is difficult today to imagine the antagonism between the United States and Russia that threatened to destroy the world as recently as the 1980s. By far the greatest sources of global conflict remain in the Balkans and Transcaucasia. Even the massive refugee movements and major border realignments of the last few decades cannot seem to satisfy the various ethnic groups of those regions for any substantial period.

In spite of the ongoing ethnic and religious unrest, however, much of the world is more peaceful than it has ever been. The EC has continued to expand geographically and functionally. Sweden, Turkey, Hungary, and Finland are now full members and have completed the substitution of the ECU, controlled by the European central bank in Brussels, for their historic local currencies. Many other European states are associate members, as are Australia and New Zealand. Canada, the United States, Russia, and Japan have begun discussions with the EC about the creation of a World Economic Community, which would gradually lower the economic barriers between those states and the EC.

The United States, Russia, and the EC have created what some call a condominium in their joint effort to limit increasingly dangerous regional conflicts in the Third World. They actively support the UN program of inspection to verify the bans on production and stockpiling of chemical and biologic weapons. Through the United Nations, and its increasingly well-financed peace-keeping forces, they were finally able to secure acceptance by the Israelis and Palestinians of a two-state solution to their conflict. The key was convincing many Israelis that the international guarantees of their borders and of Palestine's demilitarization could be enforced.

Economic leadership has come from a different combination of states: the EC, Japan, and the United States. After their joint success in finally resolving the Third World debt problems, they turned to reform of the world economic order. A key change was the restructuring of GATT, so that extensive trade preferences are routinely given to LDCs; the new Development Assessment Group (DAG) oversees the gradual process of the graduation of NICs to developed status.

The principle of national self-determination, perhaps the most powerful of all world forces in the twentieth century, appears to have prevailed nearly everywhere. China gave autonomy to Tibet after the widely publicized civil disobedience period, and, after lengthy violence, India and Pakistan accepted an autonomous Kashmir. There proved to be a strong interaction between willingness of states to support self-determination and the growth of a global community. As the pluralistic security community of the Organization for Economic Cooperation and Development countries expanded into Eastern Europe and the South, the security needs of most states became less pressing. In this somewhat safer world, the contemporary models of the EC and India, allowing great regional autonomy, while maintaining limited central governmental functions, have proved popular. It is hard to see, however, how the conflicts of the old Soviet empire will ever cool.

Global community continues to strengthen in several ways. For instance, the United Nations Human Rights Commission (HRC) now sends observer teams around the world. The HRC recommends the application of economic sanctions against countries that it finds to hold political prisoners, use torture, or violate other international human rights standards. Although some countries still ignore the sanctions, failure to redress the problems identified by the observer teams (or refusal to admit them) now confers a pariah status on states that few are willing to accept. The continued spread of democracy facilitates this strengthening of global community. Freedom House now reports that 61 percent of the world's population lives in free societies, and another 23 percent are partly free (the figures in 1990 were 39 percent and 22 percent).

In addition the global community has made some progress on environmental issues. The EC has been a leader in that arena as well. CFC production has ceased, and the ocean dumping regime has nearly eliminated the most egregious sources of ocean pollution. The Mediterranean Action Plan was a useful early model. The Amazon for the Globe organization raised billions from governments, foundations, and individuals to compensate Brazil for conversion of extensive regions of the basin into national parks.

Human beings increasingly find themselves in communities with boundaries that they can define and with institutions and the policies they can control. The complexity of overlapping legal and institutional frameworks continues to grow in ways that Grotius, Kant, or Wilson might understand, but never imagined. States have not disappeared but possess increasingly restricted freedom of action. The world appears poised on the edge of a new era.

THE GLOBAL MARKET

Two primary forces have driven the continued integration of the global economy in the first third of this century: the magnetism of the Economic Community and the dynamism of global corporations or GCs (once known as MNCs). Let us consider each in turn.

The Economic Community (EC) is a multitiered structure of states progressively removing barriers to goods, capital, and labor flows among them. That process has gone the furthest in the eighteen core states of the EC, which have not only eliminated such barriers but have adopted a common currency, and a central bank to control money supply and interest rates. The second tier, the EC Associate Group, links the core to most of the other states of the old Organization for Economic Cooperation and Development and to the NICs of the late twentieth century. These additional countries have eliminated tariffs among themselves, as well as with the core, but have yet to standardize economic policies fully (for instance, product standards and subsidies) in the way that the old Single Market had by 1992. The third tier is the EC Preference Zone, and consists of states (now sixty-two) that have undertaken to eliminate tariffs and to initiate the standardization process. This includes most of the "new NICs," such as Colombia, India,

China, and Indonesia. In 2004 Brussels regularized the procedure for entry into the structure and for graduation across tier barriers. The scope and power of this complex structure is now so great that few states are likely to remain outside of it through this century.

Participation of Russia and Eastern European countries in the third tier was contingent on the economic reforms they began seriously in the late 1980s. That process took much longer than many expected (and faced a variety of setbacks including the Eastern debt crisis), but eventually culminated in the establishment of convertible currencies throughout the region. Now that those countries have truly joined the world economy, many expect several of them to progress rapidly into the first tier.

The GCs transmit the economic energy of the EC throughout the world. Once they all had clearly established "home countries" (most originated in Europe, the United States, Japan, and the early NICs), whereas today the share holding and management of many companies is really global. There has been a slow and irregular evolution of world institutions capable of overseeing and controlling power of global corporations. The United Nations Global Corporation Center imposes uniform accounting standards on them and requires extensive public reporting. It is now reviewing charges of monopoly practices in financial services by World Visacorp.

Latin America illustrates the role corporations have played in spreading economic growth around the world over the last 100 years. Early in the twentieth century most of the companies with important presences in the region were largely primary materials (mineral and agricultural product) producers and exporters. At the end of that century, and particularly after the debt crisis of the 1980s and early 1990s, global corporations brought massive amounts of capital into the region and transformed it into a center of global manufacturing. Critics point to the tremendous pollution problems of the early twenty-first century, but local and regional regulations gradually brought these problems under control. The same kind of industrialization process, driven by the capital and technology of the GCs, is now appearing in much of Africa, and the pollution in Nigeria and Zimbabwe is the worst in the world. In recent years the large service companies have come to dominate the presence of global corporations in much of Latin America. This is particularly true in the new postindustrial countries (PICs), such as Brazil, Mexico, and Venezuela.

The impact of corporations on domestic and international political processes remains a source of debate. Cardenas (2032, 44–89) argues that the industrialization of Latin America, with the assistance of the global corporations, was responsible for the growth of pluralism and the eventual destruction of the old land-owning elites. That in turn allowed the transformation of unstable democracies and authoritarian systems (subject to frequent military coups) into stable democracies.

The inner two tiers of the EC have now been free of interstate conflict for ninety years, and the possibility of it seems remote. The world is a more prosperous place than it has ever been. The same free markets that gave humanity such material benefit also encourage a pluralism that binds countries and dampens conflict.

EVOLVING GLOBAL DIVISION OF LABOR

Although the global economy has evolved dramatically in the last forty-five years, there has been no change in the fundamental division of it into core and periphery. The most dramatic aspect of the evolution was the marginalization of Russia and Eastern Europe. As the economic reforms of those countries faltered in the late 1990s, and political unrest seemed to offer choice only between anarchy and intense repression, they turned to the West for help. German and Japanese banks organized consortia and provided nearly $200 billion by 2005. A stream of consumer and capital goods imports from the West fed the "economic miracles" of Hungary, Czechoslovakia, Poland, and Russia and created a worldwide economic boom.

Unfortunately, much of the lending sustained a high lifestyle for the new political and commercial elites in the East, without creating industrial facilities capable of facing global competition. The emergency restructuring of Polish debt in 2004 staved off imminent default but began to make the scope of the problem clear. Banks quickly ceased to make additional loans and began to attempt recovery of their principal. During the next decade there was practically no growth in the region, and debt payments actually set up a flow of capital from East to West.

As it had a generation earlier in Latin America, the IMF insisted on economic policy changes, particularly the dismantlement of the extensive welfare systems put in place during the era that aid was available. Social unrest followed, as did the establishment of military governments to keep order in several of the countries. Ironically it was the unpopularity of communism that set in motion this process of so-called reform and integration into the world economy in the 1990s; now there is a popular resurgence of Communist parties throughout the region, although most governments repress the movements actively. In the last twenty years, growth has been irregular in the region, and political instability appears endemic.

The parallels between Eastern Europe and Latin America extend beyond the similarities of their debt crises. Although both are now heavily industrialized regions, little of that industry is high-technology, and much of it (including steel, aluminum, chemicals, and automobiles) is both capital intensive and polluting. Levels of unemployment are high in both regions; air and water quality are poor. The core countries retain the headquarters and research and development centers of the MNCs that control industry in both regions, and they completely dominate the newer communications, biologic, and space industries. Many of these newer industries are relatively nonpolluting.

The Asian NICs, which showed such promise in the late twentieth century, have had difficult times in the twenty-first century. Although Taiwan and Singapore made the transition to postindustrial economies and became part of the global core economy, South Korea, Thailand, and others were weakened by competition during the economic boom of the East, and then were hit hard by the global economic crisis of 2005–2015. The intensely nationalistic regime that came to power in Korea mismanaged the economy, and the Korean experience is now reminiscent of Argentina's twentieth-century fall from economic grace and political stability.

Africa remains at the bottom of the global division of labor. Only limited industrialization has taken root on the continent, and all efforts to implant it there face the problem of competition with already beleaguered industrial producers in Eastern Europe, Latin America, and Asia. Much of the world routinely denies export markets to Africa by tariffs and quotas, and other regions simultaneously seek to flood the limited domestic markets in Africa with their own goods. To add insult to injury, Africa has again become a dumping ground for industrial and household wastes from the industrial countries.[2] Although environmentalists in the core protest both the creation of pollution in the industrial countries of the periphery and the dumping of waste in Africa, there is little question that the core societies in which they live benefit from the inexpensive industrial goods available to them, and from their privileged place in the global division of labor.

The political and economic structures controlled by the core countries appear stronger than ever. The understanding of the costs that those structures impose on the periphery, and the extent of opposition to them, has also strengthened, however. Marx and Engels or the world systems theorists would have no difficulty identifying the contradictions and tensions in the contemporary system. The question is will the capitalist world system once again prove capable of adapting and surviving, or will the pressures for drastic change this time prove too great?

TECHNOLOGICAL ADVANCE

Writers of the late twentieth century sometimes suggested that the pace of technological advance was accelerating. They did not anticipate, however, the degree to which communications and artificial intelligence technologies would further force that pace. By the turn of the century, an overlapping set of electronic networks almost completely integrated the scientific community globally, and allowed simple and low-cost transmission of messages and data.[3] Computerized language translation (still by no means completely bug free but quite serviceable) completes the ability of scientists in all parts of the world to obtain and use the latest articles, papers, and data from anywhere on the globe. Although political barriers to the free flow of such information were still common in 2000, the necessity of being tied into these networks to maintain the quality of domestic research convinced governments that it was technologically suicidal to restrict access.

Various artificial intelligence techniques gradually increased the ease with which scientists can manipulate the otherwise overwhelming volumes of informa-

---

[2]Some now refer to parts of the continent as "global sacrifice areas."

[3]These were early versions of the same networks that now allow you to access the libraries and peoples of the world with your electronic briefcase.

tion and data available to them. Although these techniques still do not deliver on the promise, once felt to be inherent within them, of allowing computers to mimic human intelligence over a broad range of intellectual functions, specialized artificial intelligence applications (such as elaborate simulation models and expert systems) continue to become more sophisticated and useful.

Biotechnology illustrates their importance. The mapping of the genetic structures of a wide variety of flora and fauna (including, of course, humans) would have been impossible without these systems. That mapping allowed an explosion during the last three decades in the numbers of genetically engineered plants and animals. In combination with slowing population growth, and despite considerably extended life expectancies, the new agricultural techniques have finally put an end to food shortages around the world. Although the hungry are still with us in a very few areas of some countries, because of failures in social policy, humanity has banished widespread famine.

Technological advance in energy systems has been no less remarkable. New materials and techniques for construction of solar cells have made those cells into what the Japanese call the "rice of the energy system." Ironically, many thought that the transition away from oil and gas would render the OPEC countries less important globally. Instead, the new solar technologies, the plentiful capital of the OPEC countries, and the extensive desert surfaces of the Middle East have transformed Saudi Arabia and Iraq into large producers of solar energy (using a hydrogen transport system to the rest of the world). The astounding advances of the Russians in small-scale fusion power plants has, however, made it somewhat uncertain exactly what the energy system of the future will be.[4]

Unfortunately, military technology has not stagnated either. Russian and American laser weapons make the successful delivery of nuclear warheads by missiles uncertain. At the same time, however, they are capable of destroying cities and industrial facilities with incredible accuracy and speed. Other states are rushing to develop them. Although the five-party (Russia, the EC, the United States, China, and Japan) joint mission to Mars illustrates the potential for the great powers to cooperate, the rivalry in military technology poses severe challenges.

ENVIRONMENTAL LIMITS

The population of the world is now 8.2 billion, more than double that of 1970. Demographers early in the century told us that it would grow to 11 billion people before stabilizing near the end of the century. Unfortunately, it appears now that global population will likely be less than 8 billion by 2100. The famines and plagues of the last decade in Asia, Latin America, and Africa have already slowed the growth rate, and greater problems loom on the horizon. Global population clearly exceeds the carrying capacity of the global ecosystem. Consider three important pieces of evidence.

[4]Theoretical physicists greatly advanced fusion research by discovering the Whippoorwillian Effect.

First, the greenhouse effect has raised the average global temperature by nearly two degrees centigrade and significantly damaged world agricultural capability. Many countries call for dramatic restrictions on the use of fossil fuels and therefore on the emission of CO_2; actual reductions have been minor, and the warming effect will inevitably intensify. Although scientists have done a remarkable job in producing plants capable of withstanding the changed conditions,[5] and a select few countries of the world (like Canada) actually benefit somewhat from the higher temperatures, global growth rates in grain production have averaged only 0.3 percent in the last twenty years, and population growth continues near 1 percent.

Exacerbating food production problems, the rising ocean levels (from ice-cap melting) have submerged many productive coastal areas around the world and caused extremely expensive relocation of people from coastal cities to still other once-productive agricultural areas inland. The brief war between India and Bangladesh resulted from the near elimination of the latter country (a former coastal delta) by higher ocean levels and from the desperate attempt by its peoples to find safe haven in India. Global refugees now number nearly 150 million, and the problem, especially in Asia, continues to worsen.

Second, the ongoing depletion of global ozone from the upper atmosphere also contributes substantially to world food problems. At one time the primary concern about ozone depletion was that it would increase the number of skin cancers substantially. In fact, Taylor (2034) estimates that it can be blamed for about 1.5 million additional cancers worldwide. Human beings can seek shelter from the sun, however. The more significant threat to humanity has proved to be the damage that the increased ultraviolet radiation does to plants. Global crop yields are now estimated to be 15 percent lower than they would be were atmospheric ozone levels comparable to those of 100 years ago.

Third, attempts to compensate for slower growth in agricultural production led to often futile and even counterproductive efforts to increase land under cultivation. It appeared early in the century that Brazil had finally controlled the deforestation of rainforests. But by 2010 demand for food grown in that region reignited the process of forest clearing. The once-lush forests of Indonesia and the Philippines are essentially gone today. These actions, in addition to eliminating precious biologic resources, have further accelerated the greenhouse effect. What were once grasslands in a belt across Africa known as the Sahel are now deserts, after futile efforts to raise more crops and animals there. The intensification of ocean fishing by fleets from a variety of Asian and Latin American countries led to substantial overfishing and a collapse of world ocean fish catch from 80 million metric tons in 2010 to 45 million tons last year. The dams that India built at such great expense on the watersheds of the Ganges, both for flood control and for irrigation purposes, have lost nearly one-half of their storage capacity already

---

[5]Their proposals to compensate for the greenhouse effect by distributing reflective chaff in the upper atmosphere, or by installing massive reflecting dishes on the ground have attracted widespread attention but are economically infeasible.

because of silt flows from the deforested slopes of the Himalayas; they could be worthless within ten years.

Population control is the top global priority of the more developed countries. Many Asian, African, and Latin American LDCs are caught in a demographic trap, however. Rapid population growth has overstrained resources and has led to environmental degradation. This has caused GNP growth per capita to decline for the Third World as a whole in the last ten years, but the populations, and the environmental pressures, continued to grow. Agricultural production per capita in the South has now declined for twenty-five years, and food imports and grants from the North are inadequate to sustain dietary standards. Death rates from malnutrition-related causes (such as diarrhea in the young, pneumonia in the old, and influenza in both groups) are increasing sharply. In several countries (including India, Indonesia, Pakistan, Peru, Ecuador, Bolivia), and in most of Africa, death rates per 1,000 population have risen substantially during the last decade, reversing declines that began nearly 100 years ago. Higher birth rates generally follow increased death rates as parents seek to replace lost children. Thus even increased starvation has not yet checked population growth. Several countries, including Ghana, now follow the path trod earlier by China, applying coercive social controls to reduce the birth rate. Many other countries appear to have lost the political capability to undertake coherent social action.

Among the international political consequences of these developments is much greater conflict in the South and along the global North-South dimension. Although the North provides considerable food and technical assistance, developed countries increasingly feel overwhelmed by the scope of LDC problems, especially in light of significant difficulties of their own (especially coastal flooding and high-energy prices).

LAST WORDS

These hypothetical futures or scenarios both complement and contradict each other. To a considerable degree, the six worldviews focus on different aspects of the world (states, communities, markets, political-economic structures, technology, and the environment). Therefore the future will exhibit some characteristics of each scenario. Yet many elements are clearly contradictory, and thus some of these scenarios must capture the future better than others.

Which images will prove most nearly accurate? Human choice *does* influence the future. Many of you who read this book will live in the world of 2035, and you have an opportunity to help shape it.

REFERENCES

Adams, Gordon. 1988. "The Iron Triangle," in *The Domestic Sources of American Foreign Policy*, ed. Charles W. Kegley and Eugene R. Wittkopf. New York: St. Martin's Press, pp. 70–78.

Adelman, Irma. 1986. "A Poverty-Focused Approach to Development Policy," in *Development Strategies Reconsidered*, ed. John P. Lewis and Valeriana Kalab. New Brunswick, N.J.: Transaction Books.

Alker, Hayward R., Jr., and Thomas J. Biersteker. 1984. "The Dialectics of World Order: Notes for a Future Archeologist of International Savoir Faire," *International Studies Quarterly* 28, no. 2 (June), 121–142.

Allison, Graham T. 1971. *The Essence of Decision: Explaining the Cuban Missile Crisis.* Boston: Little, Brown.

Almond, Gabriel A. 1987. "The Development of Political Development," in *Understanding Political Development*, ed. Myron Weiner and Samuel P. Huntington. Boston: Little, Brown, pp. 437–478.

Ambrose, Stephen E. 1988. *Rise to Globalism: American Foreign Policy Since 1938*, 5th ed. New York: Penguin Books.

Amnesty International. 1988. *Amnesty International Report 1988.* London: Amnesty International Publications.

Appleman, Philip, ed. 1977. *Darwin*, 2nd ed. New York: W. W. Norton.

Arms Control and Disarmament Agency. 1979. *World Military Expenditures and Arms Transfers 1968–1977.* Washington, D.C.: U.S.G.P.O.

Arms Control and Disarmament Agency. 1988. *World Military Expenditures and Arms Transfers 1987.* Washington, D.C.: U.S.G.P.O.

Aron, Raymond. 1966. *Peace and War.* New York: Praeger.

Aron, Raymond. 1974. *The Imperial Republic.* Cambridge: Winthrop.

Ashley, Richard K. 1984. "The Poverty of Neo-Realism," *International Organization* 38, no. 2 (Spring), 225–286.

Axelrod, Robert. 1984. *The Evolution of Cooperation.* New York: Basic Books.

Ayres, Robert U. 1969. *Technological Forecasting and Long-range Planning.* New York: McGraw-Hill.

Bailey, Thomas A. 1948. *The Man in the Street: The Impact of American Public Opinion on Foreign Policy.* New York: Macmillan.

Baily, Martin Neil, and Alok N. Chakrabarti. 1988. *Innovation and the Productivity Crisis.* Washington, D.C.: Brookings Institution.

Baldwin, David A. 1979. "Power Analysis and World Politics: New Trends versus Old Tendencies," *World Politics* 31, no. 2 (January), 161–194.

Baldwin, David A. 1980. "Interdependence and Power: A Conceptual Analysis," *International Organization* 34, no. 4 (Autumn), 471–506.

Baldwin, David A. 1985. *Economic Statecraft.* Princeton, N.J.: Princeton University Press.

Baldwin, Simeon E. 1907. "The International Congresses and Conferences of the Last Century as Forces Working Towards the Solidarity of the World," *American Journal of International Law* 1, part 2 (July–October), 565–578.

Ball, Terrence. 1988. *Transforming Political Discourse: Political Theory and Critical Conceptual History.* New York: Basil Blackwell.

Banks, Michael. 1984. "The Evolution of International Relations Theory," in *Conflict in World Society*, ed. Michael Banks. New York: St. Martin's Press, pp. 3–21.

Banks, Michael. 1985. "The Inter-Paradigm Debate," in *International Relations: A Handbook of Current Theory*, ed. Margot Light and A. J. R. Groom. Boulder, Colo.: Lynne Rienner, pp. 7–29.

Barber, James David. 1985. *The Presidential Character: Predicting Performance in the White House*, 3rd ed. Englewood Cliffs, N.J.: Prentice Hall.

Bard, Mitchell. 1988. "The Influence of Ethnic Interest Groups," in *The Domestic Sources of American Foreign Policy*, ed. Charles W. Kegley and Eugene R. Wittkopf. New York: St. Martin's Press, pp. 57–69.

Barnaby, Frank. 1986. "How the Next War Will Be Fought," *Technology Review* 89, no. 7 (October), 26–37.

Barnet, Richard J. 1984. "Why Trust the Soviets?" *World Policy Journal* 1, no. 3 (Spring), 461–482.

Barry, Brian, and Russell Hardin, eds. 1982. *Rational Man and Irrational Society?* Beverly Hills, Calif.: Sage.

Bauer, Peter, and Basil Yamey. 1984. "Adverse Repercussions of Aid," in *Leading Issues in Economic Development*, 4th ed., ed. Gerald M. Meier. New York: Oxford University Press, pp. 293–297.

Bauer, Raymond A., Ithiel de Sola Pool, and Lewis Anthony Dexter. 1972. *American Business and Public Policy*, 2nd ed. Chicago: Aldine Atherton.

Baumol, William J., and Wallace E. Oates. 1984. "Long-Run Trends in Environmental Quality," in *The Resourceful Earth*, ed. Julian L. Simon and Herman Kahn. New York: Basil Blackwell, pp. 439–475.

Bean, Richard. 1973. "War and the Birth of the Nation State," *Journal of Economic History* 33, no. 1 (March), 203–221.

Beck, Nathaniel. 1991. "The Illusion of Cycles in International Relations," *International Studies Quarterly* 35, no. 4 (December), 455–476.

Beer, Francis A. 1981. *Peace Against War.* San Francisco: W. H. Freeman.

Belassa, Bela. 1961. *The Theory of Economic Integration.* Homewood, Ill.: Richard D. Irwin.

Bell, Daniel. 1976. *The Cultural Contradictions of Capitalism*. New York: Basic Books.

Bell, Daniel. 1987. "The World and the United States in 2013," *Daedalus* 116, no. 3 (Summer), 1–32.

Bendor, Jonathan, and Thomas H. Hammond. 1989. "Rethinking Allison's Models." Paper delivered at the annual American Political Science Association meetings, Atlanta,Georgia.

Bennett, Robert William, and Joseph Zitomersky. 1982. "The Delimitization of International Diplomatic Systems 1816–1970: The Correlate of War Project's Systems Reconstructed," in *On Making Use of History*, ed. Joseph Zitomersky. Sweden: Esselte Studium, pp. 67–129.

Bergesen, Albert. 1983. "The Class Structure of the World-System," in *Contending Approaches to World System Analysis*, ed. William R. Thompson. Beverly Hills, Calif.: Sage, pp. 43–54.

Bill, James A., and Robert W. Stookey. 1975. *Politics and Petroleum*. Brunswick, Oh.: King's Court Communications.

Black, Cyril E. 1966. *The Dynamics of Modernization*. New York: Harper & Row.

Blake, David H., and Robert S. Walters. 1987. *The Politics of Global Economic Relations*, 3rd ed. Englewood Cliffs, N.J.: Prentice Hall.

Blechman, Barry M., and Stephan S. Kaplan, with David K. Hall, William B. Quant, Jerome N. Slater, Robert M. Slusser, and Philip Windsor. 1978. *Force without War*. Washington, D.C.: Brookings Institution.

Blight, James G., and David A. Welch. 1989. *On the Brink: Americans and Soviets Reexamine the Cuban Missile Crisis*. New York: Hill and Wang.

Bloomfield, Lincoln. 1988. "Foreign Policy—Backstage in an Election Year," *The Christian Science Monitor* (March 14), 14.

Bobrow, Davis B., and John S. Dryzek. 1987. *Policy Analysis by Design*. Pittsburgh, Pa.: University of Pittsburgh Press.

Bogue, Donald J. 1980. "Policy Implications of the Changing Relationship between Population and Economic Change," in *The Politics of Food*, ed. D. Gale Johnson. Chicago: Chicago Council on Foreign Relations, pp. 124–139.

Boorstin, Daniel J. 1983. *The Discoverers*. New York: Vintage Books.

Boulding, Kenneth E. 1981. *Ecodynamics: A New Theory of Social Evolution*. Beverly Hills, Calif.: Sage.

Bower, Bruce. 1987. "Extinctions on Ice," *Science News* 132, no. 18 (October 31), 284–285.

Boyd, Andrew. 1987. *An Atlas of World Affairs*, 8th ed. New York: Methuen.

Boyle, Francis Anthony. 1985. *World Politics and International Law*. Durham, N.C.: Duke University Press.

Brandt Commission. 1980. *North-South: A Program for Survival*. Cambridge, Mass.: MIT Press.

Brandt Commission. 1983. *Common Crisis*. Cambridge, Mass.: MIT Press.

Braudel, Fernand. 1979. *The Perspective of the World*. Vol. 3 of *Civilization and Capitalism: 15th–18th Century*. New York: Harper & Row.

Brecher, Michael, and Patrick James. 1989. "Polarity, Stability, Crisis," in *Crisis, Conflict and Instability*, ed. Michael Brecher and Jonathan Wilkenfeld. New York: Pergamon Press, pp. 29–42.

Brecher, Michael, and Jonathan Wilkenfeld. 1989. *Crisis, Conflict and Instability*. New York: Pergamon Press.

Brecher, Michael, Jonathan Wilkenfeld, and Sheila Maser. 1988. *Crises in the Twentieth Century.* Vol. 1 of *Handbook of International Crises.* London: Pergamon Press.

Bremer, Stuart A., and Barry B. Hughes. 1990. *Disarmament and Development: A Design for the Future?* Englewood Cliffs, N.J.: Prentice Hall.

Bretton, Henry L. 1986. *International Relations in the Nuclear Age.* Albany: State University of New York.

British Petroleum. 1988. *British Petroleum Statistical Review of World Energy.* London: British Petroleum Company.

British Petroleum. 1989. *British Petroleum Statistical Review of World Energy.* London: British Petroleum Company.

British Petroleum. 1991. *British Petroleum Statistical Review of World Energy.* London: British Petroleum Company.

British Petroleum. 1992. *British Petroleum Statistical Review of World Energy.* London: British Petroleum Company.

Brown, Lester. 1972. *World without Borders.* New York: Vintage Books.

Brown, Lester. 1981. *Building a Sustainable Society.* New York: W. W. Norton.

Brown, Lester. 1988a. "Analyzing the Demographic Trap," in *State of the World 1987*, ed. Lester R. Brown and others. New York: W. W. Norton, pp 20–37.

Brown, Lester. 1988b. "Sustaining World Agriculture," in *State of the World 1987*, ed. Lester R. Brown and others. New York: W. W. Norton, pp. 122–138.

Brown, Lester. 1989. "Reexamining the World Food Prospect," in *State of the World 1989*, ed. Lester R. Brown. Washington, D.C.: Worldwatch Institute, pp. 41–58.

Brown, Lester, Christopher Flavin, and Edward C. Wolf. 1988. "Earth's Vital Signs," *The Futurist* 22, no. 4 (July–August), 13–20.

Brown, Seyom. 1982 (originally 1973). "The Changing Essence of Power," in *Globalism versus Realism: International Relations Third Debate*, eds. Ray Maghroori and Bennett Ramberg. Boulder, Colo.: Westview Press, pp. 23–36.

Brown, Seyom. 1987. *The Causes and Prevention of War.* New York: St. Martin's Press.

Brown, Seyom. 1988. *New Forces, Old Forces, and the Future of World Politics.* Glenview, Ill.: Scott, Foresman.

Bruckmann, Gerhart. 1983. "The Long Wave Debate," *Options* 2, 6–9.

Brzezinski, Zbigniew. 1988. "America's New Geostrategy," *Foreign Affairs* 66, no. 4 (Spring), 680–699.

Buchanan, James M., and Gordon Tullock. 1962. *The Calculus of Consent.* Ann Arbor: University of Michigan Press.

Bueno de Mesquita, Bruce. 1978. "Systemic Polarization and the Occurrence and Duration of War," *Journal of Conflict Resolution* 22, no. 2 (June), 241–267.

Bueno de Mesquita, Bruce. 1981. *The War Trap.* New Haven, Conn.: Yale University Press.

Bull, Hedley. 1977. *The Anarchical Society: A Study of Order in World Politics.* New York: Columbia University Press.

Burton, Daniel F., Jr. 1989. "Economic Realities and Strategic Choices," in *Vision for the 1990s*, ed. Daniel F. Burton, Jr., Victor Gotbaum, and Felix G. Rohatyn. Cambridge, Mass: Ballinger, pp. 3–25.

Burton, John W. 1985. "World Society and Human Needs," in *International Relations: A Handbook of Current Theory*, ed. Margot Light and A. J. R. Groom. Boulder, Colo.: Lynne Rienner, pp. 46–59.

Burton, John W., ed. 1990. *Conflict: Human Needs Theory.* New York: St. Martin's Press.

Caporaso, James A., ed. 1987. *A Changing International Division of Labor.* Boulder, Colo.: Lynne Rienner.

Caporaso, James A., and Stephan Haggard. 1989. "Power in the International Political Economy," in *Power in World Politics*, ed. Richard J. Stoll and Michael D. Ward. Boulder, Colo.: Lynne Rienner, pp. 99–120.

Carbonell, Jaime G. 1981. *Subjective Understanding: Computer Models of Belief Systems.* Ann Arbor, Mich.: UMI Research Press.

Carlson, Beverly A. and Tessa M. Wardlaw. 1990. *A Global, Regional and Country Assessment of Child Malnutrition.* New York: UNICEF.

Carr, Edward Hallett. 1964 (originally 1939). *The Twenty Years' Crisis 1919–1939.* New York: Harper & Row.

Carter, Jimmy. 1982. *Keeping Faith: Memories of a President.* New York: Bantam Books.

Cassen, Robert, and Associates. 1986. *Does Aid Work?* Oxford: The Clarendon Press.

Cassese, Antonio. 1986. *International Law in a Divided World.* Oxford: The Clarendon Press.

Castells, Manuel, and Laura D'Andrea Tyson. 1988. "High-Technology Choices Ahead: Restructuring Interdependence," in *Growth, Exports, and Jobs in a Changing World Economy: Agenda 1988*, ed. John W. Sewell, Stuart K. Tucker, and Contributors. New Brunswick, N.J.: Transaction Books, pp. 55–95.

Cecchini, Paolo. 1988. *The European Challenge.* Aldershot, England: Wildwood House.

Central Intelligence Agency. 1988. *The World Factbook 1988.* Washington, D.C.: Central Intelligence Agency.

Central Intelligence Agency. 1991. *The World Factbook 1991.* Washington, D.C.: Central Intelligence Agency.

Chan, Steve. 1984. "Mirror, Mirror on the Wall...: Are the Free Countries More Pacific?" *Journal of Conflict Resolution* 28, no. 4 (December), 617–648.

Chan, Steve. 1989. "Income Inequality Among LDCs: A Comparative Analysis of Alternative Perspectives," *International Studies Quarterly* 33, no. 1 (March), 45–65.

Chandler, Clay. 1987. "Bright Lights, Big MITI," *The New Republic*, no. 789 (August 31), 11–13.

Chase-Dunn, Christopher. 1979. "Comparative Research on World System Characteristics," *International Studies Quarterly* 23, no. 4 (December), 601–623.

Chase-Dunn, Christopher. 1983. "The Kernel of the Capitalist World-Economy: Three Approaches," in *Contending Approaches to World System Analysis*, ed. William R. Thompson. Beverly Hills, Calif.: Sage, pp. 55–78.

Chenery, Hollis. 1979. *Structural Change and Development Policy.* Baltimore, Md.: Johns Hopkins University Press.

Chevron Corporation. 1987. *World Energy Outlook.* San Francisco: Chevron.

Chourcri, Nazli. 1980. "International Political Economy: A Theoretical Perspective," in *Change in the International System*, ed. Ole R. Holsti, Randolph M. Siverson, and Alexander L. George. Boulder, Colo.: Westview Press, pp. 103–129.

Chourcri, Nazli, and Robert C. North. 1975. *Nations in Conflict: National Growth and International Violence.* San Francisco: W. H. Freeman.

Christensen, Cheryl. 1978. "World Hunger: A Structural Approach," in *The Global Political Economy of Food*, ed. Raymond F. Hopkins and Donald J. Puchala. Madison: The University of Wisconsin Press, pp. 177–200.

Christensen, Cheryl. 1987. "Food Security in Sub-Saharan Africa," in *Pursuing Food Security*, ed. W. Ladd Hollist and F. LaMond Tullis. Boulder, Colo.: Lynne Rienner, pp. 67–97.

Cipolla, Carlo M. 1962. *The Economic History of World Population.* Baltimore, Md.: Penguin Books, 1962.

Cipolla, Carlo M., ed. 1970. *The Economic Decline of Empires.* London: Methuen.

Clairmonte, Frederick, and John Cavanagh. 1982. "Transnational Corporations and Global Markets: Changing Power Relations," *Trade and Development: An UNCTAD Review* 4 (Winter), 149–182.

Clark, Grenville, and Louis B. Sohn. 1960. *World Peace Through World Law.* Cambridge, Mass.: Harvard University Press.

Claude, Inis L., Jr. 1962. *Power and International Affairs.* New York: Random House.

Clawson, Marion. 1982. "Private Forests," in *Current Issues in Natural Resource Policy*, ed. Paul R. Portney. Washington, D.C.: Resources for the Future, pp. 283–292.

Cline, Ray S. 1980. *World Power Trends and U.S. Foreign Policy for the 1980s.* Boulder, Colo.: Westview Press.

Cobban, Helena. 1988. "Israel's Nuclear Game: The U.S. Stake," *World Policy Journal* 5, no. 3 (Summer), 415–433.

Cohen, Benjamin J. 1987. "A Brief History of International Monetary Relations," in *International Political Economy*, ed. Jeffrey A. Frieden and David A. Lake. New York: St. Martin's Press, pp. 245–268.

Coleman, James S. 1986. *Individual Interests and Collective Action.* Cambridge: Cambridge University Press.

Congressional Quarterly. 1979. *Energy Policy.* Washington, D.C.: Congressional Quarterly Press.

Connor, Walker. 1967. "Self-Determination: The New Phase," *World Politics* 20, no. 1 (October), 30–53.

Cook, Earl. 1976. *Man, Energy, Society.* San Francisco: W. H. Freeman.

Cooper, Richard N. 1987. "Economic Interdependence and Foreign Policy in the Seventies," in *International Political Economy*, ed. Jeffrey A. Frieden and David A. Lake. New York: St. Martin's Press, pp. 18–30.

Cottam, Richard W. 1988. *Iran and the United States.* Pittsburgh, Pa.: University of Pittsburgh Press.

Couloumbis, Theodore A., and James H. Wolfe. 1986. *Introduction to International Relations*, 3rd ed. Englewood Cliffs, N.J.: Prentice Hall.

Council on Environmental Quality. 1981. *The Global 2000 Report to the President.* Washington, D.C.: U.S.G.P.O.

Council on Environmental Quality. 1991. *21st Annual Report.* Washington, D.C.: Council on Environmental Quality.

Cox, Robert W. 1987. *Production, Power, and World Order.* New York: Columbia University Press.

Craig, Gordon A., and Alexander George. 1983. *Force and Statecraft—Diplomatic Problems of Our Time*. New York: Oxford University Press.

Crankshaw, Edward. 1978. "Europe's Reds: Trouble for Moscow," *The New York Times Magazine* (Feb. 12), 18–20, 46, 48, 50, 51, and 56, reprinted in *World Politics Debated: A Reader in Contemporary Issues*, ed. Herbert M. Levine. New York: McGraw-Hill, 1983, pp. 154–160.

Curran, John Philpot. 1790. "Speech upon the Right of Election," in John Bartlett, *Familiar Quotations*, 12th ed., ed. Christopher Morleyas, Boston, Mass.: Little, Brown, 1950, p. 277.

Curtis, Michael. 1965. *Western European Integration*. New York: Harper & Row.

Cusack, Thomas R. 1985. "The Evolution of Power, Threat, and Security: Past and Potential Developments," *International Interactions* 12, no. 2, 151–198.

Cusack, Thomas R. 1989. "The Management of Power in a Warring State System: An Evolution of Balancing, Collective Security, and Laissez-Faire Policies," in *Power in World Politics*, ed. Richard J. Stoll and Michael D. Ward. Boulder, Colo.: Lynne Rienner, pp. 209–226.

Cusack, Thomas R., and Wolf-Dieter Eberwein. 1982. "Prelude to War: Incidence, Escalation, and Intervention in International Disputes, 1900–1976," International Interactions 9, no. 1, 9–28.

Czempiel, Ernst-Otto, and James N. Rosenau, eds. 1989. *Global Changes and Theoretical Challenges*. Lexington, Mass: Lexington Books.

Dahl, Robert. 1956. *Preface to Democratic Theory*. Chicago: University of Chicago Press.

Dahlberg, Kenneth A., Nancy K. Hetzel, and Marvin S.Soroos. 1980. *Global Issues: Environment*. Columbus, Oh.: Consortium for International Studies Education.

Daltrop, Anne. 1986. *Politics and the European Community*, 2nd ed. New York: Longman.

Daly, Herman E., ed. 1980. *Economic, Ecology, Ethics*. San Francisco: W. H. Freeman.

Dasmann, Raymond F., John P. Milton, and Peter Freeman. 1973. *Ecological Principles for Economic Development*. New York: John Wiley.

Davis, David Howard. 1978. *Energy Politics*, 2nd ed. New York: St. Martin's Press.

Dawshia, Adeed. 1986. *The Arab Radicals*. New York: Council on Foreign Relations.

DeConde, Alexander. 1978. *A History of American Foreign Policy*, 3rd ed., Vol 2. New York: Charles Scribner's.

Denton, Frank H., and Warren Phillips. 1968. "Some Patterns in the History of Violence," *Journal of Conflict Resolution* 12, no. 2 (June), 132–195.

Der Derian, James, and Michael J. Shapiro, eds. 1989. *International/Intertextual Relations: Postmodern Readings of World Politics*. Lexington, Mass.: Lexington Books.

de Riencourt, Amaury. 1968. *The American Empire*. New York: Dell.

Destler, I. M. 1978. "United States Food Policy 1972–1976: Reconciling Domestic and International Objectives," in *The Global Political Economy of Food*, ed. Raymond F. Hopkins and Donald J. Puchala. Madison: The University of Wisconsin Press, pp. 41–78.

de Tocqueville, Alexis. 1945 (originally 1835). *Democracy in America*. 2 vols. New York: Vintage Books.

Deutsch, Karl W. 1961. "Social Mobilization and Political Development," *American Political Science Review* 55, no. 3 (September), 493–515.

Deutsch, Karl W. 1966. *Nationalism and Social Communication*, 2nd ed. Cambridge, Mass.: MIT Press.

Deutsch, Karl W. 1968. *The Analysis of International Relations*. Englewood Cliffs, N.J.: Prentice-Hall.

Deutsch, Karl W. 1974. "Between Sovereignty and Integration: Conclusion," in *Between Sovereignty and Integration*, ed. Ghita Ionescu. New York: John Wiley, pp. 181–187.

Deutsch, Karl W. 1979. *Tides among Nations*. New York: The Free Press.

Deutsch, Karl W. 1988. *The Analysis of International Relations*, 3rd ed. Englewood Cliffs, N.J.: Prentice Hall.

Deutsch, Karl W., and others. 1957. *Political Community and the North Atlantic Area: International Organization in the Light of Historical Experience*. Princeton, N.J.: Princeton University Press.

Deutsch, Karl W., and J. David Singer. 1969. "Multipolar Power Systems and International Stability," in *International Politics and Foreign Policy*, 2nd ed., ed. James N. Rosenau. New York: The Free Press, pp. 315–324.

Dizard, Wilson P., Jr. 1985. *The Coming Information Age*, 2nd ed. New York: Longman.

Domke, William K. 1988. *War and the Changing Global System*. New Haven, Conn.: Yale University Press.

dos Santos, Theotonio. 1984 (originally 1970). "The Structure of Dependence," in *The Gap between Rich and Poor*, ed. Mitchell A. Seligson. Boulder, Colo.: Westview Press, pp. 95–104.

Dougherty, James E., and Robert L. Pfaltzgraff, Jr. 1981. *Contending Theories of International Relations*, 2nd ed. New York: Harper & Row.

Dougherty, James E., and Robert L. Pfaltzgraff, Jr. 1986. *American Foreign Policy: FDR to Reagan*. New York: Harper & Row.

Downs, Anthony. 1957. *An Economic Theory of Democracy*. New York: Harper & Row.

Doyle, Michael W. 1986. *Empires*. Ithaca, N.Y.: Cornell University Press.

Drucker, Peter F. 1969. *The Age of Discontinuity*. New York: Harper & Row.

Drucker, Peter F. 1986. "The Changed World Economy," *Foreign Affairs* 64, no. 4 (Spring), 768–791.

Drucker, Peter F. 1986b. "New Technology: Predicting Its Impact," in *Technology and Man's Future*, 4th ed., ed. Albert H. Teich. New York: St. Martin's Press, 214–218.

Druckman, Daniel, and P. Terrence Hopmann. 1989. "Behavioral Aspects of Negotiations on Mutual Security," in *Behavior, Society and Nuclear War*, ed. Philip E. Tetlock, Jo L. Husbands, Robert Jervis, Paul C. Stern, and Charles Tilly. New York: Oxford University Press, pp. 85–173.

Durning, Alan B. 1989a. *Action at the Grassroots: Fighting Poverty and Environmental Decline*, Worldwatch Paper 88 (January). Washington, D.C.: Worldwatch Institute.

Durning, Alan B. 1989b. "Mobilizing at the Grassroots," in *State of the World 1989*, ed. Lester R. Brown. Washington, D.C.: Worldwatch Institute, pp. 154–173.

Eichenberg, Richard C. 1989. *Public Opinion and National Security in Western Europe*. Ithaca, N.Y.: Cornell University Press.

Eicher, Carl. 1982. "Facing up to Africa's Food Crisis," *Foreign Affairs* 61, no. 1 (Fall), 151–174.

Emmanuel, Arghiri. 1972. *Unequal Exchange: A Study of the Imperialism of Trade.* New York: Monthly Review Press.

Engler, Robert. 1961. *The Politics of Oil: Private Power and Democratic Directions.* Chicago: University of Chicago Press.

Enthoven, Alain C., and K. Wayne Smith. 1971. *How Much Is Enough?* New York: Harper Colophon.

Etzioni, Amitai. 1988. *The Moral Dimension: Towards a New Economics.* New York: The Free Press.

Falk, Richard. 1975. *A Study of Future Worlds.* New York: The Free Press.

Falk, Richard, and Samuel S. Kim. 1983. "World Order Studies and the World System," in *Contending Approaches to World System Analysis,* ed. William R. Thompson. Beverly Hills, Calif.: Sage, pp. 203–237.

Farnsworth, David N. 1988. *International Relations.* Chicago: Nelson-Hall.

Farrell, R. Barry. 1966. "Foreign Policies of Open and Closed Political Societies," in *Approaches to Comparative and International Politics,* ed. R. Barry Farrell. Evanston, Ill.: Northwestern University Press, pp. 167–206.

Feinberg, Richard E. 1985. "International Finance and Investment: A Surging Public Sector," in *U.S. Foreign Policy and the Third World: Agenda 1985–86,* ed. John W. Sewell, Richard E. Feinberg, and Valeriana Kallab. New Brunswick, N. J.: Transaction Books, pp. 51–71.

Feinberg, Richard E., and Gregg H. Goldstein. 1988. *The U.S. Economy and Developing Countries: Campaign 88 Briefing Papers for the Candidates.* Washington, D.C.: Overseas Development Council.

Feld, Werner. 1976. *The European Community in World Affairs.* Port Washington, N.Y.: Alfred.

Ferguson, Yale H., and Richard W. Mansbach. 1988. *The Elusive Quest: Theory and International Politics.* Columbia: University of South Carolina Press.

Feuer, Lewis S., ed. 1959. *Marx and Engels: Basic Writings on Politics and Philosophy.* New York: Anchor Books.

Finley, David J., Ole R. Holsti, and Richard R. Fagen. 1967. *Enemies in Politics.* Chicago: Rand McNally.

Flavin, Christopher. 1985. *World Oil: Coping with the Dangers of Success.* Worldwatch Paper 66 (July). Washington, D.C.: Worldwatch Institute.

Flavin, Christopher, and Alan B. Durning. 1988. *Building on Success: The Age of Energy Efficiency.* Worldwatch Paper 82 (March). Washington, D.C.: Worldwatch Institute.

Foreign Policy Association. 1992. *Great Decisions.* New York: Foreign Policy Association.

Foster, Richard H., and Robert Edington. 1985. *Viewing International Relations and World Politics.* Englewood Cliffs, N.J.: Prentice Hall.

Frank, André Gunder. 1983. "World System in Crisis," in *Contending Approaches to World System Analysis,* ed. William R. Thompson. Beverly Hills, Calif.: Sage, pp. 27–42.

Freeman, Chris. 1988. "Diffusion: The Spread of New Technology to Firms, Sectors, and Nations," in *Innovation, Technology, and Finance,* ed. Arnold Heertje. New York: Basil Blackwell, pp. 38–70.

French, Hillary F. 1990. *Green Revolutions: Environmental Reconstruction in Eastern Europe and the Soviet Union.* Worldwatch Paper 99. Washington, D.C.: Worldwatch Institute.

Fri, Robert W. 1988. "New Directions for Oil Policy," *Environment* (June). Reprinted in *Global Issues 88–89*, ed. Robert Jackson. Guilford, Conn.: Dushkin, pp. 105–112.

Fried, Edward R. 1976. "International Trade in Raw Materials: Myths and Realities," *Science* 191, no. 4227(February 20), 641–646.

Frieden, Jeffrey A., and David A. Lake, eds. 1987. *International Political Economy*. New York: St. Martin's Press.

Friedman, Milton. 1962. *Capitalism and Freedom*. Chicago: University of Chicago Press.

Frost, Ellen L. 1987. *For Richer, For Poorer: The New U.S.–Japan Relationship*. New York: Council on Foreign Relations.

Fukuyama, Francis. 1989. "The End of History?" *The National Interest*, no. 16 (Summer), 3–18.

Galtung, Johan. 1964. "A Structural Theory of Aggression," *Journal of Peace Research* 1, no. 2, 95–119.

Garnett, John C. 1984. *Commonsense and the Theory of International Politics*. Albany: State University of New York Press.

Garnham, David. 1986. "War-Proneness, War-Weariness, and Regime Type: 1816–1980," *Journal of Peace Research* 23, no. 3 (September), 279–289.

Garraty, John A., and Peter Gay, eds. 1981. *The Colombia History of the World*. New York: Harper & Row.

George, Alexander L., and Juliette L. George. 1964. *Woodrow Wilson and Colonel House: A Personality Study*. New York: Dover.

George, Jim, and David Campbell. 1990. "Patterns of Dissent and the Celebration of Difference: Critical Social Theory and International Relations," *International Studies Quarterly* 34, no. 3 (September), 269–293.

Gereffi, Gary. 1985. "The Renegotiation of Dependency and the Limits of State Autonomy in Mexico (1975–1982)," in *Multinational Corporations*, ed. Theodore H. Moran. Lexington, Mass: Lexington Books, pp. 83–103.

Gerschenkron, Alexander. 1962. *Economic Backwardness in Historical Perspective: A Book of Essays*. Cambridge, Mass: Belknap, Harvard University Press.

Gilpin, Robert. 1975a. *U.S. Power and the Multinational Corporation: The Political Economy of Foreign Direct Investment*. New York: Basic Books.

Gilpin, Robert. 1975b. "Three Models of the Future," *International Organization* 29, no. 1, 37–60.

Gilpin, Robert. 1977. "Economic Interdependence and National Security in Historical Perspective," in *Economic Issues and National Security*, ed. Klaus Knorr and Frank N. Trager. Lawrence, Kan.: Regents Press of Kansas, pp. 19–66.

Gilpin, Robert. 1979. "Three Models of the Future," in *Transnational Corporations and World Order*, ed. George Modelski. San Francisco: W. H. Freeman, pp. 353–372.

Gilpin, Robert. 1981. *War and Change in World Politics*. New York: Cambridge University Press.

Gilpin, Robert. 1984. "The Richness of the Tradition of Political Realism," *International Studies Quarterly* 38, no. 2 (Spring), 287–304.

Gilpin, Robert. 1987a. *The Political Economy of International Relations*. Princeton, N.J.: Princeton University Press.

Gilpin, Robert. 1987b. "American Policy in the Post-Reagan Era," *Daedalus* 116, no. 3 (Summer), 33–68.

Gladwin, Thomas N. 1987. "A Case Study of the Bhopal Tragedy," in *Multinational Corporations, Environment, and the Third World: Business Matters,* ed. Charles S. Pearson. Durham, N.C.: Duke University Press, pp. 223–239.

Glaser, Charles L. 1986. "Why Even Good Defenses May Be Bad," in *The Star Wars Controversy,* ed. Steven E. Miller and Stephen Van Evera. Princeton, N.J.: Princeton University Press.

Gochman, Charles S., and Zeev Maoz. 1984. "Militarized Interstate Disputes 1816–1976," *Journal of Conflict Resolution* 28, no. 4 (December), 585–615.

Goldman, Marshall I. 1987. "The Case of the Not-So-Simple Machine Tools," *Technology Review* 90, no. 7 (October), 20, 73.

Goldstein, Joshua S., 1985. "Kondratieff Waves as War Cycles," *International Studies Quarterly* 29, no. 4 (December), 411–444.

Goldstein, Joshua S. 1988. *Long Cycles: Prosperity and War in the Modern Age.* New Haven, Conn.: Yale University Press.

Goldstein, Joshua S., and John R. Freeman. 1990. *Three-Way Street: Strategic Reciprocity in World Politics.* Chicago: University of Chicago Press.

Goldstein, Judith. 1988. "Ideas, Institutions, and American Trade Policy," *International Organization* 42, no.1 (Winter), 179–217.

Goldstein, Judith. 1989. "The Impact of Ideas on Trade Policy: The Origins of U.S. Agricultural and Manufacturing Policies," *International Organization* 43, no. 1 (Winter), 31–71.

Goldstein, Judith, and Stefanie Ann Lenway. 1989."Interests or Institutions: An Inquiry Into Congressional-ITC Relations," *International Studies Quarterly* 33, no. 3 (September), 303–327.

Gordon, David C. 1989. *Images of the West.* United States [no city]: Rowman and Littlefield.

Grant, Lindsey. 1982. *The Cornucopian Fallacies.* Washington, D.C.: Environmental Fund.

Greenberg, Stanley B. 1987. "Looking Toward '88: The Politics of American Identity," *World Policy Journal* 4, no. 4 (Fall), 695–722.

Grieco, Joseph M. 1988. "Anarchy and the Limits of Cooperation: A Realist Critique of the Newest Liberal Institutionalism," *International Organization* 42, no. 3 (Summer): 485–507.

Grieco, Joseph M. 1990. Cooperation Among Nations. Ithaca, N.Y.: Cornell University Press.

Griffin, Keith B. 1987. "World Hunger and the World Economy," in *Pursuing Food Security,* ed. W. Ladd Hollist and F. LaMond Tullis. Boulder, Colo.: Lynne Rienner, pp. 17–36.

Grilli, Enzo R., and Maw Chang Yang. 1988. "Primary Commodity Prices, Manufactured Goods Prices, and the Terms of Trade of Developing Countries," *The World Bank Economic Review* 2, no. 1, 1–47.

Gurr, Ted Robert. 1985. "The Political Consequences of Scarcity and Economic Decline," *International Studies Quarterly* 29, no. 1 (March), 51–75.

Gurr, Ted Robert, and James R. Scarritt. 1989. "Minorities at Risk: A Global Survey," *Human Rights Quarterly* 11, 375–405.

Haas, Ernst B. 1953. "The Balance of Power: Prescription, Concept, or Propaganda?" *World Politics* 5, no. 4 (July), 446–458.

Haas, Ernst B. 1976. "Turbulent Fields and the Theory of Regional Integration," *International Organization* 30, no. 2 (Spring), 173–212.

Haas, Ernst B. 1983. "Words Can Hurt You; or Who Said What to Whom about Regimes," in *International Regimes*, ed. Stephen D. Krasner. Ithaca, N.Y.: Cornell University Press, pp. 23–60.

Haas, Ernst B. 1986. *Why We Still Need the United Nations: The Collective Management of International Conflict, 1945–1984*, Policy Papers in International Affairs, no. 26. Berkeley: University of California Institute of International Studies.

Haas, Ernst B. 1990. *When Knowledge Is Power.* Berkeley: University of California Press.

Haas, Peter M. 1989. "Do Regimes Matter? Epistemic Communities and Mediterranean Pollution Control," *International Organization 43*, no. 3 (Summer), 337–403.

Hagopian, Mark N. 1985. *Ideals and Ideologies of Modern Politics.* New York: Longman.

Hamburger, Henry. 1979. *Games as Models of Social Phenomena.* San Francisco: W. H. Freeman.

Hampshire, Stuart, ed. 1956. *The Age of Reason: 17th Century Philosophers.* New York: Mentor Books.

Hamrin, Robert D. 1980. *Managing Growth in the 1980s: Toward a New Economics.* New York: Praeger.

Hansen, Roger D., and the Staff of the Overseas Development Council. 1976. *The U.S. and World Development: Agenda for Action 1976.* New York: Praeger.

Hardin, Garrett. 1968. "The Tragedy of the Commons," *Science 162*, no. 3859 (December 13), 1243–1248.

Hardin, Russell. 1982. *Collective Action.* Baltimore, Md.: Johns Hopkins University.

Harf, James E., and B. Thomas Trout. 1986. *The Politics of Global Resources: Energy, Environment, Population, and Food.* Durham, N.C.: Duke University Press.

Harff, Barbara, and Ted Robert Gurr. 1988. "Toward Empirical Theory of Genocides and Politicides," *International Studies Quarterly 32*, no. 3 (September), 359–371.

Harrelson, Max. 1989. *Fires All around the Horizon.* New York: Praeger.

Harris, Marvin. 1977. *Cannibals and Kings.* New York: Vintage Books.

Harrison, Lawrence E. 1985. *Underdevelopment is a State of Mind.* Lanham, Md.: University Press of America.

Harsanyi, John C. 1986. "Advances in Understanding Rational Behavior," *Rational Choice*, ed. Jon Elster. New York: New York University Press, pp. 82–107.

Hart, Jeffrey. 1988. "Empiricism, Metaphysics and the Recovery of the Whole," *Essays on Our Times 4*, no. 1 (April), 3–21.

Hartmann, Frederick H. 1970. *The New Age of American Foreign Policy.* New York: Macmillan.

Hastedt, Glenn P. 1988. *American Foreign Policy: Past, Present, Future.* Englewood Cliffs, N.J.: Prentice Hall.

Hayami, Yujiro, and Vernon W. Ruttan. 1985. *Agricultural Development: An International Perspective.* Baltimore, Md.: Johns Hopkins University Press.

Hayek, Friedrich A. 1963 (originally 1944). *The Road to Serfdom.* Chicago: University of Chicago Press.

Hayter, Teresa, and Catherine Watson. 1985. *Aid: Rhetoric and Reality.* London: Pluto Press.

Headrick, Daniel R. 1981. *The Tools of Empire.* New York: Oxford University Press.

Heertje, Arnold, ed. 1988. *Innovation, Technology, and Finance.* New York: Basil Blackwell.

Heise, Lori. 1988. "AIDS: New Threat to the Third World," *World Watch 1*, no. 1 (January–February), 19–27.

Heise, Lori. 1989. "Responding to AIDS," *State of the World 1989*, ed. Lester R. Brown. Washington, D.C.: Worldwatch Institute, pp. 113–131.

Held, David. 1980. *Introduction to Critical Theory*. Berkeley: University of California Press.

Henkin, Louis. 1991. "Law and Politics in International Relations," *The Evolution of Theory in International Relations*, ed. Robert L. Rothstein. Columbia: University of South Carolina Press, pp. 163–188.

Hermann, Charles F. 1969. *Crises in Foreign Policy*. Indianapolis: Bobbs-Merrill.

Herz, John H. 1950. "Idealist Internationalism and the Security Dilemma," *World Politics 2*, no. 2 (January), 157–180.

Herz, John H. 1951. *Political Realism and Political Idealism*. Chicago: The University of Chicago Press.

Herz, John H. 1957. "Rise and Demise of the Territorial State," *World Politics 9*, no. 4 (July), 473–493.

Herz, John H. 1969. "The Territorial State Revisited," in *International Politics and Foreign Policy*, rev. ed., ed. James N. Rosenau. New York: The Free Press, pp. 76–89.

Hinsley, F. H. 1986. *Sovereignty*, 3rd ed. Cambridge: Cambridge University Press.

Hirsch, Fred. 1976. *The Social Limits to Growth*. Cambridge: Harvard University Press.

Hobson, John. 1902. *Imperialism: A Study*. London: Allen and Unwin.

Hollins, Harry B., Averill L. Powers, and Mark Sommer. 1989. *The Conquest of War*. Boulder, Colo.: Westview Press.

Hollist, W. Ladd, and F. LaMond Tullis, eds. 1987. *Pursuing Food Security*. Boulder, Colo.: Lynne Rienner.

Holmes, Richard. 1988. *The World Atlas of Warfare*. New York: Viking Studio Books.

Holsti, K. J. 1980. "Change in the International System: Interdependence, Integration, and Fragmentation," in *Change in the International System*, ed. Ole R. Holsti, Randolph M. Siverson, and Alexander L. George. Boulder, Colo.: Westview Press, pp. 23–53.

Holsti, K. J. 1983. *International Politics: A Framework for Analysis*, 4th ed. Englewood Cliffs, N.J.: Prentice Hall.

Holsti, K. J. 1985. *The Dividing Discipline: Hegemony and Diversity in International Theory*. Boston: Allen and Unwin.

Holsti, K. J. 1986. "The Horsemen of the Apocalypse: At the Gate, Detoured, or Retreating?" *International Studies Quarterly 30*, no. 4 (December), 355–372.

Holsti, K. J. 1988. *International Politics: A Framework for Analysis*, 5th ed. Englewood Cliffs, N.J.: Prentice Hall.

Holsti, Ole R. 1962. "The Belief System and National Images: A Case Study," *Journal of Conflict Resolution 6*, no. 3 (September), 244–252.

Holsti, Ole R. 1992. "Public Opinion and Foreign Policy," *International Studies Quarterly 36*, no.4 (December), 439–466.

Holsti, Ole R., Robert C. North, and Richard A. Brody. 1968. "Perception and Action in the 1914 Crisis," in *Quantitative International Politics*, ed. J. David Singer. New York: The Free Press, pp. 123–158.

Holsti, Ole R., and James N. Rosenau. 1988. "A Leadership Divided: The Foreign Policy Beliefs of American Leaders, 1976–1984," in *The Domestic Sources of American Foreign Policy*, ed. Charles W. Kegley and Eugene R. Wittkopf. New York: St. Martin's Press, pp. 30–44.

Holsti, Ole R., Randolph M. Siverson, and Alexander L. George, eds. 1980. *Change in the International System*. Boulder, Colo.: Westview Press.

Holzman, Franklyn, and Richard Portes. 1978. "TheLimits of Pressure," *Foreign Policy* no. 32 (Fall), 80–90.

Hook, Sidney. 1943. *The Hero in History*. Boston: Beacon Press.

Hopkins, Raymond F., and Donald J. Puchala. 1978. "Perspectives on the International Relations of Food," in *The Global Political Economy of Food*, ed. Raymond F. Hopkins and Donald J. Puchala. Madison: University of Wisconsin Press, pp. 3–40.

Hopkins, Raymond F., Robert L. Paarlberg, and Mitchel Wallerstein, 1980. *Global Issues and Food*. Columbus: Ohio State University, Consortium for International Studies Education.

Hopkins, Terence K., and Immanuel Wallerstein. 1982. "Cyclical Rhythms and Secular Trends of the Capitalist World-Economy: Some Premises, Hypotheses, and Questions," in *World-Systems Analysis: Theory and Methodology*, ed. Terence K. Hopkins and Immanuel Wallerstein. Beverly Hills, Calif.: Sage, pp. 104–120.

House, Karen Elliot. 1980. "Reagan's World: Republican Policies Stress Arms Buildup, A Firm Line to Soviet," *The Wall Street Journal* (June 3), 1, 25.

Howe, James W., and the Staff of the Overseas Development Council. 1974. *The U.S. and the Developing World: Agenda for Action 1974*. New York: Praeger.

Hufbauer, Gary Clyde, Jeffrey J. Schott, and Kimberly Ann Elliott. 1990. *Economic Sanctions Reconsidered*. Washington, D.C.: Institute for International Economics.

Hughes, Barry B. 1978. *The Domestic Context of American Foreign Policy*. San Francisco: W. H. Freeman.

Hughes, Barry B. 1985. *World Futures: A Critical Analysis of Alternatives*. Baltimore, Md.: Johns Hopkins University Press.

Hughes, Barry B., and others. 1985. *Energy in the Global Arena*. Durham, N.C.: Duke University Press.

Hume, David. 1888. *A Treatise of Human Nature*, ed. L.A. Selby-Bigge. Oxford: The Clarendon Press.

Hunger Project. 1985. *Ending Hunger: An Idea Whose Time Has Come*. New York: Praeger.

Hunger Project. 1991. *World Development Forum* 9, no. 3 (February).

Huntington, Samuel P. 1978. "Trade, Technology, and Leverage: Economic Diplomacy," *Foreign Policy* no. 32 (Fall), 63–80.

Huntington, Samuel P. 1985. "Will More Countries Become Democratic?" in *Global Dilemmas*, ed. Samuel P. Huntington and Joseph S. Nye, Jr. Cambridge, Mass.: Harvard University Center for International Affairs, pp. 253–279.

Huntington, Samuel P. 1988. "The U.S.—Decline or Renewal?" *Foreign Affairs* 67, no. 2 (Winter), 76–96.

Hymer, Stephen D. 1987. "International Politics and International Economics: A Radical Approach," in *International Political Economy*, ed. Jeffrey A. Frieden and David A. Lake. New York: St. Martin's Press, pp. 31–46.

Imbert, Gaston. 1956. *Des Mouvements de Longue Durée Kondratieff* (Ph.D. dissertation). Aix-en-Provence: Office Universitaire de Polycopie. Cited in Joshua S. Goldstein. 1988. *Long Cycles: Prosperity and War in the Modern Age.* New Haven, Conn.: Yale University Press.

Ingersoll, David E., and Richard K. Matthews. 1986. *The Philosophic Roots of Modern Ideology.* Englewood Cliffs, N.J.: Prentice Hall.

Inoguchi, Takashi. 1988. "Four Japanese Scenarios for the Future," *International Affairs 65,* no. 1 (Winter), 15–28.

Inter-American Development Bank. 1989. *Annual Report 1988.* Washington, D.C.: Inter-American Development Bank.

International Institute for Strategic Studies. 1987.*The Military Balance 1987–1988.* London: International Institute for Strategic Studies.

International Monetary Fund. 1983. *International Financial Statistics Yearbook.* Washington, D.C.: International Monetary Fund.

International Monetary Fund. 1988a. *Annual Report 1988.* Washington, D.C.: International Monetary Fund.

International Monetary Fund. 1988b. *International Financial Statistics Yearbook.* Washington, D.C.: International Monetary Fund.

International Monetary Fund. 1989a. *World Economic Outlook.* Washington, D.C.: International Monetary Fund.

International Monetary Fund. 1989b. *International Financial Statistics Yearbook.* Washington, D.C.: International Monetary Fund.

International Monetary Fund. 1992. *World Economic Outlook.* Washington, D.C.: International Monetary Fund.

Jacobson, Harold K. 1984. *Networks of Interdependence,* 2nd ed. New York: Alfred A. Knopf.

Jacobson, Jodi L. 1989. "Abandoning Homelands," in *State of the World 1989,* ed. Lester R. Brown, and others. Washington, D.C.: Worldwatch Institute, pp. 59–76.

Janis, Irving L. 1972. *Victims of Groupthink.* Boston: Houghton-Mifflin.

Jensen, Lloyd. 1988a. *Negotiating Nuclear Arms Control.* Columbia: University of South Carolina Press.

Jensen, Lloyd. 1988b. *Bargaining for National Security: The Postwar Disarmament Negotiations.* Columbia: University of South Carolina Press.

Jervis, Robert. 1976. *Perception and Misperception in International Politics.* Princeton, N.J.: Princeton University Press.

Jervis, Robert. 1978. "Cooperation Under the Security Dilemma," *World Politics 20,* no. 2 (January), 167–214.

Jervis, Robert. 1983. "Security Regimes," in *International Regimes,* ed. Stephen D. Krasner. Ithaca, N.Y.: Cornell University Press, pp. 173–194.

Joffee, Josef. 1985. "The Foreign Policy of the Federal Republic of Germany," in *Foreign Policy in World Politics,* 6th ed., ed. Roy C. Macridis. Englewood Cliffs, N.J.: Prentice Hall, pp. 72–113.

Johnson, D. Gale. 1978. "World Food Institutions: A 'Liberal' View," in *The Global Political Economy of Food,* ed. Raymond F. Hopkins and Donald J. Puchala. Madison: University of Wisconsin Press, pp. 265–282.

Johnson, D. Gale. 1980. "Increasing the Food Security of Low Income Countries," in *The Politics of Food*, ed. D. Gale Johnson. Chicago: Chicago Council on Foreign Relations, pp.183–206.

Johnson, D. Gale. 1984. "World Food and Agriculture," in *The Resourceful Earth*, ed. Julian L. Simon and Herman Kahn. New York: Basil Blackwell, pp. 67–112.

Jones, Walter S. 1985. *The Logic of International Relations*, 5th ed. Boston: Little, Brown.

Jorgensen-Dahl, Arnfinn. 1975. "Forces of Fragmentation in the International System: The Case of Ethno-Nationalism," *Orbis* 19, no. 2 (Summer), 652–674.

Kahn, Herman. 1979. *World Economic Development: 1979 and Beyond*. Boulder, Colo.: Westview Press.

Kahn, Herman, William Brown, and Leon Martel. 1976. *The Next 200 Years*. New York: William Morrow.

Kaplan, Morton A. 1957. *System and Process in International Politics*. New York: John Wiley.

Kaplan, Stephen S. 1981. *Diplomacy of Power*. Washington, D.C.: Brookings Institution.

Kedourie, Elie. 1961. *Nationalism*, rev. ed. London: Hutchinson.

Keeny, Spurgeon M., Jr., and Wolfgang K. Panofsky. 1982. "MAD versus NUTS," *Foreign Affairs 60*, no. 2 (Winter), 287–304.

Kegley, Charles W., ed. 1990. *International Terrorism*. New York: St. Martin's Press.

Kegley, Charles W., and Eugene R. Wittkopf. 1979. *American Foreign Policy: Pattern and Process*. New York: St.Martin's Press.

Kegley, Charles W., and Eugene R. Wittkopf. 1991. *American Foreign Policy: Pattern and Process*, 4th ed. New York: St. Martin's Press.

Kegley, Charles W., and Eugene R. Wittkopf. 1985. *World Politics: Trend and Transformation*, 2nd ed. New York: St.Martin's Press.

Kegley, Charles W., and Eugene R. Wittkopf, eds., 1988. *The Domestic Sources of American Foreign Policy*. New York: St. Martin's Press.

Kennan, George F. 1951. *American Diplomacy: 1900–1950*. New York: The New American Library.

Kennan, George F. 1989. "New Agenda for a Weary Europe," *Stanford Magazine 17*, no. 10 (December), 45–48.

Kennedy, Paul. 1983. *Strategy and Diplomacy: 1870–1945: Eight Studies*. London: Allen and Unwin.

Kennedy, Paul. 1987. *The Rise and Fall of Great Powers: Economic Change and Military Conflict from 1500 to 2000*. New York: Random House.

Keohane, Robert O. 1980. "The Theory of Hegemonic Stability and Changes in International Economic Regimes, 1967–1977," in *Change in the International System*, ed. Ole R. Holsti, Randolph M. Siverson, and Alexander L. George. Boulder, Colo.: Westview Press, pp. 131–162.

Keohane, Robert O. 1983a. "The Demand for International Regimes," in *International Regimes*, ed. Stephen D. Krasner. Ithaca, N.Y.: Cornell University Press, pp. 141–172.

Keohane, Robert O. 1983b. "Theory of World Politics: Structural Realism and Beyond," *Political Science: The State of the Discipline*, ed. Ada W. Finifter. Washington, D.C.: American Political Science Association, pp. 503–540.

Keohane, Robert O. 1984. *After Hegemony, Cooperation and Discord in the World Political Economy.* Princeton, N.J.: Princeton University Press.

Keohane, Robert O., ed. 1986. *Neorealism and Its Critics.* New York: Columbia University Press.

Keohane, Robert O. 1988. "International Institutions: Two Approaches, " *International Studies Quarterly* 32, no.4 (December), 379–396.

Keohane, Robert O. 1989. *International Institutions and State Power.* Boulder, Colo.: Westview Press.

Keohane, Robert O., and Joseph S. Nye, Jr., eds. 1970. *Transnational Relations and World Politics.* Cambridge, Mass.: Harvard University Press.

Keohane, Robert O., and Joseph S. Nye, Jr. 1977. *Power and Interdependence: World Politics in Transition.* Boston: Little, Brown.

Keohane, Robert O., and Joseph S. Nye, Jr. 1987."Power and Interdependence Revisited," *International Organization* 41, no. 4 (Autumn), 725–753.

Keohane, Robert O., and Joseph S. Nye, Jr. 1989. *Power and Interdependence: World Politics in Transition,* 2nd ed. Boston: Little, Brown.

Keesing's Research Report. 1969. *The Sino-Soviet Dispute.* New York: Charles Scribner's.

Kidron, Michael, and Dan Smith. 1983. *The War Atlas: Armed Conflict-Armed Peace.* New York: Pluto Press/Simon & Schuster.

Kindleberger, Charles P. 1973. *The World in Depression 1929–1939.* Berkeley: University of California Press.

Kindleberger, Charles P. 1987. "The Rise of Free Trade in Europe" in *International Political Economy,* ed. Jeffrey A. Frieden and David A. Lake. New York: St. Martin's Press, pp. 85–104.

Kirchner, Emil J. 1988. "Has the Single European Act Opened the Door for a European Security Policy?" Paper delivered at the International Political Science Association Meeting, Washington, D.C., August 28.

Kirk, Grayson, Harrison S. Brown, Denis W. Brogan, Edward S. Mason, Harold H. Fisher, and Willard L. Thorp. 1956. *The Changing Environment of International Relations.* Washington, D.C.: Brookings Institution.

Kissinger, Henry A. 1962. *The Necessity of Choice.* Garden City, N.Y.: Doubleday.

Kissinger, Henry A. 1974. *American Foreign Policy,* expanded ed. New York: W. W. Norton.

Kissinger, Henry A. 1979. *White House Years.* Boston: Little, Brown.

Klass, Rosanne. 1988. "Afghanistan: The Accords," *Foreign Affairs 66,* no. 5 (Summer), 922–945.

Kline, John M. 1985. "Multinational Corporations in Euro-American Trade: Crucial Linking Mechanisms in an Evolving Trade Structure," in *Multinational Corporations,* ed. Theodore H. Moran. Lexington, Mass.: Lexington Books, pp. 199–218.

Knorr, Klaus. 1975. *The Power of Nations: The Political Economy of International Relations.* New York: Basic Books.

Krasner, Stephen. 1976. "State Power and the Structures of International Trade," *World Politics* 28, no.3 (April), 317–347.

Krasner, Stephen D. 1978. *Defending the National Interest.* Princeton, N.J.: Princeton University Press.

Krasner, Stephen D. 1983a. "Structural Causes and Regime Consequences: Regimes as Intervening Variables," in *International Regimes*, ed. Stephen D. Krasner. Ithaca, N.Y.: Cornell University Press, pp. 1–21.

Krasner, Stephen D., ed. 1983b. *International Regimes*. Ithaca, N.Y.: Cornell University Press.

Krasner, Stephen D. 1987a. "State Power and the Structure of International Trade," in *International Political Economy*, ed. Jeffrey A. Frieden and David A. Lake. New York: St. Martin's Press, pp. 47–66.

Krasner, Stephen D. 1987b. *Asymmetries in Japanese-American Trade, Policy Papers in International Affairs*, no. 32. Berkeley: Institute of International Studies, University of California.

Kravis, Irving B., Alan Heston, and Robert R. Summers. 1982. *World Product and Income*. Baltimore, Md.: Johns Hopkins University Press.

Krickus, Richard J. 1987. *The Superpowers in Crisis: Implications of Domestic Discord*. Washington, D.C.: Pergamon-Brassey's.

Kruzel, Joseph. 1986. "From Rush-Bagot to START: The Lessons of Arms Control," *Orbis 30*, no. 1 (Spring): 193–216.

Kugler, Jacek, and A. F. K. Organski. 1989. "The End of Hegemony?" *International Interactions 15*, no. 2, 113–128.

Kuhn, Thomas. 1970. *The Structure of Scientific Revolutions*, expanded ed. Chicago: University of Chicago Press.

Kurian, George Thomas. 1984. *The New Book of World Rankings*. New York: Facts on File.

Kuznets, Simon. 1966. *Modern Economic Growth: Rate, Structure and Spread*. New Haven, Conn.: Yale University Press.

Kuznets, Simon. 1984 (originally 1955). "Economic Growth and Income Inequality," in *The Gap Between Rich and Poor*, ed. Mitchell A. Seligson. Boulder, Colo.: Westview Press, pp. 25–37.

Lake, David A. 1987. "International Economic Structures and American Foreign Policy, 1887–1934," in *International Political Economy*, ed. Jeffrey A. Frieden and David A. Lake. New York: St. Martin's Press, pp. 145–165.

Lall, Sanjaya. 1984. "Exports of Technology by Newly-Industrializing Countries: An Overview," *World Development* 12, no. 5/6 (May–June), 471–480.

Lamy, Steven L., ed. 1988. *Contemporary International Issues: Contending Perspectives*. Boulder, Colo.: Lynne Rienner.

Landsberg, Hans H., and John E. Tilton. 1982. "Nonfuel Minerals," in *Current Issues in Natural Resource Policy*, ed. Paul R. Portney. Washington, D.C.: Resources for the Future, pp. 74–116.

Lapham, Robert J., and W. Parker Mauldin. 1984 (January). "The Measurement of Family Planning Effort," Unpublished paper.

Lapid, Yosef. 1989. "The Third Debate: On the Prospects of International Theory in a Post-Positivist Era," *International Studies Quarterly 33*, no. 3 (September), 235–254.

Lauterpacht, H. 1985. "The Grotian Tradition in International Law," in *International Law: A Contemporary Perspective*, ed. Richard Falk, Friedrich Kratochwil, and Saul H. Mendlovitz. Boulder, Colo.: Westview Press, 1985, pp. 10–35.

Lebow, Richard Ned. 1981. *Between Peace and War: The Nature of International Crisis*. Baltimore, Md.: Johns Hopkins University Press.

Lenczowski, George. 1979. "The Arc of Crisis," in *Foreign Affairs* 57, no. 4 (Spring), 796–820.

Lenin, Vladimir I. 1939 (originally 1916). *Imperialism: The Highest Stage of Capitalism.* New York: International.

Levine, David. 1988. *Needs, Rights and the Market.* Boulder, Colo.: Lynne Rienner.

Levine, Herbert M., ed. 1983. *World Politics Debated: A Reader in Contemporary Issues.* New York: McGraw-Hill.

Levy, Jack. 1982. "Historical Trends in Great Power War, 1495–1975," *International Studies Quarterly* 26, no. 2 (June), 278–300.

Levy, Jack. 1983. *War in the Modern Great Power System, 1495–1975.* Lexington: University of Kentucky Press.

Levy, Jack. 1989. "The Diversionary Theory of War: A Critique," in *Handbook of War Studies*, ed. Manus I. Midlarsky. Boston: Unwin Hyman, pp. 259–288.

Lewis, John P., and Valeriana Kallab, eds. 1983. *U.S. Foreign Policy and the Third World: Agenda 1983.* New York: Praeger.

Lightbourne, Robert Jr., and Susheela Singh. 1982. "The World Fertility Survey," *Population Bulletin* 37, no. 1 (March), 1–54.

Lindgren, Karin, Birger Heldt, Kjell-åke Nordquist, and Peter Wallensteen. 1991. *SIPRI Yearbook 1991.* New York: Oxford University Press, pp. 345–380.

Lippmann, Walter. 1955. *The Public Philosophy.* Boston: Little, Brown.

Lipset, Seymour Martin. 1963. *The First New Nation.* New York: Basic Books.

Loehr, William, and John P. Powelson, eds. 1977. *Economic Development, Poverty, and Income Distribution.* Boulder, Colo.: Westview Press.

Lovins, Amory B. 1976. "Energy Strategy: The Road Not Taken?" *Foreign Affairs* 55, no. 1 (October), 65–96.

Luce, R.D., and Howard Raiffa. 1957. *Games and Decisions.* New York: John Wiley.

Machiavelli, Niccolò. 1940. *The Discourses.* New York: Modern Library.

Machiavelli, Niccolò. 1886 (originally 1513). *The Prince,* trans. by Henry Morely. London: George Routledge.

MacDonald, Stuart. 1986. "Controlling the Flow of High-Technology Information from the United States to the Soviet Union," *Minerva* 24, no. 1 (Spring), 39–73.

Macrae, Norman. 1985. *The 2025 Project.* New York: Macmillan.

Macridis, Roy C. 1985. "French Foreign Policy," in *Foreign Policy in World Politics*, 6th ed., ed. Roy C. Macridis. Englewood Cliffs, N.J.: Prentice Hall, pp. 22–71.

Macridis, Roy C. 1986. *Contemporary Political Ideologies: Movements and Regimes*, 3rd ed. Boston: Little, Brown.

Maddison, Angus. 1982. *Phases of Capitalist Development.* Oxford: Oxford University Press.

Magdoff, Harry. 1969. *The Age of Imperialism: The Economics of United States Foreign Policy.* New York: Monthly Review Press.

Maghroori, Ray, and Bennett Ramberg, eds. 1982. *Globalism versus Realism: International Relations' Third Debate.* Boulder, Colo.: Westview Press.

Mandel, Ernst. 1975. *Late Capitalism.* London: New Left Books.

Mandel, Robert. 1986. "The Effectiveness of Gunboat Diplomacy," *International Studies Quarterly* 31, no. 1 (March), 59–76.

Mansbach, Richard W., and Yale H. Ferguson. 1986. "Values and Paradigm Change: The Elusive Quest for International Relations Theory," in *Persistent Patterns and Emergent Structure in a Waning Century*, ed. Margaret P. Karns. New York: Praeger, pp. 11–34.

Mansbach, Richard W., and John A. Vasquez. 1981. *In Search of Theory: A New Paradigm for Global Politics*. New York: Columbia University Press.

Maoz, Zeev. 1983. "Resolve, Capabilities, and the Outcomes of Interstate Disputes, 1816–1976," *Journal of Conflict Resolution* 27, no. 2 (June), 195–229.

March, James G. 1966. "The Power of Power," in *Varieties of Political Theory*, ed. David Easton. New York: Prentice Hall, pp. 54–61.

March, James G. 1986. "Bounded Rationality, Ambiguity and the Engineering of Choice," in *Rational Choice*, ed. Jon Elster. New York: New York University Press, pp. 142–170.

Marx, Karl. 1959. "Excerpt from A Contribution to the Critique of Political Economy," in *Marx and Engels*, ed. Lewis S. Feuer. Berkeley, Calif.: Ramparts, pp. 42–46.

Maslow, Abraham. 1970. *Motivation and Personality*, 2nd ed. New York: Harper & Row.

Maxwell, S. J., and H. W. Singer. 1979. "Food Aid to Developing Countries: A Survey," *World Development* 7, no.3 (March), 225–247.

Mazrui, Ali. 1967. *Towards a Pax Africana*. London: Weidenfeld and Nicolson.

Mazrui, Ali. 1988. "International Stratification and Third World Solidarity: A Dual Strategy for Change," reprinted in *Global Issues 88–89*, ed. Robert Jackson. Guilford, Conn.: Dushkin, pp. 132–136.

McDermott, John. 1972. "Technology: The Opiate of the Intellectuals," in *Technology and Man's Future*, ed. Albert Teich. New York: St. Martin's Press, pp. 151–177.

McKinlay, R. D., and R. Little. 1986. *Global Problems and World Order*. Madison: University of Wisconsin Press.

McNeil, William H. 1976. *Plagues and Peoples*. Garden City, N.Y.: Anchor Press.

McNeil, William H. 1982. *The Pursuit of Power*. Chicago: University of Chicago Press.

McWilliams, Wayne C., and Harry Piotrowski. 1988. *The World Since 1945*. Boulder, Colo.: Lynne Rienner.

Meadows, Dennis L., William W. Behrens III, Donella H. Meadows, Roger F. Naill, Jorgen Randers, and Erich K. O. Zahn. 1974. *Dynamics of Growth in a Finite World*. Cambridge: Wright-Allen Press.

Meadows, Donella H., Dennis L. Meadows, Jorgen Randers, and William W. Behrens III. 1972. *The Limits to Growth*. New York: Universe Books.

Meadows, Donella H., Dennis L. Meadows, and Jorgen Randers. 1992. *Beyond the Limits to Growth*. Post Hills, Vt.: Chelsea Green.

Meek, Ronald M., ed. and trans. 1953. *Marx and Engels on Malthus*. London: Lawrence and Wishart.

Meier, Gerald M., and Robert E. Baldwin. 1957. *Economic Development: Theory, History, Policy*. New York: John Wiley.

Mendlovitz, Saul, ed. 1975. *On the Creation of a Just World Order*. New York: The Free Press.

Merrick, Thomas W. 1986. "World Population in Transition," *Population Bulletin* 41, no. 2 (April), 1–52.

Merritt, Richard L., and Bruce M. Russett, eds. 1981. *From National Development to Global Community: Essays in Honor of Karl W. Deutsch.* London: Allen and Unwin.

Merritt, Richard L., and Dina A. Zinnes. 1989. "Alternative Indexes of National Power," in *Power in World Politics,* ed. Richard J. Stoll and Michael D. Ward. Boulder, Colo.: Lynne Rienner, pp. 11–28.

Meyer, John W., Francisco O. Ramirez, Richardson Rubinson, and John Boli-Bennett. 1979. "The World Educational Revolution, 1950–70," in *National Development and the World System,* ed. John W. Meyer and Michael T. Hannan. Chicago: University of Chicago Press, pp. 37–55.

Midlarsky, Manus I. 1986. "A Hierarchical Equilibrium Theory of Systemic War," *International Studies Quarterly* 30, no. 1 (March), 77–105.

Midlarsky, Manus I. 1988. *The Onset of World War.* Boston: Unwin Hyman.

Mikdashi, Zuhayr. 1976. *The International Politics of Natural Resources.* Ithaca, N.Y.: Cornell University Press.

Mikesell, Raymond F. 1988. "The Changing Demand for Industrial Raw Materials," in *Growth, Exports, and Jobs in a Changing World Economy: Agenda 1988,* ed. John W. Sewell, Stuart K. Tucker, and contributors. New Brunswick, N.J.: Transaction Books, pp. 139–166.

Milbrand, Ralph. 1977. *Marxism and Politics.* Oxford: Oxford University Press.

Miller, Steven E. ed. 1986. *Conventional Forces and American Defense Policy.* Princeton, N.J.: Princeton University Press.

Miller, Steven E., and Stephen Van Evera, eds. 1986. *The Star Wars Controversy.* Princeton, N.J.: Princeton University Press.

Mills, C. Wright. 1956. *The Power Elite.* New York: Oxford University Press.

Mishan, E. J. 1982. *What Political Economy is All About.* Cambridge: Cambridge University Press.

Mitrany, David. 1966. *A Working Peace System.* Chicago: Quadrangle, 1966. Originally published as *A Working Peace System: An Argument for the Functional Development of International Organization.* London: Royal Institute of International Affairs.

Modelski, George. 1978. "The Long-Cycle of Global Politics and the Nation-State," *Comparative Studies in Society and History* 20, no. 2 (April), 214–235.

Modelski, George. 1983. "Long Cycles of World Leadership," in *Contending Approaches to World System Analysis,* ed. William R. Thompson. Beverly Hills, Calif.: Sage, pp. 115–140.

Modelski, George, ed. 1987. *Exploring Long Cycles.* Boulder, Colo.: Lynne Rienner.

Modelski, George, and William R. Thompson. 1987. *Seapower in Global Politics: 1494–1993.* London: Macmillan.

Moran, Theodore H. 1985. "Multinational Corporations and the Developing Countries," in *Multinational Corporations,* ed. Theodore H. Moran. Lexington Books, Mass: Lexington Books, pp. 3–24.

Morgan, Dan. 1979. *The Merchants of Grain.* New York: Viking Press.

Morgan, T. Clifton, and James Lee Ray. 1989. "The Impact of Nuclear Weapons on Crisis Bargaining," in *Power in World Politics,* ed. Richard J. Stoll and Michael D. Ward. Boulder, Colo.: Lynne Rienner, pp. 193–208.

Morgenthau, Hans J. 1965. "Another 'Great Debate': the National Interest of the United States," in *America's Foreign Policy*, ed. Harold Karan Jacobson, rev. ed. New York: Random House, pp. 107–136.

Morgenthau, Hans J. 1973. *Politics Among Nations: The Struggle for Power and Peace*, 5th ed. New York: Alfred A. Knopf.

Mortimer, Edward. 1982. *Faith and Power*. New York: Random House.

Mueller, John E. 1973. *War, Presidents and Public Opinion*. New York: John Wiley.

Myrdal, Gunnar. 1957. *Rich Nations and Poor*. New York: Harper & Row.

Naisbitt, John. 1982. *Megatrends*. New York: Warner Books.

Naisbitt, John, and Patricia Aburdene. 1990. *Megatrends 2000: The New Directions for the 1990s*. New York: William Morrow.

National Science Foundation. 1991. *International Science and Technology Data Update: 1991*. Washington, D.C.: National Science Foundation.

Nau, Henry R. 1990. *The Myth of America's Decline*. New York: Oxford University Press.

Nielsson, Gunnar, and Ralph Jones. 1988. "From Ethnic Category to Nation: Patterns of Political Mobilization." Paper presented at the 1988 meeting of the International Studies Association, St. Louis, Missouri.

Nietschmann, Bernard. 1987. "The Third World War," *Cultural Survival Quarterly 11*, no. 3, 1–16.

Ngolle Ngolle, Elvis O. 1985 (March). *The African Refugee Problem and the Distribution of International Refugee Assistance in Comparative Perspective*. Unpublished Ph.D. dissertation. Denver, Colo.: University of Denver.

Niksch, Larry A. 1983. "Japanese Attitudes Toward Defense and Security Issues," *Naval War College Review 36*, no. 4 (July–August), 57–72.

Nixon, Richard. 1962. *Six Crises*. Garden City, N.Y.: Doubleday.

Norris, Ruth, ed. 1982. *Pills, Pesticides and Profits*. Croton-on-Hudson, N.Y.: North River Press.

Nye, Joseph S. 1971. *Peace in Parts*. Boston: Little, Brown.

O'Brien, Conor Cruise. 1988. *God Land: Reflections on Religion and Nationalism*. Cambridge, Mass.: Harvard University Press.

Odell, Peter R. 1986. *Oil and World Power*, 8th ed. New York: Viking/Penguin Books.

Office of Technology Assessment. 1986. "Commercial Biotechnology: An International Analysis," in *Technology and Man's Future*, 4th ed., ed. Albert H. Teich. New York: St. Martin's Press, pp. 360–385.

Olson, Mancur. 1965. *The Logic of Collective Action*. Cambridge, Mass.: Harvard University Press.

Olson, Mancur. 1982. *The Rise and Decline of Nations: Economic Growth, Stagflation, and Social Rigidities*. New Haven, Conn.: Yale University Press.

Olson, Mancur, and Richard Zeckhauser. 1966. "An Economic Theory of Alliances," *The Review of Economics and Statistics 48*, no. 3 (August), 266–279.

Oneal, John R. 1989. "Measuring the Material Base of the Contemporary East-West Balance of Power,"*International Interactions 15*, no. 2, 177–196.

Oneal, John R., and Mark A. Elrod. 1989. "NATO Burden Sharing and the Forces of Change," *International Studies Quarterly 33*, no. 4 (December), 435–456.

Ophuls, William. 1977. *Ecology and the Politics of Scarcity*. San Francisco: W. H. Freeman.

Oppenheim, Lassa. 1908. "The Science of International Law," *American Journal of International Law*, 2, 313–351.

Organization for Economic Cooperation and Development. 1988a. *Development Co-operation 1988 Report*. Paris: Organization for Economic Cooperation and Development.

Organization for Economic Cooperation and Development. 1988b. *Voluntary Aid for Development*. Paris: Organization for Economic Cooperation and Development.

Organization for Economic Cooperation and Development. 1988c. *The Telecommunications Industry: The Challenges of Structural Change*. Paris: Organization for Economic Cooperation and Development.

Organski, A. F. K. 1965. *The Stages of Political Development*. New York: Alfred A. Knopf.

Organski, A. F. K. 1968. *World Politics*. New York: Alfred A. Knopf.

Organski, A. F. K., and Jacek Kugler. 1980. *The War Ledger*. Chicago: University of Chicago Press.

Osgood, Charles E. 1962. "Reciprocal Initiative," in *The Liberal Papers*, ed. James Roosevelt. Garden City, N.Y.: Doubleday, pp. 155–228.

Overturf, Stephen Frank. 1986. *The Economic Principles of European Integration*. New York: Praeger.

Oye, Kenneth A. 1985. "Explaining Cooperation under Anarchy: Hypotheses and Strategies," *World Politics* 38, no. 1 (October), 1–24.

Oye, Kenneth A. 1987. "Constrained Confidence and the Evolution of the Reagan Foreign Policy," in *Eagle Resurgent? The Reagan Era in American Foreign Policy*, eds. Kenneth A. Oye, Robert J. Lieber, and Donald Rothchild. Boston: Little, Brown, pp. 3–40.

Oye, Kenneth A., Robert J. Lieber, and Donald Rothchild, eds. 1987. *Eagle Resurgent? The Reagan Era in American Foreign Policy*. Boston: Little, Brown.

Page, Benjamin I., and Robert Y. Shapiro. 1983. "Effects of Public Opinion on Policy," *American Political Science Review* 77, no. 1, 175–190.

Page, Benjamin I., and Robert Y. Shapiro. 1992. *The Rational Public*. Chicago: University of Chicago Press.

Palmer, Monte 1989. *Dilemmas of Political Development*, 4th ed. Itasca, Ill.: F. E. Peacock.

Papathanasis, Tus, and Chris Vasillopulos. 1989. "Japanese Technological Superiority a Myth?" *The Christian Science Monitor* (April 27), 19.

Papp, Daniel S. 1984. *Contemporary International Relations: Frameworks for Understanding*. New York: Macmillan.

Papp, Daniel S. 1988. *Contemporary International Relations: Frameworks for Understanding*, 2nd ed. New York: Macmillan.

Parenti, Michael. 1989. *The Sword and the Dollar: Imperialism, Revolution and the Arms Race*. New York: St. Martin's Press.

Pavitt, K. L. R. 1973. "Malthus and Other Economists," in *Models of Doom*, ed. H. S. D. Cole and others. New York: Universe, pp. 137–158.

Payne, Keith B., and Colin S. Gray. 1984. "Nuclear Policy and the Defensive Transition," *Foreign Affairs* 62, no. 4 (Spring), 820–842.

Pearce, David W., ed. 1983. *The Dictionary of Modern Economics*. London: Macmillan.

Pearson, Charles S., ed. 1987. *Multinational Corporations, Environment, and the Third World: Business Matters*. Durham, N.C.: Duke University Press.

Pearson, Lester. 1965. "Democracy and the Power of Decision," in *America's Foreign Policy*, ed. Harold Karan Jacobson. New York: Random House, pp. 20–33.

Pirages, Dennis. 1978. *Global Ecopolitics.* North Scituate, Mass.: Duxbury Press.

Pirages, Dennis. 1983. "The Ecological Perspective and the Social Sciences," *International Studies Quarterly* 27, no. 3 (September), 243–255.

Pirages, Dennis. 1989. *Global Technopolitics.* Pacific Grove, Calif.: Brooks/Cole.

Plano, Jack C., and Roy Olton. 1988. *The International Relations Dictionary*, 4th ed. Santa Barbara, Calif.: ABC-CLIO.

Platt, John. 1988. "The Future of AIDS," reprinted in *Global Issues 88–89*, ed. Robert Jackson. Guilford Conn.: Dushkin, pp. 40–47.

Polanyi, Karl. 1944. *The Great Transformation.* Boston: Beacon Press.

Pollins, Brian M. 1992. "International Order, Cycles, and Armed Conflict 1816–1976." Paper presented at the annual meeting of the International Studies Association, Atlanta, Georgia, March 31–April 4, 1992.

Population Reference Bureau. 1976. *World Population Growth and Response.* Washington, D.C.: Population Reference Bureau.

Population Reference Bureau. 1986. *1986 World Population Data Sheet.* Washington, D.C.: Population Reference Bureau.

Population Reference Bureau. 1988. *1988 World Population Data Sheet.* Washington, D.C.: Population Reference Bureau.

Population Reference Bureau. 1989. *1989 World Population Data Sheet.* Washington, D.C.: Population Reference Bureau.

Population Reference Bureau. 1990. *1990 World Population Data Sheet.* Washington, D.C.: Population Reference Bureau.

Population Reference Bureau. 1992. *1992 World Population Data Sheet.* Washington, D.C.: Population Reference Bureau.

Portney, Paul R., ed. 1982. *Current Issues in Natural Resource Policy.* Baltimore, Md.: Johns Hopkins University Press.

Posen, Barry R., and Stephen W. Van Evera. 1987. "Reagan Administration Defense Policy: Departure from Containment," in *Eagle Resurgent? The Reagan Era in American Foreign Policy*, ed. Kenneth A. Oye, Robert J. Lieber, and Donald Rothchild. Boston: Little, Brown, pp. 75–114.

Postel, Sandra. 1984. *Air Pollution, Acid Rain and the Future of Forests.* Worldwatch Paper no. 58. (March). Washington, D.C.: Worldwatch Institute.

Postel, Sandra. 1987. *Defusing the Toxic Threat: Controlling Pesticides and Industrial Waste.* Worldwatch Paper no. 79. (September). Washington, D.C.: Worldwatch Institute.

Postel, Sandra. 1989. "Halting Land Degradation," in *State of the World 1989*, ed. Lester R. Brown and others. Washington, D.C.: Worldwatch Institute, pp. 21–40.

Press, Frank. 1987. "Technological Competition and the Western Alliance," in *A High Technology Gap? Europe, America and Japan*, ed. Andrew J. Pierre. New York: Council on Foreign Relations, pp. 11–43.

Puchala, Donald J. 1981. "Integration Theory and the Study of International Relations," in *From National Development to Global Community: Essays in Honor of Karl W. Deutsch*, ed. Richard L. Merritt and Bruce M. Russett. London: Allen and Unwin, pp. 145–164.

Pushkov, Alexi. 1992. "The Commonwealth of Independent States," *NATO Review* 40, no. 3 (June), 13–18.

Putnam, Robert D. 1988. "Diplomacy and Domestic Politics: The Logic of Two-Level Games," *International Organization* 42, no. 3 (Summer), 427–460.

Quester, George H. 1977. *Offense and Defense in the International System.* New York: John Wiley.

Quinn-Judge, Paul. 1989. "Latvian Moves Stir Further Unease in Moscow," *Christian Science Monitor* (June 16), 4.

Radnitzky, Gerard, and Peter Bernholz, eds. 1987. *Economic Imperialism.* New York: Paragon House.

Ramazani, R. K. 1982. *The United States and Iran: The Patterns of Influence.* New York: Praeger.

Rao, C. Niranjan. 1989. "Trade Related Aspects of Intellectual Property Rights," *Economic and Political Weekly* (May 13), 1053–1056.

Rasler, Karen, and William R. Thompson. 1989. "Ascent, Decline and War." Paper delivered at the annual American Political Science Association meeting, Atlanta, Georgia.

Ray, James Lee. 1987. *Global Politics*, 3rd ed. Boston: Houghton Mifflin.

Ray, James Lee. 1988 (November). "The Abolition of Slavery and the End of International War," Unpublished paper, Florida State University.

Ray, James Lee. 1990. *Global Politics*, 4th ed. Boston: Houghton Mifflin.

Reich, Robert B., ed. 1990. *The Power of Public Ideas.* Cambridge, Mass.: Harvard University Press.

Rejai, Mostafa, and Cynthia H. Enloe. 1981. "Nation-States and State-Nations," in *Perspectives on World Politics*, ed. Michael Smith, Richard Little, and Michael Shackleton. Chatham, N.J.: Chatham House.

Richardson, Lewis F. 1960a. *Arms and Insecurity.* Pittsburgh, Pa.: Boxwood Press.

Richardson, Lewis F. 1960b. *Statistics of Deadly Quarrels.* Pittsburgh, Pa.: Boxwood Press.

Rielly, John E. 1988. "America's State of Mind," in *The Domestic Sources of American Foreign Policy,* ed. Charles W. Kegley and Eugene R. Wittkopf. New York: St. Martin's Press, pp. 45–56.

Rifkin, Jeremy. 1984. *Algeny.* New York: Penguin Books.

Riggs, Robert E., and I. Jostein Mykletun. 1979. *Beyond Functionalism: Attitudes Toward International Organization in Norway and the United States.* Minneapolis: University of Minnesota Press.

Riggs, Robert E., and Jack C. Plano. 1988. *The United Nations: International Organization and World Politics.* Chicago: Dorsey Press.

Riker, William H. 1962. *The Theory of Political Coalitions.* New Haven, Conn.: Yale University Press.

Riker, William H. 1964. *Federalism: Origin, Operation, Significance.* Boston: Little, Brown.

Risse-Kappen, Thomas. 1991. "Public Opinion, Domestic Structure, and Foreign Policy in Liberal Democracies," *World Politics* 43 (July), 479–512.

Rogowski, Ronald. 1989. *Commerce and Coalitions: How Trade Affects Domestic Political Alignments.* Princeton, N.J.: Princeton University Press.

Rosecrance, Richard N. 1963. *Action and Reaction in World Politics.* Boston: Little, Brown.

Rosecrance, Richard N. 1986. *The Rise of the Trading State: Commerce and Conquest in the Modern World.* New York: Basic Books.

Rosecrance, Richard N. 1987. "Long Cycle Theory and International Relations," *International Organization* 41, no. 2 (Spring), 283–302.

Rosenau, James N. 1966. "Pre-Theories and Theories of Foreign Policy," in *Approaches to Comparative and International Politics*, ed. R. Barry Farrell. Evanston, Ill.: Northwestern University Press, pp. 27–92.

Rosenau, James N., ed. 1969. *International Politics and Foreign Policy*, 2nd ed. New York: The Free Press, pp. 315–324.

Rosenau, James N. 1980. *The Scientific Study of Foreign Policy*, rev. ed. London: Frances Pinter.

Rosenau, James N. 1984. "A Pre-Theory Revisited: World Politics in an Era of Cascading Interdependence," *International Studies Quarterly* 28, no. 3 (September), 245–306.

Roskin, Michael G. 1989. *Countries and Concepts*, 3rd ed. Englewood Cliffs, N.J.: Prentice Hall.

Rostow, W. W. 1971a. *Politics and the Stages of Growth*. Cambridge: Cambridge University Press.

Rostow, W. W. 1971b. *The Stages of Economic Growth*, 2nd ed. Cambridge: Cambridge University Press.

Rostow, W. W. 1978. *The World Economy*. Austin: University of Texas Press.

Rourke, John T. 1989. *International Politics on the World Stage*, 2nd ed. Guilford, Conn.: Dushkin.

Rubin, Barry. 1980. *Paved with Good Intentions: The American Experience in Iran*. New York: Penguin Books.

Ruggie, John Gerard. 1983. "Continuity and Transformation in the World Polity: Toward a Neorealist Synthesis," *World Politics* 35, no. 2 (January), 261–285.

Ruggie, John Gerard, ed. 1983b. *The Antimonies of Interdependence: National Welfare and the International Division of Labor*. New York: Columbia University Press.

Rummel, Rudolph J. 1963. "Dimensions of Conflict Behavior within and between Nations," *Yearbook of the Society for General Systems 8*, 1–50.

Rummel, Rudolph J. 1983. "Libertarianism and International Violence," *Journal of Conflict Resolution* 27, no. 1 (March), 27–71.

Rummel, Rudolph J. 1985. "Libertarian Propositions on Violence within and between Nations," *Journal of Conflict Resolution* 29, no. 3 (September), 419–455.

Rummel, Rudolph J. 1988. "From 'Political Systems, Violence, and War,'" *The United States Institute of Peace Journal* 1, no. 4 (September), 6.

Rupert, Mark E., and David P. Rapkin. 1985. "The Erosion of U.S. Leadership Capabilities," in *Rhythms in Politics and Economics*, ed. William R. Thompson. New York: Praeger, pp. 155–180.

Russett, Bruce, and Harvey Starr. 1985. *World Politics: The Menu for Choice*, 2nd ed. New York: W. H. Freeman.

Russett, Bruce, and Harvey Starr. 1989. *World Politics: The Menu for Choice*, 3rd ed. New York: W. H. Freeman.

Russett, Bruce, and Harvey Starr. 1992. *World Politics: The Menu for Choice*, 4th ed. New York: W. H. Freeman.

Russett, Bruce. 1983. *The Prisoners of Insecurity*. San Francisco: W. H. Freeman.

Russett, Bruce. 1989. "Democracy, Public Opinion and Nuclear Weapons," in *Behavior, Society and Nuclear War*, ed. Philip E. Tetlock, Jo L. Husbands, Robert Jervis, Paul C. Stern, and Charles Tilly. New York: Oxford University Press, pp. 174–208.

Saborio, Sylvia. 1992. "The Long and Winding Road from Anchorage to Patagonia," in *The Premise and the Promise: Free Trade in the Americas*, ed. Sylvia Saborio. Washington, D.C.: Overseas Development Council.

Sagan, Carl. 1983. "Nuclear War and Climatic Catastrophe: Some Policy Implications," *Foreign Affairs* 62, no. 2 (Winter), 257–292.

Saivetz, Carol R., and Sylvia Woodby. 1985. *Soviet–Third World Relations*. Boulder, Colo.: Westview Press.

Sampson, Anthony. 1978. "Want to Start a War?" *Esquire* (March 1), 58–69.

Samuelson, Paul A. 1955. "Diagrammatic Exposition of a Theory of Public Expenditure," *Review of Economics and Statistics* 37, no. 4 (November), 350–356.

Schelling, Thomas C. 1978. *Micromotives and Macrobehavior*. New York: W. W. Norton.

Schlagheck, Donna M. 1988. *International Terrorism*. Lexington, Mass: Lexington Books.

Schlesinger, Arthur, Jr. 1967. "Origins of the Cold War," *Foreign Affairs* 46, no. 1 (October), 22–52.

Schneider, William. 1984. "East-West Relations and Technology Transfer," *Department of State Bulletin* (August), 68–71.

Schneider, William. 1987. "'Rambo' and Reality: Having it Both Ways," in *Eagle Resurgent? The Reagan Era in American Foreign Policy*, ed. Kenneth A. Oye, Robert J. Lieber, and Donald Rothchild. Boston: Little, Brown, pp. 41–74.

Sewell, John W., Richard E. Feinberg, and Valeriana Kallab, eds. 1985. *U.S. Foreign Policy and the Third World: Agenda 1985–86*. New Brunswick, N.J.: Transaction Books.

Sewell, John W., and Christine E. Contee. 1985. "U.S.Foreign Aid in the 1980s: Reordering Priorities," in *U.S. Foreign Policy and the Third World: Agenda 1985–86*, ed. John W. Sewell, Richard E. Feinberg, and Valeriana Kallab. New Brunswick, N.J.: Transaction Books, pp. 95–118.

Sewell, John W., Stuart K. Tucker, and contributors. 1988. *Growth, Exports and Jobs in a Changing World Economy: Agenda 1988*. New Brunswick, N.J.: Transaction Books.

Shafer, Michael. 1985. "Capturing the Mineral Multinationals: Advantage or Disadvantage," in *Multinational Corporations*, ed. Theodore H. Moran. Lexington, Mass.: Lexington Books, pp. 25–54.

Shannon, Thomas Richard. 1989. *An Introduction to the World-System Perspective*. Boulder, Colo.: Westview Press.

Shepherd, George W., Jr. 1987. *The Trampled Grass*. New York: Greenwood Press.

Sibley, Mulford Q. 1956. "The Limitations of Behavioralism," in *Contemporary Political Analysis*, ed. James C. Charlesworth. New York: The Free Press, pp. 51–71.

Sick, Gary. 1985. *All Fall Down*. New York: Penguin Books.

Simon, Herbert A. 1957. *Models of Man*. New York: John Wiley.

Simon, Herbert A. 1985. "Human Nature in Politics: The Dialogue of Psychology with Political Science," *American Political Science Review* 79, no. 2 (June), 293–304.

Simon, Julian. 1981. *The Ultimate Resource*. Princeton, N.J.: Princeton University Press.

Simpson, Smith. 1987. *Education in Diplomacy: An Instructional Guide*. Boston: University Press of America.

Singer, J. David. 1961. "The Level of Analysis Problem in International Relations," in *The International System*, ed. Klaus Knorr and Sidney Verba. Princeton, N.J.: Princeton University Press, pp. 77–92.

Singer, J. David, Stuart Bremer, and John Stuckey. 1972. "Capability Distribution, Uncertainty and a Major War,1820–1965," in *Peace, War and Numbers,* ed. Bruce M. Russett. Beverly Hills, Calif.: Sage, pp. 19–48.

Singer, J. David, and Thomas Cusack. 1981. "Periodicity, Inexorability, and Steermanship in International War," in *From National Development to Global Community: Essays in Honor of Karl W. Deutsch,* ed. Richard L. Merritt and Bruce M. Russett. London: Allen and Unwin, pp.404–422.

Singer, J. David, and Melvin Small. 1974. "Foreign Policy Indicators: Predictors of War in History and in the State of the World Message," *Policy Sciences 5,* no. 3 (September), 271–296.

Sivard, Ruth Leger. 1976. *World Military and Social Expenditures.* Washington, D.C.: World Priorities.

Sivard, Ruth Leger. 1986. *World Military and Social Expenditures,* 11th ed. Washington, D.C.: World Priorities.

Sivard, Ruth Leger. 1987. *World Military and Social Expenditures,* 12th ed. Washington, D.C.: World Priorities.

Sivard, Ruth Leger. 1989. *World Military and Social Expenditures,* 13th ed. Washington, D.C.: World Priorities.

Sivard, Ruth Leger. 1991. *World Military and Social Expenditures,* 14th ed. Washington, D.C.: World Priorities.

Siverson, Randolph M. 1980. "War and Change in the International System," in *Change in the International System,* ed. Ole R. Holsti, Randolph M. Siverson, and Alexander L. George. Boulder, Colo.: Westview Press, pp. 211–229.

Slater, Jerome, and David Goldfischer. 1986. "Can SDI Provide a Defense?" *Political Science Quarterly* 101, no. 5, 838–856.

Small, Melvin, and J. David Singer. 1976. "The War-Proneness of Democratic Regimes, 1816–1965," *Jerusalem Journal of International Relations* 1 (Summer), 49–69.

Small, Melvin, and J. David Singer. 1982. *Resort to Arms: International and Civil Wars, 1816–1980.* Beverly Hills, Calif.: Sage.

Small, Melvin, and J. David Singer. 1985. "Patterns in International Warfare, 1816–1980," in *International War,* ed. Melvin Small and J. David Singer. Homewood, Ill.: Dorsey Press, pp. 7–19.

Smith, Adam. 1910. *An Inquiry into the Nature and Causes of the Wealth of Nations.* London: Dent.

Smith, Adam. 1937. *An Inquiry into the Nature and Causes of the Wealth of Nations.* New York: Modern Library.

Smith, Dale L., and James Lee Ray. 1989. "European Integration: Gloomy Theory versus Rosy Reality." Paper presented at the annual meeting of the American Political Science Association, Atlanta, Georgia.

Smith, Marjorie S. 1987. "Japanese Defense Spending: A Levels-of-Analysis Approach," Unpublished paper, University of Denver.

Smith, Michael Joseph. 1986. *Realist Thought from Weber to Kissinger.* Baton Rouge: Louisiana State University Press.

Smith, Sheila, and John Toye. 1983. "Three Stories about Trade and Poor Economies," in *The Struggle for Economic Development,* ed. Michael P. Todaro. New York: Longman, pp. 289–300.

Snidal, Duncan. 1985a. "Coordination versus Prisoner's Dilemma: Implications for International Cooperation and Regimes," *American Political Science Review* 74, no. 4 (December), 923–942.

Snidal, Duncan. 1985b. "The Limits of Hegemonic Stability," *International Organization* 39, no. 4 (Autumn), 579–614.

Snyder, Glenn H. 1984. "The Security Dilemma in Alliance Politics," *World Politics* 36, no. 4 (July), 461–495.

Snyder, Glenn H., and Paul Diesing. 1977. *Conflict among Nations: Bargaining, Decision-Making and System Structure in International Crisis.* Princeton, N.J.: Princeton University Press.

Somerville, John, and Ronald E. Santoni, eds. 1963. *Social and Political Philosophy.* Garden City, N.Y.: Doubleday.

Soroos, Marvin S. 1986. *Beyond Sovereignty: The Challenge of Global Policy.* Columbia: University of South Carolina Press.

Soroos, Marvin S. 1987. "Global Commons, Telecommunications, and International Space Policy," in *International Space Policy*, ed. Daniel S. Papp and John R. McIntyre. New York: Quorum Books, pp. 139–156.

Soroos, Marvin S. 1988. "The Tragedy of the Commons in Global Perspective," in *The Global Agenda: Issues and Perspectives*, 2nd ed. Charles W. Kegley, Jr., and Eugene R. Wittkopf. New York: Random House, pp. 345–357.

Soroos, Marvin S. 1989. "Conflict in the Use and Management of International Commons." Paper presented at the Tampere Peace Research Institute, Orivesi, Finland.

Sorokin, Pitirim A. 1937. *Social and Cultural Dynamics, Vol. 3: Fluctuations of Social Relationships, War, and Revolution.* New York: American Book.

Spector, Leonard S. 1988. *The Undeclared Bomb.* Cambridge, Mass.: Ballinger Publishing.

Spector, Leonard S. with Jacqueline R. Smith. 1990. *Nuclear Ambitions.* Boulder, Colo.: Westview Press.

Spero, Joan Edelman. 1981. *The Politics of International Economic Relations*, 2nd ed. New York: St. Martin's Press.

Spero, Joan Edelman. 1990. *The Politics of International Economic Relations*, 4th ed. New York: St. Martin's Press.

Sprout, Harold, and Margaret Sprout. 1971. *Towards a Politics of the Planet Earth.* New York: Van Nostrand Reinhold Company.

Starr, Harvey. 1984. *Henry Kissinger: Perceptions of International Politics.* Lexington: University Press of Kentucky.

Staviranos, L. S. 1981. *Global Rift.* New York: William Morrow.

Stoessinger, John C. 1976. *Henry Kissinger: The Anguish of Power.* New York: W. W. Norton.

Stoessinger, John C. 1979. *Crusaders and Pragmatists: Movers of Modern American Foreign Policy.* New York: W. W. Norton.

Stoessinger, John C. 1985. *Why Nations Go to War*, 4th ed. New York: St. Martin's Press.

Stoessinger, John C. 1986. *The Might of Nations*, 8th ed. New York: Random House.

Stoll, Richard J. 1989. "State Power, World Views, and the Major Powers," in *Power in World Politics*, ed. Richard J. Stoll and Michael D. Ward. Boulder, Colo.: Lynne Rienner, pp. 135–157.

Stone, Irving. 1980. *The Origin.* New York: Doubleday.

Strange, Susan. 1988. *States and Markets.* New York: Basil Blackwell.

Streit, Clarence. 1961. *Freedom's Frontier—Atlantic Union Now.* Washington: Freedom and Union Press.

Sullivan, David S., and Martin J. Sattler, eds. 1971. *Change and the Future International System.* New York: Columbia University Press.

Summers, Robert, and Alan Heston. 1984. "International Comparisons of Real Production and Its Composition: 1950–1980," *The Review of Income and Wealth,* Series 30, no. 2 (June), 207–262.

Sunkel, Oswaldo. 1979. "Big Business and 'Dependencia,'" in *Transnational Corporations and World Order,* ed. George Modelski. San Francisco: W. H. Freeman, pp. 216–225.

Swing, John J. 1976. "Who Will Own the Oceans?" *Foreign Affairs* 54, no. 3 (April), 527–546.

Sylvan, David, Duncan Snidal, Bruce M. Russett, Steven Jackson, and Raymond Duvall. 1983. "The Peripheral Economies: Penetration and Economic Distortion, 1970–1975," in *Contending Approaches to World System Analysis,* ed. William R. Thompson. Beverly Hills, Calif.: Sage, pp. 79–111.

Tabor, Charles S. 1989. "Power Capability Indexes in the Third World," in *Power in World Politics,* ed. Richard J. Stoll and Michael D. Ward. Boulder, Colo.: Lynne Rienner, pp. 29–48.

Taylor, Charles Lewis, and David A. Jodice. 1983. *World Handbook of Political and Social Indicators,* 3rd ed. 2 vols. New Haven, Conn.: Yale University Press.

Taylor, Michael. 1987. *The Possibility of Cooperation.* Cambridge: Cambridge University Press.

Thompson, Janice E., and Stephen D. Krasner. 1989. "Global Transactions and the Consolidation of Sovereignty," in *Global Changes and Theoretical Challenges,* ed. Ernst-Otto Czempiel and James N. Rosenau. Lexington, Mass: Lexington Books, pp. 195–220.

Thompson, Starley L., and Stephen H. Schneider. 1986. "Nuclear Winter Reappraised," *Foreign Affairs* 64, no.5 (Summer), 981–1005.

Thompson, William R., ed. 1983. *Contending Approaches to World System Analysis.* Beverly Hills, Calif.: Sage.

Thompson, William R. 1988. *On Global War: Historical-Structural Approaches to World Politics.* Columbia: University of South Carolina Press.

Thompson, William R., and L. Gary Zuk. 1982. "War, Inflation and the Kondratieff Wave," *Journal of Conflict Resolution* 26, no. 4 (December), 621–644.

Thurow, Lester. 1987. "America, Europe and Japan: A Time to Dismantle the World Economy," in *International Political Economy,* ed. Jeffrey A. Frieden and David A. Lake. New York: St. Martin's Press, pp. 385–394.

Tilly, Charles. 1985. "War Making and State Making as Organized Crime," in *Bringing the State Back In,* ed. Peter B. Evans, Dietrich Rueschemeyer, and Theda Skocpol. Cambridge: Cambridge University Press, pp. 169–191.

Todaro, Michael P. 1981. *Economic Development in the Third World,* 2nd ed. New York: Longman.

Todaro, Michael P. 1989. *Economic Development in the Third World,* 4th ed. New York: Longman.

Toffler, Alvin. 1970. *Future Shock.* New York: Bantam Books.

Toffler, Alvin. 1980. *The Third Wave.* New York: William Morrow.

Tollison, Robert D., and Thomas D. Willett. 1979. "An Economic Theory of Mutually Advantageous Issue Linkages in International Negotiations," *International Organization* 33, no. 4 (Autumn), 425–449.

Toynbee, Arnold. 1972. *A Study of History.* New York: Weathervane Books.

Tucker, Robert C., ed. 1978. *The Marx-Engels Reader,* 2nd ed. New York: W. W. Norton.

Union of International Associations. 1985. *Yearbook of International Organizations 1985–86.* Brussels: Union of International Associations.

United Nations. 1973. *The Determinants and Consequences of Population Trends,* Vol 1. Department of Economic and Social Affairs, Population Studies No. 50 (ST/SOA/SER.A/50).

United Nations. 1979. *World Population Trends and Prospects by Country, 1950–2000.* Department of International Economic and Social Affairs (ST/ESA/SER.R/33).

United Nations. 1980. *The World Population Situation in 1979.* Department of International Economic and Social Affairs, Population Studies No. 72 (ST/ESA/SER.A/72).

United Nations. 1988. *Statistical Yearbook 1985–86.* New York: United Nations.

United Nations Centre on Transnational Corporations [UNCTC]. 1985. *Trends and Issues in Foreign Direct Investment and Related Flows.* New York: United Nations.

United Nations Centre on Transnational Corporations [UNCTC]. 1988. *Transnational Corporations in World Development.* New York: United Nations.

United Nations Centre on Transnational Corporations [UNCTC]. 1991. *World Investment Report: The Triad in Foreign Direct Investment.* New York: United Nations.

United Nations Development Programme [UNDP]. 1992. *Human Development Report 1992.* New York: Oxford University Press.

United Nations Environment Programme [UNEP]. 1979. *The United Nations Environment Programme.* Nairobi: United Nations Environment Programme.

United Nations Environment Programme [UNEP]. 1987. *North American News* 2, no. 5 (October).

United Nations Food and Agricultural Organization [UNFAO]. 1987. *The Fifth World Food Survey.* Rome: United Nations Food and Agricultural Organization.

United States Arms Control and Disarmament Agency [U.S. ACDA]. 1991. *World Military Expenditures and Arms Transfers 1990.* Washington, D.C.: U.S. ACDA.

United States Committee for Refugees. 1989. *World Refugee Survey: 1988 in Review.* Washington, D.C.: United States Committee for Refugees.

United States State Department. 1989. *Patterns of Global Terrorism 1988,* Department of State Publication 9705. Washington, D.C.: Ambassador-at-Large for Counterterrorism.

Vadney, T. E. 1987. *The World Since 1945.* New York: Penguin Books.

Van Creveld, Martin. 1989. *Technology and War.* New York: The Free Press.

Van Deelen, Wim. 1988. "Nuclear Fusion Research in Europe," *Europe,* no. 274 (March), 26–28.

Van Dinh, Trans. 1987. *Communication and Diplomacy in a Changing World.* Norwood, N.J.: Ablex.

Vasquez, John A. 1983. *The Power of Power Politics: A Critique.* New Brunswick, N.J.: Rutgers University Press.

Verba, Sidney. 1961. "Assumptions of Rationality and Non-Rationality in Models of the International System," in *The International System,* ed. Klaus Knorr and Sidney Verba. Princeton, N.J.: Princeton University Press, pp. 93–117.

Vernon, Raymond. 1971. *Sovereignty at Bay.* New York: Basic Books.

Vernon, Raymond. 1987. "International Investment and International Trade in the Product Cycle," in *International Political Economy,* ed. Jeffrey A. Frieden and David A. Lake. New York: St. Martin's Press, pp. 174–86.

Vestal, Theodore M. 1985. "Famine in Ethiopia: Crisis of Many Dimensions," *Africa Today* 32, no. 4 (Fourth Quarter), 7–28.

Viner, Jacob. 1958. *The Long View and the Short: Studies in Economic Theory and Policy.* New York: The Free Press.

Viotti, Paul R., and Mark V. Kauppi. 1987. *International Relations Theory.* New York: Macmillan.

Walker, R. B. J. 1987. "Realism, Change, and International Political Theory," *International Studies Quarterly* 31, no. 1, (March), 65–86.

Wallace, Michael D., and J. David Singer. 1970. "Intergovernmental Organization in the Global System, 1815–1964: A Quantitative Description," *International Organization* 24, no. 2 (Spring), 239–287.

Wallerstein, Immanuel. 1976. *The Modern World System,* Vol 1. New York: Academic Press.

Wallerstein, Immanuel. 1980. *The Modern World System,* Vol 2. New York: Academic Press.

Wallerstein, Immanuel. 1981. "Dependence in an Interdependent World: The Limited Possibilities of Transformation within the Capitalist World Economy," in *From Dependency to Development,* ed. Heraldo Munoz. Boulder, Colo.: Westview Press.

Walters, Robert S., and David H. Blake. 1992. *The Politics of Global Economic Relations,* 4th ed. Englewood Cliffs, N.J.: Prentice Hall.

Waltz, Kenneth N. 1959. *Man, the State and War: A Theoretical Analysis.* New York: Columbia University Press.

Waltz, Kenneth N. 1969. "International Structure, National Force, and the Balance of World Power," in *International Politics and Foreign Policy,* 2nd ed, ed. James N. Rosenau. New York: The Free Press, pp. 304–314.

Waltz, Kenneth N. 1979. *Theory of International Politics.* New York: Random House.

Waltz, Kenneth N. 1982 (originally 1973). "The Myth of National Interdependence," in *Globalism versus Realism: International Relations' Third Debate,* ed. Ray Maghroori and Bennett Ramberg. Boulder, Colo.: Westview Press, pp. 81–96.

Wang, Kevin, and James Lee Ray. 1990. "The Initiation and Outcome of International Wars Involving Great Powers, 1495–1985." Paper presented at the 1990 meeting of the International Studies Association, Washington, D.C.

Watson, Adam. 1992. *The Evolution of International Society.* London: Routledge.

Weimer, David L., and Aidan R. Vining. 1989. *Policy Analysis: Concepts and Practice.* Englewood Cliffs, N.J.: Prentice Hall.

Weisbund, Stefi, and Janet Reloff. 1985. "Climate and Africa: Why the Land Goes Dry," *Science News* 127, no. 18 (May 4), 282–285.

White, Ralph K. 1985. "Misperception in Vienna on the Eve of World War I," in *International War,* ed. Melvin Small and J. David Singer. Homewood, Ill.: Dorsey Press, pp. 231–239.

Wiegele, Thomas C. 1990. "The Emerging Significance of Biotechnology for the Study of International Relations," *International Studies Notes* 15, no. 3 (Fall), 98–103.

Wilkenfeld, Jonathan, and Michael Brecher. 1989. "Third Party Intervention I: The Global Organizational Dimension," in *Crisis, Conflict and Instability*, ed. Michael Brecher and Jonathan Wilkenfeld. New York: Pergamon Press, pp. 57–73.

Wilkenfeld, Jonathan, Michael Brecher, and Stephen R. Hill. 1989. "Threat and Violence in State Behavior," in *Crisis, Conflict and Instability*, ed. Michael Brecher and Jonathan Wilkenfeld. New York: Pergamon Press, pp. 177–193.

Will, George F. 1983. *Statecraft as Soulcraft: What Government Does.* New York: Simon & Schuster.

Williams, William Appleman. 1962. *The Tragedy of American Diplomacy.* New York: Dell.

Wittkopf, Eugene R. 1990. *Faces of Internationalism: Public Opinion and American Foreign Policy.* Durham, N.C.: Duke University Press.

Wolf, Edward C. 1988. "Raising Agricultural Productivity," in *State of the World 1987*, ed. Lester R. Brown and others. New York: W. W. Norton, pp. 139–156.

Woodby, Sylvia, and Martha L. Cottam. 1988. *The Changing Agenda: World Politics Since 1945.* Boulder, Colo.: Westview Press.

World Almanac. 1987. *The World Almanac and Book of Facts.* New York: World Almanac.

World Almanac. 1989. *The World Almanac and Book of Facts.* New York: World Almanac.

World Almanac. 1990. *The World Almanac and Book of Facts.* New York: World Almanac.

World Bank. 1979. *World Development Report 1979.* Washington, D.C.: World Bank.

World Bank. 1981. *World Development Report 1981.* Washington, D.C.: World Bank.

World Bank. 1987. *World Development Report 1987.* New York: Oxford University Press.

World Bank. 1988a. *World Development Report 1988.* New York: Oxford University Press.

World Bank. 1988b. *Annual Report.* Washington, D.C.: World Bank.

World Bank. 1988c. *The World Bank Atlas 1988.* Washington, D.C.: World Bank.

World Bank. 1989. *World Development Report 1989.* New York: Oxford University Press.

World Bank. 1991a. *World Development Report 1991.* New York: Oxford University Press.

World Bank. 1991b. *Global Economic Prospects and the Developing Countries.* Washington, D.C.: World Bank.

World Bank. 1992a. *World Development Report 1992.* New York: Oxford University Press.

World Bank. 1992b. *Global Economic Prospects and the Developing Countries.* Washington, D.C.: World Bank.

World Resources Institute. 1986. *World Resources 1986.* New York: Basic Books.

World Resources Institute. 1988. *World Resources 1988–89.* New York: Basic Books.

World Resources Institute. 1992. *World Resources 1992–93.* New York: Oxford University Press.

Wright, Quincy. 1965. *A Study of War*, 2nd ed. Chicago: University of Chicago Press.

Yasutomo, Daniel T. 1986. *The Manner of Giving.* Lexington, Mass.: Lexington Books.

Young, Oran R. 1986. "International Regimes: Toward a New Theory of Institutions," *World Politics* 39, no. 1 (October), 104–122.

Young, Oran R. 1989. "The Politics of International Regime Formation: Managing Natural Resources and the Environment," *International Organization* 43, no. 3 (Summer), 349–375.

Zeigler, David W. 1987. *War, Peace and International Politics*, 4th ed. Boston: Little, Brown.

INDEX

SUBJECT INDEX

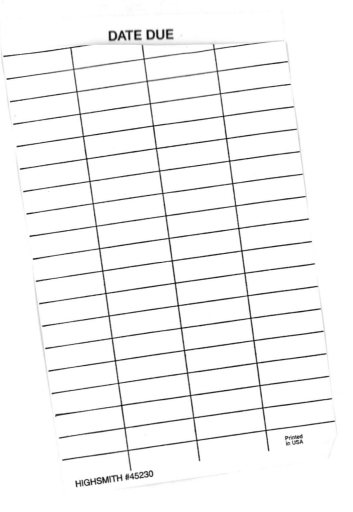

DATE DUE

Printed in USA

HIGHSMITH #45230